Ian Breward is Emeritus Professor of Church
History, United Faculty of Theology and
Senior Fellow in the History Department,
University of Melbourne.

THE OXFORD HISTORY OF
THE CHRISTIAN CHURCH

Edited by
Henry and Owen Chadwick

A History of the Churches in Australasia

IAN BREWARD

OXFORD
UNIVERSITY PRESS

OXFORD
UNIVERSITY PRESS

Great Clarendon Street, Oxford OX2 6DP

Oxford University Press is a department of the University of Oxford.
It furthers the University's objective of excellence in research, scholarship,
and education by publishing worldwide in

Oxford New York
Athens Auckland Bangkok Bogotá Buenos Aires Cape Town
Chennai Dar es Salaam Delhi Florence Hong Kong Istanbul Karachi
Kolkata Kuala Lumpur Madrid Melbourne Mexico City Mumbai Nairobi
Paris São Paulo Shanghai Singapore Taipei Tokyo Toronto Warsaw

and associated companies in Berlin Ibadan

Oxford is a registered trade mark of Oxford University Press
in the UK and in certain other countries

Published in the United States
by Oxford University Press Inc., New York

© Ian Breward 2001

The moral rights of the author have been asserted

Database right Oxford University Press (maker)

First published 2001

British Library Cataloguing in Publication Data

Data available

Library of Congress Cataloging in Publication Data

Data applied for

ISBN 0-19-826356-2

1 3 5 7 9 10 8 6 4 2

Typeset in Bembo
by Regent Typesetting, London
Printed in Great Britain
on acid-free paper by
Biddles Ltd., Guildford & King's Lynn

To Malcolm Lakwaifisi
and Hazel Keleramo
and Anna Mari

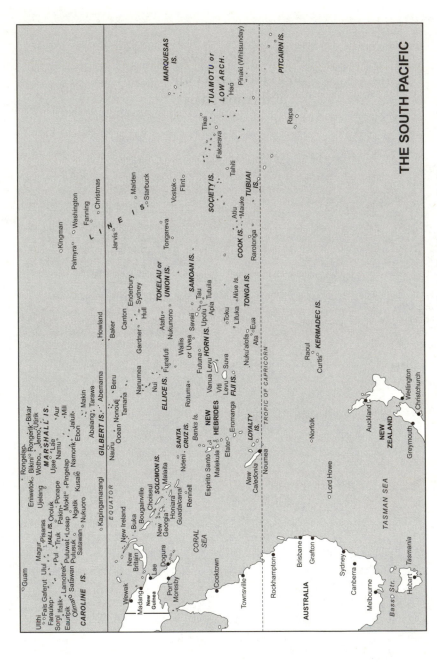

The South Pacific (1949). (*Source:* I. Shevill, *Pacific Conquest*, Sydney, 1949.)

PREFACE

Writing a history of this very complex region with huge distances between island groups is a task for several lifetimes. Populations vary from 2,000 in Niue to 4,000,000 in Papua New Guinea, with substantial populations also in Fiji (775,000), Solomon Islands (368,000), the two Samoas (223,000), French Polynesia (218,000), and Vanuatu (164,000). Many Polynesians and Melanesians have migrated to Australia, with 19 million people, New Zealand, with almost 4 million, and New Caledonia, with 200,000, and to the capitals of their own island groups. The indigenous peoples of the region had $c.1,500$ languages, and richly varied cultures shaped by particular contexts, even when there were shared regional and cultural features. Inevitably, the writing of history involves some contemporary agendas, which subordinate local attitudes to time and place, because of the need to make larger constructs like 'Polynesia' and 'Melanesia'.

The interests of colonizing powers have thus been given more historical weight than the important perspectives of micro-states, tribe, and clan, though the number of Pacific Islanders and Aborigines able to write academic history from within their own culture is growing, and is offering new perspectives. Given the secular assumptions and wide range of angles from which history can be written, the religious experience of Pacific and Aboriginal peoples can be further minimized by social scientists and historians who see little significance in religion. In this fascinatingly varied region, islands range from mountainous ones like New Caledonia and Papua New Guinea with rich mineral resources, to coral atolls where only a subsistence life is possible. Many of these islands are stunningly beautiful, but their people must live with unpredictability caused by cyclones, along with many diseases which are life-threatening, notably malaria. Understanding such societies poses many problems for those with a 'western' viewpoint.

That has been a problem since the first European explorers of the region. Study of world religions was in its infancy in the eighteenth and nineteenth centuries when thorough exploration occurred. Primal religions seemed especially primitive to Christians. Not only did some peoples, like Aborigines, appear to have no religion, but the nature of their religious knowledge was inaccessible to those who were neither initiated nor deeply conversant with the local language. At a time when European religion was moving to an emphasis on the private, intellectual, and moral significance of worship, it was hard for observers to appreciate the communal nature of primal religion. European folk Christianity actually had some similar features, where rituals provided both protection and access to sacral power. Even more important was the way in which the whole of life gained a cosmic and eternal dimension. Practice of rituals was far more important than the articulation of belief. Ironically, some of the best descriptions of religion's role have come from the study of anthropologists working with micro-communities in the Pacific. Sir Raymond Firth's classic studies of the transition to Christianity on Tikopia make that plain, despite his conviction that religion needs no revelatory explanation. 'Religion is the name for some of man's most audacious attempts to give meaning to his world, by giving his constructions a symbolic transcendental referent'.[1]

The impact of the social sciences on the writing of church and religious history has become very obvious in the interest taken in folk beliefs by historians of magical custom and practice.[2] The Marian 'picture' at Yankalilla, South Australia, and the healing spring at Bullsbrook, Western Australia, are indications that pilgrimage may be beginning in Australia. As yet, few church historians have paid such close attention to religion's role in local communities as have anthropologists in their mapping of religion in tribal communities of the Pacific.[3] They have preferred rather to concentrate their attention on the studies of denominations, and movements of national significance. One of the advantages of studying Christianity in the Pacific is that an historian is constantly reminded of the relationship of religion to issues of land ownership, titles, sickness and health, family life, social control,

---

[1] R. Firth, *Religion* (London, 1996) 70.

[2] K. Thomas, *Religion and the Decline of Magic* (London, 1973); C. Waddell, 'Magic and liturgical correctness in the Church', *AJL* 6 (1997) 5–19 for an account of a Marian shrine; A. Nutter, 'The events of Yankalilla', *Medjugorje Sentinel* (June 1997) for a description of the Marian picture which has appeared since May 1994.

[3] D. Clark, *Between Pulpit and Pew* (Cambridge, 1982); J. Obelkevich, *Religion and Rural Society* (Oxford, 1985); and H. McLeod, *Religion and Society in England* (London, 1996) show the possibilities of such study.

and the importance of initiation to deeper levels of religious knowledge and authority. Gender roles have also been deeply influenced by traditional religious ideas. Recent converts to Christianity in the Highlands of Papua New Guinea have found admission of women to the sacred space of a church building just as challenging a paradigm shift as some Anglicans have found admission of women to the priesthood.

Though nineteenth-century observers of Aboriginal and Pacific Island societies were deeply shocked by customs like cannibalism, few were able to note the similarities with their own culture. Popular European ideas of sickness and death were still only lightly touched by science. Fate, sin, and judgement served as explanations. Attitudes to sexuality, marriage, and birth were still strongly linked with ideas of purity, and contamination by female blood was a threat to male power. Though many missionary writers were appalled at the subordination and degradation of Aboriginal and Pacific women, they were culturally unable to see corrupted patriarchy in their own societies, or even in their own families.

Historians and social scientists increasingly recognize the difficulty of reconstructing the mentality of tribal peoples, and the inevitability of their own cultural priorities affecting research outcomes. Missionary reports, or occasional writings by converts, offer tantalizing hints of how the process of conversion was experienced by those who became Christians, but we know all too little about the history of religious and cultural changes at village level. Neither missionaries nor converts were interested in writing the history of local communities and churches. Missionaries wrote for European audiences about religious changes, and the attractions of western technology. Village people only handed on selected stories of the process of religious change, usually as that had affected particular families. They did not see the nation, region, or island as a key category for social memory.[4] Anthropologists have been so concerned to recover the dimensions of traditional society and religion, that they have rarely explored the results of conversion to Christianity with the same depth.[5]

[4] E. Kolig, 'A sense of history and the reconstruction of cosmology in Australian Aboriginal society', *Anthropos* 90 (1995) 49–67.

[5] P. Brown, *Beyond a Mountain Valley* (Honolulu, 1995) and B. Burt, *Tradition and Christianity* (Chur, 1994) open up the possibilities, as does M. Kahn, 'Sunday Christians, Monday sorcerers', *JPH* 18 (1983) 96–112, and J. Barker, 'We are Ekalesia', in J. Carrier, (ed.), *History and Tradition in Melanesian Ethnography* (Berkeley, 1992) 199–32. J. T. O'Meara, *Samoan Planters* (Fort Worth, 1990) 47–56, 206–10. J. Huntsman and A. Hooper, *Tokelau* (Honolulu, 1996).

Writing the history of oral tribal societies is a complex and delicate task, proceeding on assumptions about authority, gender, and race, which often make the result of little interest to such communities. This history does not deal with the way that the family story is jealously guarded from strangers lest title to land and kin ties are jeopardized, or family honour shamed. The careful evaluation demanded by historians is alien to many Pacific Island communities. Historians need tribal and language-group histories both for new nations and for micro-societies like Tokelau. Such concern is very evident also among Aboriginal communities in Australia, who face cruel dilemmas over the protection of sacred sites, and the disclosures of sacred knowledge, which they believe cannot be revealed without spiritual disaster to their community. The difficulty of these issues in the 1990s was vividly displayed in the claims to secret women's knowledge relating to land affected by a bridge to Hindmarsh Island, South Australia. The Ngarrindjerri community concerned was itself divided over whether such secret knowledge existed, with some women claiming that it was a political creation.[6] European observers in this case have also been divided, because little attention was paid in the past to the roles of women in Aboriginal communities.

Control of community memory is an important form of power. Pacific ethnocentrism is very strong, though it has received less attention from European historians than the racism of their own culture. Villages may seem unimportant in the larger historical scheme of things, but the breakdown of large national communities may make the recovery of memory about the skills needed to live in face-to-face communities very significant in the twenty-first century.[7] In a region where tribe and clan are still very important political units, historians educated in the European tradition need to challenge their own social assumptions. Larger social units are not necessarily more effective bearers of meaning than micro-societies, though that is the assumption of much writing on localism. Understanding the cultural context of meaning and social order needs both national and local history, which does justice to Islander political skills and values, as well as to the many-sided European impact. A major challenge for emerging

---

[6] D. Wilson, *The Cost of Crossing Bridges* (Melbourne, 1998). D. Bell, *Ngarrindjerri Wurruwarrin* (Melbourne, 1998) offers a counterview to Wilson's claims.

[7] B. Reay, *Microhistories* (Cambridge, 1996); G. Trompf, 'Macrohistory and acculturation', *Comparative Studies in Society and History* 31 (1984) 621–48; L. T. Smith, *Decolonizing Methodologies* (Dunedin, 1999).

Melanesian states is to develop national identity when tribal loyalties are so strong and languages so numerous. That has been easier in countries like Fiji, Samoa, and Tonga, where cultural identity and a common language pre-dates European contact.

European Christians who migrated to Australasia have their own enduring tribalisms and myths. Each religious community has its own tradition and memory, reshaped in the light of events and new questions. The experience of local Christians can be significantly different from the views of regional, national, and international leaders, which still can be of great importance in many historic churches. Laity see discipleship at very different levels from religious professionals.[8] Evidence mounts that women use their heritage very differently from men, even though the reasons for this are imperfectly understood. I have not attempted to give a complete narrative account of these variables church by church across the region, but have instead tried to illustrate wide-ranging regional issues by local exemplars. Denominational completeness is not possible, so the term 'churches' is used to include realities which cross denominational and political boundaries.

Understanding the religious impact of Anglo-Celtic, French, German, and, more recently, American Christianity, on the Polynesian and Melanesian societies of the region makes the writing of a history of the Church in the region quite challenging.[9] Christianity in the region has been modified by encounter with a physical context where the Christian year is characterized by a reversal of seasons and where many cultures are small scale and vulnerable to cultural invasion. Interactions between local cultures and imported Christianity have led to changes not only in village life, but also in the Christianity which has emerged. Local people have made use of aspects of Christianity which were socially useful to them, but not necessarily a reflection of missionary and overseas leaders' priorities. Missionaries collected stories, but did not give them the same meaning as their informants. Much research is needed to contextualize these local views historically.

Aboriginal, Polynesian, and Melanesian Christians have reacted differently to such historical questions than migrants from Europe,

---

[8] G. Davie, *Religion in Britain since 1945* (Oxford, 1994); P. Kaldor, et al., *Taking Stock* (Adelaide, 1999) 67–113.

[9] D. Denoon et al., *Cambridge History of the Pacific Islanders* (Melbourne, 1997) 3–36, 119–51, discusses the problem of Pacific historical writing in general.

North America, Asia, and the Middle East. Both groups see walking in the paths of their forebears as vital to survival in the future, but the tribal ancestors are present in a different way than for those Christians who have a linear and chronological view of history, rather than a mythological one in which the past is the present, providing justification for the social order. Few indigenous inhabitants of the region would doubt that Jesus lived, for he can be comfortably fitted into their mythological view of the past, which can take many forms—song, dance, story. Dealing with Jesus' historicity and humanity can be a formidable cultural hurdle.[10] Des and Jenny Oatridge, Bible translators living among the Binumanien tribe of the Eastern Highlands Province, Papua New Guinea, were amazed when they translated the genealogies in Matthew, for genealogies are one of the most vital forms of historical memory in the Pacific. People suddenly realized that Jesus was a person like themselves, for spirit people had no ancestors. Tribal people may only write on their own tribe. That can help to remind us of the variety of clan loyalties, and the different ways in which such communities cherish their own heritage.

On Australia Day 1988, Gary Foley and Galarrwuy Yunupingi pointed out that a bicentennial of European occupation was nothing beside the 200th Bicentenary which Aborigines claimed. Indeed they could only mourn the decline of population from *c.*350,000 and the disappearance of many of the *c.*500 languages existing in the eighteenth and nineteenth centuries. Only G. W. Rusden's histories of Australasian colonies did some justice to the brutality of dispossession and conquest. Other historians celebrated discovery, settlement, and the colonizing of the continent's empty spaces, as well as the achievement of federation, and the development of a nation. Racism was a non-issue. Much work remains to be done on understanding the depth of Aboriginal and Islander consciousness and how historical and mythological thinking interact. Ethical issues about sacred objects, photos of the dead, or reference to their names, are still hardly understood by white historians, who may have no place for the sacred in their personal philosophy.

Integrating Aboriginal and Pacific Islander memory into mainstream historical teaching and writing will mean a much franker recognition of the theme of conflict between migrants and the people of the land. We need much more intellectual engagement with

---

[10] D. B. Rose, 'Ned Kelly died for our sins', *Oceania* 65 (1994) 175–86.

indigenous ideas of the past like the Samoans' 'mornings', which mark new beginnings in their story. Such alternative rationalities are difficult to understand, but something of the possibilities of indigenous historical writing can be seen in the nineteenth-century Hawaiian histories of David Malo and John Papa I'i. The collection, editing, and analysis of indigenous history can be shaped for literate markets and filtered by religion, gender, and class so that colonialism is reinforced.[11] It is a rare historian who manages to break through this cultural barrier. In New Zealand, Judith Binney's magisterial study of the Maori prophet, Te Kooti, is a unique regional example of sensitive use of varied and conflicting family traditions, combined with the critical analysis of a historian.[12]

Protective attitudes about the past are not unknown amongst European migrants to the region. There is still a strong current of opinion that history should be celebratory, not divisive, or focused on unpleasant episodes in the past. Current controversy about 'the stolen children' in Australia and political denunciation of the 'black armband' view of Australian history, which allegedly draws undue attention to the forcible conquest and dispossession of Aborigines, are reminders of divisions over history writing.[13] Yet the controversies over native title in Australia in the 1990s, reactions to the decisions of the Waitangi Tribunal in New Zealand, and, above all, the tragic civil war on Bougainville, demonstrate that, where a community becomes divided deeply, some historical healing of memories is essential if rebuilding of village life is to occur. Such cultural truth-telling is not a Christian monopoly, but some of its most significant roots lie in the Christian Scriptures and Tradition, not least in recognition of human sin.

Consequently, a church historian must pay attention to what Christians believe about God's revelation to humanity, for that pro-vides essential criteria for assessing the integrity of translations of the Gospel into different regional cultures. Balancing the claims of the temporal and the eternal is a never-ending task for the churches,

---

[11] A. McGrath (ed.), *Contested Ground* (Sydney, 1995) 388–9 for some of the difficult cases which have arisen; 306–56 for an outline of the contrast between European and Pallawa history of Tasmania. M. King (ed.), *Tihe Mauriora* (Auckland, 1974) 9–18; S. Webster, 'Post-modernist theory and the sublimation of Maori culture', *Oceania* 63 (1992–3) 222–39; T. Van Mejl, 'Maori socio-political organisation in pre- and proto-history', *Oceania* 65 (1994) 304–20; T. P. Fanua and L. W. Webster, *Malo Tupou* (Auckland, 1996).

[12] J. Binney, *Redemption Songs* (Auckland, 1995).

[13] H. Reynolds, *Why Were We Never Told?* (Sydney, 1999); R. Marsh, ' "Lost", "Stolen" or "Rescued"?', *Quadrant* (June 1999) 15–18.

because of human inadequacies in responding to God and each other.[14] Historians can make an important contribution to communities of faith, by helping them to accept their fallibility and partiality in handing on their story. Pointing to the universality of Christianity is just as important as recognizing its particularity, especially in a time of rapid change when everything can be relativized, and faith explained as a social construct. That it can be, but there are also signs of Christian formation of culture present in the history of Australasia. They need to be identified if Christianity is to retain its capacity for bearing witness in the public forum and contributing to significant change.

November 1999   I.B.

[14] As Dr Norman wisely remarks, Christians need 'to be guardians of a timeless message which can be known about only when each successive generation changes the images in which it is represented'. E. Norman, 'Epilogue: the changing role of the ecclesiastical historian', in N. Aston (ed.), *Religious Change in Europe 1650–1914* (Oxford, 1997) 407.

ACKNOWLEDGEMENTS

In a lifetime of work as an historian, one incurs innumerable debts to students and to colleagues. My indebtedness to the writings of T. P. Boland, E. Campion, A. Cooper, R. McGinley, P. O'Farrell, and M. Press on Australian Roman Catholicism is obvious. J. Garrett, W. N. Gunson, D. Hilliard, R. Lange, H. Laracy, P. Steffen, R. Thompson, A. Thornley, and G. Trompf have similarly been invaluable guides to the complexity of Pacific Islands Christianity. On Australian religious history, K. Cable, B. Dickey, G. Griffin, M. Hutchinson, K. Manley, S. Piggin, R. Frappell, and R. Withycombe have been generous colleagues over the years. I am particularly indebted to Colin Brown, Susan Campbell, Allan Davidson, David Hilliard, Peter Lineham, Peter Matheson, and Ruth Redpath for reading drafts and suggesting many improvements.

Amongst librarians, Lawrence McIntosh has been without peer in his assistance, but I have been greatly helped by Stephen Connelly, library staff in the Joint Theological Library, Parkville; the Hewitson Library, Dunedin; the Mollison Library, Parkville; Moore College, Sydney; St Mark's, Canberra; and St John's College, Auckland. The archives and rare book collections of the various state libraries in Australia, the National Library in Canberra, the Turnbull and Hocken Libraries in Wellington and Dunedin have been invaluable, as have the archives of the Uniting Church in Darwin, Melbourne, and Sydney, the Anglican archives in Brisbane, Sydney, and Melbourne, and the Lutheran archives in Lae and Neuendetteslau.

The University of Melbourne provided a Small Research Grant, in addition to the leave granted by the Theological Hall and its generous financial assistance for typing by Mrs S. Simpson and Ms S. Tashkoff. I wish also to thank the Humanities Division of Oxford University Press for their editorial help. Ann Marie Philpott indexed.

I also wish to thank the following for copyright permissions. Some have been impossible to trace.

Anglican Church, Papua New Guinea: 'Papua New Guinea:

Anglican dioceses'

Anglican Media: 'Australia: Anglican dioceses' (permission Angela Grutzner)

Cartography Unit, Australian National University: 'Fiji'

Christian Research Association: 'Australia: Origins of Pentecostal affiliates'; 'Australia: The religious "nones"'

E. J. Dwyer: 'Australia: Catholic dioceses'

Her Britannic Majesty's Stationery Office: maps of the Pacific Islands

Institute for Pacific Studies: 'Cook Islands' and 'French Polynesia'

National Church Life Survey: 'Australian weekly attendance at church'

Open Book Publishers: 'Early Christian missions, Papua New Guinea'

Roman Catholic Church, Papua New Guinea: 'Papua New Guinea Roman Catholic dioceses'

United Church, Papua New Guinea: 'Papua New Guinea and Solomon Islands: United Church Regions'

Uniting Education: 'Samoa'

Vision New Zealand: 'New Zealand: who goes where'; 'New Zealand: No religion/not stated'; 'New Zealand: Major denominations' changing affiliation, 1956–96'

Fr Wiltgen: 'Australia: Vicariates Apostolic, 1842'

CONTENTS

MAPS, FIGURES, AND TABLES

MAPS

FIGURES

TABLES

ABBREVIATIONS

ABM	Australian Board of Missions
ACS	*Australian Cultural Studies*
ACQ/CQ	*Anglican Church Quarterly/Church Quarterly*
ACR	*Australasian Catholic Record*
ADB	*Australian Dictionary of Biography*
AHS	*Australian Historical Studies*
AJL	*Australian Journal of Liturgy*
ARSR	*Australian Religion Studies Review*
BCHS	Brisbane Catholic Historical Society
CBRFJ	*Christian Brethren Research Fellowship Journal*
CIM	China Inland Mission
CMS	Church Missionary Society
GANZ	General Assembly of the Presbyterian Church of New Zealand
GAQ	General Assembly of Queensland
GSA	General Synod Australia
GSNZ	General Synod New Zealand
JACHS	*Journal of the Australian Catholic Historical Society*
JHSSA	*Journal of the Historical Society of South Australia*
JPH	*Journal of Pacific History*
JPS	*Journal of the Polynesian Society*
JRAHS	*Journal of the Royal Australian Historical Society*
JRH	*Journal of Religious History*
JRHSQ	*Journal of the Royal Historical Society, Queensland*
LMS	London Missionary Society
LMS Chronicle	*London Missionary Society Chronicle*
MLS	Mitchell Library, Sydney
NZJH	*New Zealand Journal of History*
NZMW	*Neue Zeitschrift für Missionswissenschaft*
PCNZ	Presbyterian Church of New Zealand
PS	*Pacific Studies*

PUCHSV	*Proceedings of the Uniting Church Historical Society, Victoria*
SCH	*Studies in Cultural History*
SMH	*Sydney Morning Herald*
SMR	*St Mark's Review*
SPG	Society for the Propagation of the Gospel
SPJMS	*South Pacific Journal of Mission Studies*
SSEM	South Seas Evangelical Mission
SVD	Societas Verbum Divini
TOP	*Trinity Occasional Papers*
TPNZI	*Transactions and Proceedings of the New Zealand Institute*
UCA	Uniting Church in Australia
UCNA	United Church of North Australia
UCS	*Uniting Church Studies*
ZMW	*Zeitschrift für Missionswissenschaft*
ZMRW	*Zeitschrift für Missions und Religionswissenschaft*

FROM MISSIONS
TO CHURCHES

The expansion of Christianity into the Pacific Islands, Australia, and New Zealand is inseparable from the colonial expansion of the Spanish, British, French, and Germans. On 15 July 1681, the Apostolic Prefecture of Terra Australis was established in Manila with Fr Vittorio Riccio OP as the first appointee. He died in 1685 before taking any initiative. This is a reminder that boundaries were created by Europeans which bore no relation to cultural and linguistic realities.[1] The papacy had noted the discovery of unevangelized islands in the Pacific, but the French Revolution and Napoleonic Wars had prevented any action until Propaganda Fide was revived by Cardinal Bartolomeo Cappellari, prior to his election as Pope Gregory XVI in 1831. Rome had a long missionary history but France and Germany in the nineteenth and twentieth centuries provided the dynamism, previously given by Spain and Portugal, for missions to the heathens. Large numbers of new congregations and institutes were founded such as the Congregation of the Sacred Hearts of Jesus and Mary, the Marists, and the Society of the Divine Word.

Roman Catholics had long experience in converting peoples from other religions and providing them with the necessary instruction to make a transition to life in the Church. They understood the importance of what is now called enculturating Christianity. While certain aspects of converts' previous religious culture were rejected, great care was taken to ensure that recognizable continuities made growth into Christian community life an attractive alternative. Some of the realities of change were brutal, when they were linked with conquest, but the development of churches created possibilities for construction of a new culture. Protestants did not have the same heritage to draw

---

[1] J. Dunmore, *Visions and Realities* (Waikanae, 1997); W. P. Morrell, *Britain in the Pacific Islands* (Oxford, 1960); R. Wiltgen, *The Founding of the Roman Catholic Church in Oceania* (Canberra, 1979) 1–88; B. Stanley, *The Bible and the Flag* (Leicester, 1990); A. Walls, *The Missionary Movement in Christian History* (Maryknoll, 1996).

on. Learning how to develop churches in the Pacific was full of trial and error, especially in the first missionary decades. This chapter explores that process.

Missionary service was a very masculine activity to begin with. Women religious were not expected to be missionary pioneers. Protestant societies were initially not prepared to send young women, even as wives. That changed as experience showed that married men were much more stable. Many of those recruited were not ordained to ministry, had very limited education, but satisfied their employers that they had the required spiritual maturity and insight, as well as practical skills. Millennial evangelical optimism led them to believe that conversion of the heathen would be rapid. They had no notion of how difficult it would be to gain fluency in unknown languages, or how powerful cultural barriers would prove. They believed implicitly that unless the heathen were converted, they were condemned to eternal damnation. They were optimistic because Christianity, which is, in 'every sense of the word, the religion of civilisation, has gone forth among them, attended by literature and the arts and it is not possible that she should not eventually be triumphant over all the ignorance, prejudice, with which she has here to contend'.[2]

Missionaries often confused Christianity and their own culture. They assumed that the only way for other peoples to become Christian was to accept a total religious and cultural package.[3] In some regions that pattern lasted for generations. Local Christians then began to make changes, once missionary presence thinned out. Missionary dismay was moderated by the increasing conviction amongst both Protestants and Roman Catholics that missions must become indigenous and self-supporting churches, rather than remaining under permanent tutelage. Many of the earliest sources about the process of conversion were written by missionaries who gave a Eurocentric shape to historical narrative, which is now being challenged by Islanders well versed in their own heritage.[4]

Reports from native catechists and teachers were rarely kept, even when they were sent to mission headquarters. Those writings that

---

[2] M. Russell, *Polynesia and New Zealand* (Edinburgh, 1843) 372–3.
[3] J. Samson, *Victorian Mission Ethnography* (Cambridge, 1996).
[4] C. W. Newbury (ed.), *The History of the Tahitian Mission* (Cambridge, 1959). Dr U. F. Nokise has shown that, with his study of Samoan missionaries, 'The role of the London Missionary Society Samoan missionaries in the evangelisation of the South West Pacific', Ph.D. thesis (Canberra, 1992); D. Munro, and A. Thornley (eds.), *The Covenant Makers* (Suva, 1996).

Society Islands (1943). The small uninhabited islands of Mopihaa, Fenua Ura, and Motu One, lying well to the west, have been omitted. Based on Admiralty chart no. 767. (*Source:* Naval Intelligence Division, British Admiralty, *Pacific Islands*, 5 vols., London, 1939–45, vol. 2, pp. 130. © British Crown Copyright/MOD. Reproduced with the permission of Her Britannic Majesty's Stationery Office.)

remained in villages usually perished through damp, insects, rodents, or carelessness. Reading between the lines, to deconstruct missionary diaries, letters and reports, and books, requires considerable skill, and empathy for local culture. Over the last fifty years an increasing number of such studies have been written, as Christians recognize that the history of an indigenous church is based on different priorities and questions than the writing of a mission history.

The contrast is vividly seen when the writings of the London Missionary Society (LMS) missionaries in Tahiti, who landed in 1797, are compared with the reflections of Tahitian Christians on their bicentenary in 1997.[5] Sensitivity about the importance of distinguishing between Gospel and culture has grown in countries which historically were the senders of missionaries. International migration has not only brought large numbers from the great world religions into the heartlands of Christianity in Europe and North America, but also members from newer churches which are now independent. They express a distinctive voice outside their own homeland, and have helped sending churches to understand that mission and being Christ's Church are inseparable.

[5] Église Évangélique de Polynésie Française, *1797–1997. Une Vie Polynésie* (Papeete, 1997).

ABORIGINES AND EUROPEANS

The story of these developments of Christianity must begin chrono-logically in Australia where the first religious contacts occurred. There convict beginnings and British cultural blindness made mutual religious learning between Aborigines and invaders all but impossible. Two centuries later, there are encouraging signs that Aboriginal and migrant Christianities are at last discovering one another, so that the churches can contribute to a pluralist nation with an important enculturated Christian heritage.

The encounter of Aborigines with the British settlers in New South Wales from 1788, and then in Van Diemen's Land, was largely a story of exploitation and catastrophe, relieved occasionally by hints of partnership which never matured.[6] Population estimates vary widely, but there may have been a quarter to half a million people scattered over the continent. They were changing internally, not frozen in a time warp. In northern Australia there were regular contacts with Macassan fishermen and traders, including some intermarriage. Though most Aboriginal communities were accustomed to using stone, bone, and wooden tools and weapons, they quickly adopted Asian and European technology, prizing metal and glass.

The term 'Aborigine' should not be taken to mean a sameness across the continent, any more than calling someone a 'European' excludes the cultural and linguistic variety of a Russian and a Belgian. There is no national indigenous term acceptable to all Aborigines. Tribal names have to be used for precision. For many early settlers, Aborigines looked the same, and appeared to live the same hunter-gatherer lifestyle. In reality, tribes saw themselves as very different. They were very fearful when they moved outside their traditional lands, except on very carefully defined trading and ceremonial occasions. Differences in climate, geography, flora, and fauna imposed their own constraints, but it is clear that Aborigines had considerable skill in using fire to keep a balance of grassland and forest, which aided their hunt-ing and harvesting of seasonal foods. Complex fish traps and beauti-fully crafted spears and boomerangs indicated highly developed craft skills. Their skill in bushcraft and tracking was enhanced by unusually

---

[6] J. Harris, *One Blood* (Sydney, 1990) 19–144; H. Reynolds, *This Whispering in our Hearts* (Sydney, 1998); L. Ryan, *Aboriginal Tasmanians*, 2nd edn. (Sydney, 1996).

sharp observation, long-distance vision, and great powers of physical endurance.

Distance and different languages ensured that they did not develop large-scale political alliances and confederations like Polynesians. They developed small-scale communities in which elders were the guardians of law and lore. Their poetry and mythology were astonishingly rich.[7] Tragically, much has been lost, because European settlers destroyed so many tribal communities that hundreds of the *c.*500 languages have died out, with their heritage lost for ever. By 1850, only *c.*10,000 Aborigines were left in New South Wales and Victoria. Few early settlers successfully learned an Aboriginal language. The first serious books like R. B. Smyth's *The Aborigines of Victoria* did not appear until 1876. Religion and mythology were closely bound together in complex and arcane initiation rites, which made sacred knowledge largely inaccessible to curious and interested Europeans.[8] Some were fobbed off with information which was not of real significance.

Many European observers concluded that the Aborigines were so primitive they did not even have a religion. For the Wesleyan James Dredge in Victoria, 'The awful predominance amongst them of sins of the most obscene and revolting description . . . demonstrates that they are without God in the world.' In 1805, Te Pahi, a Maori chief from the Bay of Islands, New Zealand, found Aborigines contemptible because of their nakedness, and their refusal swiftly to dispatch their enemies.[9] It was culturally impossible for most Europeans to move outside their ideas of religion as public and book-related, to understand that Aborigines had a vastly different understanding of the sacred. Equally it was very difficult for Aborigines to understand the invaders' strange new religion. Nevertheless, there is fascinating evidence that they soon adapted religious ideas. Missionaries' reports of Aboriginal questions indicate sharp minds at work, but the cultural mores of the invaders were repulsive at many points to Aborigines. There were no mass conversions comparable to those in Polynesia by the end of the 1820s. Aborigines soon learned that the invaders had weapons and techniques which made them dangerous enemies, without in any way fitting into the conventions of Aboriginal clan warfare.

[7] T. Swain, *A Place for Strangers* (Melbourne, 1993).

[8] T. Swain, *Interpreting Aboriginal Religion* (Adelaide, 1985); W. Stanner, *On Aboriginal Religion* (Sydney, 1959–61); E. Kolig, *The Silent Revolution* (Philadelphia, 1981).

[9] J. Dredge, *Notices of the Aborigines of New South Wales* (Geelong, 1845) 11.

In addition, the Europeans brought diseases to which Aborigines had no resistance, nor knowledge of the rudimentary treatment which could be given to measles, influenza, and various intestinal disorders. All were helpless before smallpox, cholera, typhoid, and tuberculosis. The British government of George III attempted to lay down guidelines for the administrators of New South Wales to promote Christian religion and education of the natives. They included recognition of the free enjoyment of their possessions, their conversion and advancement in civilization, and the need for justice, but did not take into account the brutality of the military government, and the convicts starved of sexual outlets. Nevertheless, the 1837 British Parliamentary Select Committee on Aborigines showed continuing concern for their territorial rights, warning against violence or oppression in taking land.[10] Attempts to found schools for Aboriginal children, in accord with government policy, failed because of deep cultural differences, and the slight interest Aborigines showed in the value of literacy.

Richard Johnson, the first convict chaplain in New South Wales, took some interest in the welfare and conversion of Aborigines, but his other duties made sustained missionary work impossible. His work with Aborigines bore no fruit. Samuel Marsden, Johnson's successor, was a strong advocate of missions and adopted a boy called Tristan, who lived with their family for 13 years, but fitted neither the new society nor his own. Marsden also employed some Aboriginal servants, persuaded that this would open them to the civilizing influences which he believed should precede acceptance of the Gospel. His gesture failed, and the servants returned to their nomadic life-style. Increasingly, he came to believe that there was little point in attempting to evangelize Aborigines. The Church Missionary Society (CMS) eventually sent missionaries to work in the Wellington area of New South Wales in 1832. Personal rivalries did not help, but their territory was constantly invaded by men in search of sexual favours, or anxious to sell liquor and tobacco to the mission community. Farmers tried to get Aborigines to work for them as casual labourers, which was often more attractive than the regular discipline of work on the mission. Eventually, in 1843, the missionaries gave up, and their small Christian community vanished.

William Walker was appointed by the Wesleyans to work amongst

---

[10] H. Reynolds, *Dispossession* (Sydney, 1989); *The Fate of a Free People* (Melbourne, 1995); *Aboriginal Sovereignty* (Sydney, 1996).

Sydney Aborigines in 1821. He was the most successful of the early missionaries and was persuaded that two young men were ready to be baptized. The son of Bennelong, a local leader, was given the baptismal names of Thomas Walker Coke, a successful Methodist missionary, in the hope that he might become a missionary to his own people. Unfortunately, he was carried off by illness. Walker fell out with Marsden, and the Wesleyans, and was regularly attacked in Sydney papers. The Methodists dismissed him in 1826. This small beginning joined the list of failures.[11] The only other baptisms were by Father J. J. Therry, which were not followed up. A number of Aborigines learned something of Christianity, but sadly were not deemed worthy of baptism, because they did not reach missionary standards of Christianity.

This failure occurred when Polynesians were becoming Christians in their thousands, and building strong Christian communities under missionary guidance. Added to the racist ideas which were common in New South Wales, the brief episode of resistance there, led by Pemelwuy, who showed considerable guerrilla skills, aroused great fear among outlying settlers. This enhanced settler suspicion of blacks, and justified for many the appalling massacre of twenty-eight Aborigines at Myall Creek in 1838. It was remarkable that the murderers were brought to justice and executed in November, for public opinion was in their favour, but the Catholic Attorney-General, John Henry Plunkett, insisted on a second trial, after they were initially acquitted.

It was extremely difficult for Aborigines to defend their territories against white incursions. They had few legal rights in courts, and could not serve on juries, for they could not swear on the Bible, let alone follow legal argument. They had little to trade, and thus were precluded from buying muskets, in contrast with the Maori. Aborigines were also not easily gathered into coalitions to resist invaders. Nor did they have the skills like the Maori to build forts able to withstand not only muskets but also cannon. Their patterns of leadership were local and familial, and not easily developed into the kind of generalship and diplomacy practised by the greatest Maori *rangatira*. Many settlers looked forward to their dying out as soon as possible, and sought to assist this by organizing hunting parties.

In Van Diemen's Land, settled from 1803, another guerilla leader nicknamed 'Mosquito' harried and occasionally killed outlying

[11] Harris, *One Blood*, 47–51.

settlers, but was unable to prevent constant British expansion into Aboriginal territory.[12] Colonial Office humanitarian admonitions were powerless against land hunger and racism in the migrant communities. Appalling and inhuman behaviour, which can only be called genocide, characterized settlement in Tasmania. The numbers of Aborigines steadily diminished, and the attempt by the Evangelical Governor Arthur to sweep the island in late 1830 and eliminate any threat to settlers yielded little, despite the expense. Survivors were exiled to Flinders Island in 1831. Others survived in sealing communities. Missionary work was virtually non-existent, and the absence of any clergy or lay advocacy for Aborigines was a silent testimony to the power of racism at every level of Tasmanian society. Officially, the Pallawa died out with the death of Truganini in 1876. Not until the 1980s did their descendants begin to have land claims and identity recognized.[13]

In Victoria, illegal development of a new frontier by Tasmanian pastoralists, like the Henty family at Portland from 1834, promised a repeat performance of what had already happened across Bass Strait.[14] At Port Phillip, John Batman 'purchased' a huge area of land for a few tools and garments. Though his purchase was disallowed because the Crown preferred to monopolize the proceeds of land sales, it was a sign that some settlers were willing at least to use the rhetoric of a treaty, rather than simply assert the right of possession on the grounds that the land had no owners, and was unoccupied. Most others simply killed Aborigines, and took the land for sheep. Once again, humanitarian influences were present, but Protectors had little impact. Buntingdale, a Wesleyan settlement near Geelong, lasted until 1848, but collapsed because of missionary differences, Aborigines' dislike of confinement, and settler hostility. The rapacity of colonists, for grazing land and quick profits, soon ensured that the Aborigines were driven off their traditional lands, deprived of the freedom to hunt, and excluded from access to water and sacred sites, despite government pastoral leases which explicitly safeguarded such rights.

The British settlement at Swan River in Western Australia, founded in 1829, saw a repetition of the same patterns of misunderstanding, racism, and murder of Aborigines for the sake of peace and land for

---

[12] N. J. B. Plomley, *The Aboriginal/Settler Clash in Van Diemen's Land, 1803–31* (Hobart, 1992).

[13] L. Ryan, *Aboriginal Tasmanians*, 263–89; Harris, *One Blood*, 86–100.

[14] Harris, ibid., 126–38

settlers.[15] Aboriginal resistance was crushed by 1838. Though Western Australia had only a tiny British population, some settlers were interested in the spiritual welfare of the surviving Aborigines. The Wesleyans found it difficult to get any missionary to come to such an isolated part of the Empire, but to their credit, they kept up pressure on London both to have someone to minister to them, and also to work amongst the Aborigines. John Smithies arrived in 1840 and ran a successful school for a time. Like other missionaries, John Smithies found deaths of promising protegées hard to explain. Captain Frederick Irwin, a strong Evangelical who was briefly Deputy-Governor, used his connections in Glasgow and Dublin to have a missionary sent. Dr Louis Giustiniani proved too much for the Anglican elite of the colony. Not only was he an Italian convert, but he speedily established a reputation for Aboriginal advocacy which was most unwelcome to those who saw 'clearing' Aborigines as essential to the struggling colony's prosperity. He named people to the Colonial Office in 1838. Settlers did not object to limited charity for the deserving Aborigines, so long as they did not expect equal rights before the law, or security of title on desirable land.

A different path was later followed by the Spanish Benedictines, led by Bishops Salvado and Serra, who created a community north of Perth at New Norcia in 1847.[16] While both shared common assumptions about European superiority, they had a rare empathy for Aborigines, carefully and thoughtfully observed their customs and culture, and imparted European skills to their people. The standards of education reached by a number of their pupils enabled two of them to go to Italy to study for the priesthood. It was a tragedy that both died, unable to resist European diseases. Salvado's work, despite its paternalism, showed what might be accomplished with long-term and deep personal commitment. He even had a good Aboriginal cricket team, a remarkable achievement considering Spanish ignorance of the game. These missions everywhere had failed to create churches, but Aboriginal religions appear to have changed significantly in some regions.[17]

---

[15] Ibid., 255–81; W. McNair and H. Rumley (eds.), *Pioneer Aboriginal Mission* (Perth, 1981).

[16] Harris, *One Blood*, 281–306; E. J. Stormon (ed.), *The Salvado Memoirs* (Perth, 1977).

[17] Harris, *One Blood*, 126–38 analyses the failures. Swain, *Place for Strangers*, shows that Melanesians, Indonesians, and Europeans all contributed to such developments. Aboriginal communities were never static.

COLONIZATION AND RELIGION

Christianity's future in Australia lay rather in the development of the colonists' churches. Aboriginal Christians were too few to shape the churches of their conquerors. Occasional signs of humanitarian initiatives showed that the campaign against slavery, the ideals of some British public figures, and the policy of the Colonial Office (largely ignored by colonial administrators) were not entirely forgotten, alongside the general racism and popular mythology of peaceful expansion in an empty and undeveloped continent that had been given to the British by a beneficent providence to civilize and Christianize.

Such civilizing can be seen in John Molloy and his talented wife, Georgiana, who arrived in Western Australia in March 1830.[18] He became magistrate at Augusta for nine demanding years, before moving onto land at Busselton. She had enjoyed a fascinating circle of friends before marriage and migration, including Edward Irving, John McLeod Campbell, Robert Story, and Alexander Scott, each of whom moved beyond the narrow bounds of the Calvinist Orthodoxy in Scotland. Her letters back to Scotland not only tell vividly of her struggles in Western Australia, but also of her keen interest in affairs back in Britain. She kept a strong tradition of family worship and Sabbath-keeping, founding and leading a small church, as well as having a deep interest in botany, which made her one of the most important early naturalists in Western Australia. One of her daughters, Sabina, was to marry Matthew Hale, the first Anglican Bishop of Perth, continuing the tradition of a cultivated and humane family life. Georgiana was also close friends with John Wollaston, one of the earliest Anglican clergy in Western Australia, who ministered to her in the period up to her death following complications from childbirth, giving her communion in a manner which showed that frontiers between denominations were not the barriers they often later became.

In New South Wales, Anglicanism was legally defined as the official religion on 26 January 1788 when Captain Arthur Phillip, the commandant, took an oath at the proclamation of the settlement to uphold the Protestant succession, and to reject popery, and transubstantiation. The oaths taken by officers to the Crown reflected

[18] W. J. Lines, *All Consuming Passion* (Sydney, 1994).

the fact that the United Kingdom of England, Scotland, and Ireland was Protestant by law. Political office, ordination, citizenship, and church membership were seen to be interrelated parts of the sacral and political order, along with public fasts, days of humiliation, and public prayers.

Though this sacral framework for community life tenuously existed in the convict colonies of Australia, some of the authorities and their families remembered that order, attended church parades, or read services from the *Book of Common Prayer* or the Catholic Missal to their family until congregations were established. Others used Sunday for socializing, drinking, gambling, and hunting. For convicts, church parades could be compulsory, for Sunday supposedly was a rest day, except for those on special punishments. Enforcement of attendance at worship was spasmodic, indeed impossible in outlying farms. London officials believed that religion was essential for social order and morality and set aside 400 acres of land for the maintenance of each minister. Their representatives in Australia did not interpret that public commitment too rigidly. The brutalizing of Christianity by its links with unjust laws and cruel punishments left a bitter legacy.[19]

Religion, at home or overseas, was not only a consciously chosen option, but also part of the cultural observance of rites of passage, explanation of the mysteries and tragedies of life, along with folk beliefs about fate and luck which contributed to popular religion. Most English and Scots were resolutely hostile to Roman Catholicism. Similarly, Irish Catholics regarded Protestants with deep distrust. Memories of persecution were embedded in folk memories, for British patriotism and Protestantism were inseparable. Many educated Britons were shocked at the excesses of the French Revolution, and saw the established churches as bulwarks against revolution. This view was often inseparable from class interest, for few of the ruling classes had any conscience about the oppression by which their position and power were sustained, and were fiercely resistant to any reformist challenges to their interests.

Impressive though the national churches were, with influence at every level of society and formidable social control, there were other currents flowing strongly. Dissenters were an economically important minority. In Ireland, Roman Catholicism was the majority religion, but had severe legal disadvantages. Many thousands had been touched

[19] R. Hughes, *The Fatal Shore* (London, 1988).

by the Methodist societies with their fervent commitment to new birth and vital religion.[20] By contrast, the established churches seemed cool, moralistic, and less interested in the spiritual and educational needs of the rapidly growing industrial towns and cities, in which refugees from enclosure, and those seeking to better their lot, lived in crowded and unsanitary housing. Disease, drunkenness, violence were symbols of an order which was breaking down and had not yet been remade. Terrible poverty, homelessness, hunger, and oppression were characteristic of urban communities where employment was fitful, and often dangerous to life and limb of adults and children alike. Life expectancy was short. Churches provided some resources for people who wanted to construct another social reality than that provided by the slums. Conversion was believed to be a key to living a new life, because it changed relations with God and other people. Its virtue applied among the heathen at home and abroad.

Evangelicals in Britain and North America were conscious of the large parts of the earth which were untouched by the Christian faith. In 1732, the Moravians in Saxony had been the first Protestants to take overseas missions seriously, though their impact was small compared with that of the missionary orders of the Roman Catholic Church. Hopes for a worldwide spiritual revival leading to Christ's second coming were strong among Evangelicals.[21] When government discussions about a penal colony in the Australian continent gained momentum in the wake of the loss of the American colonies, a small but influential group of Evangelicals brought pressure to bear on the British government to commission a chaplain in October 1786. They saw in this penal settlement a base for sending missionaries to Asia, and to the Pacific Islands which were just becoming known to the literate public because of the writings of explorers like Cook.

DENOMINATIONAL BEGINNINGS

Working with convicts did not offer much social prestige, but Richard Johnson, a Cambridge graduate, took the invitation seriously, and sailed with the first fleet to Sydney in 1787–8.[22] The Christianity of the

[20] M. Watts, *The Dissenters* (2 vols., Oxford, 1978–96); T. Larsen, *Friends of Religious Equality* (Woodbridge, 1999).
[21] W. R. Ward, *Protestant Evangelical Awakenings* (Cambridge, 1992).
[22] N. K. Macintosh, *Richard Johnson* (Sydney, 1978).

soldiers and officials sent to run the settlement did not shine brightly. The due observance of religion was conventional, focusing on correct doctrine, and political loyalty. Johnson held the first service on 3 February, near a spot now officially marked in Martin Place, Sydney. Johnson was treated very casually, even rudely, by the authorities. Providing for the due celebration of public worship was low on the list of their priorities. A church for worship seemed unimportant, when buildings needed to be provided for officials and convicts. Goods and services were short, and food often scarce. Johnson was given a block of land, but no labour to clear it. Nevertheless, he managed to become a successful small farmer. When there was any surplus, he generously shared. The distances he had to travel on foot, horse, or boat up to Parramatta were large, and the harsh climate took its toll on his health and energy. Services were held in the open air until Johnson, fed up with official delays, built a simple church/school with his own hands in 1792 which seated 500. That was soon burned down by disgruntled convicts, possibly by some who resented his magisterial sentences, though the offenders were never caught.

Neither he nor his successor, Marsden, communicated effectively with convict counter–culture. A significant percentage were Irish and Roman Catholic, including some highly educated political prisoners. Some Gaelic speakers could not understand English. Those who did were not disposed to listen to a Protestant telling them the way to heaven, and passively endured the compulsory services. In these early years we cannot speak of a church, only of a military chaplaincy which included limited pastoral care of convicts, some education, and the provision of last rites, plus regular services, mostly attended poorly. There was little time for education or working with those near to the end of their sentences to prepare them for a measure of freedom. Johnson was a solid preacher. Many of his sermons were on themes of divine judgement, which did not persuade those who had already experienced more than their fair share of human punishments, even though Prayer Book language reconnected some convicts to their Christian memories.

Though many of his flock were regarded by officials as beyond redemption, he visited them in their primitive huts, caring for the sick and dying. Little has survived to indicate what convicts thought about Christianity. Nor did many in authority leave journals or letters which illuminate their attitude to religion. Manning Clark's suggestion that the influence of the Enlightenment was strong is too flattering a judgement for soldiers and officials who read little, and whose interests centred on career and survival, rather than on the ideas which shaped the American and French Revolutions.[23] They were cynical conformists who did what had to be done in religious observance, and little more.

Scepticism about authority, a firm belief in the value of punishment of offenders, contempt for women, and a preoccupation with material gain characterized many colonial societies in their frontier period. These views were more strongly rooted in New South Wales and in Van Diemen's Land because of the sheer numbers of the convicts and emancipists (those who had served their sentence) in relation to total population. Until 1868 around 160,000 were transported, of whom almost a fifth were women. Feminist historians have argued that this distorted gender ratio, and the attitudes to women in this tragic period of Australia's history, continued to poison gender relations and family life into the twentieth century.[24] Other historians have suggested that scepticism about religion was deeply embedded in this segment of Australian society, and their descendants. That was little different from scepticism in the British lower classes.[25] Once free, some former prisoners were anxious to live a life unconstrained by rules and laws. Alcohol-induced euphoria was an escape route which many followed. The binge drinking of bush workers left a legacy which generations of socialization only partly tamed. Excessive drinking and gambling was not simply a lower-class phenomenon. It had regional origins in Britain. Elites could be just as destructive in their behaviour. Such *mores* have to be seen as part of wider cultural patterns, for they can also be seen amongst officials and convicts in New Caledonia.

Sexuality in Georgian and Victorian England was both indulged and closely restricted. Such ambivalent attitudes left deep imprints on Australian society at every level. The brutality of many sexual encounters in the convict period reflected life in the cities and prisons of England, as well as the exploitation of women, which was common in all classes. It was not distinctively Australian, but was vividly displayed amongst the convicts who escaped to Polynesian societies.

[23] C. M. H. Clark, *History of Australia* (6 vols., Melbourne, 1962–87) 1. 109.

[24] A. Summers, *Damned Whores and God's Police* (Melbourne, 1975); P. Grimshaw, et al., *Creating a New Nation* (Melbourne, 1994).

[25] Recent research has suggested that religion was deeply embedded in the United Kingdom even if it was not orthodox in terms of official formularies. S. Green, *Religion in the Age of Decline* (Cambridge, 1996); A. M. Grocott, *Convicts, Clergymen and Churches* (Sydney, 1980).

There the opportunities for exploitation were wide, and the demands of marriage and conformity not easily enforceable, for they did not fit within the rules of Polynesian behaviour. The gap between the ideals of Christian marriage, with all their limitations, and the long-term effects of extra-marital relationships where women were so few in number, and so highly in demand, took many generations to bridge.

The ecclesiastical authorities in Britain paid no attention to the shortage of clergy to do the necessary pastoral work in a penal colony. The responsibilities were unattractive, and almost certainly ruled out the possibilities of preferment if a chaplain returned to England. Johnson discovered that one could be forgotten both at home and abroad. Some of the chaplains like Marsden made the colony their home, founding dynasties on the wealth they accumulated by shrewd farming and land investments.[26] Most of the early chaplains were young Evangelicals with no patrons to provide comfortable livings, with slender education, and no social status.[27] The salary of a chaplain looked attractive, though the cost of living in New South Wales was in many respects higher than at home. Some clearly found chaplaincy offered more possibilities than the hazards of curacy in Britain with poor pay and little security. They enjoyed the challenges of the frontier.

Ministry to the free settlers was dominated by Evangelicals, beginning an ethos among significant groups of the laity in New South Wales and Van Diemen's Land, which was to make life hard for clergy who were seen as High Church. This Evangelical ethos was reinforced by the arrival of London Missionary Society refugees from Tahiti and Tonga in 1798.[28] Marsden was delighted to have their help with far-flung services and pastoral care. In turn, their energy and their freedom from association with the penal establishment made them acceptable to the slowly increasing numbers of free settlers, and to some emancipists. Though often Independents or Presbyterians, they had little difficulty adapting to Anglicanism, creating networks of Protestant co-operation which were to be an enduring feature of the colonies. Thomas, the son of Rowland Hassall, one of these refugees,

---

[26] A. T. Yarwood, *Samuel Marsden* (Melbourne, 1996).

[27] Robert Knopwood was an exception. His diary gives a vivid insight into his work in Hobart.

[28] G. L. Lockley, 'An estimation of the contribution made in New South Wales by missionaries of the London Missionary Society', MA thesis (Sydney, 1949); S. Piggin, *Evangelical Christianity in Australia* (Melbourne, 1996) 17–18.

became the first colonial to go to England to prepare at Lampeter for ordination. He returned to ministry in New South Wales in 1827.

Australian clergy had to possess a number of attributes which were not essential to success in Britain. Good birth, education, and even wealth were still needed for those who became archdeacons like Thomas Scott, William Broughton, and William Hutchins.[29] The clergy who gathered and planted enduring congregations often had humble origins, but had the physical toughness and endurance to cope with a severe climate, long distances, no roads, and the tasks of survival in the bush when snakes, fires, drought, and floods could make travel hazardous. Whether they walked or rode, they needed to cope with loneliness, have ability to meet all sorts of settlers, and willingness to adapt their convictions.[30]

In 1815 another strand of Evangelicalism arrived with Samuel Leigh, a Wesleyan missionary sent by Connexional authorities in London. Initially Governor Macquarie was annoyed, for he distrusted enthusiastic religion. Soon he was persuaded of Leigh's competence and integrity. So initially was Marsden. Some Methodists were not so sure. Leigh was not only responsible for gathering the small group of Methodists into classes, but also had been ordered to explore the possibilities of missionary work in Polynesia.[31] Marsden had begun work in New Zealand the previous year and was glad to share that field. Numbers in Sydney stayed pitifully small, making the authorities in London wonder about the competence of their agent, and the value of giving continued financial support. Some emancipists found Methodism a re-entry to free society, which was still very judgemental about the 'convict stain'.

Success gradually came with adaptable missionaries like Walter Lawry, who married Mary Hassall, and whose energy helped to create a credible Methodist cause, especially in Van Diemen's Land. Partnership in a common Christianity between Evangelical Christians saw the creation of various societies for moral and religious improvement. Business skills were needed to raise money, give publicity, and recruit supporters. Financing publication of Bibles, moral

[29] G. P. Shaw, *Patriarch and Patriot* (Melbourne, 1978); D. B. Clarke, *William Hutchins* (Hobart, 1986).

[30] R. S. M. Withycombe (ed.), *Anglican Ministry in Colonial Australia* (Canberra, 1993); *Anglican Ministry in Colonial Aotearoa–New Zealand* (Canberra, 1993); G. Strickland, *The Australian Pastor* (London, 1862) for an Anglican bush ministry.

[31] A. H. Wood, *Overseas Missions of the Australian Methodist Church* (5 vols., Melbourne, 1975–87) I. 20–1.

improvement, temperance, literacy, benevolence were amongst the objects covered by such societies. In addition, businesses like those founded by the Congregationalists John Fairfax and David Jones, which provided essential services to the small community in Sydney, were based on strong moral and religious convictions about the sacredness of daily work, and the importance of integrity in business.

The harsh environment shrivelled the faith and religious observance of many colonists. With some exaggeration, Alexander Harris claimed that 'The labouring population are universally lost to all sense of moral duty and religious obedience.'[32] It brought out the best in others and developed resourcefulness, generosity, and help to neighbours in ways that the settled environment of Britain could not. Indeed, the colony offered opportunity to talented but little-educated settlers to rise in the social scale, and to develop gifts that would have remained hidden at home, where there were already many to give that kind of moral and religious leadership.

The arrival of the Revd John Dunmore Lang in 1823 brought a different kind of Evangelical radicalism into the young colony.[33] From the Church of Scotland, Lang came to join members of his family who had already taken up land in the Hunter Valley. Initially, he hoped to create a congregation which included members both of the Church of Scotland and of groups which had broken away on issues of church–state relations, but his abrasive personality made that impossible. He had the financial resources to return to England, and successfully lobbied the Colonial Office for assistance in building a church, and in getting a government contribution to his stipend, after that had been rejected by Sydney officialdom.

Far better educated than most other clergy, he soon showed that he was a force to be reckoned with in every aspect of the colony's life. He had a vision for Australia as a new nation of the free, Protestant in religion, and democratic in government. His promotion of his new homeland ran to thousands of pages. He also wrote about New Zealand. As an editor and journalist, he gave no quarter, fought many libel suits, and was briefly jailed in 1850 for refusing to pay a fine.

Along with many others, Lang argued powerfully for the end of transportation of convicts, and the fostering of immigration of free

[32] A. Harris, *Settlers and Convicts* (Melbourne, 1953; first published 1847) 190 for the effect of Bible teaching. 'Their manners were altered, their very features seemed humanized.'

[33] D. W. A. Baker, *Preacher, Politician, Patriot* (Melbourne, 1998); A. Gilchrist (ed.), *John Dunmore Lang* (Melbourne, 1951).

settlers with the skills needed for the colony's development. Distinguishing between public money and family funds was not Lang's strong point. Considerable criticism was the result, though there is no evidence that he personally profited. In addition to his many public activities, which included election to the Legislative Council in 1843 for Port Phillip and Moreton Bay, and frequent trips to Britain, he was an energetic pastor to his people at Scots Church, though his sermons often shared the faults of his writing—repetition, wordiness, and denunciation of his enemies. The latter were numerous, but some had a grudging respect for his adversarial powers. He dominated early Presbyterianism, leaving a legacy of division and quarrelsomeness which outlived him, but, with Bishops Polding and Broughton, he was one of the dominant forces in both religion and the public forum.

Thomas Scott, the first Anglican archdeacon, was a well-educated clergyman who had served as secretary to the Bigge Commission, which made important recommendations about New South Wales's future in 1822–3. Scott's lack of experience of leadership, and his inability to work with New South Wales clergy of churchmanship different from his own, limited his usefulness in his four years of office from 1825 to 1828, as did his political ineptitude in robust local politics. Marsden had pioneered the development of a church, but Scott set up the beginnings of an education and parochial system which his successor, Broughton, effectively built on. On his way home to England, he stopped in Perth, and was well-regarded for his work.[34]

The beginnings of Roman Catholicism in Australia were much more troubled than for pioneer Protestants, because of the heavily discriminatory legislation of the Penal Code in England and Ireland, the severe disadvantages stemming from the absence of bishops, and prohibitions of various activities in education and politics. English Catholicism was inward-looking and aristocratic, with little concern for co-religionists in Ireland.[35] Levels of religious ignorance were high there, but Catholic loyalty was socially deeply embedded, even if practice was erratic.[36] Catholics were resistant to any hint of Protestant proselytism, though the co-operation of Catholics and Protestants in

---

[34] His *Letters* to the Revd F. Wilkinson in 1829 give useful insight into the life of clergy. *Despatches of Governor Darling* No. 21, 11 Feb. 1831, 848–9, 855–61, Mitchell MS.

[35] J. Bossy, *The English Catholic Community* (London, 1975) 323–33.

[36] D. Fitzpatrick (ed.), *Oceans of Consolation* (Melbourne, 1995); N. Turner, *Catholics in Australia* (Melbourne, 1992) 1. 29–51.

the risings of 1798 indicated that national identity could bring them together, as did celebration on St Patrick's Day.[37]

Catholic authorities in England and Ireland were not interested in convict well-being. The Protestant authorities rejected early requests in 1792 and 1796 to send priests as chaplains. Early settlers, like James Dempsey, a lay Carmelite, held simple services, and ministered to the sick and dying in their homes. Others prayed privately in places where they would be unobserved and so avoid ridicule.[38] One of the most moving early requests for help is found in a letter from Michael Hayes to his brother, a Franciscan priest in Rome.[39] Nothing happened. Some priests had been sentenced for alleged rebellion, but they could do little to meet the spiritual needs of their convict colleagues. When Fr James Dixon was permitted to hold services in 1803, some of the Irish convicts used that as cover to plan an uprising in March 1804. That confirmed the worst fears of the Protestant authorities, who were suspicious that Catholics were inevitably traitors.

Fr Jeremiah O'Flynn, who arrived in 1817, approved by Rome, appears to have also deceived the authorities about having official British credentials. When it ultimately became clear that he could not produce them, he went into hiding, but was then deported in 1818, apparently leaving the Blessed Sacrament at the Dempsey house. Such events fed religious myths about Protestant oppression, and Catholic deceit. Finally, Governor Macquarie recognized that it was both impractical and unjust to deny Irish Catholics the consolations of religion, especially at death. The result was that in 1820 the British government approved the appointment of Catholic convict chaplains.

In the absence of effective oversight, some early chaplains, like John Joseph Therry and Philip Connolly, who came in 1820, were involved in long quarrels with parishioners, and each other. There were disputes over money. Some of the chaplains were too inclined to seek the solace of alcohol. Most were deeply respected for their pastoral work, going out in all weather to attend to crises. Therry and John MacEnroe could be storm centres. At times, the Catholic community, of 15,000 in 1820, was sharply divided, for Therry's actions were divisive and authoritarian. That could be tolerated by emancipists and convicts, but was unacceptable to many free colonists, especially those with some status in the colony, who found their priests' actions very

---

[37] P. O'Farrell, *Vanished Kingdoms* (Sydney, 1990).
[38] E. Campion, *Australian Catholics* (Melbourne, 1987) 4–9.
[39] Turner, *Catholics in Australia*, 1. 41.

difficult to put up with.[40] They welcomed the establishment of a hierarchy.

Though the settler churches were short of ministers and priests, and had a small membership with straitened financial resources, they had laid important foundations for future expansion.[41] The seating of congregations strictly reflected the social order. In St Paul's, Cobbity, pews cost three shillings and ninepence a seat, but forms were fivepence a year. This supplemented income from 200 acres of glebe. Some fine Anglican buildings, like St James's, Sydney, and St Matthew's at Windsor, had been erected by convict labour by the early 1830s. St James's even had a paid choir, though it could not rival the sound of the Catholic choir and band in the nearby Castlereagh Street schoolroom. Energetic and committed laity expected to be thoroughly consulted about finance and policy, but ministry to the convict majority of the population was largely a failure, if success was measured by changed lives, and active participation in worship.

Though these small denominational bodies were replicas of their parent bodies in Britain and Europe, with the same cultural limitations, the social climate made possible limited co-operation beyond what was occurring in the British Isles. A stronger lay leadership developed than was possible where clergy had secure social status, and were constitutionally accountable to colleagues and superiors. Relationships with colonial authorities were also, of necessity, much closer than with government in Britain, because of the small size of communities, and the emergence of a more democratic and egalitarian temper which limited possibilities for social distance. Whether welcomed or not, the churches were a significant part of the colony's public life, and contributed substantially to the development of a free citizenry.

THE AUSTRALASIAN REGION

In the nineteenth century the term 'Australasia' was sometimes used of the Australian and New Zealand colonies. It also included neighbouring Pacific Islands, especially those which were within the spheres of

[40] Turner, *Catholics in Australia*, 1. 41. Dempsey's letters to Therry reprinted in P. Chandler, *Lay Carmelites* (Rome, 1985).

[41] I. Breward, *A History of the Australian Churches* (Sydney, 1993); R. Thompson, *Religion in Australia* (Melbourne, 1994); J. Woolmington, *Religion in Early Australia* (Sydney, 1976); J. D. Bollen, *Australian Baptists* (London, 1977).

influence of these British outposts. For convenience, this shorthand regional label has been taken to include French territories, but not Irian Jaya, despite the fact that this is culturally part of Melanesia. The terms Melanesia, Micronesia, Oceania, and Polynesia all reflect Europeans' perceptions, imposed in a misleadingly unitive way. The term 'Australasia' does not include the Polynesian and Micronesian islands north of the equator, despite the links of some of these islands with Samoa, and the European forms of Christianity which also shaped the islands to the south. Though there are common linkages, there is also astonishing variety. Many islanders resent being given an identity constructed by outsiders which makes them part of a wider reality to which they feel no allegiance, but Australasia is a useful label.

The origins and datings of the migrations to the region are still debated. The navigation involved is astonishing, and still only imperfectly understood. Archaeologists have only explored a few sites, but the current consensus suggests migration when Australasia included a much larger land mass 40–60,000 years ago, making sea crossings relatively simple. There is currently a lively debate about the dating of new finds in Australia, with some suggesting a date of 100,000 years ago for settlement. Settlement in Papua New Guinea may date back 40–60,000 years, while in New Ireland it appears to be 33,000 years ago. Proto-Polynesian migration along the sailing corridor began almost 4,000 years ago through New Britain to Fiji, Tonga, and Samoa around 1500-1000 BCE, judging by distribution of Lapita pottery. Major voyages appear to have ended by the sixteenth century.[42] Heyerdahl's and Langdon's theory of migration and Spanish influence from South America cannot be entirely ruled out, for the *kumara* (or sweet potato) could not have swum unaided to Polynesia. South East Asia appears a more likely major source of migration.

Linguistic similarities stretch across Polynesia, the Philippines, Indonesia, and Malaysia, to Madagascar. Melanesia and Australia have an astonishing variety of languages, falling into two groups labelled Austronesian and non-Austronesian, with little relation to the Polynesian-Malay family. Migration to the north of New Zealand occurred from the eleventh to the thirteenth centuries, moving into

---

[42] J. Golson (ed.), *Polynesian Navigation* (Wellington, 1972) must be complemented by G. Irwin, *The Prehistoric Exploration and Colonisation of the Pacific* (Melbourne, 1992); *The Cambridge History of Pacific Islanders*, ch. 2, discusses the complex archaeological and linguistic evidence; M. Spriggs, 'Pacific archaeologies: contested ground in the construction of Pacific history', *JPH* 34 (1999) 109–22.

the southern islands by the twelfth century. The theory of a great fleet is rejected. Linguistic similarities between the Cook Islands, French Polynesia, and New Zealand suggest that at least some of the migrants had their origins in the two former groups.[43] A protein-rich diet ensured rapid population growth. Polynesian navigators certainly had the skills to make return journeys across vast expanses of ocean. These migrations helped to explain the cultural unity of the societies encountered by the first explorers and missionaries.

The Polynesian communities which were reached by European sailors from the sixteenth century onwards proved well able to adapt to the newcomers, and the advantages of metal-based technology over traditional tools of wood, stone, and bone.[44] They had highly organized tribal communities, and a rich mythology and religious life. Even though some communities were ravaged by European diseases, Polynesians were convinced of their superiority to the incomers, and were skilled at managing change on their own terms. Even more important was their skill at adapting European weapons to pursue internal wars, extend political power, and repel incursions. The diseases, smallness, and isolation of many Melanesian and Polynesian islands did not make them attractive for European settlement. Spanish attempts at colonization in the Solomon Islands in the late sixteenth century were defeated by disease, Islander hostility, and poor planning.

Polynesians had a pantheon of deities who ensured social harmony, adequate food supplies, defence from enemies, and healing within a framework of cosmic meaning.[45] Every part of life was interrelated with spiritual reality. Complex rituals existed to ensure that the sacred and the common were rightly related. Chiefs and priests focused sacred power (*mana*) and there were strict rules to ensure that their power was not defiled by contact with what was common (*noa*). Breaking the boundaries of the sacred (*tapu*) was as dangerous to the whole community as to the individual who transgressed. Death was the almost certain outcome.

A large body of complex mythology was handed on orally, and

---

[43] Irwin, *Prehistoric Exploration*, 214–15; J. Davidson, *The Prehistory of New Zealand* (Auckland, 1984).

[44] P. Bellwood, *The Polynesians* (London, 1978); D. Teilhet (ed.), *Dimensions of Polynesia* (San Diego, 1973).

[45] R. W. Williamson, *The Religion and Cosmic Beliefs of Central Polynesia* (Cambridge, 1933); E. S. C. Handy, *Polynesian Religion* (Honolulu, 1927); J. Siikala, *Cult and Conflict in Tropical Polynesia* (Helsinki, 1982); H. Nevermann, *Götter der Südsee* (Stuttgart, 1977).

celebrated in song, dance, oratory, and sacred objects. The stories of the gods offered important clues to Islander worldviews, but few missionaries took advantage of such connections because their theology precluded linkages with traditional religion. In some islands, the *marae* was a sacred space for the performance of essential rites, which could include human sacrifice.[46] War often led to the eating of enemies in order to defile them, or to absorb their *mana*. Enslavement was a living death which reduced one to the status of a non-person.

Polynesian religion shaped both personality and community, but was not static. Contact with Europeans demonstrated the ability of religious leaders to adapt their cult by incorporating elements from Christianity. Missionaries did not explore Polynesian religion with the same depth as the Baptists in India, such as William Carey, explored Hinduism.[47] The absence of sacred books, defined doctrine, or master-pieces of sacred architecture appeared to imply a religious system greatly inferior to Christianity, which could be entirely replaced without loss. Sacred objects were defiled, burnt, or sometimes sent back to Britain and France to museums, or kept to demonstrate the superiority of Christianity over heathenism.

For their part, Polynesians found Christianity hard to understand. Its invisible deity, who could neither be seen nor heard, simply did not fit their religious world of *atua*, who appeared, spoke, and acted predictably. Christian morality was puzzlingly restrictive, its worship strange, and its explanations of evil, hell, and disaster offensive. The idea of keeping sacred days, however, connected with traditional religion, as did daily prayer for blessing and guidance. The sacred book of the missionaries clearly had remarkable power. Desire for literacy was one of the major motives for experimenting with the new religion, whose God was clearly more powerful than their own gods in important areas like technology, war, and healing. The new religion provided an alternative language for religious aspirations, and provided for a new construction of religious and political community.

Missionaries also had much to learn about Polynesian religion, and the problems of communicating their own religion effectively. Sharp

---

[46] Teilhet, *Dimensions of Polynesia*, 38–47 for a discussion of religious sites and buildings in Polynesia.

[47] See, however, W. Ellis, *Polynesian Researches* (2 vols., London, 1831); W. W. Gill, *Gems from the Coral Islands* (London, 1866); W. T. Pritchard, *Polynesian Reminiscences* (London, 1866); G. Turner, *Nineteen Years in Polynesia* (London, 1861); J. Williams, *Narrative of Missionary Enterprises* (London, 1838).

dispute occurred over policy and methods for several decades.[48] The relationship between civilizing and evangelizing, translation methods, linguistic issues, testing conversion, pastoral policy in matters of marriage and sexuality, attitudes to traditional religion, all had to be discussed outside the framework of conventional Protestant wisdom, whereas Roman Catholics had a heritage of mission experience. The boards of the London Missionary Society (LMS) and the Wesleyan Methodists were quite out of touch with the realities faced by their employees, and were very authoritarian in dealing with problems. They were even more unrealistic in expecting speedy results for their investment. It was to take a generation of failure and tribulation before some religious movement towards Christianity was discernible, and a theology of mission across cultures slowly began to emerge among the missionaries.

The twenty-nine missionaries plus five wives who landed in Tahiti from the *Duff* in March 1797 were ill prepared for the culture shock which awaited them.[49] The population appears to have been approximately 60,000. The Maohi (the term for Tahitians) were bitterly disappointed by missionary poverty, and their interfering ways. The missionaries did not appreciate Maohi expectations, or how difficult it was going to be to learn a new language without any linguistic aids. They did not understand that the land at Matavai Bay ceded to them was given in expectation of reciprocal benefits. The unfortunate young men landed in the Marquesas were stunned when local women examined their sexual parts, for how could men fail to accept the customary offer of sexual hospitality? Those landed in Tonga found their situation impossible. Tribal wars, physical danger, missionary divisions, and inability to cope with isolation, all conspired to lead most of the initial party to sail gratefully to Sydney in 1798.

The small group which remained in Tahiti persevered with language study, even though they were regarded with a mixture of contempt and amusement by the Tahitians. They brought few of the

[48] Newbury, *History of the Tahitian Mission*, 150–1, 305 for examples; J. Nicole, *Au Pied de l'Écriture* (Papeete, 1988); J. Elder (ed.), *Marsden's Lieutenants* (Dunedin, 1934) 175–82 for Kendall and Marsden's differences in 1821–2; W. N. Gunson, *Messengers of Grace* (Melbourne, 1978) 195–214.

[49] J. Wilson, *A Missionary Voyage* (New York, n.d.) 410–20 for their Articles of faith. Observations of religion are given 343–52; E. De Bovis, *Tahitian Society before the Arrival of the Europeans* (Laie, 1980 (1844)); R. Thomson, *Description and History of the Marquesas* (Laie, 1980 (1841)); T. Henry (ed.), *Ancient Tahiti* (Honolulu, 1928); A. J. Moerenhout, *Voyages* (Paris, 1837). The standard modern account is D. Oliver, *Ancient Tahitian Society* (3 vols., Honolulu, 1974).

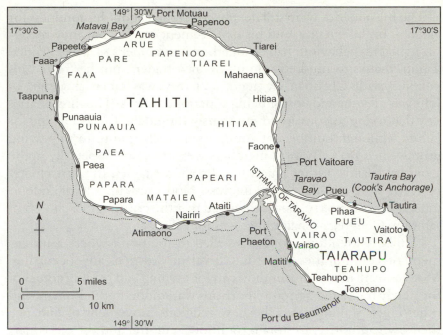

Tahiti: roads and principal settlements (1943). (*Source:* Naval Intelligence Division, British Admiralty, *Pacific Islands*, 5 vols., London, 1939–45, vol. 2, p. 139. © British Crown Copyright/MOD. Reproduced with the permission of Her Britannic Majesty's Stationery Office.)

benefits of trade. Their attempts at communication of Christianity brought more mockery than conversions. Political changes slowly worked in their favour. The important chief, Pomare II, was forced to retreat to Moorea in 1808 where his friendship with Henry Nott, a missionary who had determined to stay, led him to see more clearly some of the advantages of Christianity, notably literacy. Nott was a fair linguist, who became fluent in Tahitian. By 1810, the first part of the Bible had been translated. Pomare had learned writing quickly and by 1804 wrote spirited letters to the missionaries, even though his lifestyle caused them grave concern. The arrival of new missionaries like the Welshman John Davies in 1801 helped the tasks of translation greatly, despite the disputes on how to write Tahitian. A catechism was finished in 1801. By October 1812, Pomare left the cult of Oro and requested baptism, but despite careful teaching was not granted his wish until 16 May 1819.[50]

[50] J. Garrett, *To Live among the Stars* (Suva, 1982) 13–31.

The missionaries were still deeply concerned about his fondness for alcohol, his bisexuality, and his involvement in war, but they recognized that his behaviour had changed. In November 1815, he regained Tahiti, thanks to muskets sold by Sydney traders, but he treated his enemies with Christian clemency. Victory was taken as a sign of Jehovah's favour and power being superior to Oro's. The missionaries saw that trying to convert commoners without chiefs was a recipe for failure, although numbers of young men had begun to form praying groups since 1813. By 1815 members were over 500, especially in the Leeward Islands. Other chiefs like Paofai a Manua, the first chiefly convert, were also displaying interest. Nott drew up a legal code to guide Pomare in 1819, but recognized that the creation of a church of saints on Congregationalist lines was unrealistic.

Numbers attending worship swelled to the point where a movement of communities towards Christianity was clearly occurring. Motives were mixed, but enthusiasm for owning and reading copies of the newly translated Scripture portions was undoubted.[51] Pomare and other chiefs skilfully used the new religious movement to enhance their own authority, to sustain traditional culture, and the sacredness of their office. This pattern of conversion through chiefly example was repeated in other parts of Polynesia. Missionaries relished the political power and status which alliances with Christian chiefs conferred. They rarely understood how skilfully the chiefs used Christianity to enhance their political power. Rivalries between tribes and clans often led to religious conflict.

In 1817 a fresh group of missionaries arrived, including future leaders like William Ellis, John Orsmond, Charles Barff, and John Williams. They were critical of the older missionaries, and determined to make their own mark, with strong opinions about the task of Christianization. They were very successful in channelling the energies of converts in the Leeward Islands, producing legal codes for Raiatea and Huahine in 1820 and 1822 respectively. Even more important was the way they used their converts' gift of seamanship to spread the Christian message, capturing their commitment by skilful use of biblical dramas and religious activities, which moved people from their old religious loyalties. The Directors of the LMS were impressed by the changing order, sending Tyerman and Bennett to visit and report in 1821. Pomare received them shortly before he

---

[51] G. S. Parsonson, 'The literate revolution in Polynesia', *JPH* 2 (1967) 39–57.

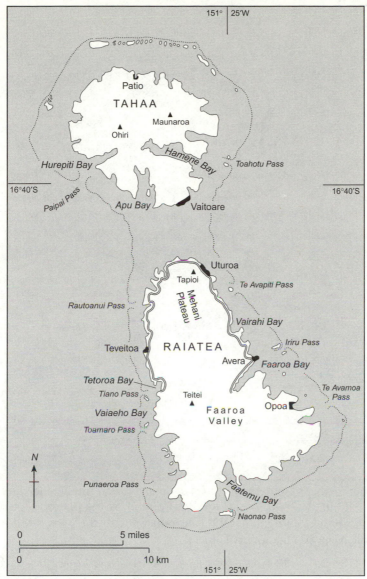

Raiatea/Tahaa (1943). (*Source:* Naval Intelligence Division, British Admiralty, *Pacific Islands*, 5 vols., London, 1939–45, vol. 2, p. 175. © British Crown Copyright/MOD. Reproduced with the permission of Her Britannic Majesty's Stationery Office.)

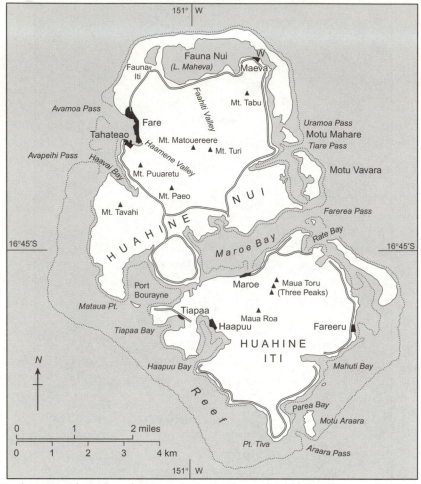

Huahine: roads and settlements (1943). (*Source:* Naval Intelligence Division, British Admiralty, *Pacific Islands*, 5 vols., London, 1939–45, vol. 2, p. 169. © British Crown Copyright/MOD. Reproduced with the permission of Her Britannic Majesty's Stationery Office.)

died in December 1821. William Ellis, later to become a notable missionary administrator in London, was taken to Hawaii to advise the struggling American missionaries.[52] Not only did he give them useful

[52] While the conversion of the Hawaiians is properly part of the history of American Christianity, there are many parallels to the conversion of other Polynesians and their missionary work. David Malo, *Hawaiian Antiquities* (Honolulu, 1971) and John Papa Ii, *Fragments of Hawaiian History* (Honolulu, 1973) describe pre-contact society. A. Loomis, *Grapes of Canaan* (Honolulu, 1972) and *For All People* (Honolulu, 1970) are popular histories

insights, he became one of the most important recorders of Polynesian custom in *Polynesian Researches*. The experience of missionaries in the Pacific was used by the LMS Directors to organize their work in South Africa and India more effectively, as well as being noted by other societies, whose members were keenly interested in missionary intelligence and news. The Tahitian conversion offered precedents which helped missionaries elsewhere in Oceania.

By the 1820s, Maohi Christians had grasped Christianity firmly as an extension of their traditional religious ideas, and were ready to share their insights with other Polynesians. Even though there were signs of creative synthesis of old and new in the Mamaia movement (1826–41), which alarmed missionaries as reversion to paganism, missionaries like Williams were captivated by the possibility of spreading Christianity to other islands by using converts as teachers and pioneer evangelists. Tahitian missionaries like Auna travelled to Hawaii, and on 30 May 1822 he noted in his diary, 'many of them said, what I told them was very good, and that as soon as the King turned to the religion of Christ, they should be very glad to follow him'. In the following month another Tahitian, Ruahine, burnt 102 idols. There has rarely been a more rapid induction into the task of Christians as missionaries, or greater willingness to send out young men and their wives with little formal preparation for their task, except the testimony of a changed life and a simple understanding of the message of the Bible.

In part, that reflected the LMS tradition of selecting promising young men who were soundly converted, and possessed of a variety of practical skills, which they could hand on to converts, and thus aid the work of induction into European civilization. It was also Williams's vision and restlessness, and his unwillingness to stay with the routine of nurturing a church on a single island, which led to expansion of the LMS churches. Despite the Directors' ruling that mission churches should not have their own ships, because they had no desire that the spiritual task of planting churches should be compromised by the profits and losses of trading, Williams travelled to Sydney and purchased an old ship, the *Endeavour*, in 1822, having dropped off Papeiha and Vahapata on Aitutaki in 1821 *en route*. Tahitian and Cook Island language and culture were very similar to one another. In a little over a year, the old religion's symbols on Aitutaki had gone,

of the mission and the recent history of the Conference of the United Church of Christ. Garrett, *To Live Among the Stars*, 32–59, gives a fine overview. He discusses the work of Hawaiian missionaries, 139–55.

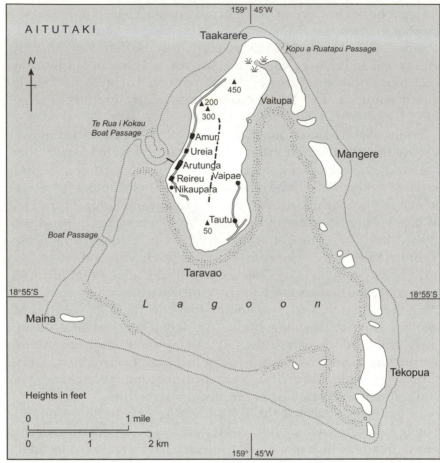

Aitutaki (1943). (*Source:* Naval Intelligence Division, British Admiralty, *Pacific Islands*, 5 vols., London, 1939–45, vol. 2, p. 550. © British Crown Copyright/MOD. Reproduced with the permission of Her Britannic Majesty's Stationery Office.)

thanks to the young Tahitians who had responded to Williams's leadership.

Williams had all the strengths of the Victorian entrepreneurs whose energies and boldness helped to expand the Empire so dramatically in the nineteenth century. Dynastic problems in Tahiti and the succession of the erratic Queen Pomare IV in 1827 hampered the consolidation of the mission, and on Williams's own island, chiefly rivalries, and inadequate leadership as the church took root, led to Christianity being absorbed within traditional religious practices for a time. His own family was neglected during his frequent absences from Raiatea, and his colleagues resented his long periods away. The LMS directors unsuccessfully attempted to control him, but his return to England in 1834 was triumphant, for he was a skilled publicist. He persuaded the missionary public to support his Christian outreach, and purchased the *Camden*, for he demonstrated that expansion of Christianity in the Pacific was dependent on ships, as well as the ability to persuade chiefs to lead their people into the *lotu* (the name given to Christianity).

In 1830 he visited the Cooks again, where there were an estimated 20,000 people. Niue with an estimated 3,000 people, the Tokelau group with 2,000 people, Tonga with an estimated 50,000 people, and Samoa with an estimated 50,000 people were also fields for mission. In Samoa he left eight teachers under the protection of Malietoa, a most influential chief, whose interest in the *lotu* was reinforced by the Tongan experience of his relative, Fauea. He had observed the beginnings of Christianity in Tonga, which owed much to Tahitians between 1822 and 1827. Nearer at hand, Tongan teachers had arrived on Manono, because the chief Matetau's daughter had married Taufa'ahau, a Tongan chief, and converted to Christianity. The *Lotu Tonga* (the Wesleyans) was also meeting at Satupaitea. There were almost 2,000 there observing the *lotu*. By 1835, there were forty villages on Savai'i and twenty-five on Upolu with members following the *Lotu Tonga*. Samoan interest in the new religion may have been stimulated by sailors who had taught a mixture of Christianity and their own ideas, but Polynesian skill at making a new religion their own was demonstrated by Siovili, who appears to have visited Tahiti.[53]

He combined Christianity with traditional religion, and promised his followers that they would receive European goods, an early example of the adjustment cults that were to be so influential in twentieth-century Melanesia. New religious patterns spread rapidly. On Tutuila, people were keeping the Sabbath, dressing in white and worshipping in a mixture of Samoan and Tahitian, even though there were no teachers on their island. Williams had no intention of leaving Manono to Tongans, and left a talented Rarotongan called Teava to establish a *lotu* with more direct connection to the *mana* of the Europeans. The LMS pattern quickly became dominant, but the

[53] D. Freeman, 'The Joe Gimlet or Siovili Cult', in J. D. Freeman and W. R. Geddes (eds.), *Anthropology in the South Seas* (New Plymouth, 1959).

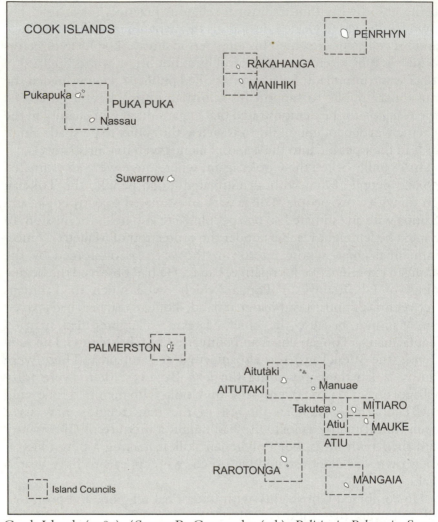

Cook Islands (1983). (*Source:* R. Crocombe (ed.), *Politics in Polynesia*, Suva, 1983, p. 155. With permission of the Institute for Pacific Studies.)

Tongan Wesleyan District countered by sending Peter Turner to Manono in 1835. By 1839, when he was withdrawn, he had been so successful that he reported 3,000 members and 13,000 hearers attending eighty chapels. Reading classes were very popular. Williams, and other LMS missionaries from England who had come in 1836, were alarmed at this Wesleyan growth and appealed to London to enforce an informal comity agreement which had been drawn up in 1830

Tokelau group (1943). (*Source:* Naval Intelligence Division, British Admiralty, *Pacific Islands*, 5 vols., London, 1939–45, vol. 2, p. 505. © British Crown Copyright/MOD. Reproduced with the permission of Her Britannic Majesty's Stationery Office.)

between Williams and the Wesleyans W. Cross and N. Turner.[54] This reflected their shared Evangelicalism and desire to avoid competition, a policy which lasted until the twentieth century. It gave Tonga and Fiji to the Wesleyans, and Samoa to the LMS. On instructions from London, the Wesleyans reluctantly withdrew from Samoa in May 1839, but the Tongans remained, seeing no reason to ignore their ties of kinship with Samoa.

Samoan converts also saw no reason to accept an agreement made without them. At a meeting on Manono, attended by several thousand Methodists, chiefs emphasized their ties with Turner and Tonga. 'And shall we be separated by the *lotu*, or by our *lotu* relatives in England? No, No, No. Never let it be thus. But what do we know of Tahiti? What communications had the Tahitians with us, or with Tonga? We

[54] M. Dyson, *My Story of Samoan Methodism* (Melbourne, 1875) 21–37.

Tonga (1944). (*Source:* Naval Intelligence Division, British Admiralty, *Pacific Islands*, 5 vols., London, 1939–45, vol. 3, p. 14. © British Crown Copyright/MOD. Reproduced with the permission of Her Britannic Majesty's Stationery Office.)

only heard of Tahiti last night.'[55] Tongans like Barnabas Ahogalu and Maika Tongia were indispensable in the rebuilding of Methodism when British Wesleyans withdrew. A small Wesleyan group remained until 1855, when the Australasian Conference in Sydney took over the Pacific from London.[56] Martin Dyson was sent from Tonga reluctantly to resume Samoan work in 1857. The LMS staff were displeased at the end of their monopoly, but recognized that Wesleyan

[55] Dyson, *Samoan Methodism*, 30–1.
[56] Ibid., 37–50 discusses the disagreement between LMS and Australian Methodists.

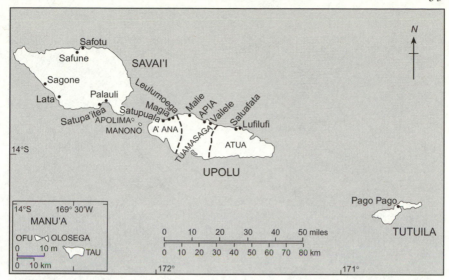

Samoa (1975). (*Source:* A. H. Wood, *Overseas Missions of the Australian Methodist Church*, 5 vols., Melbourne, 1975–87, vol. 1, p. 250. With permission of Uniting Education.)

villages would lose status by becoming LMS. Wesleyans had kept their identity for twenty years and were unwilling even to use the same Bible and hymnal as LMS churches. The reasons for religious choice often lay in family rivalries, and jockeying for titles which were a vital part of the Samoan and Tongan status system.

Under Dyson and George Brown, Samoan Methodism consolidated, and became a separate District in 1863. Dyson and Brown acted decisively to return the Samoans to authentic Methodism once it became clear that union of the two missions was unacceptable to their Samoan colleagues. Ministry was reorganized by Dyson into *leoleo* (overseers), *aoao* (teachers), *failauga* (local preachers), and *taitai* (class leaders). This action in 1858 was accompanied by rules for regular giving. By 1873 this had grown to £376. 11*s*. 2*d*. or 1*s*. 6*d*. for every Methodist.[57] A training institution began in 1864. While their leaders were discouraged from proselytism, denominational tensions at village level were considerable, because of the dynamics of family rivalries.[58] Apart from forbidding night dances, the annual assembly in 1862 laid

---

[57] Ibid., 69.
[58] Ibid., 98 narrates how a request from Tutuila was refused, in order not to offend the LMS.

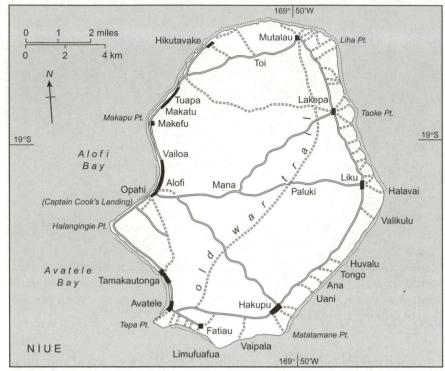

Niue (1943). (*Source:* Naval Intelligence Division, British Admiralty, *Pacific Islands*, 5 vols., London, 1939–45, vol. 2, p. 563. © British Crown Copyright/MOD. Reproduced with the permission of Her Britannic Majesty's Stationery Office.)

down that traditional stories should not be used in preaching, thereby cutting off an effective form of communication with Samoans.[59] Nor should Bible readings be selectively arbitrary. The whole biblical narrative needed to be heard. The missionaries also laid down limit on ceremonial exchange, because of the consequent quarrels. Members were also forbidden to share in Catholic services.

With Samoa settled, Williams demonstrated his vision for Christian expansion by planting Samoan teachers in Vanuatu in 1839, the first Protestant incursion into Melanesia. His death along with James Harris at Islander hands on 20 November 1839 on Erromanga, may have been pay-back for traders' misbehaviour, but it sealed his reputation as a missionary giant and church planter. Williams's martyrdom confirmed stereotypes of cannibal savagery, but did not lead to

---

[59] Dyson, *Samoan Methodism*, 79 for an example of this preaching style.

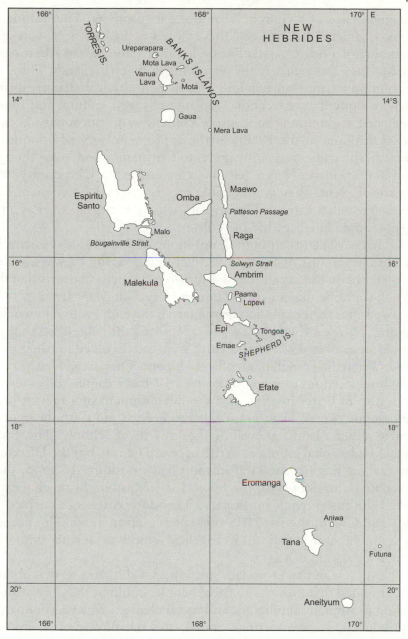

New Hebrides/Vanuatu (1944). (*Source:* Naval Intelligence Division, British Admiralty, *Pacific Islands*, 5 vols., London, 1939–45, vol. 3, p. 512. © British Crown Copyright/MOD. Reproduced with the permission of Her Britannic Majesty's Stationery Office.)

the emergence of a church. That was left to others. The Tahitians,
Cook Islanders, and Samoans he enlisted as his partners were the
beginning of a tide of 1,100 Pacific Island missionaries to Micronesia
and Melanesia, as well as to the remaining Polynesian islands. They left
a profound imprint on religious life, shaped political change, introduced rudimentary education, and interchanged cultural and food-
producing techniques. Solid stone churches and missionary houses
spread throughout the Pacific as the appropriate way of honouring
Jehovah, the name frequently given to Christians' God, even though
British missionaries often felt the conversion to Christianity was
superficial. What they were unable to see was that Polynesians had
rapidly created a form of Christianity with a European overlay, but
deeply rooted in village life and culture.

Tahitians lacked the political ambitions of Tongans and Fijians to
establish hegemony over other island groups. Pomare IV was not able
to capitalize on the expansion of Tahitian influence. The arrival of the
French Catholic missionaries Caret and Laval on Mangareva in 1834
followed after their expulsion from Hawaii through Protestant machi-
nations. This was followed by a foray into Tahiti, which led to their
expulsion in 1836. LMS missionaries were too involved for their own
good. When the French naval officer Dupetit-Thouars arrived in 1838
to uphold freedom of religion, Pomare IV had to agree to his terms,
the return of Caret in 1841, and the establishment of a French pro-
tectorate in 1842.[60] That, in turn, led to French and Catholic expansion to other islands, as well as the growth of schools. The LMS
retained substantial influence in the Leeward Islands, but the Directors
saw that an English-speaking mission had no future. In 1860, they
negotiated a transfer with the Société des Missions Evangéliques in
Paris. The first French missionary, Theodore Arbousset, arrived in
1863 and Green, the last LMS missionary, left in 1886. The French
government authorized an Evangelical synod in accord with the
French legislation of 1851.

The success of the Protestant mission to Tahiti and its neighbours
demonstrated that missions to tribal peoples could be very rewarding,
leading to substantial religious and social change. War was dramatically reduced, human sacrifice ended, and the power of traditional
chiefs modified. Despite the missionaries' cultural limitations and
personal failings, Protestantism remained a powerful ingredient in

---

[60] P. Hodée, *Tahiti 1834–1984* (Papeete, 1983) is the best account of the growth of the
Roman Catholic Church in French Polynesia.

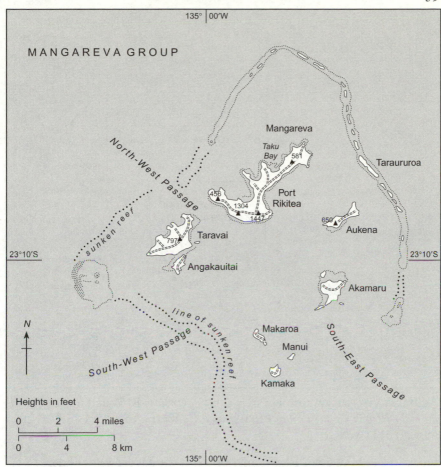

Mangareva group (1943). (*Source:* Naval Intelligence Division, British Admiralty, *Pacific Islands*, 5 vols., London, 1939–45, vol. 2, p. 228. © British Crown Copyright/MOD. Reproduced with the permission of Her Britannic Majesty's Stationery Office.)

Maohi identity, aided by the insight with which talented French missionaries built on the foundations provided by the LMS. They created a tightly knit community of faith which encompassed every aspect of life not directly subject to French control, in spite of a dramatic decline of population to something like 10,000 by 1900.

The Picpus Fathers (the Congregation of the Sacred Hearts of Jesus and Mary), founded by Pierre Coudrin, one of the great French missionary pioneers, gained papal recognition in 1817. They began

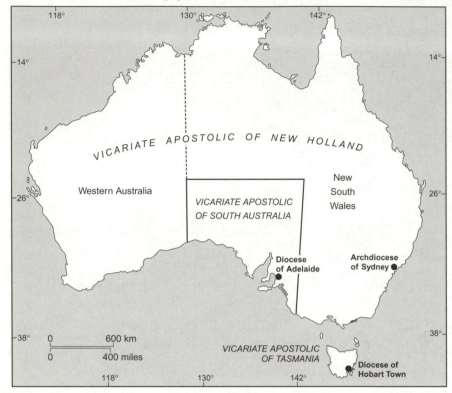

Australia: Vicariates Apostolic, 1842 (1979). (*Source:* R. Wiltgen, *The Founding of the Roman Catholic Church in Oceania*, Canberra, 1979, p. 353. With permission of Fr Wiltgen.)

work in the Hawaiian Islands in 1827, but they were expelled in 1831. De Solages, the Prefect Apostolic for the region based in Réunion, far away in the Indian Ocean, gave them most of what was to become French Polynesia. Caret, Laval, and Murphy began their work on Mangareva in 1834 and in the Marquesas in 1838.[61] Aided by their isolation, the missionaries baptized dying children, kept their congregation's discipline faithfully, learnt the local language, and began translation. Their musical gifts were an attraction. Christian songs were an important teaching aid, and the use of local music helped their acceptance. Medical skills also helped to establish good relations, and a simple hospital underlined the association of healing and evangelism.

[61] H. Laval, *Memoires pour Servir à La histoire de Mangareva* (Paris, 1968) is fundamental. See also Hodée, *Tahiti*, 125–8 for background to the congregations who came to French Polynesia; Wiltgen, *Catholic Church in Oceania*, 28–51 described the Roman background. I am indebted to Garrett, *To Live Among the Stars*, 88–96.

Like their Protestant counterparts, they saw no place for bringing the old religion into Christianity. In 1835, they desecrated the sacred place they had been given by Matua, an influential priest. No punishment from the gods followed this important demonstration of the power of the new religion. Other *marae* were destroyed and sacred objects smashed. Gradually baptisms increased, then first communions, Christian marriages, and funerals. Leaders cut their hair, breaking the *tapu* on their head, and speedily identified with Catholic views. Laval created a total Christian community, firmly disciplined in Tridentine style. His very success undermined the long-term viability of the community. A Catholic commentator described it as 'one of those marvellous triumphs of religion, which Protestants do not pretend to emulate, even at home, much less amongst savages, and which only the immense power of divine grace can explain.'[62]

By the 1840s, strong Polynesian churches greatly outnumbered the small settler churches in Australia and New Zealand. The process of conversion has many similarities throughout the region, shaped by differences in tribal organization and size of communities, but always heavily dependent on indigenous pioneer missionaries. Their energy, bravery, and compelling explanation of the Gospel irrevocably changed the region.

NEW ZEALAND

In New Zealand's islands, the original migrants, who probably numbered a few hundred, had grown to somewhere between 85,000 and 100,000 by the mid-eighteenth century, when the remarkable voyages of James Cook made these remote islands better known. Dutch and French explorers also added to European knowledge of the Maori, who were predominantly settled in the warmer parts of the North Island, with less than 5 per cent living in the southern islands, where traditional food crops could not survive, but where fish and the giant *moa* provided abundant alternative food.[63]

The Maori[64] had developed a rich stone-tooled culture, with many

[62] T. Marshall, *Christian Missions* (2 vols., Brussels, 1843) 2. 278.

[63] K. Sinclair (ed.), *Oxford Illustrated History of New Zealand* (Auckland, 1990) 1–20; J. Belich, *Making of Peoples* (Auckland, 1996) 13–116.

[64] E. Schwimmer, *The World of the Maori* (Wellington, 1974) gives an overview; E. Best, *Maori Religion and Mythology* (Wellington, 1924) surveys the evidence, 81–101; *The Lore of the Whare-Wananga*, ed. S. P. Smith, 1913–15, was critically and negatively examined by

mythological elements shared with other parts of Polynesia, but with distinctive features which may have included in some tribes an esoteric high god cult of Io, jealously guarded by a few initiates among the *tohunga,* who were guardians of all knowledge. War was an art consuming a great deal of energy, but without too much loss of life, until European weapons increased killing power dramatically in the 1820s and 1830s. The Maori swiftly adapted to European contacts, and highly prized sealers, whalers, deserters, and escaped convicts from Eastern Australia, who numbered almost 2,000 by the 1830s. Maori drove increasingly hard bargains for the flax, timber, and food desired by visiting ships, especially seeking metal tools and muskets.[65]

Not all were interested in the new faith. John Logan Campbell, writing from a Scottish upbringing where right doctrine was indispensable for Christian identity, recounted how the chief, Kanini, had rejected missionary preaching.

I am now an old man; why change my religion, or allow my people to change theirs, and so risk my power over my tribe. The *tapu* has served my purpose—will serve for my day. Your religion may be good—may be better—but how know I what my people may learn with it? Perhaps not respect for me and obedience to their chiefs. No, No; the religion of my fathers is good enough for me, good enough for my people, and if they only pray to the evil gods to leave them alone, no fear of the good ones doing them any harm—you don't require to pray to *them.* And when I die . . . my spirit will pass away from Muriwhenua and I shall eat *Kumara,* and smoke my pipe, I hope, and be happy forever.[66]

Many Maori joined ships to see the strange, new world from which the *Pakeha* came. Moehanga was one of the first travellers. He went to London with Surgeon Savage in 1805. Te Pahi visited Sydney for several months in the same year, meeting Governor King, and returning with pigs which supplemented those left by Cook. That helped the flourishing trade in pork which had developed with Sydney by 1808. Belich estimates that as many as 1,000 Maori had travelled overseas by

D. Simmons and B. H. Biggs, who suggested that much of the material in vol. 2 was late and less authentic than that in vol. 1.'The source of the lore of the Whare Wananga', *JPS* 79 (1990) 22–42. J. P. Johansen, *The Maori and His Religion* (Copenhagen, 1954) is valuable, as is J. Irwin, *An Introduction to Maori Religion* (Adelaide, 1984).

[65] Belich, *Making of Peoples,* 148–55; R. Crosby, *The Musket Wars* (Auckland, 1999).

[66] J. L. Campbell, *Poenamo* (Auckland, 1961) 119–20. A similar account can be found in W. Yate, *An Account of New Zealand* (London, 1835) 283–5 for the death of Paru, contrasted with Ann Waiapu, 296–304, who died believing in Christ.

1840, including influential chiefs like Patuone, Pomare, and Te Rauparaha. At least one Tahitian was living with the Aupori people in the far north of New Zealand. Named Jem, he could have told Maori about missions in Tahiti.

A number of Maori stayed with Samuel Marsden in Sydney, including Ruatara whom Marsden nursed back to health in 1809 after he was abandoned by an unscrupulous captain.[67] Marsden also ran a technical school for young Maori. Ruatara was to be decisive in persuading Marsden to send missionaries to the Bay of Islands, and translated the first sermon that Marsden preached on Christmas Day 1814, at Oihi. Ruatara and Hongi were both dressed in regimentals, and marched their men in as they had seen in Sydney. Marsden's writings show he had shrewd insight into some Maori aspirations. Another of Marsden's guests, Maui, went to London in 1816, and spent a good deal of time with Dandeson Coates, Secretary of the Church Missionary Society, before he died at the end of the year. He is reported to have taught Sunday school.

Marsden's concerns for the evangelization of the Maori went back many years. In 1808 he had contacted the Church Missionary Society (CMS), which had been founded for less than a decade by Church of England Evangelicals. His intimate connection with the LMS, and knowledge of their precarious situation in Tahiti, and their failure in Tonga and the Marquesas, gave him little confidence that their Directors in London would have either the will or the resources to open up a new mission in northern New Zealand. Convinced that successful evangelism required a certain level of civilization before the Gospel could be effectively heard, Marsden had recruited several godly artisans to teach agricultural and technical skills to the Maori. Enquiries in 1813 convinced Marsden that the time was right to respond to Ruatara's invitation.

He invested a substantial amount in the venture from his own funds, for his farms were profitable. Even though he had significant contact with the Maori visitors, his recruits had little inkling of the culture shock they would experience from the Maori and lawless Europeans. Kendall, King, and Hall were married, but soon were quarrelling

---

[67] J. Elder (ed.), *Letters and Journals of Samuel Marsden* (Dunedin, 1934) 134–5, 145 for Ruatara and Hongi's impressions of Parramatta which Marsden hoped 'will excite all their national powers to improve their own country'. Marsden also noted Ruatara was very anxious that the Europeans did not invade and leave the Maori like Aborigines, 141–2. The account of Maui in London is found in the above volume, 70–8.

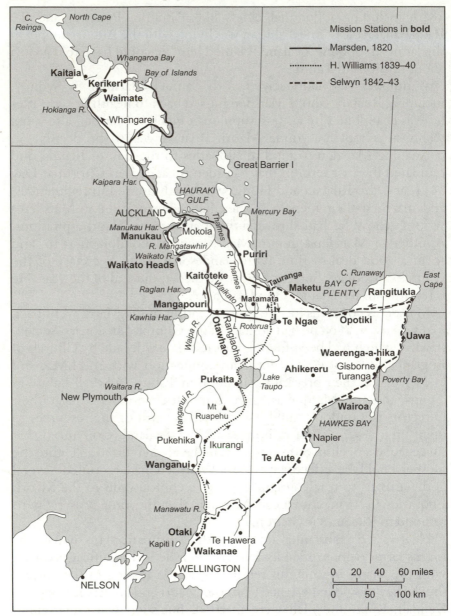

New Zealand: North Island mission stations and journeys (1914). (*Source:* H. T. Purchas, *A History of the English Church in New Zealand*, Christchurch, 1914, p. 17.)

among themselves. The arrival of Henry Williams in 1823 and his brother William in 1826 transformed the struggling and divided mission.[68] They were highly educated and disciplined, and speedily won respect amongst the Maori, who saw in them the cultural equivalents of the *rangatira*. When William Williams reached Turanga in 1839 he found that 3,000 people had already been instructed by Putoko, a returned slave. By mid-1841, Williams reported 8,000 worshippers in his East Coast region.

Both also had very gifted and educated wives, who put up with rudimentary housing, constant lack of privacy, and the challenge of parenting while their husbands were away. Their family letters and journals tell something of the cost they paid. They spent a great deal of time in the education of young Maori women, which was emotionally draining for both sides because of differing expectations. Nevertheless, their part in the turnaround of the mission's fortunes was considerable. Marianne Williams and her sister-in-law, Jane, were trained teachers with some nursing skills as well. In between chores, Jane still found time to read books like Southey's *History of the Church*. On 10 October 1840, Jane Williams wrote 'A very fatiguing day, doing little or nothing myself, but chiefly engaged in overlooking my men and maidens.'[69]

Other examples of missionary wives' input can be seen in Sarah Selwyn, the Bishop of New Zealand's wife, who later gave some help with correcting proofs for the Maori Bible, as well as writing simple readers for the school under her care. Also Lady Mary Martin, wife of the Chief Justice, and Margaret Kissling helped Archdeacon Kissling to run a school in Auckland. Maori mothers did not approve of their children, often in their late teens, being taught domestic skills like slaves. Mrs Williams noted, 'They all require to be taught the very first principles of religion and to be trained in the decencies of Christian life.'[70]

Other factors were also working in favour of the mission. The horrific scale of the destruction brought by the introduction of muskets shook Maori tribes to the foundations in the 1820s and 1830s. Belich estimates that something like 20,000 were killed. Some 6,000

---

[68] L. M. Rogers (ed.), *The Early Journals of Henry Williams* (Christchurch, 1961); F. Porter (ed.), *The Turanga Journals* (Wellington, 1974) 173.

[69] *Turanga Journals*, 133.

[70] Ibid., 567. See also F. Porter, 'All that the heart does bear,' in R. Glen, *Mission and Moko*, (Christchurch, 1992) 134–51.

guns were imported from Sydney in 1831 alone. Many captives were enslaved, and the economic bases of tribal life seriously weakened through shortage of labour. In addition, many in high contact areas died through European diseases like measles, mumps, and flu, which were triumphant over traditional prayers for healing. Venereal diseases may have reduced the birth rate, for the hospitality of Maori women to visiting crews was an important economic activity. Europeans could apparently violate *tapu* without consequences from the gods, further shaking traditional beliefs.

Even though Maori asked sharp theological questions of missionaries, and enjoyed debates between Protestants and Roman Catholics, they were often sceptical about the answers given, for they had a very pragmatic religious attitude.[71] Clearly their own Maori religious practices failed to meet expectations. In a very pragmatic way, Maori experimented with aspects of the new religion in order to test its efficacy. Some broke *tapu*, others adopted Christian prayers, and sought the secrets of reading the sacred book. Others saw the social disasters created by war, and were inclined to take the message of the missionaries about the virtues of peace very seriously. Yet others released their slaves, who, in turn, carried news about the new religion far beyond missionary presence, for some of them had taken the Christian message as a way of rebuilding their status, lost irrevocably in Maori eyes because of their enslavement.

Progress of a visible kind was slow in the 1820s. Kendall baptized Maria Ringa in 1823 before she married Phillip Tapsell, a Danish sailor. Christian Rangi (possibly one of the first converts) was baptized on his deathbed by Henry Williams in 1825. The first children were baptized in 1829, followed in the next year by a few adults. Invitations came to found mission stations in the Waikato, the Bay of Plenty, and the East Coast, and as far south as Otaki. The latter was due to the testimony of a freed slave, Ripahau, A mission press had been set up in 1834 by William Colenso, and the New Testament had been translated by 1837. The demand for printed material was insatiable as Maori clamoured to learn to read. By 1845, about half the Maori population was worshipping regularly.

---

[71] *Turanga Journals*, 180. On 13 October 1841, Williams and Fr Baty, SM, debated for four hours on disputed points like the Catholic worship of idols and Protestant clergy being adulterers. Williams carefully gave biblical references and in conclusion gave Baty a New Testament in Maori. Many of the Maori audience carefully followed up texts given by Williams, for they had their Testaments with them; J. M. R. Owens, 'Religious disputation at Whangaroa, 1823–37', *JPS* 79/3 (1970) 288–304.

Harrison Wright, Judith Binney, and John Owens have debated the social and economic reasons for the move towards Christianity in the 1830s and 1840s, underlining that the move occurred for Maori reasons.[72] Great interest was taken in the Old Testament, because of the similarities in dealing with sacred power, even though few of the missionaries were fluent enough in Maori to explain such matters. In South Taranaki, Wiremu Nera Ngatai, another returned slave, was such an effective evangelist that many local tribes renounced idolatry, built churches, and kept the Sabbath. While few Maori accounts of conversion have survived, some suggest real heart-searching. Paratene wrote to Mrs Coleman on 25 January 1834.

Here I am sitting with my evil nature, thinking upon God for us and for my people. Here lives evil in the innermost part of my heart. I must think towards God for the salvation of my soul. Here I am praying daily to God for us all. Does the Word of God grow in my tribe, or does it not? My thoughts are lifted up to you every day. I am praying to God to reveal to me the hidden evils of my heart, that I may not deceive myself and lose my soul.[73]

Not only does the letter indicate a fine grasp of English, but Paratene has also clearly internalized Evangelical language in his search for the source of religious power. Missionaries and Maori had clearly learnt from one another, and chiefs vied with one another to obtain a resident missionary.

Emergence of Maori religious movements which incorporated Christian elements was another sign of major religious shifts. Papahurihia in Northland from 1833 was one of the earliest of these adjustment cults, led by a *tohunga*, Te Atua Wera, demonstrating the religious creativity and initiative of the Maori. It included many Christian ideas, along with Maori traditions, and shut missionaries out from heaven. The coming of the Wesleyan missionaries in 1822-3 to Whangaroa gave some Maori an alternative to the CMS, but Leigh was not a suitable pioneer and left in 1823.[74] The early missionaries suffered the same problems of acculturation and quarrelsomeness as their Anglican colleagues, not to mention being plundered and facing serious physical danger when caught between warring factions. They

---

[72] H. Wright, *New Zealand, 1769-1840* (Massachusetts, 1959). R. Glen, *Mission and Moko* (Christchurch, 1992) 14-55 discusses missionary ideas and motivation; P. Lineham discusses the Maori Bible, 152-78.

[73] J. Caselberg, *Maori is My Name* (Dunedin, 1975) 39. See also the letters in W. Yate, *An Account of New Zealand* (London, 1835) 250-81.

[74] J. M. R. Owens, *Prophets in the Wilderness* (Auckland, 1974).

moved out of Northland in 1833. Like the CMS, they were hard-pressed to cope with the dramatic escalation of interest in the 1830s, especially after successful Maori evangelists publicized the benefits of Christianity.

MARIST INITIATIVES

A further religious alternative was available after the arrival in 1838 of French missionaries from the Society of Mary, led by Bishop Jean-Baptiste Pompallier, a man with great presence and keen intelligence, sympathetic to Marists.[75] The Marists were one of the numerous congregations and institutes which emerged after the destruction of traditional Catholicism in the 1790s by French revolutionaries. The Society of the Faith of Jesus had been allocated the region from the Cape of Good Hope to Japan in 1798, but nothing eventuated until 1829, when the jurisdiction of the Prefect Apostolic in Réunion was extended to the South Sea Islands of the Pacific. A Vicariate of Eastern Oceania was created in 1833. The Marists were placed under the jurisdiction of Pompallier, who had been consecrated Bishop of Maronea at the end of June 1836. The Marists looked forward to the saving of thousands of souls from heathenism and Protestantism. A significant part of their funding came from the French Society for the Propagation of the Faith, founded in Lyons by Pauline Jaricot and businessmen in 1822 from the gifts of the poor.

By 1849, the Marists had sent 117 missionaries to the Pacific. Administrators in Rome and France had no way of knowing the real costs of setting up a mission in the Pacific. Fr Jean Claude Colin, the founder of the Marists, had grand ideas of blending trade and mission through the Oceanic Company. They failed. Between 1836 and 1845, Pompallier received £37,156, which was a large sum of money.[76] Spread between forty missionaries scattered over a huge territory it did not go far, and Pompallier was constantly in financial trouble. But France, thanks to Colin's lobbying, was anxious to protect French missionaries. The priests who worked in New Zealand with Pompallier suffered great hardships, despite living very modestly. Like their later colleagues in New Caledonia they had to walk large

    [75] L. Keys, *Life and Times of Bishop Pompallier* (Christchurch, 1957); E. Simmons, *Pompallier* (Auckland, 1984).
    [76] E. Simmons, *In cruce salus* (Auckland, 1982) 20.

distances, showing that muscular Christianity was ecumenical. Shoes and clothes quickly wore out and Maori villages were not always willing to give hospitality to strangers who looked little able to confer any benefits. It was hardly surprising that Fr Servant should send seven pages of criticism of Pompallier's leadership to Colin on 26 April 1840. Tensions about the boundaries of religious and ecclesiastical obedience were a continuing problem for Catholic missions.

Pompallier had more insight than many Protestant contemporaries into the complexities of relationship between religion and culture. His *Instructions* (1841) were wise and practical. He soon began composing hymns in Maori. He speedily built good relationships with some chiefs, despite bitter opposition from Anglican and Wesleyan missionaries, for he saw the importance of gift exchange. 'In practice, it is well to make gifts with a kind of distributive charity.'[77] He also underlined that there should be no taking of land, that people should come to worship in native dress, and that the spiritual gifts of grace and poverty should be central. His personal charm, aristocratic bearing, and religious integrity commended him also to the small group of Irish settlers such as Thomas Poynton, a political deportee, who had tried vainly in 1835 to get a Catholic priest from Sydney, and whose example had led to several Maori travelling to Sydney for baptism in 1835. Pompallier arrived early in 1838 and speedily learnt Maori. Poynton's local knowledge and support, while a house was being built for Pompallier on the Hokianga in 1838, was important to the struggling mission, and a reminder of the importance of laity in introducing Roman Catholicism into New Zealand.

Pompallier's strategy in the Pacific was also shaped by conversations with Captain Peter Dillon, a Catholic trader. The Marist missionaries made some impact in the north, but strategic new centres were in the Bay of Plenty/Waikato, where the impact of Protestantism was recent. Priests like Garavel, Bezant, and Servant were astute observers of Maori custom and effective communicators of Christianity through teaching and example. By 1841, there were twelve stations in New Zealand and three in Polynesia. The contacts and friendships they patiently built up were bridges across which new ideas travelled to lodge among curious Maori, though Pompallier's claim of 45,000 catechumens in 164 tribes by 1841 was wildly exaggerated.

Like the Protestants, the Roman Catholic missionaries saw the

[77] P. McKeefry (ed.), *Fishers of Men* (Auckland, 1938) 3–20 contains extracts from the *Instructions*.

importance of literacy, and set up a printing press in Korarareka (now Russell). By 1847 a Prayer Book, *Ko te ako*, had been published, as had an interesting chart displaying the family tree of Catholicism.[78] Rome was the trunk, Protestantism was merely among the twigs. This appealed to the Maori love of genealogy. Baptisms and conversions grew steadily, despite the financial and administrative problems of the mission worsening. Letters were slow and often crossed, so that misunderstandings between Colin and Pompallier multiplied, with each charging the other with bad faith. In 1842, Epalle went to Europe and Petit-Jean to Sydney to try and sort out the problem.

Part of the answer was found by Rome creating more vicariates apostolic.[79] Pierre Bataillon was given Central Oceania in 1841. Micronesia and Melanesia were separated off in 1844, New Caledonia in 1847, and Samoa in 1851. Even with more focused responsibilities, Pompallier's financial and administrative problems did not cease. Money arrived late, and that meant borrowing at high interest. Epalle's account of the problems to Colin was quite unacceptable to Pompallier, who disowned his colleague. Visits from French ships underlined Pompallier's status in the eyes of the local Maori, and caused anxieties in Sydney about French designs. Pompallier, however, was quite scrupulous about being politically neutral. He insisted that he had 'been sent by the Prince of Bishops of Mother Church to devote myself exclusively to the ministry of salvation'.[80] Plans along lines pioneered in Algeria for a settlement in the South Island at Akaroa were completed in 1840 by the arrival of colonists in August,[81] who found to their dismay that Hobson, the lieutenant governor appointed to bring New Zealand into British control, had previously proclaimed sovereignty on 21 May over the territory. Governor Gipps in Sydney had proclaimed that New Zealand was part of New South Wales on 14 January 1840, before the Treaty of Waitangi was signed on 6 February.

Progress in the Waikato and Bay of Plenty was substantial both for the CMS and for Catholics. At Otumoetai, Phillippe Viard and a Maori catechist called Romana set up a station where numbers grew rapidly, and justified the erection of a church decorated with *tukutuku* panels, an early example of the blending of European and Maori

[78] M. King, *God's Farthest Outpost* (Auckland, 1997) 51, 58–9.
[79] Wiltgen, *Catholic Church in Oceania*, 224–45 for the negotiations.
[80] McKeefry, *Fishers of Men*, 124.
[81] P. Tremewan, *French Akaroa* (Christchurch, 1990) 1–101.

traditions. At Whakatane, Tautari was received in 1840, and Fr Jean Lampila came as resident priest in 1844. By 1847, nearly 400 had been confirmed. By 1846, Viard claimed 600 baptized at Whakatane (which also had a fine reed church) and Opotiki, 1,200 in Rotorua, and 1,000 among the Tainui in Waikato. In the north, by comparison, there were 550 baptized at Hokianga, and 222 at Whangaroa.[82] Maori were skilful at playing off Protestant and Roman Catholic missions in order to exact the most satisfactory deal for the prestige of their tribe by obtaining a resident missionary.

Pompallier's capacity for grand designs was shown again in 1846 when he proposed to Propaganda that Viard be created Archbishop of Western Oceania, with dioceses in the Bay of Islands, at Auckland, Tauranga, Wellington, Samoa, Fiji, New Caledonia and the New Hebrides, and New Guinea. Colin fought this determinedly and sought to bring Pompallier down by scurrilous accusations that his rival was a drunkard. Rome finally solved the problem in 1848 by creating dioceses in Auckland and Wellington, where the Marists could work with Viard, and Pompallier be left to build a new set of alliances with settlers and the priests and seminarians he brought from Europe in 1850, along with eight Irish Sisters of Mercy. Pompallier also became a British citizen. He had played a notable part in the foundation of Roman Catholicism in New Zealand and the Pacific Islands, though his hopes for an indigenous Maori church were not realized. The withdrawal of Marists in 1850 was a fatal blow, for he did not have the resources to staff the stations with European clergy. There were no Maori priests, and the catechists were too slenderly equipped to cope with the pastoral needs of converts so that promising beginnings were eroded.[83]

POLYNESIAN MISSIONARIES

Three other island groups need briefly to be mentioned, for they provided considerable numbers of missionaries to other parts of the Pacific, and strongly shaped the emergent Christianities in other unreached groups. In the Cook Islands, the pioneering work of the

[82] Simmons, *Pompallier*, 25.
[83] Wiltgen, *Catholic Church in Oceania*, 405–24, 496–510 describes the complex negotiations; M. C. Goulter, *Sons of France* (Wellington, 1958) gives an account of the work of several of the early priests.

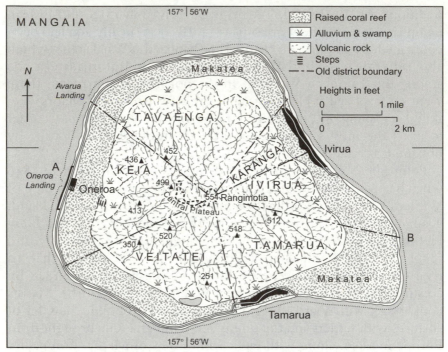

Mangaia (1943). (*Source:* Naval Intelligence Division, British Admiralty, *Pacific Islands*, 5 vols., London, 1939–45, vol. 2, p. 543. © British Crown Copyright/MOD. Reproduced with the permission of Her Britannic Majesty's Stationery Office.)

deacon, Papeiha, was complemented by Maretu's work on Mangaia.[84] Translation of the Bible into Maori was accomplished by the LMS worker Charles Pitman and Ta'unga, who was to become a notable pioneer missionary to New Caledonia. Aaron Buzzacott, who followed Pitman on Rarotonga, was a fine carpenter. He taught the Cook Islanders to build durable dwellings against cyclones, and also boats for inter-island travel. His most lasting contribution was the building (from local resources) of Takamoa College on Rarotonga in 1839, which still stands, and continues to educate for ministry.

[84] Maretu wrote a detailed history of the Church in the Cook Islands in 1871, *Cannibals and Converts*, ed. M. T. Crocombe, 1983. It contains vivid accounts of cannibalism, and the struggles over Christianity. People were greatly interested in Jesus' death and resurrection and wanted to see the place where he ascended to heaven. Conversion of the chiefs was vital to the expansion of Christianity. P. H. Buck, *Mangaia and the mission* (Suva, 1993); and J. Siikala, *Akatokamanava* (Auckland/Helsinki, 1991) explore the issues of conversion. R. P. Gilson, *The Cook Islands* (Wellington/Suva, 1980) is the standard history, but valuable material is contained in E. Beaglehole, *Social Change in the South Pacific* (London, 1957).

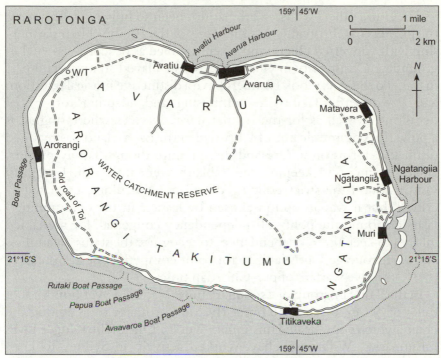

Rarotonga (1943). (*Source:* Naval Intelligence Division, British Admiralty, *Pacific Islands*, 5 vols., London, 1939–45, vol. 2, p. 540. © British Crown Copyright/MOD. Reproduced with the permission of Her Britannic Majesty's Stationery Office.)

Buzzacott gave students a strong biblical foundation, a simplified Calvinist theology, and practical skills in building, gardening, and education which stood them in good stead as they planted and developed churches in their own islands, and elsewhere in the Pacific. Student wives were taught domestic skills, which they carried to many other parts of the Pacific. By 1857, out of a population of a few thousand, there were 61 teachers from the group. Six teachers had been martyred, 36 had died, 10 had retired, and 21 had to be removed, for they had adjusted too comfortably to a new environment, and were deemed to have lapsed.[85] That may have been too much a British missionary judgement. Workers like Teava in Samoa, and Maretu on Mangaia and other Cook Islands were skilful contextualizers of Christianity, and lived out their discipleship in a very compelling way.

[85] Garrett, *To Live Among the Stars*, 118.

They, and others whose work has not been so fully recorded, were the planters of Christianity in other parts of the Pacific. Their partnership with converted chiefs who often doubled as deacons was vital in grounding Christianity in village life. Music played an important part in this. To this day, Cook Islanders have a distinctive musical tradition, and a wonderful facility in composing and adapting for special occasions, as well as for the regular *uapou* services where singing is a powerful communicator of Christian faith. Each island has retained distinctive forms of culture and discipleship, though family prayers, Bible reading, and keeping the Sabbath were universal. European visitors found the strict policing of villages ridiculous, even hypocritical, but it was an option chosen by leaders in the communities. Islanders found the polity of Independency congenial, for it enabled villages to keep their independence, to recognize the status of families, and to encourage Christianized forms of competitiveness, instead of the destructive warfare of pre-Christian times.

In the Tongan group of 259 square miles scattered over hundreds of miles of ocean, there were bitter rivalries for major titles among the chiefs, which complicated missionary work.[86] One of the refugee LMS missionaries, William Shelley, worked actively in Sydney to keep interest in Tonga alive. His widow continued that concern. The Evangelical network in Sydney gave additional support. The Wallis, Waterhouse, Fletcher, and Watkin families were part of this network, which provided a succession of ministers and missionaries throughout Australasia. Lawry went to Tonga in 1822–3, but was quite unsuccessful. The pioneer work was done by Borabora, Hape, and Tafeta, Tahitian Christians, who arrived at Nuku'alofa in 1826. Supported by the Tu'i Kanokupolu, Aleamotu'a, near Nuku'alofa, they introduced literacy, Sabbath-keeping, and the worship of Jehovah. Other Tahitians went to Vava'u unsuccessfully in 1822.

In 1826 John Thomas and John Hutchinson began work on Tongatapu under the patronage of Ata, but he became uncooperative when missionary benefits seemed few, and died without converting in 1833. Thomas was a self-educated blacksmith with great energy and perception who worked devotedly till 1859. His alliance with the Tupou family on Ha'apai was decisive for the development of Methodism, and a Christian kingdom without parallel in the Pacific. In addition to mastery of the language which enabled him to play a

---

[86] S. Latukefu, *Church and State in Tonga* (Canberra, 1974) 1–49; Wood, *Overseas Missions*, 2. 19–82; N. Rutherford (ed.), *Friendly Islands* (Melbourne, 1977) 114–53.

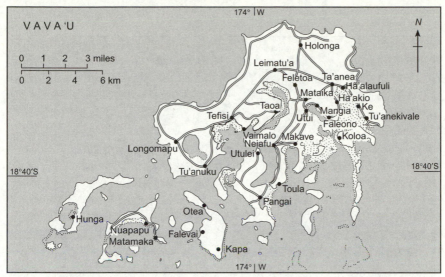

Vava'u (1944). (*Source:* Naval Intelligence Division, British Admiralty, *Pacific Islands*, 5 vols., London, 1939–45, vol. 3, pp. 104–5. © British Crown Copyright/MOD. Reproduced with the permission of Her Britannic Majesty's Stationery Office.)

major part in the translation of the Bible, he nurtured gifted converts like Peter Vi, and gave them leadership tasks quickly. He acted as District Chairman in 1831–50. By 1830 Aleamotu'a was baptized Josiah, together with five children.

More missionaries arrived in 1827, including Nathaniel Turner, whose experience in New Zealand gave him a head start, until ill-health forced his departure in 1831. He gave the despondent Thomas fresh hope and brought three Maori helpers. When Taufa'ahau of Ha'apai pleaded with Thomas for a missionary, no European was available. Pita Vi, who had been baptized in 1829, was sent.[87] Of chiefly family, he worked closely with Taufa'ahau, who defied a resident priestess, as well as sharing in a shark hunt without coming to any harm from the shark god. The *mana* of the new god was clearly demonstrated and many of the *marae* on the island were defiled and made places of Christian worship. Vi also threw stones into the volcano on Tofua without the gods killing him.

[87] Wood, *Overseas Missions*, 1. 44 notes 505 members, 528 on trial, 14 schools, 35 teachers, 953 scholars on Tongatapu. On Ha'apai there were 8 schools, 77 teachers, and 1,037 students by the time Turner left.

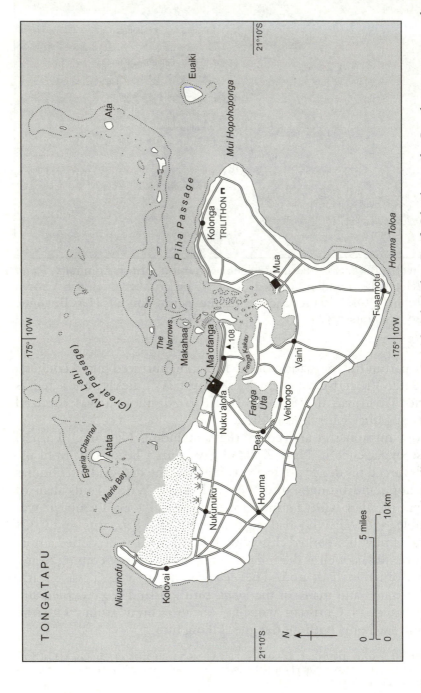

Tongatapu (1944). (*Source:* Naval Intelligence Division, British Admiralty, *Pacific Islands*, 5 vols., London, 1939–45, vol. 3, p. 86. © British Crown Copyright/MOD. Reproduced with the permission of Her Britannic Majesty's Stationery Office.)

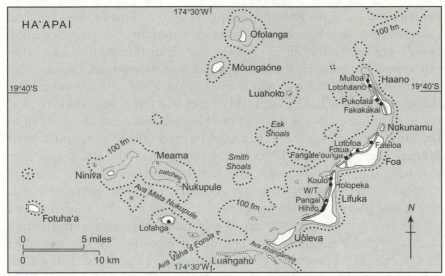

Ha'apai (1944). (*Source:* Naval Intelligence Division, British Admiralty, *Pacific Islands*, 5 vols., London, 1939–45, vol. 3, p. 97. © British Crown Copyright/MOD. Reproduced with the permission of Her Britannic Majesty's Stationery Office.)

Though Thomas could claim few converts, he had baptized Lolohea, a nephew of Tupou, holder of the Tu'i Kanokupolu title which had come to overshadow the Tu'i Ha'atakalaua and Tu'i Tonga titles. Chiefly baptisms ensured that their people would follow in a mass movement. Taufa'ahau was baptized George in August 1831 and Finau named Zephaniah in 1833. Their baptismal names were powerfully symbolic as their people learned biblical and English history. George became a lay preacher, and in his church the communion rail was made of spears. Carved clubs were placed below the pulpit, both symbols of peace. The sacred prestige already attached to their titles was enhanced by conversion. By 1833 Taufa'ahau was ruler of both the Ha'apai and Vava'u groups.

Fresh missionaries arrived, but despite personal rivalries, the church grew dramatically, especially when a 'revival' broke out in 1834 and spread rapidly through the Tongan Islands with some of the same phenomena which had marked the early stages of the Wesleyan movement in Britain. Taufa'ahau's commitment to Christianity deepened dramatically and he was admitted as a local preacher in 1834. Undoubtedly, some of the mass movement was a cultural transposition of Tongan love for communal singing and dancing, but the preaching and teaching of missionaries like Peter Turner, who had had their hearts strangely warmed, also contributed to conversions such as Bulu's. His search for 'life among the stars' transformed him and made him one of the most notable of Polynesian missionaries. Converted by a sermon on the tares and wheat in 1834 on Vava'u, he found release through Peter Turner's words. 'My heart was full of joy and love, and the tears streamed down my cheeks.' He then had a call to go to Fiji to help the missionaries there.'My soul burned within me, and a great longing sprang up in my heart to go away to that land and declare the glad tidings of salvation to the people that knew not God.'[88]

Missionaries were elated at the collapse of the traditional religious order, and ill-prepared for the wars of 1835–40, in which religion and chiefly rivalry were interwoven. Wesleyan missionaries were alarmed at the visit of Pompallier in 1837, and even more by the arrival of Fr Chevron on Tongatapu in 1842 from Fiji. Tupou and Taufa'ahau were also nervous about French activities in Tahiti, and sought to keep Tonga independent. Chevron's coming was not French imperialism. Tongans with close kin ties with parts of Fiji had invited him. Moeaki of Pea, who was a key opponent of the Tongan Wesleyans, was baptized with his wife, Fietoa, in 1844. The Tu'i Tonga was baptized by Bishop Bataillon in 1851. The French imposed a treaty in 1855 for the protection of the Marists and their converts, for there had been inter-tribal wars, aggravated by Christian rivalry. Chevron worked energetically, despite poor health, in the Tongan group for forty-two years and when he died, in 1884, a church of some 17,000 members had emerged.[89] His coffin was carried by one Catholic chief and three Protestants. Many of those who came into the Roman Catholic orbit did so as a way of retaining some of their status against the Tupou forces, while, at the same time, appropriating the power of Christianity. George inherited the prestigious title of Tu'i Kanokupolu in 1845, following the death of Aleamotu'a. Enthroned as King of Tonga on 4 December he, despite further war, had to learn to live with Roman Catholics.

King George learnt quickly about the possibilities of Christian kingship. In 1850 he wrote to Chief Justice Martin of New Zealand, seeking advice about appropriate laws and was advised to consult the Tahitian codes. The 1850 code which resulted was precursor to the 1875 Constitution, which combined Christianity and Tongan custom

---

[88] Wood, *Overseas Missions*, 1. 56–8; *The Autobiography of Joel Bulu* (1871) 15, 18.
[89] Rutherford, *Friendly Islands*, 136–54.

in a lasting way.[90] In addition, George sought to strengthen his relationship to Samoa. Peter Turner, from 1835, with the help of Tongan local preachers, spread the message, and underlined that Christianity was not an exotic European import, but a religion grounded in Polynesian culture. British missionaries accused Tupou of being too political, a sign that he did not recognize their boundaries between church and state.

Another promising field for Tongan Methodism was Fiji, where significant numbers of Tongans lived in the eastern islands, especially on Lakeba.[91] Tahitian missionaries had visited in 1827, but left few lasting results. William Cross and David Cargill arrived in 1835, sent by their colleagues in the enthusiasm generated by revival. They were reinforced by Tongans sent by King George in 1838, including one of the greatest Pacific Islander missionaries, Joeli Bulu. King George himself visited Samoa and Fiji in 1842, to support Tongan missionaries. Ma'afu, King George's cousin, carved out a fiefdom for himself for 30 years and was known as Tu'i Lau. Such religious and political expansionism was a reminder that Europeans were not the only players in the Pacific whose political ambitions were reinforced by religious convictions. Tongan missionaries carried their style of Christianity to Melanesia, as well as Samoa and Fiji.

A cluster of over 200 islands, Fiji and Rotuma included large and small communities with powerful chiefs, some of whom were closely linked with Tonga. Many young Fijian men had also begun to explore the wider world opened by visiting ships. Takai, from Lakeba, had visited Sydney, and returned through Tahiti. There, John Davies taught him to read, along with a Tongan, Lagi. Such contact encouraged Davies to send some teachers to the territories of Tui Nayau. The first missionaries came from Tahiti in 1830. Taharaa, an experienced teacher, Faaruea, and Hatai began work at Narocake on Lakeba, but after two years' failure they moved to Oneata, where about twenty joined the *lotu*, keeping the Sabbath, singing Tahitian hymns, and learning the Ten Commandments. European traders were also bringing new developments. The Fijians were skilled canoe builders and navigators, produced fine pottery and durable houses, and

[90] Latukefu, *Church and State in Tonga*, 221–51 prints the *Code* of Vava'u 1839 and the *Code* of 1850.

[91] Wood, *Overseas Missions*, 2. 1–11 sketches pre-Christian Fiji. Other important studies are R. A. Derrick, *History of Fiji* (Suva, 1950); G. K. Roth, *Fijian Way of Life* (Melbourne, 1953); D. Scarr, *History of Fiji* (Sydney, 1984); B. Thomson, *The Fijians*, (London, 1908); T. Williams and J. Calvert, *Fiji and the Fijians* (2 vols., Suva, 1982).

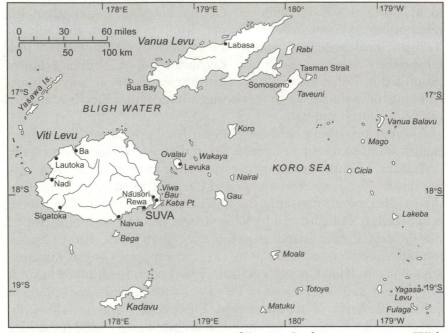

Fiji (1967). (*Source:* D. Scarr, *Fragments of Empire*, Canberra, 1967 p. 61. With permission of the Cartography Unit, Australian National University.)

were formidable warriors, whose savage treatment of their enemies was a byword. Land was crucial to identity, and its fertility was closely linked through sacred places with their religion, in which spirit possession was common among the priests. The serpent god, Degei, was greatly feared, but there were numerous other local gods, totems, and deified ancestors, whose power was awesome. Sorcery was widespread, as was human sacrifice.

It could be argued that the absolute power, cruelty, and violence of the chiefs was a mirror image of the arbitrary and destructive power of the gods. Cannibalism and torture were widely practised as part of tribal warfare, and chiefs' wives were put to death to keep their deceased husbands' spirits company in Bulotu. Abortion and infanticide were common. The reverse side of this was passionate loyalty to chiefs, great bravery, and courage in the face of suffering. As in New Zealand, the impact of endemic warfare was multiplied by the use of firearms. The tiny island of Bau was the centre of chiefly power, where the Vunivalu title was based. Tanoa held this title from 1829 to 1852, followed by Seru (or Cakobau), born in 1817; and when the first

Wesleyans arrived from Tonga in 1835, chiefly Fijians showed little interest in the message of David Cargill and William Cross.[92] Fijian culture is a unique blend of Polynesian and Melanesian cultures. The pioneer missionaries were greatly helped by the chief Josua Mateinaniu, who had been converted in Tonga. He helped Cross and Cargill to understand the basis of chiefly power and their fear of adopting the *lotu*, lest it gave their rivals an excuse to invade. While a few marginal people became Christians, no significant change could occur without the conversion of the major chief. Working-class Wesleyans often found it hard to understand the chiefly and tribal ethos. The help of missionaries like Bulu was indispensable, though that was of little help in countering the tropical diseases which seriously weakened the missionary contingent.

Yet their physical courage was respected by Fijians, who despised their religion. When Waterhouse had a prayer meeting disrupted by warriors, they dispersed when they found they could neither frighten him, nor cause him to run.[93] Late in 1838, more Tongans and several new missionaries arrived, including James Calvert and John Hunt, both of whom went on to give long and distinguished service. Hunt, in particular, was well able to hold his own in negotiations with chiefs. He was willing to take part in the exchanges of goods, which other missionaries saw as theft, and showed great insight into Fijian culture and religion, talking with priests, and shrewdly noting his observations in his very valuable diary. In addition, he mastered the Bau dialect, which was to become the standard for language, and made a fine translation of the New Testament and part of the Old.

Cross died of local diseases. Cargill, a brilliant Scottish linguist, lost his wife and child, and died of an overdose of laudanum in Tonga, while deeply depressed after dengue fever.[94] Personal rivalries were aggravated by ill-health, tiredness from the unfamiliar tropical climate, and primitive living conditions. It was uphill work trying to persuade chiefs of their need for Christ, and the repentance that missionaries believed was visible proof of inner change.

An example of the process can be seen in Varani, a famous warrior and man-eater, who was touched by Hunt's reading of his translation of Matthew. He began to pray and then, struck by Jesus' death,

[92] Wood, *Overseas Missions*, 1. 1–124; Garrett, *To Live Among the Stars*, 102–15.

[93] D. Routledge (ed.), *The Fiji and New Caledonian Journals of Mary Wallis* (Salem, 1994) 183. Wallis also wrote *Life in Feejee* in 1851.

[94] A. Schultz (ed.), *The Diaries and Correspondence of David Cargill* (Canberra, 1977) 245.

announced he would become a Christian. Not only did he put away all his wives but one, he took instruction for baptism along with commoners in 1845. This was a crucial breakthrough. Later that year a revival like that earlier in Tonga occurred, which grounded the new faith firmly in the community, as well as connecting with pre-Christian ecstasy.

Varani continued to fight with Cakobau, but refused to share in the killing and eating of prisoners of war. Cakobau had threatened to eat Varani if he converted, but prudently saw that he was of more value as an ally than a meal. He, himself, had mockingly rejected Hunt's attempts to persuade him, but he knew Hunt and others were praying for him, something that was unsettling, for the missionaries clearly had *mana*. Hunt died in 1848, still a young man, but one whose work laid the foundations for Fijian Christianity by his translation in partnership with Noa, a great authority on the language. With Lyth, Hunt used local chants and dances to celebrate the Gospel and dramatize the biblical message for those who were still shaped by orality, rather than literacy. Even more important, the District meeting ordained four Tongans to the ministry, opening the way for Fijians to do similar work. Christian ideas of holiness accorded with aspects of *tapu,* and the work of ministers was shaped by popular expectations of the *talatala* as they were called, which linked with the pre-Christian priests.

Cakobau was a complex person, ruthless and cruel, sharp-witted, contemptuous of the missionaries. Yet he could see that the world he knew was changing with European influences, and that in partnership with Christians he might save values he cherished, rather than see his people ruled by Tongans or Europeans. He knew what had happened in Tahiti in 1842. When Bataillon visited Cakobau in 1851, backed up by a French warship, Cakobau rejected his pleas to recognize the protection of the Virgin Mary, and was installed as ruler of Bau in 1853. Two Marist priests were landed at Lakeba in 1844 with two Wallisian catechists, Apolonia and Pako. Wesleyan missionaries and their converts were hostile. The small mission, however, survived and by 1861 there were 600 converts, and an estimated 4,000 catechumens, thanks to the work of Fr Breheret.

There were danger signals. Ratu Mara of Rewa stirred up revolts which Varani tried to settle by mediation, but he failed, and lost his life. Waterhouse came to live on Bau, on what had been the rubbish dump. He was tough and resilient. His work was greatly aided by a visit from Taufa'ahau, in November 1853, travelling to Sydney, who also urged Cakobau to convert, as well as pointing out that one of the strongholds of his enemies was takeable. Taufa'ahau reinforced his plea to *lotu* in a letter from Nuku'alofa in February 1854. Even more vital, his troops helped Cakobau to victory at Kaba in 1855, thus seeming to confirm the power of Jehovah. Joseph Waterhouse was also pressing hard, and on 30 April, Cakobau attended worship with wives and entourage. Sacred trees were felled, all but one wife put away, family prayers begun and after the usual instruction, he was baptized on 11 January 1857. The killing stone on Bau became a baptismal font.

Pockets of resistance remained, but increasing numbers of Fijians became Christian in a communal way, by renouncing their traditional deities and spirits, and opening themselves to personal faith in a Methodist church. The mix of attachment to land, acceptance of chiefly authority, and *lotu* formed a matrix for the emergence of Fijian Christianity which combined sacred and secular in an enduring way that was quite different from the ethos of British Methodism. Fijian missionaries carried these values to Melanesia.

While a unified monarchy did not emerge because of chiefly rivalries and regional differences, the Christian kingdom which resulted gave missionaries significant influence, and prevented major alienation of land to commercial interests. Its ethos was quite distinctive, another reminder of the way local languages and culture decisively shaped reception of the Christian message into a modified sacred society. Methodist language gave Fijians a way of speaking about a dramatically new way of life, which has retained its power for over a century. One account of conversion must suffice, filtered by a European recorder but still conveying a note of authenticity, underlining that conversion was both communal and personal.

Mary Wallis described the conversion of Marama, who initially hated the *lotu* after the death of her husband. After mourning was over, she described how

'I prayed to Jesus, not because I loved to pray to Him but I knew it was the fashion for "*lotus*" to pray. After a little while I began to love prayer. When I prayed I felt less unhappy and I began to think more about Jesus Christ than of Nalela and then I prayed very often that Jesus would make me good, that I might go to heaven and be forever happy. Jesus has made me see how foolish my former doings were, and I now hate my wicked conduct.'[95]

Some of the depth with which Christianity penetrated traditional

---

[95] M. Wallis, *Life in Feejee* (Suva, 1983) 168–9.

culture can be seen in Bulu's setting of the Creed, Lord's Prayer, and Te Deum to traditional chants. Churches were also built to the accompaniment of Christianized building songs. The first hymns in Fijian used traditional forms with great effect. Proverbs and riddles were another part of traditional culture adapted to the Christian message. Lorimer Fison adapted pre-Christian story forms in *Tales of Old Fiji*. Others were written by Fijians, and published in church papers. At funerals, dirges drawing on pre-Christian formulae honoured the dead, but combined these with Christian imagery. Ceremonial giving and exchange was also Christianized. In all these ways we can see how traditional culture and Christianity interacted to give a compelling version of the Gospel.[96]

[96] I am indebted to A. Thornley, 'Fijian Methodism 1874–1945', Ph.D. thesis (Canberra, 1979) and to A. R. Tippett, *Fijian Material Culture* (Honolulu, 1968).

2

ORGANIZING CHRISTIAN CHURCHES FROM THE 1830s TO THE 1870s

This period was marked by the expansion and consolidation of churches, both in settler colonies and in Polynesia. The evangelization of Melanesia was begun, assisted by changes through inclusion into the growing trade networks. Strong foundations for Christian societies were laid by Protestants and Roman Catholics alike. The Pacific Islands churches, which had emerged by the 1830s, were self-supporting communities where land was the source of life and identity. They had local leaders who did not normally have the right to administer the sacraments, or to determine major policy issues. Protestant pastors and chiefs shared authority, with many chiefs serving as deacons or local preachers. Care had to be taken in worship and government to ensure clan and tribal balance. In Tahiti, for example, clan groups led congregational singing. A deacon was in charge of each group. Rivalry could be keen, but was part of the dynamism of Pacific Christianity. Final power remained with missionaries. Many of these island churches had already a strong self-supporting missionary force, far larger proportionally than that of the European sending churches. Simple village schools gave adults and children the rudiments of literacy so that the Bible could be read and culturally adapted.

Village churches were usually built according to missionary memories of British or French models. They accommodated the whole population, with seating reflecting gender, family, and status. Often they were built in stone and plastered with lime, laboriously gathered from the reef, and then burnt to powder. Teachers' and pastors' houses were similar to village houses, but on a larger scale, emulating spacious missionary houses. Protestant churches were plain, and have remained so because of the sacred authority of the conversion period. Polynesian Christians were in the majority in the region until European migration gathered momentum in the 1840s and 1850s. In 1830, there were only 70,000 inhabitants in the Australian colonies. Their enculturation of Christianity endured for over a century. Missionary publicists had 'the Gospel invariably humanising the heathen whom it Christianizes. The Gospel contains the germs of true civilization.'[1] Those who were Protestants were strongly influenced by Evangelicalism. The Melanesian mission had a different ethos. Catholics reflected resurgent French Roman Catholicism and its patterns of clergy–lay relations.

In the settler churches of Australia and New Zealand demographic variations between colonies were significant for denominational patterns. Anglicans were in a majority, followed by Roman Catholics in most Australian colonies. Within each colony there were ethnic and denominational enclaves, like German Lutherans in South Australia and Victoria, which remained culturally important throughout the twentieth century. By 1840 something like 20 per cent of the population were regular church attenders. Anglicans were proportionally strongest in Tasmania, New South Wales, Victoria, and Western Australia, as well as having a strong cultural influence in New Zealand provinces like Canterbury, Nelson, Marlborough, Hawkes Bay, and Poverty Bay. In the latter two regions were large numbers of Maori converts not involved in the destructive land wars. Strong Roman Catholic groups were found in South East Queensland, where many became prosperous farmers and pastoralists, giving that colony a different history of Protestant–Catholic relationships than that in working-class suburbs of Melbourne and Sydney, where the proportion of Catholics was strong enough to exert significant influence in local government. Irish Catholic identity was reinforced by parish life and the need to support schools, as well as religious orders and institutes. Protestant individualism was reinforced amongst mostly urban Baptists and Congregationalists by the more gathered nature of their religious life and the need to have strong inner resources to cope with the absence of a ready-made natural community. Methodists and Presbyterians were sometimes present in sufficiently large numbers to create a religious–ethnic subculture, as were German and Scandinavian Lutherans in Queensland.

Some historians see secular societies developing early in the settler colonies. This thesis needs to be heavily qualified, for its supporters often ignore the influence of religious groups which do not fit their

---

[1] J. Beecham, *Colonization* (London, 1838) 15.

concepts of contemporary relevance. The admittedly imperfect statistics on church attendances and Sunday school rolls indicate that the Protestant churches, which covered almost three-quarters of the population, had levels of attendance not too different from many parts of Britain by the end of the nineteenth century because of steady numerical increase.[2] What made that growth significant was the increased involvement, as churches included both migrants and native-born in their activities. Roman Catholics also markedly increased participation rates in Australia and New Zealand, just as they did in Ireland and North America.

Church leaders were important in public life, and had close ties to the elites in their colony. If religious pluralism made the construction of a traditional Christian society impossible, many settlers thought of themselves as Christians even if their definition did not satisfy church leaders. Archdeacon Broughton argued that 'as a community, then, which is irreligious, can afford but precarious support to liberty, prosperity, peace or life, it is no better, perhaps it is even worse, than no society at all; for when the laws which are in operation do no good they must do mischief'. The Presbyterian John Gillie in Hobart was more optimistic, believing that a Presbyterian minister should be involved 'in all movements for social advancement, in all attempts to suppress vice, immorality and crime: in all attempts to elevate the people, he should be foremost'.[3]

The small settler denominations in Sydney, Hobart, and Launceston were heavily dependent on the church buildings, schools, and clergy subsidized by the authorities, though Catholics, Presbyterians, and Wesleyans were beginning to develop their giving. Settlers wanting a church built used local materials to erect simple buildings in remote districts, but travelling clergy often held services in settlers' homes, or crude hotels. Emancipists and free laity knew that their co-operation was essential to the future of the denominations, but governors and officials were still important because of their political and financial power. Religious and educational change in Eastern and Southern Australia was inescapable because of growth of the free settler population.

The coming to Sydney of the gifted William Grant Broughton to succeed Scott as Archdeacon of New South Wales in 1829 marked

    [2] W. Vampley and W. Phillips, *Historical Statistics and Australians* (Sydney, 1987) 421 ff.
    [3] W. G. Broughton, *Religion Essential to the Security of Nations* (Sydney, 1834) 4; J. Gillie, *An Address* (Hobart, 1884) 16.

a decisive new beginning for the town of over 12,000 people. He was experienced in leadership, had formidable social connections, and was both intelligent and well educated. Representing all that was best in the High Church tradition, he was a committed Protestant with a clear vision of the duty of the Church of England to shape the life of the whole community. The dissolution of the financial basis for that came when the Church and Schools Corporation was ended in 1833 and its lands sold.

A skilled defender of the principle of establishment, Broughton was an important member of the colony's Executive Council, giving wise counsel, while upholding the privileges of the Church of England. He won the confidence of key laity, and travelled energetically around his far-flung territories, even to Paihia, New Zealand, in 1838, for confirmations, making shrewd observations on the clergy, and planning for the expansion of church schools and parishes.

He believed that a strong Church of England was the best solution to the needs of the Australian colonies, and that Christianity was essential to social stability and morality. He worked hard to encourage colonists to fulfil their religious and civic obligations. Some watched his growing influence with alarm, fearing that he was working to plant a religiously tyrannical Established Church. In actuality, expansion of settlement, religious demography, and Catholic Emancipation in 1829 were working against him, not to mention the development of Port Phillip, and the foundation of South Australia in 1836. Anglicans in Hobart who disputed Presbyterian claims to equality were dismayed by a letter from Sir George Grey in London to Principal MacFarlane in Scotland in 1836, which laid down that the Church of Scotland was equally entitled with the Church of England to share in the public funds applicable to the general objects of religious instruction.

A DIFFERENT CATHOLICISM

Greatly helped by the Society for the Propagation of the Faith, which provided £26,000 between 1837 and 1849, Roman Catholics formed somewhere between a fifth and a quarter of the population in undivided New South Wales. They were led by clergy who were not content to be religiously and socially subordinate, even though many of their people fell into the latter category. Their religious loyalty and obstinate piety in face of Protestantizing pressures were a precious resource. The arrival of William Ullathorne, as vicar general, later to become a notable bishop in England from 1846, marked a further stage in the development of local Catholicism.[4] He intervened decisively in the bitter disputes between clergy and laity. The colonial authorities could not ignore someone so well educated and talented. To make up for decades of indifference and neglect, Rome bestirred itself and took a dramatic initiative, appointing the Englishman John Bede Polding in 1834 as Bishop of Sydney, the first diocesan English Catholic bishop to be appointed since the reign of Mary.

Arriving in 1835, he proved a very gifted and dedicated pastor, an energetic writer and publicist for Catholicism, who gave huge energy to the task of bringing religious consolation to convicts, especially to the newly arrived. Recidivism fell sharply, which pleased the authorities. Anglicans were chagrined at the development of such episcopal leadership, for their nearest bishop was in Calcutta. Broughton protested without avail to the Colonial Office against Polding taking the name of Sydney for his diocese.

Polding had only Roman episcopal models to guide him, but he was never anything other than a very English gentleman. The normal structures of diocesan life did not exist, and his task as a pioneer bishop was very difficult, for he lacked financial resources. Many of his clergy were passionately Irish. He disliked their money-raising enthusiasm. His vision of a Benedictine Australia was noble but unrealistic. Relationship with his Irish suffragans was soured by his insensitivity to Irish aspirations, and their returned animosity. Though Australia remained a mission country under Propaganda Fide till 1976, his order was never able to provide the men and money that the Marists drew on for their Pacific missions. A hierarchy was set up in 1842. Polding's capacity for taking tough decisions was limited and he was too easily persuaded by the last person to speak to him. His pastoral duties took him away from Sydney too much, and his subordinates were liable to make decisions which he regretted. He attempted to set up a seminary to meet the huge pastoral need for clergy, but was, like Broughton, frustrated by the absence of an adequate educational system. One of his best decisions was to invite the Sisters of Mercy to start a religious community. In 1857 he also founded the first local religious order—the Good Samaritan Sisters.

---

[4] W. B. Ullathorne, *From Cabin Boy to Archbishop* (London, 1941); J. B. Polding, *Letters* (2 vols., Sydney, 1994–6); F. O'Donohue, *The Bishop of Botany Bay* (Sydney, 1982).

Though Roman Catholic Irish had great deference for their priests, especially when they were attacked by Protestants, they also had their ways of taking initiatives, and disregarding authority. A succession of bishops found that they had to face public criticism from their own people, of a kind that they were unaccustomed to, even if they and the clergy were spiritually indispensable in ministering sacramentally. Catholic laity had a long period in which to imbibe the democratic and anti-authoritarian attitudes which were so potent in colonial life, and which modified their religious obedience.

Polding had little effective control over missionary priests or laity pushing out beyond the boundaries of law and order.[5] Many laity became accustomed to taking services of their own, reading the Missal and saying the Rosary, so that when a network of religious authority was set up by resident priests and the creation of dioceses in Hobart, Adelaide, Perth, and Melbourne, a great deal of work was needed to fill in the gaps in priestly authority bred by years of self-reliance. In addition, educated Catholics like W. A. Duncan, despite their small numbers, soon established their civic influence through the press.

There was deep disagreement in the Irish community about how to relate to British hegemony. For the significant Protestant group, there was no problem. For Catholics it was more difficult. One group moved into political and professional leadership. Some wanted to avoid antagonizing the Protestant majority, and gradually to improve Catholics' position in society. Others were for a policy of confrontation regarding the injustices which had too long been inflicted by the English. A Catholic convert from the Church of England who was enormously significant for both New South Wales and Victoria was Caroline Chisholm, whose deep Christian convictions, political acumen, oratorical and literary gifts, and social status gave her concern for migrants considerable impact.[6] Arriving in Sydney in 1838, she was deeply concerned about the exploitation of young women. She provided hostels, and acted as employment agent, and marriage broker, for thousands of ordinary people in a quite unsectarian way. She was unique in her lobbying of officials in Sydney and London, which was seen by some as quite unladylike. Though her officer husband had

---

[5] R. Wiltgen, *The Founding of the Roman Catholic Church in Oceania* (Canberra, 1979) 346–57 points out the way Polding negotiated to secure both episcopal power and the authority of a vicar apostolic. Polding, as Vicar Apostolic of New Holland, remained responsible for Aborigines.

[6] C. Chisholm, *Female Immigration* (Sydney, 1842); *Comfort for the Poor* (London, 1847).

only a modest pension, she demonstrated that riches and power were not the only resources to bring about social and legislative change.

She and her supporters achieved significant changes in the regulations governing emigrant ships. When she returned to Victoria in 1854, she saw how greatly migrants and their families needed temporary accommodation, and set up hostels on the route to the goldfields. Though she died impoverished in London in 1877, her humanitarian achievement was astonishing. Even though Dr Lang saw her as a threat to the Protestant character of New South Wales, many whom she helped were Protestants. In her later years she was an advocate of radical causes like universal male suffrage, abolition of state aid, and ending squatter privilege, as well as pleading for better housing for the poor.[7]

Clergy could be even more difficult to deal with than assertive laity, as Bishop Robert Willson found to his cost when he came to Hobart in 1844. Not only did he have to deal with Anglican antagonism, Fr Therry did everything possible to make his bishop's life miserable. Polding had promised to recall him, and alternately supported and attacked Willson in his struggles with Therry, despite the mounting evidence for Therry being almost totally without scruples in financial matters, and bringing the church into disrepute by his refusal to settle debts. Yet he was greatly respected by many of his parishioners. Willson had great problems because of the poverty of the small Catholic community (only 14 per cent of the colony in 1851). Religious observance was low, partly because of shortage of priests, partly because Protestant employers still had power to compel their servants to attend Protestant services, and partly because the community was so poor that it was hard put to provide churches and schools.

Few Catholics were elected to parliament, or were respected members of the clannish elite dominated by Protestants. Willson imaginatively used lay catechists, and in 1854 founded a lay sisterhood for works of mercy. He was alone among Catholic bishops in his ministry to the whole community through pleas for penal reform on Norfolk Island, which was closed because of his telling submissions. He did remarkable work in Tasmania, Victoria, and New South Wales to improve the often barbarous treatment of the mentally ill and permanently insane. He demonstrated that Catholic commitment to

[7] *Sydney Morning Herald*, 9 July 1859; 22 Feb. 1861; 14 June 1861.

liberty was not only the monopoly of clergy like Therry, who posed as martyrs to episcopal tyranny but were unrepentant autocrats where their own interests were concerned.

In Perth, there was an even more deplorable example of factionalism inspired by the irascible Bishop Brady whom Polding had appointed vicar general in 1843. His ambitions totally outran his ability and the finances of his tiny diocese. He had proposed in 1845 the creation of three vicariates apostolic—Perth, Essington, and King George Sound—and was consecrated Bishop of Perth in 1845 while in Rome. When Rome appointed Serra in response to Brady's plea for a co-adjutor in 1849, Brady then engaged in a series of unjustified lawsuits against his colleagues. Rome again intervened. Pius IX suspended Brady and made Serra his representative. In December 1851, Brady returned to Perth in defiance of Rome and tried to unseat Serra. Polding went to settle the matter. Brady submitted, and some of his supporters were excommunicated. It was one of the few occasions when Polding showed that he could act decisively.

While Serra dreamt of a great network of Benedictine missions, it was Salvado who gave the vision local substance at New Norcia from 1847. The abbey later was exempted from episcopal control, and flourished. Rome still saw Australia as a mission country, and Pius IX exhorted the Australian hierarchy in 1868 to do more for the needs of the Aborigines. Polding's vision for Aborigines was a noble one, but it never took flesh. Unlike Pompallier, who had the opportunity to focus on mission, Polding had too many other responsibilities.

EXPERIMENTS WITH ESTABLISHMENT

In the wake of the Reform Act of 1832, the English authorities recognized that a local bishop was needed for the Church of England. Governor Bourke was pressing them to regularize the situation. Broughton was the obvious candidate, but he was deeply embroiled in debates about the future of education. He did not want to accept the office, if it would limit his freedom to criticize the government. Speaking to the General Committee of Protestants in 1836, he emphasized that the Church of England must have the primary responsibility for educating the colony's children. 'I think you will have perceived it is my determination, whether with the Government or without, to stand on the proper ground of the Church of England. . . . I take that course for the advantages of Protestants generally.'[8]

Archdeacon William Hutchins in Hobart took a similar position against general religious education in *A Letter on the School Question* (1839). Broughton was equally adamant that the teaching office of the Church of England should not be undercut by a common Christianity taught in schools. He rejected the non-denominational Irish solution, which Bourke saw as the best way to educate youth in Christianity while at the same time aiding the main churches financially, and thus entrenching religious division. Broughton was equally hostile to Gipps's proposals for the British and Foreign School Society system, for the church's schools 'are to her as to her right hand, by means of which she is to execute the work which is given to her to do.'[9]

Despatches from the colonies pushed the British authorities to recognize that an Anglican monopoly was politically not sustainable. There were similar pressures for equality before the law, and in sharing financial assistance, in Ontario, Canada. The result was a decision to grant aid to each of the major religious bodies, using a formula for stipends and buildings which encouraged self-help, and the gathering of viable congregations. The Acts were passed in 1836 in New South Wales, in 1837 in Van Diemen's Land, and in 1840 in Western Australia. Most Baptists and Congregationalists refused on ground of conscience to take any aid, or to accept grants of land which the governments of both colonies made very generously to the major churches.[10] Anglicans, Presbyterians, Roman Catholics, and Wesleyans all greatly benefited by this assistance. In virtue of numbering over 50 per cent of the population, the Anglicans with some wealthy donors were best placed to organize new congregations, and thus received a proportion of the funds greater than their proportion of the population. The structure of the system of grants favoured urban churches against rural areas with scattered settlers. The British government wished to create a Christian society, but on different bases than in the United Kingdom. Divisions over education suggested some very articulate settlers wished the state to curb clerical pretensions.

The strain on the colonial budgets became such that the subsidy

[8] A. Austin (ed.), *Select Documents in Australian Education* (Melbourne, 1963) 50–1.

[9] Ibid., 73–4.

[10] E. O. Cox (ed.), *Journal of Frederick Miller* (Hobart, 1984); J. West, *The Voluntary Support of the Christian Ministry* (Hobart, 1849); A. C. Nelson, *History of the Effective Establishment of Congregationalism* (Hobart, 1930) 71–2.

amount was capped in 1842. Migration from Van Diemen's Land and New South Wales to what became Victoria grew rapidly in the 1830s and 1840s, and there were a few settlers venturing into Queensland, or Moreton Bay as it was then called. No aid was given there after 1859, when it was detached from New South Wales. Settlement in Western Australia remained small and sparse, but similar assistance was given from the colonial treasury for the building of churches, and the payment of stipends for the scattered clergy.

The consecration of Broughton as Bishop of Australia on 14 February 1836 was well deserved, but he had no legal basis to create a diocesan system of government. Acting unilaterally as bishop, when there was no legal definition of the rights of clergy, would not have worked even in England or Ireland. In Australia it was a prescription for conflict, and suspicion. Nor was the position of the laity adequately defined. The Church of England Temporalities Act of 1837 created elected property trustees and churchwardens, and thus gave a legal basis for parishes and congregations to operate in the new environment created by the Church Acts. Similar legislation was passed for other churches, but Anglicans had no voice in the choice of clergy, for that was Broughton's responsibility alone. Lay patronage was virtually unknown, but laity soon came to feel they ought to have a part in the choice of their clergy, and in their education. Attempts by Broughton to train ordinands at St James's College in Sydney were ridiculed by *The Atlas* in a scurrilous letter purporting to be from students there. 'Without glory for him and slavishness for us, what would be the use of our learning?'[11]

The Acts were enormously important in shaping the future of Christianity for the rest of the century, just as was similar legislation in Canada. They entrenched the dominance of the Church of England, and yet ensured that its establishment status was weakened because of the financial help to Wesleyans, Presbyterians, and Catholics. Christianity was given a public role which made it partner with colonial governments in the creation of a righteous and educated nation. Church leaders were expected to contribute to public debate on all kinds of subjects, as well as to those matters which were deemed to be central to the churches' concerns. Yet the Acts meant that the public identification of the Church of England as the legal guardian of the Christian tradition had ended. The colonial governments opted

---

[11] *Atlas*, 6 Feb. 1847.

for an inclusive definition of Christianity which was abhorrent to many Anglicans. Their leaders, however, grasped the financial assistance offered, and began a modest building boom which saw church buildings of the favoured four churches double in number. A quite respectable church could be built with the pound-for-pound subsidy offered, up to £1,000. Similarly, stipends were subsidized up to £200 providing that a congregation could be gathered. Wealthier congregations paid more, but struggling ones paid lower stipends well into the twentieth century.

Presbyterians had formed a presbytery in 1832 in New South Wales, and three years later in Van Diemen's Land.[12] Compared with parent bodies in Scotland, their membership was tiny, but they took themselves with great seriousness, and gradually shepherded their constituency into cohesion. Dr Lang found to his dismay that ministers whom he had recruited for ministry in Australia were not disposed to be his clients. They displayed independent minds, and were critical of Lang's administrative shortcomings and personal vindictiveness. The 1843 Scottish Disruption deeply divided the colonial Presbyterian community.

SOUTH AUSTRALIA

In South Australia, where Dissenters were strongest, the governor's attempt to place a modest sum on the estimates for church purposes in Ordinance No. Ten of 1847 aroused their strong opposition.[13] As soon as a parliament was elected in 1852, legislation was passed to prevent any further state aid for religious purposes. A total of £15,424 had been distributed. Despite this self-denial, Christians there managed to build many fine churches, and also gave generously for church extension. Significantly, the Church of England never had the dominance it did in other parts of Australia. Methodists were the dominant body, so far as effectiveness was concerned, and Anglicans declined steadily from 53 per cent in 1846 to 29 per cent in 1901, while Methodists grew from 10 per cent in 1846 to 25 per cent in 1901.

It was in South Australia that Congregationalists were most strongly

---

• [12] J. Heyer, *Presbyterian Pioneers of Van Diemen's Land* (Hobart, 1935); J. Cameron, *Centenary History of the Presbyterian Church of New South Wales* (Sydney, 1905).

[13] D. Pike, *Paradise of Dissent* (Melbourne, 1957) 383; D. Hilliard, *Godliness and Good Order* (Adelaide, 1986) 4–21.

represented, and their first minister, T. Q. Stow, was a fine choice, for he quickly adapted to the hardships of the colony, built a simple church, and provided important leadership in the community, especially on church–state partnership. His confidence in the emergence of a free community without the problems of old England helped to sustain settlers in the first difficult years. Similarly, the influence of the lay philanthropist George F. Angas ensured that from the beginning there was an organized Baptist presence.[14] Their church in Flinders Street, Adelaide, became one of the most important in the Australian colonies. Angas's generosity to persecuted Lutherans from Prussia gave South Australia a distinctive strand in its mosaic of denominations. He was one of the most notable laymen in the colonies, a philanthropist, and advocate of spiritual liberty as a foundation for Christian society. Though he had many financial setbacks in the 1840s, he migrated to Adelaide in 1851 to safeguard his investments, and became exceedingly wealthy. His radical nonconformity, shared by many other settlers, gave South Australia a distinctive Christian tone though Anglicans remained significant. Holy Trinity Church in Adelaide is one of the oldest surviving Anglican parishes in Australia.[15]

Its first minister, Charles Howard, was an Irish Evangelical. The parish was endowed with one urban acre and forty rural acres to provide a glebe, and had a carefully drawn trust deed of 27 June 1837. Howard was active in the Temperance Society, the British and Foreign Sailors Society, the Adelaide Savings Bank, the South Australian Schools Society, and the Board of Aboriginal Protection, as well as fulfilling parish duties through a District Visiting Society. Governor Gawler supported him enthusiastically, underlining just how important establishing a Christian society was for many of the colonial leaders. A Sunday school was opened in 1838.

Howard even put together 105 hymns in the *South Australian Hymn Book*—a thoroughly evangelical selection. They were accompanied by a seraphine, a precursor of the harmonium. Howard found that being a parish priest and ministering as chaplain to the colony had its problems, for the parish's finances were precarious. A debt of over

---

[14] E. Hodder, *George Fife Angas* (London, 1891). H. Hussey, *More than Half a Century of Christian Life and Colonial Experience* (Adelaide, 1897) 308 ff. gives a lively account of his role as private secretary to G. F. Angas and controversies with Roman Catholics.

[15] B. Dickey, *Holy Trinity* (Adelaide, 1988) 15–64. I am indebted to him for permission to quote from his history. Hussey, *Christian Life and Colonial Experience*, 81–104 gives a member's perspective on Trinity membership.

£2,000 and other expenses were not covered by an income of only £400 in a time of financial crisis in the colony in the early 1840s. Howard died in June 1843, with the threat of the buildings being seized for debt. To make matters worse, the church developed severe structural problems which brought further expense. James Farrell, another Irish Evangelical, succeeded as the colony's chaplain, and married Mrs Howard. He was a much better financial manager, and the debt gradually fell. The history of the parish until the early 1850s shows what a financial struggle it was to fund the buildings thought necessary for a Christian colony, even though many of the colony's elite worshipped there. Some of the leading parishioners were hostile to the synod set up by Bishop Short, one of the bishops appointed in 1847, because they did not want to weaken common Christianity, or undermine democratic rights by accepting voting in 'houses'. They were also at the centre of a spirited debate about polity after the 1850 Conference of Bishops in Sydney.[16]

LUTHERAN BEGINNINGS

An important strand of European Protestantism arrived in South Australia late in 1838—Lutherans, who were refugees from an attempt by Frederick William II of Prussia to create a united Church of Lutheran and Reformed Christians.[17] Pastor Augustus Kavel (1798–1860) was initially in favour of the royal policy, but came to the conviction that union would lead to indifferentism. He resigned at Easter 1835, and was re-ordained by Lutherans. The result was severe persecution. He investigated several possible destinations for migration, and was attracted by South Australia where Angas was sympathetic, and also willing to give financial help. The Prussian government was obstructive about granting passports, but the migrants finally departed from their homes on 8 June 1838. Angas advanced £8,000 for, though he had reservations about Lutheranism, he believed that their willingness to suffer persecution meant that they should be given the right hand of fellowship. He also hoped that they would be of great value to his total investment in the colony.

[16] Anon., *An Account of the Proceedings of the Laity and Clergy of the Church of England* (Adelaide, 1851).

[17] A. Bauer, *Under the Southern Cross* (Adelaide, 1956); E. Leske, *For Faith and Freedom* (Adelaide, 1996); T. Hebart, *The United Evangelical Lutheran Church in Australia* (Adelaide, 1938).

Astonished by the dryness of Adelaide, pestered by flies, and puzzled by the strange vegetation on arrival, they nevertheless gave thanks to God on 25 November, rejoicing that they could worship according to conscience and educate their children in the Lutheran tradition. Like many British migrants, they named their area after familiar sites. They called their first village Klemzig. Another group arrived on 30 December and yet another at the end of January 1839. They settled further inland and called their settlement Hahndorf after Captain Hahn. All speedily proved their worth as farmers.

In May 1839, the three groups held a church convention. They adopted a constitution, decided to buy land in the Barossa Valley, and invited G. D. Fritzsche to join them. His conscience had led him to resign from the state church in 1835. He conducted a secretive under-ground ministry, believing that emigration was wrong, but a break-down in health, and invitations from both the United States and Australia, led him to reconsider his options. Angas could not help, but others helped finance the migrants who arrived on 27 October 1841, and settled at Bethania and Lobethal. The first 800 settlers provided the spiritual care for a much larger German community who came for economic rather than religious reasons. By 1860, almost 9,000 German migrants had arrived.

In addition to adjusting to a new land with a dramatically different climate, they had to finance churches and stipends without state aid, and learn how to deal with pastoral and theological disagreements over eschatology which erupted into confrontation at the Bethany con-vention of August 1846. Kavel and Fritzsche separated, and the schism lasted 120 years, despite attempts to negotiate on the churches' con-stitution, Kavel's *Protestations*, and eschatology. Further schisms occurred, reflecting little credit on any of those involved. Personalities and doctrine were dangerously confused. Church members played a part in these disputes in a way that would not have so readily occurred in Germany, but it was their Lutheran heritage rather than their new environment which shaped their construction of a denomination. The same was true of Lutherans in New Zealand whose first congregation was founded in 1846 in Upper Moutere, Nelson.

Other Lutherans migrated to Victoria. Pastor M. Goethe united varied groups of Lutherans in Victoria from 1852. He had been a student for the Roman Catholic priesthood, but became a Protestant, and was ordained by J. D. Lang. He was installed as pastor of Trinity Lutheran Church, on Good Friday 1853, by other Protestant clergy, none of whom were Lutherans. The Lutheran population had grown sufficiently to establish a Lutheran Synod of Victoria in 1856, which to the strict confessionalists of South Australia was fatally tainted by unionism, links with German state churches, and the interdenominational Basel Mission Society. Attempts to establish links with Fritzsche's Synod led to splits in Victoria. Other groups migrated from South Australia to Western Australia and the Wimmera. A more lasting presence was established in the Riverina, led initially by laymen, with strong parishes such as Walla Walla still flourishing over a century later.

The first Lutherans in Queensland were sponsored by Lang, who was fluent in German.[18] He recruited missionaries in 1837 from the interdenominational Gossner Mission Society to work among Aborigines. In early 1838 they established themselves at Zion Hill near Breakfast Creek, Brisbane, but their missionary effort failed. The Society also sent missionaries in 1842 to the remote Chatham Islands in New Zealand, where they had only limited impact despite their energy and dedication. C. F. A. Schirmeister's health forced his retirement from this isolated mission after a decade, and he began ministry in central Brisbane, founding St Andrew's Lutheran Church, and was a key figure in the formation of the Lutheran Synod of Queensland in 1885. Another group formed a German and Scandinavian Synod later that year. Rivalry was keen. The North German Mission Society also sent A. Honoré, A. Riemenschneider, and J. F. H. Wohlers to New Zealand to work among German settlers, but they preferred to work among the Maori.[19] Wohlers worked on Ruapuke from 1844.

ESTABLISHING DENOMINATIONAL IDENTITY

Such divisions were not a problem for Roman Catholics once a hierarchy was set up, and the first council held in 1844.[20] The canonical powers of bishops were carefully defined, though in a mission territory they had fewer checks on their authority than in Ireland, where the

---

[18] F. D. Theile, *One Hundred Years of the Lutheran Church in Queensland* (Adelaide, 1985).

[19] S. Natusch, *Hell and High Water* (Christchurch, 1977). *Brother Wohlers* (Christchurch, 1969) gives a useful overview, but Wohlers' own writings are worth consulting, *Memories of the Life of J. F. H. Wohlers* (Dunedin, 1905). He also wrote 'On the conversion and civilization of the Maoris in the South of New Zealand', *TPNZI* 14 (1881) 123–34.

[20] *Acta et decreta concilii primi* (Sydney, 1844).

historic legal rights of clergy could be an embarrassment to bishops. In Australia, clergy of the mission had no rights of tenure until later in the century, and could be freely moved by their bishops.[21] There were also tensions over expenditure, for articulate Catholic laity resented the assumption of some bishops and priests that the spending of God's money was not the business of church members. In Melbourne there were robust lay criticisms of Bishop Goold's financial management in the 1850s, but these did not carry the day, for there was no legal requirement that his accounts should be published as was normal in the Protestant churches.

Though bishops from time to time held consultations with their priests, tensions between bishops, and the mission status of Australia, prevented the emergence of synodal meetings on a regular basis. Polding and his successor held provincial councils which later included New Zealand bishops, but these trans-Tasman relationships were never strong. The focus of unity was Propaganda in Rome, not the region of Australasia. The French Marist bishops in the Pacific took little interest in the doings of their southern brothers, apart from attending major ceremonies if they were travelling through.

By contrast, the Wesleyans in the Australian colonies had a close relationship with their co-religionists in New Zealand and the Pacific. Considerable exchange of ministers occurred between districts, and between mission territories. Even though London retained considerable authority and often exercised it most insensitively, devolution of responsibility occurred as Methodism grew in the colonies, and needed less financial assistance from London through the Missionary Society. In 1844, Walter Lawry became superintendent of both mission and home work. While in Auckland, Lawry became a wealthy man. Joseph Fletcher prayed that 'we may see his face no more, unless he got reconverted'.[22]

An Australasian Conference (with forty ministers and 20,000 members, of whom only 7,000 were Europeans) was set up in 1855, including districts in Tonga, Fiji, and New Zealand, as well as Victoria, Tasmania, South Australia, and later Queensland. A general Committee met annually, but an Executive in Sydney dealt with the ordinary business of the missions. Pronouncements on Sunday schools, education, and state aid were issued by the Conference.

---

[21] I. B. Waters, 'Stability of parish priests: the Australian history', *ACR* 74 (1997) 307–14.

[22] J. Colwell (ed.), *A Century in the Pacific* (Sydney, 1914); J. Fletcher, *A Voice from New Zealand* (Auckland, 1850) 2.

Formal addresses were sent to the societies, to the British Conference, and to the governor. A careful list of all Methodist properties had been compiled. Income in 1855 was estimated to be £6,300, but estimated expenditure was likely to be £8,228, with the deficit being made up by Britain. That financial dependence soon ended. Energetic preachers and committed members combined to take Methodism into expanding districts, as well as building a formidable network of urban circuits and associations with strong philanthropic, educational, and mission commitments.

As Congregationalism grew in Australia, links developed with LMS workers in the Pacific, some of whom began to take furloughs and undertake deputation in Australia. Strong lay leadership in Sydney, Melbourne, Hobart, Launceston, and Adelaide made local context formative of identity. In Sydney there was quite a network of retired Pacific missionaries like Aaron Buzzacott and William Barff, who played significant parts in congregations, and helped to foster regional awareness. In Hobart, George Clarke at Davey Street Chapel built a congregation which included premiers such as W. R. Giblin and Sir Philip Fysh and other leading citizens. Clarke himself was vice-chancellor of the university from 1890 to 1907. He shared the great optimism for congregational growth with Stow in Adelaide. Stow had a vision for expanded Congregationalism. 'We look far into a *third* world—forming under the brilliant lights of expanded science, the rapid processes of modern improvement, the surprising impulse of universal commerce, the meliorations of widely extended philanthropy and the awakened and gathered energies of the church of God.'[23] Despite their small size, Congregationalists powerfully shaped the emerging Christian ethos, as well as being politically, culturally, and economically influential.

Broughton with an eye to expansion visited New Zealand in 1838 at the request of CMS missionaries, and wrote to the Archbishop of Canterbury about the need for bishops there, and in other Australian colonies. Lambeth was increasingly interested in colonial church affairs. An imperial vision for the Church of England was slowly emerging. High quality candidates were found such as George Selwyn as Bishop of New Zealand in 1841, and Francis Nixon as Bishop of Tasmania in 1842. Further steps were taken in 1847 to divide Broughton's gigantic diocese of Australia. He became Bishop

[23] T.Q. Stow, *Congregationalism in the Colonies* (Sydney, 1855) 5.

of Sydney.[24] Augustus Short, William Tyrrell, and Charles Perry were appointed respectively to Adelaide, Newcastle, and Melbourne. The last was a strong Evangelical. The others were all influenced by the continuing High Church tradition represented by Broughton. That was to have important consequences for the development of the Church of England's government, ethos, and relation to the state in Australia.[25]

A network of clergy and bishops co-operated with powerful laity like W. E. Gladstone, and Miss Angela Burdett-Coutts, to staff churches in the Empire with suitable clergy who could live out a more apostolic ministry than was possible at home. Edward Coleridge of Eton was a key figure in recruiting gifted and idealistic clergy ready for some sacrifice. Bishop Selwyn, a member of the Camden Society, had already thought carefully about the role of the Church of England before going to New Zealand, and written a perceptive account of the role that reformed cathedrals could play. He took with him a group of talented, well-educated clergy to help him put the Church in New Zealand on a proper basis, in which the CMS missionaries had only a minor part. Selwyn disapproved of their theology, their churchmanship, their landholdings, and was slow to ordain them, for they were mostly not educated to the standard he desired for his expansionist vision in the Pacific. The Archbishop of Canterbury had charged Selwyn 'to regard New Zealand as a fountain to diffuse the streams of salvation over the coasts and islands of the Pacific Ocean'.[26]

A bishop of enormous physical energy, he learnt Maori speedily, and from his arrival in 1842 walked and sailed the length and breadth of the country in the best traditions of muscular Christianity. In addition, he travelled into Melanesia, which had been mistakenly included in his diocesan boundaries. The Maori respected him as one with chiefly characteristics. No other Anglican bishop could match his feats of endurance (though he always rested on Sunday), which frequently took him away from his family for months on end while he acted as a Victorian Paul.[27] He even signed affectionate letters to his

[24] J. H. Evans, *Churchman Militant* (Wellington, 1964); G. Philipson, 'The thirteenth apostle', Ph.D. thesis (Dunedin, 1992); J. M. Brown, *Augustus Short* (Adelaide, 1974); A. de Q. Robin, *Charles Perry* (Perth, 1967); A. P. Elkin, *The Diocese of Newcastle* (Newcastle, 1955).

[25] B. Porter (ed.), *Colonial Tractarians* (Melbourne, 1984); R. Border, *Church and State in Australia* (London, 1962); J. Davis, *Australian Anglicans and their Constitution* (Canberra, 1993).

[26] *Church Record* (1861) 111.

[27] W. Limbrick (ed.), *Bishop Selwyn in New Zealand* (Palmerston North, 1983) 11; H. Hogan (ed.), *Renate's Journey* (Christchurch, 1994) 65 describes some of the frustrations from a Maori perspective.

wife episcopally. At times he was overweeningly authoritarian, and unreasonable to those who saw the purposes of God differently, but he arrived at a crucial time for creating a Church of England with spiritual independence, even though Anglicans behaved as the Established Church. After an earthquake in 1848 the Lieutenant Governor Eyre asked the Revd Robert Cole in Wellington to lead a day of solemn fasting and humiliation for the whole community, as though the Church of Scotland there did not exist.

TOWARDS A MAORI CHURCH

The CMS missionaries had also played an important part in the negotiations which led to the signing of the Treaty of Waitangi in 1840, for they had long been concerned at the lawlessness of British subjects in the Bay of Islands and elsewhere. Though a British Act of 1817 purported to give courts jurisdiction over offences by British nationals overseas, and the missionary Thomas Kendall was appointed a magistrate in 1814, there was no way of enforcing British law. A petition by some northern chiefs for British protection led to the appointment of the worthy James Busby as Resident in 1833. He achieved some order by negotiation, but more was needed at a time when tribal wars were at their most destructive. Baron De Thierry, a French adventurer who arrived in 1837, caused some alarm by his claims to sovereignty. The Confederation of United Tribes in 1835, created by Busby, was incapable of dealing with such incursions if they had been backed by French vessels or of punishing the offences of their own members.

Skilful appeals to the Evangelical networks in London led by the CMS, the Select Committee on Aborigines in 1837, the dispatch of New Zealand company colonists in September 1839, and commercial interests, combined to push the British government to seek through a treaty sovereignty by cession, control of land sales and leases, while the Maori retained control of their resources. Already huge land claims had been made by Sydney land sharks, and some missionaries. Richard Taylor claimed 50,000 acres but was ultimately granted only 2,000. Captain William Hobson arrived on 30 January 1840. After brief discussion and lively debate, the treaty was signed by forty-three local chiefs on 6 February and then taken around the remainder of New Zealand for further signatures, totalling around 500. Surviving records of the discussions for and against signature show that many chiefs were aware that there were dangers in signing. Rewa asked pointedly, 'Is this land to become like Port Jackson and all other lands the English have come to? No! Return! Governor, I, Rewa, say to you, go back.'[28]

At Taupo, the great Te Heuheu Tukino bluntly rejected the treaty emissaries, Iwikau and Te Korohiko. 'Is it for you to place the *mana* of Te Heuheu beneath the feet of a woman? I will not agree to the *mana* of a strange people being placed over this land. Though every chief in the island consent to it, yet I will not.'[29] Other chiefs in the North Island from tribes like the Arawa also did not sign, raising interesting questions about their legal status when they claimed that they were not bound by the provisions of the treaty. From the outset there were serious doubts about the status of the document and the meaning of the key terms, for it was quickly drafted, and there were significant differences between Maori and English versions. Henry Williams, who was responsible for the translation, was competent in Maori, but not so fluent as his brother, William. 'Sovereign authority' was rendered as 'kawanatanga katoa', the term used for the office of Pontius Pilate in the Maori translation of the Gospels. The Maori version of the (*te tino rangatiratanga*) treaty guaranteed chiefly authority over their land, villages, and treasures (*taonga*). The English version did not mention chiefly authority, but spoke of 'the full exclusive and undisturbed possession of their lands, estates, forest, fisheries and other properties', which conveys a rather different meaning.

For Hobson and his superiors, the treaty clearly meant Maori subordination to the Crown, but for Maori the symbolism was rather protection and recognition of chiefly status. Before signing, frank comment about missionary land purchases was made, for Maori debate could be very confrontational before a consensus was reached.[30] The CMS missionaries were clearly in favour of a treaty, believing that without it, the Maori were doomed. Pompallier, who was present, did not actively participate, but sought to ensure that all denominations were treated equally. William Colenso published a very thoughtful account of the proceedings in 1890, when all the other participants

---

[28] J. Caselberg, *Maori is My Name* (Dunedin, 1975) 45.

[29] Ibid., 50; Hogan, *Renate's Journey*, 90. When Selwyn visited Te Heuheu, he drew a map of the North Island with emphasis that 'Taupo is mine and mine it shall remain'.

[30] C. Orange, *Treaty of Waitangi* (Wellington, 1987); J. Belich, *Making of Peoples* (Auckland, 1996) 193–211; J. Crawford (ed.), *Church and State* (Auckland, 1998) 4–6 for analysis of *kawanatanga* in the Maori Bible.

were dead. With the benefit of hindsight he suggested that explanations of the treaty's implications were not careful enough and that the Maori would later accuse the missionaries of complicity in loss of land. While the Treaty did not have direct bearing on the legal status of Christianity it gave the missionaries a more secure framework.

Compared with other treaties signed by colonial powers, its vagueness was not unusual. Certainly Hobson's resources were minimal. Maori consent was essential, and CMS missionaries were vital in securing further chiefly signatures. Its intention was humanitarian, and Lord Stanley, in 1845, curtly repudiated the view of New Zealand Company officials who claimed that it was merely a device for pacifying savages. Many chiefs welcomed courts and a few settlers. They did not expect swamping. Mr Justice Chapman ruled in 1847 in Symonds *v.* Regina that native title was not extinguished except by the free consent of the occupants. From 1846 to 1853 over 30 million acres were alienated for the expenditure of a mere £62,000. For all its limitations, the treaty was one of the foundations for partnership between the Maori majority of 70–100,000 and a very small settler community. British sovereignty meant little until the arrival of troops in 1846, and the defeat of substantial Maori tribes in the New Zealand Wars of the 1860s.

Selwyn, influential laity, and some Wesleyan missionaries, were able to persuade London to uphold the Treaty of Waitangi. Joseph Fletcher made the same point that a wide interpretation of the treaty was in the best interest of the colonists. He claimed that missionaries had been assured that surrender of sovereignty of the Maori did not mean surrender of 'their original claims on any part of the soil'[31]. The demand by Earl Grey, the Colonial Secretary, in his despatch of December 1846 that all land not used by Maori should be declared waste land, and fall to the Crown indicated how divided opinion was. Maori suspicion of European intentions grew, especially as the number of settlers increased beyond Maori control. The appointment of protectors on both sides of the Tasman was a failure, despite the commitment of the appointees to justice in race relations. In New Zealand, George Clarke, the son of the Protector of Aborigines, was fluent in Maori and a very articulate advocate of Maori interests. He resigned his post in 1846 and migrated to Hobart, where he had a notable ministry in the Davey Street Congregational Church, and

---

[31] J. H. Fletcher, *Sermons* (Sydney, 1892) 12.

became one of the most influential Tasmanians in the nineteenth century.

Sir George Grey, coming from South Australia to New Zealand in 1845, was deeply interested in the Maori, and learnt a great deal about their culture, one of the few governors who became fluent in Maori. With the help of Te Rangikaheke, he published *Polynesian Mythology* in Maori in 1854. It remains an important collection. Once he had brought northern chiefs like Heke and Kawiti under control militarily, he aimed to win them by demonstrating the benefits of civilization, providing schools, hospitals, and courts. Strongly religious, Grey could also be very devious, but was always sure of his rightness. Provincial government in 1852, and responsible government by 1856, marked a decisive change in race relations, for the governor's powers were now significantly limited. Many of the new parliamentarians were hostile to the Maori. Continuation of their traditional way of life seemed a needless obstacle to economic progress. Where Maori became successful farmers and traders, settlers were jealous.

Missionaries were placed in a difficult dilemma for they could see Maori were divided over policy towards Pakeha. They were often in a position to minister to newly arrived colonists, who then expected missionaries to give them priority. Yet the growth of Maori committed to Christianity was such that 60 per cent were regular worshippers,[32] though other estimates ended up with more Christians than there were Maori. Emergence of a number of prophetic movements (perhaps as many as fifty in the nineteenth century) under Maori leadership demonstrated the religious creativity of the Maori, and their refusal to accept denominational boundaries. In 1845, Tikanga Hou emerged in Taranaki led by Hakopa Nikau, who rejected the Bible, sin, hell, Devil, and Sabbath. Movements like Kaingarara, led by a Wesleyan, Tamate Te Ito, during the 1850s in the same region sought to break the hold of traditional *tapu* in order to modernize, and absorb suitable European techniques.

These movements indicate that many Maori were willing to make religious changes, but on their own terms rather than simply accepting missionary definitions of Christianity.[33] Maori continued to reshape

---

[32] Belich, *Making of Peoples*, 212–23 for a stimulating account of conversion.

[33] B. Elsmore, *Mana from Heaven* (Tauranga, 1989); *Like Them that Dream* (Tauranga, 1985); B. Mikaere, *Te Maiharoa and the Promised Land* (Auckland, 1988); D. F. McKenzie, *Oral Culture, Literacy and Print* (Wellington, 1985); R. Rakena, *The Maori Response to the Gospel* (Auckland, 1971); A. R. Tippett, *People Movements in Polynesia* (Chicago, 1971) 40–75 offers a

their religious and communal identity using Christian ideas, but missionaries were slow to incorporate Maori leaders. A number of Maori identified with the Jews, because of the cultural resonance of the Hebrew Scriptures, translated by 1840. Like other Polynesians they saw change of religious practice in pragmatic terms of worshipping Jehovah, a more powerful god than their traditional deities. The numerical superiority of the Maori in many parts of the North Island, their permanent villages, their skill in adapting European beliefs and techniques, their formidable military skills, and their literacy, challenged the inherent racism of many settlers, and made impossible the destructive behaviour of settlers to nomadic Aborigines in the Australian colonies.[34]

Many Maori chiefs were at home in English, and even when race relations were at their lowest in the 1860s, many influential tribes like the Arawa, Ngapuhi, and Ngati Porou chose to stay out of the wars, and to stress the importance of peace between the two cultures. Maori parliamentary representation granted in 1867, for all its inadequacies, also gave pause to public racism. The view of Maori members may initially have been often ignored, but they exerted an influence which is still impossible for Aborigines in Australia, even though their English was limited and parliamentary procedure opaque. Important books and articles about Maori and their culture were written quite early both by colonists and by the Maori themselves.

MISSIONARY DEVELOPMENT

Selwyn already had more than enough responsibilities within New Zealand, but his love of adventure and sailing led him to make long trips to the New Hebrides and Loyalty Islands, making contact with the islanders, seeking to bring boys away for education, and hoping that some of them would return to their people as evangelists and pastors, because of the impossibility of Europeans learning all the requisite languages.[35] He saw New Zealand as a missionary base for the

useful comparative perspective. T. Van Mejl, 'Historicizing Maoritanga', *JPS* 105 (1996) 311–46.

[34] E. Howe, 'Caught in the crossfire', M.Th. thesis (Melbourne,1998) gives a good account of the philo-Maori. Limbrick, *Bishop Selwyn*, 94–120; G. Lennan, *Sir William Martin* (Christchurch, 1961); Lady Martin, *Our Maoris* (London, 1884); R. Taylor, *Past and Present of New Zealand* (London, 1868) 111 underlines how common racist attitudes were.

[35] Limbrick, *Bishop Selwyn*, 121–54 for Selwyn in the Pacific.

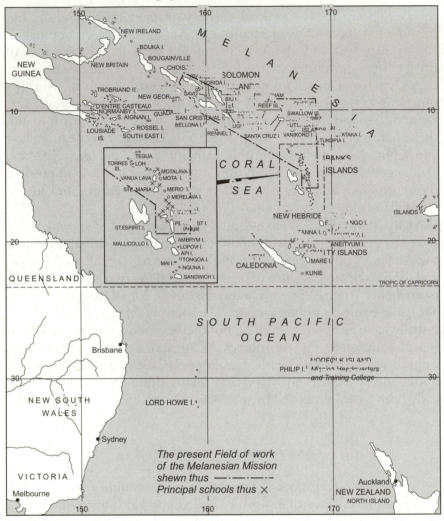

Anglican Diocese of Melanesia (1900). (*Source:* E. S. Armstrong, *The Melanesian Mission*, London, 1900, p. xxviii.)

conversion of the Pacific and he also purchased extensive land around Auckland to support this mission. Selwyn was deeply concerned about the beginnings of the labour trade which he observed from the *Dido* on which he served as chaplain in 1847–8. While travelling he met Captain James Paddon, a sandalwood trader on Aneityum, who shared his insights on Melanesians. In 1849 Selwyn set out in his own ship, the

Undine of 21 tons, to begin the work of conversion, and recruiting potential missionaries, without any reliable charts and a crew of four. He covered over 3,000 miles. He brought back five young Loyalty Islanders listed in St John's College records as George Siapo, Isaka Valu, Waderulu, George Apale, and John Thol. Committed to the one Church, he refused to work where others had already begun. Thus, he made informal agreements with the LMS and the Presbyterians not to work in the Loyalty Islands, or the southern New Hebrides, where John Geddie and Samoans were working.

The formation of the Australasian Board of Missions following the meeting of bishops in 1850 gave Selwyn access to more resources. He saw his sphere as New Britain, New Ireland, and New Guinea. Colonial dioceses gave him the *Border Maid* of 100 tons, in which he took Bishop Tyrrell of Newcastle. They returned with thirteen islanders, after an incident at Malekula on 25 August 1851 which was potentially dangerous, but which was dealt with very coolly by the bishop and his companions. Some settlers were sharply critical of the morality and utility of missionary work. Logan Campbell of Auckland, writing of the 1840s, called it a vain thing, and argued the money would have been better spent on the heathen in the British Isles.[36] He was critical of the romantic glow cast over painful antipodean realities by missionary reports, arguing that it was not possible for missionaries of limited education to teach their converts the truths of Christianity. 'Oh! Ye Foreign Missions that only make your heathen change one form of incantation for another, and that so miserably fail to imbue your converts with any true idea of the guiding principles of the Christian faith, I pray ye stay at home.' When even a Selwyn had to admit to failure after the tragedy of the land wars, 'how could the simple primitive "mechanic" missionary ever have succeeded?' Such comments could equally have been applied to nominal settler Christians.

Harsh settler judgements about the integrity of Maori Christianity increased after the New Zealand wars, especially amongst those who spoke no Maori and had little personal contact, a feature of much New Zealand life until late in the twentieth century. Various forms of Maori Christianity persisted regardless, and have in the last thirty years been interpreted much more generously, by scholars like Binney, than as reversions to paganism, or hardness of heart as William Williams

---

[36] J. L. Campbell, *Poenamo* (Auckland, 1952) 170–2.

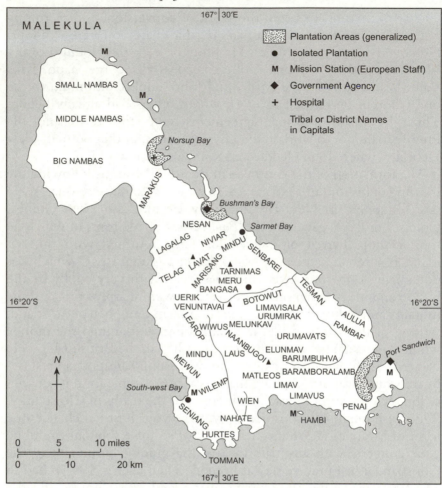

Malekula (1944). (*Source:* Naval Intelligence Division, British Admiralty, *Pacific Islands*, 5 vols., London, 1939–45, vol. 3, p. 579. © British Crown Copyright/MOD. Reproduced with the permission of Her Britannic Majesty's Stationery Office.)

claimed. Settlers found it difficult to hear Maori Christians' appeals on ethics and land. So far as the Maori leaders were concerned, they were aware of the contradiction between what they understood of Christianity, and the greed of successive governments and their agents. Renata Tamakihi Kurangi wrote a long and eloquent letter to Hawkes Bay's superintendent, T. Fitzgerald, in 1861, taking the self-interest of the British case apart, pleading for an independent administration.

Wiremu Tamihana Tarapipipi also wrote in similar vein towards the end of his life on 24 July 1866, petitioning Parliament for redress.[37]

A few missionaries such as Richard Taylor in Wanganui developed a deep knowledge of Maori mythology and religion, but most, like Richard Davis, insisted that converts learn a completely new religious language and practice, rather than seeking contact points from which Maori life could be transformed from within.[38] 'Satan endeavours to revive and strengthen the pernicious lessons of evil inculcated in their youth, to enslave their minds, and ensnare their souls.' Davis consequently did not think a native ministry possible. There were strict rules about preparation for baptism and admission to communion, but Wesleyans made intelligent use of local preachers and catechists, some of whom had considerable biblical knowledge, and founded prophetic movements in Taranaki.

Most missionaries were unable to build on this. Selwyn was not opposed to Maori clergy, but he had educational demands which made entry very difficult. Rota Waitoa was not deaconed till 1853 and priested in 1860. That restrictiveness, which also applied to CMS staff, meant that, when the Maori entered a period of disillusion with missionaries and Selwyn, there were few to uphold the official teaching of the Church against those prophets who claimed direct inspiration from Jehovah. The Wesleyan John White wrote scathingly of Maori superstitions in 1856, but his words were intended for the Pakeha, not the Maori. William Bolland, an Anglican, wrote differently saying 'their knowledge of the New Testament is amazing'.[39]

Selwyn had initially seen himself as a missionary bishop to the Maori and Melanesians, but the steady growth of British settlers, many of whom were connected with the Church of England, meant that he had to devote increasing attention to their pastoral care, provision of clergy, and to education of their children. The College of St John the Evangelist, which began life at Waimate North in 1843, was initially intended for the liberal education of young men, including missionary

---

[37] Caselberg, *Maori is My Name*, 184–96; Taylor, *Past and Present of New Zealand*, 244–50; W. Williams, *Christianity among the New Zealanders*, 2nd edn. (Edinburgh, 1989) 319, 366.
[38] P. Munz, *The Feel of Truth* (Wellington, 1969) 197–220. See also Wohlers, *Memories*, 122–56, 193–6; J. N. Coleman, *Memoir of the Rev. Richard Davis* (London, 1865) 348. Karepa Hiaro, who died late in 1849, left a vivid account of his conversion in A. G. Bagnall and G. C. Petersen, *William Colenso* (Wellington, 1948) 463.
[39] Turnbull MS, 2004/1&2, *Bolland Family Papers*.

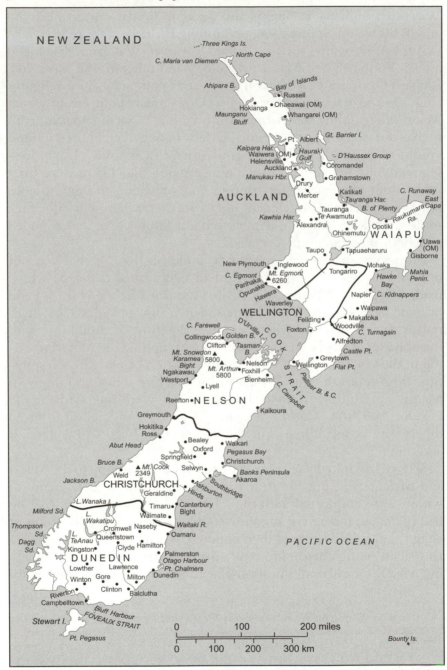

New Zealand: Anglican dioceses (1887). (*Source:* H. Jacobs, *New Zealand*, London, 1887, p. xvi.)

clergy in full connection with the Church of England.[40] Moving it to Tamaki near Auckland, which became the first capital, gave the college a wider function from 1844. It was for a time genuinely inter-racial until homosexual practices led to its temporary closure during 1852–9.

Selwyn's conviction that Maori deserved the same standard of education as Pakeha was a noble goal, but neither he nor his associates appreciated how demanding the establishment of such education could be. St Stephen's College, near Pokeno, provided an interim education for some Maori ministers from 1853, but attempts to found another college at Porirua came to nothing. Maori leaders were thus deprived of the educational opportunities like those offered at Malua and Takamoa, where goals were lower, but which educated generations of ministers very effectively. Te Aute College in 1855 and the later establishment of Te Rau Kahikatea in Poverty Bay in 1883 partly remedied this. Wesleyans also set up a college which combined secondary and ministerial education at Three Kings, near Auckland. Formal education was still suspect in the Wesleyan community, which relied on practical experience as local preachers, limited education, and then probation, which led to ordination. This college trained a number of ministers.

In other contexts like the United States and Africa, some mission-aries drew their converts into Christian villages where they were less in danger of reverting to previous customs. That rarely happened in New Zealand, but one of the most interesting examples was Te Tapiri in the Waikato, inspired by the leadership of Tamihana or Tarapipipi. It was carefully laid out in 1838 on CMS land, and possibly owed something of its genesis to the teaching of A. N. Brown, the CMS missionary at Tauranga. Unlike the traditional *pa* it was completely without defences, for Tarapipipi was deeply committed to peace, much to his formidable warrior father's dismay. A church was built 80 feet long, 40 broad and 30 high. Many of the Ngati Haua were still not Christian, and Tarapipipi frequently thwarted the missions of the war-like by warning their enemies. They, in turn, brought considerable pressure on him to return to traditional ways.

By early 1839 there were 400 in the village. Brown suggested a code of laws. Tarapipipi drew up a list of expulsion offences—adultery, theft, Sabbath breaking, swearing, tattooing after entering the village.

---

[40] A. K. Davidson, *Selwyn's Legacy* (Auckland, 1993).

'Listen, my friends, because of these things God's anger has come upon us. Let us put them away that he may be appeased.'[41] A very knowledgeable Bible student, and ardent asker of theological questions, he was baptized on 23 June 1839 as William Thompson. Taking a British name underlined the new identity. A *tohunga* attempted to shake his commitment by challenging him, and threatening death from the old gods. He did not die, but like many converts, retained his belief in the reality of the *atua*, even though he denied their power.

At times it was difficult to move his people from traditional practices like *utu* (compensatory revenge) into more Christian dispute resolution. Believing themselves to have been cheated out of payment for land by other Waikato in 1844, some of his tribe plundered some completely innocent settlers. Tarapipipi wrote a contrite letter to Governor Fitzroy.

I cannot describe the load of shame I feel on account of this plunder; but you must not suppose that this sort of conduct is a new thing. No, it is of old; like my own dispositions for mischief formerly . . . but when Christianity came I was taught to be kind, and to protect my fellow creatures, which I continue to do to this day.[42]

The tribe made reparation. In 1846, he moved the village to Peria (Berea) on his own land, dividing it into *hapu* (or families). A church, school, post office, and flourishing gardens provided a very congenial environment. He had applied to enter St John's College, but when told he would have to give up his pipe, he decided that the sacrifice was too great.

Racist attitudes were common among new settlers, who frequently called Maori 'niggers', but Selwyn, Grey, missionaries, and senior officials were unfailingly courteous and committed to equality before God and the law. Friendship with chiefs, ability to converse in Maori, and willingness to respond to some of their concerns with a mixture of paternalism and autocracy, kept race relations on a relatively even keel. Though they were strongly committed to Maori interests, in the last resort they saw the future of the Maori in assimilation within British culture. Recent arrivals were inclined to dismiss the Maori as ignorant savages, and to see them as obstacles to progress. That was especially the case in Maori-controlled parts of the North Island. In the South Island, the more severe climate meant that Maori numbers were much

---

[41] L. S. Rickard, *Tamihana the Kingmaker* (Wellington, 1963) 41.
[42] Ibid., 48–9.

fewer, and far more open to European influence and intermarriage. Vast areas of pastoral lands were available for lease and sale, and there seemed ample room for both communities to co-exist. Yet Ngai Tahu were deeply aggrieved at unjust loss of their land.

That was not the case around New Plymouth, where the 1841 settlers were confined to a small area near the coast, while much of the rich volcanic soil remained under Maori control. The situation was complicated by the defeated Atiawa migration to the Wellington area earlier in the century, and the return of substantial numbers in the 1840s to reoccupy their land. Some were willing to sell, but Wiremu Kingi stood fast against alienating their tribal heritage, and was branded as a troublemaker by leading settlers who simply did not understand Maori custom and decision-making. In 1855 Selwyn was asked to mediate by the governor, but found himself in an extremely difficult position. He recognized the right of Kingi to take the stand he had, but encouraged the Maori to sell land they were not using. Kingi was not persuaded, but the government went ahead with purchases from Te Teira, who claimed to have the right to sell. That was not recognized by the rest of the Atiawa. Survey and occupancy followed. The agonizing conflict of interest for missionaries was illustrated by John Whiteley, a Wesleyan missionary to the Maori, who also ministered to the settlers. He honestly believed that it was in the best interests of the Maori to sell so that land could be developed, and played an important part in the sale of the Waitara block by translating for the Land Purchase Commissioner.

Selwyn, Hadfield, and Sir William Martin, who were fluent Maori speakers, wrote hard-hitting letters, published later as booklets, on the injustice of the Waitara purchase and they were, for their advocacy, branded as traitors by most colonists and their newspapers.[43] *The Argus* in Melbourne ran a tendentious article on the missions in New Zealand and the war, to which Bishop Perry vigorously replied. Though the purchase was ultimately disallowed, colonists' feelings were running high as a result of the war which followed the government's seizure of the disputed lands. The establishment of the Maori Land Court in 1856 did not resolve the deeper problems of settler desire for Maori land. Selwyn and Hadfield were seen by some Britons, with no understanding of the Maori attitudes to land or the deviousness of local politicians and officials like Sir Donald Maclean,

---

[43] *The Argus*, 29 Apr. 1860.

as troublemakers who were forsaking their spiritual role to meddle in politics. For Maori, nothing was more spiritually important than defending their land. Maclean was seen as a Pharoah figure by Ringatu members. Rewi Manipoto insisted, 'we are fighting under the religion of Christ',[44] though the settler churches rejected that, teaching that unused land was a gift of God for all.

SETTLER CHURCHES

British and European settler numbers grew rapidly in New Zealand from 1851 to 1901, from 37,306 to 772,210. In Australia, the comparable figures were 405,356 and 3,765,339. The 1851 religious census in England and Wales gave some clues about the religious patterns which would prevail in Australasia. One-third attended the Church of England, one-third other denominations, and the remainder did not attend on this particular Sunday. There is no easy way of determining how many of those counted were twicers. Many of the non-Anglicans could have been. The figures also show significant regional variations. Urban working-class areas were lower in attendance, as were some rural areas where there was antagonism between farm workers and their employers. So the churches in Australasia had not only to retain their own members and adherents against the loosening impact of migration. There were also substantial numbers to recover, whose links to the churches' institutions were slight, but who still saw themselves as Christian. By the end of the century, success was considerable, based on the denominational foundations of the 1850s and 1860s.

Scottish Presbyterians hoped to avoid this erosion by a colony on Free Church principles. In 1847, the Otago Association was formed in Scotland, with the object of founding a Free Church settlement, using the help of the New Zealand Company, dominated by the Wakefields, who had already influenced the settlement of Adelaide.[45] A fascinating combination of desire for profit, and religious hopes for creating a Christian community for the nineteenth century comparable to the Puritan settlements in New England, the settlement had gifted leaders like Captain Cargill, the Revd Thomas Burns, and John

---

[44] J. Cowan, *The New Zealand Wars* (2 vols., Wellington, 1922–3) 1. 381.

[45] E. Olssen, *History of Otago* (Dunedin, 1984); 'The great escape, Wakefield and the Scottish settlement of Otago', in Friends of the Turnbull Library, *Edward Gibbon Wakefield* (Wellington, 1997) 123–34. T. Brooking, *Captain of Their Souls* (Dunedin, 1984).

McGlashan. The settlers were much more ordinary, and included a number of English migrants who showed little sympathy with Scottish attempts to create a godly community with strictly observed Sabbaths, fast days, communion seasons, and stern moral discipline by the kirk session. That was shown on the first anniversary of the landing, in March 1849. The English celebrated with races, sports, and a ball. The Scots had services of humiliation and prayer. The relation between Presbyterians and Anglicans was civil, but the differences in religious culture remained strong.

The development of Anglicanism rested on settler initiative and the generous financial help of the two great Anglican missionary societies. The Society for Propagation of the Gospel (SPG), and the Society for Promoting Christian Knowledge (SPCK) provided chaplains for migrant ships, grants towards buildings and literature, and some missionary salaries. The SPG gave £75,000 to New Zealand between 1840 and 1880.[46] The idealistic hopes of the Canterbury Association for a Church of England settlement at Christchurch indicate how closely colonial expansion and loyalty to the Church of England were interwoven.[47] Four ships left for Canterbury in September 1850, after a sermon from the Archbishop of Canterbury, commending their enterprise to God. Some 3,500 migrants came out under the Association, but, like most of the Wakefield colonies, hopes and realities were far apart. Land sales were far smaller than estimated, so that schools, vicarages, and churches simply could not be built. Financing public works was a great burden on the small settlement, and voluntary contributions were essential for the erection of schools and churches.

New Zealand was a collection of isolated coastal towns and small cities, connected by boat, each place with its own strongly held identity, and suspicious of the capital Wellington. The absence of metropolitan cultures like Sydney's and Melbourne's shaped the New Zealand churches in a different way from their trans-Tasman counterparts, as did differences in migrant groups, with Scots outnumbering the Irish, and shaping New Zealand settlement decisively.

The major churches had both to provide money for their own denominational organization and buildings, and come to terms with a frontier society where few of the traditional social controls were in

---

[46] A. K. Davidson, *Christianity in Aotearoa* (Wellington, 1991) 51.
[47] S. Parr, *Canterbury Pilgrimage* (Christchurch, 1951); J. Hight, et al., *History of Canterbury* (3 vols., Christchurch, 1957–71); S. Eldred-Grigg, *New History of Canterbury* (Dunedin, 1982).

place.[48] Clergy livings were much less adequate than in Britain and their energies more far-flung. In Victoria, where there was one minister to each 2,500 Anglicans, Perry wished to halve that ratio. There was much goodwill until money was requested, but also much apathy from settlers struggling for the basic necessities of life. There was little emotional energy for parish activities. There were few wealthy benefactors. St Mark's, Fitzroy, in Melbourne, was an exception. It had a debt of over £11,000 which Mr R. Grice gave £10,000 to reduce.

Many of the early buildings were very simple, often made of wooden slabs with bark roofs. On the goldfields, canvas churches made it possible to keep pace with the constant movements of population. Gradually more dignified buildings were erected. In both Australia and New Zealand, wood was used very skilfully by architects like the Revd F. W. Thatcher in Wellington, whose St Paul's Church is a masterpiece. Though distance was not such a problem as in Australian colonies, the isolation and loneliness of settlement in the bush was very oppressive. Many lost their lives because there was no medical help within several hours walking or riding. Home missionaries and itinerant priests were vital for both Protestants and Roman Catholics.

Congregationalist and Baptist beginnings were equally untidy, because they had no missionary organization to found churches in a colony of settlement.[49] In Hobart, Frederick Miller came to a small Congregational cause begun by the businessman Henry Hopkins. He was followed to Tasmania by Charles Price and John West, both of whom made notable contributions to the colony. In 1840, Barzillai Quaife ministered briefly in Korarareka, New Zealand, but left no lasting congregation. When he came to New South Wales, he ministered to Presbyterians, indicating the fluidity of church boundaries in the colonies. In Sydney, the formation of the Pitt Street congregation was confused by the late arrival of a minister called from Britain. His journey took so much longer than expected that Charles Price was invited from Launceston. When William Jarrett finally arrived, Price generously vacated the charge and worked as chaplain

---

[48] W. P. Morrell, *Anglican Church in New Zealand* (Dunedin, 1973); R. D. McEldowney, *Presbyterians in Aotearoa* (Wellington, 1990); E. Simmons, *Short History of the Catholic Church* (Auckland, 1978); M. King, *God's Farthest Outpost* (Auckland, 1997); E. W. Hames, *Out of the Common Way* (Auckland, 1975).

[49] P. Tonson, *A Handful of Grain* (4 vols., Wellington, 1982); J. D. Bollen, *Australian Baptists* (London, 1975); J. B. Chambers, *A Peculiar People* (Wellington, 1984).

for the Australian Land Company, to the chagrin of some Anglicans who felt that the post should have been filled by one of their own.

The first Sydney Baptist minister, John McKaeg, had problems with alcoholism, but a small group persisted and called James Saunders in 1835, who proved an outstanding minister. New Zealand Baptists began in 1851, with the first Brethren arriving in 1852. Baptists in Melbourne were deeply divided between Particular and General Baptists. The Scotch Baptists were in communion with neither, preferring to keep their own identity. All denominations were deeply dependent on lay energy, generosity, and initiative for the development of self-government of colonial churches.

LAITY AND POLITY

As well as cutting new paths in race relations and Christian partnership, Selwyn sought to create a church unambiguously apostolic with appropriate lay participation. In 1842 he had refused government assistance for buildings and stipends, arguing that the early church had depended on the gifts of the faithful. He wished to do the same. His New Zealand stipend of £1,200 was paid by the CMS, the SPG, and the Colonial Office, but when the New Zealand government proposed to increase that by £200, Presbyterians and Roman Catholics protested. Selwyn accepted this. He also believed that an apostolic church was self-governing. In September 1844, and in September 1847, he called synods, without the royal approval that was legally required, insisting that episcopal authority was sufficient. Similar views were being discussed in Canada and in New South Wales. From 1846 Broughton no longer served on the Executive Council.

Selwyn was fortunate in the quality of laity who were willing to share this important beginning, like William Martin, the Chief Justice, William Swainson, the Attorney General, and John Robert Godley of the Canterbury Association. When Selwyn was invited to attend a bishops' conference called by Broughton in Sydney during 1850, a group of laity presented him with an address encouraging him to support the inclusion of laity in councils of the church, a view not shared by Broughton.

Perry in Melbourne pulled off parliamentary support for his synodical proposals in a way which Broughton longed for, but was unable to achieve. He withdrew a bill from the New South Wales parliament for fear that it would be amended at a number of points by his political enemies and Anglicans who distrusted his leadership. That legacy, combined with suspicions of other churches, ensured that it was to be many years before the dioceses of Sydney and Newcastle had their legal status clarified. Getting rid of the legacy of establishment was almost as difficult as exercising its privileges. Broughton had already found that trying to use ecclesiastical discipline against refractory clergy was extremely hard.

Not only were there doubts about the status of canon law in Australia, but other Protestant churches were nervous that, if some enabling legislation was passed, they would find it used against them, for discrimination against them in England was still very real. Baptists such as Henry Dowling, for example, joined the protest in Hobart against Bishop Nixon's proposals for a consistorial court in Tasmania. 'Your petitioners emigrated hither, in the reasonable expectation that the equality assured by the laws of their country, would secure to themselves and their posterity, the blessings of complete religious liberty—they therefore contemplate with much alarm the efforts to establish Courts, from which, by Your Majesty's protection, your Petitioners hoped to escape forever.'[50]

Perry knew that there were those in London who were uneasy about such legislation by colonial parliaments affecting the exercise of the Crown's prerogative, as well as limiting the authority of Westminster. He took no chances that those who saw such legislation being used as precedent to upset the privileges of the British established churches would prevent the act receiving royal assent. He travelled to London, lobbied skilfully and assiduously, and was delighted when Queen Victoria finally signed. The result was a diocese securely operating in a legislative framework which clearly established the place of laity in church government, defined the powers of the bishop and clergy, and set out clear procedures for holding property and exercising disciplinary procedures. The rights of other denominations were in no way affected. His church assembly in Victoria was a very powerful body because of the abilities and status of many of its early members.

In Adelaide and New Zealand, another solution was adopted which was widely copied elsewhere in the Empire.[51] Consensual compact

[50] Anon., *The Equal Legal Status of all the Churches of the Australian Colonies* (Hobart, 1851) 49.

[51] Morrell, *Anglican Church in New Zealand*, 58–67; Brown, *Augustus Short*, 92–104.

was a process by which the bishop called together clergy and laity to decide on a constitution which was then recognized by Parliament as part of the requirements for holding property, and making trusts. Selwyn visited England and consulted widely after attempts to legislate for some of the problems at Westminster had failed between 1852 and 1854. He believed that he could legally hold a diocesan synod. On 14 May 1857, he called a conference followed by a Constituent Assembly on 2 June at St Stephen's Church, Auckland, which hammered out a constitution based on voluntary compact. The laity included E. W. Stafford, the premier, and other parliamentarians like Haultain, Tancred, Whitaker, and Swainson. Clergy included C. J. Abraham, later a notable bishop, A. N. Brown, and O. Hadfield, plus the Williams brothers. The 1611 version of the Bible, the 1662 *Book of Common Prayer*, and the Thirty-nine Articles were made fundamental provisions, changeable only if the Church of England had modified them through Crown and Convocation. The place of trusts and endowments was clarified, making it clear that there was no way to change doctrine or practice without breaching trust, and threatening title to property. Other eventualities provided for were disestablishment of the United Church of England and Ireland, and the separation of New Zealand from Britain. The 1869 end of establishment in Ireland showed how wise this provision was. General Synod had limited power to make unilateral changes, which was remedied in the 1928 Church of England Empowering Act.

Diocesan synods were set up alongside a General Synod, each with three houses, which could vote separately. Legislation by the General Synod was not binding until it was accepted by individual dioceses. That reflected the provincial structure of the New Zealand politics, the difficulty of communication, and a strong sense of local identity. It entrenched localism, to the chagrin of those who wanted stronger national power. The constitution served the church well. Selwyn had to resign his letters patent. He, Abraham of Wellington, Williams of Waiapu, and Hobhouse of Nelson were then all issued with fresh instruments of authority by the Crown on 27 September 1858.

By such actions, the colonial churches set very important precedents for the English mother church in synodal government, with strong involvement of laity and clergy in decision-making. The emergence of synodal government made it possible for all the dioceses to address both church and community problems. The debates were as fully reported by papers as those of colonial parliaments and provincial councils. Some of those involved were talented citizens and dedicated churchmen, and their deliberations enhanced the leadership of the Church of England in colonial society. Yet there was a fundamental break with the past. The church had no official voice in colonial parliaments. Church members had to take up that role individually, but few had the education or status to make the contribution of English bishops. Colonial parliaments steadily became more secular bodies, a process hastened by religious pluralism. Bishops' roles were denominationalized as they lost their link with government.

MELANESIAN BEGINNINGS

As part of his vision of a regional church, Selwyn was also interested in the Loyalty Islands and New Caledonia as a sphere of interest for the New Zealand church, but his removal of young men from the Loyalty Islands to Auckland in 1849 did not bring any fruitful result on their return. Nor did the placement of William Nihill on Maré in 1852. Negotiations with the LMS about a comity agreement came to nothing in 1853, because of French annexation. When Nihill died in 1855, he was not replaced, and Selwyn focused on other Melanesian islands.[52] Once again, when British authorities said they could not found a diocese outside the Empire, Selwyn, with the bishops of Nelson and Wellington, acted apostolically without government authority, and consecrated Bishop John Coleridge Patteson in 1861, who was a shrewd leader, and a marvellous teacher of Christianity to Islanders in the decade he served as bishop.

He had great gifts as a linguist, speaking over 20 languages, and made important advances in pushing out the frontiers of missionary contact at the same time as the sugar planters in Queensland and Fiji were seeking cheap labour from the islands, and employing recruiters who were brutal and unscrupulous. Many Melanesians lost their lives and any European was a target for payback for recruiters' brutality.

Unlike Presbyterians, who created a theocracy on Aneityum and Tanna, Patteson was deeply committed to making the Gospel part of the Melanesian way of life, not turning them into English Christians. His schools, first at Kohimarama, Auckland, and then at Norfolk Island from 1866 till 1920, were influential. Despite serious malaria in

---

[52] Morrell, *Anglican Church in New Zealand*, 143–50.

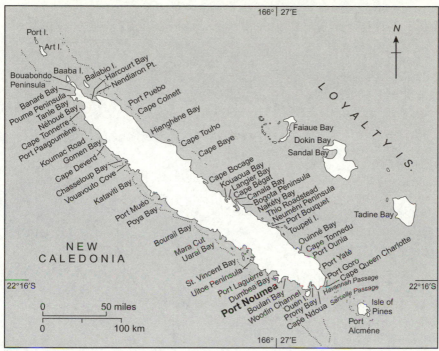

New Caledonia (1944). (*Source:* Naval Intelligence Division, British Admiralty, *Pacific Islands*, 5 vols., London, 1939–45, vol. 3, p. 420. © British Crown Copyright/MOD. Reproduced with the permission of Her Britannic Majesty's Stationery Office.)

1870, he returned to the islands where the misdeeds of some of the labour ships made any white person a target. At Nukapu, a Polynesian outlier in the Santa Cruz group, several boys had been forcibly abducted by a captain. Patteson was killed by a relative of one of the boys on 20 September 1871. His death, interpreted as martyrdom by devout Anglicans, forced the British government to curtail the worst of the trade by the Pacific Islanders Protection Act of 1872, but in varying forms it continued until the end of the century because it met Islander and employer needs.

Protestantism had already moved into Melanesia. In 1839 the LMS landed Lalolagi and Salama on Tanna, then in the Loyalty Islands in 1841, and in 1842 on New Caledonia, where Ta'unga, Taniela, and Noa had begun work.[53] They had some advantages, for there were

---

[53] K. Howe (*The Loyalty Islands* (Canberra, 1977); J. Garrett, *To Live Among the Stars* (Suva, 1982) 189–205.

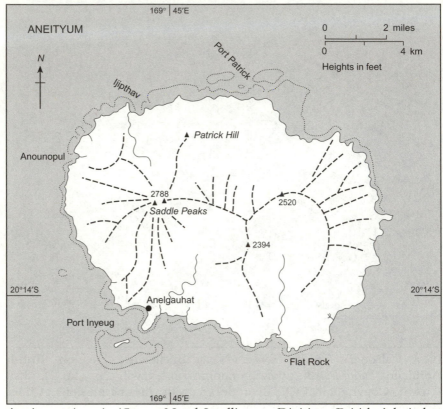

Aneityum (1944). (*Source:* Naval Intelligence Division, British Admiralty, *Pacific Islands*, 5 vols., London, 1939–45, vol. 3, p. 600. © British Crown Copyright/MOD. Reproduced with the permission of Her Britannic Majesty's Stationery Office.)

distant links with Tonga. These cultures were similar enough for the missionaries to gain a working knowledge of the language, and understand the customs and religions of their hosts. On some islands, Christianity was adopted quite quickly because of chiefs' conversion. Ta'unga, a remarkable Rarotongan of chiefly ancestry, wrote a full account of this work at Tuauru, and on the Isle of Pines. He and his colleagues moved around the south of New Caledonia, but Ta'unga's ability to deal with chiefs, and his skill in translating Christian ideas into local idiom, aroused some jealousy from his two Samoan colleagues. They appear to have had something of the authoritarianism that often marked their people in contact with others' cultures, and lacked his grace in dealing with chiefs and commoners.

Ta'unga was born about 1818 in Ngatangiia on Rarotonga, and by his early teens had become actively associated with the LMS mission, writing a statement of faith in 1833 which showed that he had understood very clearly missionary teaching about the atonement. His admiration for the courage of Jesus was obvious, and he wanted Jesus' sacrifice remembered throughout the world. 'In order for this remembrance to come about, the word of God must be spread through every single island so that every person may reach heaven and sit at the side of Jesus so that there might be boundless joy.'[54] He was educated at Takamoa and then travelled to Western Polynesia on the *Camden* via Niue, Rotuma, Samoa, and the New Hebrides, finally reaching the Loyalty Islands. Polynesian teachers had experienced limited success on Maré and the Isle of Pines. War had stopped, but Christianity had not been accepted. *En route*, Ta'unga had been invited to stay on several islands, but he gained no peace in his prayers, and was finally placed at Yate on New Caledonia with Taniela in mid-1842. His account of his work is unique, the most detailed analysis of the process of conversion by a Polynesian missionary.

The story of Jesus and the love of God was central to Polynesians' message, but they also exhorted people to keep the Sabbath. When their message did not bear the expected fruit, at Ta'unga's insistence they set two days aside for prayer. There was a great change for the better. The onset of illness on the Isle of Pines led to the expulsion of teachers, because people feared that Jehovah was killing them. Ta'unga gave another explanation—that it was because of their refusal to obey the Word of his God. Keen discussion took place about the name of God, and Ta'unga's hearers were impressed by his account of creation and the soul, which had no parallel in their myths. His chiefly lineage was helpful, for he knew how to meet and converse with chiefs, to work through them, and to elicit their support for the building of churches.

Ta'unga was taken to Maré in 1846, where cannibalism was common and where he was mocked by women for wearing clothes, their mockery presumably accompanied by derisory sexual comments. Once again, he taught the message of God's love, but that was hard for people to hear, because of the epidemics of European diseases which were raging. Neither the old gods or new could deal with them. Getting rid of the newcomers seemed a solution. His vivid

---

[54] M. Crocombe, *The Works of Ta'unga* (Canberra, 1987) 6.

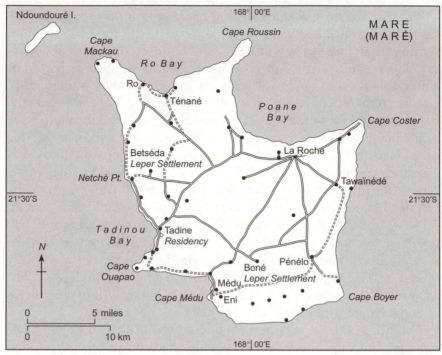

Maré (1944). (*Source:* Naval Intelligence Division, British Admiralty, *Pacific Islands,* 5 vols., London, 1939–45, vol. 3, p. 499. © British Crown Copyright/MOD. Reproduced with the permission of Her Britannic Majesty's Stationery Office.)

descriptions of cannibalism are horrific but 'compassion grew in my heart for them, for they are so addicted to these evil customs'. A Maré priestess, with ancestral rights to victims' hands, said 'there is no food so sweet and savoury as that of human flesh'. He was not persuaded to accept her gift, but Ta'unga also noted that it was also a hereditary right of chiefs, who believed that, if custom was interfered with, the guilty one would die.[55]

In addition, he gave careful description of funeral rites and sorcery, marriage, customs, prayers for the planting of crops, and the pervasive nature of vengeance, adding that he had left out some things lest his mentor Pitman's sensibilities be offended. When he returned to Rarotonga and described his experiences, his compatriots were fascinated. Ta'unga thanked them for their prayers, which he believed had

[55] M. Crocombe, *The Works of Ta'unga,* 73, 91, 94–5.

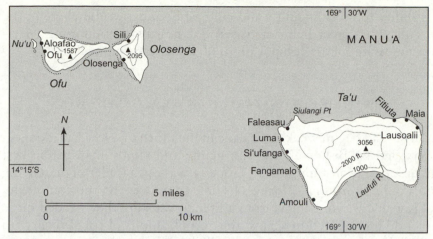

Manu'a group (1943). (*Source:* Naval Intelligence Division, British Admiralty, *Pacific Islands*, 5 vols., London, 1939–45, vol. 2, p. 674. © British Crown Copyright/MOD. Reproduced with the permission of Her Britannic Majesty's Stationery Office.)

preserved him against tremendous odds. While on furlough he wrote two books in the language of Tuauru to use when he returned via Samoa. Negotiations were taking place between Bishop Selwyn and George Turner at Malua about who should have responsibility for New Caledonia. No agreement was reached by 1849, and Ta'unga went to Manu'a, Samoa. The LMS could not supply a British missionary and the people were unhappy at having a Cook Islander. They thought him culturally inferior, and did little to support him until, by 1862, it had become clear he was to stay. Despite other offers, he decided to marry Ngapoko, from a chiefly family in Rarotonga, whom he met in 1847.

The churches on the island prospered under his leadership, with many joining the church, and the communities energetically making coconut oil to fund the LMS. He continued to stress the good work of Jesus, and his wife ran a very successful class for church membership. She also introduced regular prayer meetings. A colleague introduced hat-making to complement traditional weaving. Unfortunately, by 1870 war had broken out. Ta'unga retired to his home island in 1879, then worked for a time on Mauke, where stories are still told about his great *mana* and miraculous powers. He and his wife died in 1898. They are splendid examples of the depth of Cook Islands Christianity, and its ability to cross linguistic and cultural boundaries elsewhere in the Pacific. His career helps us to see Polynesians encountering Melanesians, without the complications of European colonialism.

FRENCH COLONIZATION IN NEW CALEDONIA

Marists had begun work[56] at Balade in the north of New Caledonia in 1843, led by Bishop Douarre, a gentle and saintly man in the best tradition of Marist spirituality. Douarre was not a leader of men living on a difficult frontier. Nor was he able to understand the complexity of Kanak custom. Landed from a French warship, they needed more than divine protection against the complications of tribal rivalry. In 1847, Brother Marmoiton was killed, and the houses looted and burned. After travel south, they finally found refuge on the Isle of Pines, and then on Futuna and Aneityum. Wallis and Futuna were to become solidly Catholic.

Douarre wanted annexation so the protection of the state could be extended to their work, but he bravely returned to Hienghene, where Bwazat was the paramount chief. Douarre died in April 1853, and his hope for annexation was realized a few months later. Marist presence remained fragile for several years, until they learnt that more was needed for the conversion of the heathen than diligence, observance of their rule, and private prayer. Small churches down the east coast of Grande Terre still bear witness to the pioneer Marist missionaries and their attempt to create a more authentic Catholicism than was possible in a divided, and increasingly anti-clerical, France.[57] By the end of the century they claimed around 20,000 converts, although it was expected by many French administrators and settlers that the Kanaks would soon die out.

After French annexation in 1853, there were occasions when French punitive expeditions reminded the warlike tribes that they must grudgingly respect greater military and naval might. Kanaks were also skilled at cultural and religious innovation which gave them some control over the process of acculturation and colonization. That was particularly so in the Loyalty Islands, whose churches sent evangelists

---

[56] Wiltgen, *Catholic Church in Oceania*, 425–45, 463–73 on Marist beginnings; G. Delbos, *L'église Catholique en Nouvelle-Calédonie* (Paris, 1993).

[57] J. Dauphine, *Christianisation et politique en Nouvelle Calédonie* (Noumea, 1996); J. Izoulet, *Mekete poun* (Paris, 1996).

to eastern Grande Terre, disregarding French authority. Allegiance to Christianity followed the lines of tribal relationships and conflicts, often unrecognized by European missionaries, administrators, and settlers.[58] Beliefs in the spirit world were strong, ancestors were important, and each clan had its own totem. To Bishop Douarre, all this spoke of a people in cultural infancy. Serious study of local custom did not begin until late in the century. Though chieftainship was hereditary, there were significant checks on their authority, not least that land was held by the clan. French authority in the Loyalty Islands was not complete until the end of the nineteenth century.

LMS missionaries from Britain came permanently to Maré in 1854, to Lifou in 1859, and Ouvéa in 1864, building on the pioneering work of Polynesian teachers. Paoo from Aututaki was the first teacher to land on Maré and on Lifou. His life hung in the balance but he was adopted by Bula the southern chief as his *enehmu*, whereby a stranger was adopted as an intimate friend, and religious adviser. Paoo's talk of Jesus was incorporated into existing polytheism, but when Bula died and an epidemic occurred, for which Christians were blamed, Paoo returned to Maré, but was eventually invited to return to Lifou. He worked there for 18 years until he died in 1860, making places like Chépénéhé and We important Protestant centres, as well as graciously welcoming Marists in 1859.

Within a year of the arrival of John Jones in 1854, and of Stephen Creagh, most of the people of Maré, about 3,000, became active worshippers. The new moral order enhanced the authority of the Northern chief, Nasiline Nidoish, who was crowned in 1862 by the missionaries. Other important chiefs stood outside the new order, because they did not want to lose their authority to rivals. To make the point emphatically they welcomed Marist missionaries. The Marists had also arrived on the Isle of Pines (Kounie) in 1848, and converted many of the people by 1857. On Lifou, where Samoan and Rarotongan teachers had been present since 1842, a rival chief, Ukeneso, wanted to check the influence of Bula and Wainya, chiefs in LMS areas, and welcomed Montrouzier's pioneering work. By 1859, there were a little over 10 per cent of the population of 6,000 who were sympathetic to Catholicism.

The arrival of Samuel MacFarlane and William Baker in 1859 on

---

[58] A. Bensa and A. Goromido, 'The political order and corporal coercion in Kanak societies of the past', *Oceania* 68 (1997) 84–106.

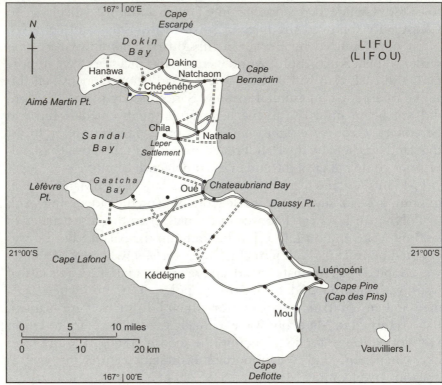

Lifou (1944). (*Source:* Naval Intelligence Division, British Admiralty, *Pacific Islands*, 5 vols., London, 1939–45, vol. 3, p. 500. © British Crown Copyright/MOD. Reproduced with the permission of Her Britannic Majesty's Stationery Office.)

Lifou dismayed the Marists, for they consolidated a following for Protestantism, strictly organized, with local church police to enforce Christian morality. On Ouvéa, where Catholics were numerous, a system of Christian laws was also created which enhanced the authority of the Catholic Bazit, one of the major chiefs.

Indigenous rivalries, LMS–Marist conflicts on Lifou, and misunderstandings produced a complex religious and political situation with international ramifications. Unlike his colleagues, MacFarlane was a formidable lobbyist when French pressure against British missionaries increased in 1864. Not only did he write letters of protest to the authorities in Noumea, he wrote to Napoleon III demanding religious liberty and lobbied in London. In Sydney his contacts in the Congregationalist-owned *Sydney Morning Herald* publicized the issues there. Dr Lang thought that New Caledonia and its islands should be part of the coming Australian republic. The LMS and its allies brought pressure to bear on the French government, fearing French encroachment on British spheres of influence. Early in 1865, Napoleon told Guillain, the governor in Noumea, that MacFarlane could take up his work again and re-open schools. Chépénéhé on Lifou became a centre for training evangelists, both locally and in Papua, and the French troops were reined in. In 1887 French Protestants secured the release of imprisoned pastors and teachers in the Loyalty Islands.

The French authorities in Noumea were unhappy about the influence of British missionaries in the Loyalty Islands. A series of problems led to military interventions, and the subjugation of Protestants. Governor Guillain had MacFarlane recalled in 1871 because he was unwilling to moderate his activities. Jones was also expelled from Maré in 1887 for foolish political acts in support of the Nasiline chiefs. Even though the British government pressed the French government successfully to moderate Guillain's actions, he had an unenviable task, for the Marists suspected him of being pro-English, and resented his insistence that some of the militantly anti-Protestant Marists be withdrawn from Ouvéa. Nevertheless, when Samuel Ella of the LMS left the island of Ouvéa, a solidly Catholic community emerged in some villages. Some of the tensions were resolved by the LMS handing over to the Paris Missionary Society in 1898 its work on Maré and in 1920 on Lifou and Ouvéa. The religious boundaries laid down in the nineteenth century have endured to the present.[59]

The Christianity of the Loyalty Islanders was congruent with their traditional culture and cosmology, so far that some missionaries lamented the extent to which 'heathenism' had infiltrated Christianity. Buildings were cherished as symbols of unity, and the extent of community commitment to Christian observance amazed visitors. Though literacy was highly valued and was fostered by the LMS ability to print in the vernacular languages, schools were not so successful. Support of Protestantism and Catholicism was closely related to pre-Christian tribal and regional divisions. Giving was a way of gaining prestige. On Lifou, between 1879 and 1886, Protestants gave £2,700, which represented an enormous amount of labour and trade.[60] The Loyalty Islands also provided the first eight pioneer

[59] Garrett, *To Live Among the Stars*, 189–205.
[60] Howe, *Loyalty Islands*, 109.

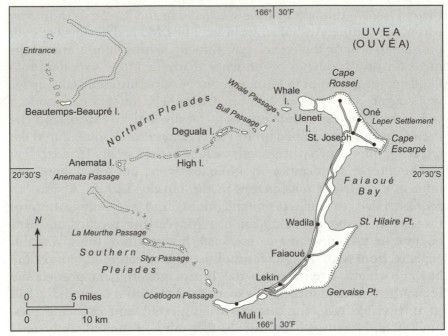

Ouvéa (1944). (*Source:* Naval Intelligence Division, British Admiralty, *Pacific Islands*, 5 vols., London, 1939–45, vol. 3, p. 501. © British Crown Copyright/MOD. Reproduced with the permission of Her Britannic Majesty's Stationery Office.)

missionaries to the Torres Strait Islands in 1871. When they were told of the fierceness of the people, they were undismayed, saying that wherever there are men, missionaries are bound to go. By 1884 Loyalty Islanders had provided many of the 300 teachers and wives who had served in Papua.

SAMOAN CHRISTIANITY

Another Christian ethos emerged in Samoa, where different aspects of the LMS culture were taken over. Lacking the professional priesthood of many other Polynesian societies, without highly sacred *marae*, heads of family had significant religious status in the *nu'u* (village), where kin lived together in varying degrees of amity and rivalry. As in Tonga, there was fierce rivalry over the great titles—Tui Alua, Tui A'ana, Gatoaitele, Tamosoali'i. One great chief, Malietoa, combined the

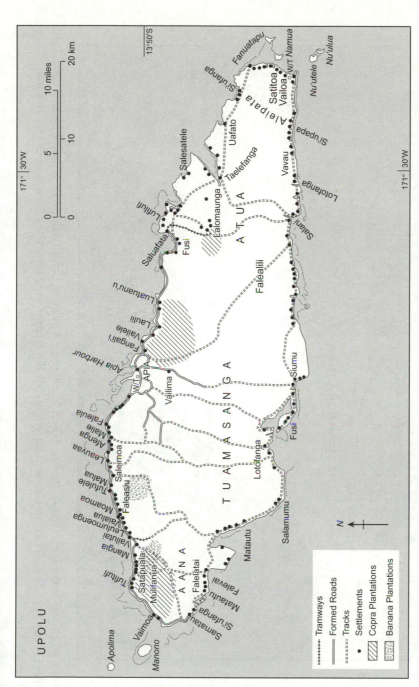

Upolu (1943). (*Source*: Naval Intelligence Division, British Admiralty, *Pacific Islands*, 5 vols., London, 1939–45, vol. 2, p. 668. © British Crown Copyright/MOD. Reproduced with the permission of Her Britannic Majesty's Stationery Office.)

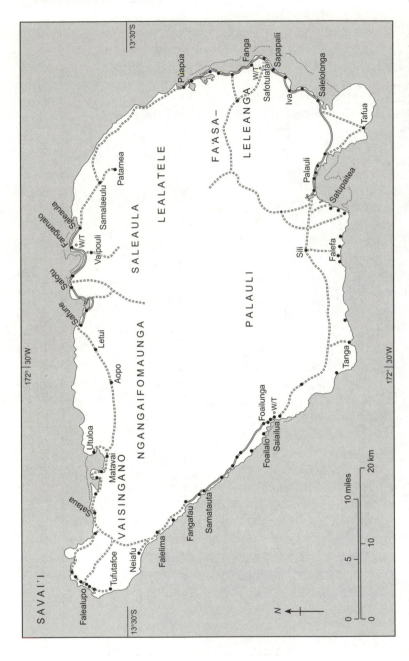

Savai'i: roads and settlements (1943). (*Source:* Naval Intelligence Division, British Admiralty, *Pacific Islands*, 5 vols, London, 1939–45, vol. 2, p. 663. © British Crown Copyright/MOD. Reproduced with the permission of Her Britannic Majesty's Stationery Office.)

titles in his own person, but he did not establish a dynasty like Tupou. When he died in 1841 he was the last Tafa'ifa—one who combined all titles, and he, according to tradition, decreed on his deathbed that they should not be so united again. According to oral tradition, Malietoa's dying charge to his followers was to cherish the Gospel of Jesus Christ and have God as King.[61]

Samoan culture was a powerful entity and absorbed many features of Christianity, without itself being changed markedly. Many Samoans did not regard the Tahitian teachers highly, but were disposed to take Tongans more seriously. The authority of the *matai* and *tulafale* (chiefs and orators) was modified by the emergence of *faife'au* (teachers and then pastors) who acquired considerable *mana*, were generously supported by their village by a covenant, and exercised considerable spiritual authority. Though the LMS missionaries were honoured, it was the pastors and their wives who were the local face of Christianity, which unified the islands, despite fierce village rivalries.

They saw the advantages of regional oversight and by the end of the century had developed a distinctive polity as well as a degree of financial independence by two collections—one for themselves, one for the LMS. Districts had elder pastors, or *toea'ina*, appointed on both seniority and ability, a position zealously sought, to a certain extent paralleling that of the LMS missionaries, but advisory in matters still controlled by the Samoan District Committee, of which only missionaries were members. The *Fono Tele* (or Assembly) held in May became a national occasion with meetings, dancing, choir competitions, and money-raising. Pastors and deacons from the whole of Samoa gathered, along with their wives and supporting parties, even when there were inter-district wars, and seeming political chaos. Though this had the potential to become a national parliament, local rivalries, and the London Missionary Society attachment to separation of church and state, ensured this did not happen. The Mé also remains important in French Polynesia and the Cook Islands.

Not only did teachers take successful industrial action in 1853 to secure better pay, they also won the right to ordination before many of the missionaries believed they were ready for such a privilege. By 1875 they had won the right for the *Fono Tele* to advise the District Committee. They had been well educated at Malua, which opened in 1844 and produced hundreds of pastors, many of whom became

[61] P. Culbertson (ed.), *Counselling Issues and South Pacific Communities* (Auckland, 1997) 174.

missionaries. Pastors' wives were also given education in domestic crafts, and Sunday school teaching, and were entrusted with the oversight of the village virgins, who were so important in marriage alliances that enhanced the status of the village, and its leading title-holders. The recognition of *au toea'ina* in 1906 gave senior pastors enhanced power in both church and district.

LMS and Wesleyan congregations speedily took on board biblical teaching in some cultural areas. Wars decreased, tattooing disappeared, as did the sexually explicit night dances, and the Sabbath was kept with diligence by congregations dressed in white. Cricket, locally adapted, was an important outlet for village rivalry. Every night families gathered for prayers. Every village took pride in its substantial church and pastor, who was generously supported by gifts. The carpenters, who built churches with village help, showed remarkable ability to adapt their skills to erection of large European style stone buildings, very few of which collapsed because of defects in construction, or because of cyclones. These cultural patterns were taken by Samoans to other parts of the Pacific, notably to Melanesia later in the century.

Europeans who settled in the group as traders and beachcombers found life difficult because of the shifting boundaries of chiefly alliances. There were wars in 1869–73, and a good deal of European meddling until 1889, when Malietoa Laupapa was installed as an ineffective ruler. Finally, the islands were divided between Germany and the United States, with Germany taking the western islands until 1914.

A number of the missionaries became well-versed in Samoan culture and language. George Pratt was a key figure in producing the Bible which was translated by 1855, and also produced a dictionary and grammar which is still invaluable. George Turner wrote acutely on Samoan custom. A.W. Murray, who worked mainly on Tutuila, wrote extensively on his experiences, and aroused considerable interest because he shepherded a revival between 1839 and 1842 which had some similarities to awakenings in Scotland about the same time.[62] The intensity generated gave the Samoans an outlet for their emotions which hymns and sober worship did not satisfy. A notable convert, Penisimani, wrote hymns which were regarded as too Samoan by some missionaries, who had all the printed copies

[62] A. W. Murray, *Forty Years Mission Work* (London, 1876); G. Turner, *Nineteen Years in Polynesia* (London, 1861); Mitchell MS 2259 Penisimani papers.

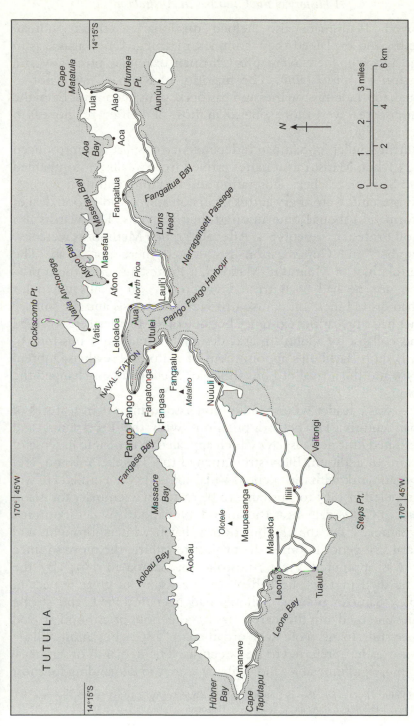

Tutuila (1943). (*Source:* Naval Intelligence Division, British Admiralty, *Pacific Islands*, 5 vols., London, 1939–45, vol. 2, p. 672. © British Crown Copyright/MOD. Reproduced with the permission of Her Britannic Majesty's Stationery Office.)

destroyed. Penisimani also helped missionaries collect Samoan proverbs, and explained their complex meaning. Once again, as in Tonga and Fiji, there were pre-Christian examples of ecstasy and possession by spirits (*aitu*). The majority of Samoans were not so touched, for their missionaries and pastors kept tight control. Even the Methodist areas were more sober than those of their co-religionists in Tonga and Fiji.

A further outlet for Samoan independence of spirit was introduced in 1845 when Marist missionaries arrived from Wallis, accompanied by two Samoan teachers, Kosetatino and Ioakimo, and their wives.[63] The Protestants were angry at this incursion and spread a good deal of disinformation about Rome amongst their converts. The Marists also lived off Protestant stereotypes. After all, French Methodists were few in number, and Congregationalists existed there not at all. The powerful chief of Mulinu'u, Mata'afa, a Protestant, gave them protection, for he had been treated generously on Wallis when his ship had drifted there off course in 1842. The priests and the solitary brother had a precarious existence because of the financial crisis caused by the collapse of Colin's grand design for trade and missions in 1849. Bishop Bataillon's appointment of Antoine Freydier-Dubreul in 1850, and the arrival of Louis Elloy of Metz in 1856, changed the situation.

Elloy was a leader who speedily understood important features of Samoan culture. He held disputations with the Protestants, and orchestrated liturgical displays which appealed to the Samoan sense of occasion. In addition, Elloy strengthened the Tokelau mission, and also began work with the talented Vidal at Leone on Tutuila. He was then recalled in 1863 to Australia, to be rector of a seminary for island students at Clydesdale, near Richmond, New South Wales. Fourteen were Samoans, but the combination of harsh winters, drought, and financial stringency doomed the project to failure, the more so since Elloy was appointed Vicar Apostolic for Samoa in 1864. By the time he died in 1878, he had become a figure of great respect in complex Samoan politics. Schools had been founded, and strong parishes emerged, but the search for an indigenous priesthood proved unsuccessful. Ioane Tofe was ordained in 1892, but most village Catholic leaders preferred to be catechists. The demands of seminary discipline, rigid timetable, and celibacy were too demanding for most

[63] J. Heslin, *History of the Roman Catholic Church in Samoa* (Apia, 1995) 24–30; F. Angleviel, *Les Missions à Wallis et Futuna au XIXème siècle* (Bordeaux, 1994).

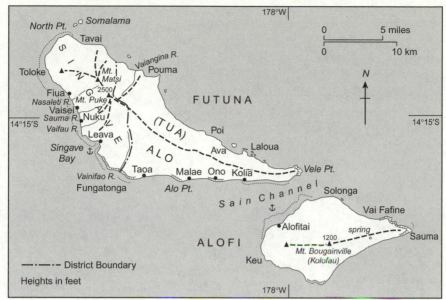

Futuna and Alofi (Hoorn Islands) (1944). (*Source:* Naval Intelligence Division, British Admiralty, *Pacific Islands*, 5 vols., London, 1939–45, vol. 3, p. 291. © British Crown Copyright/MOD. Reproduced with the permission of Her Britannic Majesty's Stationery Office.)

Polynesians, and alien to their culture. The priesthood and hierarchy were to remain expatriate until late in the twentieth century, but many of the Marists were very knowledgeable about Samoan culture.[64] The church steadily consolidated under Bishops Lamaze, Broyer, and Darnand.

WORSHIP

When missionaries travelled to proclaim the Gospel in the scarcely known regions of Australasia, they brought with them a cluster of practices, attitudes, and theologies which left a significant legacy among the communities which became Christian. Those who heard and responded to their message also made a contribution to the Christianities which developed, bringing their own cultural

[64] Heslin, *Catholic Church in Samoa*, 37–8, for their rule of life; A. Hamilton, 'Nineteenth century French missionaries and Fa'a Samoa', *JPH* 33 (1998) 163–77.

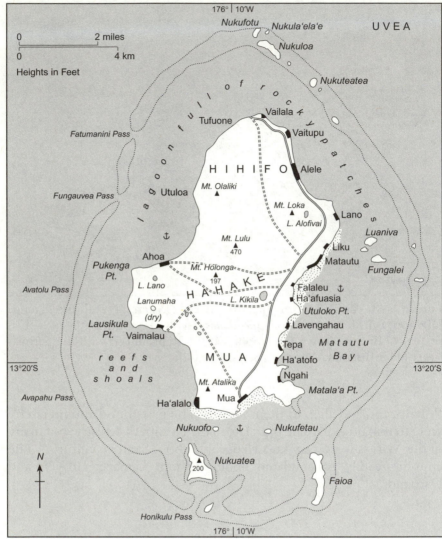

Uvea (Wallis) (1944). (*Source:* Naval Intelligence Division, British Admiralty, *Pacific Islands*, 5 vols., London, 1939–45, vol. 3, p. 277. © British Crown Copyright/MOD. Reproduced with the permission of Her Britannic Majesty's Stationery Office.)

perceptions to what functions religion should have in their village communities, for they were active participants in the process of conversion and acculturation. Sometimes there was conservative rejection. Christian worship was a source of great amazement in Aboriginal and Pacific Islander communities. Logan Campbell, in Auckland, gave a patronizing account of Maori Christians near Maraetai at worship, with no awareness of the use of traditional *waiata*.

As the sun dipped behind the distant hills an old woman could be seen holding in one hand a three-legged pot, suspended by a blade of flax, which she struck with a stone held in the other hand, and thus tolled a chime which called the tribe to evening prayers. The *whare* filled immediately with devout worshippers, who, muffled in their mats and blankets, strewed themselves over the floor in a promiscuous manner. The conductor of the religious ceremony then gave out a psalm, upon which all assembled forthwith gave out in song what I supposed to be some *Pakeha* tune which doubtless the *mihinare* had endeavoured to teach them.

But alas for the extraordinary noise that fell upon my ear—I utterly failed to recognise it, or from what tune it was a falling away. The imitation was not to be traced to any tune religious or profane—in fact, the sound was quite terrible, even in the low suppressed tone in which—fortunately for me—it was given. It had nothing either European or Maori about it; of the former element the instructing Missionary had utterly failed to impart any resemblance. If it had only been allowed to assume the latter, any Maori lament and chant or song, save the war song, would have been better than the hideous incongruity into which the ill-used psalm tune had drifted.

It was, however, decorously given, and after it a chapter from the New Testament was read, winding up with the Lord's Prayer—all in the Maori language, of course. Even at that date the Scriptures had been translated into Maori, and were in the hands of the missionaries for distribution. On the Amen being pronounced the whole meeting-house, as if by a stroke of an enchanter's wand, was instantaneously converted into a gossiping hall again, with accompanying incense proceeding from innumerable pipes, all hard at work before the parson had stuck his Testament behind one of the rafters overhead—a sort of depot for storing away things.

At Hick's Bay, J. W. Stack gave a rather more positive account of the way in which a congregation of 500 Maori gave thunderous liturgical responses which blended with the noise of the surf outside the church.[65]

Missionary expansion occurred at a time of liturgical aridity amongst Protestants. Liturgical changes have been unwelcome in island churches, who see liturgy possessing a sacred stability which has deep historical roots. The long prayer of eighteenth-century Dissenting worship is still alive and well in churches of London Missionary Society and Wesleyan origin, as is suspicion of anything that might be

---

[65] Campbell, *Poenamo*, 167; A. H. Reed (ed.), *Early Maoriland Adventures* (Dunedin, 1933) 129.

seen as popish. In some places adaptation occurred. Breadfruit, coconut pulp, water, and coconut juice were used instead of bread and wine for the Lord's Supper. Such adaptation goes back to the very beginning of Protestant missions in Tahiti in 1797.

The traditional *kava* ceremony has many sacred associations which underline village unity and social gradations through speeches and drinking *kava*, but has been kept separate from Christian worship. Status from ceremonial exchange, in the form of gifts to the missionary societies, was, however, quickly incorporated into the life of Pacific churches. There are parallels to the offerings to Tangaloa in pre-Christian times. Occasionally pre-Christian symbols found novel uses. At Mbau the baptismal font had been used as a skull-crusher in pre-Christian days. The social status of chiefs was recognized by their sitting near the pulpit, and in some cases the chiefs had special seats erected so that their heads were higher than those of the missionaries.

Amongst those who welcomed Roman Catholic missionaries, the corporate character of worship, the pomp and colour, the congregational responses, the sacred spaces, and definite priestly authority had some significant connections culturally. There was no desire to challenge the way worship was conducted by the ordained clergy, but important developments occurred in family worship which became near universal, at a time when it was beginning to decline among the generality of British Protestants. The 'priesthood of all believers' was focused in the head of the family, and prayers were observed by the whole community at a curfew time, which lasts to this day. This may reflect patterns of pre-Christian worship of household gods.

The opening of churches with large feasts associated is another sign of how tradition and Christianity have been integrated. Burials often included gifts to propitiate the soul of the deceased as in pre-Christian times, with graves usually close to the family house. Singing is enormously important in all Polynesian and Melanesian churches, and the singing patterns of Samoa and the Cook Islands have been particularly important as Christianity spread into Melanesia. Occasional hints in missionary reports, visitors' accounts, and the few surviving diaries of Pacific Island Christians, suggest deep personal piety, but with currents which often ran in different directions from mission approved liturgical and doctrinal practice.

Polynesian cosmology slowly changed, but traditional ideas of death, and the afterlife as a shadowy version of this life, remained significant long after the process of conversion had begun. It would be misleading to call this syncretism, for there was no real meeting of cosmologies. Each existed alongside the other, being given different primal meanings such that they were heard with very different resonance by Polynesian hearers, even though the language might have appeared very biblical. A moralistic and practical approach to theology persisted with undiminished authority in all the islands, and is still a significant force.

ARCHITECTURE AND MUSIC

The building of churches was an important attempt to recreate sacred space in the new world of the converts and settlers. In New South Wales Francis Greenaway, a former convict, built a number of fine churches, but the first sign of an Antipodean architectural idiom emerged in New Zealand. Around Auckland, Bishop Selwyn and Frederick Thatcher designed and built a number of wooden churches which were beautifully proportioned neo-Gothic structures, most of which still stand 150 years later. Roman Catholics happily built in Gothic, and those in Sydney were soon involved in the building of St Mary's Cathedral, well before Anglicans built St Andrew's Cathedral. Lutherans in South Australia erected churches that were replicas of those which they had known in Prussia.

Polynesian converts built Christian meeting houses in their traditional styles, often decorated with intricate carvings which symbolized some continuity between the old religious world and the new. Some of these seated several hundred worshippers. The most impressive Maori church was at Rangiatea, north of Wellington, which was destroyed by arson in 1995.[66] The Congregationalist and Wesleyan missionaries built churches along the lines of the chapels they remembered from Britain, just as Picpus and Marist missionaries built churches and dwellings reminiscent of the French countryside.

In some colonies where an old building was converted to a Sunday school and was not demolished, the different styles of architecture can still be seen side by side, with a Gothic style replacing the earlier classical and Georgian styles. Decoration was minimal in early Protestant churches, for the Word was expected to carry the whole weight of liturgical meaning. Some churches had texts painted on the

---

[66] R. Sundt, 'On the erection of Maori churches in the mid-nineteenth century', *JPS* 108 (1999) 7–38; National Library, *Rangiatea* (Wellington, 1997).

arch of the chancel, or tablets bearing the Decalogue and Lord's Prayer, sometimes accompanied by the Apostle's Creed. As the Oxford Movement gained momentum in Anglicanism, carved wood-work appeared, decorating pulpits, altars, communion tables, and choir stalls. Initially clear glass, or geometrically patterned glass, filled Protestant windows, but as stained-glass techniques improved, bene-factors gave generously to remember family or relatives by scenes from the Gospels or church history. Figures from the Old Testament were much less common. Occasionally, real people were portrayed, if they had been important to the congregation.

Catholic churches were more lavishly decorated with statues of the Saviour, Mary, and the saints. The stations of the cross were often vividly portrayed, and wealthier parishes sometimes had lavish murals and frescoes, or even portrayals of biblical scenes and saints to remind worshippers that they were heirs of a long and rich history of devotion to God. In Noumea, the cathedral built with the help of convict labour dominates the city. Protestants and Catholics sought to out-build each other in many parts of the Pacific, with large churches making emphatic statements about the importance of the villages that had erected them. Candles, from the 1860s, and incense, from the 1890s, came slowly into Anglican churches where the clergy were sympathetic to the Oxford Movement. Evangelical parishes were resolutely undecorated and plain, lest worshippers be distracted from the Word and corrupted by Romanism and Ritualism.[67]

Choirs initially were rare, for few had the expertise to sing classical settings. Protestants also were suspicious of Popish music. J. W. Stack of New Zealand in 1846 attended St James Anglican Church in Sydney, where his parents worshipped on their arrival in 1834. 'I heard a pipe organ for the first time in my life, and when the Te Deum was sung by the choir to Jackson's music, I was so overpowered by the beauty of it that I nearly fainted. I never remember a service that has left a deeper and more abiding impression upon my memory.' The Anglican musical heritage came to Christchurch's cathedral in 1881, together with a cathedral school for choristers.

Choir leaders and organists in major cities were often also active in civic music-making, or connected with opera companies. Their soloists welcomed opportunity to sing solos with church choirs of standing. Musicians were not over-constrained by denominational

---

[67] J. Dickson, *Shall Ritualism and Romanism Capture New Zealand?* (Dunedin, 1912) 29.

boundaries. A Protestant, W. J. Cordner, served at St Mary's Cathedral, Sydney, from 1856 to 1872. George Rutter, another Protestant, who was Director of Music at St Francis', Melbourne, even composed a Mass setting, though he was not as prolific as Paolo Giorza, another Director.

The choir in St Mary's Cathedral, Sydney, began through Catherine Fitzpatrick, who arrived in 1811 to join her convict husband, and who gathered a group of singers to assist with Mass. She was the first and only woman to direct the choir, but she was dismissed in 1829 by Fr Power, because she supported Therry. Isaac Nathan, a significant composer, was the first organist in 1841, though J. Cavendish had played a seraphine from 1834. Disputes over the nature of the choir were long-standing, for some wanted it to be a monastic choir. Those with more comprehensive musical tastes prevailed and the choir developed a fine reputation for its singing of the wide range of Mass settings by major composers.[68] Some found the theatricality of some performances distasteful, judging by a description of the choir of St Stephen's Catholic Cathedral in Brisbane. 'The choir sang more than its fair share of jumping kyries, savage roaring credos, shrieking offering solos and rude street marches which had begun to offend even the untrained ear.'[69]

Many Protestant congregations still sang psalms unaccompanied, usually with a precentor's help, sometimes singing after him line by line. Anglicans and Wesleyans, at this early stage, were sometimes aided by local winds and strings, or by the increasingly popular seraphine, a precursor of harmoniums and organs. In the Polynesian churches, congregations sang lustily, by ear rather than from printed music. British hymns were quickly translated and singing was one of the attractions of the *lotu,* especially when hymns were set to traditional chants.

The music of Polynesian churches was more melodious, but equally reflected a particular culture, symbolizing the manner in which Christianity had become part of the Pacific way. Hymnody and music reflected both the divisiveness of Christianity, as well as the permeability of denominational boundaries as laity switched without odium to a different religious environment.

[68] P. O'Farrell (ed.), *St Mary's Cathedral* (Sydney, 1971) 157–8.

[69] N. Byrne, 'The music and musicians of St Stephen's Cathedral, the first 60 years', *BCHS* 2 (1989) 15–29.

3

THE MAKING OF CHRISTIAN SOCIETIES

Throughout the region from the 1850s to the 1880s there was a variety of attempts to create societies which were Christian in law, ethos, and priorities. Competing elites devised new metaphors for their vision of emerging nations within greater Britain, but drew heavily on lay Protestant assumptions about what was Christian. Even as late as 1868, governments were still setting days aside for humiliation before God because of drought. In a number of British colonies of settlement, this vision meant developing a new relation between the churches and the government, each with its own divinely given responsibilities, because there was a sufficiently strong coalition of churches to abolish establishment.

Presbyterians, Methodists, Baptists, and Congregationalists wanted pluriformity within a broadly defined Protestantism rather than uniformity. Though there was a considerable amount of unofficial religious discrimination, there was never a significant majority willing to entrench denominational privileges legally, and to use those powers to harass and persecute. Protestantism had significant influence at every level of society. As Alexander Thomson of Geelong put it, 'Let it never be forgotten that it is to her Protestantism that England owes her greatness and it is by Protestantism alone that she can maintain and preserve her Empire'.[1] The granting of responsible government to most of the colonies in the early 1850s speedily brought new groups into political power, because of the generous provisions for male suffrage.

Many in the early colonial parliaments were strongly Christian and determined that religious tests would have no place in their colony. Separation of religious and political authority ensured this, even though the pattern was different from the United States. Care was taken not to intrude denominational issues into political debate. Educational issues in the 1870s were an exception. From the outset,

[1] La Trobe MS 9345 Box 1034 2a.

Roman Catholic members were elected by a cross-section of voters, not just by their co-religionists. When O'Shanassy looked like becoming premier in Victoria one Protestant, however, felt that 'the idea of an English colony ruled by an Irish rebel! That is rich'.[2]

Some Protestant clergy, like Dr Lang, who regularly topped the poll in Sydney from 1859, were also elected. It was not long before the prohibition on Anglican clergy being elected was repealed, without their having to resign their orders. When the Anglican Revd G. D. MacCartney, a member of the Victorian Legislative Assembly, committed suicide, the Anglican newspaper spoke of 'the nemesis that waits upon abandoned orders'.[3] Thomas Reibey, in Tasmania, a former archdeacon, became premier, despite a legal case alleging sexual misbehaviour.

The experience that members had already gained in their parishes and congregations stood them in good stead. The importance of accountability was clear. They knew how to debate, how to use procedure, and how to scrutinize finances. Many of the urban newspapers they read like *The Argus* and *The Age* in Melbourne, and *The Sydney Morning Herald*, were published and edited by Christians who shared the same aspirations. Members with legal backgrounds also had advantages in drafting and amending bills. Many of the issues which had to be settled were concerned with public works, land distribution, and education. The major issues of law, foreign policy, and defence were still controlled from London.

With the exception of South Australia and Queensland, the Australian churches were treated generously with grants of land for glebes, burial grounds, education, and worship, plus subsidies for stipends and buildings so they could play a key role in nation-building. Such aid enabled them to cope much better with the rapid expansion of population from the 1850s to 1870s than would have been possible if they had had to rely solely on slowly rising voluntary giving. Only occasional wealthy colonists gave money to build churches and provide endowments. Sir Richard Dry endowed Hagley in Tasmania with £400 a year. Bishop Tyrrell of Newcastle left £200,000 to his diocese in 1879. In Melbourne, the Presbyterian Francis Ormond gave £5,000 to help the building of St Paul's Cathedral, if Anglicans raised another £25,000, and they did.

Even so, ministers of the former established churches found it an

---

[2] La Trobe MS NS/3D1, McLure-Fenton, 19 Sept. 1857.
[3] *Messenger*, 14 June 1878, 3.

uphill struggle to persuade their congregations to give systematically. Gifts from the wealthy were not enough. Nor were pew rents. When some congregations democratically abolished these, for other forms of money-raising, there were just as many complaints. Regular direct giving had not been universally necessary at home, and schemes like Sustentation Funds seemed to some ardent Protestants too close for comfort to Rome's long experience of collections. Some clergy deplored bazaars as fundraisers, though many laity, especially women, enjoyed the sociability they and tea meetings fostered.[4] Vital local networks were reinforced by such activities, even if clergy felt they were secular rather than religious.

EDUCATION FOR CITIZENSHIP

Creating a citizenry, with a majority committed to broadly Christian values, was a vital contribution to the development of freedom and mutual responsibility, where persuasion was more influential than persecution and elimination of political rivals. Beneath the bitter confrontations of the public square was a commitment to social solidarity, justice, and truthfulness which helped to create some of the most stable democracies in the world. Government assistance in this society building was especially important through education, which had been dominated by the churches for centuries. Catholics were insistent that parental and religious authority must not be impaired by public education, because parents and clergy were commanded by tradition and revelation to form children for moral living in society and for service of God. By the 1860s and 1870s, it had become clear that, even with government assistance, the churches were unable to meet the educational needs of rapidly growing and expanding communities.[5] Some of their schools were most inadequate in facilities, in the quality of their teaching, and curriculum. Some thoughtful citizens argued for secular government schools, to set standards, serve the whole community, and also to overcome needless competition. They suggested ministers should not even visit schools to give religious instruction, so that no

---

[4] St Mark's Library, William Chalmers' Diary, 29 Jan. 1865, noted that the adults at his services in Inglewood, Victoria, had contributed an average of fourpence each, whereas a tea meeting had brought in £16.

[5] A. G. Austin, *Australian Education* (Melbourne, 1961) 164–9; J. Mackey, *Making of a State Education System* (London, 1967).

religious group was disadvantaged. Sunday schools were the place to inculcate religious ideas.

Anglicans and Catholics, in particular, were very hostile to this, because some of their leaders believed that public schools would seriously weaken the essential link between the dogmatic teachings of their church, and the inculcation of morality.[6] Some wealthy Christians feared the re-emergence of Chartism in the 1850s in Victoria following the influx of goldminers. In 1853 there were 115,000 on the Victorian goldfields, and only three Anglican clergy to maintain sacred order. Some Anglicans worried that society would collapse under the strain of such numbers, and that divine institutions like the Sabbath would disappear. The Revd H. B. MacCartney saw the Sabbath as payment of homage to God and 'the tenure on which we hold our right to the world around us'.[7] Bishop Perry was hostile to indiscriminate state aid, which he believed 'would deprive us of the character of a Christian nation', but he had no solution to the numbers of children attending no school at all. If school was compulsory, it had to be free and non-denominational. It was politically impossible for governments to continue subsidizing church schools.[8]

The Catholic Bishop Goold in Melbourne, possibly with an eye on France and Germany, argued that it was religious persecution to impose a godless and compulsory system of education, which could heathenize Christian nations. 'But it is not possible to have good government, which politics pretend to give, without religion. Politics without religion we should deprecate as a great evil and a public calamity.'[9] Similar Catholic convictions were forcibly expressed in New South Wales by Archbishop Vaughan's 1879 *Pastorals*.

Pope Pius IX, and Cardinal Cullen in Ireland, both emphasized the importance of church schools to counter liberalism, rationalism, and indifferentism. For Cullen it was vital to counter Protestantism and its allegedly neutral relative—'common Christianity'—which transcended denominations. Earlier attempts to create a national school system in Ireland had failed because of Catholic opposition. The emergence of teaching congregations was the answer to bishops' concerns about education. Not only were they much cheaper than lay

---

[6] A. G. Austin (ed.), *Select Documents in Australian Education* (Melbourne, 1963) 164–8, 220–1.

[7] *Church of England Messenger* (1851) 102.

[8] Ibid., 165.

[9] *The Age*, 14 June, 1872. A. Cunningham, 'Under the banner of the cross', Ph.D. thesis (Sydney, 1998) discusses the reasons for Vaughan's hostility to government schools.

teachers, they were seen as a much more reliable source for an all-encompassing religious education on Catholic principles. Attendance at Catholic schools was part of the strengthening of discipline and identity, which can be seen in the legislation of the 1869 Provincial Council in Australia. The Catholic bishops in Australia, like the Quinn brothers, and Bishop Murray of Maitland, were closely connected with Cullen and Croke of Auckland in their campaign to strengthen Catholic identity.

The New Zealand provinces had varied systems of financial partnership with major churches, but, in Dunedin, Bishop Patrick Moran ran a confrontational campaign from 1871 against the public schools, which were substantially Presbyterian in ethos.[10] He argued in *The Tablet* against the injustice of Roman Catholics paying taxation for schools to which, in conscience, they could not send their children. Bishop Goold, in Melbourne, made similar interventions once serious discussion began about the ending of state aid to church schools.

Population growth had important consequences for the Anglican position on education, especially after the death of Broughton in 1853. Finding a successor proved difficult. To make matters worse, continuity in educational policy was impossible because no acceptable High Church candidate was available. In 1854, Sir George Grey, Secretary of State for the colonies, persuaded the Evangelical Frederick Barker to accept. That was a decisive shift in party balance in Australia, which strengthened Sydney's Evangelicalism. Though without Broughton's learning, he was very suitable for the times.[11] Strongly Protestant, he was not interested in politics, but focused on developing worshipping and witnessing congregations with a variety of organizations to involve and inspire laity. Sunday schools grew rapidly during his later episcopate, taking up some of the religious education which closure of Anglican schools had ended, placing it in lay hands.

He was more successful than Broughton and Tyrrell in utilizing a strong laity because he did not challenge their political power, seeking instead to encourage them to increase voluntary giving and to take advantage of missionary responsibilities within the Empire and the colony. He recruited eighteen clergy from Ireland and the north of

[10] H. Laracy, 'Paranoid popery: Bishop Moran and Catholic education in New Zealand', *NZJH* 10 (1976) 212.

[11] W. M. Cowper, *The Episcopate of Frederick Barker* (London, 1888); G. S. Maple, 'Evangelical Anglicanism', MA thesis (Sydney, 1992).

England, but saw this could not be a long-term solution to provision of clergy. Moore College was his answer in 1856, supported by Perry, who provided half the ordinands.[12] It monopolized Anglican theological education until the foundation of Trinity College in Melbourne in 1872. But even so, it did not produce enough graduates for the expanding needs of Sydney, and other Evangelical dioceses. To staff outlying districts, Barker skilfully developed the office of lay reader from the 1860s, providing them with an Institute in 1875 to give them more adequate preparation. Enabling clergy and laity to deal with new currents of thought was to prove a more difficult matter. Barker and his gifted wife Jane believed that conversion, not education, was the best answer to doubt,[13] and to the development of good citizens.

Most Protestants happily sent their children to government schools. Catholic bishops, by contrast, were willing to deny the sacraments to parents who sent their children to public schools by choice or financial necessity. Some leading Catholic laity resisted, but were out-manoeuvred, because many parents genuinely wanted a religious education for their children, rather than the secular one which was proposed by some Protestants as a solution to sectarian rivalries. The problem was money, for many Catholic families were poor with large families. A creative local answer developed in South Australia at Penola, where Fr Tenison Woods and Mary MacKillop joined forces to provide low-cost Catholic education.[14]

She was from a gifted Scottish family which was in serious financial straits. They had well-off relatives and connections, and she had already had some experience of teaching before she went to teach pastoralists' children in Penola. Deeply religious, energetic, and with high ideals, she took simple vows in 1866. Tenison Woods was an unusually talented priest, well educated, with interests in science which made him one of the leading amateur scientists in nineteenth-century Australia. A rousing orator, whose revival sermons were spellbinding, he also had a mystical side to his personality, and guided Mary into deeper religious commitment. His appointment as Director of

---

[12] M. Loane, *Moore College* (Sydney, 1955); G. Treloar (ed.), *The Furtherance of Religious Beliefs* (Sydney, 1997).

[13] S. Judd and K. J. Cable, *Sydney Anglicans* (Sydney, 1987) 80.

[14] P. Gardiner, *Mary MacKillop* (Sydney, 1994); M. Foale, *The Josephite Story* (Sydney, 1995); T. P. Boland, *Quiet Women* (Deception Bay, n.d.) for Wood's later career; M. Press, *Julian Tenison Woods* (Sydney, 1986); E. Pickering (ed.), *Mary and Julian: Their Letters 1862–1868* (Sydney, 1989).

Education in the Adelaide Catholic diocese, and MacKillop's conviction that God had called her to teach the children of the poor at little cost by founding a community committed to poverty, led to the formation of the Sisters of St Joseph.

A timely initiative, it soon attracted other young women. They did not have to pay a dowry as in other congregations, and were prepared to live in rented houses and great poverty in order to carry out their mission, refusing to offer students frills, like music, so that they could concentrate on a truly Catholic education. Tenison Woods was a charismatic leader, and not always a good judge of others' spiritual maturity and integrity. His rather romantic personality, inadequacies in administration, and poor judgement of excessive religiosity made life difficult for the young community, the more so because Mary was determined that her sisters would not be the servants of parish priests or bishops with other educational priorities.

The Josephite community grew steadily and attracted pupils. Other bishops were anxious to secure their services, including James Quinn in Brisbane.[15] Mary had already had problems with her local bishop and some priests who were jealous of her success, and hostile to her independence of spirit. Fearing divided educational effort, they believed that Catholic unity demanded unambiguous obedience to episcopal and priestly authority, for schools were crucial in developing Catholic identity. In Brisbane, the issues of control came to a head and Mary withdrew her sisters, for Bishop James Quinn and his episcopal brother, Matthew, in Bathurst, were convinced that nuns should be subject to the local ordinary, not to the superior of the community. Mother Mary refused to weaken the Institute's central government and the related control of its schools.

In Adelaide, matters reached a crisis in 1871, with Mary being excommunicated by an ill-advised and authoritarian Bishop Sheil. Another confrontation occurred in 1883, when she was expelled from the diocese by Bishop Reynolds. She bore her tribulations with great patience and dignity, and never wavered in her commitment to appropriate obedience.[16] Bishops and priests were not willing to accept that feminine definition of obedience. The Quinns did succeed in splitting a small group of sisters away into diocesan congregations—the black Josephites, as distinct from the brown habit Mary and her sisters wore. After a long struggle, which involved a stay in Rome during 1873–5,

---

[15] A. McLay, *James Quinn* (Toowoomba, 1989).
[16] M. Press, *From Our Broken Toil* (Adelaide, 1979).

Mary finally achieved official recognition for her central government, and accepted a somewhat modified version of poverty.

The sisters were invited in 1883 to New Zealand by an enthusiastic Marist priest, Fr Favuel, who wanted a school in Temuka. In 1884 they entered Auckland, after Bishop Luck gave legally binding assurances to respect the rules of the Institute. Mary spent a considerable amount of time in New Zealand visiting isolated places like Matata in the Bay of Plenty. This was their first school with Maori pupils. She continued writing innumerable letters and circulars, to encourage and inspire her sisters in their vocation. They won the affection of Catholics and Protestants alike wherever they went, for it was clear that they were enduring considerable hardship.[17] Money for buildings, gifts of food, and supplies flowed, and a large network of houses and schools had been created by the time Mary died in 1909.

At times, she could also be unyielding, and had some failures in relationships in the community. A number of talented women joined the order, and gave fine leadership when she was unable to function officially as superior, while always making it clear that her spiritual guidance was to be taken with the utmost seriousness. Her letters and circulars are full of spiritual insight, and clearly mark her out as one of the outstanding founders in the nineteenth century.[18] Her beatification in 1995 is a reminder of how effectively she embodied the best in Catholic spirituality, and demonstrated that women could, without official encouragement, contribute to the discipleship of other lay Catholics. She and her sisters retained the spirit of poverty and commitment to the children of the poor, and grew into one of the largest women's religious congregations in Australia and New Zealand, with a formidable network of schools financed entirely by Catholics.

The Mercy, Brigidine, and Presentation Sisters were other important women's congregations helping to provide low-cost teachers— the only way to counter increasing numbers of government schools. Nor were Catholics content with giving religious instruction to Catholic children in state schools. They saw such schools as culturally

---

[17] A. M. Power, *Sisters of St Joseph* (Auckland, 1983) 14 noted the comment that Sister Raymond was so dreadfully seasick that 'she will turn *schismatic* rather than cross the Southern Ocean again'. Power, ibid., 52, notes a leading Methodist was so impressed he became a regular supporter. D. Strevens, 'The Sisters of St Joseph, N.Z. 1880–1965', M.Th. thesis, (Melbourne, 1995).

[18] S. M. Denis (ed.), *Mother Mary's Circulars to the Sisters* (Sydney, 1976).

Protestant. They wanted authentically Catholic schools. The exclusion of religious teaching from Victorian schools from 1872, and New Zealand after 1877, and the minimal instruction allowed in South Australia and Queensland from 1875, were a further warning of how precarious such religious instruction could be.[19] A number of women's congregations also began educational work in the Pacific Islands, providing otherwise unavailable opportunities for girls to have some education.

Only in New South Wales was there reasonable clergy access to pupils, of which Barker's clergy took full advantage. For Roman Catholics that was simply not Christian education, for 'common Christianity' was to them a Protestant moralism without spiritual roots. In order to rally their people, in case government aid disappeared, the Catholic bishops began an aggressive campaign against the alleged deficiencies of state schools. Protestant anger was great, which confirmed what many Catholics maintained—public schools were Protestant, and misleadingly labelled state or public schools. In 1882 New South Wales ended aid for denominational schools, with general religious instruction and clergy entry to state schools as compensation. Only eleven Anglican schools survived the abolition of state aid. Barker had fought for the old dual system in the 1860s, but also had time to prepare clergy and people for the new order. Education of conscience had to take new forms in all the colonies. That significantly changed the functions of colonial church bodies and expanded the role of religious congregations involved in education.[20]

Before compulsory primary education the Protestant churches also provided a significant percentage of the children of the colonies with basic literacy and religious instruction through Sunday schools and Ragged schools, 'which is the only provision that we can make on any large scale to prevent the education of our youth from becoming merely secular'.[21] These schools were also very influential in North America and in Britain, which provided models for Christians in the antipodes. They provided for children who had to work in normal school hours, as well as for those from poorer families who could

---

[19] D. Grundy, *Secular, Compulsory, Free* (Melbourne, 1975); I. Breward, *Godless Schools?* (Christchurch, 1967) discusses the New Zealand developments.

[20] P. Gallagher, *The Marist Brothers in New Zealand* (Auckland, 1976); C. Larkin, *A Certain Way: An Exploration of Marist Spirituality* (Rome, 1995); K. K. O'Donoghue, *P. A. Treacy and the Christian Brothers* (Melbourne, 1983).

[21] C. E. Walch, *Sunday School Teaching* (Hobart, 1883) 15.

not afford any school fees. Many of the Sunday schools provided a strongly evangelistic lay environment, libraries, clubs, and annual occasions such as the picnic and anniversary, which involved families and friends. Involvement of members in teaching provided an important way of demonstrating parish vitality and handing on the Christian heritage.[22] The Whit walks, which were so common in the Northern England counties, did not transplant to Australasia. In Sydney, Bishop Barker founded a diocesan Institute in 1851 to increase Sunday school effectiveness. In Victoria Mr Robert Allan of Buninyong gave generously of time and energy to set up a Sabbath-school Institute.[23] In the Pacific Islands, Sunday schools were also an important contributor to literacy and evangelism. Samoa developed an interesting custom— White Sunday. Each year, children were feted for this one day, with parents reversing roles and serving children, as well as providing them an opportunity to wear special white clothes for worship.

Sunday schools were usually controlled by church members rather than ministers, and were a vital source of Christian influence among many who did not normally attend church services and who had no strong denominational identity. They were important in working-class districts, where many men rarely attended worship, but were glad for their children to have an introduction to Christianity, and its morality.[24] Huge annual rallies of thousands of children led in singing by choirs of hundreds gave the movement a high public profile. An added bonus was that it could provide parents with a little free time for themselves, important when long hours were worked and houses were crowded. Male superintendents often were leading citizens. In Trinity Congregational Church in Perth, the Hon. George Randell was a Sunday school superintendent who also served 33 years in Parliament, read widely, and was passionately concerned for education, but resolutely opposed to state aid.[25] Women also played an important part in teaching and administration, even though the system was male-controlled. As a result, many young women gained experience in leadership, which was important in later phases of the women's movement in the nineteenth century, and transferred to the YWCA,

[22] F. Hanson, *The Sunday School in New Zealand Methodism* (Auckland, 1998); D. Keen, 'Feeding the lambs: the influence of Sunday schools on the socialization of children in Otago and Southland 1848–1901', Ph.D. thesis (Dunedin, 1999); J. Graham, *My Brother and I* (Dunedin, 1991) 12–15 for the importance of religious organizations for New Zealand youth.

[23] R. Sutherland, *The History of the Presbyterian Church of Victoria* (Melbourne, 1877) 508–16.

[24] R. Howe, *A Re-appraisal of the Relationship between the Churches and the Working Classes 1880–1910* (Melbourne, 1989). [25] S. H. Cox, *Memorial Sermon* (Perth, 1915).

the temperance movement, and other para-church networks and organizations, particularly foreign missions. As Keen points out, many went on to teach in state schools which grew steadily in numbers in the 1860s, contributing a religious perspective to teaching.

Children were encouraged to give to missions through specially written magazines and collections. Multiplied, their pennies could be a significant addition to missions' tight budgets, as well as giving children a feeling of involvement in preaching to the heathen, complemented by the visits of missionaries on furlough, or retired because of ill-health. LMS ships in the Pacific were partly financed from this source. The drama of salvation and deliverance was fostered by the singing of hymns specially composed for children. Their words were often a lifelong framework for understanding the complexities of life, and a foundation for naming different facets of religious experience.[26] Only a small portion of the attendees went on to church membership, but they, nevertheless, provided an important link with the wider community, keeping some Christian connections and upholding a broadly Christian morality which was generally accepted even by those who rarely entered a church door.

In the missionary churches of the Pacific, the convictions about the importance of education for morality and development of a deeper Christian faith, held by both Protestants and Roman Catholics, were also embodied in simple village schools. The Anglican Bishop Patteson believed that 'the surest and quickest way in the end is to get hold of some few intelligent fellows and teach them *thoroughly*, not neglecting the mass of the people . . .'.[27] Pastors and their wives played an important part in the provision of such facilities, drilling children in catechism, encouraging the acting out of biblical incidents and stories, as well as teaching the skills of reading and writing. Priests and religious also gave a great deal of time and energy to schooling converts and their children in a new history.

Both Catholic and Protestant traditions produced tightly knit communities in which sacred knowledge was appropriately passed on in this new and accessible way. Educating girls and boys together was a radical change. So was the introduction of formal teaching of Christian history in schools. Family heads were also able to take over the task of telling biblical stories and proverbs, alongside handing on traditional mythology and proverbs about their ancestors. James Stack in Kaiapoi

---

[26] I. Bradley, *Abide with Me* (London, 1997) 49–52, 110–18.
[27] V. Browne-Wilkinson, *The Far Off and the Near* (Florence, 1983) 223.

kept morale high while his congregation built a new church, by telling them Christian stories, 'for there is no subject the Maori takes more interest in than history'.[28] Pacific Islanders, who were unused to thinking historically in a western way, did not place past figures in a chronological context, for that was not an important issue in their culture. They remembered instead what was formative for their identity, and such informally told stories reshaped the community's awareness.

Traditional mythological thinking and history are not easily aligned, but Judith Binney's life of Te Kooti breaks new ground because of the depth of her insight into the various stories remembered by his followers. Though some are contradictory, and others are complementary, they can be woven into a conventional historical narrative.[29] Such blending of oral and written sources demonstrates how such history can be vital for contesting European perspectives and enhancing local Christian identity.

In order to retain their identities, some denominations' curricula had significant historical content. They also tried to establish educational and social activities for their youth, like Bible classes, mutual improvement societies, and sports clubs. These were never as successful as the Sunday schools, which in New Zealand attracted 20 per cent of school-age children by 1858, compared with 31 per cent actually at primary schools. This folk Christianity is now hard to delineate, but useful research has been done in Britain and Europe which suggests that different forms of lay Christianity were much more influential in the nineteenth century than the published laments of clergy would lead one to believe.[30] This cultural Protestantism transcended denominational boundaries, focusing on morality, not church attendance and clerically defined discipleship. Laity heard something of the former, but were less interested in the latter. Many congregations had organizations which reached out into the community, culturally and recreationally, giving it a Christian ethos. They included people who did not see the need to be involved heavily in worship and 'spiritual' activities.[31]

Two other forms of education into heritage and identity were strongly supported by church elites who could afford secondary and

---

[28] J. W. Stack, *More Maoriland Adventures* (Dunedin, 1936) 189.

[29] J. Binney, *Redemption Songs* (Auckland, 1995); L. T. Smith, *Decolonizing Methodologies: Research and Indigenous People* (Dunedin, 1999) 28–33.

[30] H. McLeod, *Piety and Poverty* (New York, 1996); S. Green, *Religion in the Age of Decline* (Cambridge, 1996).

[31] H. Jackson, *Churches and People in Australia and New Zealand* (Wellington, 1987) 167–73.

university education for their children. Grammar or high schools were clearly important for education of those entering professions, or hoping to become community leaders through university education. The churches, like their British parent bodies, played a crucial part in founding such schools, which were sometimes affiliated to the British Headmasters' Conference. A number of schools were founded by individuals. Even though many of them had rocky financial beginnings, and some collapsed, they created influential networks of old pupils.[32] Girls' schools followed a little later, but a number had been established by the end of the nineteenth century.[33] Usually with male headmasters, and a female deputy, they provided employment for talented young women, and widened horizons and opportunities for many girls who otherwise would have found marriage their only option.

The other aspect of education to which Protestants gave high priority was the foundation of university colleges, governed by leading members of their denomination. When theology was excluded from the fledgeling universities of Sydney (1852) and Melbourne (1853), St Paul's in Sydney was the first residential church college to be founded. Anglicans founded it to give moral and religious teaching, and to repress 'every deed and word of an immoral, dishonourable, or ungentlemanly character'.[34] It also was lay controlled. Here young men could live in a Christian atmosphere which complemented, even countered, university teaching. Not being able to teach theological disciplines at university level was a real problem for the churches, who were increasingly aware that local recruitment for ministry was inescapable. In Melbourne and Sydney the churches built such colleges next to the university, with the New South Wales and Victorian governments giving land to the churches for such purposes. Unlike major North American churches, those in Australia and New Zealand did not found church-related liberal arts colleges, though Christ's College in Christchurch began in 1855 with that intention, as did St John's College in Auckland.

Finance for the fledgeling University of Otago's (1869) first chairs in Arts came from Presbyterian church endowments until 1945, but the formation of the University of New Zealand, with a number of deter-

---

[32] W. Bate, *Light Blue Down Under* (Melbourne, 1990); G. Dening, *Xavier Portraits* (Melbourne, 1993); V. Braniff, *The Quest for Higher Things* (Kilmore, 1992).

[33] M. Theobald, *Knowing Women* (Melbourne, 1996).

[34] Mitchell Library, W. B. Clarke MS 139/19x, 1–3.

mined secularists on its council, made the establishment of separate theological colleges the only option, as had already happened in Australia, using English and Scottish models.[35] In both Melbourne and Sydney, church-related university colleges were later permitted to admit divinity students eligible for matriculation.[36] Such courses for ministerial education had no connection with the university, but they gave ordinands opportunities for study in a tertiary-related context, which gave them invaluable contacts with future professional, business, and political leaders, as well as influencing some of the latter for Christian service, and shaping their worldview within their chosen vocations.

Broadly speaking, Protestants saw their colony as a Christian society, but one without an established church. They believed that the religion of the Bible was fundamental to the maintenance of morality, political freedom, commercial wealth, and material greatness.[37] All the churches believed their Gospel nourished conscience and morality. Clergy were also expected to be present on major and local public occasions, to offer prayer, to speak, and perhaps to lead some simple act of worship. Meetings of colonial parliaments and some local bodies opened with prayer, though that had been a struggle in Victoria.[38] Baptists, the Congregationalists, and some Presbyterians summarized this in the phrase 'a free church in a free state', by which they meant that both spheres had their own God-given responsibility and that their respective roles ought not to be confused by making the church political, or the state involved in matters spiritual.[39] Smaller Protestant groups like the Brethren, the Churches of Christ, and the Lutherans made similar points from different theological perspectives. Some Evangelical and Broad-Church Anglicans had similar views, but were willing to allow Parliament, as representative of the people, to have some functions in approving doctrinal formularies and worship. They nevertheless distanced themselves from other denominations. Bishop Perry deplored Wesleyan doctrinal errors and spiritual methods which 'lead many to deceive themselves with the show of Godliness'.[40]

[35] S. McIntyre (ed.), *Ormond College Centenary Essays* (Melbourne, 1984); J. Grant (ed.), *Perspective of a Century* (Melbourne, 1972); A. Dougan, *The Andrews Book* (Sydney, 1964); O. Parnaby, *Queen's College* (Melbourne, 1990).

[36] Treloar, *Furtherance of Religious Beliefs*, 8–71; C. Turney, et al., *History of the University of Sydney* (Sydney, 1991); I. Breward, *Grace and Truth* (Dunedin, 1976).

[37] *Messenger*, 15 July 1868.

[38] A. Cairns, *The Inauguration of the Political Independence of Victoria* (Melbourne, 1856).

[39] J. S. Gregory, *Church and State* (Melbourne, 1973).

[40] C. Perry, *A Letter from the Lord Bishop of Melbourne* (London, 1850) 126.

High-Church clergy also had subtle arguments to stress the ways in which state and church were both agents of God, as did Roman Catholics, and establishment Presbyterians. Such views have rarely received the historical attention they deserved, for their nineteenth-century detractors saw them as an attempt to justify a society in which religious privilege was entrenched. Such views on the centrality of religion for social health were taken for granted by many citizens, and underestimated by many modern historians, so that colonial societies have been read as more secular than they were. The roles of the Christian laity need to be much more carefully scrutinized in business, politics, civic issues, and education, if the construction of colonial societies is to be understood adequately. The laity also contributed notably to the development of the churches' ethos. Bishop Nixon of Hobart found that out in his struggle for tolerance of more Catholic views in the Church of England.[41] Episcopal attempts to shape identity did not always evoke compliance.

The arduous travel, the constant struggle to find sufficient clergy, battles to finance expansion, and the familiarity with which they were treated by other denominations, made the lot of a colonial bishop difficult indeed.[42] Bishops like Thomas in Goulburn were extremely conscientious, and his correspondence gives a vivid insight into the energies which he had to expend on matters which would be of little concern to an English counterpart with well-established parishes, ample clergy, and loyal laity who treated his views with great deference, as well as responding well to appeals for finance. On the other side of the continent in Western Australia, Bishop Parry and his successor, Bishop Riley, had even more difficult struggles, because of the huge distances which they had to travel, sometimes on foot, more often on horseback or camel, and rarely in the comfort of a ship, let alone a coach, or train, when roads and bridges were so rare.[43] Riley was once lost for four days. Entrepreneurial and public relations skills, which few English bishops needed to acquire, were essential for survival in the colonies.

[41] Anon., *Papers and Correspondence Relative to the Ordination held at Campbelltown* (Hobart, 1866).

[42] J. T. R. Border, *The Founding of the See of Goulburn* (Canberra, 1956) contains a selection of the correspondence; R. T. Wyatt, *History of the Diocese of Goulburn* (Sydney, 1937).

[43] A. E. Williams, *West Anglican Way* (Perth, 1989); Battye Library MS 614/181/2467a; C. Holden, *Ritualist on a Tricycle* (Perth, 1997).

WOMEN'S PLACE

The role of women in the establishment of colonial churches, as well as in Pacific churches, has not yet been fully and adequately dealt with. A number of women helped to establish congregations, founded voluntary societies, and shared in the tasks of education and pastoral care. Those of high social status have sometimes been remembered, especially if they have left journals, letters, and books to remind later generations of their achievements.[44]

Bishops' wives also needed to have physical and emotional stamina during their husbands' frequent absences, sometimes for many weeks on end. If they were without children, and occasionally accompanied their husband on his visitations, they needed to be able to rough it in accommodation that their peers in England would never have dreamt of enduring. Frances Perry, Sarah Selwyn, and Jane Barker left vivid descriptions of their travels and hardships, as well as their pleasures. So did missionary wives like Mrs Watt and Mrs Paton in Vanuatu.[45] While only a small number of young women went on to university and the professions, many women who went to these church secondary schools became important leaders in their community, churches, and para-church organizations of many kinds. Horizons for women were gradually expanding, even though the discrimination against women had strong foundations in the Christian churches, as well as in colonial society.[46]

Clerical and lay males alike argued powerfully (in their own eyes) for the indispensable moral and spiritual influence of women in family, church, and community. Women were portrayed as more delicate creatures than men, of altogether finer sensibility, and able to appeal to men's highest ideals.[47] To weaken these divine gifts by action in the public realm, where male aggression, brutality, and immorality reigned, restrained only by strong laws and powerful community sanctions, was seen as a body blow at the health of society. New

[44] J. West, *Daughters of Freedom* (Sydney, 1997) provides a good introductory overview.

[45] K. Cable, 'Mrs Barker and her diary', *JRAHS* 54 (1968) 67–105. G. Cox (ed.), *Notes on Gippsland History*, No. 38, includes material from Mrs Perry's journals of 1849–56. M. W. Paton, *Letters and Sketches* (London, 1905); A. C. P. Watt, *Twenty-five Years Mission Life* (Paisley, 1896).

[46] K. Daniels and M. Murnane, *Uphill All the Way* (Brisbane, 1980) 59–61; R. Teale (ed.), *Colonial Eve* (Melbourne, 1978); M. Quartly, et al., *Freedom Bound* (2 vols., Sydney, 1995).

[47] R. D. McEldowney, *Presbyterians in Aotearoa* (Wellington, 1990) 64 for Dr James Wallis on 'Women's True Beauty' in 1874.

women's roles would undermine spiritual and moral foundations ordained by God. Some Christian men lived these ideals, and cherished their wives and daughters, providing inspiring ideals of masculinity to them, and their sons and family circle. Others did not.

Social and family historians have for some time drawn attention to the dark side of Victorian masculinity, its oppression of women through domestic violence, sexual politics, and stigmatizing of women who did not fit approved roles, especially those of the working classes and those trapped in the cycle of poverty, and sexual and economic exploitation, through no fault of their own. Feminist historians of Australia and New Zealand have tellingly stripped away other dimensions of gender stereotyping, and the crippling effect it had not only on women, but also on oppressive males.[48] Australians and New Zealanders shared many of the sexist assumptions of British and European societies, though in a few areas like divorce reform, family law, and the right to hold property independent of husbands, changes were made which predated those in Britain. Some shipboard diaries by women are most illuminating, and family letters can throw vivid light on church life and the challenges of Christian discipleship.[49]

Women were a majority of church attenders in Britain and the USA, where the figures were two-thirds by the end of the nineteenth century. While colonial church statistics are not very detailed, there is some anecdotal evidence for a similar gender profile in Protestant settler churches, not least because constant efforts were made by leaders to find ways of attracting men to services, and to involvement in church life. There is no evidence for campaigns to attract more women. They were indispensable for fundraising, catering for church functions, cleaning and decorating churches with flowers, and for education and charitable work.[50] The history of the Young Women's Christian Association shows what a significant force they could be in temperance and suffrage movements, even though leadership of such organizations was middle to upper class.

Wives of prominent men, like the Baptist Louisa Ardill, or the Wesleyan Euphemia Bowes, were also very active in community charitable activities, which were an important part of feminine

---

[48] J. Simpson, 'Women, religion and society in New Zealand', *JRH* 18 (1994) 198–218; T. McLaughlin (ed.), *Irish Women in Colonial Australia* (Sydney, 1998).

[49] D. Fitzpatrick (ed.), *Oceans of Consolation* (Melbourne, 1995); F. Porter and C. Mac-Donald (eds.), *My Hand will Write what my Heart Dictates* (Auckland, 1996).

[50] J. West, *Daughters of Freedom*, 134–67; S. Willis (ed.), *Faith and Fetes* (Melbourne, 1977).

discipleship. Ardill was an evangelist, rescue worker, nursing educator, and matron of the South Sydney Women's Hospital. Bowes was an ardent temperance worker, evangelist, advocate of women's suffrage, campaigner against child prostitution, and rescuer of the unfortunate. Eliza Hassall the daughter of the Revd Thomas Hassall was a founder of the Scripture Union in 1880, gave her home as the Anglican Missionary Training College in Sydney, 1892–1917, and was its first superintendent. Matilda Evans was a teacher, Baptist deaconess, and writer in Adelaide whose novels were deeply religious with strong female characters.

The most significant Catholic women leaders were superiors of Roman Catholic religious communities.[51] Mother Ignatius, a Mercy Sister in Bathurst, was the sister of Bishop Croke of Auckland, and then Cashel. Mother Teresa Molloy, of the Dominican Convent in Maitland, was a relative of Cardinal Cullen in Ireland. Though they were canonically lay, their religious authority in their church, and in the community, was powerful. Those who were relatives of bishops and leading clergy and laity had an edge, but office conferred significant status. They were formidable fundraisers and ambassadors for the church, presenting a different face from that of the male leaders. They were skilful recruiters of men to advise them in the running of schools, hospital, orphanages, and refuges. The hospitals founded and administered by women's religious orders were always for the service of the whole community, never just for Roman Catholics, and were a widely respected aspect of Catholic presence. They pioneered high standards of nursing care and education, developing alliances with medical schools and leading doctors, and created a demand for better hospitals and medical services which ultimately could only be filled by government action.[52]

Sisters could be skilled at requesting assistance within and beyond their faith community, though little historical attention has been paid to their finances. Many Protestants discreetly donated, sometimes being reminded that if they failed, Roman Catholic custom would dry up, a significant issue in country towns where Catholic presence was strong. The impressive convent buildings on prominent sites which

[51] West, *Daughters of Freedom*, 99–133; M. Oliver, *Love is a Light Burden* (London, 1950); M. M. O'Brien, *Mother Mary Patricia O'Neill* (Melbourne, 1976).

[52] V. Allen, *Nurse Maude* (Christchurch, 1996) 10–11 for the links between Sybilla Maude and the Anglican Community of the Holy Name in Christchurch, leading to the development of district nursing.

were found in every significant town in Australia and New Zealand, and in some insignificant ones as well, were a very powerful sign of the presence of women religious. In many places, they made a major contribution to musical life, for their music teaching was an important part of their financial viability.

Bigoted Protestants were sometimes persuaded that unmentionable crimes went on behind high convent walls, and that secret passages connected presbyteries and convents. Such scurrility was naturally highly insulting to loyal Catholics who understood very well what hardships many sisters uncomplainingly suffered for their love of God. They were fierce assailants of those who attacked the sisters' honour, as ex-Father Chiniquy from Canada found when he attempted in 1878–9 to lecture in Australia on the shortcomings of the Roman Catholicism he had rejected. On a number of occasions, meetings could not be held because of the threat of riot from enraged Catholics. Many Protestants were also uneasy about his stirring of sectarian hostility. The Congregationalist George Clarke, in Hobart, remarked that religion cannot be revived by 'inflaming the mutual resentments of Protestants and Catholics'.[53]

MAORI RELIGION

In New Zealand, Tonga, and Fiji, there were important moves to enculturate Christianity without surrendering to a European religious, cultural, and political invasion. Apart from the Hawaiian Islanders, there was no group more vulnerable to settler dominance than the New Zealanders, a name applied to the tribes of New Zealand. The term 'Maori' has often been used by Pakeha to imply that they have an overriding cultural identity which transcended tribal realities. Nothing could be further from the truth. Granted that they had a common language, they felt differences from other tribes as keenly as Scottish clans did before they were broken after the 1745 rebellion, even though they had common grievances over land confiscations and government failure to honour promises to create reserves.

Acting together against the Pakeha was not always possible given the strength of the remembered enmities, both before and after the musket wars of the 1820s and 1830s, though substantial groups combined against the government. Religiously too, there were a

---

[53] G. Clarke, *Quiet Godliness* (Hobart, 1879) 11.

number of responses to Christianity after the New Zealand Wars of the 1860s which so deeply affected some tribes. Attention has focused on those tribes which opposed the Pakeha. Developments in about half the tribes which were neutral, or who used the wars to settle old scores with rivals, have often been ignored by historians.[54]

Pai Marire, meaning 'good and peaceful' was one of the first attempts to incorporate Christianity in a more Maori traditional framework during the disruption of the 1860s and 1870s. This religious movement built on earlier attempts to free Maori from *tapu* and *makutu* in Taranaki in the 1850s. Pai Marire remains an important part of the King Movement. Led by former slave Te Ua Haumene, who had been strongly influenced by Wesleyan missionaries, the movement gathered momentum in Taranaki from 1864, where conflicts over land had been sharpest. Well-versed in the Bible, Te Ua also had visionary experiences of Gabriel, and had acted as *tohunga* to Maori warriors fighting against government forces.

His recorded messages had a strongly biblical flavour and were intended to lead to peace. One chant ran, 'God of peace! God of love, Son of universal peace, Honour and Glory be to Thee, Holy Ghost, Spirit of Love, Spirit of Peace, Spirit of Universal love, Glory and honour be to Thee.'[55] Rituals of dancing, chanting, and marching were much more in accord with traditional religion than the decorous services of Christianity, though settlers and missionaries mocked them as savage reversions. That stereotype was reinforced by the Hau Hau use of the head of Captain Lloyd as a symbol of triumph over Pakeha. The head was the most sacred part of the body. Settlers with appalling lack of knowledge of their own military history in Australia, or the British massacre of Maori women and children at Rangiaowhia, took it as a sign of barbarism unredeemed. Te Ua claimed that angels would expel the Pakeha from Canaan.

The killing of the CMS missionary Carl Volkner in St Stephen's Anglican church at Opotiki in March 1865 further confirmed Pakeha fears about the movement. Those, like Kereopa Terau, who were responsible for the gruesome death were only loosely linked with Pai Marire. Local Maori suspected rightly that Volkner was reporting to the government on Maori movements. Spies are rarely treated

[54] J. Binney, 'Ancestral voices', in K. Sinclair (ed.), *Oxford Illustrated History of New Zealand* (Auckland, 1990) 153–84.

[55] P. Clark, *Hauhau* (Auckland, 1975) 118; D. Jones, 'Response to Steve Taylor's paper on Pai Marire', *Baptist Research* 3 (1998) 84–9; L. Head, 'The Gospel of Te Ua Haumene', *JPS* 101 (1992) 7–44.

mercifully, and Volkner paid a high price for his loyalty to the government. English Christians saw him as a martyr. Only some of those allegedly responsible for his death were tried. Others, like Mokomoko, were executed after an inadequate trial in 1886, and buried in unmarked prison graves, a source of deep grief and shame to their relatives. Not until 1988 were members of the Ngati Awa tribe pardoned for their alleged rebellion at this time and an attempt made to get a posthumous pardon for Mokomoko in 1990. Their remains were disinterred in 1992 and returned to their lands, so that the long shadow cast by the tragic event has been partly removed. The confiscation of 440,000 acres that followed Volkner's murder is still unresolved for the Whakatoea tribe.[56]

Te Ua repudiated the violent aspects of the movement after his capture by Grey's troops early in 1866, but he influenced a number of other Maori Christians, such as Tawhiao among the Waikato people, Te Kooti, Te Whiti, and Tohu. They later were at the heart of resistance to the confiscation of the rich Waimate plains around Hawera in South Tarankai. The movement was one of the most successful pan-tribal movements. There is some evidence that Titokowaru, one of the most brilliant strategists the British troops met, was also influenced by Te Ua, for he acted as a peacemaker, until forced into a devastating resistance movement, in 1868–9, by what seemed to his people government intransigence. He came close to reversing British military dominance. A similar shock was administered in 1878 in New Caledonia, where Atai led a campaign against settlers on unjustly taken land. Initial success was followed by brutal French repression, over a thousand Kanak deaths, and further confiscation, the injustice of which is still keenly felt.[57]

Another movement, which was not in any sense military, was linked with remarkable religious leaders like Te Matorohanga, Nepia Pohuhu, and others within the Whare-Wananga in the 1860s. Despite sharp disagreement amongst scholars as to whether the teaching on the high god Io was post-European, or an ancient and esoteric cult known only to a few *tohunga* in particular tribes, the reworking of traditional mythology and cosmology was a striking religious achievement in the context of the 1860s.[58] Io is placed at the apex of twelve heavens,

---

[56] E. D. Howe, *Bring Me Justice* (Auckland, 1992) discusses this.

[57] J. Belich, *I Shall Not Die* (Wellington, 1989); A. Bensa, *Nouvelle Calédonie* (Paris, 1998) 89–92, 148–9.

[58] M. P. K. Sorrenson, *Maori Origins and Migrations* (Auckland, 1979); *Manifest Destiny* (Auckland, 1992) sees the development of Pakeha myth.

where lesser deities order their cosmos. A vivid account of the conflict of good and evil is linked with Tane and Wairo. Clearly parallels with Christianity exist, but the religious system is cosmology in Maori terms, despite the filtering by Pakeha editors to accord with their uncritical views on religion.[59] Simmons accepts that the book accords with Te Matorohanga's ideas, but is not substantially his actual words.

Another aspect of Maori adaption of Christian symbols can be seen in the movement to appoint a king for the Maori. This was important amongst the Waikato tribes, with some support from Taupo, and owed much to the perceptiveness of Tarapipipi (also known as Wiremu Tamihana), whose study of the Bible led him to the conclusion that a king would unify his people and enable them to control their own affairs under Queen Victoria.[60] He had taken soundings over much of the North Island from 1855. There was a strong religious commitment in the movement, both Christian and traditional, summed up in the term Tariao (morning star). The king was to be a fountain of justice for Maori, seen as God's appointed, a symbol of authority rather than an executive ruler, for tribal rivalries would not permit that. It took some time to find a suitable and willing candidate.

The Waikato Maori were aware of related developments towards kingship in Tonga. The aged Te Wherewhero was proclaimed as Potatau I in June 1858. Tawhiao (Encircle the World) was baptized by Te Ua and succeeded in June 1860, as Potatau II. He was both *Ariki* and prophet, whose authority was widely respected. He identified himself with widows, orphans, and other people of lowly origin.[61] Many of his associates were related to those who had not signed the Treaty of Waitangi and wished to create an enclave in which they could continue unhindered their traditional life. As Tarapipipi put it, 'He will be a covering for the lands of New Zealand which still remain in our possession.'[62] The king exhorted his followers to hold fast to love and to kindness and was advised by a council of twelve, perhaps a reflection of the twelve apostles of Jesus.

[59] E. Best, *Maori Religion and Myth* (Wellington, 1924). J. M. R. Simpson, 'Io as supreme being: intellectual colonization of the Maori?', *History of Religions* 37 (1997) 50–85 reviews the literature skilfully. M. P. Shirres, *Te Tangata* (Auckland, 1997) argues for the pre-contact cult of Io. D. R. Simmons, 'The words of Te Matorohanga', *JPS* 103 (1994) 115–71.

[60] L. Rickard, *Tamihana the Kingmaker* (Wellington, 1963) 74 for Tamihana's explanation of his reasons for seeking a king. J. Gorst, *The King Movement* (Hamilton, 1959, repr.) is a perceptive contemporary account.

[61] K. Sinclair, *Kinds of Peace* (Auckland, 1991) 43–8.

[62] Rickard, *Tamihana the Kingmaker*, 74.

Few settlers could see that Maori attempts to govern themselves were quite consistent with the Maori version of the treaty. After all, they had no place in the colonial parliament, or provincial councils, until four parliamentary seats were set up in 1867. Unfortunately, there were no models of parallel political indigenous institutions existing in a colony of British settlement. Sir William Denison, the Governor of New South Wales, however, saw it as an opportunity to introduce good government among the Maori. 'Give that body the means of deciding what their interests are, and of submitting them in proper form for your consideration.'[63] Places for consultation with Maori by the settlers were very limited. There was no place for Maori leadership in the churches. The Maori had not been consulted on the constitution in 1857. Rota Waitoa was only deaconed in 1863, and numbers of Maori clergy grew very slowly.

Many in the colonial government did not trust Tarapipipi, misinterpreting his pleas for negotiation as devious resistance. They did not agree with his view that there was a difference between the authority of the colonial parliament, and that of the Crown. Not for the first or last time, differing understandings of sovereignty were politically divisive. Tarapipipi tried to make peace in Waitara, but was accused by the government of aggression. Gore-Brown made matters worse by a bombastic Declaration on 21 May 1861. Tarapipipi replied acutely and carefully.[64]

War was proclaimed on 15 July 1863, accompanied by the threat that those who took up arms against the Queen would forfeit the possession of the lands guaranteed to them by the treaty. Some 14,000 British troops were involved, including a number from the Australian colonies. Tarapipipi and other Waikato chiefs had long discussions about response to government policy, and its provocative plan for a road into their heartland. Selwyn attempted a meeting at Peria, in late October 1862, with representatives from many tribes. On Sunday 26, Tarapipipi had preached on unity from Psalm 133. Selwyn preached a counter sermon against the idea of a king on the same text in the afternoon.[65] The following day he met with the assembly again, and pleaded with them in Christ's name, but the suspicion on both sides

    [63] H. R. L. Wiley and H. Maunsell, *Robert Maunsell* (Dunedin, 1938) 58–65, 186–7; W. Swainson, *New Zealand and the War* (London, 1862) 38.
    [64] Rickard, *Tamihana the Kingmaker*, 108–15; J. Belich, 'The government and the Maori', in Sinclair, *Oxford Illustrated History*, 75–97.
    [65] Rickard, *Tamihana the Kingmaker*, 139–42.

was growing. Tarapipipi's influence was declining, for he was seen by many Maori as too moderate. Provocations on both sides and erosion of trust led to renewal of war in Taranaki.

Nor could the magic of Grey, who had replaced Gore-Browne, work again. Many Maori weighed his actions against his words and refused to trust him. Tarapipipi took up arms, but made peace in May 1865. He saw this as a covenant. Pakeha saw it as a surrender. He petitioned Parliament on 18 July 1865, pleading for arbitration, and the forwarding of his petition to the Queen.[66] Nothing was done. Nor was his plea heard for return of unjustly confiscated land.[67] Ignored by the victorious settlers and with much of his *mana* among his own people gone because he had surrendered, he died on 27 December 1866 with Bible in hand, but his achievements in ruins. His last words were, 'Obey the laws of God and man.'[68]

His life shows how deeply the Christian message had changed him, without weakening his commitment to the land as a source of identity. Differences with settlers never led him to deviate from his commitment to peace, and the conviction that both races could live together under the Queen's authority, even though he had not signed the Treaty. It was a tragedy that he was not treated with the respect he deserved, for the course of New Zealand history may have been rather different. The issues of sovereignty with which he wrestled still remain unresolved. Sir John Gorst, who observed the King movement from its outset and then returned to high office in Britain, said simply, 'I have met many statesmen in the course of my long life, but none superior in intellect and character to this Maori chief, whom most people would look upon as a savage.'[69] Long-lasting memories on both sides poisoned relations for generations, and the depth of Maori grievances over unjust confiscation of over three million acres of land was not understood, and was still not comprehended by many Pakeha in the 1980s and 1990s, when they re-emerged before the Waitangi Tribunal.[70]

When the New Zealand wars finished, the older generation of missionary leaders were either dead, or limited in influence to their region. In 1864, Bishop Selwyn was despondent. 'Our native work is a remnant in two senses—a remnant of a decaying people, and a

[66] Ibid., 166–70.
[67] Ibid., 184–91, for another petition of 24 July 1866.
[68] Ibid., 178.
[69] J. Gorst, *New Zealand Revisited* (London, 1908) 141.
[70] D. Graham, *Trick or Treaty?* (Auckland, 1997) discusses the processes of negotiation.

remnant of a decaying faith.'[71] Some, like B. Y. Ashwell in the Waikato, had to leave their station, despite the affection in which they were held. T. S. Grace of Taupo had unusual insights during his long ministry there, but the CMS and bishops did not take notice of his comments on the need for encouraging Maori leaders. Bishop Hadfield still retained the trust of many Maori in the Wellington diocese, especially around Otaki, where a notable Maori church had been built at Rangiatea, close to the spot where soil from Hawaiki was said to be buried. Full of religious symbolism of Maori origin, its out-wardly European appearance and Maori interior indicated how creatively Christianity had been integrated with Maori insights.[72] Hadfield used some Maori clergy, including Riwai Te Ahu, Riwai Ranui, and Henare Te Herekau, of whom the latter two were ordained in 1872, in an attempt to counter Maori versions of Christianity. By 1900, seventy Maori clergy had been ordained by the Church of England, which helped it to retain some influence in the new century.

A combination of drastic falls in numbers of Maori worshippers, and the spiritual needs of settlers, led to former Wesleyan missionaries moving to settler circuits. After the war, 90 per cent of Methodist Maori members had left. Presbyterians were so little involved in Maori ministry that the wars had no influence on their numbers, except to underline their commitment to the government cause. The Presby-terian church near Pukekohe was used as a fort. Early Presbyterian services in Hawera and Opunake were held in the blockhouse and barracks in 1874 and 1884 respectively. The symbolism was not lost on the Maori, who were angered by the confiscation of the rich Hawera block in Taranaki.

Though many Maori left the Anglican and Wesleyan churches, they were still deeply committed to Christianity. The whole Bible had been translated by 1868. Feeling marginalized in the major churches, many Maori refused even to use Pakeha prayers. Catholics were much less affected. Pompallier's letters underline how much more con-sistently some Maori Catholics retained their faith, because they had not been involved in the land wars.[73] The connections between the

[71] *Church of England Gazette* (1864) 29.
[72] S. J. Brittain, et al., *A Pioneer Missionary among the Maori* (Palmerston North, 1928) 258–89, on T. S. Grace; C. Lethbridge, *The Wounded Lion* (Christchurch, 1993) for Hadfield; G. E. Ramsden, *Rangiatea* (Wellington, 1951).
[73] L. Keys, *The Life and Times of Bishop Pompallier* (Christchurch, 1957) 328–31.

faith imparted by the missionaries, and the Maori alternatives, are now much clearer than at the time. Most Christian leaders then dismissed these renewal movements as superficial, satanic, and heathen. Some missionaries saw Maori love for their land as idolatrous. Certainly, many Maori were anti-missionary, and perhaps even anti-settler.

James Stack was one CMS missionary who saw how significant Maori Christianity had become. He did not dismiss the prophetic movements so confidently as others did.[74] In those parts of New Zealand where tribes remained neutral, or even fought out old grievances on the British side, there were still possibilities for partnership. The diocese of Waiapu was unique in the number of Maori clergy, and the leadership of Bishop William Williams ensured real sensitivity to their concerns.[75] Maori was used freely in the early synods, and it was no accident that one of the renewal movements— the Young Maori party—originated at Te Aute College in Hawkes Bay, which developed largely because of the generosity and stewardship of Samuel Williams.[76] Hukarere Girls' School began in 1875.

Yet even among these strongly Christian communities, there were stirrings which British leaders found hard to understand. When Bishop Williams's replacement was being considered, questions were raised about the reasons for not considering Maori candidates. In 1877, pleading for a Maori Bishop of Waiapu, James Martin, a Maori Christian, wrote somewhat cynically, that an evilly disposed mind might think that Bishop Crowther had been appointed in West Africa because the climate was unsuitable for Europeans, whereas in the genial climate of New Zealand, the episcopate was restricted to Europeans. 'But let such a man think as he pleases. It is the right we are seeking for; the right according to Scripture, and according to the custom in other lands, and some way, also, whereby the union between European and Maori may be quite complete.'[77]

Another influential Maori religious leader was Te Kooti (1814– 93).[78] Baptized around 1852 with the name of Coates, the CMS secretary, he had been instructed by William Williams. Of chiefly lineage, and somewhat wild in his youth, he became a successful trader and

[74] A. H. Reed (ed.), *Early Maoriland Adventures of JW Stack* (Wellington, 1933); J. W. Stack, *Koro* (Christchurch, 1909) gives an account of a remarkable churchwarden at Kaiapoi.

[75] W. Williams, *Christianity among the New Zealanders*, 2nd edn. (London, 1989) 355.

[76] S. M. Woods, *Samuel Williams of Te Aute* (Christchurch, 1981) 89.

[77] J. Caselberg, *Maori Is My Name* (Dunedin, 1975) 120.

[78] G. Mizur, 'From prophet cult to established church', in I. H. Kawharu (ed.), *Conflict and Compromise* (Wellington, 1975) 97–115.

seaman who fought for the government, but did not forget his kin obligations to those on the other side, for many in his tribe became followers of Pai Marire. Unjustly accused of spying for the Hauhau, he and other suspects were deported to the Chatham Islands without trial in 1865. He became seriously ill, but underwent some dramatic visions and trances between 21 March and 30 May which enhanced his *mana*. He and his followers executed a daring escape on 30 June 1868, capturing a boat and landing on an isolated part of the East Coast, leaving the crew unharmed. Moving north with nearly 300 followers, he took vengeance on his betrayers, and settlers whom he considered to have taken his land.

He conducted a brilliant guerilla campaign for the next four years, gaining a mythical reputation for elusiveness, riding a white horse which may have had links with the white horse in Revelation, ridden by one faithful and true. Unsuccessful in gaining refuge among the Taupo people after he had to leave Tuhoe territory, he found refuge among the Kingites from 1872 to 1873, when an amnesty was declared. For the next decade he lived at Te Kuiti, developing a church with a distinctive liturgy. Special services were held on the 12th of each month, with large gatherings on 1 January and 1 July. Upraised hands in homage to God became the symbol of the new faith. He stressed peace and unity across tribes, performed healings, and uttered numerous prophecies, for he drew heavily on the Hebrew Scriptures. 'You shall be a mouthpiece for me, and they shall write it down; and let there be many to search all the books; but do you not take heed of any books, for they are the work of men, and unintelligible. But I will speak to you, and you to them, that they may know that I am a voice from God. If there is any saying they do not understand, do you call upon God, and I will disclose it.'[79] Te Kooti was insistent that his movement, Te Hahi Ringatu, was not a replacement for other forms of Christianity, but he claimed equality for his movement, to the chagrin of some church leaders.

He offered a powerful interpretation of the suffering and exile his people had experienced. Some of his followers gave him godlike status, but he always disclaimed this.[80] The leaders of the movement

[79] Waikato Museum, *Te Kooti Rikirangi Te Ruraki* (Hamilton, n.d.) 10. This contains a number of his prayers and utterances.

[80] Dr James Irwin shared a piece of oral tradition, about Te Kooti announcing that he would walk on Ohiwa harbour. His followers gathered. He asked them if they believed that he could walk on the harbour. They shouted, Yes! He reportedly said, then I do not need to demonstrate it.

had no formal training, but were expected to have extensive biblical knowledge and to be able to recite prayers precisely, as was the case with traditional *karakia*. Some in government regarded him as a troublemaker, but he did nothing to disturb the peace, even though he had fallen out with the Kingites, and the leaders at Parihaka. Granted 600 acres at Wainui on the shores of Ohiwa Harbour in the Bay of Plenty, he died there and was buried secretly.

The other notable renewal movement which indicated Maori ability to rework Christianity in their own cultural context was developed at Parihaka in South Taranaki by Te Whiti and Tohu. They had become Christians through Wesleyan missionaries, were influenced by Pai Marire, but rejected war. Following war and confiscations, they developed a model Christian community which kept Europeans and their corrupting ways at a distance. Their town had running water and public lighting, but no corrupting Pakeha school. Te Whiti had a superb command of the Bible and was a compelling orator. Coming to see that Maori would not win a war against the increasingly numerous Pakeha, he organized his followers into skilful non-resistance when the government attempted to purchase land against their will. The prophets and their followers identified with the Jews and the Old Testament. Special services were held on the 17th of each month, attended by up to 2,000 people, with feasting, prophecy, and dancing. Their struggle for retention of their land was related to the history of Israel. They refused to negotiate over land, claiming it was theirs—'the land is dearer to us than life'. Given the succession of broken government promises over reserves and return of land, their stand had some point.

When the surveyors put in pegs, they were removed, with people being told to rest quietly upon the land. On 7 November 1881, Te Whiti said in poetic and biblical language,

I stand for peace. Though the lions rage, still I am for peace. I will go into captivity. My aim will be accomplished, peace will reign. I am willing to become a sacrifice for my aim . . . Though I am killed I yet shall live; Though dead, I shall live in the peace which will be the accomplishment of my aim. The future is mine; and little children, when asked hereafter as to the author of peace, shall say—Te Whiti—and I will bless them.

Sinclair, on rather questionable grounds, suggests he had a paranoid personality.[81]

---

[81] Caselberg, *Maori Is My Name*, 135–6. See also D. Scott, *Ask That Mountain* (Auckland,

Bryce, the bellicose and insensitive Minister of Native Affairs, who did not appear to have the word 'negotiate' in his vocabulary, decided that force had to be used to break resistance, and enforce British law. Backed by a force of 1,600, Bryce read the Riot Act, in November 1881, to a peacefully seated community. Te Whiti and Tohu were arrested, and deported without trial to the South Island for two years. Others also were arrested, and the surveys and land sales went ahead. The prophets split in the 1890s, and they both died in 1907. No compensation was paid, and the injustice still rankles. It was hardly surprising that many Maori were disillusioned with Parliament, and experimented with their own political structures in the 1880s and 1890s.

PACIFIC CHURCHES

Polynesians had a very different approach to government from the pragmatic division between the sacred and secular in the British colonies of settlement. Government and church life were village-based. Chiefs retained something of the sacred authority of pre-Christian times, Christian law acquired associations of *tapu*, and particular forms of Christian religious practice such as Sunday observance became deeply embedded in island life. This made for significant acculturation of the new religion, which reduced some missionaries to despair, for they found that their invitations to change were ignored.[82] The converts had accepted Christianity on their own terms, and used it for their own social, family, and political goals. Few missionaries had the insight to see that European versions of Christianity were not the norm worldwide. Their writings frequently suggest that they were unsympathetic to Polynesian versions of Christianity, for they displayed very different priorities. Bishop Stewart of Waiapu had met with some Maori at Tauranga, who could not bear 'that we should be directing them to heaven while we were robbing them of their land'.[83] Such attitudes indicated a fundamental divergence.

In Tonga, these developments assumed their most striking form,

1975). D. P. Lyons, 'An analysis of three Maori prophet movements', in Kawharu, *Conflict and Compromise*, 55–79; D. P. Gadd, 'The teachings of Te Whiti o Rongomai', *JPS* 75 (1966) 452.

[82] E. T. Ta'ase, 'The Congregational Church in Samoa 1818–1928', Ph.D. thesis (Pasadena, 1995).

[83] *Messenger*, 10 Aug. 1878.

not only because of Tongans' missionary work in Fiji and Samoa, which took no account of Wesleyan directors' decisions in London, but even more so because George Tupou skilfully used biblical precedent and missionary advice to create a Christian kingdom.[84] The developments were assisted by British transfer of authority to the Australasian Wesleyan conference based in Sydney from 1855. John Thomas had been one of the strongest supporters of the change, hoping that it would make possible the re-establishment of a missionary presence in Samoa. What he had not foreseen was Tupou's consolidation of his authority by creating an independent Wesleyan church as the spiritual foundation of a kingdom which would keep colonial powers at bay.[85] When Thomas lost the king's favour in 1859, he left Tonga, and was replaced by Shirley Baker in 1860. From Victoria, he had considerable ability, as well as a high estimation of himself, and skills in being devious about his own interests. Fluent in Tongan, and friendly with the king, he helped to draft the 1862 Constitution. Other missionaries' strictness in moral matters was causing tension with the king and chiefs. Baker also encouraged Tongan competitiveness in fundraising to what some deemed burdensome levels. In 1869, Tonga sent almost £5,500 to the Conference Mission Board. In that year, he became chairman of the Tonga district to the dismay of the far abler John Egan Moulton, who had established Tupou College, but who also behaved very independently. Moulton was also a fine hymnwriter and Bible translator. Their rivalry lasted until Baker's death.

Baker also significantly influenced the 1875 Constitution, which has entrenched royal and noble power until the present, but intrigues by his rivals, who distrusted his ambition and financial probity, led to his recall by the Conference in 1879. J. E. Moulton, too, fell out with the king, partly because of his refusal to compromise on educational and ethical standards, but also since the missionaries were scandalously divided, and that affected Tongan political unity. Tupou wanted to become part of a New Zealand Conference, but that was rejected in 1884 by the Australian majority. A schism on Ha'apai the following year gave Baker his chance for settling scores. He and the king, who had invited him back as premier, created the Free Church of Tonga on 4 January 1885, and cut all ties with the Australasian Conference.

[84] S. Latukefu, *Church and State in Tonga* (Canberra, 1974).
[85] N. Rutherford, *Shirley Baker and the King of Tonga* (Melbourne, 1971); A. H. Wood, *Overseas Missions of the Australian Methodist Church* (5 vols., Melbourne, 1975–87) 1. 133–206.

Baker resigned his ministry in order to become premier, and so was beyond the reach of their discipline. King George brutally persecuted the minority loyal to Sydney, led by Moulton and some dissident chiefs, but they remained faithful to the Wesleyan Conference. Other missionaries, like J. B. Watkin, a former chairman, joined the royal church and became its chairman until 1924. He had grown up in New Zealand and was fluent in Maori and Tongan. Baker was not popular with many Tongans, and some from Mu'a attempted to kill him in January 1887, which led to appalling further persecution, and execution of the alleged assailants. J. B. Thurston, the High Commissioner for the Western Pacific, was disturbed by reports of Baker's behaviour.

When it became clear that the Australasian Conference's attempt at conciliation by sending George Brown to mediate had failed, Thurston took note of confidential comments by Brown and deported Baker in 1890 for two years, on grounds of endangering good order. As a British subject, Baker had to comply and went to Auckland, where his business ventures failed, and he returned to Ha'apai in 1897. Without royal support, he had little influence. King George had died in 1893. He attempted to capitalize on a dispute among the chiefs over Tupou II's marriage by forming his own church—The Church of Victoria—and sought Anglican orders to regularize his status. He died, a sad and marginal figure, in 1903. New Zealand bishops were unimpressed by his pleas, apart from the expansionist Nevill in Dunedin. Baker's leadership was finally destroyed by the arrival of Bishop Alfred Willis of Honolulu, who had been replaced by an American and who went to Tonga in 1902 at the request of this little group of disaffected Wesleyans. He appointed himself Missionary Bishop of Tonga, until his status was regularized in 1908 by the formation of the Diocese of Polynesia, within the jurisdiction of the New Zealand Anglican Church.

The Kingdom of Tonga was under British protection from May 1900, but retained considerable independence. Christianity was a vital part of Tupou's consolidation of his authority. The creation of an independent church which was financially self-supporting was unique and gave the kingdom a sacral quality which included every aspect of life. Though the French Marists were an anomaly in this Methodist kingdom, they became expert in Tongan culture. Their flock was utterly loyal to the king, without accusations of dual loyalties to local rulers and the Bishop of Rome, which Protestants used to discredit Catholics in Australia and New Zealand.

In Fiji, Cakobau failed in his attempt to emulate his ally Tupou in Tonga by creating a Christian kingdom. There were too many other powerful chiefs for that, but the Fijian Methodist churches developed into powerful village institutions. In 1855, Fiji also came under the Australasian Conference. Authoritarian colonial Methodists were influenced by their experience of failure in Tonga, and were not inclined to allow Fijian preachers and Tongan missionaries the same exercise of authority which Joseph Waterhouse had allowed. Policy divisions between missionaries ended with Waterhouse's death in 1881.

Political circumstances changed in 1874, when Cakobau and other major chiefs ceded sovereignty to Queen Victoria, but they did not have to contend with the same influx of British settlers as poured into New Zealand. Basically, they kept their own land, and with it maintained a traditional way of life, reshaped at particular points by the new faith.[86] Gradually memories of war, cannibalism, and human sacrifice faded, largely due to the work of Fijian catechists inspired by the Tongan missionary Joeli Bulu, who in later years was Cakobau's chaplain till he died in 1877. Parts of the Fijian Islands remained pagan until the end of the nineteenth century. In other parts elements of traditional religion coexisted with Christianity.[87] A number of traditional customs correlated with Christianity. Sermons included traditional oratory and fables, prayers had similarities with ancient invocations, and hymns drew on ancient chants. Respect for, and fear of, ancestral spirits remained below the surface of village life, as did traditional healing. Some of the custom of traditional religion featured in the Tuka messianic adjustment movement begun by Dugumoi, which is still present in some parts of Fiji despite its forcible suppression. The new society was notably different from pre-Christian communities, but it seemed only partly Christian to British observers, some of whom wished to Anglicize the natives.

Views of what constituted a Christian society could differ quite sharply between the colonial governors, Fijian chiefs and pastors, and the Australian missionaries. The tension between Tasmanian-born

[86] J. Garrett, *To Live among the Stars* (Suva, 1982) 279–88; Wood, *Overseas Missions*, vol. 2: *Fiji*. J. W. Burton, *The Fiji of Today* (London, 1910) 59–256 gives an account of the way in which life had changed for Fijians, with Britain's remedies for their problems at the turn of the century.

[87] A. Thornley, 'Fijian Methodism 1874–1945', Ph.D. thesis (Canberra, 1979). C. W. Whonsbon-Aston, *Pacific Irishman* (Sydney, 1970) gives an account of Anglican beginnings in Fiji.

Frederick Langham, who was the leader of the mission in the latter part of the nineteenth century, and the aristocratic governor, Sir Arthur Gordon, was not helped by his contempt for colonials, or by Langham's authoritarian style. Gordon resented Langham's power, resting on close knowledge of village life, and use of rivalries which financially benefited the mission, which Gordon could never hope to equal. Langham was not prepared to share authority with Fijians and Tongans, because he feared a chiefly takeover of the church, and believed that strict missionary control was vital for spiritual purity and power. Nor did he like what he saw as government interference in the mission's work. Despite these tensions, Fiji provided hundreds of missionaries to Melanesia and workable models of village Christianity.

By contrast, Lorimer Fison, one of the first British missionary anthropologists of the nineteenth century, made important contributions to understanding village life and attitudes to land, and looked for a gradual transition to Fijian participation on equal terms. He helped Gordon to see the importance of indigenous ownership of land.[88] Events in Tonga gave Langham some justification for his hard line against evolution and partnership, especially in 1874 when Bulu, in charge of the training institution for catechists, led a campaign for participation in the District Meeting by Fijians and Tongans.[89] In 1879, a very important change occurred with far-reaching consequences. That was the introduction of Indians to work on cane plantations under indenture. Fijians were simply not interested in such labour and workers available from the Solomon Islands were insufficient. They had, however, provided the nucleus for a small Anglican community alongside the white settlers who had a Tractarian chaplain, William Floyd in Levuka. Though he had a comity agreement with the Methodists not to seek Fijian converts, a few chiefly families became Anglicans, in order to escape the moralistic restrictions of Methodism on alcohol, and Sabbath-keeping. These groups, plus those in Tonga, were part of the justification for the later formation of the Diocese of Polynesia.

It took time for the Methodists to decide whether to undertake any mission work among the Hindu, Muslim, and Sikh labourers. An

---

[88] I. S. Tuwere, 'Making sense of *vanua* in the Fijian context', Th.D. thesis (Melbourne, 1992).

[89] A. Thornley and T. Vulauno, *Mai Ki Vei: Stories of Methodism in Fiji and Rotuma* (Suva, 1995) 33–49.

Indian called John Williams began work in 1892, but it was an Australian, Hannah Dudley, beginning work in 1897, who made some impact amongst the families of the cane workers. She had gone to India in 1891–6. Health restored, she went to Fiji, became a vegetarian, and gave herself unstintedly till 1913, with little encouragement from the male missionaries who saw their work to be amongst Fijians.[90]

Roman Catholic work in Fiji began in 1844, when Bataillon put Fathers J. B. Breheret and F. Roulleaux-Dubignon ashore. They were to be helped by two catechists Pako and Apolonia from Wallis, and two converts from Fiji who had been baptized in Tonga when on the point of death, but recovered. They were refused permission to settle at Lakeba and Namuka, and underwent all sorts of hardships and illness, for Bataillon had left them virtually resourceless. Fortunately, humanity triumphed over anti-popery among the Methodist missionaries, and the Marists were given medical treatment which saved their lives. They persisted despite chiefly hostility, and in 1861 there were 500 baptized, and several thousand under instruction. Despite his limitations as an administrator, Breheret was a lovable and effective missionary, whose funeral in 1898 was an ecumenical event attended by the whole populace of Levuka. In 1882, the Missionary Sisters of Mary arrived, and opened schools in 1885/6. Julien Vidal from Samoa, who became the first bishop from 1888 until his death in 1922, brought in additional religious orders, built a cathedral in Suva, and began missionary work among the Indians in 1895. There were vigorous controversies with Protestants, notably over the burning of Bibles in 1900 by Father Rougier. Slowly the work of Catholic mission expanded into villages, creating an alternative kind of Christian society.

COLONIAL RELATIONSHIPS

A number of factors showed just how closely the worlds of Australasia interacted, even though they were constitutionally separate. Colonialist trading companies run by Christians such as Burns Philp created important economic links. New Caledonia was strictly controlled from Paris, with no self-government at all for the small body of settlers, which included some Australians. British colonies, however,

[90] Wood, *Overseas Missions*, vol. 3: *Fiji-Indian*, 1–54; E. H. Smith, *Yesterday and Today* (Suva, 1979); Burton, *The Fiji of Today*, 257–364; M. Sidal, *Hannah Dudley* (Suva, 1997).

shared a common experience of responsible government within loyalty to the Crown, drawing from their own memories of Britain, and responding with equal vigour when the ministers and civil servants of Westminster gave directions which colonists felt were unrelated to reality. Governors like Sir George Grey, and Sir Frederick Weld, who had served as a New Zealand parliamentarian before becoming governor of Western Australia, brought an inter-colonial perspective to their responsibilities, for Grey had served in South Australia before going to New Zealand, as well as being shaped by his experience in South Africa. Even though responsible government reduced the political power of governors, they were still very influential.

Another regional link was provided by a number of Australians who served in the British forces which helped to subdue the Maori, and were granted confiscated land. It was Australians' first experience of overseas combat. Huge numbers from Australia had also moved across the Tasman, to seek their fortune when gold was discovered in Central Otago in the 1860s, and then later in Westland and Coromandel. They took with them technology, architecture, and attitudes to politics and religion which decisively changed the isolated Wakefield settlements of Otago and Canterbury. A number of families had relatives on the opposite side of the Tasman as a result, and there were close commercial ties between Auckland, Dunedin, Sydney, and Melbourne as well as exchanges of Congregational, Methodist, and Presbyterian ministers, and Catholic clergy and religious. Labour leaders also criss-crossed the Tasman.

Australian Catholicism was Irish, with an English overlay in Sydney until the 1880s, because English support was politically important for Rome. Benedictine bishops were a useful counter to the influence of Irish bishops. The Irish bishops' lobbying skills, however, became increasingly strong in Rome by the end of the nineteenth century, especially after the division of Sydney Diocese into five new dioceses in the 1860s.[91] In New Zealand, Irishness was tempered by a strong French influence through the Marists in the Wellington and Christchurch dioceses. Until 1869, the bishops and a majority of clergy were French, though the laity were Irish, with some French devotional practices. Increasing numbers were entering professions and the public service, defending their religion strongly against Protestantism.

[91] Cunningham, 'Under the banner of the cross', gives an illuminating account of Roman lobbying.

Pompallier had resigned from Auckland in 1869 while in Europe, and died in 1871. Bishop Goold of Melbourne was asked to report on the diocese's affairs in 1869, while he was travelling to Vatican I, and did so scathingly. For all Pompallier's many weaknesses in leadership and administration, he made an important contribution to partnership between Maori and Pakeha. St Mary's College in Auckland produced twenty-five clergy during 1850–69 but, unfortunately, none of the fifteen Maori seminarians was ordained. The last of Pompallier's priests, Fr Thomas Walsh, died in 1926.

Bishop Philippe Viard, in Wellington, had worked in New Caledonia before coming to New Zealand, and never lost his Pacific vision. He struggled with limited finances, a shortage of clergy, and was unable to do justice to the pastoral needs of both settlers and Maori. Twelve priests put up with severe privations as they travelled huge distances, but were sustained by their Marist spirituality as they travelled the area between Taupo and Stewart Island. The rapid growth of population in the gold rushes, and assisted migration, made the creation of new dioceses urgent. In 1863, almost 27,000 migrants arrived in Otago. Patrick Moran from Grahamstown in South Africa was appointed to Dunedin late in 1869, and Thomas Croke to Auckland in 1870–4. These appointments did something to satisfy the Irish laity before Viard died in 1872, greatly respected by Protestants as well as Catholics.

Moran had to turn roving missionaries into settled parish priests, though some roving was still necessary to keep up with rapidly moving mining populations. By his death in 1895, he had won the grudging respect of some Protestants, created a network of twenty-nine schools staffed by Dominican Sisters and Christian Brothers, founded fifteen parishes and developed passionate loyalty among his 20,000-strong flock.[92] A cathedral was opened in 1886. Moran travelled widely, whatever the weather, and attacked Protestant injustice in denying state aid for Catholic schools, for he claimed the public schools were seedbeds of immorality, and inappropriate for Catholic children. He founded *The Tablet* and edited it from 1873 until 1881, using the city's newspapers as well at every opportunity to attack Protestant intolerance, and an alleged international conspiracy of Freemasons against the true church. His people loved this fighting spirit. He stood for Parliament in 1883, so that he could dramatize Protestant hostility

[92] E. Simmons, *Brief History of the Catholic Church in New Zealand* (Auckland, 1971) 68.

to Catholics, and attack the irreligion of the secular system set up nationally in 1877. He fought hard, but failed to secure an Irish bishop for Christchurch, despite that being approved by the 1885 Council in Sydney. Some Irish laity were bitter about having to be subject to an English bishop, for they saw the English historically as oppressors. Ethnicity was more vital than Catholicity.

In Wellington, Viard was followed by a New Zealand-educated Marist, Francis Redwood, who had no need to be confrontational, or an uncritical supporter of Irish nationalism. His English family had migrated to Nelson in 1841, and prospered. He was educated by Fr Garin, one of the most notable Marist priests, before being sent to France, and professed as a Marist in 1864. An outstanding student and musician, he taught for a time in Ireland before becoming Bishop of Wellington in 1874. He mixed easily, and encouraged the foundation of a Marist seminary at Meanee in 1890.[93] He did not approve of the militant Irishness of *The Tablet* and founded *The Catholic Times* in 1888 to serve the whole Catholic body, irrespective of party and nationality. By 1900, there were 26,000 members in Wellington, making it the largest diocese. Three-quarters of its clergy were Marists, and 236 nuns staffed schools and charitable institutions. Roman Catholics were found at every level of society in Wellington. St Patrick's College was founded in 1885, and staffed by Irish Marist Brothers, led by Fr Felix Watter.[94]

To Moran's dismay, Wellington became the primatial see in 1887, not Dunedin. Wellington was further divided in 1887, and a new diocese established in Christchurch, under the English Marist Bishop John Grimes, consecrated in 1887. Dunedin gained one triumph—the establishment of a national seminary at Mosgiel in 1900–97, named after Holy Cross in Ireland, until its removal to Auckland to join Mount St Mary's in training priests in 1998. Michael Verdon, who had been Vice-Rector of the Irish College in Rome, and Rector at Manly Seminary in Sydney, set the college on solid foundations, ending the sending of some New Zealand ordinands to Sydney. A nephew of Cardinal Cullen, he strengthened that network in the Antipodes when he became Bishop of Dunedin.

In Auckland, Croke restored financial sanity by taking some hard decisions before he returned to Ireland, becoming one of the most

[93] E. Simmons, *Brief History of the Catholic Church in New Zealand* 84; F. Redwood, *Reminiscences* (Wellington, 1922).
[94] M. King, *God's Farthest Outpost* (Auckland, 1997) 115.

strong supporters of Irish nationalism.[95] The Marist succession was broken by the consecration of Bishop John Luck, 1882–96, an English Benedictine who had already gained a fine reputation as a parish priest. Clergy still had a part in episcopal appointments, and some of the Irish priests lobbied very intensely to fulfil their dream of the New Zealand Roman Catholic Church becoming Irish in leadership, as well as in membership, thereby expanding the Irish Empire and fighting Protestant discriminatory practices.

Mission to the Maori was not a high episcopal priority, but in Auckland Fr Walter MacDonald moved from a parish to missionary work, and kept some Catholic loyalties alive where promising beginnings had collapsed. The coming of the Mill Hill Fathers in 1885 to work amongst the Maori was important, but they never had sufficient priests. In 1894 there were only four priests for 4,000 scattered Maori Catholics in the Auckland diocese.[96] One of the most important workers in Maori communities was Sister Suzanne Aubert, a Marist tertiary and nurse.[97] A woman of small stature, large heart, and great compassion, she visited in all weathers. Her upper-class French social background was a great asset, enabling her skilfully to resist bishops and parish priests when she thought it necessary.

When Pompallier left Auckland, Aubert was not at home with Croke's new regime, and moved to Hawkes Bay in 1871, where her medical and pastoral work was widely respected. She then moved to Jerusalem on the Wanganui River, to work with the Josephites amongst the isolated Maori communities along the river. In addition, she founded an orphanage, before going to Wellington and setting up a Home of Compassion. In spite of episcopal disapproval, she founded a women's religious institute of Our Lady of Compassion in 1892 to staff it and other institutions. She wanted Marists to take it in. They refused and, after a long struggle, papal approval for an independent congregation was given in 1917. A formidable fundraiser, she travelled all over Wellington's hills and flats collecting goods and money for her homes. She lived to a great age and died in 1926. Her funeral involved a large proportion of the city's population, for she was

[95] M. O'Meeghan, *Held Firm by Faith* (Christchurch, 1988); P. Norris, *Southernmost Seminary* (Mosgiel, 1999).

[96] Mill Hill Fathers, *Our Maori Mission* (Auckland, 1933); W. Gibbons, *History of Matata Parish* (Edgecumbe, 1991); Anon., *The Story of Mill Hill in New Zealand* (Putaruru, 1966).

[97] J. Munro, *The Story of Suzanne Aubert* (Auckland, 1996). The story of her community is told in *Audacity of Faith; Sisters of Compassion Centennial 1892–1992* (Wellington, 1992).

known by thousands for her compassion. She embodied the best in French Catholicism, giving it unstintedly to her adopted land.

New Zealand Catholicism was on a smaller scale than that of Australia's, with 12 per cent of the population. Nevertheless, it had established itself as an important part of New Zealand Christianity by the end of the century. Its energy was symbolized by a number of notable buildings, especially F. W. Petre's superb Cathedral of the Blessed Sacrament in Christchurch, Sacred Heart Church in Wellington, and St Patrick's Cathedral in Dunedin. The French connection gave it a different kind of internationalism and spirituality which in many parishes interacted very fruitfully with Irish laity.[98] The French settlement at Akaroa remained small, but a number of the families, like the Le Lièvres, spread throughout the country, and took strong Catholic loyalties with them. Catholic Dalmatians came from the Austro-Hungarian Empire and settled in the north of the North Island, digging for kauri gum, some planting vineyards which were to become the basis for a flourishing wine industry in the twentieth century, and playing an important part in Auckland Catholicism by their generosity and loyalty. A Bohemian settlement at Puhoi still retains roadside shrines, common in Europe, but otherwise unknown in New Zealand.

Australian Catholicism was an important part of Irish ecclesiastical politics by the end of the nineteenth century, heavily dominated by Irish bishops, priests, and religious, as well as the vast majority of laity. The Cullenite network was influential. In Sydney, however, they had been resisted by Archbishop Vaughan, who disliked his Irish suffragan bishops, and despised many of the Irish clergy. When Vaughan foolishly refused to attend his deceased colleague Bishop O'Quinn's Month's Mind Mass, his suffragans' dislike of Vaughan escalated into hostility, fuelled further by his appointment of Cani as administrator of Brisbane. When Vaughan died, bishops both in New South Wales and in Ireland energetically lobbied Rome for an Irish successor. Occasional European bishops of other origins were found in smaller dioceses, like Bishop Torregani in Armidale (1875–1904). An unbalanced Irishman attempted to assassinate him on Christmas Day in 1884. Irish clergy, like the Horan brothers in Queensland, nephews of the Quinns, made life miserable for the Italian priest Cani when he was administrator of Brisbane.

[98] M. C. Goulter, *Sons of France* (Wellington, 1958).

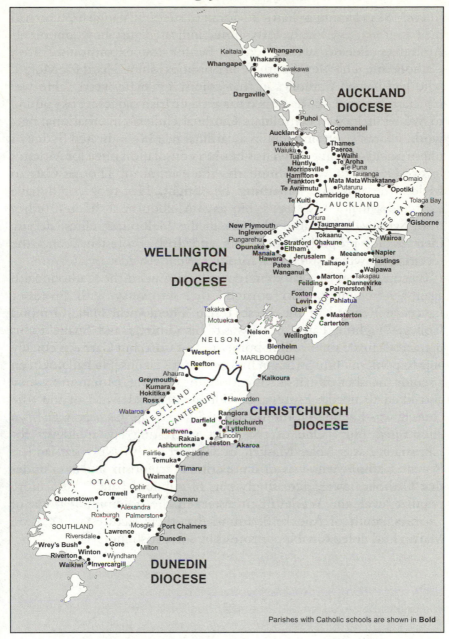

New Zealand: Catholic dioceses (1938). (*Source:* P. B. McKeefry (ed.), *Fishers of Men*, Wellington, 1938, frontispiece.)

The 1884 election of Patrick Moran to succeed Vaughan, who had died in 1883, aged only forty-nine, indicated just how important Australian dioceses were seen to be for the expansion of Irish Catholicism. The New South Wales bishops lobbied hard for Moran, who had helped Catholics in that colony for many years.[99] He was reluctant to come, for he hoped for a major Irish diocese. His coming to Sydney helped to consolidate Cardinal Cullen's international network. Moran's appointment as a cardinal in 1885 indicated Sydney's importance for Rome, as well as being a consolation prize for Moran's loss of Dublin to Walsh. Similarly, the election of Thomas Carr to Melbourne was not something he sought. He, too, could have expected a major Irish see.[100] He gave Melbourne a different ethos from Sydney, for he moved easily in the Melbourne elites, despite their strong proportion of Scots and Irish Protestants, and the sectarianism which lasted well into the twentieth century.

Bishops, clergy and laity energetically defended the Catholic faith against its enemies. Carr engaged in controversy with Professor Laurence Rentoul of the Presbyterian Theological Hall, Ormond College. 'Fighting Larry', as he was to his admirers, and 'Snake' to his detractors, made some telling points against Carr, but Carr was equally able to point out limitations in his opponent's claims. He had not been a senior member of staff at Maynooth for nothing. Moran in Sydney also liked to needle Protestants, but his major defence of the true church was his huge tome on the *History of the Catholic Church in Australasia*, 1897. One of the most interesting lay apologists for Christianity was Miles Maskell of Canterbury in New Zealand, a Roman Catholic who was an acute critic of scientism, and a reminder that Catholics were increasingly part of public debate.[101] At a more popular level, the Wesleyan ministers in the goldmining town of Thames, south of Auckland, found that their lectures in 1871 on Martin Luther led to violent protests by local Irish miners.

---

[99] D. H. Akenson, *Half the World from Home* (Wellington, 1990). Cunningham, 'Under the banner of the cross', 334 ff. for Moran's appointment.

[100] T. P. Boland, *Archbishop Thomas Carr* (Brisbane, 1997).

[101] J. Stenhouse, 'Catholicism, science and modernity', *JRH* 22 (1998) 59–82.

ABORIGINES OPPRESSED

The prosperity of colonists and the construction of Christian churches and societies was in striking contrast to the destruction of Aboriginal communities. Whole tribes, their language, and their culture disappeared. Where survivors remained, often with a tenacious grasp of their tribal memories, they lived on Lutheran or Moravian mission stations and were expected to adopt European ways, cut off from their traditional lands and ceremonies.[102] Some converts adopted Christianity and European culture, and demonstrated their cultural skills. David Unaipon, of Point McLeay in South Australia, was not only an extraordinary inventor, and a custodian of traditional law, he had deep insight into Christianity. It was a tragedy that people like him were denied opportunity for the full use of their gifts, because of the ingrained racism of many settlers who could not believe that Aborigines were anything but savages on the lowest scale of civilization. His treatment by police and frequent arrests for alleged vagrancy were a disgrace.

In Queensland, where the brutality of frontier conflict lasted late into the nineteenth century, there were occasional examples of what might have been, if settlers had not been so hostile to Aboriginal culture. Fr Duncan MacNab shrewdly exploited opportunities to apply for government grants of land for hereditary owners. His bold scheme was defeated by a combination of settler greed, Protestant fears that Catholicism would gain a large amount of land, and political chicanery. In the far north, tribes continued to live as they had for millennia, because they were so isolated, and the tropics were too discouraging for pastoralists or agriculturalists. In the far south in Tasmania, the remnants of a significant community eked out a difficult and isolated existence of a different kind, exiled from the mainland to Flinders Island and a Christian half-life.[103] Bishop Nixon's 1855 charge claimed that it was part of Nature's law 'that wherever the white man settles, the native heathen should fade and wither before his presence'. That was true in Australia, but would also happen in New Zealand and

---

[102] A. McGrath, *Contested Ground* (Sydney, 1995) gives a detailed account of racist legislation and administration in each state and the Northern Territory. It is essential reading. G. Russo, *Lord Abbot of the Wilderness* (Melbourne, 1980). C. Mattingly and K. Hampton (eds.), *Survival in Our Own Land* (Adelaide, 1988) is an attempt to write an Aboriginal history in South Australia.

[103] L. Ryan, *The Aboriginal Tasmanians*, 2nd edn. (Sydney, 1996).

the Pacific islands. Nixon believed it was vital, therefore, to 'make the evangelisation of this unhappy class one main object of our work and prayers'.[104] That was to prove a very mixed blessing to Aborigines.

Few Australasian Christians were able to offer a critical analysis of racism, for it was too deeply ingrained. Some Christians campaigned against the Pacific labour trade in the 1870s and 1880s, but most justified the religion of development, which offered enormous financial rewards to the successful, and entrenched their power, politically and socially.[105] This they did with great success in the upper houses of each colony, in control of key newspapers, and in the law courts. Dr Reynolds has shown with dismaying clarity how Australian courts, staffed by judges of great integrity and deep faith, nevertheless resiled from the policy of the British government about Aboriginal ownership of land, and instead developed the legal fiction of *terra nullius*, even though there was an important body of case law which led in a different direction.[106]

The courts in New Zealand did not recognize the legal status of the Treaty of Waitangi, but Maori title to land was never in question. The Land Court, however, seemed more expert at separating Maori from their land than protecting their recognized title, because fighting for their claims was a costly business, and even when title was granted to families and individuals, much land had to be sold in order to meet legal expenses. Reining in European greed for land was also a source of tension in Papua and New Guinea, where Sir William MacGregor and Albert Hahl firmly protected indigenous owners, to the chagrin of Australian and German capitalists.

CONSTITUTIONAL CHANGES

The churches played an important part in fostering inter-colonial unity, by meetings of Anglican and Catholic bishops and large conferences of clergy and laity. Catholic congresses met in 1900, 1904, and 1909. Congregationalists, Wesleyans, and Presbyterians exchanged representatives. Anglican Church congresses between 1882 and 1947 attracted clergy and laity from Australia and New Zealand. Presbyterians and Methodists were also part of world bodies. Roman

---

[104] F. Nixon, *Charge* (Hobart, 1855) 10.
[105] K. Howe, *Race Relations in Australia and New Zealand* (Wellington, 1977).
[106] H. Reynolds, *The Law of the Land* (Melbourne, 1992); *Dispossession* (Melbourne, 1989); *This Whispering in our Hearts* (Melbourne, 1998).

Catholic Eucharistic Congresses from 1934 also were powerful witness to the strength of Catholicism in the colonies and their ties with a universal Church. Some Anglican bishops were frequently in touch with Lambeth Palace. The Lambeth Conferences from 1867 were another source of confessional identity.

The Anglicans formed a General Synod of the dioceses in Australia and Tasmania, meeting every three years from 1872. Regarded by Anglo-Catholics as a failure, it was actually a realistic solution to the problems of distance and independent colonies. The constitution lasted until 1961 and entrenched diocesan authority. Legislation was binding only when it was agreed by the individual dioceses. Much Anglican life was not covered by the constitution, such as missionary societies, social service providers, and schools. They did not even fit within diocesan constitutions, which also assumed that the apostolic form of the church was historically given, with liturgy, law, and polity in place. Whether that gave Anglicans a consistently theological view of the church is arguable.[107] Nor did it provide an adequate basis for re-examination of the role of the church, which was undergoing rapid change towards a plurally religious community, shaped by the needs of colonial society rather than by the Gospel and the Scriptures. Much was still left to the local faith community to fill out the constitutional blueprint, as Christians contributed to the creation of a society which looked British, but was already beginning to shift into a new identity.

From 1866, Sydney's Anglican Synod was especially interesting because of the place given to laymen—up to three from each parish. Many of those elected were community leaders, respectful of episcopal authority, but determined to share in government with clergy and the bishop. The diocese's financial resources were slender. The registry lived off fees, the Synod expenses came from parish levies. Endowment income was minimal, so the Church Society (1856) was crucial for the foundation of new parishes, even before state aid was abolished in 1863. The last recipient, the venerable Dean Cowper, received his allowance until 1902. Abolition of these grants made co-operation of clergy and laity essential. With about half of the population related in some way to the Church of England, the impact of its leaders was considerable. Anglican laity were often intellectually and culturally more impressive than most of the nineteenth-century bishops, and did much to give colonies a Christian shape.

---

[107] R. Border, *Church and State in Australia* (London, 1962); B. Kaye, *Church Without Walls* (Sydney, 1996) explores these issues.

Bishops and clergy alike stressed the importance of community obedience to the Holy Scriptures, the right of private judgement, the sanctity of marriage, the sacredness of the Sabbath as a pledge of national obedience to God, the duty of generosity, integrity in vocation, the intertwining of politics and ethics, and the duty of helping those in need. England was believed to be a maker of great nations because her people loved freedom, had the power to practise it, and were willing to share their knowledge with more primitive peoples. Sometimes this imperial ideology was used in a racist way to justify keeping Asiatics out of these British colonies.

Josiah Firth, an Auckland businessman, however, argued that if 'we do our duty rightly and wisely, with kindness and consideration for others in our hearts, then, we are building up a nation after Christ's pattern'.[108] On public occasions and Sunday services, in Masonic lodges, as well as in countless schools, this Protestant ethic was rehearsed and celebrated. Even among those who attended church hardly at all, this cultural framework provided boundaries and directions, underlined in many newspaper editorials. W. G. Cowie, Anglican Bishop of Auckland, believed that 'the federation of the Empire, and close and firm alliance with the English-speaking American nation, are the main grounds of hope to many, for the lasting peace of the world'.[109]

Though Protestants were theologically, ethically, and politically divided, their common convictions provided a cultural substratum, which for all its ambiguities remained a potent cultural force until the 1950s. For Dr Lang, in Sydney, this cultural Protestantism was seen as vital to colonization, which was a divine ordinance. A sense of emergent nationality was God's gift, for Lang believed that God at Mt Sinai had set out the spiritual foundations for republican government, resting on universal suffrage, political equality, and popular election. Such foundations, Lang considered, would make Australia a vital centre of Christian influence. 'I believe it is destined, in the counsels of Infinite Wisdom, to be the seat of one of the first of the Christian nations of the earth.'[110]

---

[108] J. C. Firth, *Nation Making* (London, 1890) 279.
[109] W. G. Cowie, *Our Last Year in New Zealand* (London, 1888) 392.
[110] J. D. Lang, *The Coming Event* (London, 1870) 39–41, 136, 470.

HYMNODY AND CONGREGATIONAL LIFE

Such convictions were reinforced by the worship and parish life of countless Christians, whose political and economic views were biblically and theologically nourished Sunday by Sunday. Though some Anglicans and Presbyterians continued to sing only psalms up until the 1870s, the popularity of hymns was steadily growing and creating a new language for piety. By the mid-1850s, Melbourne Anglicans were discussing the possibility of a diocesan hymnal, with sharp disagreement over what was suitable. Anglicans produced locally composed hymn collections as early as 1855 without any episcopal encouragement. R. Bentley Young collected *78 Australian Hymn Tunes* in 1892, but Anglo-Catholics preferred *Hymns Ancient and Modern*, which was used in Dunedin by 1861 and in Brisbane before 1880. In evangelical dioceses and parishes, less 'advanced' hymnals were preferred. All Protestants valued hearty singing, but Catholics were more inclined to listen to choirs rather than sing for themselves.[111]

The rediscovery of the musical heritage of the Western Church was slow in reaching Australia and New Zealand. Many churches were installing pipe organs from the 1850s. As a Launceston Presbyterian remarked, regarding St Andrew's Presbyterian Church in Hobart, which had bought an organ in 1858, 'if it were good for David to use instruments in praising God, when anticipating a Saviour, surely it is neither unseemly nor unscriptural on our part to imitate his example after that Saviour has come'.[112] Choral music was immensely popular in colonial communities, but it was amateur, for even notable musicians rarely made enough to live on. It provided another area in which laity could take initiatives.

Many congregations were uneasy about choirs becoming dominant in worship. The Wesleyan conference in 1863 issued a *Digest of Laws* which included rules for controlling choirs in Sunday worship. Choirs retaliated by holding mid-week sacred concerts. Imposing musical taste was as futile as trying to control lay theology. In the YMCA and YWCA people sang lighter Christian music, often from the United

---

[111] *Weekly Advance*, 8 May 1880, 41, has a fine description of Wesleyan worship. R. White, *Joy in the Singing* (Dunedin, 1989); K. J. Hastie, 'Music making in the Wesleyan churches of New South Wales, 1855–1902', M.Phil. thesis (Sydney, 1991); D. Gome, 'Australia's Catholics and Congregational Singing', *ACR* 74 (1997) 417–31.

[112] A. Priestley, *The Mode of Conducting the Praise of God in Presbyterian Churches* (Launceston, 1858) 27.

States, without needing to be accountable to conservative clergy and office bearers. By the 1870s, lining out of hymns by a precentor was in decline, for literacy rates were increasing, and hymnals becoming widely owned. Organists were in considerable demand for recitals, for continuing orchestras were non-existent.

Congregationalists, Lutherans, and Wesleyans had a lively choral heritage, but Presbyterians suspected that hymns and anthems were merely human, rather than inspired, compositions. At First Presbyterian Church in Dunedin, the congregation first stood for singing psalms in September 1875, but no hymns were sung until 1884. Hostility to 'instrumental music' divided many congregations until late in the nineteenth century, when many began choirs and installed organs. At Knox Presbyterian Church in Dunedin, the Sunday school began using a harmonium in 1881, although the congregation had rejected the introduction of an organ a decade earlier. Once the Sunday school had led the way, and some prejudices had been removed, Knox installed an organ in 1882.

At St Peter's, Eastern Hill, Melbourne, under their vicar H. P. Handfield, a pipe organ was installed in mid-1855 and a paid choir begun, which attracted Bishop Perry's ire, because its members not only chanted but also were surpliced from 1862. Perry's injunctions against this innovation in 1867 had to be withdrawn, for they were not upheld by English lawyers. Pressure for improved music came from parish members, and not from Handfield alone.

DISSENTING OPTIONS

Another example of lay leadership of congregational life can be seen in Melbourne. Collins Street Independent Church, begun in September 1839, had a covenant of membership, but interpreted this liberally. Henry Hopkins and John Fawkner, both members, determined to find a minister. Hopkins sent the requisite money for the Revd William Waterfield's passage and his stipend, instead of waiting until the congregation was large enough to qualify for assistance under the Church Act. The worshippers included seven pastoralists, one banker, four merchants, two clerks, a lawyer, eleven artisans, and two labourers. The building, opened in 1841, was unpretentious and the congregation decided not to install an organ.[113]

---

[113] C. Wood and M. Askew, *St Michael's Church* (Melbourne, 1992) 9.

John Fawkner, the entrepreneurial son of a convict, was a member and also ran the *Port Phillip Patriot,* which attacked any signs of privilege, stressing instead hard work and merit as bases for status and leadership. Church workers took a leading role in providing a Mechanics' Institute in 1840. Waterfield found the robust factions of Melbourne hard to bear. Add financial problems, the foundation of a Baptist cause, criticisms of his ministry, and his resignation can be understood. He ministered another twenty-five years in Tasmania. His successor, Alexander Morrison, trained in Dublin and London, found twenty-three members when he arrived, but gave such effective leadership that the membership grew to 103 in 1849. The debts were cleared, school buildings begun, and he also became an influential community leader. He also led the expansion of Congregationalist churches in the turbulent gold years. Many Congregationalists contributed to the community by their probity in business, their commitment to citizenship, and membership in representative institutions.

By 1854, there were fourteen Congregational churches in the colony. Attempts to help expansion by seeking government grants brought strong reaction from purists. The arrival of John Poore and Richard Fletcher, in March 1854, both talented and experienced, led to the formation of a Union and Home Mission. A financial crisis led to their collapse in 1856, but inter-colonial conferences were held from 1855. A recruiting tour by Poore brought fifteen new ministers to Victoria and New Zealand, so that by 1860 there were forty-two chapels, thirty-three ministers, and over 12,000 members.[114] Among the recruits was the notable Thomas Binney, who led the Victoria Parade church to considerable prosperity from 1857. Promising beginnings, based on a broadly Protestant appeal, withered as denominational loyalties consolidated in the 1860s and 1870s. Collins Street Independent Church struggled, and Morrison resigned in 1864, unable to stem the flight to the suburbs, and dissatisfaction in the congregation with his ministry. He was also marginalized in the Union because of his acceptance of state aid. In Ipswich, Queensland, the Congregational church there founded twenty-eight other congregations in the colony.

Though Congregationalist churches are difficult to categorize, they nourished an important lay Christian ethos in business and community service. The Balmain church in Sydney included in its membership Sir Thomas Henley, and Josiah Mullins, founder of the Sydney

---

[114] Ibid., 27.

Stock Exchange. In South Australia, between 1857 and 1882, Congregationalists provided one-third of the members of the Legislative Council and 15 per cent of the Legislative Assembly. Not all congregations were happily united. The combined Presbyterian–Congregational church in Balmain, which opened in 1855, split in 1857. T. A. Gordon, their minister, described Congregationalists as 'the bond-slaves of a usurping and irresponsible oligarchy'—a reference to the influential laity in the Pitt Street congregation.[115] He left to become a Presbyterian, believing that tradition better secured the liberties of all. By contrast, Thomas Forsaith, briefly Prime Minister in New Zealand, was a Presbyterian, and then became a Congregational minister in New Zealand, before founding the Congregational church in Parramatta, New South Wales.

Under Anketell Henderson (1866–76), Collins Street Independent Church became the flagship of Melbourne Congregationalism.[116] A fine preacher, originally from the Church of Ireland, and briefly a Wesleyan until he was convinced by Scripture that the autonomy of the local congregation was the polity God most approved, he then ministered in London at Claremont Chapel, which he restored to vigorous life, as well as being involved in theological education, journalism, and outreach. Equipped with a lucid mind, a strong personality, and a persuasive debating style, he became very influential in both city and denomination, especially in the doctrinal and educational debates of the 1870s. His deacons complemented his leadership, and they planned and built the present church, designed by Joseph Reed, which is one of the most original buildings in Melbourne. It was debt-free by 1869 and had cost £16,000. Similar Congregational churches in Auckland, Wellington, Sydney, Adelaide, and Perth nourished a strong business and professional ethos.

Presbyterians on both sides of the Tasman were strongly affected by the Disruption of 1843, but in both Victoria and New South Wales had worked hard to overcome this and earlier divisions over relations with the state. The latter colony was not so successful as Victoria in healing splits, and the tiny Presbyterian Church of Eastern Australia continues into the present. Victorian Presbyterians achieved union in 1859 after some tough negotiations both in Melbourne and Edinburgh, with an intransigent handful of clergy staying out because

---

[115] T. A. Gordon, *Congregational Independency in New South Wales and Presbyterianism* (Sydney, 1858) 9.
[116] Wood and Askew, *St Michael's Church*, 19–27.

of personality conflicts and theological differences.[117] The reunited churches were actively involved in home and overseas missions, the latter beginning in the New Hebrides, where Nova Scotians, Scots, New Zealanders, and Australians all supplied workers and money. Attempts to unite New Zealand Presbyterians, especially for more effective mission work, began in the 1850s, and looked likely to conclude with the agreed Basis of Union. Otago and Southland, however, were not happy with minor changes to the Basis, and formed their own synod in 1866. Union had to wait another thirty-four years.

Building a church was seen as a catalyst for other civilized institutions, and Presbyterians were concerned for both, especially schools. Few fought more energetically for this kind of development than Dr Lang in Sydney, even after he retired from the pulpit of Scots Church in Sydney. Although ministers were a source of community pride, work and family piety were the bedrock of Presbyterian culture, with elders giving leadership with or without their minister. They believed that the strict observance of the Sabbath not only restored the foundations of Britain's greatness in a raw new society, it testified to the grace and purpose of creation, and inspired the labours of the week.

Capitalists like James Macandrew in Dunedin saw commerce and Christianity as allies, though his flexible ethics suggested business was king of his conscience. Sir Donald McLean typified the possibilities of colonial life for a Presbyterian. He left Scotland for New South Wales in 1838 to join relatives and then moved to New Zealand, where he had a checkered early career and then settled down as a skilled land purchaser and negotiator with the Maori. His diaries show a deep religious side to his personality, which did not always integrate with his political and economic activities. He died a wealthy livestock farmer, thankful to the Almighty for his prosperity. Dr Sidey, his minister in Napier, preached an eloquent memorial sermon in 1877 about McLean's success in the light of God's purposes. Sir George Reid, a minister's son and premier of New South Wales, at the end of the century linked free trade and Christianity as inseparable partners.

Presbyterians were strongly represented among the prosperous by the 1870s as runholders, businessmen, and professionals. The best ministers were also handsomely paid—as much as university professors. In Christchurch, the congregation of St Andrew's wrote home

---

[117] Sutherland, *Presbyterian Church of Victoria*, 487–508, for the key documents.

for a clever minister who was not only a good preacher, but capable 'of giving an occasional week evening lecture on Astronomy, Geology, Natural History or other secular subjects of popular and instructive interest'.[118] Such lectures were very popular and often an important source of fundraising. Not all clergy were well read, but some Anglican and Presbyterians, such as Rutherford Waddell in Dunedin, had extensive libraries, and encouraged the formation of public libraries.

With their elders in parishes, they exercised strict discipline, like their counterparts in Scotland and Ireland, though this was in terminal decline by the 1870s, judging by representative session minutes. Presbyteries and Assemblies set firm ethical standards for the community. Presbyterians were strong on civic virtue, resting on eternal values given by God. Though emphatically not teetotallers, they sought regulation of alcohol abuse. Sabbath-breaking and gambling, as well as sexual licence, were also frequently rebuked in statements designed to inform and jolt the Christian conscience of the community. In the south of New Zealand, Presbyterians behaved like an established church, reflecting a sober conservatism which was as suspicious of political radicalism as it was of showy piety. They were little interested in the welfare of the Maori, or the feckless poor.

One unexpected missionary responsibility came with the discovery of gold on both sides of the Tasman. Some Protestants were determined to evangelize Chinese miners. The impact of Christianity in China was still slight, but Chinese catechists were employed by Anglicans, Presbyterians, and Wesleyans, who gathered small congregations of lonely men, some of whom were baptized. They did not always follow denominational rules. Lo Sam Yuen was disciplined by Bishop Perry for attending a Wesleyan service of the Lord's Supper in 1859 at Ballarat. In 1870, Paul Ah Chin, a Methodist, was employed by Presbyterians to minister to the Otago Chinese. Little attempt was made to translate the Christian message into Chinese cultural idiom. One church paper claimed that it was sophistry 'if an attempt to raise the moral condition of these benighted strangers should be interpreted as sympathy with an alien race, whose presence among us threatens to be a festering plague sore'.[119] Dr Lang, on the other hand, was a firm

---

[118] McEldowney, *Presbyterians in Aotearoa*, 31.

[119] Diaries of several Chinese ministers are in the Victorian archives of the Uniting Church. J. Ng, *Windows on a Chinese Past* (4 vols., Dunedin, 1993–9) is a rich portrait of the New Zealand Chinese. *Church Record* (1857) 11; J. Stenhouse and B. Moloughney, 'Drug besotten, sin begotten friends of filth. New Zealanders and the Oriental other', *NZJH* 33 (1999) 43–64.

opponent of anti-Chinese racism, and brought about repeal of discriminatory legislation against the Chinese which he had earlier helped to enact, thereby winning great respect in the Sydney Chinese community. They were expected to conform to British customs as part of the price of becoming Christians. Many converts moved easily across denominational boundaries which had little relevance to them. Fr James Cheong, at St Peter's, Eastern Hill, Melbourne, had a Presbyterian father who disapproved of his becoming an Anglican, let alone an Anglo-Catholic.

Presbyterians combined, somewhat uneasily, Evangelical piety and confessional Calvinism. For the Irish, the Welsh, and some Scots, the former was influential. It was Scots who most strongly upheld the latter. As a result they took a leading part in early Protestant ecumenism, and in the development of both Evangelical and liberal Protestantism which eschewed intolerance and persecuting principles. In their Scottish/Irish way they laid important foundations for nationhood, even though they saw themselves as part of Greater Britain. They rejected the idea that nationality had to be linked with religious exclusiveness. The Queensland General Assembly welcomed the liberal and unsectarian constitution of the colony as a liberal basis for a Christian society.[120]

The Methodists who came to Australasia were just starting to develop an independent ethos. They drew heavily on the Puritan heritage of morality and social responsibility, and were committed to reform of church and nation by spreading scriptural holiness over the land. Like their founder, many were politically conservative, and could not contain more radical groups like Primitive Methodists, the New Connexion, or Bible Christians. They retained close relations with Evangelical Anglicans, but were not always comfortable with Dissenters. Strongly committed to evangelism, they sought to create a church of the soundly converted which was biblical, spiritual, disciplined, and progressive, for they believed that God was with them. Ministers were servants of the Conference, but one of the great strengths of Methodism was the energy of its independent-minded laity, who initiated class meetings and schools, preached, and pastored before ministers were available. The Methodist hymnals were basic to their piety, and singing essential to their worship.

In South Australia, such laymen as John Colton, who was a Member

---

[120] GAQ *Proceedings* (1863–73) 5.

of Parliament for twenty-three years, and the Stephens brothers, who were sons of a Conference President, gave Methodism a public face which was generous, public-spirited, and sometimes at odds with ministerial orthodoxy and discipline.[121] Bitter divisions in the 1840s suggested other dynamics than scriptural holiness, but under Daniel Draper, between 1846 and 1855, the church grew tenfold. He demonstrated his capacity as a builder in the fine new church in Pirie Street. The smaller Methodist churches also flourished with notable leaders like James Way, James Maughan, and laymen like John Dunn. Francis Faulding, Thomas G. Waterhouse, and George Harris were all wealthy supporters of Prince Alfred College (1869), the educational flagship of the colony's Methodism.

As minister in Pirie Street, Thomas Williams, a notable former Fijian missionary, helped widen missionary horizons, and convince Methodists of the need to bring light to the heathen. Ironically, his artistic Lindsay grandsons tried to bring alive the pagan heritage of the classical world. The Waterhouse family was also prominent in business and missionary service. John Watsford was another ex-Fiji missionary who had a powerful influence in the colony. The energy of the Methodist community was shown in its expansion into the new farming districts, and the Adelaide suburbs, and its influence at every level of society. Sir Frederick Holder was the first speaker of the Federal parliament.

Similar influence could be seen in Tasmania, New South Wales, and New Zealand. In Western Australia and Queensland, the Methodist churches were much smaller because the population was much lower, but were still important because of the Conference networks. Nathaniel Turner, a notable Pacific missionary, was also a founder of Queensland Methodism, underlining how important that experience was in nurturing the evangelistic and conversionist ethos of Methodism. The Anglican newspaper in Victoria attacked Wesleyan Camp Meetings at Queenscliff as 'an undesirable United States import likely to be subversive of home discipline and social order'.[122] Conversionism could lead to unpleasant religious imperialism, hostility to other forms of Christianity, and expectations which burnt out many ministers and members. For those who could survive,

---

[121] A. D. Hunt, *This Side of Heaven* (Adelaide, 1985) 25–104 gives an admirable survey of the period up to 1870.

[122] J. G. Turner, *The Pioneer Missionary* (Melbourne, 1872) 296–34 for Turner's Queensland ministry. *Messenger*, 10 Jan. 1882, 2.

the joyous optimism and strong fellowship contributed to an expansionist mentality, which was an important ingredient in Australasian Protestantism for two centuries.

The Churches of Christ are not a group which frequently make headlines, but they were a significant part of Evangelical Protestantism in the Australian and New Zealand colonies. Their first recorded service, led by Thomas Jackson, was in Nelson, New Zealand, on 2 March 1844, followed by expansion to Auckland in 1845 and later to Adelaide the same year through Thomas Magarey. Many of the congregations were small, but large congregations developed in Dunedin, Auckland, Adelaide, Melbourne, and Sydney. They stood for a tradition of restoration of apostolic Christianity and, though they were similar to Baptists in many respects, kept a separate identity believing that they alone were authentic disciples. Their ministers were termed 'evangelists' and came both from the United States and from Britain. For example, M. W. Green came with the Albertland settlers in 1862 to New Zealand before moving between Dunedin, Sydney, Melbourne, and Adelaide, and back to Dunedin in 1902. It was believed that ministerial success 'was achieved by consecrated energy, absolute faithfulness to principle, and a total absence of the temporising spirit'.[123] Australians and New Zealanders were less responsive than Americans to this ethos.

Lutheran churches also had a different tradition. They were strongly supported by German and Scandinavian migrants, for whom their churches were central to community identity and cultural memory. Choirs and brass bands kept their musical heritage vigorously alive in both rural areas and urban congregations, such as Walla Walla in New South Wales, and those in the Barossa Valley in South Australia. They remained strongly European in their liturgy, but were proudly Australian. Though they were not often represented in politics, they were citizens of great integrity whose theology separated the roles of church and state very sharply. At times deeply divided theologically, they were an important representative of a major European Protestant tradition.

---

[123] J. Wright, *Churches of Christ in New Zealand* (Wellington, 1903) 351; H. R. Taylor, *History of the Churches of Christ in South Australia* (Adelaide, 1959) 1–35. G. Chapman, *One Lord, One Faith, One Baptism* (Melbourne, 1979) has produced a valuable history of the Australian Churches of Christ. C. Ma, *History of the Swanston St Church of Christ* (Melbourne, 1995) gives a valuable account of the dynamics of an inner city congregation founded in the nineteenth century.

English influence in the region has been so extensive and normative that it has rarely been historically discussed in the same detail as the contributions of other ethnic groups.[124] In addition to providing the bases to law, parliamentary government, farming, and business practice, English influence in the media, education, the arts, and sport has been enormous, and helped to create two of the most stable popular democracies in the world, where principle and compromise were interwoven. Though adherence to the Australian Anglican Church has diminished by almost half, from just over 40 per cent in 1901 to 23 per cent of the population in the 1990s, the Church of England remained influential until the 1970s when the influence of all the major churches eroded dramatically.

After a period of quasi-establishment, the Anglican Church became only the largest denomination, assisted on the same basis as other churches. It lacked the social strength of its parent in England and Ireland, it lost dominance in primary education to publicly funded schools, and had to struggle for the retention of its nominal adherents against the proselytizing evangelism of other churches like the Methodists. Its leaders, however, had a large vision of a Christian society. J. D. Mereweather believed that the Englishman, from infancy, was reared on the word of God. 'He early forms a habititude of judging for himself in religious matters, biased perhaps, but not peremptorily dictated to, by any man or body of men.' Bishop Barry, of Sydney, believed that the future of Australian Christianity depended largely on the Anglican Church, because it represented, most fully, English culture. Loyalty to the Crown was seen by many English migrants as an instinctive virtue, leading on to other civic virtues. 'The extinction of slavery, the elevation of woman, the humanizing of war, the deepening of compassion, the worship of gentleness, the creation of the feeling of universal brotherhood—all these are positive gains, absolutely secured and reached under the sanctifying influence of the Gospel.' That, of course, was embodied particularly by the life of the Anglican Church.[125]

The social status of Anglicanism was reinforced by the role played by colonial governors, bishops, and the secondary schools to which the social elite sent their children in each colony. Anglican clergy

---

[124] J. Jupp (ed.), *The Australian People* (Sydney, 1988, new edition forthcoming) 'English' 367–464 gives a very important overview.

[125] J. D. Mereweather, *Diary of a Working Clergyman* (London, 1850) 19; *Messenger*, 23 Mar. 1872, 1; *Messenger*, 9 Sept. 1885, 5; *Messenger*, 2 Dec. 1878, 10–11.

continued to baptize, marry, and bury a majority of the community, without resolving the problem of nominalism which is perhaps better described as non-clerical piety. For most Anglicans, the party struggles of the nineteenth-century church in Britain and the colonies were irrelevant. On public occasions, however, the English experience of Anglican liturgy, with its dignity and beauty, provided an important focus for social unity, and reinforced the link between church and society. The language of the *Book of Common Prayer* provided for everyday life as well as crises and tragedies. Its language was as deeply embedded in popular consciousness as that of the Bible. While colonial elites did not necessarily attend worship regularly, they believed that the Anglican Church's role was essential for the well-being of the community and that it was theirs, not just the clergy's. Anglicans also contributed to distrust of showy religion which was better at talk than action.[126]

The slow growth of public conviction in the nineteenth century that Christianity, public service, and compassion for the weak and needy were inseparable, owed much to the leadership of the English churches, which included Baptists, Congregationalists, and Methodists as well as Anglicans. In addition, the English churches slowly reinforced the notion that holders of public office should avoid nepotism, payment for favours, and economic favouritism. These ideas were reinforced in the press, frequently owned and edited by English Christians, and in sermons which underlined the importance of vocational integrity, good citizenship, generosity, and the partnership between government and non-established churches. The energies of the Scots, and the Irish passion for equality and justice, were also important ingredients in the creation of these democracies. Government was not experienced only as power imposed by elites, but as an agent of transformation for the whole community.

Churches also played a vital part by offering an account of society which was not just the creation of the market or of government. They insisted on the importance of spiritual priorities such as faith, hope, and love as foundations for local communities which fostered fairness, compassion, and loyalty, both to what was local and to what was imperial. English capacity to struggle with injustice in a plural way through diverging visions of a Christian society created crucial associations which carried values transcending both the market and

---

[126] D. Hilliard, 'Anglicanism', *ACS* (1988) 64–82 with a response by R. T. Ely, ibid., 83–5.

politics, moderating both individualism and ethnic tribalism, contributing to a popular ethos which had lost the servility of the British poor and which created solid, decent societies, albeit lacking the cultural creativity of European societies and their massive injustices. There were no saints, but few demons either.

Unlike the left-leaning transformers of the late twentieth century who devalued family, church, and nation in the name of individual freedom, nineteenth-century church members and church leaders alike saw these associations as the bases of the nation and freedom, without idolizing them. They believed responsible community and personal freedom intersected in shared commitment to God. They did not achieve a perfect synthesis. Many malign distortions can be seen with the benefit of hindsight, but there was a solidity of civic responsibility, political realism, and business integrity at the core of these new societies, which endured across classes as a unifying mythology until the 1960s, strongly influenced by Protestant and Catholic Christianities. Secular perfectionism was just as destructive of this consensus as religious perfectionism, but neither could gain political power. In both Australia and New Zealand, most distrusted this and opted for untidy pragmatism which was community-oriented and tolerant, except when the foundations were threatened by egotistic visionaries who cared nothing for community, only for the triumph of their own fantasies.

It is important neither to exaggerate the impact of the churches on colonial societies nor to write them out of history. Some commentators in the nineteenth century recognized that there were serious weaknesses, which boded ill for the future. In Auckland, the Revd Samuel Edger deplored 'the utter inability of all sectarian systems in maintaining a religious tone in the community. The moral character of the church here is not one shade above the moral level of the people generally; sometimes I fear it is below it.' Edger argued that the solution to this problem was to find a new integration between religion and common life. All things must be made holy, a spiritual reality he called secular Christianity.[127] Unfortunately, most remained content with the limits of sectarianism, which hindered the more generous impulses of early ecumenism.

Whether historians examine politics, economics, law, education, newspapers, health, or popular culture, the influence of the churches was pervasive for both good and ill. Christians reflected the blind-

---

[127] S. Edger, *Sermons* (Auckland, 1870) xii 24.

spots of their heritage, which at times made them destructive and insensitive, quarrelsome and expert at demeaning opponents. They also were responsible for many of the foundations of contemporary society and transformed decisively some of the disastrous features of the societies from which they had emigrated. Australasia provided the space for Christian generosity to grow out of the bitter religious enmities of Britain and Europe, although change was slow in the nineteenth century.[128]

[128] P. O'Farrell, 'Sectarianism: imagination's stain', in D. Cameron (ed.), *Imperfect Communion* (Sydney, 1998) 87–96.

4

NEW OPPORTUNITIES
FOR MISSION AND SERVICE

The period from the 1880s to the end of the First World War was marked by a number of important religious developments. There were significant changes in worship in all the major Protestant churches, especially in the use of hymnody, chant, organs, and choirs. Changes in a more Catholic direction spread in the Church of England, so that what had been 'advanced' in the 1860s had become mainstream by the end of the period. Likewise, in all the major Protestant churches, national patterns of government and unity had begun to emerge, despite the power of local loyalties. Liberal ideas on progressive change in society were widely accepted. 'The great aim of the changes must ever be to regenerate society.' Christianity was seen by many Protestants as vital for social change. 'Christ is at the root of all progress and where men revere Him there civilisation marches with the most rapid strides.'[1] Important ideological opposition was emerging amongst the working classes in the form of socialism, expressed in a variety of ways, but frequently hostile to Christianity as a religion of the rich and powerful.

The place of women was changing. Fewer were content to raise money for men to spend for God, and more were beginning to find ways to attain financial control. Women's suffrage began in New Zealand in 1893 and spread to all the Australian states by 1914, but with little immediate effect on legal disabilities in both church and community. The Women's Temperance Movement and the National Council of Women, which began in 1885 and 1896 respectively in New Zealand, both had Christian origins but were inclusive of other viewpoints. They became very powerful agents for change, alongside national youth organizations. Political and theological liberalism were growing in influence, and some notable social reforms for the most needy were pioneered, especially in New Zealand in the 1890s.[2]

[1] *Tasmanian Congregational Yearbook* (1886) 24; (1898) 11.

[2] M. McClure, *A Civilised Community: A History of Social Security in New Zealand, 1898–1998* (Auckland, 1998).

Missionary interest grew significantly in all the churches, encouraged by the formation of national assemblies, synods, and unions. Interest in the spiritual welfare of the Aborigines reawakened. New work was started in India, China, Korea, and South America, with Anglicans going east to Africa, which had been opened up by people like David Livingstone. It was in Papua New Guinea, however, that some of the most dramatic changes occurred, spreading into other areas of Melanesia, one of the world's last missionary frontiers.

Sectarianism remained an ugly feature of church life, occasionally flowing over into politics, though many Christians began to question whether ancient hatreds and suspicions deserved to be taken seriously.[3] Important political events, like moves to federation in Australia, played an important part in widening denominational horizons, and modifying relations between governments and churches. So did awareness that greater challenges existed than upholding denominational identity. The impact of economic depression in the 1890s, and the emergence of militant trade-unionism, posed another set of divisive problems with which the churches found it hard to deal. In Dunedin, the Revd W. Saunders, a Congregational minister, strongly supported the Seamens' strike in the 1890s, as did some influential Australian clergy such as Cardinal Moran. Most either opposed strikes on principle, or pled for negotiation. Finally, the problems of war raised ethical issues which neither nation nor churches were adequately able to resolve, either before or after federation. The churches were deeply enculturated without recognizing it. In Western Australia in 1899, some leading Anglican clergy wanted to change the name of the Church of England to the Church of Australia in order to develop a national character, and unite Anglo-Saxon Christians. 'What would do the utmost to bind them to the Empire, and make them feel they were all of one blood and belonged to the same Empire would be when they could feel they were all united and belonged to one branch of the Catholic Church of Christ.'[4]

In many ways, the churches in the region reflected the values and priorities of the societies in which they were situated. Polynesian Christians similarly contributed to the interaction of religion and culture. In the Tahitian group, administered by France, the pre-contact population of about 35,000 had fallen to 7–8,000 by 1810 and remained there for the rest of the century. French missionaries were

---

[3] M. Hogan, *The Sectarian Strand* (Melbourne, 1974).
[4] *West Australian*, 19 Oct. 1899.

deeply concerned at Roman Catholic expansion, and pled for more missionaries to come from France. Missionaries such as Charles Vienot, Frederic Vernier, and Theo Arbousset helped the Maohi Christians to develop a strong religious and community network, symbolized by the opening of a large new church in 1908 in Papeete. In villages, Protestant services took up most of Sunday. The deacons were elected by the whole district community, according to the 1884 church constitution. By 1918, there was a theological school which had trained the thirty-four pastors of the Evangelical Church, which had 4,500 communicant members, 2,500 Sunday school pupils, and fifty-one churches guided by four French missionaries. Missionary commitment remained strong despite the numbers of deaths from sickness. Teina-Ore wrote

And now my kindred at Raiatea, I ask you this, surely we are not to be the last to come to New Guinea from Raiatea! Oh, Friends at Raiatea, if anyone should say, 'I will go to New Guinea as a substitute for the dead,' don't let your hands hang down, but hold up your hands (and support him). New Guinea is being harvested. Some ungathered fruit is dropping off the tree. The vine has been pruned, seed is growing. Oh, friends at Raiatea, look with your own eyes at this field, wherein the ground is digged and softened. Make the Mission Institution grow once more. Send to me here in New Guinea reapers for the harvest. Be up and doing. Don't sever the rope by letting the Institution fall through. The Gospel rain is falling now. Men are coming over to God, and oh, nearly all the missionaries are dead. Oh, Raiatea, now you must go forth and collect fresh men for the Mission Institution. This is the request I send to you, O people of our Islands.—Your affectionate son, Teina-ore, at New Guinea.[5]

Churches still saw themselves as moral guardians, for they were interpreters of the Christian ethic for a Christian people. Sorting out the nature of that symbiotic relationship is an exacting task which can only yield impressionistic results. The churches provided some values, which could be called counter-cultural, but in many other ways they offered a Christian version of values and customs deeply embedded in the ethnic and regional cultures of the British Isles. Pastor McCullough in Tasmania, arguing as a Baptist, suggested that Christian interference in politics was unavoidable. 'When law touches morality, or religious freedom, we are going to have a finger in the pie.'[6] The Scots and Welsh identified with the majority culture of England in many

[5] F. Paton, *The Kingdom in the Pacific* (London, 1913) 92–3.
[6] *The Daystar*, April 1886.

respects, and readily shared in the colonies' elites. By and large, the churches had secured freedom from state interference, with politicians and church leaders alike believing this was to their mutual benefit. Alexander Gosman saw this as 'true secularity' as distinct from surrender to secularism.[7]

The Salvation Army was an interesting Protestant variant. After arrival in Adelaide in 1880, it rapidly carved out a place in other colonies in the 1880s, on both sides of the Tasman, and attracted a large number of adherents and supporters who valued charitable activism, compassion for the forgotten down-and-outs, and the commitment of its leaders and soldiers to holiness. Its growth was astonishing. Initially a Methodist New Connexion offshoot, many of its early members were former Methodists who saw in its fiery preaching and battles against evil a resurrection of the early Methodist spirit. Captain Edward Wright and Lieutenant G. A. Pollard came to Port Chalmers in New Zealand in 1883, and were speedily followed by other officers, whose earthly rewards were small, for the Army demanded great personal and family sacrifice.[8]

Criticized by mainline Protestants for their emotionalism, sensationalism, and noisy music, they were mocked by the classes they came to serve. Parodies of Salvationist meetings by Skeleton Army parades did not dissuade them, any more than occasional arrests for disturbing the peace. The Salvationists speedily won a respected, but minority, place in the Protestant community through their prison-gate ministry and other forms of service. Determinedly counter-cultural, they were not interested in becoming members of governments at any level, regarding their spiritual responsibilities to the overlooked as a priority. They were convinced that, just as they worked with anyone in need, they could ask the community for financial support, whether people were active Christians or not. General Booth's visits to Australia in 1891 and 1905 were triumphant Evangelical celebrations, but the black and brown poor were still largely ignored.

While Aborigines and Maori appeared to be dying races, locally born and migrant population in all the colonies was increasing rapidly because of the pull of mineral discoveries on both sides of the Tasman, as well as the steady expansion of farming and industry. In New

[7] *Victorian Independent*, 10 Jan. 1883.
[8] B. Bolton, *Booth's Drum* (Sydney, 1980); C. R. Bradwell, *Fight the Good Fight* (Wellington, 1982).

Zealand, assisted migration under the Vogel government in the 1870s added to the momentum of gold discoveries in the South Island, and then in the North. The defeat of the Maori in the New Zealand Wars, and the unjust confiscation of huge areas made available large new tracts for settlement, at a time when new techniques for food preservation made the development of dairy factories and freezing works feasible. By the 1890s even remote Western Australia had its own gold rush, lifting the colony out of any need for convict labour, and dramatically increasing the opportunities for the churches.

Churches played a vital part in the social, sporting, and cultural life of the towns, as well as offering religious consolation and inspiration in a harsh environment. Dean Moore, of Perth, described his first committee meeting as a new arrival in the Kanowna pub. The chair-man began with, 'Well, gentlemen, we'll start the meeting with a shilling in, and the winner shouts.' This was rather different from the decorous meetings of Belfast from which Moore had come.[9] Church building boomed in the expanding suburbs from the 1870s. They were important sources of care for the victims of illness, loss of employment or a breadwinner, and natural disasters.

Ministers' and missionaries' diaries illuminate the wide range of duties they performed, as well as the piety that inspired them. J. H. Davies, one of the pioneer Presbyterian missionaries in Korea, wrote in his diary, 30 March 1889, about his fears of declining faith, 'I am afraid my Christianity is made up very largely of ambition.'[10] Services could be held in a variety of places in the bush. In a Gippsland railway camp, services were held in the local pub, but in order not to offend parsons' sensibilities, it was renamed 'Coffee Palace' for Sundays. Church members could at times make sharp criticisms of their clergy. Sir Thomas McIlwraith, a member of St Paul's Presby-terian Church, Wickham Terrace, Brisbane, spoke of the dangers of leaving ministers to change things by sensational preaching, 'The church will degenerate into a theatre.'[11]

By the turn of the century, all the major cities had a network of suburban churches, as well as major central missions, some of which were beginning to find difficulties in competing with suburban ministers. Anglicans, likewise, created an unsuccessful mission zone in central Sydney. Occasional ministers such as R. B. S. Hammond later

---

[9] Battye Library MN129/120A, Moore papers.
[10] La Trobe MS 10411, J. H. Davies.
[11] Sydney *Daily Telegraph*, 21 Mar. 1891.

managed to build city congregations like St Barnabas, which reversed the trend, by creating a reputation for preaching excellence, with attractive ancillary activities. William Taylor pioneered a Methodist Central Mission in Sydney. David Shearer in St Andrews Presbyterian church, Perth, created a thriving congregation as well as taking on important educational responsibilities. Such ministers were not only active in church affairs, but took a leading role in the whole community and often gained an inter-colonial profile. James Gibb, after a successful ministry in Footscray, Victoria, moved to First Church, Dunedin, and then to St John's Presbyterian church, Wellington, becoming an influential national leader.

Local parishes and congregations had their own dynamism and ethos, which can provide a very important window into religious activities and changes. In the 1860s Holy Trinity, Adelaide, had visits from Bishop Patteson in 1864/65, and gave modest sums to the Melanesian Mission. The tenor of parish life was even, with organizations running smoothly, and regular attention being paid to building maintenance. The Sunday school had 300 scholars, many of whom gave to the Melanesian Mission. A Teachers' Union was formed in 1872 to raise standards of teaching. Other improving Societies were a Band of Hope, a Girls' Friendly Society, and a Temperance Society. Debates over a new hymnbook ended with the choice of *Church Hymns*, edited by A. Sullivan, rather than *Hymns Ancient and Modern*. A strong mixed choir had a vital role in worship, as well as having a strong social identity. From 1880 to 1900, South Australia's economy was in decline and the Rector's salary went down to £200 a year, but by 1889, the church had been extended sympathetically, and extensions also made to the school buildings. But drift to the suburbs and an ailing parson meant that the parish was losing members, despite its strong Evangelical ethos.

The next rector, Frederick Webb, was a Melbourne Evangelical who served from 1895 to 1925.[12] At his communion services in 1896, an average of 43 men and 107 women attended each Sunday. By the end of his ministry, the figure was nearer 200. The number of marriages grew, but baptisms and Sunday school attendance fell to 100. Income remained at around £400 a year. Adult education was not forgotten and a literary society, led by William Shakespeare, lasted forty years, till its death in 1899. A Mother's Union began in 1899 due

---

[12] *Quiz and the Lantern*, Adelaide, 84–5, for comments on Webb.

to the energy of the governor's wife, Lady Buxton, exercising an influential ministry.[13]

St Peter's, Eastern Hill, in Melbourne, which was mildly Anglo-Catholic, consolidated that tradition during the incumbency of E. S. Hughes. There were stand-offs with the bishop during 1900–6, though Hughes made a few concessions, but fundamentally the parish was moving to a gathered church, a feature of many city and suburban congregations at the turn of the century. The high social status of many parishioners declined, as the suburban churches creamed off those seeking more congenial living than the crowded suburbs of Carlton, Fitzroy, Collingwood, and Richmond. E. S. Hughes came as a curate in 1894, and attendances boomed. Tall, Australian-born, and a sportsman, he not only pushed ahead with Anglo-Catholic ritual, he was active in work amongst the poor, like many of his counterparts in England, and developed a reputation as a confessor, and a Christian socialist. He hammered opposing churchmen in *The Mitre,* treating Protestantism and Roman Catholicism as spent spiritual forces. Until his death in 1900, Handfield restrained Hughes's more florid hopes for a full Catholic ritual.

Once installed as vicar by a reluctant Bishop Field Flowers Goe, who gave him a tolerance which few Anglo-Catholic bishops extended to Evangelicals, Hughes introduced vestments and, in 1906, incense. This did not harm attendance, for working-class people appreciated his advocacy, but he became a figure of concern to Evangelicals. They instituted proceedings against him, but he had married, become independently wealthy, and could afford to disregard critics. A number of parish members became missionaries, or members of religious orders. Clergy from other states visited to experience 'advanced' worship. The musical reputation of the parish also was enhanced by A. E. H. Nickson, a notable organist and choirmaster.[14] C. E. Perry, a convert from Evangelicalism, went to St Michael's, in Christchurch, taking it significantly further in an Anglo-Catholic direction.

Another kind of gathered church emerged in Ponsonby, Auckland. A Baptist church was founded in 1880, after a Sunday school, begun in 1876, had proved successful. By 1900, there were 203 scholars and twenty-three teachers. To keep the faith, members signed a covenant

[13] B. Dickey, *Not Just Tea and Biscuits* (Adelaide, 1995) 65–80.

[14] C. Holden, *From Tories at Prayer to Socialists at Mass: A History of St Peter's, Eastern Hill, Melbourne* (Melbourne, 1997) 76–94.

accepting the Bible as the inspired word of God, confessing a Trinitarian faith including the following doctrines—original sin, Christ's atonement, justification through faith, repentance towards God, regeneration and sanctification by the Holy Spirit, salvation by grace, good works as evidence of saving faith, the resurrection of the dead, eternal rewards, and punishment.

The congregation grew rapidly, forming a choir, a Tract Society, and a Vigilance Committee to watch for new members. In 1886, a church seating 400 was opened, with Thomas Spurgeon preaching. Strong laymen like J. S. Bigelow made ministers' lives difficult, and three left in six years. The congregation founded the first New Zealand Christian Endeavour Society in 1891, following a Band of Hope in 1887. Pew rents ended in 1909.

Baptists could have strong views on social issues. In 1892 the Revd A. H. Collins came to Ponsonby from Birmingham. He had been a supporter of Joseph Chamberlain, and was a passionate critic of exploiters of the poor. 'The time will come when the capitalist will cease out of the land. The skilled manager will remain at the head of the industrial army; but the capitalist who lives only on the fruit of other men's toil, will be as extinct as the dodo.' The congregation also had members who fought the reintroduction of the Contagious Diseases Act in 1882. Linking Evangelistic energy and care for the needy, Alfred North ministered there from 1902 to 1911, after retirement from Dunedin's thriving Hanover Street.[15]

Many Christians were still isolated from regular pastoral care. In New Zealand's Southland, Fairlie Evans recalled that 'it was hardly possible to find a people more neglected by the church than we.'[16] People in the Australian bush echoed that comment. Bible reading was all the more important as the rule of life in such geographical isolation. 'The Bible is the only infallible authority visible on earth. It is the sole depository of saving truth in the world . . . and is destined to effect changes among the nations, greater than fleets or armies, art, science, philosophy and merely human literature.'[17] Yet alongside family worship, which was important for all Protestants, an educated ministry shaped the future. Michael Watt, Presbyterian minister of Green Island near Dunedin, insisted that 'we are engaged in laying in the consciences of our people, the solid foundations on which reformers

[15] M. Davison, *Ponsonby Baptist Church* (Auckland, 1990) 3–8.
[16] W. F. Evans, *The Day Thou Gavest*, TS Hewitson Library, 24.
[17] A. N. Somerville, *The Bible for the World* (Hobart, 1877) 5.

of all sorts, legislators, commercial men build up the fair fabric of national prosperity'. In Christchurch, Charles Fraser saw Presbyterianism as 'identified with every movement and measure which was calculated to promote the wellbeing of mankind. It has always been favourable to the vindication of liberty, and a bulwark against the inroads of revolution. It has been the stoutest advocate for the education, not of one or two classes of society, but of all the members of the human family.'[18] Each denomination's leaders made similar claims.

Across the Tasman, in 1901, the South Australian Methodists had grown to almost 25 per cent of the population. Among the miners, piety could foster union solidarity. In 1891, a miners' delegation to the directors was mostly Methodist. John Verran, Labour premier in 1910–12, was a Primitive Methodist local preacher. Cornish mining congregations were also known for periods of awakening, such as in 1875, but despite such movements and regular visits by evangelists, including women, the Methodist churches did not find the longed-for revival.[19] Instead they had to cope with spreading liberal theological ideas, as well as sharing the reformist ethos in South Australian society. Voting in elections was taken as a sacred responsibility, but political reform was not confused with conversion. Only that was the basis of lasting social change.

While novels like Clarke's *For the Term of his Natural Life* explored the issues of convictism, Joseph Furphy in *Such is Life* wrote vividly about the ups and downs of a settler's life in the north of Victoria. Steele Rudd, in a series of evocative short stories, described the problems of a small farmer trying to make a living on the leavings of the big pastoralists, who kept the best of the land when their properties were broken up for closer settlement. Furphy was from a devout and enterprising Methodist family who made farm machinery, but all the authors make clear what a struggle it was for many barely to survive in their new homeland. For many, religion was marginal. Catherine Spence, a Unitarian and social reformer, in Adelaide gave the same impression in her novel, *Clara Morison* (1854), though her own faith was solidly grounded.

Life could be very different for those who managed to acquire huge

[18] *New Zealand Presbyterian*, 2 Feb. 1880, 146; *Canterbury Presbyterian* (1873–4) 55.
[19] A. D. Hunt, *This Side of Heaven* (Adelaide, 1985) 124–6; *The Newsletter*, No. 1 (1978) of the South Australian UCA Historical Society contains extracts from Serena Thorne's diary of her missions.

tracts of land, and survive the unpredictability of Australian seasons, or the cruel winters in high country New Zealand. Some Christians saw a new kind of Briton emerging from this struggle, with 'patience in the face of misfortune, resourcefulness in difficulties, energy and grit when occasion demands'.[20] Disease could also ravage flocks and herds, but the huge homesteads erected by successful pastoralists on both sides of the Tasman are still a reminder of the wealth of a minority. Others made fortunes from developing new suburbs, from the professions, business, and from manufacturing household essentials. Some Christians read this as divine blessing, but trade-unionists differed in their interpretation. A number of wealthy Christians were generous philanthropists. They included Walter and Eliza Hall, and Francis Ormond, but such generosity alone could not overcome economic injustice and unsafe workplaces.

The optimism bred by colonial possibilities was celebrated in many books inviting people from the old world to make a new beginning under God, blending faith and works. Dr James MacGregor, of Edinburgh, believed that, with the exception of North America, God had given no greater trust to a people 'than when he committed New Zealand and the mighty Australian continent into the hands which now hold them, and . . . would hold them forever'.[21] Writing on Western Australia in the 1840s, Wildey painted a picture of how, with modest capital and energy, 'There, the anxious father of a family exchanges the corrosion of doubt and anxiety for their future provision, for a quiet and secure feeling that God has placed him in a beautiful region, so vast, that thousands of years will elapse before it feels the same pressure of numbers, and want of occupation, as the old and noble country from which he came.'[22] That secular eschatology was to sound hollow even by the 1890s, when depression, caused by wanton and unprincipled speculation, brought the economies of New Zealand and the Eastern colonies of Australia to a crushing contraction of opportunity.

That social disaster was compounded by drought in parts of Australia, which delayed recovery until the beginning of the new century. Rural bishops and clergy dealt with great hardships and physical strain from travel in all weathers. The hardship faced by ordinary people was laconically chronicled by Bessie Lee and Albert Facey,

[20] J. W. S. Tomlin, *Australia's Greatest Need* (London, 1914) 98.
[21] *New Zealand Presbyterian*, Feb. 1890, 148.
[22] W. B. Wildey, *Australasia and the Oceanic Region* (Melbourne, 1876) 225.

for whom there was no consolation in religion.[23] Survival meant tough resourcefulness and making the most of what little one had, with fragments of a Christian ethic and mateship to evoke care for others even worse off.

THEOLOGICAL CHALLENGES

By the 1870s and 1880s the churches in Australia and New Zealand were caught up in the larger movements of ideas in Britain, Europe, and North America. Regional theological writing was more than a footnote to developments elsewhere. The changes in historical enquiry soon spilled over into a more critical Protestant approach to the Bible, starting with the Pentateuch, and then moving into the New Testament, and scrutinizing the ways in which the significance of Jesus could be understood. Thoughtful Christians saw both the possibilities, and the problems, of peeling away revered dogma in order to understand the strange appeal of the man, Jesus of Nazareth. J. R. Seeley's *Ecce homo* (1865) caused great unease among the orthodox. Searching questions were being asked about Christian origins, sharpened by the development of evolutionary theory. Relationships between species raised troubling questions about the nature of the biblical narratives, and the extent to which they could be understood as scientific or historical. For many Christians that spelled the end of the traditional view of biblical authority for daily life, with significant consequences over the next century.

Nor was there agreement about the nature of science, or the methods used by historians. What was becoming clearer was that the era of the generalist was over, and that clergy could no longer speak with authority on scientific and historical questions, unless their work was the equal of laity whose lives were devoted to such issues. Issues of how to test evidence, and how to understand development and evolution, led to violent controversies. In Hobart, Bishop Bromby claimed that 'the varieties of belief are bringing a state of unbelief. Belief in *anything* will, sooner or later, end in belief in nothing.'[24]

Theological booksellers were not common, but George Robertson

---

[23] M. I. Lee, *The Not So Poor* (Auckland, 1991); A. Facey, *A Fortunate Life* (Harmondsworth, 1981); D. Hulme-Moir, *Edge of Time* (Sydney, 1998) for her parents' ministry in the bush.

[24] Diocesan Synod, *Opening Address* (Hobart, 1865) 14.

in Melbourne had a huge stock of books, which included a large selection of the most recent British theology, for he was keenly interested himself.[25] Melbourne scholars like the Anglican Robert Potter, and the Congregationalist Alexander Gosman, argued for revelation which was adapted to different historical contexts. Lively discussions on miracles, inspiration, authenticity of biblical books, and the scope of reason were found in the church press, daily newspapers, and weekend reviews, as well as in sermons, lectures, and pamphlets. The colonists were part of vigorous theological discussions occurring in metropolitan Britain and North America. William Anderson, a Wesleyan lay preacher in Melbourne, wrote about his own theological struggles, and the inability of many ministers to deal adequately with modern thought. Yet he was convinced of the need for ministers to be 'in the van of progressive thought'.[26]

Was Christianity best defended by a reassertion of the past theological heritage? That was the position taken by many conservative and Evangelical Christians, who saw in apologetics a major task. The 1904 Model Trust Deed of the Congregational Union of Western Australia annexed a schedule of classical doctrines which its ministers must preach. Or was the faith once delivered to the saints capable of such reinterpretation that it could be accepted by thoughtful people who were excited by the advances in science and technology, developments in the humanities, and who were willing to recognize the human character of the Scriptures? Drawing a boundary between the divine and human in the Bible was not a task readily to be solved, but a number of clergy in the colonies were beginning the task, as were some laity who were not persuaded by dismissive comments about infidel biblical critics in Germany. The New Zealand Methodist W. Anderson argued for the importance of a godly life and deplored the refusal of Conference to reject modern views of the Bible which he believed undermined redemption.[27]

John Langford, a respected Wesleyan local preacher in Adelaide, dealt with such matters in an address to his class in the Norwood circuit in 1866, emphasizing the distinctively religious authority of the Bible, and the reliability of its historical and scientific pronouncements. A more sophisticated approach, based on textual criticism, was

---

[25] J. Holroyd, *George Robertson* (Melbourne, 1968).
[26] La Trobe MS 12517, Anderson Papers.
[27] W. Anderson, *How Methodists Meet Heresy* (Dunedin, 1912); J. Hosking, *The Elements of Christian Theology* (Christchurch, 1894).

offered by James Martin, the talented Baptist minister of Collins Street, Melbourne.[28] Martin had a knowledge of middle-of-the-road German scholarship which was unmatched in Australia. He had translated a large number of Old Testament commentaries from German into English for T. & T. Clark of Edinburgh, one of the most important theological publishers in Britain. He wrote a short, but insightful, book, *The Origin and History of the New Testament* (1871), for the members of his congregation. In Auckland, and then as Bishop in Wellington, T. H. Sprott, an Irish Anglican, popularized the best contemporary scholarship in his modern study of the Old Testament, which was published in 1909.

In Melbourne, an Evangelical paper, *The Southern Cross*, which was edited by W. H. Fitchett, the founder and principal of Methodist Ladies College, and the Presbyterian paper, *The Messenger*, contained some of the most judicious writing on controversial issues. Melbourne compared with Toronto in Canada for the extent and liveliness of its theological discussions. The Anglican *Messenger* was more cautious. It paid little attention to *Essays and Reviews* (1860) or to *Lux Mundi* (1889), which caused great theological and ecclesiastical turbulence in England in the latter part of the nineteenth century. Even though some of the theological foundations of Protestant Evangelicalism were being eroded from within by those who were persuaded that Christianity must be restated to survive, its moral and crusading fervour was undiminished. Its problem was retention of unity when doctrine, ethics, and education were all changing. In Wanganui, C. H. Garland, a Wesleyan, argued that 'my authority in religion is my conscience, which is illuminated by Holy Scripture, as it is energised by the Holy Ghost'.[29] He did not suggest how to reconcile divisions over the guidance of conscience.

That diversity was reinforced by the revival of personal piety that occurred through the visits of international evangelists, like Dr Somerville or Dr Chapman, in the 1890s and 1900s, and the expansionist mood prior to, and after, Federation in Australia. Bodies like the YMCA and YWCA, youth organizations like the Boys' and Girls' Brigade, Christian Endeavour, and Bible classes all contributed to this. Quite considerable attention was paid to last things, a favourite topic of Freethought lecturers who sought to discredit the irrationalities

---

[28] H. Willoughby, *The Critic in Church* (Melbourne, 1872) 72 ff. gives a comment and critique of Martin's preaching.

[29] C. H. Garland, *Authority of the Bible* (Wanganui, 1893) 19.

of Christianity. They were vigorously answered by defenders of orthodoxy in all the major centres of the colonies.[30] Anglican bishops such as Perry and Moorhouse in Melbourne, or Barry in Sydney, were influential apologists who rebutted the ideas of a sceptical Justice Turner.[31] Some clergy, like the Anglican C. Fetherstonhaugh, supported drastic restatements of Christianity. He was unrepentant about protesting 'against doctrines being taught which are contrary to reason and with that moral sense implanted in our human nature by Him in whose image we are made'.[32]

A number of clergy took a keen interest in natural science and made important contributions to geology, botany, and zoology through the various societies set up in each colony to discuss such scientific matters. Increasing Protestant rejection of biblical infallibility led the Congregationalist George Clarke, in Hobart, to argue that 'God's revelation has never been absolute, but always relative.'[33] Moral commitment to truth and goodness were essential for the sense of what had been revealed. Others, like Lorimer Fison, a former missionary in Fiji, wrote discerning accounts of Victorian Aboriginal life, as did John Mathew, who drew on his recollections of Queensland Aborigines from the time he worked there on stations. His *Eaglehawk and Crow* (1899) is an important pioneer ethnography. Julian Tenison Woods, who was a many-sided figure, not only founded religious orders, and made vital contributions to the development of Catholic education, but was also a competent scientist, who travelled to Malaya in his later years to gather information. A number of missionaries, like R. H. Codrington in Melanesia, made important contributions to ethnography and linguistics, describing local customs and compiling dictionaries of languages in the regions in which they worked.

Finding a method of theological enquiry which enhanced a sense of divine authority, rather than its erosion, preoccupied many Christians for another century. By 1914, liberal Evangelicalism, which stressed the right of private judgement, the authority of the Jesus of the Gospels, and the duty of restating Christianity in terms of modern knowledge, had become influential on both sides of the Tasman in all

---

[30] P. Lineham, *New Zealanders and the Methodist Evangel* (Auckland, 1983); 'Christian reaction to free thought and rationalism in New Zealand', *JRH* 15 (1988) 236–50; G. Duke, 'Science, biblical criticism and the Protestant churches in Victoria, 1850–1900', D.Theol. thesis (Melbourne, 1999).

[31] H. Williams, *Religion Without Superstition* (Melbourne, 1884).

[32] *Messenger*, 4 Feb. 1875, 7.

[33] G. Clarke, *Inspiration Not the Ground of Our Faith* (Hobart, 1885) 9.

the major Protestant churches. Some Anglicans argued that 'the man who limits his belief as to what is in accord with his reason, will also limit his obedience to what is in accordance with his inclination'. The publication of *Essays and Reviews* seemed to some colonial Anglicans to indicate that so far as the authors were concerned 'in their hands the fabric of Christianity crumbles under the touch'.[34] That was important for political as well as religious leaders.

Mapping the religious allegiance of parliamentarians is a complex task, for some resolutely kept their religion private, in order to avoid sectarian problems. Others were very public. In New Zealand, James Fitzgerald, a scion of Anglo-Irish gentry, was a stalwart Anglican, though his political career was erratic. Two of his sons became clergy.[35] Alfred Deakin, an important liberal politician from Melbourne, showed how deeply religious conviction of an unorthodox kind, which could be called spiritualist, could interact with both colonial and federal politics. He served as Prime Minister for three terms after 1903.

Some federal and state politicians were quite open in their commitment to particular denominations, but only rarely did that allegiance shape the way they spoke publicly and voted. They shared in the responsibilities of nation- and community-building like many other settlers from Britain and Europe. They were aware of the ways in which religion could corrupt and divide national life, and were determined to safeguard the liberty of conscience from intrusive political and social pressures. And many saw their nation as broadly Christian with spiritual foundations in no need of political enhancement. So they worked for a society in which religious tests for office were illegal, sectarian conflict was deplored, and there was a modicum of justice and ample opportunity for religious diversity.

One of the few political figures who kept a detailed personal journal was Alfred Deakin, who was involved in spiritualism, and fascinated by Swedenborg and Freethought. His journal shows a deep sense of God's grace, and a large gap between his hopes and the unworthy reality of his experience. He was active in the Victorian Association of Progressive Spiritualists and Dr Motherwell's seances. 'Almost always I realise the existence of God. Always I believe in Him with my intellect and turn to Him with my heart, but I am anxious for a closer

---

[34] *Church Record* (1857) 66; (1861) 95.
[35] O. Fitzgerald, *Leaves from the Life of a Colonial Parson* (Wellington, 1943) gives fine insight into the Anglican ethos.

and more permanent relationship.'[36] Deakin had a growing sense of a divine mission and guidance, and great insight, as well as political flair and ruthlessness, but his contempt for Aborigines showed in the Half-Caste Act 1886. Attendances in the first half of 1887 at the London Colonial Conference confirmed his sense of divine call, and a prophecy of seven years before led him to become an apostle of Federation. He played an important part in shaping legislation on immigration, tariffs, and defence, and in defining a basic wage.

In both Australia and New Zealand a number of clergy were reading liberal, even infidel, books. The doctrine of the Trinity, biblical inspiration, and understanding of prayer and miracles were all vigorously discussed. In March 1882, Bishop Moorhouse of Melbourne refused requests to authorize prayers for rain, saying it was God's will to dam the rain. At the Australian Church in Melbourne, the Revd W. E. Addis rejected the doctrine of the Trinity, for it 'entangles the reason in hopeless contradictions, and it wounds religion, because it demands servile adhesion to a dogma'.[37]

In Christchurch, the Anglicans J. W. Stack and George Cotterell were reading Darwin, Huxley, and Tindall and discussing them privately. Henry Jacobs, another leading Anglican, had one child who became an atheist, another a Theosophist, another a Christian Scientist, while still another later joined Moral Rearmament, a reminder of the difficulty of handing on faith. There were vigorous discussions in Dunedin over what were the boundaries of orthodoxy for membership of the YMCA. A number of rationalists, like Robert Stout, a former Presbyterian, kept more conservative Christians in a state of turmoil by sharp and well-directed ridicule of traditionally expressed faith, while, at the same time, seeking a just and righteous society.[38]

Important cultural shifts were taking place in the community on both sides of the Tasman, reflecting and sometimes preceding changes in Britain, notably in the disappearance of deference to superiors and the aggressive individualism which dismayed genteel bishops' and clergy wives. Holding together a doctrinal consensus defined by educated elites in such a social climate was to prove increasingly difficult.

[36] A. Gabay, *The Mystic Life of Alfred Deakin* (Melbourne, 1992) 40.

[37] W. E. Addis, *Lectures on the Trinity* (Melbourne, 1893) 28.

[38] J. Stenhouse, 'The war between science and religion in nineteenth century New Zealand', *Pacifica* 2 (1989) 61–86; *Encyclopedia of Unbelief* (2 vols., Buffalo, 1982): 'Unbelief in Australia', 'Unbelief in New Zealand'; R. Dahlitz, *Secular Who's Who* (Melbourne, 1994); B. Cooke, *Heathen in Godzone* (Auckland, 1998).

The churches had lost the will to hold moral boundaries on the Sabbath and on integrity in business. Usury as a sin was replaced by the virtue of high dividends. In addition the scientific method of establishing truth by experimenting, and questioning received wisdom, also proved a challenge to traditional ways of theological thinking. An increasing number of clergy celebrated the possibilities of moral and doctrinal freedom to bring in the Kingdom of God. That meant that the historical tradition came to be pruned in accord with the shifting contours of modernity. The social sciences, especially psychology, and the disciplines of philosophy and history, lost their connection with dogmatic and moral truth, as the relativist critique gained momentum. Their development appeared to lie in becoming value-free.

Those who cherished the past appeared to have no defence but reassertion of the theological formulae of previous eras. That apologetic was done intelligently in some divinity faculties, by Charles Hodge and B. B. Warfield at Princeton Theological Seminary, and in some of the articles in *The Fundamentals* (1910), which was an American attempt to hold the line on Protestant orthodoxy. In the Roman Catholic Church, the so-called modernists were severely dealt with after *Lamentabili* in 1907. The anti-modernist oath required of all clergy from 1910 until the 1960s ensured that the dogmas of the faith were strongly defended, reinforced by the catechism taught in parish schools. Catholics took pride in the unity of their faith compared with the disarray of liberal Protestantism, which seemed but the logical outworking of the emphasis on freedom of conscience. The same diversity appeared in worship.

TENSIONS OVER WORSHIP

Church buildings were often very basic, lacking space and furnishings for worship according to the best practice of the British Isles. The Anglican Church in Castlemaine, Victoria, had no font, for example. A teacup filled with water from the nearby creek was used instead. Buildings were often stiflingly hot in the summer, and freezing in winter, and worshippers needed great stamina to plough through muddy bush tracks and unbridged streams to reach the house of God. There were strong clashes in the Church of England over the theological implications of worship, especially in Sydney and Melbourne, where there were many Irish Protestant clergy and laity suspicious of

Romish tendencies. In Hobart also, over 800 laity petitioned Bishop Bromby against the introduction of Romish books and practices in 1872.

The first serious case in New Zealand over innovations in Anglican worship occurred in Kaiapoi under the Revd H. E. Carlyon in 1875–7. His bishop ruled against him on several points and he returned to Britain, where there were more opportunities for innovations in liturgy. By the end of the century, several parishes in Wellington and Auckland had adopted elements of Catholic worship. Methodists and Presbyterians remained hostile to such practices, which they feared would undermine Protestantism. Isaac Harding said Methodists would rather wear shrouds than 'don the fashionable frippery borrowed by her sister Anglicans from the wardrobe of the scarlet whore of Babylon'.[39]

There were also some significant developments in the music used in worship. Anglo-Catholics drew on patristic and medieval hymnody. Towards the end of the century, Negro spirituals were introduced to New Zealand and Australia. Revival hymns, popularized by evangelists, were widely used, and undermined the monopoly previously held by psalms. In Melbourne, the Collins Street Baptist Church introduced the chanting of psalms in June 1870, despite the unease of many of the congregation. Some Australians and New Zealanders began to compose hymns, anthems, Mass settings, and even oratorios. In 1882, in Melbourne, Dr Torrance had composed and led the performance of *The Revelation*. Some church leaders attempted vainly to keep church and worldly music separate. In 1884, Bishop Hale in Brisbane protested violently against the performance of *HMS Pinafore* by choirboys in a Sunday school hall, arguing that they were in danger of corruption if they were introduced to the stage.[40] Choirs had their own ways of pushing their views. In Wagga Wagga, New South Wales, in 1866, the choir went on strike when their minister refused permission to sing 'Kyries'.

The foundation of the Bush Brotherhoods from 1897 to minister to outback Anglicans had a major impact, showing how frontiers can affect other areas. Adventurous young English clergy agreed to come as missionaries, to live very plainly, and to travel widely. Wearing

[39] I. Harding, *High Churchism or Semi-Popery* (Auckland, 1867) 26–7; J. Dickson, *Shall Ritualism and Romanism Capture New Zealand?* (Dunedin, 1912).

[40] A. H. McLeod, 'The introduction of the spiritual to New Zealand', *Baptist Research* 2 (1997) 47–58; *Church of England Gazette* (1862) had lively discussions on the place of music in worship.

full clericals they rode, cycled, and walked hundreds of miles in all weather, to carry the full Catholic liturgy to the outback. They found surprising additions to their congregations, like dogs, horses, not to mention flies and mosquitoes. They had their counterparts in Melanesia, seeing such hardships as part of their calling. Many returned home after their term, but continued to act as agents and ambassadors for the Australian church. A significant group stayed, and became bishops of bush dioceses, and then of major sees like Brisbane, ensuring in the process that the liturgical tradition in large areas of rural Australia was strongly Anglo-Catholic by the 1930s.[41] Laity either stayed away, joined other churches, or gradually came to value the new ways, which underlined the spiritual authority of the Church, and its divine responsibility to order its own life without compromise with the world, creating another sectarianism. In parts of rural Queensland, Protestant hostility to printed liturgy remains influential in the Uniting and Pentecostal Churches, a century later.

Liturgical differences were reflected in church architecture. Initially, many Protestant churches were quite unadorned. 'High' Anglicans and Roman Catholics were much less inhibited. Some very fine Victorian glass can be found throughout Australia and New Zealand, often from English studios like Hardman's of Birmingham. This can be seen in St Andrew's Cathedral, Sydney, and St Patrick's, Melbourne. In St Barnabas's, Norfolk Island, there are fine Burne-Jones/William Morris windows. Local craftsmen, such as Ferguson and Urie in Melbourne, provided quality stained-glass windows.[42] There is beautifully crafted woodwork in the pulpits, pews, and communion tables of some churches, and in the choir stalls of the larger Anglican churches and cathedrals. Where limestone or sandstone of suitable quality was used for windows, archways, and doors, some fine carved stonework can be found, even in Presbyterian churches which might have been expected to eschew such decoration. First Church in Dunedin is a good example.

In a number of places, colonial architects demonstrated what could be achieved by large wooden churches, like St Mary's pro-cathedral in Auckland, built in 1886. Analysis of these sacred spaces is not enough

[41] C. H. S. Matthews, *A Parson in the Australian Bush* (London, 1907); R. Frappell (Teale), 'Anglican ministry to the unsettled rural districts of Australia *c.*1890 to 1940', Ph.D. thesis (Sydney, 1991).

[42] J. Phillips and C. MacLean, *In the Light of the Past* (Auckland, 1983) and B. Sherry, *Australia's Historic Stained Glass* (Sydney, 1991) 90–114 discuss stained-glass. See also F. Ciaran, *Stained Glass Windows of Canterbury* (Dunedin, 1998).

to fill out our understanding of the material piety of the nineteenth century. Pictures in homes, Sunday schools, and church halls, and illustrated family Bibles, all created imagery amongst Protestant Christians. Popular portaits of Jesus could carry important theological messages, giving a sense of divine presence, and conveying emotional messages about Jesus' sympathy and friendship. They also fostered the ideal of a Caucasian Christianity, giving powerful hints on racial purity. Many Protestant hymns portrayed Jesus as a friend, and reinforced the move away from divine transcendence which had characterized earlier centuries. In some Pacific Island churches, such European religious pictures also conveyed a powerful message that Christianity was a religion for Europeans in the first place, with brown-skinned Christians implicitly being seen as inferior.

TRIBAL PIETIES

Owning a Bible was a priority for many Pacific Islanders. In Samoa, for example, the local version of the Bible had sold 20,000 copies by the end of the century, though some missionaries believed that it was not always rightly understood. J. Marriott deplored the fact that few Samoans 'feel deep contrition for sin and the duty of the assurance of pardon'.[43] Strongly Evangelical denominations expected that souls would be saved each Sunday, and appeals were made for sinners to come forward to the penitents' bench to receive the gift of salvation. Christians in this evangelistic milieu longed for Australia and New Zealand to have a mighty revival, such as those which swept through Ireland in 1851, or Wales in 1904–5. Anxiety over irresponsible youth focused in calls for strong religious and moral education to comple-ment conversion from evil ways. Piggin makes clear that there were some districts in Australia where there were local awakenings that influenced Christian witness for two or three generations.[44] Similar impact can be seen in parts of Southland, the Manawatu, or Taranaki in New Zealand, where lay leaders, like Andrew Johnston and Gordon Forlong, continued the tradition through house meetings,

---

[43] *LMS Chronicle*, Oct. 1900, 248.

[44] S. Piggin, *Evangelical Christianity in Australia* (Melbourne, 1996). The diary of E. P. Field (1855–1928) of Sydney gives sharp insight into the spiritual world of an Evangelical layman (Mitchell MS 2435). The Margaret McIntyre papers include moving letters on Presbyterian piety in New England (Mitchell MS 1158). The Vickery papers embody the faith of a notable Methodist family (Mitchell MS 3092).

prayer meetings, and special services. In Clear Lake, Victoria, the whole community, mostly Methodists, gathered for district prayer meetings up until the 1950s.

Roman Catholic piety was centred differently, with a religious universe peopled by saints and angels available for all kinds of needs, who encoded meaning at different stages of life. Pilgrimages were not important in Australasia, till travel to Lourdes became popular, for there were no regional Christian sacred places. Nor were there any local saints, though churches were still so named, and some had stones from associated sites or relics of saints giving a sense of continuity. The rosary was an important devotional aid, sodalities and novenas provided extra opportunities for focused prayers. Marian devotions were also very important for both men and women. Mary presented an ideal of compassion and gentleness, which was complementary to the saving work of Jesus, whose presence on personal and communal crucifixes, statues, and pictures was an essential feature of the Catholic religious landscapes. Until recently, such popular religion has been seen as less authentic than theological and liturgical texts, and left to sociologists and folklorists. Reports of signs and wonders, healings of the New Testament type, and saints' lives reflected experience of transcendent power, but were easily dismissed as subjective. Yet they were influential bearers of sacred messages.

Catholics often prayed privately during the obligatory weekly Mass, treating this as a context for private devotion. Adoration of the Blessed Sacrament was another important focus for parishioners' devotion, as well as for those in religious communities and seminaries. It was a powerful symbol of the presence of Christ. Other symbols, like the Wounds of Jesus, or the Sacred Heart, around which important cults of devotion grew, sanctified the place of pain and assured devotees of divine sympathy, and were signs of Catholic renewal. Bishop Murray, of Maitland, fostered devotion to the Sacred Heart, so that God's order could be restored by prayers of reparation.[45]

Fasting was an important discipline before Mass, and as a way of taming the desires of the flesh. The eating of fish on Fridays was another way of reducing dependence on animal flesh and reminding Catholics of their distinctiveness. There was still strong emphasis on poverty as a great spiritual virtue, which was socially useful for a

---

[45] K. Massam, *Sacred Threads* (Sydney, 1997); D. Morgan, *Material Christianity* (New Haven, 1995); R. Orsi, *Thank You St Jude* (New Haven, 1996); L. Fraser, *To Tara via Holyhead* (Auckland, 1996).

community where many of its members were still unskilled and in the lowest income groups, and where the work of religious was so important. Obedience was inculcated from childhood, being directed not only to parents, but also to religious, clergy, and bishops, who were seen as essentially close to God. As a result, the Catholic community had an inclusiveness and unity, which Protestants could not match. While marriage was still understood as a spiritual second best to virginity and celibacy, the Holy Family was the model for the Catholic family. The ways in which this family was depicted artistically represented the convictions of those who portrayed them, with dress and setting vital in conveying meaning.

The shaping of personal morality and piety by Protestant and Catholic culture had failures as well as successes, but the virtues of faith, hope, and love nurtured disciplined, tough, self-sacrificing people who lived for more than the present, and endured hardship, disaster, and tragedy with a quiet certainty that God would sustain them. The pastorals of Catholic bishops such as Willson and Polding make these links powerfully. The duty of caring for the needy, the ill, and the broken was deeply embedded in colonial cultures, by both secular and religious impulses, as was the importance of honesty, integrity, self-effacement, generosity, and service to the community. Such themes were foundations for the ideals of citizenship and honest government that were becoming dominant by the early twentieth century. For a significant Protestant and Catholic minority, converting others was *the* priority, drawing them into home or overseas missionary work.

In the metropolitan cities, bishops and well-educated clergy, especially Jesuits and Dominicans, could be expected to enter the fray to defend Catholicism, but in country towns there were also some gifted priests who used such views to underline the importance of loyalty to the Church as the ark of the faithful, fostering the fervour with which the authority of the one true Church was administered.[46] Though not the official teaching of the Church, some priests were understood to say that civil and Protestant marriages were not valid in the sight of God, a substantial change from Trent. Some went so far as to speak of children of such marriages as bastards. Strict demarcation lines between Catholic and Protestant meant that, if marriage meant one left the tribal fold, or even dropped into non-observance, such an

---

[46] T. Le Menant des Chesnais, *The Church and the World* (Dunedin, 1905) 204.

errant mortal became a non-person to many in their family. For Catholics, attendance at Protestant funerals was permitted, but not participation in any form of prayer, so that Catholics stayed outside church buildings and heard the service through open windows, or satisfied church law by standing just out of hearing of the minister when he prayed. Strict Catholics invited to Protestant relatives' weddings could enjoy the wedding breakfast, but not share in the service, lest they be contaminated by error.

The sectarian divide between Roman Catholic and Protestant tribalism was one of the most obvious features of the social landscape at the turn of the century. Protestant defence associations had large memberships, but little electoral impact. Many Protestants would have agreed that 'Romanism is the natural and implacable enemy of all forms of freedom' and that 'the Papacy is the deadly enemy of our Empire'.[47] Protestants could not, however, sustain a confessional political party. Nor could Catholics. Occasional sectarian eruptions into colonial and federal politics were still occurring, as well as in local government. It was a reminder that religion reached into many areas of life even for the religiously inactive.

It was specially evident in the Orange Lodges, Masonic lodges and friendly societies, which were very important for Protestants, but are still little-researched bodies. Not only did they provide important support for members and their families in illness, disaster, and death, including participation in funeral services, they also provided religious-style rituals and regalia for laity and clergy. Ironically, many grand masters, senior officials, and members were sturdy opponents of any elaboration of Protestant worship which suggested Roman influences, especially clerical vestments of any kind. Many clergy from the Protestant churches were active lodge members and leaders, because of the social advantages, contacts with men, insurance benefits, and the attraction of belonging to an organization with an aura of secrecy. There is strong anecdotal evidence that, on occasions, Masons actively discriminated against Roman Catholics in employment, and prompted growth of the Catholic Knights of the Southern Cross with similarly secret meetings and rituals.

[47] J. J. North, *Roman Catholicism* (Napier, 1922) 138; T. De Hoghton, *Shall the Church of England be Protestant or Roman Catholic?* (Hobart, 1919) 11.

GODLY WOMEN

Ideas of femininity and masculinity were significantly influenced by the priorities of colonial elites, but were also deeply embedded in the consciousness of the working classes. In Britain and North America, middle- and upper-class women were active in philanthropy, and charitable work. At times they were very independent. In 1872, the Ladies Committee of the Blind Institute in Melbourne was dismissed, because they had appointed a Catholic and a Jew to their number. Miss Margaret Ogg, the daughter of a Presbyterian minister in Brisbane, founded the Sailors' Mission, the Brisbane Women's Club, and the Lyceum, was secretary of the Women's Electoral League for thirty years, and was on the committee of the Queensland Deaf and Dumb Mission. She also fought to raise the age of consent to seventeen, and to gain better provisions for widows.[48] A huge amount of practical help was given locally by women to the poor, outcasts, orphan and neglected children, prisoners, victims of alcohol abuse, and the homeless. Help ranged from money, clothing, and meals to accommodation in specially built institutions.

Though Christian compassion was strong, it was shaped by class perspectives, theological convictions, and moral priorities. Protestant women had considerable freedom to pioneer such work, but lay Roman Catholics were more limited. Not only were women's religious orders responsible for such works, but bishops were uneasy about financially independent movements among the laity.[49] In 1800, there were only 120 nuns in Ireland. A century later there were 8,000, plus thousands who migrated. Catholic lay women were thus often reduced to fundraising and advice, or working as tertiaries. Protestant women were also indispensable and sometimes independent fundraisers. There were some wealthy Protestant benefactors, but in every parish and congregation, women raised money for furnishings, repairs, and charity, even when their efforts were not appreciated. In Inglewood, the Revd William Chalmers deplored bazaars for undermining self-denial 'though they do bring out the zeal and liberality of the female element in our society'.[50] Sectarian boundaries were still important in such benevolent work, though some attempted to be

---

[48] Oxley MS 83/1 M.A. Ogg papers.
[49] M. Luddy, *Women and Philanthropy in Nineteenth Century Ireland* (Cambridge, 1995) 23.
[50] *St Augustine's Occasional papers* No. 88 (1865) 11.

non-sectarian. All denominations were shaped by the reformist ethos, and the desire to control the potentially dangerous behaviour of marginal groups. British, European, and North American initiatives were rapidly copied here.

The most striking example of a nineteenth-century woman leader of a new denomination in Australia was provided by Ellen White, of the Seventh-day Adventists, who was very active in New South Wales between 1891 and 1900, sharing in the purchase of the property at Cooranbong which now houses their key educational institutions, and the Sanitarium health foods factory. She was already writing voluminously, and forging the mix of milliennialism, prophetic ministry, and concern for healthy diet and living, based on vegetarianism, which made the Adventists rather marginal, but respected for their hospitals, schools, and sanatoria.

By the latter decades of the nineteenth century, various new organizations had emerged, like the Anglican Mothers' Union, which came to New Zealand in 1886 and Tasmania in 1892, to foster the sacredness of marriage and enhance the spiritual well-being of children, so that they, in turn, could be adequate parents. Faith missions like the China Inland Mission (1865) enthusiastically accepted single women workers. They were not prisoners of the violent hatred many male British settlers had for Chinese. One Anglican clergyman even claimed that the Chinese were 'the most abominable sensualists in the world. I cannot conceive it to be any advantage to any country to be so over-run with them as Australia is.'[51] Women working in China helped to counter such stereotypes by telling accounts of converts' new life as individuals and in families. Morality seemed the key to personal freedom and achievement, and personal conversion the foundation of morality. Women mission workers accepted low income and poor living conditions, and were then replaced by cheaper local people.[52]

Individual women pioneered new developments without changing the position of women in general. Originally from Nelson, Florence Young, from a wealthy Brethren family with Queensland plantations, began her mission work by teaching in Sunday schools on her brothers' estate. Such initiative was welcomed by some employers, and Melanesian labourers. Other employers were opposed, in case their indentured labourers protested after reading unsuitable books. Some planters made huge profits, and clergy who protested at the ill

[51] J. D. Mereweather, *Diary of a Working Clergyman* (London, 1850) 251.
[52] R. Gooden, 'Awakened women', M.Th. thesis (Melbourne, 1998).

treatment on some plantations were driven out. The Queensland Kanaka mission resulted in many Christians. Some lapsed on return to their islands because of isolation, but others founded Christian groups, and asked Miss Young to send workers. She visited Malaita, Solomon Islands, in 1904–5, and the South Seas Evangelical Mission began.[53]

Others, from the working classes, worked for the Biblewoman's Mission, which began in Melbourne in 1865, a decade after beginning in London. They taught the Scriptures in private home gatherings, or in women's Bible classes in church buildings. Others with more boldness were evangelists. Primitive Methodists and Baptists were prominent. Mrs Margaret Hampson conducted missions on both sides of the Tasman in the 1880s. At Hanover Street, the leading Baptist congregation in Dunedin, Catherine MacDougall was city missioner, undertaking much personal evangelism. Selina Sutherland, a Presbyterian, who had worked for a time in New Zealand before coming to Melbourne, fell out with the Presbyterian authorities in Scots' Church, because she wished to do her social work on a less sectarian basis than just caring for Presbyterians.

A different kind of feminine initiative can be seen in the Anglican Mission to the Streets and Lanes, founded in 1894, in Auckland, following the example of Melbourne in 1885. In both cases, the mission developed into a women's religious order. In Melbourne, a group of deaconesses became the Community of the Holy Name. Led by Mother Esther, it preceded the development of the similar Anglican Order of the Good Shepherd in Auckland, in 1905. In Christchurch, the Community of the Sacred Name arrived in 1893. They provided an important stimulus for the district nursing pioneered by Nurse Maude in 1896. In Sydney, another group, the Sisters of the Church, came from Kilburn, without the invitation of the bishop, and founded a school for girls. They founded other schools in Hobart, Adelaide, and Dunedin in the 1890s. The Dean of Hobart, J. B. Kite, believed that such sisterhood life was 'the exactest expression of the mind, the closest imitation of the life, and the highest embodiment of the spirit of Christ Jesus'.[54]

The deaconess movement, which had been founded at Kaiserswerth in Germany by Pastor Fliedner and his wife, inspired similar

[53] F. Young, *Pearls from the Pacific* (London, 1926). A. Sayven, *Seven Sermons* (Mackay, 1913) exemplifies the preaching of a converted Islander.

[54] *Hobart Church Congress* (1894) 101; R. Fry, *Community of the Sacred Name: A Centennial History* (Christchurch, 1993) 15.

communities of service in other parts of Germany, Britain, Europe, and North America.[55] Mrs Selma Schleicher, a deaconess trained in Dresden, married a CMS missionary in India, came briefly to Sydney, and then returned to Germany to educate their gifted children. Their son became principal of Moore College, and his sisters the first two deaconesses in Australia, from 1885 and 1890 respectively. 'Bethany', a deaconess training house, with a two-year course, was set up in Balmain in 1891, by the Anglican rector Mervyn Archdall and his deaconness wife, Martha. He gave a quarter of his income to fund the venture, which soon included a school, and various forms of compassionate outreach. This initiative suited Sydney well, because sisterhoods were suspected of Popery, while deaconesses were firmly under clergy control. Canon Spencer of Goulburn believed that 'without the female diaconate, the ministry of the Church is imperfect, the Church is maimed in one of her hands'.[56] Sister Maspero, from the Mildmay Training Institution, came to give leadership, bringing another strand of women's ministry to New South Wales.

Methodists in New Zealand opted for a deaconess movement in 1908, unlike their counterparts across the Tasman. There, the Sisters of the People, founded in Sydney in 1884, were diaconal in all but name, spreading to New Zealand in the 1890s. Deaconesses did not gain Australian Conference recognition until the 1930s, as a consolation prize for refusal to admit women to circuit ministry.[57] Presbyterians in Melbourne followed the example of Professor Charteris of Edinburgh, in developing a deaconess training centre, through the persistence of the Revd W. Rolland, a New Zealander who had migrated to Victoria.

One of their first graduates, Christabel Duncan, was invited to Dunedin by Rutherford Waddell of St Andrew's Presbyterian Church, to work in difficult streets with serious social problems. Though his office-bearers were not enthusiastic about an extra financial commitment, Sister Christabel soon won them over, and Waddell's willingness to pay for her first year's salary was soon justified, many times over, by the enthusiasm and insight which she showed. Other congregations, in Christchurch, Dunedin, Wellington, and Auckland, soon

[55] J. E. Olson, *One Ministry, Many Roles* (St Louis, 1992); L. Strahan, *Out of Silence* (Melbourne, 1988); N. Tress, *Caught for Life* (Araluen, 1993); Anon., *The Vision Unfolding: Deaconess Institution 1891–1991* (Sydney, 1991).

[56] *Adelaide Church Congress* (1902) 37.

[57] W. Chambers, *Not Self But Others* (Auckland, 1987); B. Champness (ed.), *The Servant Ministry* (Melbourne, 1996).

followed Waddell's initiative, using Melbourne graduates until a training centre was established in Dunedin. A flow of recruits was inspired by the notable ministries of the young Australians who pioneered this ministry in New Zealand.[58] These young women worked in pastoral, medical, educational, and evangelistic tasks. Many were strongly Christ-centred in their piety, and their diaries give a vivid picture of life among the underclasses in New Zealand and Australia.[59]

Another example of the way women pioneered comes from the South Australian and New Zealand Baptists who worked in the Zenana missions of India, which had grown from the initiative of British missionary wives of the 1860s. Ellen Arnold and Marie Gilbert went to East Bengal in 1882 and died there, in 1931 and 1926 respectively. They preached, taught hygiene, vaccinated, started girls' education, provided homes for widows, and established child care centres. By 1885, young women from Victoria and Queensland had joined them in the Ladies Zenana Mission Society. Rosalie Macgeorge from New Zealand went to Ceylon in 1886 and died there five years later. Three others had gone by 1890—Annie Newcombe, Hopestill Pillow, and Annie Bacon. No formal missionary training was given. Missionaries like these young women were required to resign on marriage, but they usually continued as active, but unpaid, missionaries.[60] Newcombe, who became Mrs H. H. Driver, played an important part in preparing missionaries for service, from her training centre in Dunedin, from 1899 until 1904, when it was taken over by Presbyterians.

Arnold and Gilbert were teachers from Flinders Street Baptist Church, where Silas Mead, a visionary minister, was an influential advocate for foreign missions. Donovan Mitchell saw the significance of women's initiative. 'In Christ the female, placed last by Paganism, has frequently become the first. Mary Magdalene was the pioneer witness of our Lord's resurrection. Lydia was the pioneer convert in Europe. Ellen Arnold was, with Marie Gilbert, the first Australian Baptist missionary to India. Her holy daring secured the honour for Australian women.' At this time there were about 12,500 Baptists in

[58] C. Ritchie, *Not to be Ministered Unto* (Melbourne, 1998); J. D. Salmond, *By Love Serve* (Christchurch, 1962).

[59] Mabel Cartwright's diary from 1907–11 is in the PCNZ archives, Dunedin; M. Tennant, 'Sisterly ministrations', *NZJH* 32 (1998) 3–22.

[60] R. Gooden, 'Awakened women'; H. M. Carey, 'Women's peculiar mission to the heathen: Protestant missionary wives in Australia', in M. Hutchinson and E. Campion (eds.), *Long Patient Struggle* (Sydney, 1994).

Australasia. South Australia had many gifted women, such as the Unitarian Catherine Helen Spence, who created a climate of affirmation and challenge for women in South Australia.[61] Laura Fowler, the first female Adelaide medical graduate, and her husband, Charles Hope, went as independent missionaries to India.

A number of the women who worked for the Baptists did so because their own denomination would not accept women, or because they had been baptized as adults. Particular churches, like Hanover Street, Dunedin, Baptist Tabernacle, Auckland, and Aberdeen Street, Geelong, had strong missionary interests, as did certain families like the Meads, who influenced both Australian and New Zealand Baptists. Many of the women who went to India exercised far wider roles than they would have at home, as well as being less expensive than married couples. They certainly were the majority of serving missionaries. Girls could also take initiatives. In the Bluff Presbyterian Manse near Invercargill, Muriel and Dorothy Laishley raised money and formed the Busy Bees, which involved hundreds of Presbyterian children in learning about missions, and fundraising. The CMS founded training homes for women in Sydney and Melbourne. Helen Plummer, their first woman missionary, went to Ceylon in 1892, and founded girls' schools. The CIM sent out 198 women and 122 men from Australia between 1888 and 1918.

Many reminders remained that women were expected to adorn the private sphere, rather than interfere in the public realm and thus lose the delicate femininity which was regarded by some men as essential to civilization. Girls' schools, such as the Ladies Colleges in Melbourne and Sydney, were still led by male principals, though there were signs of some change as gifted teachers with private means founded schools like Fintona Girls' School in Melbourne in 1896, which employed mostly female staff, under a female principal. Men were often on the governing body of girls' schools, because their skill in finance, building, and maintenance was important. Here and there, churches were permitting women to participate in church government. The Wellington Anglican Synod rejected a proposal, in 1891, permitting women to vote at church meetings, but after women's suffrage was granted, they had changed their mind by 1919. Women could then vote for both synod and parish representatives, but not be elected themselves, until that was approved nationally in 1923.

[61] D. E. Mitchell, *Ellen Arnold* (Adelaide, 1932) 9; S. Magarey, *Unbridling the Tongue of Women* (Sydney, 1983).

Apart from a few evangelists and lay preachers in the smaller Methodist groups and in the Salvation Army, freelance women evangelists would have been unthinkable at mid-century. A number had emerged after the 1850s. By the end of the century, Sister Laura Francis of Sydney and Mrs Emilia Baeyertz had become widely recognized among Evangelical Protestants as credible expounders of the Christian faith. The latter had already broken with her Welsh family's orthodox Judaism when she married an Anglican in Melbourne, and began seeking a deeper experience of God over many years.[62] After his death in 1881, she came into an experience which gave her deep assurance. Beginning by sharing in small groups with the YWCA, she moved into a more public role in Bendigo and Ballarat, then conducting meetings throughout churches in New Zealand, in 1889, and the west coast of the United States, Canada, and Britain, in 1892. Such commitment also nourished pioneers of temperance and women's franchise.

Bishops' and ministers' wives were also important role models in their communities. Many were well educated and idealistic, who saw their role as an opportunity to lead other women into deeper religious commitment. Margaret Herring, a vicar's wife in Upper Hutt, Wellington, wrote vivid letters of her struggles and joys.[63] Mrs Cross in Victoria wrote a number of novels as Ada Cambridge. These spouses chaired meetings of women's organizations, assisted in religious education, gave generous hospitality, and also brought up children. Often they read widely, and were as well equipped as their husbands to lead study groups, and to create networks for service. Retired missionary wives also were an important source of unpaid expertise and energy.[64] Some clergy deplored this growing feminine influence, fearing that women's role as nurturers of piety and morality in the home would be threatened. Even worse, there was a danger 'that the clergy may become less virile, and the influence of women, if it shall have undue sway, is likely to maximise a tendency to inordinate display'.[65]

In the bush, at a lower social level, the wives of home missionaries performed similarly supportive roles on miserable and sometimes

---

[62] Anon., *From Darkness to Light: The Life and Work of Mrs Baeyertz* (n.p., n.d.); E. Baeyertz, *Three Lectures* (Auckland, 1890).

[63] La Trobe MS 8466 MSB 989/6 Margaret Herring papers, 1857–95; M. Broadstock and L. Wakeling, *Rattling the Orthodoxies* (Melbourne, 1991).

[64] J. West, *Daughters of Freedom* (Sutherland, 1997) 201–4.

[65] *Perth Church Congress* (1910) 38.

long-unpaid stipends. The diary of Emma Elizabeth Dau, 1868–1947, reveals this. One of seventeen children, she was married to Alfred Coates, a Methodist home missionary. Her sense of God's presence sustained her in a semi-independent ministry.

On 3 July 1904, she wrote from Chiltern, Victoria,

I conducted the service here at night, had the church full. God helped me wonderfully. I felt his power. We had a good meeting after. I delivered my soul. I gave the message as straight as God gave it to me. I long to see the salvation of souls—it is what I live and work for. O God, save the people is my constant prayer. Two of my class have been converted to God—Mabel and Ruby, for which I give God all the glory.

She was comforted by the thought that when she was tired, Jesus had been weary for her, for she frequently recorded her utter weariness.[66] This Methodist religious passion declined as the movement became more middle-class and economically secure. Methodism moved from being counter-cultural to subcultural, but women's leadership expanded.

EXPANDING COMMUNITY SERVICE

The boom years of the 1880s saw the establishment of many important church-related schools, the beginning of many more hospitals and philanthropic institutions, and the expansion of the parish school networks of the Roman Catholic Church. The suburbs became more attractive to the rich, who sought escape from the noise, smell, and overcrowding of the central city. Ministers of prosperous suburban churches increasingly provided denominational leadership. Protestants and Catholics alike had hopes for reforming society through colonial parliaments and welfare initiatives.[67] New Zealand church leaders had the same large hopes, even though federation with Australia was rejected. Wesleyans, and the smaller Methodist groups on both sides of the Tasman, were negotiating for union. In New Zealand this ended in 1896, though the process was not completed until 1913, when New Zealand gained its own Conference.

---

[66] I am indebted to John Morley for access to this diary.

[67] Hunt, *This Side of Heaven*, 179–209, for reformism in South Australia; C.H. Pearson, *The Higher Culture of Women* (Melbourne, 1875); J. Godden, 'Philanthropy and the women's sphere in Sydney, 1870–1900', Ph.D. thesis (Sydney, 1983); R. D. McEldowney (ed.), *Presbyterians in Aotearoa* (Wellington, 1990) 68–78.

Presbyterians were able to unite on both sides of the Tasman by 1901.

Both churches looked to widen the prospect of reunion by working for a united Evangelical Protestant Church for each nation. The Australian scheme drew heavily on Canadian models, and was ambitious enough to contemplate including the Church of England. A talented Scot, James Gibb, formerly from Footscray, Victoria, led New Zealand Presbyterians in this search. Church leaders tried to inspire their members about the religious possibilities of the Commonwealth, but little changed. Brian Wibberley, of Adelaide, claimed that Methodism had an interpretation of Christ specially suitable for the new era, helping God to make mankind anew by being in touch with the everyday life of the masses. He believed that Methodism had ever found culture

an ally and not an enemy. Unless you live and rule through the people, the end of all our boasted progress will be chaos, vanity and evil. . . . Our future usefulness will be largely determined by our competency to meet the test of social exigency. The followers of Him whose aim was the reconstruction of human society on the basis of a reasonable love can never hold themselves aloof from the problems of social wellbeing.[68]

Reunion in Australia fell through, because some key Anglicans were Anglo-Catholics who detested non-denominationalism, and did not recognize the negotiating churches as anything but Protestant sects, without a valid ministry or sacraments. Those who were Evangelical or Broad Church, and sympathetic, found that there were large legal obstacles, for their church was still an integral part of the Church of England. Initial interest by some Baptists soon waned. That did not mean that Evangelical ecumenism was dead. It assumed new forms in co-operation in missions, in backing evangelistic campaigns, in state councils of churches which attempted to speak on public issues with a united voice, and in foundation of Bible colleges.

Political divisions were also emerging because of divided attitudes to socialism, and the emerging Labour parties on both sides of the Tasman. Many Protestants claimed to see parallels between the teaching of Jesus and socialist hopes for a more just society. In his presidential address to the Congregational Union in Perth, W. F. Turton of Trinity Church spoke of the need for aggressive work. 'The church

---

[68] B. Wibberley, *The Marks of Methodism* (Adelaide, 1906) 105, 186–7, 188; A. Black, 'Church union in Canada and Australia', *Australian–Canadian Studies* 1 (1983) 44–56.

declares its interest in everything that is for the uplifting of Man . . . just as He who is the Church's Master and King showed himself interested.'[69] Significant numbers of Australian and New Zealand Protestants voted Labour, even though there were still distracting confessional and sectarian loyalties. Leaders of the labour movement, like W. G. Spence, often had strong cultural Christian links, and admired Jesus' ethics, but were often sceptical about the churches' support, seeing them as too deeply aligned with the interests of the bosses. J. S. McGowen, Labor premier of New South Wales, was strongly convinced that socialism and Christianity could be inter-related, and he was very active in his local Anglican parish of Redfern. Significant numbers of tradesmen and labourers were worshippers in all churches, as parish registers show.

Depressions and Australian drought hit all the churches hard, prior to the outbreak of war in 1914, but there were some imaginative initiatives, undertaken with minimal financial resources. In Queensland, the energetic and gifted Anglo-Catholic Canon David Garland co-ordinated a campaign and coalition of churches which wore down the state government, so that they were forced to recognize that there was a majority in favour of introducing reading of the Bible in state schools, despite Roman Catholic opposition. Sunday schools did not always bring adequate educational results, though they had significant impact on lay piety, and the way Christian idioms could be reinterpreted. One Sunday school scholar in Dunedin wrote of New Zealand as the promised land, 'we get there by steamer', a recognition that forty years in the wilderness was not necessary in the twentieth century.[70]

In New Zealand there had been similar concerns, since the 1880s, about the absence of the Bible from state schools, but no progress had been achieved until Garland agreed to visit New Zealand, an example of trans-Tasman co-operation, and to run a similar campaign to that in Queensland. He swiftly built a similar coalition of Anglicans, Methodists, and Presbyterians and, by organizing referenda in local regions, began to build up pressure on the government. Some teachers were alarmed that success of the programme could lead to a revival of sectarianism in schools, and disadvantage teachers if they were not in conformity with the local religious feeling. By 1913, the campaign had gathered considerable momentum, but, before the government had

---

[69] W. F. Turton, *The Immediate Work of the Churches* (Perth, 1897).
[70] *Otago Daily Times*, 3 Dec. 1907.

time to waver, the outbreak of war made it necessary to stop the campaign. The funds remaining were used to buy ambulances.[71] The churches in Victoria looked enviously at what had happened in Queensland and almost in New Zealand, but they took no significant action and the situation there remained unchanged.

Another important initiative in the late nineteenth and early twentieth centuries was the expansion of missions to Aborigines, especially in Northern, North Western, and Central Australia. Lutherans and Moravians had never stopped missionary work, but the big three Protestant churches started afresh. So did the Jesuits and Sacred Heart missionaries, at Daly River and on Bathurst Island, in the Northern Territory. British ideas about their right to Aboriginal lands were still strongly held. Bishop Moorhouse of Melbourne rejected the right of Aborigines to occupy land without fencing or tilling. 'God did not make the earth simply for the savage tribes to wander over; He made it to be the scene of happy homes which were supported by honest industry, and if a set of men stood in the way of another set of men doing that work it was the order of divine Providence that the hinderers should be swept away.'[72]

A variety of reasons lay behind this renewed concern for Aboriginal souls, including awareness that the decline in Aboriginal population was serious, and that government policies were unjust. Some Christians felt that reparation for appalling treatment needed to be made, while governments were glad that missions took over responsibility for limited health care and education, thereby saving expenditure. They also welcomed the social control that missions gave to the remnants of tribes which defended their territory against pastoralists and hunters. Missions to the Queensland Aborigines were of little interest to Presbyterians there. Their financial contribution to the welfare of the dispossessed and exploited tribes was minimal.

It was Moravians from Britain and Europe who pioneered work in the far north, financed by Victorian Presbyterians. The work at Ramahyuck in Gippsland, and at Ebenezer in the Wimmera, offered some haven to tribal people whose lands had been taken. The Revd F. Hagenauer at Ramahyuck did all his teaching in English for he believed that 'their own dialects are entirely insufficient to express spiritual things'.[73] Methodists did little for Aboriginal remnants in

[71] McEldowney, *Presbyterians in Aotearoa*, 86–8.
[72] *Messenger*, 14 June 1879, 4.
[73] La Trobe MS 3343 F. Hagenauer letter books, 1 July 1870. N. Hey describes the work of

New South Wales, South Australia, and Victoria, but were willing, in conformity with the romantic vision of missions, to work in the Northern Territory. Western Australian Christians connived at the appalling treatment of Aborigines in the Carnarvon region—in some cases, worse than slavery. When the Revd John Gribble exposed this, after his arrival in 1885, he was rejected by the Anglican establishment which employed him. Bishop Parry found him insubordinate and threatened to withdraw his licence. When he sued the *Western Australian,* edited by a leading Anglican, Winthrop Hackett, for libel over the claim that he was 'a lying canting humbug', Gribble lost his case, was unable to pay costs, and returned east a broken man, which was the message the leading families and graziers wanted to send to whistleblower missionaries.[74] Bishop Parry believed that Aborigines needed to be dependent on station owners rather than regarded as British subjects.

The expansion of smaller denominations can be illustrated by the development of Churches of Christ and Baptists in Western Australia, from 1892 onwards. The first Churches of Christ conference was held in 1898, when there were 289 members in the colony. Baptist beginnings were troubled. Andrew Lambert gathered a small group in his home, but it lasted less than a year, because several members left Perth. George Johnston, an architect and Presbyterian, went to New Zealand for his health, became involved with Baptists, and then went to Victoria. Arriving in Perth in 1894, he worked for Presbyterians, and then worshipped in the Church of Christ before becoming a Baptist evangelist. James Cole of Melbourne, an accountant, arrived in 1895. He supported himself and formed an open membership church on 25 June 1895 which called the Revd Alfred Wilson, a noted writer of devotional books in later life. Cole also founded churches in Fremantle and Katanning. A union was formed in 1896, and exercised a significant role from the outset because the revenues were so slender, and the colony so isolated. Baptists were active in partnership with other denominations, had good contacts with visitors from ships, and grew as the colony's population expanded, but were divided, like Victoria and South Australia, over the nature of membership, until

the Moravians at Mapoon in Queensland. Moravian Archives Herrnhut R15 viib nos. 3–7. Bishop Peter La Trobe was also in regular contact with Sir Henry Barkly, the governor of Victoria, about missions to Aborigines.

[74] Harris, *One Blood* (Sydney, 1990) 381–501; Battye MS MN73, Parry papers; MN134, Parry–Gegg, 9 July 1886; H. Reynolds, *This Whispering in our Hearts* (Melbourne, 1998).

Silas Mead returned to Perth to be with his daughter, Blanche, the Revd Alfred Wilson's wife. Though the Wilsons went to Wanganui, New Zealand, from 1906 to 1913, the schism was ended with Mead's help, by agreement to leave each church to decide the basis for membership. Inspired by the state's optimism after the discovery of gold, Baptists looked to expand. By 1907, 1,066 members were recorded.

CHURCHES AND FEDERATION

The move to Federation of the Australasian colonies demonstrated the determination of leaders to reject sectarianism. Some were willing to create a secular constitution rather than see the possibility of a persecuting establishment.[75] That led to some vigorous discussion on the desirability of 'God' being mentioned in the proposed constitution. Some opponents were strong Christians, who saw no need for any formal relation between religion and politics. Indeed, they argued, with a considerable amount of historical justification, that the freedom of the churches to carry out their mission came from God, and did not need any constitutional foundation, apart from the liberty of individual conscience, and the prohibition of any religious tests for the holding of public office. Seventh-day Adventists, with American precedents in mind, were determined that they should not be the victims of Protestant Sabbatarians who denied them the right to work on Sunday. Some Jews felt equally strongly, even though the number of Orthodox Jews was not great.

Other Protestant groups, like the New South Wales Council of Churches, were not only pressing for the recognition of God, but also for Parliament to be opened with prayer, and for the governor-general to have the power to call days of national thanksgiving and humiliation. The Seventh-day Adventists managed a very effective counter campaign. They were painfully aware that William and Henry Firth had been sentenced to the stocks in Parramatta on 22 April 1894. They had been prosecuted by the New South Wales Council of Churches for working on Sunday.[76] In addition to their

[75] R. T. Ely, 'Australian federation, religion and James Bryce's nightmare', *ACS* (1997/8) 151–69.

[76] R. T. Ely, *Under God and Caesar* (Melbourne, 1976) gives a valuable account of the lead-up to the Constitution. G. and H. Metcalf (eds.), *Parramatta Adventist Church* (Parramatta, 1992) 16–17.

in-house paper, the *Bible Echo*, they also published the quarterly *Sentinel*, and *Herald of Liberty*, modelled on a similar journal in the USA. It reached a circulation figure of 4,000 and its emphases were welcomed by some of the major dailies.

The small Seventh-day Adventist church was able to exercise such leverage because it reaffirmed principles which had already been used by Baptists, Congregationalists, and some Presbyterians to defeat a dual system of education. It distributed tracts door-to-door in tens of thousands and, as a result, won over 22,000 signatures to their petition against any religious clause or declaration of belief in the Constitution. Even the *Bulletin* approved of their common sense, but the recognition petition still managed to gain more than twice the number of signatures, as well as some weighty political supporters.

The first referendum on federation failed on 3 June 1898. Cardinal Moran, who had unsuccessfully stood for the Convention in 1896, carefully intervened in the late stages of the campaign prior to the second referendum, with the result that many priests urged their parishioners to vote for the bill. In Brisbane, the Revd William Higlett, a Baptist minister, argued that federation would enhance Australia's ability to fulfil its missionary responsibility to the Pacific islands.[77] The *pro* vote increased by 36,000, giving the bill a comfortable majority over the almost 83,000 who voted against. Sir George Reid, premier of New South Wales, had also changed sides, and some modest changes were made to the bill, but the churches were clearly influential. Both Moran and the Anglican archbishop, Saumarez Smith, were in favour of Section 116 of the Constitution, which prevented Sabbatarian legislation, and ensured that the governor-general could not proclaim days of humiliation and thanksgiving. The issue of prayers in Parliament, and questions of ecclesiastical precedence, caused some discussion, but the latter was a prerogative matter. Nevertheless, it caused considerable tension, because of the symbolic importance of the issues involved.

Moran refused to share in the official inauguration ceremony when his claim to precedence on seniority was rejected. Smith read the prayer on 1 January. Presbyterians also had some claim to precedence because of links with the Church of Scotland, but failing that they argued for equality. At the opening of Parliament, Lord Hopetoun read a prayer, which created an important precedent. W. Knox and J. T. Walker moved, in each house, that prayer begin each session.

[77] Oxley Library OM 84.47, Higlett Papers.

They had support from all major church leaders in Victoria, and though some argued that this would break S. 116 of the Commonwealth's Constitution, the majority agreed that a standing order was not a law. But the prayer was theist rather than Christian, showing, yet again, that lay Christianity was non-sectarian and not interested in issues of dogma. The prayer was read by the Speaker. There has never been a chaplain to either house, unlike the practice in the US Congress. Only a New Zealand delegate asked about the constitutional position of the Aborigines, who were completely ignored in the final drafts.

EXPANSION INTO MELANESIA

With over 1,200 languages, Melanesian communities have a long history in their region.[78] Archaeology is only in its infancy, but settlement in Papua New Guinea goes back perhaps 50–80,000 years. Agriculture developed in the Highlands as early as *c*.7000 BCE, so that culture contact with Europeans is only a tiny part of the region's heritage. Complex irrigation systems in New Caledonia also indicate very ancient agriculture. Though small in numbers, tribal groups on island coasts showed considerable adaptability, often making very intelligent choices about what parts of the invaders' culture they would use, even though ignorant Europeans dismissed them as savages. Religion was interwoven with all other aspects of their societies, and resulted in Christianity being taken into an existing social system, where spiritual forces were believed to have enormous power for life and death. The depth and sophistication of these cultures was rarely understood in the nineteenth century, or even until the latter part of the twentieth, when many anthropologists studied tribes, and had written up the richness and complexity of cultures which often only had a few hundred people.

Myths about a creator god were found in some areas, though how far they were responses to Christian ideas is uncertain. In others, heroes have divine power, while totems and totemic mythology have great importance in many communities. Important elements of secrecy are preserved in initiation. Group identity was bound up with

[78] P. Swadling, *Papua New Guinea Pre-history* (Port Moresby, 1981); R. H. Codrington, *The Melanesians* (Oxford, 1891); W. Flannery (ed.), *Introduction to Melanesian Cultures* (3 vols., Goroka, 1983–4); M. Leenhardt, *Do Kamo* (Chicago, 1977); G. Trompf, *Melanesian Religion* (Melbourne, 1991).

place, and the well-being of the community always came before that of individuals. Moral codes existed, but their relation to ancestors varied. Trade was widespread, even though hostility to neighbouring clans was endemic, with great emphasis on payback.[79] Reciprocal exchange could be important, and 'big men' gained status by their capacity to give. While men had strong systems of bonding, women also had their own cultural formation, which has not always been given due weight by male missionaries and anthropologists. Much remains to be done to understand how these millennia-old patterns integrated with a Christianity shaped by its European origins. The acceptance of Christianity in Melanesia had many parallels with the process in Polynesia, but was much more dangerous to missionaries and their families.[80]

There were some advantages in being a second stage of mission, because conversions in Polynesia had provided insights into strategy, the tasks of cultural and biblical translation, and church planting. Such learning was not always taken seriously by far-away missionary administrators, with the result that mistakes were frequently repeated as new groups came into Melanesia to evangelize. Missionaries had to draw boundaries between the old culture and the new one they sought to introduce. Whether they were Polynesians, Fijians, or Europeans, they sought to stop warfare, infanticide, sorcery, cannibalism, ritual rape, and the taking of slaves. They had to demonstrate that the Christian God was stronger than traditional deities and spirits and thus to undermine the power of sorcery. They offered healing of diseases, literacy, new technology and crops, longer life expectancy, and, above all, peace, which improved the length and quality of life markedly, as did rudimentary sanitation, better food, and public health measures. In the absence of a clearly defined hereditary chiefly group, it was possible to persuade marginal people to become enquirers, and even to be baptized, though group identity was strong.

Many young men went to work on plantations in Queensland, hastening the process of entering a Pacific economy centred in Australia, and took Christian ideas home when their contract expired. Even though they were often brutally exploited, and at times treated like slaves by unscrupulous and cruel captains who forcibly kidnapped them, others went voluntarily, hoping to acquire the possessions and

[79] A. W. Murray, *Martyrs of Melanesia* (London, 1885).
[80] G. Trompf, *Payback* (Melbourne, 1994); M. Crocombe et al., *Polynesian Missions in Melanesia* (Suva, 1982) 55–78, 131–4.

experience of the wider world which would enhance their status when they returned. Mercer estimated that 62,475 were recruited to Queensland between 1863 and 1904, of whom nearly 40,000 came from Vanuatu and almost 18,000 from the Solomons, especially Malaita. Much smaller numbers, about 3,000, came from Papua New Guinea, and from the Loyalty Islands, around 1,100.[81] Germans in New Guinea also recruited vigorously.

Methodists from Australasia created churches in Papua, and the North and West Solomons. LMS missionaries from Britain, Melanesia, and Polynesia planted the Christian message and a number of cultural changes in the Torres Strait Islands and Papua.[82] Roman Catholics from France, Belgium, Holland, Italy, and Germany pioneered in Melanesia. Lutherans began work in New Guinea and brought another Christian tradition into the region. Anglicans from Australia, New Zealand, and the United Kingdom slowly expanded their outreach in Vanuatu, the Solomons, and Papua.

There had been a long gap since the first recorded contacts between Europeans and Melanesians in 1568, on Santa Ysabel in the Solomon Islands, when Alvara De Mendana was greeted by a local chief, Bile Bangara.[83] In 1595, Mendana returned in the hope of founding a colony, but that was a disastrous failure. No further European Catholic missionary work began until 1844, when Rome carved up the West Pacific, and appointed J. B. Epalle, who had some experience with the Maori, to be vicar apostolic for Melanesia. There were no Protestant rivals, and the Eastern Solomons looked a strategic place to plant the faith, preserve natives from Protestant heresy, and then move on into Papua New Guinea. The attempt was a tragic failure, with killings in 1845 and 1847. No further Catholic missionary initiatives occurred until 1898. 'The blood of the martyrs could not be relied on to be the seed of Christians.'[84] Quinine was to prove a more effective saver of Christian lives.

Anglicans and Presbyterians had more success, building on the pioneering work of Polynesian missionaries.[85] The peace brought

<hr />

[81] P. Mercer, *White Australia Defied* (Townsville, 1995) 33–4.

[82] D. Munro and A. Thornley, *The Covenant Makers* (Suva, 1996); L. Early, 'If we win the women: the lives and work of female missionaries in the Solomon Islands, 1902–42', Ph.D. thesis (Dunedin, 1998).

[83] A. O'Brien, *A Greater than Solomon is Here* (Honiara, 1995) 18–22.

[84] H. Laracy, *Marists and Melanesians* (Canberra, 1976) 30.

[85] D. Hilliard, *God's Gentlemen* (Brisbane, 1978); J. G. Miller, *Live* (7 vols., Sydney, 1978–90) 1. 107.

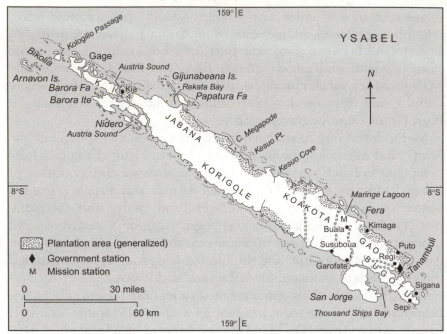

Ysabel (1944). (*Source:* Naval Intelligence Division, British Admiralty, *Pacific Islands*, 5 vols., London, 1939–45, vol. 3, p. 681. © British Crown Copyright/MOD. Reproduced with the permission of Her Britannic Majesty's Stationery Office.)

about by the missionaries was greatly valued, and people melded their culture of generous ceremonial exchange with Christian love. Though elements of the old sorcery survived, the new religion gave a different way of coping with illness, raised the standard of family life, and offered access to European skills and knowledge through schools. In 1848, Roman Catholics came to Aneityum and built a chapel at Angelhaut to the dismay of Presbyterian missionaries. John Geddie, however, received Bishop Douarre courteously when he visited in September 1849, but missionary deaths led to the Marists' withdrawal between 1850 and 1877. The Marists returned from New Caledonia at the urging of the Anglican capitalist John Higginson, who had scores to settle with Presbyterians, but progress in developing a Catholic community was slow.

Christian villages in the New Hebrides provided refuge from oppressive custom, access to trade, schools, and simple medical care. Former slaves, men detribalized by the labour trade, and widows could find a new life. Though some missionaries saw the disadvantages of such villages in making a too sharp disjunction between the old spiritual world and the new, they offered an alternative to intractable clan disputes. Indigenous Christians were certainly under missionary oversight, but they also used the villages as a safe haven in which to experiment with attractive aspects of European culture. Similar phenomena could be observed in parts of Africa. Being free from the association with traditional sacred sites was also liberating, for the fear of sorcery was very powerful in many Melanesian societies. Some indigenous clergy like the Anglican George Sarawia, on Mota, secretly combined the old religion and new. A Christian place for worship, and the sacred power of the Bible and the sacraments, provided a unifying ritual space for the construction of a different kind of society.

PAPUA NEW GUINEA

Papua New Guinea was the last major area in the Pacific to be colonized and evangelized.[86] As recently as 6,000 years ago there appears to have been a land bridge to Australia. The large populations of the Highlands were unknown to outsiders until the 1930s, and many of them were not effectively under Australian control until well after the Second World War. Marist missionaries had a brief stay on Woodlark Island from 1847 to 1855. Samuel MacFarlane, from Lifou, and A.W. Murray, from Samoa, reconnoitred in 1871, and the first missionaries were landed in the same year from the Loyalty Islands.[87] They ceased work by 1889, often accused of causing bad crops. Some local chiefs wished to eat the teachers. At Kiwai, in Papua New Guinea, the chief said, 'Why seek pigs in the bush or across the river whilst we have some here with us? Do you not see that we have had more sickness amongst us since the missionaries came with their God? They are the proper pigs to kill for the feast.'[88] The teachers were tipped off and escaped. There were strong differences among the British LMS missionaries about the best strategy. MacFarlane wanted to use the offshore islands as a base, and educate young men from the mainland, before sending them back to evangelize among their own people. Others wanted to begin on the mainland.

[86] D. Langmore, *Missionary Lives* (Honolulu, 1989) xi lists 327 missionaries to Papua between 1874 and 1914.
[87] N. Sharp, *Stars of Tagai* (Canberra, 1993) 99–125.
[88] *LMS Chronicle* (1885) 207.

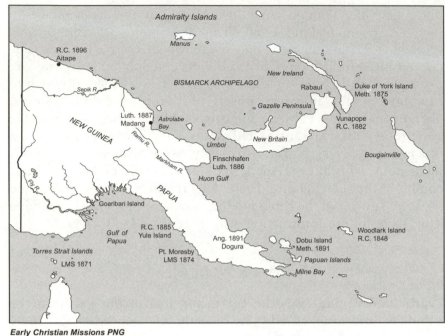

Early Christian Missions PNG

1848	Rom. Cath.	Woodlark Island		1885	Rom. Cath.	Yule Island
1871	LMS	Torres Strait Islands		1886	Luth. (ND)	Finschhafen
1874	LMS	Hanuabada/		1887	Luth (Rh)	Astrolabe Bay/
		Pt. Moresby				Madang
1875	Methodist	Duke of York Islands		1875	Methodist	Dobu Island
1882	Rom. Cath.	Gazelle Peninsula/		1891	Anglican	Dogura Plateau
		Vunapope		1896	Rom. Cath.	Aitape

Papua New Guinea: missions (1987). (*Source:* H. Wagner and H. Reiner, *History of the Lutheran Church*, Adelaide, 1987, p. 320. With permission of Open Book Publishers.)

A formidably experienced team arrived in the 1870s, including William Lawes from Niue, and James Chalmers from Rarotonga. They adapted quickly to Papua, along with Polynesian teachers, of whom Ruatoka was an outstanding example. He was a fine linguist and quickly learnt Motu, which was widely used by the tribes of the south coast. Marrying a local woman after the death of his first wife gave him a secure social place, but his ability in teaching the significance of the *lotu*, in terms that were readily understood, was even more vital for the adoption of Christianity. Ruatoka responded to Chalmers' murder by challenging his home church to send twelve young men to replace Chalmers so that 'the blood of Tamate and his party . . . may result in great good'.[89] Intense competition between

---

[89] *LMS Chronicle* (June 1902) 133.

villages in giving transferred Polynesian custom into a new context. Polynesian singing and dancing were very popular. The Sabbath took root quickly. Ruatoka worked round what is now Port Moresby for thirty years, until he died, greatly honoured, in 1906. An adopted son, Teine Materua, became the first indigenous senior civil servant. The work of such Pacific Islanders was fundamental to the planting of Christianity in Papua, and then in the northern islands. The personal cost was heavy. By 1891, around a hundred had died, many of them wives. By 1906, there were seventy-two Papuan pastors and evangelists, but neither they nor the Polynesian missionaries could provide adequately for the needs of their area.

Polynesian missionaries understood the importance of power encounters with traditional religion.[90] These underlined the helplessness and falsity of the traditional gods. The missionary Timoteo, from Karo in Papua, reported to the Samoa District Council in 1894 that he had cut down a sacred tree, and used its timber to build a church, despite the villagers' fear they would be punished with death. Timoteo replied that 'you must all know there is one true God and He lives in the heavens. Because of His authority we are alive; it is also His authority that will make us die.'[91] Coming from the Cook and Leeward Islands, Samoa (1884), and Niue (1874), and then from Tonga and Fiji, such missionaries left a lasting religious and cultural imprint.[92] Between 1890 and 1942, 150 Fijians also came to Melanesia. Some Islanders failed, many died, and some were very authoritarian, even physically brutal. Some British and French missionaries disliked Samoans for their insistence on status and their sense of equality with Europeans.

New styles of housing, better hygiene, superior fishing and gardening techniques, and new foods like mango, taro, and breadfruit, underlined the advantage of Jehovah's religion, as did the peace which followed the adoption of Christianity, with forgiveness and reconciliation replacing payback. At Saguane, Hiro from Rarotonga described how he told the people that 'I had come to bring them words of peace'. They then planted a peace tree after smoking tobacco together.[93] Villagers were introduced to an elementary cash economy.

[90] D. Wetherell, *Charles Abel and the Kwato Mission* (Melbourne, 1996) 80–95.

[91] *LMS Chronicle* (1894) 349.

[92] U. F. Nokise, 'The role of the London Missionary Society Samoan missionaries in the evangelisation of the South West Pacific', Ph.D. thesis (Canberra, 1992) 349, 363 for ministerial recruiting songs to attract missionaries to join them.

[93] *LMS Chronicle* (Aug. 1900) 196.

Stiff fines, and penalties for breaking the Christian moral code, made it necessary for people to obtain cash. Competitiveness in fundraising and sport partly replaced fighting. As C. S. Abel at Kwato put it 'We transformed our spears into wickets and our shields into cricket bats.'[94] Local people thought that the missionaries were either desperately poor, or fugitives from their native land, for what normal person would leave their tribal land, and the security that gave?

By 1890, Australasian Methodists led by W. E. Bromilow had also begun work on Papua's south-east islands and in the Solomons under J. F. Goldie, following initiatives in New Britain and New Ireland in 1875, thanks to the persuasive powers of George Brown, who was Secretary of the Conference Missions Committee.[95] After putting the Wesleyan mission in Samoa on a firm basis, George Brown wished to emulate the LMS in their expansion into the Melanesian Islands and Papua. He had his eyes on New Britain, and shared his vision, on deputation in Australia and New Zealand. Henry Reed, already a generous benefactor to a number of worthy causes, gave a boat, bearing his own name, and Brown recruited Samoan and Fijian Christians to assist the pioneering venture, which began in 1875.

The proposed mission was not under any European political jurisdiction. Germans were beginning to trade there, as Brown knew from contacts in Samoa. He was excited by the potential for adventure and fresh achievements. He mixed easily with administrators and businessmen, had a keen intellect, was a good linguist, and was fascinated by native customs. His ability to trust his island colleagues enabled them to explain the new *lotu* in readily understandable terms. Brown could also be an impossible colleague, brutally tactless and unsympathetic, overreaching himself. He saw that the people with whom he wished to make contact were already keen traders. He stayed for fourteen months, making contacts, but malaria hit them hard. Most of the wives died, and the teachers were reluctant to occupy the places he allocated, possibly sensing that, while he was absent in Australia and New Zealand, they were at risk without a white protector. By the end of 1877 he had established twenty-three stations. A volcanic eruption added excitement, but did not check their mission.

Despite illness, Brown and his colleagues worked to establish churches, but the local people were suspicious, and the chief Talili determined to end the missionary incursions. Five Fijian missionaries

---

[94] *LMS Chronicle* (Oct. 1900) 252.
[95] W. E. Bromilow, *Twenty Years among Primitive Papuans* (London, 1929).

were killed and eaten, in April 1878. A punitive expedition led by Brown burnt Talili's house, and destroyed his canoe. The missionaries' bones were recovered. Another party led by traders killed a number of people. These actions caused a storm of disapproval back in Victoria and New South Wales, but Brown also had powerful and articulate defenders in the Conference. Despite an almost fatal illness, Brown was never one to run for cover. He went to Fiji to place himself at the disposal of the Western Pacific High Commission, where a charge of manslaughter was to be heard by Chief Justice Gorrie. Sir Arthur Gordon was sympathetic to Brown, and, the night before the trial, withdrew the charges on the grounds that there was inadequate evidence. Gorrie fumed, but the trial was aborted, and Brown departed, discreetly refusing a congratulatory dinner from settlers.[96]

Australian Anglicans did not have the same missionary relations with the Pacific as their counterparts in New Zealand, and responded unenthusiastically to MacGregor's invitation in 1909 to work in Papua. MacGregor's challenge was met in a piecemeal way. Australian Anglicans' giving was derisory for many years. The SPG gave £1,000, but the Australian Board of Missions merely gave Albert Maclaren permission to raise money, to fulfil his vision of a new mission field. Maclaren's meeting with Copland King, a descendant of an early governor of New South Wales, was a decisive event. King was an Evangelical, who longed to work in Papua. He was a fine linguist. Maclaren romantically wanted to create a truly Catholic and apostolic church amongst the tribes of New Guinea, freed from the corruptions of Rome and Protestantism. When the party landed, they met Abrieka Dipa, who had worked in Queensland and begun teaching Christianity in Bartle Bay. He was dismissed by Maclaren for sharing in the proceeds from the sale of land, an act which showed Maclaren had no grasp of Melanesian ideas of exchange.

Maclaren died of malaria and Copland King did not wish to become bishop. He wanted to be a frontier missionary. Stone-Wigg was consecrated, and brought great strengths as a fundraiser and networker with the powerful, for he had married Elsie Mort of Sydney. He had substantial private means, and excellent connections with governors and premiers, but could rough it with the toughest. Fascinated by mythology, he saw the importance of making Christian connections,

[96] J. Garrett, *To Live among the Stars* (Suva, 1982) 224–9.

and encouraged his staff to embrace celibacy, poverty, and hardship as a way of modelling Christ, and identifying with the material poverty of their people. He joined his people at 5 a.m. to work in gardens. Others taught carpentry and boat-building. Priests received £24 a year, whereas LMS staff and Wesleyans were paid over £100. Most, however, had comfortable houses, and were generous in their hospitality to visitors.

Curiously, this group of Anglo-Catholics had almost no relationship with their counterparts in the Melanesian mission, despite the fact that they could have learned much from each other. The sea was too formidable a barrier. To begin with, over forty teachers from Queensland plantations worked for the mission. James Nogar was an impressive Tannese, but other significant teachers were Harry Mark, Bob Tasso, Willie Holi, and John and Timothy Gela. The mission did nothing significant to remedy their educational deficiencies, and was unsympathetic about the failure of some to live up to the early ideals of celibacy. Some of them were very articulate, and resented the patronizing manner and racism of some of the English missionaries. A. K. Chignell was very mocking of their limited English, and Wilfred Abbott told one, 'We don't like black men',[97] which suggests a class-based racism which would make it difficult to trust local Christians with leadership. English missionaries refused to use pidgin, but made little attempt to teach adequate English. Language about 'a child race' illuminates the mindset of such missionaries.

People had ways of showing resistance like teaching missionaries obscenities, urinating in their gardens, and staying away from services, but the elders did not totally oppose young people receiving a missionary education, or the rescue of abandoned children. Missionaries were seen as more powerful priests, with their prayers having magical powers. False teeth seemed very powerful magic, for no sorcerer could trump that. Dreams and visions remained important, and many found the teaching of Christianity on life after death very compelling and attractive. Adaptations of Christianity appeared as early as the 1890s.

---

[97] D. Wetherell, *Reluctant Mission* (Brisbane, 1977) 119.

CATHOLICS AGAIN IN MELANESIA

Following the expulsion of religious orders from France in 1880, Propaganda in Rome persuaded the Sacred Heart fathers to undertake mission work in Melanesia in 1881. The Marists already had a significant presence in New Caledonia. Henri Verjus, an impetuous and independent priest, who undertook mortification to win souls from Satan for the sake of Mary, went to Yule Island in 1885, hoping to reach the mainland quickly, for Rome was anxious to evangelize Papua. Sisters from the Daughters of Our Lady of the Sacred Heart came the following year, and provided an important complement to the male missionaries. The LMS opposed these Catholic incursions, but the Sacred Heart fathers ignored what they saw as illegitimate Protestant comity agreements in which they had no part, believing that Protestants were as much in danger of eternal damnation as the heathen. In 1889 André-Louis Navarre's huge vicariate of Melanesia–Micronesia was divided three ways.

Despite the reluctance of some of the missionaries to learn English, they built up good relations with the natives and some traders, and won the grudging respect of MacGregor and his administration, even though Navarre read the worst into MacGregor's actions, and was implacable about Protestants and Freemasons.[98] His experience of an anti-clerical government in France led him to read the same kind of hostility to the true church in the neutrality of the British administration, for how could Protestants be trusted? Though not a good administrator, he was perceptive about the tasks of mission, and in 1896 published a very practical work called *Handbook for Missionaries*. Not all the difficulties were of his own making, but stemmed from tensions between being bishop, and yet not being allowed the role of a religious superior. This conflict between episcopal power and religious obedience was to remain a problem well into the next century.

Alain De Boismenu, a notable bishop from 1900 to 1945, was totally opposed to the Papuan administration's policy of allotting spheres of influence to missions, and attempted to expand as much as possible, even though his staff was overstretched, and there were constant financial deficits. He and his clergy explored the region, braving great

---

[98] J. Waldersee, *Neither Eagles nor Saints* (Sydney, 1995) 188–9, 234, 644; M. Venard, *History of the Daughters of Our Lady of the Sacred Heart* (Gordon, 1978) 15.

dangers from hostile tribes. By 1900 progress was obvious, in an area with six languages, and over 4,000 linked with the mission. Progress in literacy was slow. By 1916 only 115 children could read.[99] Many were nominal, and did not see the importance of attending Easter communion. There were still deep fears of spirits, and Father Guis claimed that Papuans were the most superstitious people in the world.[100] Schools were used to attract former Protestants and to build up converts. De Boismenu insisted on a long catechumenate, so that a strongly sacramental community could be built. He also had deep insight, and set out the duties of catechists in 1916, though expecting they would always be under European guidance. The mission's work was bedevilled by differences between De Boismenu and Navarre, who had resigned in 1907 but still hung on to the remnants of power until his death in 1911.

Further problems were caused by the difficult religious situation in France, which almost destroyed the Daughters of Our Lady of the Sacred Heart, by poor administration in the order, and by the juris-dictional problems of boundaries between bishops' and religious superiors' authority. A Papuan society, the Handmaids of the Lord, complemented the work of the French sisters from 1918, while the Little Brothers, formed in 1920, included among their number Louis Vangeke, who was later to become the first Papuan bishop.

In New Britain, the Sacred Heart fathers had serious problems because, being French, they were not approved by the German authorities. Couppé, based at Vunapope, however, made skilful use of the society called the Anti-slavery Work of Cologne to redeem slaves, and provide them with special new villages. In addition, he expanded into Methodist territory, and claimed that 90 per cent of the people of the Gazelle Peninsula had moved from Methodism to Roman Catholicism, even though he neglected communities in his official territories. Like Navarre and De Boismenu, he had constant problems with superiors who refused to allow him to combine the role of religious superior and vicar apostolic. In 1912, he set up the indigenous Sisters of the Immaculate Heart, in part because he found European sisters were unwilling to learn local languages. Chronically short of funds because of his focus on expansion, and the inability of people in Europe to understand how costly it was to live in New Guinea, he

[99] Waldersee, *Neither Eagles nor Saints*, 240, 644.

[100] J. Guis, 'Have the Papuans a religion?', *Proceedings of the First Australasian Catholic Congress* (Sydney, 1900) 829–42.

nevertheless laid the foundations of a strong indigenous church. Priests like Joseph Meier made significant contributions to the journal *Anthropos* on the rich cultures of the region and the possibilities of enculturation.

German colonial aspirations for New Guinea provided an opportunity for missionaries from both Protestant and Catholic regions of the newly united country, where strong currents of religious renewal inspired young men to work in this dangerous new territory.[101] The first Lutheran missionary came from the South Australian Synod, where he had served at the Bethesda Mission to Aborigines in Central Australia. Johann Flierl and his wife, Louise, arrived at Finschafen in July 1886, after some delays while the authorities decided what to do with a missionary. Educated at Neuendetteslau, Bavaria, with its strict Lutheran confessonalism and warm piety, Flierl had fitted in well with the similar emphases in South Australia, and had useful contacts with other graduates who had gone to Iowa in the USA, and from whom important help for the mission was to come in later years.

Another group, the North West German Rhenish Mission, had also been seeking entry.[102] It was also deeply influenced by pietism, but was willing to co-operate with other missions because it accepted the ecclesiastical unity which was an anathema to the strict Lutherans. The first missionaries, Wilhelm Thomas and Friedrich Eich, were both experienced missionaries from Indonesia and South West Africa respectively. They arrived at Madang early in 1887 and, after consulting Methodists in New Pomerania, began a station at Bogadjim late in 1887. Both were forced to leave because of severe malaria. They were associated in the minds of the local people with the colonizing activities of the New Guinea Company, which had seized considerable areas of land for plantations, without any adequate compensation. The first baptism occurred in 1903, but instead of being the beginning of progress, was quite atypical.

The real feelings of the people were shown in July 1904, when a plot to murder all Europeans was discovered. One of the missionaries, Helmich, served on the court which sentenced six leaders of the plot to death. Others were involved in brutal punishments, and attempts to

[101] J. Garrett, *Footsteps in the Sea* (Suva, 1992) 24–4; P. Steffen, *Die Anfänge der Rheinischen, Neuendettelauer und Steyler Missionsarbeit in Neuguinea* (Rome, 1993); H. Wagner and H. Reiner (eds.), *The Lutheran Church in Papua New Guinea* (Adelaide, 1987) 35–9.

[102] H. Schutte, 'Magie und Volkskultur: Zu Briefen Rhenischer Missionare aus Neuguinea', in U. van der Heyden and H. Liebau (eds.), *Missiongeschichte* (Berlin, 1996) 215–24.

stamp out initiation cults, but, despite these follies, some of the communities saw that the mission offered possible protection, and a group in 1907 came with their sacred artefacts to surrender them in exchange for instruction in the Bible. Hymns were a novelty. In one village the elders told schoolchildren, 'Stop that new-fashioned howling. You crow like the leatherhead birds. Climb up and join them in the trees but spare us from that in our houses.'[103]

The German annexation of Western Samoa in 1900 opened the way for Samoan missionaries to come in 1912–13, because of the co-operation of the LMS and the Barmen mission. They were able to understand elements of local language, were culturally close, and understood something of German ways. Their evangelistic and pastoral effectiveness weakened hostility to German missionaries, and led to the formation of a significant church by 1932, when the Barmen mission withdrew, and handed over to a branch of the Lutherans. The Samoans' authority was helped amidst all the confusing stages of colonial change after 1918, by their sense that they were missionaries of the Samoan church with its strong tradition of independence, and the status accorded to pastors. They broke the institution-centred educational approach of the mission, and recognized the importance of power encounters in breaking the hold of the primal spirit world and demonstrating the superior power of the new God. Faea, the wife of Asafo, dealt with one of the local sorcerers, Masar, by giving him some of her hair and challenging him to do his worst. He failed, gave up his sorcery, and became a friend of the missionaries.[104]

Hanke, Blum, and Willenkord made important advances along the Rai coastline, including the education of local evangelists, the adoption of Graged as the mission language, and coping with the complications of the Australian mandate after 1918. Their work was absorbed by the Neuendetteslau Mission in partnership with Australian and American Lutherans, for which the Brisbane pastor, Otto Theile, deserves much credit. He played a crucial role in the difficult war and post-war years, underlining that good administrators can be worth their weight in gold in troubled times.

The Bavarian ethos of the other mission, and the strict separation of functions of church and state, led Flierl to distance himself from German colonizing activities. In late 1886, Flierl began a station at Simbang, living very simply and assisted by Methodist volunteers. He

---

[103]   M. P. B. Felde, 'Song and stance', Ph.D. thesis (Chicago, 1994) 68.
[104]   Wagner and Reiner, *Lutheran Church in Papua New Guinea*, 122–3.

was accustomed to hard work and roughing it. In addition, he had a keen strategic eye, and saw the possibilities of the hill settlements, which also had the advantage of being more free from malaria, a fact underlined by his wife when she arrived two years later. In 1892, Flierl moved to Sattelberg, inland from Finschafen. He saw the value of both the Kate and Jabem languages, and sought to understand local culture. He could be easily identified as a 'Big Man', a source of trade goods, education, and a new kind of spiritual power. Word about returning ancestors played some part in disposing local people to look favourably on the missionaries, especially since they were clearly not landgrabbers. Flierl's experience in, and links with, Australia were very significant. In 1889, Freda Goertz joined the mission and acted as a much-needed nurse, once she was freed from her obligations as housekeeper to her brother, who worked for the New Guinea Company. Medical mission work developed from the 1890s, and made a deep impression on the natives.

The five pioneer missionaries laid vital foundations, and began wrestling with translation issues, such as the best word to use for 'God', and how to explain atonement and incarnation. By 1899, Tobias Kaboing and Silas Kamungsanga had demonstrated that they understood that Jesus was their Saviour, and had mastered the basics of Lutheran doctrine. They were the first to be baptized. Flierl also began plantations, sawmills, and mission ships, as well as a printery at Logaweng, where Jabem missionaries were prepared. This helped finances, and also provided valuable employment. A similar school was founded at Heldsbach for Kate speakers.

Christian Keysser, who arrived in 1899, was to become one of the most notable missionaries of the twentieth century, quickly learning the Kate language. He also saw very early that people lived in a strongly communal world, and did not make individual choices like Europeans. As knowledge of local languages grew, missionaries came to appreciate their richness and flexibility. Keysser, therefore, insisted that natives could not be converted as individuals, but must come as a people. Group evangelization was a new concept for many missionaries, though there were similar movements in India and Africa, and many Polynesians had become Christians in the same way. Keysser became a partner with Zake of Bare, with whom Flierl had also established good relations. They hunted together, and talked. Gradually, Keysser persuaded his friend that sorcery and war were not effective ways of solving tribal disputes, that past misdeeds must be confessed, and the instruments of the old religion publicly repudiated. The result was a meeting and feast at Bare in November 1903, where the guests put aside their spears. Zake confessed his sorcery and murder. Others followed his example, and weapons and aids to sorcery were buried beneath a tree. It was a classic power encounter, which underlined the status of Keysser and other missionaries, for other similar ceremonies took place in the Huon region.

Keysser did not think it was necessary to spend a long time preparing individuals for baptism. Group baptisms were another act in the visual drama of salvation. The first among the Kate took place in May 1905. The leaders of the community remained, but with new responsibilities. They disciplined offenders, were encouraged to discuss suitable forms of worship, administered baptism, and sent missionaries to tribes which were traditional enemies. A major earthquake in September 1906 was understood as a warning from Anutu, the name given to God, and hundreds began attending worship, and savouring a life without constant danger of death by payback. In addition, local religion strongly linked worship and material blessing. Some expected miraculous access to European goods from their experience of working for Europeans. Cargo cults (or adjustment cults as they are more accurately called) were a very important religious phenomenon throughout Papua New Guinea in the twentieth century. Local leaders attempted to link old convictions and a strange new world, on their terms, rather than rely on the disappointing response of missionaries. They were often seen as having concealed secret knowledge, which they had not passed on to the local people in order to secure their own wealth and status. Keysser also prepared the first young men as missionaries in 1907.[105]

During the First World War, Flierl's Australian experience made it easier for the Australian authorities to recognize the spiritual independence of the mission, and not to react too heavily to German staff as potential traitors. Only Steck and two others were interned in Australia. The work of the mission continued with a strong indigenous emphasis, but with Australian–American partnership, as well as sympathetic help from the Anglican mission whose territory adjoined. Australians were working towards some interdenominational partnership in mission, following the great missionary conference in Edinburgh in 1910. London Missionary Society missionaries were keenly

[105] Wagner and Reiner, *Lutheran Church in Papua New Guinea*, 47–8.

interested in its implications, especially since the Society had a serious deficit by 1913. That led to the handover of the Torres Strait Islands region to the Anglican diocese of Carpentaria. Despite this excision, the work of the LMS throughout the Pacific was considerable. There were 22,000 members, 48,000 adherents, 400 schools catering for 21,000 pupils. In Papua itself there were fourteen missionaries, and 112 native teachers, indicating that the development of an indigenous church there was not far away.

A number of the Neuendetteslau staff were quite outstanding in their grasp of local culture, language, and ethnology.[106] Their learned articles and books were unique in the region and still provide remarkable insight into a world that has been lost, even though their observations are inevitably coloured by their own cultural assumptions. Their translation of the Bible, hymns, and educational materials gave their converts an important entry to the strange new world of the Europeans, as well as resourcing a church which has become very significant in the Christianization of Papua New Guinea.

One other important strand of mission remains to be described— that of the Divine Word fathers, who also took no notice of Protestant boundaries, and travelled anywhere there was an opening, from their arrival in 1896. There were also serious problems with the German authorities in New Pomerania. After complicated negotiations with the German government and the New Guinea Company, the first Divine Word missionaries from Germany arrived in August 1896, at Madang, to work in the prefecture of Wilhelmsland under Fr Eberhard Limbrock, an experienced missionary.[107]

Initially the Divine Word fathers' request to the German government was coolly received, but the position of Catholics improved with the ending of the *Kulturkampf*. The desire to counter French missionaries also helped their case. Father Limbrock, two other priests, and two brothers arrived at Wilhelmshafen on 13 August 1896. With thirteen years of experience in China behind him, and a close identification with the pastoral and practical emphases of the Divine Word founder, Arnold Janssens, Limbrock had the task of preparing for a bishop.

Their work began on Tumleo Island, an important trade centre.

---

[106] Many important papers are in the Lutheran archives at Lae in the Neuendetteslau mission file, vol. 1, no. 55/10 Conference papers 1899–1938, 55/20 J. Flierl MS.

[107] H. Bettscheider et al., 'Divine Word missionaries in Papua New Guinea 1896–1996', *Verbum* 37 (1996) 41–70.

The missionaries set quickly to work on the task of language-learning, and the creation of plantations which would help to make their mission self-supporting. Limbrock believed that 'Christianity without work is of little value. It will become superficial and contaminated. For idleness is the beginning of all vices. But without Christianity there can be no decent living culture and no sound progress.'[108] Schools were founded, with children being given to the mission as they were according to custom, so that communication between tribes would be kept open. Sometimes those who had taken an interest in the mission expressed surprise that they were not being rewarded, according to their understanding of mutual exchange.

Limbrock's policies created a powerful link between the new religion and material progress. The Divine Word fathers from the beginning had a deep respect for the customs of the local people and did not seek rapid cultural change into black Germans. They refused to use pidgin, arguing that it was demeaning, and that those associated with the mission needed to know German if they were to play a role in the colony. Understanding the culture of those to whom they ministered was a basic commitment. Fr Wilhelm Schmidt believed that such study was greatly assisted by the study of anthropology. His congregation was one of the first to do this systematically, and has published *Anthropos* from 1906 to further this aim. A group of dedicated priests like Holtker, Gerstner, Erdweg, and Puff gathered a variety of ethnographic and linguistic information which remains an invaluable source about cultures, especially from the Sepik region.[109]

Limbrock's strategy did not find acceptance in Rome, and in 1913, the region was divided between the Divine Word and the Picpus fathers. Limbrock resigned, but the outbreak of war delayed the arrival of new colleagues. For a time he continued as a solitary missionary, but died before he could be dispensed from his vows, a step which he had undertaken out of frustration with his situation. He was one of the most influential missionaries in the region, for the Catholicism he transplanted to New Guinea with his colleagues took root in a variety of cultures, creating a Catholic diversity in unity, and liberating energies for meeting the challenges of the twentieth century.

Throughout the region, a variety of Christianized societies had developed in the Pacific Islands, enabling Islanders to deal with Euro-

---

[108] H. Bettscheider et al., 'Divine Word missionaries in Papua New Guinea 1896–1996', *Verbum* 37 (1996) 235.

[109] Ibid., 71–8.

pean challenges to their way of life, and to develop substantially indigenous churches. That was not so obvious in the settler churches of Australia and New Zealand, but they were developing priorities and emphases which diverged from parent bodies. Even more important, they were major contributors to the core Anglo-Celtic culture of the colonies and its significantly Christian lay ethos. Dismissed by church leaders as nominalism, it was much more, notably a redefinition of Christianity in lay terms.

5

WARS AND DEPRESSION

The churches in Australia and New Zealand faced common problems after the end of the 1914–18 war.[1] Many had argued that British patriotism was ever sacrificial in upholding treaties, and the war therefore a spiritual enterprise. The Presbyterian minister at Killara in New South Wales, A. P. Campbell, dealt with these issues on Empire Sunday 1917, affirming that, 'It has stood for the defence of Justice, Freedom, and Truth. And not for the first time in her long history is the body of her being bled that their eternal verities perish not from the earth.'[2] Many who had served overseas found such theology unbelievable when they returned with physical and emotional wounds which would never heal. The influenza pandemic was a further reminder of the fragility of life and the inadequacies of health care, and a challenge to theodicy. Numbers of families continued to grieve for the dead, or found coping with the returnees very demanding, for knowledge about dealing with trauma was scant.[3]

Some of the lessons of war, however, could be applied in more constructive ways. The Royal Flying Doctor Service, which was established in 1928, transported patients from outback Australia. One of the founders, John Flynn of the Australian Inland Mission, embodied the vision of the young airman Cliff Peel, killed in 1918, who saw the potential in aircraft as a means of saving outback lives in peacetime for people hundreds of miles from medical help. By 1998, flying over 9 million kilometres, the service dealt with 159,000 patients.

---

[1] T. H. Sprott, *Redeeming the Time* (Wellington, 1948) 295–308, for a statement on Christian citizenship in wartime.

[2] A. P. Campbell, *Why Do These Men Thus Die?* (Killara, 1917) 8.

[3] J. Damousi, *The Labour of Loss: Mourning, Memory and Wartime Bereavement in Australia* (Melbourne, 1999).

THE FIRES OF WAR

The outbreak of war in 1914, and the following years of struggle, showed that the churches' leaders on both sides of the Tasman were strongly identified with the passions of patriotism, and infrequently able to distinguish between the claims of national self-righteousness and justice. Chaplain Major William Grant of New Zealand wrote proudly of his Gisborne boys, 'The sacrifice is necessary for the world's life and well being, and our hearts beat high with pride that men in multitudes are ready to volunteer for this high service.'[4] Sermons and official pronouncements were full of calls to sacrifice, and service of nation. Identification with the perceived interests of the Empire and the need to resist German aggression ensured that those who volunteered were strongly supported by every level of the community, yet Australian voters twice rejected conscription. Archbishop Mannix's opposition was influential and he was demonized as a traitor by many Protestants.

Huge crowds attended farewells, and many found it natural to commend their loved ones by attendance at special church services, and more regular prayers. Most of the young men who so boldly volunteered had no idea of the horror of what awaited them and how many of them would be buried far from home, or maimed for life. Those who failed to volunteer were sent white feathers, and ostracized by 'patriots'. That should not obscure the importance of well-informed church leaders, like the Anglican Archbishop of Brisbane, St Clair Donaldson, who were able to integrate patriotism with a sense of sin, and see that God's judgement covered all the combatants in war. They saw the ambiguity of defending the moral order by war, but reluctantly saw no alternative.

The Gallipoli Campaigns, following the landing on Sunday 25 April in 1915, soon reminded the volunteers of the huge cost of war. Between 1914 and 1918, 60,000 Australians died, out of 332,000 who went overseas. The New Zealand deaths were 16,000 out of 100,000 who served. The courage and initiative of the young men, who fought so bravely against the determined Turks for no strategic gain, won admiration on both sides of the Tasman. Commemoration of Anzac

---

[4] M. McKernan, *The Churches at War* (Sydney/Canberra, 1980). R. M. Lang, *Shall War and Militarism Prevail?* (Christchurch, 1911) 32 argued that producing good citizens was far more productive than making soldiers. W. Grant, *In Memoriam* (Gisborne, 1915) 32.

Day, which began in 1916 through Canon Garland of Brisbane, and which spread quickly to New Zealand, and became a national day in Australia in 1922, touched deep chords of religion beyond denominational boundaries. The virtues of compassion for the wounded, loyalty to comrades, and courage in the face of suffering and adversity were frequent themes in the sermons and addresses of chaplains.[5] Yet, the more thoughtful chaplains came to recognize that these were also secular values among the troops, which were not explicitly connected with the churches' life and worship. That was seen in war memorials with strong classical, rather than Christian, associations.[6] Women's contribution to the war effort was excluded in both the Anzac services, and in writing about the troops, which has attracted strong criticism from feminist historians.

It was something of a shock for clergy, accustomed to life of the churches, to be forcibly reminded that a significant proportion of the men they came to know in the trenches were scarcely interested in the priorities of the churches, and happily ignorant of the teaching of the denomination to which they claimed official allegiance in the forces' lists. A folk fatalism was reinforced by the arbitrariness of death and wounding. It was hard to keep hopes for a better world alive in atrocious trenches, polluted by the stench of unburied corpses, with gastro-enteric disease endemic, rats everywhere, water short, and leave infrequent. Men lived an hour at a time, but most welcomed the ministry of chaplains, even though it was mocked and put down at times with laconic humour and sharp insight into their inadequacies.[7] Was it a substitute religion? 'The digger had real religion deep down in his heart, and would lead one to believe he was an unmitigated pagan . . . He had indeed much of the spirit of Christ. True his Christianity was most inarticulate.'[8]

    [5] I. Benson, *The Man with his Donkey* (Melbourne, 1965) for an idealized religious interpretation of John Simpson Kirkpatrick, whose courage became legendary. P. Cochrane, *Simpson and the Donkey* (Melbourne, 1992) and T. Curran, *Across the Bar* (Brisbane, 1994) present the events with a greater degree of realism.

    [6] J. Lack (ed.), *Anzac Remembered: Selected Writings of K. S. Inglis* (Melbourne, 1998) 97–119 on war memorials, and 171–93; J. Phillips, 'War memorials in Australia and New Zealand', *AHS* 96 (1991) 179–91; C. Maclean, *For Whom the Bells Toll* (Wellington, 1998) on the National War Memorials; Oxley Library OM 64–14 Garland Papers; K. Inglis, *Sacred Places* (Melbourne, 1999).

    [7] E. Crane, *I Can Do No Other* (Auckland, 1986) 13–51; W. H. Downing, *To the Last Ridge* (Melbourne, 1920; rept. 1998).

    [8] D. B. Blackwood, *A Padre's Confession* (n.p., n.d.) 16–17; M. McKernan, *Padre* (Sydney, 1986); J. B. Haigh, *Men of Faith and Courage* (Auckland, 1983).

Little training was given. As a result, chaplains found that they had a good deal of freedom to share their ministry to all ranks, for detailed rules and regulations did not exist to begin with, or were not taken too seriously. Chaplains went for both short and long terms. Some soon acquired a reputation for courage in ministering to troops and the wounded in situations of great danger, as well as lending aid in letter-writing, recreation, and pastoral counsel. Ernest Merrington had been a notable Presbyterian minister in Brisbane, whose 'activities touched all, or nearly all, the moral and religious agencies of those years in Brisbane'.[9] He adjusted to a new comprehensiveness, and with others became used to the absence of the cautious deference of civilian life, the peculiar respect due to their officer status, and their duty to mix with all ranks.

Like their men, they carried the physical and spiritual wounds of war to their graves. Chaplains' diaries are an invaluable resource for understanding denominational tensions, and the ways in which the larger-minded clergy learned to labour with men from denominations they would not have worked with at home. That was especially true of some Anglicans and Roman Catholics, who came to see that denominational arrogance had no place in the realities of war. Some chaplains wanted *one* church, 'We want a strong, united, bold, aggressive Church to act as *guide* and *soul* to this great people.'[10] Such hopes were not speedily realized.

In the Protestant churches some minor figures pleaded for a pacifist interpretation of Jesus' teaching, but were treated with contempt and ostracism.[11] A few brave men resisted by declaring that they were conscientious objectors to war. While magistrates had to sort out the insincere who simply wished to avoid service, the weight of official pressure was brutal, and a denial of justice. The appalling story told simply by Archibald Baxter about his treatment in New Zealand, and then at the front in France, shows how shallow was the commitment to liberal principles when nationalist prejudices corrupted even elementary justice.[12] Christians were far more interested in Prohibition, which was almost voted in by New Zealanders in 1919.

---

[9] The *Memoirs* of Chaplain E. N. Merrington are held in the Gibson Library, Emmanuel College, University of Queensland, 110.

[10] Blackwood, *Padre's Confession*, 24.

[11] J. Poynter, *Doubts and Certainties* (Melbourne, 1997) for a patriotic view through the eyes of Dr Leeper of Melbourne.

[12] A. Baxter, *We Shall Not Cease* (Christchurch, 1968); P. Baker, *King and Country Call* (Auckland, 1988).

PATRIOTS AS PERSECUTORS

Lutherans had another experience of the brutalities of British patriotism. They were exemplary citizens, thoroughly law-abiding, deeply committed to being Australians, with pride in their German heritage, and seeing nothing incongruous in using German in worship and in their church publications. Some Germans had not been naturalized, even though they had been settled in Australia for many years. Their loyalty was to Australia, even though they retained German citizenship. Mr E. Elkan's dilemma was poignant. He had been in Australia for thirty years, his wife and children were Australian, and he had no wish to live anywhere else. But he had relatives in the German army, others in the Russian army, some in the French and British armies. He refused combatant duty, but was willing to serve as a non-combatant. Yet he could only wish it were all over. For writing about these issues frankly in the Adelaide *Register* in September 1914, the super-patriots classified him as disloyal.[13]

Some German citizens were unjustly interned. Many Lutherans suffered abuse, and had their windows smashed and their businesses boycotted, even though their sons were serving with the Australian forces. In Queensland, several churches were defiled. Two churches in South Australia and two in Victoria were burned. Despite protests from Lutheran church leaders, who had made their loyalty quite plain, the South Australian government closed forty-one schools in 1917, leaving open only two colleges and a mission primary school. There was no similar action in Victoria, or Queensland. A number of place names were also anglicized, the South Australian government only restoring a few in 1935. A number of Lutheran congregations had already introduced English services for young people. The pressure of war completed that process. Even the newspapers of the churches were closed, which forced publication in English. Some families changed their names, for virulent anti-German hysteria was fostered by a number of newspapers and community leaders. The South Australian Labour parliamentarian John Verran, a leading Methodist, and former premier, claimed that the German settlers were 'as full of disloyalty as hell is of sinners'.[14]

Such actions demonstrated all too clearly the dark side of Christian patriotism among British Australians, and the inability of the Gospel to

[13] E. Leske, *For Faith and Freedom* (Adelaide, 1996) 152.   [14] Ibid.

redeem such deep irrationalities, which also affected Asians. Sir George Reid rejected the criticism that the related White Australia Policy aimed at offending other races, 'it is purely and simply the out-come of instinct that is at the heart of every race, that of trying to retain its racial integrity and to develop its own national ideals'.[15] There were other consequences of the war that brought Lutherans out of their isolation. Occupation of New Guinea made it essential for the Australian and American churches to take over the staffing of the German missions there. American Lutherans from Iowa helped to fill the gaps, together with the Immanuel Synod. The Queenslander F. O. Theile became the full-time director of the mission, and gave notable leadership. The stresses of war underlined commonalities and, in 1921, five groups came together in the United Evangelical Lutheran Church in Australia. A further union occurred in 1926, but wider negotiations stalled on dogma and personalities.

ASSIMILATING THE DISADVANTAGED

The indigenous minorities in both countries were still gravely marginalized, and disadvantaged by internal colonialism. A few families managed to escape the poverty trap imposed by discrimina-tory legislation, lack of education, and community racism. In New Zealand, it was less and less possible to live a traditional Maori life, because land continued to be alienated or locked up in long leases.[16] Many lived in real poverty as a result and were not interested in the definition of *Maoritanga* by elite Maori. The size of the Australian con-tinent meant that where pastoralism and mining were absent, Aboriginal clans could continue their immemorial way of life in very isolated places. Politicians' schemes and missionaries were hard to escape, bringing changes which most elders deplored, but many young people accepted. Oral history has underlined how ambiguous assimilation was. In 1961, the Queensland Protector of Aborigines Dr J. W. Bleakley argued for government missions 'to preserve the purity of the white race from the grave social dangers that always threaten where there is a degraded race . . . at its back door'.[17]

Brutal repression continued on some stations, such as those run by

---

[15] J. W. S. Tomlin, *Australia's Greatest Need* (London, 1914) 35.

[16] R. T. Kohere, *Autobiography of a Maori* (Wellington, 1951) for life on the East Coast.

[17] J. W. Bleakley, *The Aborigines of Australia* (Adelaide, 1961). Human Rights and Equal Opportunity Commission, *Bringing Them Home* (Sydney, 1997) 124.

the Vestey family, and missions. The cat-o'-nine-tails was still being used at Moore River in Western Australia in the 1950s. A terrible massacre took place in Central Australia after a runholder had been killed by Aborigines. At least 31 Aborigines were killed, perhaps 100, but the Board of Inquiry later in 1928 said that the shooting was justified. Many families had children removed to dormitories with restricted access to parents, or taken away physically, and adopted into white Australian families, as late as 1980 in Western Australia. Some were fortunate, but many were tragically scarred, even destroyed, by this well-meant paternalism. Recent reports like *Bringing Them Home* (1997) have underlined how long-term and bitter were the consequences for some Aborigines. Others triumphed over their hardships.[18]

Orphans and children from broken or dysfunctional families, as well as child migrants from Britain, suffered similarly on both sides of the Tasman in government and church institutions well into the 1970s, where physical and sexual assault was far too common, and rarely dealt with by responsible authorities.[19] Records were lost, even falsified. The tensions between the realities of (mostly) male brutality, and the ideals of justice and love which were common in public discourse about the standards expected in a Christian society, were rarely discussed in the churches. Coldrey's history of the homes at Clontarf, Castledare, and Bindoon, run by the Christian Brothers in Western Australia for orphans, child migrants, and delinquents, underlined what a difficult task those in charge had, to cope with such a variety of physical and emotional needs. On 24 May 1996, an out-of-court settlement of $35 million was offered to 263 abused claimants by the Christian Brothers. Kingsley Fairbridge set up farms in New South Wales (1937–73), Western Australia (1913–81), South Africa, and Rhodesia for many hundreds of children. Some staff were Rhodes Scholars, and highly idealistic. The Salvation Army was also active

---

[18] *Bringing Them Home*, 115–18; F. Alcorta, *Marjorie Harris* (Palmerston, 1998) for an Arunta story; J. Harris, *We Wish We'd Done More* (Adelaide, 1998) 311–428; Battye Library MN 545/1–37/2389A Superintendents' diaries 1921–50 give a vivid picture of tensions at Forrest River, Western Australia; *Bringing Them Home*, 159; R. Brunton, *Betraying the Victims* (Melbourne, 1998) offers an alternative view.

[19] A. Gill, *Orphans of Empire* (Sydney, 1997); F. Hicks, *Neerhol* (Laidley, 1993) for comments on some Mercy orphanages; R. Howe and S. Swain, *All God's Children* (Canberra, 1989); K. Davies, *When Innocence Trembles* (Sydney, 1994); R. Sinclair, *All God's Children* (New Westminster, 1993) is an account of such abuse in New Zealand. See also I. A. Knight, *Out of Darkness* (Fremantle 1998) 365–7 for Alex MacDonald's memories. B. Coldrey, *The Scheme* (Perth, 1993) offers a defence.

in child rehabilitation, for some institutions met real needs com-passionately.

Migration from Britain to Australia and New Zealand continued in the interwar years. Mechanization of labour on farms steadily under-mined the viability of small country towns, and fostered the growth of cities, which has been one of the major themes in the history of the region. In addition, Anglicans, Presbyterians, and Methodists took seriously the need for ministry to isolated people in the inland and out-back. Kirby, Flynn, and Holden respectively built up the organization necessary for this mission, which included flying doctors, patrol padres, nurses, pedal radio, and bush hospitals which saved many lives. Little changed economically for Pacific Islanders in their villages. They lived with a subsistence economy in which copra was the main cash crop, where education was limited and medical care often unavailable. It was missions which provided these services. Colonial regimes had slender revenues and left the natives alone unless crimes were committed.

Steady suburban growth demanded the building of new churches, housing for clergy and religious, halls for social and educational activities.[20] Youth groups of various kinds, like the Methodist Order of Knights and Girls Comradeship, helped to socialize part of the next generation into Christian discipleship, and citizenship. The churches continued to be indispensable for charitable work in their communi-ties. Women did most of the labour, but, despite being a numerical majority, had little authority in policy. Women's organizations were extraordinary in their range, and wide community membership, and were financially indispensable. Some of their leaders were beginning to ask questions about equality.

Church leaders experimented in vain to find organizations which could similarly capture men's commitment, without ever asking if women had fundamental lessons to teach them.[21] The Church of England Men's Society, however, never matched the Mothers' Union.[22] Some Anglican laymen nevertheless found such a society

[20] B. Lewis, *Sunday at Kooyong Road* (Melbourne, 1976); M. Roe, *Australia, Britain and Migration* (Melbourne, 1995).

[21] G. Bederman, 'The women have had charge of the Church work long enough', in S. Juster and Lisa MacFarland (eds.), *A Mighty Baptism* (Ithaca, 1996) shows this concern was true of North America as well as Australia and New Zealand. A. O'Brien, 'A church full of men', *AHS* 102 (1993) 437–57.

[22] *A Report of the First New Zealand Church Congress* (Christchurch, 1923) 120–32 for these societies' ideals.

supportive of their faith and wrote eloquently about its foundations. In Palmerston North, New Zealand, H. B. Warne, the Anglican editor of the *Manawatu Daily Times*, wrote, 'There is nothing I treasure in earth so much as the Bible.' When pressed by care, fifteen to twenty minutes spent over a Gospel passage 'will send me about my work again like a new man . . . To me it is one of the mysteries of my religion', a reminder that the resonances of the Bible were still influential for Protestants.[23]

Whether such Protestantism could be classified as civic religion, in the North American sense, is doubtful. Catholics distanced themselves from it, the Jewish community was small in Australia, and tiny in New Zealand. Culture Protestantism is a better term, for between 70 and 80 per cent of the population was Protestant for census purposes, even though there were regional variations. Many of those who listed themselves denominationally as Protestant, or Christian, knew little about the Christian faith as defined by clergy and church leaders, but they should not be dismissed as nominals. While historical research into popular religion is not as far advanced as in Europe or North America, there is significant evidence that many people saw themselves as living a Christian life, regarding that as the real test of integrity, rather than loyalty to a denomination or a creed.[24]

Many believed that life after death was for all, and devoid of judgement. Little active anti-clericalism existed, but many Australians and New Zealanders were cynical about clergy. That did not exclude great respect for individual clergy, like the Methodist C. G. Scrimgeour in Auckland, the Anglican R. B. S. Hammond in Sydney, or John Flynn of the Australian Inland Mission, who broke out of this stereotype, and whose work for the community was seen as transcending churchianity and suspect religiosity.[25] The Presbyterian moderator-general made an appeal in 1933 for broadly based Christianity. 'We can never have a genuine democracy without a real religion . . . We have an unparalleled opportunity to shape a Commonwealth which might be an ideal for the rest of the world.'[26] Such hopes seemed empty in the wake of the 1929 crash.

The destructive experience of economic failure and depression that

---

[23] Oxley Library OM 64/14/3, Garland Papers, H. B. Warne–D. J. Garland.

[24] C. H. Lippy, *Popular Religiosity in the U.S.A.* (Westport, 1994).

[25] L. Edwards, *Scrim* (London, 1971); *The Scrim-Lee Papers* (Wellington, 1976); B. Judd, *He that Doeth* (London, 1951).

[26] G. R. S. Reid, *The Service of the Church to the Nation* (Sydney, 1933) 21–2.

dominated the 1930s left deep social wounds and feelings of helplessness in the face of uncontrollable forces. E. Burgmann's *Justice for All* (Morpeth, 1933) was a powerful Anglican tract on the needs of the unemployed, but many Christians were still content to use the rhetoric of blame. Roman Catholics were still deprived, with a higher percentage in lower socio-economic groups, and over-represented in crimes of poverty. Some Protestants blamed this on bad religion. Yet, if such fatalistic attitudes were distant memories of Calvinism for Protestants, and Jansenism for Roman Catholics, the 1920s and 1930s also saw minorities' passionate hopes for a new world order in which Christianity would have a dominant place. Some Christians placed their hopes in the League of Nations, others in radical pacifism, others in schemes for the renewal of society. The Anglican Bishop Halford of Rockhampton, Queensland, took a different way—renouncing his position as bishop so that Jesus could be better manifested to others by his living in poverty and under rule.[27]

Socialism attracted many political Christians, such as Arthur Calwell, Walter Nash, and Arnold Nordmeyer, especially in its British form, which had some deep Christian roots.[28] From the other side of politics, Sir Thomas Henley, a Congregationalist, wrote an open letter to premiers and captains of industry based on John 11: 44. He asked for the dismantling of arbitration, so youth could work. 'Australian industry is suffering more from unreasonably excessive taxation and meddlesome arbitration awards than anything else.'[29]

Communism, which offered a total reconstruction of society as dramatic in its sweep as any of the Christian eschatologies, promised likewise to eliminate all evil by removing the exploiting classes and inculcating new ethical goals which overcame individual and social selfishness.[30] Many idealistic youths became Communists, without seeing the price exacted by the Party in the Soviet Union. Some influential Australians, who believed in the virtues of capitalism, were attracted by the Fascist-style solutions in Germany, Italy, and Spain,

[27] Oxley Library OM 79–17/23 Halford–Garland, 28 Feb. 1928.

[28] L. H. Barber, 'The social crusader', Ph.D. thesis (Palmerston North, 1970) examines the work of James Gibb, a notable Presbyterian. E. Crane, *I Can Do No Other* (Auckland, 1986) describes Ormond Burton, a brave soldier who became an equally courageous pacifist. A. Calwell, *Be Just and Fear Not* (Melbourne, 1978); C. Holden, *From Tories at Prayer to Socialists at Mass: A History of St Peter's, Eastern Hill, Melbourne* (Melbourne, 1997) 191–216; P. Hempenstall, *The Meddlesome Bishop* (Sydney, 1993); K. Sinclair, *Sir Walter Nash* (Dunedin, 1977) (see also *First New Zealand Church Congress*, 75–81, for Nash's ideals).

[29] T. Henley, *Loose Him and Let Him Go* (Sydney, 1933) 13.

[30] S. McIntyre, *The Reds* (Melbourne, 1998).

where a strong leader allegedly brought salvation by discipline, unity, and sacrifice. The influential Sydney Baptist preacher T. E. Ruth attacked premier Jack Lang's repudiation of New South Wales debt, as part of the Red menace.[31] In Australia, the White Army and the New Guard were serious danger signals on the extent of these convictions, and fear of Communism. Unlike the Christian account of redemption, where the bringer died in order to defeat evil, these secular mythologies of redemption relied on imprisonment and death of victims to secure the power of the leader.

Few observers were willing to see the hideous costs of contemporary totalitarian solutions. They saw only the achievements in buildings, and statistics. No one in Australasia had the insight of the American ethicist Reinhold Niebuhr into the evil results of misapplied goodness, and specious nationalism. Though a number of theological books were published in Australia between 1920 and 1945, they lacked depth, and added little to the churches' message to the nation. Bishop Burgmann was the one who came closest to the realities. A new political consciousness developed in New Zealand through the rise of the Labour Party, some of whose leaders like Walter Nash had strong Christian convictions. In Kurow, North Otago, Dr McMillan, and the Revd Arnold Nordmeyer, the Presbyterian minister, developed a local model for public health care and social security, which transformed New Zealand after the election of the Labour Party in 1935. They still assumed a society shaped by Christian ideals.[32]

PROTESTANTISM MILITANT

Sectarian tensions had been strong in New Zealand, as well as in Australia, during the First World War. The distractions of sectarian misunderstanding were still powerful in New South Wales, where Protestant pressures brought a confrontation over proposed legislation to validate marriages which were allegedly called into question by the 1908 *Ne Temere* decree of the Roman Catholic Church in the 1920s. The church naturally resisted what it saw as an unjustified and sectarian attack on its religious freedom to define a sacrament. Arch-

---

[31] T. E. Ruth, *Australia at the Crossroads* (Sydney, 1933) 23; S. Thwaites, 'The Rev. T. E. Ruth, a controversial pastor', *Our Yesterdays* 4 (1996) 19–46.

[32] C. Van der Kroght, 'More a part than apart: the Catholic community in New Zealand society 1918–40', Ph.D. thesis (Palmerston North, 1994).

bishop Kelly, in Sydney, declared his willingness to go to gaol, rather than conform to state legislation on a sacrament. Though a measure passed the lower house, it was destroyed in the New South Wales upper house.[33] That was to be the last serious eruption of the Protestant political sectarianism in Australia. In New Zealand, the Protestant Politician Association, led by a former Australian Baptist minister, Howard Elliott, sought to keep New Zealand Protestant, but only a minority were willing to politicize their religion in that way, even though Parliament passed a Marriage Amendment Act in 1920.

In Auckland, Protestant suspicions of the Catholic community were aired in the charges of sedition levelled against Bishop James Liston, Bishop Cleary's co-adjutor. Born in Dunedin, with post-graduate theological education in Ireland and Rome, he taught at Holy Cross College, Mosgiel, from 1904, and became rector in 1910. Somewhat reclusive, and certainly not a firebrand, he spoke feelingly about Ireland at the St Patrick's Day concert in 1922, and suffered from a badly reported speech. The militant Protestants who laid charges brought discredit on themselves and were taken apart by P. J. O'Regan in court. An all-Protestant jury acquitted Liston, adding a rider that he had been indiscreet.[34] Dr Liston's repute was enhanced, although he had difficulties with his bishop, Henry Cleary, who attempted unsuccessfully to get rid of him. Cleary's own episcopate from 1910 to 1929 had been notable, not least for his important book on the Loyal Orange Lodges and editing *The Tablet*. He also spoke good Maori, but he found handing over authority very difficult.[35]

Protestant concern for the teaching of common Christianity in state schools re-emerged in the inter-war years, especially in New Zealand and South Australia.[36] The so-called Nelson system spread steadily in New Zealand from 1899, relying on the energy of ministers and some laity to give lessons outside legal hours about the Bible, where that was permitted by the local school committee. That was not a problem in most areas. Children, whose parents were opposed to such religious

[33] M. Hogan, *The Sectarian Strand* (Melbourne, 1987); J. Dixon, *Shall Ritualism and Romanism Conquer New Zealand?* (Dunedin, 1912) 176–96 for a New Zealand Presbyterian comment on *Ne Temere*.

[34] R. Sweetman, *Bishop in the Dock* (Auckland, 1997).

[35] M. King, *God's Farthest Outpost* (Auckland, 1997) 141.

[36] Sprott, *Redeeming the Time*, 168–83, pleaded for the rights of Protestant children and Bible reading in schools. In Queensland, George Vowles, head of Petrie Terrace State School, wrote to Garland about the very positive effect of Bible lessons. Oxley Library 66–5/1–7 B. S. League Box 2 5/3 17/6 1912; I. Breward, *Godless Schools?* (Christchurch, 1967) 74–88.

education, were permitted to opt out, but even many who were rather unsympathetic left their children in on the principle that it could do little harm. Mostly the assumption was that the lessons would not be denominational, so that the classes did not need to be split. At Howick, near Auckland, Catholic children were banished to the shelter shed for lessons by the local priest in the early 1940s. Some regarded all religious teaching as a blight on education. Catholic teaching was even worse. 'To pay money for separate schools for Roman Catholics would be to subsidize fraud and lying in education, to support breeding grounds of hatred and sectarianism, and to subject free children to a tyranny that has ruined every country in which it [was] rooted.'[37]

In Roman Catholic schools, it was very different. Religious education was in the context of a liturgical life. Catechetical instruction was led by religious or by the local parish priest, who was expected to keep a close eye on the religious ethos of the school.[38] Religious instruction was not left to the conscience of the individual. It was a matter of salvation or damnation. That did not mean that Catholic schools had a 100 per cent success rate. Large classes of up to seventy students, and poor facilities, meant they had their share of failures, and rote learning was too common, but school frequently reinforced family beliefs, and helped to contribute to the effective support of a strong Catholic subculture. In Queensland there was a strong Catholic Taxpayers Association campaign for educational justice, which was resisted by the Protestant majority in 1937. The *Courier Mail* opined that if the Catholic claim was granted, 'disintegration of the present state instruction would be inevitable'.[39]

Lutheran schools took time to recover from the war years before they had something of the same impact, but have been little studied. Protestants continued to have large Sunday schools and youth groups, to complement what was taught by precept or example at home.[40] Many churches upgraded their Sunday school buildings, and were also more aware of the importance of a graded curriculum following

---

[37] Arthur Student, *A New Social Policy* (Melbourne, 1916) 21–3.

[38] R. Park, *Fence Around the Cuckoo* (Auckland, 1993) 30–1 gives a vivid account of the effect of her Josephite education.

[39] J. Woodward, 'The turmoil of state aid', *BCHS* 1 (1988) 57; R. Fogarty, *Catholic Education in Australia* (2 vols., Melbourne, 1959).

[40] R. L. Cooper, *A Good Heritage* (New Plymouth, 1950) gives an account of the Methodist Sunday school. M. A. R. Pratt, *A Jubilee Story of Endeavour* (Christchurch, 1890–1940) gives a brief account of the North Canterbury Sunday School Union. M. Williams, 'Aspects of Sunday school training', *JRHSQ* 16 (1997) 281–4.

North American trends. This was assisted by the formation in 1914 of the ecumenical, and trans-Tasman, Joint Board of Christian Education, based in Melbourne (closed in 1996), and a comprehensive system of Sunday school examinations.

For some Anglicans, education was not enough. They wished to shape the processes of synodal government to support their party. The Anglican Church League was formed to hand on the faith in a very specific way, and to keep liberal theology and Anglo-Catholic liturgy out of Sydney. It operated discreetly, but its purpose was to ensure that Evangelicals dominated the key Synod committees. It had the numbers to elect Howard Mowll, an avowedly Evangelical bishop, in 1933. The diocese also felt the influence of W. J. G. Mann, the chancellor, a tough and uncompromising Low-Churchman, who was very suspicious of Lambeth and Prayer Book changes, and was a skilled opponent of Anglo-Catholic attempts to change the General Synod Constitution. H. Minton-Taylor, another legal battler from the diocese's firm of solicitors, drafted the constitution of the tiny Church of England in South Africa, which had separated from the main body of Anglicans, but was seen in Sydney as a partner in faith.

The few parishes which had liturgical sympathies deemed to be 'advanced' were held on a tight rein. Their clergy were forbidden to wear fully Catholic vestments, though John Hope at Christ Church-St Laurence ignored the rules deliberately.[41] That he was not brought to book was perhaps due to his ability as a priest, and reluctance to make him a martyr. But the Anglican Church League was determined that such calculated disobedience to the formularies, as they understood them, would not be allowed to spread in the name of comprehension. They refused to recognize that the Anglican Communion was moving away from the view of the *Book of Common Prayer* still dominant in Sydney. Archbishop Mowll and T. C. Hammond discreetly encouraged the Church of England in South Africa, which was seen by many Anglicans, including the Archbishop of Canterbury, as a schismatic body.

Evangelicals had seen some dioceses move towards the 'High' end of a worship scale and proscribe Evangelical clergy, not to mention imposing Anglo-Catholic clergy on congregations with a significant number of Evangelical communicants, with no consultation with parishioners about imposing 'advanced' liturgy. Anglo-Catholics might justly complain about Evangelical authoritarianism and

[41] L. C. Rodd, *John Hope* (Sydney, 1972).

persecution, but they could be just as tyrannous, as in the capture of St Mary's Anglican Church, Maitland, from Evangelicals in 1921. 'Consultation' was not a priority in Anglo-Catholicism. Clergy were expected to rule. In Queensland Alex Perkins, of the Church of England Defence Association, in 1932 wrote of action needed 'if we are not to be deprived of our Evangelical Protestant Church Worship, which has brought our British nation such rich blessings in the past; even to being the leading Nation, both morally and financially, in the world'.[42]

Anglo-Catholicism did have its peaceable side.[43] In parishes like St Peter's, Melbourne, All Saints, Wickham Terrace, Brisbane, St Michael and All Angels in Christchurch, and Christ Church-St Laurence in Sydney, the clergy had supportive vestries and parishioners, with the result that they gave leadership far beyond the boundaries of their parish, even if they were not to be the wave of the future. Indeed, where Anglo-Catholics were in a majority, as in Brisbane and Adelaide, they tended to become complacent and conservative, with little of the theological learning and social passion which characterized the movement at its best in Britain and North America.

PROTESTANT DIVISIONS

Evangelicals continued to be a significant, if embattled, part of Protestantism. Bible Colleges were founded in all Australian states, to safeguard historic Evangelicalism, for theological colleges were seen as liberal. In Auckland, a Bible Training Institute was set up largely through the energies of Joseph Kemp, minister of the Baptist Tabernacle.[44] He was deeply concerned at the inroads of liberal theology into the Protestant churches. With help from Presbyterians, Brethren, and some Anglicans and Methodists, he gathered together a group of ministers and businessmen to finance buildings next to the

---

[42] University of Queensland, Fryer MS F1452, Church of England Defence Association; W. T. Nelson, *T. C. Hammond* (Edinburgh, 1994).

[43] J. S. Reed, *Glorious Battle* (Nashville, 1996); J. Moses (ed.), *From Oxford to the Bush* (Canberra, 1996); M. Peters, *Christchurch St Michael's* (Christchurch, 1986). C. Holden, *Tories at Prayer to Socialists at Mass*, 169–244, gives a fine analysis of the ministry of Farnham Maynard from 1926 to 64. A. P. Kidd (ed.), *Halford: The Friar Bishop* (Brisbane, 1998).

[44] J. O. Sanders, *Expanding Horizons* (Auckland, 1971); J. M. R. Simpson, 'Joseph W. Kemp: prime interpreter of American fundamentalism in New Zealand in the 1920s', in D. Pratt (ed.), *Rescue the Perishing* (Auckland, 1989).

Tabernacle. He played an important part in the initial lecturing, and helped to foster an Evangelical ethos with significant millennial overtones in Auckland. This exerted a powerful influence in congregations, through young men and women who became local leaders, teachers in youth groups, and workers in Christian education. Many became missionaries overseas.

In the universities, teachers colleges, and schools, the Student Christian Movement split over theological differences. The visit of Howard Guinness in 1930 to Australia and New Zealand gave Evangelical tertiary students an alternative religious network. In tertiary institutions, the Inter-Varsity Fellowship was modelled on British precedents, and deliberately rejected the ecumenism, and theological and ethical study, which characterized the Student Christian Movement, for Bible study, personal evangelism by missions, and prayer meetings. They were reinforced by annual conferences addressed by Evangelical clergy, like Canon Orange in Christchurch.[45] In high schools from 1930, Crusaders fostered Evangelical piety, while the Scripture Union, expanded by Dr John Laird, provided a foundation for Bible reading in congregations. In Sydney and Melbourne, these Evangelical groups had a strong link with the Great Public Schools. Squashes and Drawing Room Meetings fostered this elitism which reached its apogee in the holy networks dominated by the Grant and Neill families in Sydney and Melbourne.[46] In Melbourne, this group, now known as The Family, has seen bitter disputes between its members. Its powerful influence in the Presbyterian churches of Canterbury and Camberwell is an example of religion both liberating and oppressive.

Few dioceses had leadership capable of breaking out of the existing polarization and creating a new consensus. One of the few bishops who did was Ernest Burgmann of Goulburn, but he was seen by most of his episcopal colleagues as a dangerous socialist and radical, because of his concern for social justice in the terrible years of the Depression.[47] He was almost alone among the bishops in being Australian, and coming from a very modest rural background in New England. Most Anglican bishops were English, public school, upper class, and quite

[45] P. J. Lineham, *No Ordinary Union: History of Scripture Union in New Zealand* (Wellington, 1980); J. Laird, *No Mere Chance* (London, 1987); H. Guinness, *Journey among Students* (Sydney, 1978); J. Prince, *Tuned into Change* (Sydney, 1979); *Out of the Tower* (Sydney, 1971).

[46] D. Millikan, *Imperfect Company* (Sydney, 1991); J. Stasse, *Fractured Fellowship* (Melbourne, 1999).

[47] P. Hempenstall, *The Meddlesome Bishop* (Sydney, 1994).

impatient of his concern for Anglicanism to become Australian. As Warden of St John's Morpeth from 1918 to 1934, he exercised remarkable influence, along with his gifted colleagues, Roy S. Lee, and A. P. Elkin, later Professor of Anthropology at the University of Sydney. The college had strong links with St Johns, Auckland, with A. B. Catley and R. E. Sutton going from Morpeth as wardens. Burgmann often clashed with Batty, his erstwhile bishop, who thought him heretical. Burgmann, however, had a vision for the national church shared by few of his peers. Not only did he press for a national university in Canberra, but he also argued powerfully for a national theological centre, finally established as St Mark's Library towards the end of his episcopate.

There was one Anglican in Melbourne, C. H. Nash, who had some of the same abilities to build new institutions, widen horizons, and create influential coalitions of laity.[48] Tragically he was not able to do this within the Anglican Church. He had fallen out with Archbishop H. L. Clarke over allegations of professional misconduct, which Clarke read in the worst possible light. It is possible that he wanted to get rid of Nash, whose popular influence in Geelong and Melbourne was quite unique. Clarke's heavy-handed use of his episcopal power did him no credit, and alienated some very important laity.

Though Nash was given a licence to minister in neighbouring Gippsland, his heart was in Melbourne, and he ministered for a time in a Congregational church in Prahran. There his capacity as an unusually gifted preacher and Bible teacher was greatly valued, and made it possible for him to begin the Melbourne Bible Institute, which was to produce hundreds of missionaries and lay leaders. In addition, Nash ran a businessmen's Bible class each week, which was attended by hundreds, and had an extraordinary influence in creating an Evangelical business network in Victoria. Including Lee Neill, Ralph Davis, Charles Sandland, and H. P. Smith, it touched almost all the Protestant denominations, and had a deep influence through the numerous missionary bodies based in Melbourne. Their energies were not confined to the Anglican Church, so that the Melbourne network never exercised political power like the Anglican Church League, and acquired a more inward and less political character than Sydney Evangelicals. The number of Evangelicals is not accurately known. There were divided views of providence and eschatology, which shaped attitudes on the need for government amelioration of social

---

[48] D. Paproth, *Failure is Not Final* (Sydney, 1997).

problems, or letting a mysterious divine future take its course. Saving souls was seen as more vital than reforming society. Evangelical moral hegemony in many parts of the region was quite striking, a fruit of earlier Puritan codes.

Nash, in his particular way, widened the appeal of Evangelicalism by his teaching on relationship to Christ and holiness, which was reinforced by the Upwey Convention (later Belgrave Heights), where every year hundreds gathered to hear the Bible expounded, missionary appeals, and calls to discipleship and holiness made. Similar conventions at Katoomba in the Blue Mountains were also influential in sustaining Sydney's Evangelical networks. In New Zealand conventions were held at Easter at Ngaruawahia and Pounawea, collecting hundreds of all ages, imparting a powerful lay ethos, and missionary vision. Nash also was seen as a powerful defender of the authority and inspiration of the Bible. He was one of the founders of the Bible Union in 1923, formed to meet the assaults of liberal Protestantism, seen to be growing dangerously strong in the major Protestant churches, both in Australasia and in North America.[49] A New Zealand Evangelical Bible League followed in 1936, but supporting ministers like P. B. Fraser and T. Miller were seen as cranks by Presbyterian leaders, with nothing to contribute to the questions of the day. Pentecostals were universally dismissed, despite the crowds attending Smith Wigglesworth's missions in the 1920s.

Liberalism was influential, and yet was out of touch with the religious experience of a significant part of its constituency, on which it sought to impose a modernizing version of Christianity. One opponent, the Very Revd R. G. Macintyre, was an elder statesman in the Presbyterian Church of New South Wales, and a weighty defender of revealed religion, while at the same time abreast of contemporary scholarship. He provided a counterbalance to the widely published Samuel Angus' public influence in the 1930s, intellectually and politically. He showed the shallowness of liberal optimism, 'Christianity stands or falls by its belief that Jesus belongs essentially to the Godhead and that faith accepts no compromise.'[50] Liberal Protestants, like E. S. Kiek and J. S. Griffiths, were especially influential in the Congregational Unions, where creeds counted for little. Lionel Fletcher, however, was an influential Congregational

---

[49] S. Piggin, *Evangelical Christianity in Australia* (Melbourne, 1996) 91–4.
[50] R. G. Macintyre, *The Substance of the Christian Faith* (Sydney, 1936) 38; S. Emilsen, *A Whiff of Heresy* (Sydney, 1980) on Angus.

evangelist in Port Adelaide, Auckland, and Cardiff, who provided a theological alternative to the liberal ethos of Australasian Congregationalism.

Liberal clergy were also influential in parts of the Anglican Church and amongst a considerable body of Presbyterians and Methodists. Those graduates influenced by the Student Christian Movement were also a significant liberal network. Among Methodists, Principal Arthur Albiston, of Queen's College in Melbourne, and Sir Irving Benson of Wesley Church, Melbourne, were interesting combinations of evangelical heritage and modernizing tendencies. Liberal impact was moderated by the warm-hearted piety which was still dominant.[51] It was possible to sing Wesleyan hymns and still appreciate their spiritual power, while being open to the restatement of theological ideas, when there was no confessional heritage enforced to act as a yardstick of orthodoxy. The attempts of Dr Fitchett to uphold the historic doctrine of Methodism in the 1920s failed, and Principal Albiston's revisionist liberalism dominated the Victorian Conference. Nevertheless, the cultural and religious importance of historic Protestantism remained significant, despite questions on its relevance.

Anglicans had the Thirty-Nine Articles as a doctrinal standard, but they were increasingly treated as a dated formula for faith, or reinterpreted in ways which would have amazed their authors.[52] Anglicans who could be labelled as 'Low Church' or 'Broad Church' were underestimated, because they were scornful of Anglo-Catholics, Evangelicals, and others who tried to make Anglicanism in their own image. One of the region's most notable liberals, H. D. A. Major, had left New Zealand, and become influential in England. The liturgy was seen as the norm for authentic Anglicanism, nurturing the spirit in which reason and tradition were to be understood.

Roman Catholics took no significant part in these Protestant debates, except to point out that these modernist views were the natural result of Protestant individualism.[53] Catholics were instructed to avoid contamination, and to trust the infallible teaching role of the church. The condemnations of Modernism were still taken very seriously. Influential Protestants like Principal Hammond of Moore

---

[51] C. Pearson, 'H. D. A. Major and English modernism, 1911–48', Ph.D. thesis (Cambridge, 1989). A brief account of his views is given in *Thirty Years After: A New Zealander's Religion* (Auckland, 1929) 95–106.

[52] Sprott, *Redeeming the Time*, 208–29.

[53] H. Johnston, *The Church Built upon the Rock* (Melbourne, 1934); L. Rumble, *Dr Angus or Christ* (Sydney, 1934).

College remained resolutely suspicious of Rome and its supposed desire to impose its way on others. 'It is well known that Romanism positively hates Protestants and would love to see all England brought low so the Pope may get his power back in that country.'[54] He could not see that his hostility to liberalism had much in common with Rome's insistence on historic Christianity.

MAORI AND MELANESIAN INITIATIVES

In New Zealand an important Maori renewal movement emerged, led by T. W. Ratana near Wanganui. Late in 1918, he had a dramatic vision which gave his troubled life new direction as religious leader and healer. He founded the Ratana Church at Pentecost 1925, and took many Maori from the Anglican diocese of Wellington, with a combination of prophecy and healing, at a time when interest in the religious side of healing was re-emerging following the flu pandemic of 1918. North Island bishops issued a heavy-handed pastoral letter at the beginning of July 1925, warning that any who signed Ratana's covenant excommunicated themselves from the Church of Christ, a neat way of avoiding the odium of taking formal action. Some of Ratana's followers used exuberant language, which suggested to those who knew little Maori that he was claiming status equal to Jesus, but Ratana himself never claimed more than being a divine mouthpiece (*Te Mangai*).

The Anglican bishops were in a dilemma. They could see Ratana's attraction to their Maori community, but they did not see the need for Maori clergy to participate in General Synod. Paternalism reigned supreme. Maori pastorates covered wide areas, and rarely were self-supporting. Some dioceses, like Auckland and Waiapu, had Maori Synod members and church boards for Maori ministry until 1913, but there was no national network set up until 1934, and that did not work. When the Archbishop of Canterbury, Randall Davidson, was consulted about separate Maori leadership, after a meeting in Rotorua during June 1925, he replied at the beginning of 1926 that the Church's unity overrode racial distinctions. 'I should regret the necessity, if it be a necessity, of your making such arrangements, but I do not go further than that.'[55] This admirable sentiment took no account of

---

[54] *Record*, 19 July 1960.
[55] *Proceedings of General Synod* (1928) 14–15.

the realities of power, and lack of partnership. However, such communications were a reminder of the closely-knit episcopal networks in the Anglican communion, and the important consultative role the Archbishop of Canterbury had.[56]

There was no agreement about a Maori bishop at the special General Synod held late in 1925. The North Island bishops initially felt no Maori was suitable. Their proposal for a Maori diocese, centred at Te Aute, was rejected by Maori members, because the nominee, Herbert Williams, was a Pakeha. Another attempt was made in 1928, and a novel form of suffragan episcopacy set up, covering the Maori all over New Zealand. Finding a candidate was not easy. Ngata was not pleased with the consecration of F. A. Bennett, arguing that he was too deferential, and that better candidates were available, like P. Tamahori, who had been passed over.[57] Made assistant bishop in Waiapu, which still had the largest number of Maori members and clergy, Bennett had a very anomalous position. He had to ask bishops' permission to enter their dioceses. Some, like Bishop W. J. Simkin of Auckland, who had earlier opposed the idea of a Maori bishop, were actively unhelpful. Bishop Cherrington of Waikato did little to foster ministry to the large Maori community in his diocese.

Bennett had few financial resources, no way of developing lay leadership nationally, no real input into theological education, and no way of formally keeping other bishops in touch with issues which were pressing for the Maori in his care. Nor did he have effective relationships with Anglican schools for Maori pupils. The Maori clergy in all churches were dependent clients of the Pakeha majority, and any adaptations of liturgy, or contextualizing of ministry and theology, were almost impossible. A proposal for a Methodist Maori Synod had been rejected in 1896. Miserably paid deaconesses, and lay workers from Britain and Australia, worked in isolated Maori communities such as Ruatoki in the Bay of Plenty. A group of English ladies worked at their own expense in Te Araroa from 1936 to 1945.

Some Catholic, Methodist, and Presbyterian missionaries were the exception to this neglect. H. J. Fletcher of Taupo was fluent in Maori, and an authority on their astronomy. Princess Te Puea respected Methodist leaders such as Becker, Haddon, and Seamer.

[56] R. Teale, R. Withycombe, L. Frappell, R. Nobbs (eds.), *Anglicans in the Antipodes* (Westport, 1999).

[57] M. P. K. Sorenson, *Na to hoa aroha* (3 vols., Auckland, 1986) 1. 124–5. This first volume has an excellent introduction on both Ngata and Buck. J. Paterson, (ed.), *He Toenga Whatiwhatinga: Essays concerning the Bishopric of Aotearoa* (Rotorua, 1983).

J. G. Laughton, a Presbyterian recognized as an authority on *Maori-tanga*, also played an important part on the revision committee with Ngata which, in 1946, significantly modified the nineteenth-century Maori Bible. But other churches were just as paternalistic as the Anglicans, and had no effective channel through which Maori concerns could be voiced. The governments of the day were equally insensitive. When Methodists sent a deputation to the government about statutory recognition of the Treaty in 1940, they were treated dismissively.[58] Maori feelings of betrayal over the Treaty were widespread, far beyond Ratana's followers, and went back into the nineteenth century, when King Tawhiao took a treaty petition to Britain in 1884 without success. King Koroki and Princess Te Puea boycotted centenary commemoration of the Treaty in 1940, and did little to encourage recruitment to the Maori Battalion when war broke out in 1939.

The other major indigenous form of Christianity among the Maori was the Ringatu Movement centred among the Tuhoe, and modified by the enigmatic Rua Kenana.[59] It continued along the path laid down by Te Kooti. After a clash with the government in 1916, Rua suffered a very inadequate trial, and then a prison sentence. Rua rebuilt religious loyalties, and the Maungapohatu community, from 1927. Its system of holy days, and the deep knowledge of the Scriptures among some of its leaders, suited a movement led by men who had no formal training for leadership, but who adapted the Christian message to their Maori context with notable insight. Ringatu had lost its initial missionary impulse, and remained somewhat isolationalist because of suspicion of Pakeha and other tribes. The local county councils could not levy rates on communal land, so with no roads, Tuhoe attempts at farming were futile. Tuhoe was content to live to itself amidst its isolated valleys in the Urewera. Reluctantly they admitted Presbyterian missionaries, including John Laughton, who gradually won the trust of Rua and his associates, and persuaded the Tuhoe to allow schools into their region.

Sister Annie Henry, one of the first deaconesses to work there, remembered the material poverty of the people, and their unwillingness to break out of their ancient customs and become Pakeha-style farmers living in separate houses. They preferred simple huts built

[58] G. I. Laurenson, *Te Hahi Weteriana* (Auckland, 1972) 234–5.
[59] J. Binney, *Mihaia* (Wellington, 1979); P. Webster, *Rua and the Maori Millennium* (Wellington, 1979).

of bush materials, with elaborate meeting houses for all important functions, and for communal sleeping. Traditional beliefs about the power of the spirits were still strong, and those with gifts of *makutu* (sorcery) were greatly feared. People still died believing that they had been cursed, and that no Pakeha medicine could heal them. Gradually Sister Annie taught women simple hygiene, to complement strict *tapu* rules about the handling of food and bodily wastes. In Whakatane, a remarkable Anglican Maori doctor, Golan Maaka, slowly broke down Tuhoe prejudice about European medical care.

Timu Tioke and Hemi Potatau were the first Maori to be ordained by Presbyterians, in 1931 and 1933. The educational gap was huge, for many Maori had only limited primary education, and to attend institutions like Knox College, Trinity College, Holy Cross College, or St John's College was an isolating step to take. There was no alternative after the 1920 closure of Te Rau Kahikatea, until the 1950s. Wiremu Te Awhitu became the first Maori Roman Catholic priest in 1944.[60] Takuira Mariu, the first Catholic bishop, was only consecrated in 1988. The leaders of the Pakeha churches decreed that partnership could only occur by assimilation. There were few who considered that there was anything to learn from Maori ways of being Christian, despite the strength of Pacific churches. Burton, a Methodist mission leader, described Maori Christianity as 'a woeful jumble of Christian ideas, of superstitious practices, and of unhealthy customs that bear little resemblance to any form of Christianity'.[61]

Similar views about Melanesian Christians were present in New Caledonia, where there was a significant number of settlers, some of them descendants of the 20,000 convicts sent by the end of the nineteenth century. The French community (or Caldoches) assumed that the Kanaks were doomed to die out. They had been confined to ludicrously small reserves, after another rebellion in 1917. The Caldoches justly complained of neglect by Paris, were often uninterested in religion and were hostile to pro-Kanak missionaries, as well as resenting government aid to Kanak coffee growers in the 1930s. Kanaks resented the growing number of Wallis Islanders working in the nickel industry.

Between 1902 and 1926, one of the most remarkable missionaries of the era, Maurice Leenhardt, made notable contributions to the

---

[60] S. A. Carney, *Story of Mill Hill to New Zealand 1886–1966* (Putaruru, 1966); Kohere, *Autobiography of a Maori*, 94–100, for Te Rau College for Maori students.
[61] J. W. Burton, *Missionary Survey of the Pacific Islands* (London, 1930) 19.

development of the Protestant Church, and a renewal of Kanak confidence in their future, despite inadequate landholdings, forced labour,
no access to adequate education, and substantial inequalities. Kanak
population had fallen by one-third to 27,000 since 1887. Roughly one-
third of the remaining population was Roman Catholic, but many of
the majority had little Christian connection. Pastors from the Loyalty
Islands began work among related tribes on the mainland, which
refused to be Roman Catholic both for tribal and for religious reasons.
The administration did not object, but the Caldoches were unhappy
because this weakened their control. They wanted to reduce the
Kanak reserves to a mere 60,000 hectares. Some Protestant churches
were illegally burnt.

Maurice Leenhardt's education of indigenous pastors changed
that subordinate status and led to the emergence of a significant
Protestant Church on Grande Terre. Colonists were suspicious of
these developments, and branded Leenhardt as pro-native. Members
of the colony's administration also were resentful of his advocacy
on land issues, civil rights, and labour. He did not fit the Catholic
culture of deference. One of his major contributions was to show
Kanaks that the French democratic ideas could be used in their
search for equality. He was crucial in the acquittal of alleged rebels in
1918.

His major contribution was to explore Kanak mentality and world
view in such a way that it could become a powerful resource against
colonial oppression, and a source of deep pride. In this he was greatly
helped by Bwesou Erijisi, the first New Caledonian pastor, and other
leading Kanaks like Pwagatch. Leenhardt believed that 'Through
them, we rediscover elements of the affective life, the aesthetic life,
and the mythic life, which we had forgotten, and which were lacking
in the balance of our thought.'[62]

By the time Leenhardt left, the proportion of Protestant population
on Grande Terre had grown to a third of the total, with a growing
number of well-prepared pastors. Do Neva, Houailou, where his
seminary was situated, was a place to learn self-reliance, though there
was struggle between advocates of this pattern and the more institutional style of the Lifou Seminary. By contrast, the Roman Catholic
Church was content with its French priests. The first indigenous

[62] J. Guiart, *Maurice Leenhardt* (Noumea, 1997) 70 for the names of Kanak pastors;
R. Dousset-Leenhardt, *A Fleur de Terre* (Paris, 1984); J. Clifford, *Person and Myth* (Berkeley,
1982) 198; G. H. Anderson, et al., *Mission Legacies* (Maryknoll, 1994) 494–9.

Catholic priest was not ordained until 1946, the same year that Kanak confinement to reserves was ended.

When he returned to France in 1926, the Paris Mission did not know what to do with him, for there were sharp missiological divisions over his insistence on indigenous leadership and criticism of missionary colonialism. He became the founding Director of the Institut Française d'Océanie in Noumea in 1948, despite bitter local opposition, and continued to be very influential in shaping French Protestant missionary work, in both Oceania and Africa. Even the Marists, who had been rivals, came to see the importance of his anthropological work on Melanesian culture. He is one of the few twentieth-century missionaries whose work influenced other anthropologists like Lévy-Bruhl and Mauss, together with students at the École Pratique des Hautes Études.

IMPERIAL VISION

One of the most attractive advocates of the imperial patriotism and worldwide Christian vision, which was so important for most Protestants and some Roman Catholics, was Archbishop St Clair Donaldson of Brisbane. His views are set out in *Christian Patriotism* (Brisbane, 1915). He also saw missions as 'true Imperialism' and the evangelization of the world as necessary for human progress. 'I cling to my conviction that the Empire is of God.'[63] He was also an embodiment of the upper-class connections of so many of the Anglican bishops. His father had been first premier of New South Wales. His statesmanlike attributes helped his translation to Salisbury, which was a reminder that Australia was still seen as part of the English ecclesiastical network.

Independently wealthy, unmarried, and with strong Australian connections, he believed that the Church of England should have stronger local roots. In addition to energizing the construction of a cathedral, he enlarged St Francis' theological college in Brisbane, and increased the number of Australian clergy, as well as fostering the Bush Brotherhoods. At a crucial stage he supported Canon David Garland's campaign for Bible in schools which was embodied in the Act of 1910, permitting such teaching. Donaldson also built up a more effective

[63] A. P. Kidd, 'The Brisbane Episcopate of St Clair Donaldson 1904–21', Ph.D. thesis (Brisbane, 1996) 198; *ABM Review*, 21 June 1922, 56.

church secondary school system, with five new schools, and founded a university college as well as St Martin's war memorial hospital. The constitution for the province of Queensland pointed the way to a judicious exercise of authority by General Synod. Donaldson also worked hard to get General Synod in 1921 to agree to seek autonomy. His close connections with Canterbury were a help, but Sydney resisted constitutional reform.

He had a keen interest in social issues, even though his privileged upbringing made it hard for him to appreciate the problems of workers and their families. His offer to mediate in the 1912 strike in Brisbane was well-intentioned, but not acceptable to either side. His concern for missions was part of his imperial vision, but he did not succeed, as he had hoped, to make the Anglican Board of Missions (ABM) more effective. Though his idea that Queensland was the Antioch of Australia seems odd, he did at least deal with some of the problems of the ABM Aboriginal mission at Yarrabah. The 1920s saw expansion of orphanages, hospitals, and homes for the aged as an expression of the churches' compassion for the needy, and a conservative social ethic.[64]

Aboriginal institutions came at the bottom of the list. They were run on minimal budgets by staff with little or no professional training, who often solved problems by punishment, and were influenced by what T. G. Strehlow described as 'that pathetic and unscientific belief in white supremacy'. The Aborigines on such missions were used as unskilled labour as part of their redemption.[65] The dilemmas faced by mission staff are vividly seen in the career of the Revd Ernest Gribble,[66] at Yarrabah in Queensland, and then in Western Australia. Gribble was a very complex personality, a skilled mythmaker about himself, with ambiguous commitment to Aborigines. He despised their culture as 'very low in the scale of humanity'. Gribble was a stern disciplinarian, yet the father of a girl by an Aboriginal woman, Janie Clark. Transferred to Forrest River, Western Australia, he exposed the brutal murder of a number of Aborigines (perhaps as many as 50) by police and trackers in 1926, who disposed of the bodies by burning. The resulting Royal Commission had no effect. None of the police

[64] S. Rae, *From Relief to Social Service* (Dunedin, 1981).

[65] T. G. H. Strehlow, *Assimilation Problems* (Adelaide, 1964) 35; *ABM Review* (1922) 57; (1923) 172.

[66] I owe this information to C. Halse, 'The Rev. Ernest Gribble and race relations in Northern Australia', Ph.D. thesis (Brisbane, Queensland, 1992) which discusses the complexity of Gribble's personality. J. Thomson, *Reaching Back* (Canberrra, 1989) for Yarrabah memories.

were ever brought to account. Gribble's marriage and impossible personal problems, corrupt colleagues, financial mismanagement, and brutal discipline led to his dismissal in 1928.

Bishop Feetham of North Queensland generously took him on as Chaplain at Palm Island, 1930–57. He remained authoritarian, but won respect of many Aborigines for his battles against authority on their behalf. Obsessed about duty, he refused to leave the island even for award of an OBE. Bishop Shevill finally had him forcibly carried off when it was clear he could no longer perform his duties. The stresses of acculturation and coercion gave Aborigines little choice. Gribble gave them an alternative authoritarian world, but one which cut them off from traditional culture. Paradoxically, he was one who provided the beginnings of an Aboriginal church. Yarrabah nurtured the first Aboriginal bishop—Arthur Malcolm.

WOMEN'S WORK

Australian and New Zealand schools were still very sexist. Schools focused on domestic or home science. The number of women undertaking university and professional education was small. Even girls' schools often had male principals. Nurses were dominated by male doctors in hospital hierarchies. Homemaking was assumed to be the normative feminine role, a message reiterated by bishops, clergy, teachers, and politicians. The Mothers' Union had 1 per cent of Anglican women as members, but had high social prestige and sought to strengthen families with work in children's courts, homes for unwed mothers, and district nursing. They were strongly opposed to any widening of grounds for divorce.[67] The pattern set down in the Victorian era remained dominant. Some women were deaf to that. Kate Cocks, a South Australian Methodist, pioneered a women's police group. Muriel Heagney, a Melbourne member of the Catholic Women's Social Guild campaigned for equal pay. Evidence that this male dominance was often violently oppressive was ignored and women were advised to win over their men by sweet submission.

Aboriginal women were the most tragically exploited and culturally misunderstood of their gender, hampered by poor education, poverty, discriminatory legislation, and sexual predators. They were often out

---

[67] Sprott, *Redeeming the Time*, 184–98, on marriage and divorce in 1922. T. Le Menant des Chesnais, *The Church and the World* (Dunedin, 1904) 236–9 for a Catholic view.

of sight and out of mind and yet despite this, women like Margaret Tucker and Kath Walker showed what strength Aboriginal women had.[68] Countless others who did not write about their life showed the same resourcefulness and courage, remembered only by their clan and family. The history of significant women in the Pacific churches remains to be researched and written. Everywhere, women were vital for church fundraising and care of buildings and as caterers. The churches reinforced gender stereotypes at every level of their life.[69] Attempts to give women a constitutional place in church bodies was often met with mockery and hostility, despite the equality before God conferred by baptism. Mary Salmond, a New Zealand Presbyterian, visited Europe in 1936, and noted how much more activity there was there. Attempts to admit women to eldership failed, as did pleas for equality of opportunity in ordination. Methodists in Australia between 1929 and 1935 deemed ordination of women inappropriate, but began the ministry of deaconess in 1935. There was no change until 1966.

Australian Anglicans were reluctant to take any action which might open up pleas for ordination to the priesthood. When Maude Royden visited Australasia in 1928, her ministerial gifts were obvious, but she was denied access to many pulpits, because of her gender. St Mark's, Darling Point, Sydney, Christchurch Cathedral, and St Peter's Cathedral, Adelaide, were exceptions. Winifred Kiek of Adelaide, the first woman to gain a Bachelor of Divinity, in 1922, was ordained as a Congregational minister on 13 June 1927, in Colonel Light Gardens, a new housing area, and speedily built an effective congregation which exercised an impressive pastoral ministry to the poor and unemployed. In touch with women leaders in the United States and Britain, she broke down many stereotypes, followed by women ministers in the Churches of Christ in the 1930s.

Catholic women's organizations like the Catholic Women's Association, founded in Sydney in 1913, were carefully controlled by clergy and limited to devotional and charitable activities. The Women's Social Guild, founded in Melbourne in 1916 by Dr Mary

---

[68] M. Tucker, *If Everyone Cared* (Sydney, 1977); K. Walker (Oodgeroo Noonuccal), *We Are Going* (Brisbane, 1984).

[69] M. Rose, *Freedom from Sanctified Sexism* (MacGregor, 1996); M. Porter, *Women in the Church* (Melbourne, 1988); B. Dickey, *Not Just Tea and Biscuits* (Adelaide, 1996); S. Willis (ed.), *Faith and Fetes* (Melbourne, 1977); B. Feith, *Women in Ministry* (Melbourne, 1990); J. Crewther, *My God is Logical* (Melbourne, 1996) covers the Methodist story; J. West, *Daughters of Freedom* (Sutherland, 1997) 296–330.

Glowrey and Anna Brennan, had a more radical edge. Archbishop Mannix forced the Guild to break ties with the National Council of Women in 1920, because he distrusted their concern for issues of justice. A change came with The Grail in the 1930s, pioneered by gifted Dutch members who came to Australia and worked independently of bishops. In 1936, Archbishop Gilroy of Sydney brought them and the Catholic Women's Association under control, by appointing chaplains to both. He expelled The Grail from running the Catholic Central Library.

They and Catholic Action groups widened some horizons, as did the Campion Societies which emerged in universities and attempted to show that Catholics had all the answers to difficult issues. The Society of the Sacred Heart in Sydney secured permission to found Sancta Sophia as a university college for women. There was a struggle with the hierarchy and Fr Maurice O'Reilly of St John's College, who lost the battle to control the new college, which became incorporated in 1929. Mother Margaret MacRory was a formidable opponent, and had invaluable support from influential laity. Women religious began to study in universities in the 1930s, with very guarded episcopal permission, so that they could be better qualified for secondary teaching and teacher education. That meant sisters did not have to attend state teachers' colleges.

Numbers steadily increased, with 10,000 Catholic women religious in Australia by 1940. Women in religious congregations still had great prestige in the Roman Catholic community, attracting a steady flow of vocations from their schools, and continued to expand their charitable, educational, and medical work. Dr Glowrey's lobbying in Rome ended the ban against being in a religious order and practising a profession in 1936. Canonical restrictions remained on sisters becoming midwives, on the grounds that their sexual desire would be roused, but they were not inhibited as persuasive fundraisers, with well-organized networks of supporters, both male and female, which ensured that Catholic hospitals grew in importance. St Vincent's, Melbourne, became a teaching hospital in 1910, while St Vincent's in Sydney achieved that status in 1923. Superiors of institutes, headmistresses, and hospital administrators continued to remind men that women could command and organize.[70]

---

[70] S. Kennedy, *Faith and Feminism* (Sydney/Melbourne, 1985); H. Carey, *Truly Feminine, Truly Catholic* (Sydney, 1987); R. McGinley, *A Dynamic of Hope* (Sydney, 1996); E. Campion, *Great Australian Catholics* (Melbourne, 1997).

Women continued to dominate numerically in Protestant mission work overseas as doctors, nurses, and teachers. They were trained separately from men except in the Melbourne Bible Institute from 1921. Some missionaries like Mary Andrews returned from China to head Deaconess House in Sydney, where she had an influential ministry. Deaconess Dorothy Harris had a notable ministry in Pyrmont in inner Sydney, in the Bush Church Aid Society in western New South Wales, and in India, before returning to Sydney to become a pioneer social worker. Ruth Minton-Taylor was recruited by Bishop George Chambers for CMS service in Tanganyika. He had built up an impressive diocese with many Australian staff. Women nurses like Elizabeth Burchill and Ina Currey were pioneers of medical care for the Presbyterian Australian Inland Mission. The Bush Church Aid Society, the United Aborigines Mission, and the Aboriginal Inland Mission had numerous women staff, as did the CMS in the Northern Territory.[71]

DEALING WITH SOCIAL CHANGE

A few Christians saw the possibilities of radio as a medium for communicating the Gospel. In Auckland, 'Uncle Scrim' (the Revd Colin Scrimgeour, a Methodist) established a phenomenal audience for the Church of the Friendly Road on 1ZB. A more staid, but influential, innovation was Irving Benson's broadcast of Wesley Church Melbourne's Pleasant Sunday Afternoons. Sydney's 2SM and 2CH, and Adelaide's 5KA were church-related stations, but without the impact of similar stations in North America, where priests like Fulton Sheen, Evangelicals like Charles Fuller, and Bible teachers like William Aberhardt in Alberta, captured large audiences. The development of national radio networks in Australia and New Zealand, modelled on the BBC, prevented paid religious broadcasting, though only the Australian Broadcasting Corporation developed professional religious broadcasters. Led by Kenneth Henderson, they were initially Anglicans with a sense of mission to the whole community.[72]

There were some who saw business as well as religious opportunities

---

[71] M. Lamb, *Going it Alone* (Sydney, 1995); West, *Daughters of Freedom*, 249–52, on Minton-Taylor; D. Harris, *God's Patience* (n.p., 1990).

[72] A. M. Healey, 'Spirit and substance: religious broadcasting on ABC radio', Ph.D. thesis (Sydney, 1993); L. Edwards, *Uncle Scrim, Radio Rebel* (London, 1971); A. Pratt, *Sidney Myer* (Melbourne, 1978).

in these difficult years. Some Christians who saw business as a vocation, wealth creation as a virtue, and philanthrophy as a duty, founded new businesses, or expanded existing ones. Broken Hill Proprietary grew rapidly, under its leader Essington Lewis, an Anglican. James Fletcher, a Presbyterian, established a construction business in Dunedin which has become a large international company. In Melbourne, the Nicholas family, with Methodist links, built a major company out of Aspirin, and Sidney Myer, a converted Jew, built a great department store. William Goodfellow, an active Presbyterian with rare business flair, was a key figure in the development of the Waikato dairy factories into the New Zealand Co-operative Dairy Company in 1920, the development of ancillary enterprises like Glen Afton colliery, butterbox packing, and the Challenge Phosphate Company, which substantially reduced the price of fertilizer.

A CONGREGATION RESPONDS

Many congregations struggled during the Depression years. Some were closed. Others reduced their already modest budgets, but were still seen as centres for community life. In a suburban church like St Leonard's Presbyterian, Brighton Beach, the task of creating a Christian network from nothing can be seen.[73] It was founded in 1891. A primary school was set up in 1915. Numbers at worship and other activities necessitated the appointment of a deaconess in 1920. Hugh Kelly in the 1920s was an experienced editor, and also a leader writer for *The Age* who emphasized the connection between the Gospel and current affairs. Youth clubs, both religious and recreational, flourished, and missionary work was generously supported by a membership of 297, plus a larger number of adherents, a Presbyterian way of combining comprehensiveness with strict criteria for membership.

The parish was closely linked with the Melbourne Orphanage, with its Presbyterian children regularly attending worship. A strong social network flourished, together with a parish magazine, and a couple of magazines from youth groups. Minister and congregation supported a 'No licence' vote in 1930, but Session vetoed a proposal for a youth anti-war group to be set up. Little interest appears to have been taken in justice issues during Depression years. The congregation was preoccupied with its own financial woes, though its members gave

[73] V. Byrne, *The People of St Leonard's* (Melbourne, 1991) 18.

generously to relief, as they did to the war effort: 160 men and women served in the forces. Furnishings, memorial tablets, and windows tied families and buildings together, giving the sacred space deep community roots. The same story of salvation interacting with the joys and sorrows of daily life could be told from different angles in thousands of congregations throughout the region.

GROWING SECULARITY

The nineteenth-century ending of state aid, and the separation of Christianity's leaders from the responsibility of government, helped to secularize politics, privatize religion, and turn the churches inward. Nevertheless, the cultural and religious influence of the Bible and its moral teaching remained powerful.[74] Liberal theology also fostered individualism, especially in the pressures of Depression, refusing to allow any written creeds to come between people and the mind of Christ. Some liberal Christians looked for a Parliament of Man, with law replacing war. In Melbourne, the Anglicans Farnham Maynard and 'Brother Bill' Nichols saw the importance of addressing these issues. In Sydney, the Evangelical R. B. S. Hammond suggested, 'It is not what we do for the poor, but what we stimulate and encourage them to do for themselves that makes a difference. Most of our "poor relief" merely increases and perpetuates poverty.'[75] Oswald Barnett, a Methodist, and an ecumenical group of Melbourne businessmen met regularly to study difficult social and economical issues. R. W. Macaulay, an influential Melbourne Presbyterian, was involved in various groups idealistically seeking a new economic order, but they did not have the popular participation of Catholic groups with similar aims. Their political influence was important.

Using North American material, the reports of the Life and Work movement, and the COPEC conferences of the 1930s, they sought to apply insights on justice to the misery of the unemployed, the homeless, and the hungry, rather than stay content with handouts and soup kitchens. In Newcastle, Burgmann argued that there must be a Christian revolution or there will be some other form of revolution. Russia's model only need be feared 'if our efficiency, our zeal, and our

---

[74] P. O'Farrell, 'Bible reading and related mental furniture', *ACS* (1992) 16–27.
[75] *Southern Churchman*, Nov. 1935, 5.

humanity are less than hers'.[76] He articulated a radical vision of social justice to give the unemployed a chance for a new life. In his sermon after enthronement in Goulburn, he claimed the Anglican Church must find 'the making of the Australian nation is her special task . . . She must become a focus where the best religious forces of the nation can meet and find articulation and expression.' He also believed in the importance of developing the continent, so it was not occupied by Asian hordes. 'We must give ourselves to this continent as our only earthly home . . . This continent will become to us a sacramental expression of God's trust and love.'[77]

In 1930 a group of the Anglicans in Newcastle, and then in Melbourne, founded a religious community led by R. S. Lee and G. K. Tucker. The community's aim was to live with the poor, and as the Brotherhood of St Laurence, it was to become a major social service agency. In Auckland, Uncle Scrim of the Church of the Friendly Road founded in 1933, and in Wellington, the Anglicans Fielden Taylor and Jasper Calder, did notable work for the disadvantaged. Many congregations found it difficult to help the poor and survive financially. The Rector of Wagga Wagga said, 'We have cut down everything to the bone, yet we are in debt.'[78] Urban agencies for the poor were thus doubly important, but many congregations were vital sources of help in the Depression years.

A different approach emerged among educated Catholics, through Australian adaptations of the insights of Pierre Cardijn, which led to the formation of the Jesuit Institute for Social Order and the Catholic Social Study Movement in Melbourne as an expression of Catholic Action. A National Secretariat was set up in Melbourne by the Bishops' Conference, with F. Maher and B. A. Santamaria as staff. Differences soon emerged, with Sydney bishops wanting to keep the movement spiritual, and exercise much more direct control than Mannix did in Melbourne. An additional complication was how best to deal with the threat of Fascism and Communism. Amongst the large Italian community in Melbourne, Fr Modotti SJ felt that tension keenly. The threat of Communism greatly exercised a number of Catholics in touch with the trade union movement, where Communist officials were strategically placed in key unions. Both in the Catholic Social Study Movement and in the Knights of the Southern

[76] E. H. Burgmann, *God in Human History* (Morpeth, 1931) 31.
[77] *Southern Churchman*, June 1934, 3; ibid., Dec. 1937, 2.
[78] Ibid., Sept. 1933, 7.

Cross there were secret cells to counter this threat. That gathered momentum in the 1940s and early 1950s, deeply dividing both the Roman Catholic Church and the Australian Labor Party.[79]

If some Christians feared for the future, others expressed their optimism in building for a future not unlike the past. After the 1914–18 war, building resumed in most denominations. St Andrew's Presbyterian, Creek Street, Brisbane, and First Church Presbyterian, Invercargill, were fine examples of contemporary architecture. In Western Australia, a number of parish churches and the most original Roman Catholic cathedral, in Geraldton, which was completed in 1938, were designed by John Hawes, a gifted architect and priest who combined original form and liturgical appropriateness. St Brigid's, Red Hill, Brisbane, built in 1914, had architectural links with the cathedral at Albi in France, expressing the solidity of true faith in an unbelieving world. Some made concessions to the Australian climate, as in the verandahs on Tamrookum Chapel at Beaudesert, Queensland. Pews continued to keep worshippers in their place. Electric lighting was almost universal, but cooling was less successfully handled.

In South Australia, by 1940, almost £500,000 had been spent by Methodists on building, mostly by circuits. A Memorial Hospital, extensions to church schools, and an office block in central Adelaide further indicated the optimism and generosity of Methodists. Missionary giving reached £12,700 in 1928, a figure not surpassed until the 1950s. City missions were a vital part of Methodist witness in the Depression years. Members gave generously in goods, inspired by Tom Williams and Samuel Forsyth, both Irish, who had met in New Zealand. Both became remarkable city missionaries whose response to the Depression was immensely practical. They believed that to do nothing for human need was a great sin. Some attempts were made to reach workers through industrial mission, but little was gained, because the cultural context of such evangelism was little understood by church leaders.

Campaigns against alcohol abuse and gambling continued on both sides of the Tasman. National days of prayer, and the silence observed when Big Ben struck before war bulletins, were reminders of residual convictions about Christian nationhood. That was reinforced by amendment to the South Australian Education Act in 1940, which permitted thirty minutes of teaching on religion by ministers, or their

---

[79] P. O'Farrell, *Catholic Church and Community* (Sydney, 1985) 392–403.

representatives. Roman Catholics did not object. Two leading Methodists, Robert Richards, leader of the Labor Party, and Shirley Jefferies, the Minister of Education, saw the legislation through.[80]

Preaching was still considered an essential form of Christian communication, but has been little analysed compared with North American studies. In all the major cities, central churches were usually led by impressive preachers with congregations of many hundreds each Sunday. In provincial towns, and suburban churches in more prosperous suburbs, large congregations also were frequently led by gifted ministers whose preaching and teaching left a lasting community impact. F. W. Boreham of Mosgiel, and then Melbourne, was an ecumenical Baptist, with a flair for writing essays and editorials. His collections sold in tens of thousands far beyond Australasia, even though the market for published sermons was in decline. Metropolitan newspapers still ran Monday columns to report notable sermons, and Boreham wrote regularly for the Hobart *Mercury*, with gentle Christian perspectives. Such interchange underlines how significant the churches were in focusing important community aspirations, sustaining Anglo–Celtic identity, and at the same time enhancing community action in good causes.

PACIFIC CHANGES

Despite many colonial officers and missionaries treating Islanders as inferiors, many communities had adapted Christianity to their own cultural priorities in exchange, authority, and gender. Women's roles were as carefully defined in religious contexts as they were in daily life, so that they enhanced rather than undermined the sacred order defined by chiefs and clergy. In the Pacific many of the churches had moved a long way towards local control.

Local control by chiefly families was most obvious in the Free Wesleyan Church of Tonga, which in 1924 reunited with most of the old Wesleyan Church which had earlier refused to cut its ties with Australian Methodism. The union was a contribution to national unity. Queen Salote played a vital role. A small Free Church remained outside the union because some family rivals to the Tupou dynasty wished to keep power from Salote. Under Rodger Page, the relations between the two churches had slowly improved from 1905. As presi-

[80] A. D. Hunt, *This Side of Heaven* (Adelaide, 1985) 303–44.

dent from 1925 to 1946, his authority was wide-ranging. Page was able to win the confidence of Tongans, for he had no desire to impose his own agenda. He had important supporters among the nobility, especially Tungi, who was to become the consort of Salote in 1917, after her return from schooling in Auckland at the Anglican Queen Victoria College. She was a gifted woman of imperious temper, great personal charm, and artistic ability, who had potent *mana* and sacred authority because of her lineage. She skilfully ensured the weakening of potential rivals to her children, by marrying them to families of lower status, but her steady growth in political wisdom was a major reason for her stature.[81]

The union of the two main strands of Methodism underlined the close relation between social stability, Tongan identity, and this form of Christianity.[82] The sense of the sacred which is so important in Polynesian religion was retained, but modified by the warm piety of Methodism, and reinforced by the high quality of many Tongan ministers, who combined good education and commitment to all things Tongan. Salote chose the Conference presidents who often doubled as royal chaplains. She founded Christian Endeavour in 1935, and was an example of nation-building by women. Many missionaries continued to go to other parts of the Pacific, sharing their experience of self-support, cultural pride, and the importance of generous giving, never losing their sense of coming from Tonga, but able to create a partnership of faith which transcended island, tribal, and family loyalties, without denying them authority.

Under the leadership of Bishop Joseph Blanc, Vicar Apostolic of Central Oceania, 1912–37, and then of Tonga, 1937–53, the Roman Catholic Church became a respected part of Tongan Christianity, with good schools for boys and girls, and a slowly increasing number of Tongan clergy and religious. The partnership with New Zealand Marists was very fruitful, for it opened up possibilities for priestly education, fitted with the New Zealand schools syllabus, and helped Catholicism to appear less foreign. The Marist connection no longer needed to be dominantly French, for the congregation had grown significantly in both New Zealand and the United States. The French connection had, however, given Catholics different horizons from Methodists. They did not fruitfully interact until after Vatican II. Seventh-day Adventists and Mormons had a small presence, linked

[81] E. Wood-Ellem, *Queen Salote of Tonga* (Auckland, 1999).
[82] C. Forman, 'Tonga's tortured venture in church unity', *JPH* 13 (1978) 3–21.

specially with schools. A small Anglican Church was also present. Each of these benefited from occasional quarrels and schisms within the Methodist establishment, but Tonga remained predominantly Methodist.

Following the union of 1924, a number of Australian Methodists and occasional New Zealanders worked in the Tongan Church. Two of the most notable, A. Harold Wood and Cecil Gribble, both had long terms of service in education, and had great status because of their empathy with Tongan language and culture. Both returned to Australia, Wood to be principal of Methodist Ladies College in Melbourne, and Gribble to the post of Secretary to Overseas Missions. Both became presidents of the General Conference, and influential national leaders.

SAMOANIZING THE CHURCH

In Samoa, there was a different set of church and cultural relationships. J. E. Newell and Vanessa Schultze played vital roles in smoothing the transition to German rule from 1900. The latter had founded a girls' school at Papuata in 1892, which educated many of the wives of the pastors and chiefs.[83] Newell learned the importance of direct relations with German missionary societies, and became fluent in German as well as in Samoan. He came to understand the complexities of German ecclesiastical politics, and the ways in which Protestant and Catholic rivalry there impinged on affairs in Samoa. As principal of Malua, he was a key person in educating pastors for leadership, for he had deep insight into Samoan culture, and knew that the future of the Congregational Church lay with Samoans. In addition, he was a trusted adviser to Solf, the German governor, was close to leaders of many of the German Protestant missionary societies, and was thus able to make possible the work of Samoan missionaries in New Guinea, as well as recruiting pastors from other islands—Kiribati, Tuvalu, and Niue, and occasionally Micronesians from as far away as the Marshall Islands.

In 1909, Newell played a vital role as mediator between Solf and Lauaki, a powerful London Missionary Society deacon on Savaii and *tulafale,* who was a leader of the Samoans increasingly disillusioned

---

[83] J. Garrett, *Footsteps in the Sea* (Suva, 1992) 186–215. E. A. Downs, *Daughters of the Islands* (London, 1944) describes the ethos of the school. J. Charlot, 'Aspects of Samoan literature', *Anthropos* 85–7 (1990–2) 127–50, 415–74, 33–48.

with German policy. There was real danger of an uprising, but Newell persuaded Lauaki and his followers to place themselves in Solf's hands. They were exiled, until 1914, to the Marianas. In addition, Newell persuaded his colleagues to establish a council of *toeaina* (elder pastors) to give advice to the missionary-controlled Samoan District Council. Newell ultimately looked forward to the *Fono tele* becoming the ruling body of the Samoan church, where Samoans could organize affairs in their own way, given that the church was self-supporting. That change came sooner than the new group of missionaries who worked under New Zealand's rule in the 1920s had expected. A strong Samoan independence movement emerged, called the Mau, involving thousands of armed men pressing for much more control of their own affairs.[84] Some historians have argued that insensitive New Zealand officials pushed a significant number of Samoans into rebellion. O. F. Nelson, a Samoan Methodist businessman, was imprisoned for his leadership in the Mau. The issues were more complex, with the United States sternly repressing dissent in its Samoan territories.

The LMS sent two experienced missionaries, Hough and Parker, to report on the situation where missionaries had unilaterally dismissed the 1928 *Fono tele*, fearing it was controlled by Mau supporters. They consulted carefully, and produced a report which was very critical of the District Council, but also made some very important suggestions about admitting Samoans into more responsibility, so that communications could not break down again. In particular, they recommended a clearer explanation of financial affairs, hitherto mission-controlled, and a Samoan co-Treasurer, while making it clear that, though the Samoans paid the missionary stipend, this did not give them the power to direct missionaries. It was an important moment of transition, which set the Congregational Christian Church of Samoa, with almost 23,500 members, on the path to self-government.[85] It had long been financially self-supporting.[86] Not until the Labour government came into power in 1936 was O. F. Nelson freed, the Mau

[84] J. W. Davidson, *Samoa mo Samoa* (Melbourne, 1967). T. W. Reid, *A Man like Bati* (London, 1960) describes the important role played by Reginald Bartlett in ending the rebellion of 1929–31. M. J. Field, *Mau* (Wellington, 1984) gives a good account of the follies of the New Zealand regime, but must be read in conjunction with I. C. Campbell, 'New Zealand and the Mau', *NZJH* 33 (1999) 92–110.

[85] J. Heslin, *History of the Roman Catholic Church in Samoa* (Apia, 1995) 59. Methodists numbered 6,500 and Catholics almost 6,000.

[86] A. J. Hough and A. Parker, *Deputation to Samoa August–December, 1928* (London, 1928) gives a thorough report.

reorganized, and leaders given a limited role in government. So far as Methodists were concerned, they continued to retain strong links with Tonga and Australia, especially in centres of influence like Manono, and Southern Savaii. Tongan ministers had status above Samoan colleagues, but there was no move for an independent conference.[87]

Relations between Solf and the Roman Catholic Bishop Broyer had been tense, especially over the issue of education. The outbreak of war in 1914, and the New Zealand invasion of this German territory, left the Catholic Church in an uncertain situation so far as the Marist minor seminary at Moamoa was concerned. The Marists left in 1913. At village level, the missionary sisters of the Society of Mary had won deep respect for their quiet dedication to the well-being of their people. The girls they educated became resourceful leaders in village and parish life. Roman liturgy and customs merged with *fa'a Samoa*. Bishop Darnand worked comfortably with the New Zealand administration. Saints replaced ancestors, and the awe which was evoked by the Mass corresponded with ancient notions of *tapu*. Once again, French Catholic influences were strong in popular piety.

FIJI

In Fiji, with about 145,000 people, another form of indigenous Christianity with very influential chiefs had emerged, reflecting a different social structure, and the influence of Australian and New Zealand Methodists.[88] They emphasized outward conformity to moral rules, with rejection of such important customs as kava drinking and night dancing, both of which continued unofficially. Village Methodism met many of the religious and social needs of its people, but its leaders were not able to prepare their people for change. The centuries-old rhythms of village life were Christianized, but villagers showed no ambition to become a part of a new economic world. Fijians still held over 80 per cent of land in the 1920s. It was not

[87] R. W. Allardice, *The Methodist Story in Samoa 1828–1984* (Malifa, 1984); F. T. Fa'alafi, 'A century in the making of the Samoan church, 1818–1928', D.Theol. thesis (Melbourne, 1994); E. T. Ta'ase, 'The Congregational Christian Church in Samoa', Ph.D. thesis (Pasadena, 1995).

[88] A. H. Wood, *Overseas Missions of the Austrlian Methodist Church* (5 vols., Melbourne, 1975–87) vol. 2: *Fiji*, 341–73; vol. 5: *Fiji-Indian and Rotuma*, 1–95. A. Thornley, 'Fijian Methodism 1875–1945', Ph.D. thesis (Canberra, 1979).

surprising that some chiefs, like Ratu Sir Lala Sia Kune, who were close to colonial officials and benfited from indirect rule, found the Church of England more accommodating to pastoral liberty, and use of alcohol. They fostered a strong emphasis on British loyalty, and sports like rugby and cricket. Paternalist British governors and missionaries were united in preferring to import and exploit Indian plantation labourers, rather than disrupt Fijian village life and its strong Methodism, for the sake of economic development through the sugar industry.

It was John Burton, a New Zealand missionary, who analysed the system of indentured labour and publicized its abuses in a way the authorities could not ignore.[89] Burton deserves credit for his courageous advocacy and his missiological thinking about work in the Pacific, but his later attitudes were often patronizing, and, as Secretary for Missions, he could often be dictatorial. He later recognized that his opposition to delegating authority to Fijians and encouraging indigenous leadership was mistaken, but he did not have public critics among the Methodist staff. Most were convinced of the unreadiness of Fijians for control of the church. That was not granted until 1964. Part of the problem was the success of the extensive institutions which contributed so much to the impact of Methodism at every level of Fijian society.[90] For Fijians to finance them unaided was impossible.

The Catholic Church expanded its influence. Father Rougier exploited the dissatisfaction of Methodist chiefs, and succeeded in planting a church on Bau, to the anger of the Methodists. He had a strong entrepreneurial streak, and eventually was forced to leave the Marists, for wheeling and dealing in ways which profited his family. He eventually retired to Tahiti, living off his investments, until death claimed him in 1932. The Catholic Church grew steadily, especially through the work of girls' schools run by Sisters of St Joseph and the Third Order Regular of Mary. They advised on health and hygiene, and did something to reverse the decline in Fijian population. At Magokai, Mother Marie Agnes and a dedicated team of nurses cared for leprosy patients, winning admiration far beyond Fiji for their work.

Methodists also began to employ single women from Australia and New Zealand to work as nurses and teachers, but many missionaries were remote from Fijian aspirations, dismissing them as childlike. The Adventists exploited Fijian disillusion successfully, with the help of

---

[89] J. W. Burton, *The Fiji of Today* (London, 1910) 277 ff.
[90] J. W. Burton, *The Weaver's Shuttle*, TS Mitchell Library, is an autobiographical reflection.

Ratu Aporosa and Pauliasi Bunoa, both former Methodists. Another important leader, Apolosi Nai, was educated by the Methodists, but appears to have had some contacts with the pre-Christian *Tuka* cult which re-emerged in 1914 and the 1930s.[91] His attempt to set up a Viti company to market produce, without foreign middlemen's interference, was attractive to many of his people. Like Ratana, he broke out of the constraints of title and district, roused nationalist aspirations, and gave voice to the Fijian desire to regain land from Europeans. He died in 1946 after periods of exile by authorities who saw him as a troublemaker. He was a striking example of Fijian aspirations for control of their religious and economic destiny, even though he was unable to deliver his promises because of his own limitations, government opposition, and inability to replace the chiefly system. He demonstrated how powerfully Christianity could reinforce such aspirations, and provides an interesting comparison with the Ratana movement in New Zealand. His impact was immense, because he pleaded for Fiji for the Fijians, and attracted many Methodists to his movement. Some of Nai's leaderless followers were attracted by Seventh-day Adventists' preaching which capitalized on their disillusion, especially in the Wainibuke Valley.[92]

EXPANSION INTO THE HIGHLANDS

In New Guinea, the major event of the period was the discovery by miners and missionaries that there were tens of thousands of people living in the hitherto unknown Highlands.[93] They were opened up to European contact, after 1926, by gold prospectors willing to face fearsome climbs and great physical dangers from tribes for whom warfare was a way of life. Lutherans and Divine Word missionaries were well placed to deal with this challenge to evangelism. There were already 700 indigenous workers among the Lutherans, and when it was decided to enter, 200 volunteered immediately. Leonard Flierl,

[91] D. Scarr (ed.), *More Pacific Island Portraits* (Canberra, 1979) 173–92.

[92] A. J. Ferch (ed.), *Adventist History in the South Pacific 1885–1918* (Sydney, 1986) 174–88.

[93] A. Schaefer, *Cassowary of the Mountains* (Rome, 1991) is an account of Schaefer. J. Nilles, *They Went Out to Sow* (Rome, 1957) discusses the SVD expansion into the Highlands. M. Mennis, *Hagen Saga* (Boroko, 1982) on Fr Ross; G. Pilhofer, *Geschichte der Neuendettelauer Mission* (2 vols., Neuendettelau, 1961–3); A. C. Frerichs, *Anutu Conquers in New Guinea* (Columbus, 1957); G. F. Vicedom, *Church and People in New Guinea* (London, 1961); G. Apo, *Recollections and Experiences of a New Guinea Evangelist* (Columbus, 1937).

Georg Pilhofer, and Wilhelm Bergmann were the first German missionaries to enter. The latter and his wife, Louise, began a station in Kambaidam in 1931, following the pioneering journeys of Geyammolo and Gapenuo Ngizaki. The Australian government was also sending in patrols and district officers, who imposed a rough justice on the warring tribes with little concern for tribal perspectives. That made life less dangerous for prospectors and landseekers, who soon discovered the fertility of the valleys. The enterprising Leahy brothers began putting in airstrips to make the movement of supplies easier and cheaper, ultimately becoming influential business owners, and supporters of Catholic missionaries.

Missions were vital in the process of modernization because government agencies were few, and were so poorly financed. Enterprising missionaries sought strategic sites for stations. In 1934, the killing of two Divine Word workers led the government to ban further missionary work for a decade, and even indigenous evangelists were pulled out. A number of New Guineans were upset by this decision. Sekung wrote, this is 'our, the brown Papuans' country, and not that of the whites. If the brown heathen want us brown Christians, how then can the whites, strangers to the country, put up a barrier between us and forbid us to settle with our friends?'[94] Bergmann stayed, using the methods pioneered by Keysser, and not baptizing until communities were ready to act together.[95] He stayed for forty years, writing extensively on the customs of the Chimbu, and their language, before retiring to Brisbane. Vicedom wrote important studies of the communities around Mt Hagen. Hermann Strauss at Ogelbeng was also a notable ethnographer and linguist. Even more important, he saw the value of teaching people about Jesus from the beginning, rather than using the Old Testament, as Keysser had, as the basis for pre-baptismal instruction.

Though a number of the Lutherans were intensely patriotic, and

[94] H. Wagner and H. Reiner (eds.), *The Lutheran Church in Papua New Guinea* (Adelaide, 1987) 200.
[95] W. Bergmann, *The Kamanuku* (1971, Archives MLS); H. R. Hannemann, *Mission Work* (Lutheran Archives, Lae); W. Hannemann, *Vierzig Jahren in Neu Guinea* (11 vols., Lutheran Archives, Lae); J. Flierl, *Wunder die gottlichen Gnade* (Tanunda, 1931); W. Fugmann, *Christian Keysser* (Stuttgart, 1985); C. Keysser, *Bai the Sorcerer* (Madang, 1986); *Sanggang, Cannibal Chief to Christian* (Madang, 1986; 1st edn. 1949). Similar stories from other denominations give an indigenous perspective, even though written by missionaries. R. C. Nicholson, *Son of a Savage* (London, 1925); G. C. Carter, *David Voeta* (Auckland, 1973); and *Ti e Varane* (Rabaul, 1981); A. H. Voyce, *Peacemakers: The Story of David Pausu* (Coromandel, 1979).

some were members of the Nazi Party, they were much less racist than many of the Australians, who brought attitudes shaped by encounter with Aborigines.[96] The Australians saw the locals as 'coons' who needed stern discipline. Huge numbers were indentured between 1919 and 1939—about 280,000. They were paid three shillings monthly, which bought some trade goods and paid the poll tax of ten shillings annually. Women kept village economies alive. Australians used pidgin, while the Lutherans still insisted on the use of local languages and maintained correct relations with their German Catholic rivals, who adopted similar methods, and had a deep respect for local customs. They were not interested in turning their adherents and converts into brown Europeans.

Local understanding of Christianity had powerful links with pre-Christian worship and beliefs, where initiates had secret knowledge. Converts believed that missionaries had kept from them the secrets of obtaining goods. Perceptible cooling of commitment on the Huon Peninsula and in the Madang areas was followed in the 1920s by what seemed a promising movement of revival called Eemasang, led by Selembe and Desiang. The mission had become very institution-centred, with plantations, sawmills, and shipping. It is not surprising that the links between religion and material goods, always strong in Melanesian religions, were drawn by converts into conclusions which the missionaries found hard to understand, except in terms of reversion to heathenism. The movement developed cargo elements, which died down, but re-emerged in the 1940s.[97]

In Papua, the London Missionary Society was quietly expanding and consolidating its work, though the individualism of the missionaries and their often liberal theology produced some surprising results, giving birth to an elite who expected equality with whites. A number of women gave very distinguished missionary, educational, and medical service. They included Suzanne Ellis, a talented Welsh double graduate, who was the first ordained woman in the region. Ordained in 1926, she preceded by a year the ordination of Winifred Kiek, in South Australia. When Ellis married Robert Rankin, an LMS colleague, in 1937, she was no longer listed as an active missionary, though she continued her work in Papua until 1976, known as Sinabada. She taught people to pray Christian prayers before they cleared new gardens, for she saw how powerful the world of the spirits

[96] *Smiths Weekly*, 20 Mar. 1937, 'How German missionaries are white-anting Australia'.
[97] Wagner and Reiner, *Lutheran Church in Papua New Guinea*, 474–5.

was.[98] She did much for the advancement of village women. One violent husband was himself beaten by Ellis, which had a salutary effect on local levels of domestic violence. Constance Fairhall, who was called 'Paul' by colleagues, arrived in 1931, and in 1937 began a hospital for TB and leprosy victims at Gemo with a notable Samoan couple called Auana and Vaiiga, who spent 30 years in Papua. Samoans were still important partners in LMS work. Nemaia and his wife, Initia, worked at Lawes College, where village pastors were educated, as partners with Maurice Nixon, who was principal during 1939–49.

At Kwato, Charles Abel and his sons, who were strongly entrepreneurial Evangelicals, and then influenced by Moral Rearmament, withdrew from the LMS.[99] They insisted on a total break with the old culture and established new financial support from the USA between 1923 and 1942. They produced the first Papuan nursing trainees, the first lawyers, and key public servants, and created a very distinctive partnership between themselves and the Papuans by their industrial methods.[100]

In their own way, both Sacred Heart and Divine Word fathers were localizing like the Protestant missions, developing training and opportunities for catechists, though never in sufficient numbers to meet the needs of rapidly growing congregations. By 1930 there were over 16,000 Catholics. Sacred Heart priests such as Dubuy and Trompf were very influential among the Fuyughe. Their members increasingly saw the advantage of Christianity, and were willing to make some sacrifices of their heritage.[101] The first Papuan priest, Louis Vangeke, was ordained in 1938, after education overseas. He was the son of a high-ranking sorcerer, and his authority as a priest was enhanced by people's knowledge of his family. Christianity was seen as a superior form of spiritual power, with educational and technological advantages. Though village churches looked outwardly Catholic and controlled by missionary priests, other dynamics from traditional custom remained influential, though without formal institutional power.

---

[98] L. Gray, *Sinabada, Woman Among Warriors* (Melbourne, 1988) 78; S. C. Keays, 'Sinabada or Misis', Ph.D. thesis (Brisbane, 1995).

[99] D. Wetherell, *Reluctant Mission* (Brisbane, 1977); *Charles Abel and the Kwato Mission* (Melbourne, 1996).

[100] P. Chatterton, *Day that I have Loved* (Sydney, 1984); B. T. Butcher, *We Lived with Headhunters* (London, 1963).

[101] J. Waldersee, *Neither Eagles nor Saints* (Sydney, 1995) 278; G. Delbos, *The Mustard Seed* (Port Moresby, 1985).

Bishop De Boismenu persuaded Carmelite nuns to join him in 1934. They were an invaluable addition to the religious team. The Daughters of Our Lady of the Sacred Heart had inspired a group of young women to live outside their clan community and became auxiliaries of the sisters. Such a dramatic change in familial authority had a strong ripple effect. With a simple rule, the Handmaids of the Lord were practically very helpful to their European mentors.[102] The superiors of the sisters were able to adapt to very different conditions than those in their native France. Marie-Thérèse Noblet, Solange Dazin De Jesay, and Genevieve De Massingnac provided powerful models of Christian ministry and grounded Catholicism firmly in the lives of women in their areas. In the post-war years, Australian sisters and priests joined the French pioneers.

Anglicans began work in a relatively homogeneous area of Papua. By 1930 there were three priests, five deacons, forty-two Papuan catechists, plus eighty-eight teachers and 165 lay preachers.[103] Repatriated Melanesian converts from Queensland plantations were valuable workers, despite their lack of formal training and the patronizing refusal of the English missionaries to speak pidgin with them on grounds that it was a bastard language. The Melanesians could not always cope with English or local languages, but even as late as 1939, there were five still working in the diocese. Women were also treated as inferiors by male colleagues, but despite their lack of authority made notable contributions in schools and medical services and thereby modified local perceptions about gender roles.

Despite hostility and cultural misunderstandings, baptisms began in 1896 and growth became steady between 1910 and 1920. At Dogura, a large cathedral was built over a number of years. Romney Gill created a fascinating Christian community, and pioneered very effective monthly village councils which dealt with all kinds of issues. The mission did not develop the range of institutions and enterprises that neighbouring missions did. Its finances were limited and its workers expected to live a life of poverty. Unlike some other missions, Bishop Henry Newton was willing to ordain Papuans—the first in 1919, with seventeen ordained to the priesthood by 1942. The invaluable village teachers were expected to be self-supporting, but were

---

[102] M. Venard, *The History of the Daughters of Our Lady of the Sacred Heart in Papua New Guinea* (Port Moresby, 1978); M. Winowska, *Le Scandale de la Croix* (Montsurs, 1973) for a life of Noblet.

[103] Waldersee, *Neither Eagles nor Saints*, 289.

paid two shillings a month, plus sixpence a child, while Methodist teachers received £11 a year. Education and health care were still very inadequately funded, but Anglicans, like other missions, provided services which governments could not afford.

A spirit of independence was emerging among the Papuans. Two priests, Aidan Uwedo and Clement Wadidika, deeply offended Bishop Strong in 1936, when they raised the issue of wages in discussion of his Charge after his enthronement. He was to do better than that in later years, revealing a deeper pastoral sensitivity. Such cross-currents were Pacific-wide, indicating that the days of paternalism were numbered, even though such views remained powerful in Australia and New Zealand, where people were ignorant of the strength and integrity of village churches.

In the New Hebrides, the 1906 Condominium between the British and the French was a clumsy and unsatisfactory arrangement for administration. Its sole advantage was that, because it had so little money and decisions were so difficult to make, the lives of the islanders changed very little. Missions continued to provide services through churches, schools, medical care, and some technical education, without paying much attention to the dynamics of custom and the ceremonial authority of chiefs. Presbyterians were 40 per cent of the population, Anglicans and Roman Catholics 15 per cent each, while the Churches of Christ and Adventists covered another 5 per cent. Many islanders remained committed to custom, while on Tanna there was a dramatic revolt from the Presbyterian Church to follow the leadership of the mysterious John Frum. This movement had many of the features of an adaptation by the Tannese of their culture to take aspects of Christianity to create a new identity, but entirely on their terms.[104] Some of the missionaries simply saw it as a regression to traditional religion, inspired by Satan. Others with more insight saw that it had much to do with the failure of the mission to trust local people and to give them real responsibility.

The Solomon Islands, with a population of almost 100,000, were also politically divided by European powers with no interest in local aspirations. After 1918, Australia took over Buka and Bougainville.

[104] J. G. Miller, *Live* (7 vols., Sydney, 1978–90) vol. 5; R. Adams, *In the Land of Strangers* (Canberra, 1984); G. S. Parsonson, *The Gospel in the Southern New Hebrides* (Dunedin, 1985); P. Monnier, *Cent ans de Mission L'Eglise catholique au Vanuatau, 1887–1987* (Port Vila, 1987); K. Bowes (ed.), *Partners: One Hundred Years of Mission Overseas by Churches of Christ* (Melbourne, 1991) 55–85 for Vanuatu.

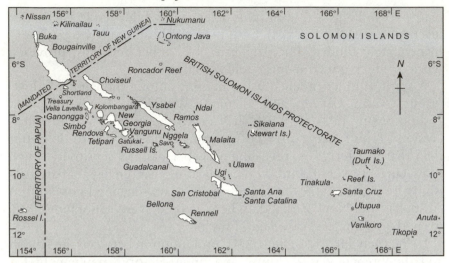

Solomon Islands (1944). (*Source:* Naval Intelligence Division, British Admiralty, *Pacific Islands*, 5 vols., London, 1939–45, vol. 3, p. 608. © British Crown Copyright/MOD. Reproduced with the permission of Her Britannic Majesty's Stationery Office.)

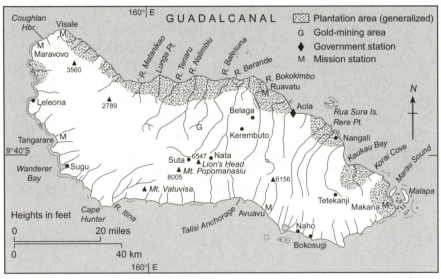

Guadalcanal (1944). (*Source:* Naval Intelligence Division, British Admiralty, *Pacific Islands*, 5 vols., London, 1939–45, vol. 3, p. 688. © British Crown Copyright/MOD. Reproduced with the permission of Her Britannic Majesty's Stationery Office.)

Britain administered the remainder of the Southern islands, but trade and church links with Australia were strong. Political dissent flared on Malaita in a tax revolt in 1927. Melanesia's diocesan headquarters moved from Norfolk Island to Siota in 1919. The bishops of Melanesia were English gentlemen, who mixed easily with the small body of colonial officials because they shared the same paternalist values. The Christians they ruled were occasionally turbulent, but the formation of the Melanesian Brotherhood by a former policeman, Ini Kopuria, in 1926, was an example of local initiative and concern for the still unreached tribes in the mountains. Bishop Steward helped to draft the Brotherhood's rule.

They vowed celibacy and service on an annually renewable basis, and travelled two by two, living very simply on donations, and spreading the message into New Guinea and New Britain, starting schools. Some became priests, but some of the British clergy of the diocese were sceptical of the value of the Brotherhood, charging it with elitism, which was rich, stemming as they themselves did from a very self-conscious public school elite. Charles Fox, a great New Zealand priest, joined the Brotherhood in 1932, but such identification was seen to be demeaning for a white man. Bishop Frederick Molyneaux forced him to leave, but was himself forced to resign his office because of his homosexual activity. It was a tragic failure of vision, which slowed the development of an indigenous priesthood.

Even the appointment of church headmen on Ysabel by Richard Fallowes in 1931 was seen as dangerous. He had a breakdown in 1935. Invalided home, he returned without Mission permission, in 1938. He helped to organize meetings which became the basis for petitions to the government in 1939. Fallowes was deported by Sir Henry Luke for his part in the Chair and Rule movement which sought a basis for local decision-making, but he saw much more clearly than his colleagues that white paternalism was based on distrust of Melanesian potential. The leaders of a post-war movement, Maasina Rule, looked back to Fallowes as one of their heroic forebears.[105] By 1946, there were sixty Melanesian clergy, who were far more in touch with village hopes than the British administration.

Amongst the Marists, Ronald Paves also took the side of local Christians, and pleaded with Bishop Raucaz for an increase in pay for

[105] H. Laracy (ed.), *Maasina Rule* (Suva, 1983) 47–52. Laracy also prints earlier letters asking for more Christian treatment, 44–8. C. Fox, *Kakamora* (London, 1962); A. Tippett, *Solomon Islands Christianity* (New York, 1967); D. Hilliard, *God's Gentlemen* (Brisbane, 1978).

the catechists. The bishop refused and closed down the school for catechists on grounds of economy, and sent Paves back to Europe to do penance for disobedience.[106] The people among whom Paves worked at Tanagrine and Visile stayed away from school and services in protest from 1933 to 1936, but without changing the bishop's mind. The American Marist Bishop Wade, in the North Solomons from 1930 to 1959, was much more encouraging in developing local leaders.

On Malaita, the SSEM, which had begun in Queensland as a faith mission on the sugar plantations, was led by Plymouth Brethren, who had imbibed attitudes from the raj in India before they moved south. They drew a sharp distinction between salvation, which was spiritual, and the way in which the Young family plantations were run in Queensland. Florence Young was a notable missionary, but could see little in the Solomons' culture that was redeemable. Solomon Islanders did not appreciate the difference between white and black wages and conditions. As early as 1912, Peter Ambuofa and Benjamin Footaboori petitioned King Edward VII through the governor, asking for equal wages, since they were all one in Jesus. This independent spirit was not appreciated by mission or government.

Adventist missionaries, intensely disliked by other missions, had taken their message to many parts of the Pacific by the 1920s. It was in Papua New Guinea, from 1908, that their work was to take deepest roots, though they also became strong in the Solomon Islands from 1914. Their work was helped by their Fijian missionaries, who were able quickly to make effective contact with Papuans. Many had been educated by John Fulton in Fiji. Only four Solomon Islanders were ordained by 1942, from 1,423 members. Villagers were skilled at playing off missions against one another for their own advantage. Adventists were no respecters of comity agreements.

A high turnover of their expatriate staff was due to inadequate education in faith and its relation to culture. Their position on diet might have appeared at first sight to be a recipe for failure, for their vegetarian diet and teaching that pigs were unclean cut right across some of the most fundamental features of Melanesian culture. Yet they brought

---

[106] D. Munro and A. Thornley, *The Covenant Makers* (Suva, 1996) 276–89 for a study of Catholic catechists. J. Luxton, *Isles of Solomon* (Auckland, 1955); J. A. Bennett, *Wealth of the Solomons* (Honolulu, 1988); A. K. Davidson (ed.), *The Story of my Life* (Suva, 1996) is a Tongan's account of his pioneering work on Ontong Java. D. Steley, 'Juapa Rane, The Seventh-day Adventist Mission in the Solomon Islands, 1914–42', MA thesis (Auckland, 1983).

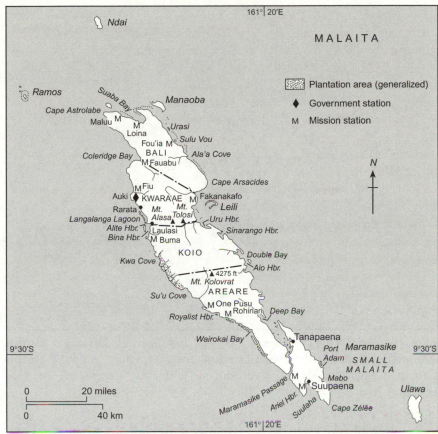

Malaita (1944). (*Source:* Naval Intelligence Division, British Admiralty, *Pacific Islands*, 5 vols., London, 1939–45, vol. 3, p. 686. © British Crown Copyright/MOD. Reproduced with the permission of Her Britannic Majesty's Stationery Office.)

about a remarkable cultural transformation in some villages, providing a cultural package of health, education, and religion which was an effective substitute for the old ways. Missionaries left much custom untouched, because of their sharp distinction between sacred and secular. Even the distinctive teaching on the Second Coming connected with some of the aspirations for 'cargo', and convictions about the power of ancestors, while tithing connected with exchange. Funeral practices also changed dramatically. One of the major reasons for change was the impact of children educated in the mission's schools.

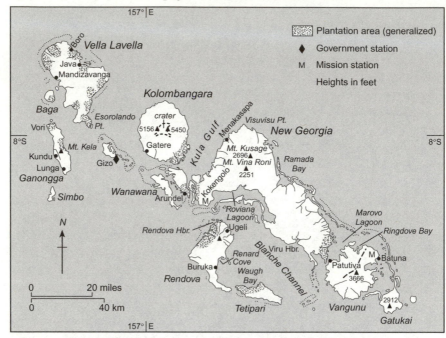

New Georgia (1944). (*Source:* Naval Intelligence Division, British Admiralty, *Pacific Islands*, 5 vols., London, 1939–45, vol. 3, p. 677. © British Crown Copyright/MOD. Reproduced with the permission of Her Britannic Majesty's Stationery Office.)

Vangalo of Marovo, New Georgia, described the change. 'They returned and began to teach us things they learned, and to tell us that our parents and forefathers were not helping us to catch fish, to make large gardens, or take us safely on head-hunting expeditions, but they were asleep in the earth. For some time we could not believe, but our boys and girls kept instructing us and, as you know, we gave up everything.'[107] By 1940, there were 1,780 members in Papua and around 4,000 in New Guinea, sustained in their identity by their eschatology and strong missionary leadership.

---

[107] Ferch, *Adventist History in the South Pacific*; N. Clapham (ed.), *Seventh-day Adventists in the South Pacific 1885–1985* (Sydney, 1985); D. Steyley, 'The Adventist package deal', in P. H. Ballis (ed.), *In and Out of the World: Seventh-day Adventists in New Zealand* (Palmerston North, 1985) 157.

ABORIGINAL CHRISTIANITY

The sesquicentenary of British arrival in Sydney in 1938, and the centenary of Waitangi in 1940, brought forth an outpouring of self-congratulatory reflection by the descendants of triumphant settlers, who were praised for their development of empty spaces and clearance of mighty forests. The indigenous people were largely ignored in this celebration. William Ferguson and William Cooper reminded the few Australians willing to listen, that it was a day of shame not celebration. Their pleas for justice for Aborigines went unheeded, even by the National Missionary Council.

Aborigines were much studied by anthropologists, but these were little less influenced by pervasive paternalism than the missionaries they sometimes criticized. Those who ventured criticisms were speedily brought into line. Ralph Piddington's critique of Western Australia's Aboriginal policy produced a violent reaction from A. O. Neville, the government Protector. Professor A. E. Elkin of Sydney University, an Anglican clergyman originally from New Zealand, did nothing to defend Piddington's independent research.[108] Elkin was an optimistic and frequent adviser to governments and the Anglican Church on Aboriginal and Pacific issues, and wrote 'We really now have an understanding of the Aborigines which should enable us to help them adjust themselves to the new conditions which have come upon them.'[109] Some of his students became missionaries to the Aborigines and, like the Methodist T. T. Webb, sought to find connections between traditional culture and Christianity. From a different theological position, Fr E. Worms, vicar apostolic from 1935 in North West Australia, a German Pallottine whose order arrived in 1901, wrote detailed reports on the culture of the people he lived amongst, as did Carl Strehlow, a Lutheran in Central Australia. His studies of Aranda culture are classics.

It was among these people that the first significant Aboriginal ministry emerged, led by the famous evangelist, Uraiakurai, or 'Blind Moses', who was deeply grounded in tribal culture and the world of

---

[108] T. Wise, *The Self-Made Anthropologist* (Sydney, 1985) studies Elkin. *ABM Review*, Sept. 1937, 150; G. Gray, 'Piddington's indiscretion', *Oceania* 64 (1993–4) 217–45; T. T. Webb, *From Spears to Spades* (Sydney, 1944); E. A. Worms, *Australian Aboriginal Religions* (Melbourne, 1986); B. Henson, *A Straight Out Man* (Melbourne, 1992); T. G. H. Strehlow, *Central Australian Religion* (Adelaide, 1978).
[109] *ABM Review*, Sept. 1937, 115.

the Bible. A white observer condescendingly described a Hermanns-
burg service at which Blind Moses preached. 'How much the natives
understood it was hard to see, but they seemed to do it all in a parrot
kind of fashion, without a trace of animation.'[110] Missionaries and
administrators disagreed deeply about the best methods of equipping
Aborigines for the new world, which pressed remorselessly on fragile
resources and small tribal communities. State government spending
on Aboriginal education and health was miserly, and administration
brutal, especially to children of cross-cultural marriages. Many in
government still expected the Aborigines would die out, and believed
that those with European parentage would be more readily assimilated
if they were removed from reserves and forced to work and live in
mainstream Australia. Funds for Aboriginal health and education
were miserably inadequate, and Aborigines Protection Boards were
more often destruction boards. Catholic missions expanded. In 1906,
Benedictines began work in Kalumburu, the St John of God Sisters
went to Beagle Bay in 1907, and Sacred Heart priests to Darwin in
1906, the Centre in 1935, and to Wilcannia in 1936, each creating lasting institutions and small communities.

Occasional white Australians attempted to publicize the injustice to
which Aborigines were almost universally subjected. Margaret
Bennett, the daughter of a Queensland pastoralist, wrote eloquently
about this, but Dr Charles Duguid of Adelaide was the most effective
in his advocacy, arguing powerfully that the Pitjantjatjara people in the
north of South Australia should have their lands protected so that they
could come to terms with Australian society at their own pace.
Paternalism was present in Duguid's gradualist approach, but his
concern for health and education was passionately argued, and
uncomfortable to the authorities. A diary of J. E. Owen, a
Presbyterian minister from Victoria, about his visit to Ernabella in the
1930s, shows how struck he was by the depth and integrity of tribal
culture.[111] It was to take decades before such attitudes were to become
part of many Australians' world-view.

Significant parts of Aboriginal culture remained little understood by
'whitefellas'. Even missionaries fluent in local languages missed seeing

[110] *Melbourne Herald*, 13 Sept. 1923.

[111] M. M. Bennett, *The Australian Aboriginal as a Human Being* (London, 1940). When
criticized by J. S. Needham in *The ABM Review*, she replied in a scorching letter, April 1932,
9–10. C. Duguid, *The Future of the Aborigines* (Melbourne, 1941). J. E. Owen, I owe access to
this diary to Dr Davis McCaughey and Dr M. Owen. *ABM Review*, Feb. 1942, 21–6, had an
obituary for Noble. J. Harris, *We Wish We'd Done More* (Adelaide, 1998) 265–309.

important parts of Aboriginal culture. Aborigines gave up some custom, but kept initiation and ceremonies related to land and identity.[112] Many Australians thought the Aborigines incapable of civilization, despite the contrary evidence in people such as James Noble, who died in 1941, a great Anglican, learned in custom, a fine athlete, and associate of E. Gribble. He was the first Anglican Aboriginal deacon, though several Torres Strait Islanders had been ordained in the inter-war years, beginning with Joseph Lui and Poey Passi in Advent 1919, followed by their priesting in 1924. They retained important links with custom and were important in an Islander strike against the Queensland government in the 1930s.[113]

In 1939, Fuata Taito from Rotuma went to Arnhem Land as a Methodist missionary. People were amazed, for they thought Christianity was a white man's religion. It would be several decades before many Australian Christians had to deal with issues of Christianity and their culture, which forced them to scrutinize their faith's cultural foundations. An interesting font at St Mary's, Mabuiag, in the Torres Strait, was made from a large clam shell on a basalt stone which offenders had once had to carry for punishment—a vivid evocation of removing the burden of sin. The link of Christianity and traditional culture was potent, and though the Torres Strait Islanders were only a small ethnic group, their conviction that they had title to their land had religious roots. The legal case later begun by the Anglican Eddie Mabo and others to have their title recognized succeeded in 1992, despite legislation to the contrary by the Queensland government, and was to change the course of Australian legal history in the 1990s.

WAR AGAIN

As in the 1914–18 war, only a tiny minority of Christian pacifists deplored the recourse to war when Hitler's unending last demands drove Britain and France to resist militarily. In the Student Christian Movement, there had been fierce debates about the morality of war in the 1930s, but some of the leading theological pacifists, such as Professor John Allan of Knox College, Dunedin, who had served in

---

[112] A. A. Yengoyan, 'Religion, morality and prophetic traditions', in R. W. Hefner (ed.), *Conversion to Christianity* (Berkeley, 1993) 233–58.
[113] N. Sharp, *Stars of Tagai* (Canberra, 1993) 204–8.

the First World War, gradually came to see that in some tragic situations war was a necessary evil. Christian leaders did not preach fiery patriotic sermons or act as eager recruiting agents, even though young men were still signed up with a sense of adventure as well as idealism. Archbishop Wand, the Anglican Archbishop of Brisbane and later Bishop of London, compared Australian troops to crusaders 'going out to defend the sacred places of the human spirit'. The Presbyterian Assembly was more circumspect, and produced a carefully balanced statement on war and peace.[114] Some Evangelicals saw the crisis as a lead-up to the Second Coming in which Mussolini was a key figure. Knowledge of millions wiped out by the monstrous regime of Stalin and his associates was only slowly emerging until the 1960s.

The Methodist Church in New Zealand came down heavily on Ormond Burton, who had been decorated by both British and French governments for his bravery in the First World War. Some thought he deserved a Victoria Cross. He became a pacifist, and in 1941 was imprisoned for speaking against the war. In 1942, the Conference in secret session withdrew his recognition as a minister, after some strong presidential pressure from William Walker. Half the conference abstained from the vote. Burton remained a prisoner as a conscientious objector for the duration of the war in Europe. Burton's *Testament of Peace* puts his view succinctly.[115] After the war he had a notable second career as an educator, before he was eventually readmitted to the Methodist ministry.

All the churches provided chaplains. Once again, they met a cross section of men and women, far wider than regular church attendees. They saw how war could debase and ennoble. Those to whom they ministered also experienced the horror of war, the destructive boredom of prison camps, and the freedom from constraints of civilian life. The churches' life continued much as before, except for the absence of ministers and members, the constraints of war effort, and the curtailing of evening activities. As well as serving in the forces, women, once again, maintained the war effort in essential occupations, as well as generously providing canteens and comforts for troops. For some, war brought discovery of faith. Archbishops Gilroy and Mowll produced joint statements on Christian principles

[114] *Church Chronicle*, Feb. 1940, 44; GAQ *Proceedings* (1940) 17.
[115] E. Crane, *I Can Do No Other* (Auckland, 1986) 49–60, 166; ibid., 157–73, for the conference debate; R. D. McEldowney (ed.), *Presbyterians in Aotearoa* (Wellington, 1990) 116 for Presbyterian attitudes.

for reconstruction.[116] For others it increased scepticism about the role of Christianity in society and its inability to transcend national boundaries to prevent war. Principal Hammond of Moore College, Sydney, saw in German capitulation to Nazi ideology the bitter fruit of Enlightenment rejection of revelation in Jesus Christ. 'A heathen hope comes down to this, we hope in ourselves, and we are a sorry lot of mortals to put our trust in.'[117]

Such theological judgements were more pessimistic than the hopes for Christian unity and reunion. In New Zealand, a National Council of Churches was founded in 1941.[118] One of its major programmes was the Campaign for Christian Order begun in 1942. Though there was disagreement about the definition of both words, important discussions took place on every aspect of the nation's life. In 1944, this ecumenical partnership made possible the formation of the Council of Organizations for Relief Service Overseas (CORSO) by the Methodist Revd Haddon Dixon, and the sending of peace teams to Greece, China, and Egypt.[119] In Australia also, Christians radicalized by the Depression with a vision for a new world founded the Campaign for a Christian Social Order inviting governments to be more actively interventionist economically and socially. The churches also attempted to re-establish their missionary work in war-torn areas, without fully realizing how greatly the context had changed. They also took an important role in caring for refugees.

While Rome still strongly influenced regional Catholicism, the tide flowed the other way when Australian Catholic bishops lent their weight to pleas to the Allies not to bomb Rome. The Apostolic Delegate had considerable influence on this, but it was Arthur Calwell and Dr Herbert Evatt who actually drafted the final wording of the appeal.[120] Clashes over censorship brought conflict about the boundaries of press freedom. Both Australia and New Zealand admitted some Jewish refugees, though not as many as were requested by Australian Jewish leaders. Official documents and parliamentary debates demonstrated that crude anti-Semitism was alive and well in the community. Though many church leaders made it plain that Jews and Christians had much in common, Victorian Presbyterians still

---

[116] *Sydney Morning Herald*, 3 July 1943.

[117] T. C. Hammond, *Fading Light* (London, n.d.) 117; *Sydney Morning Herald*, 3 July 1943.

[118] C. G. Brown, *Forty Years On* (Christchurch, 1981).

[119] R. T. Thompson, *New Zealand in Relief* (Wellington, 1965). M. Lovell-Smith, *No Turning Back* (Christchurch, 1986). K. P. Clements, 'The churches and social policy', Ph.D. thesis (Wellington, 1970). [120] I owe this point to Ms Mary-Elizabeth Calwell.

retained a committee for Jewish evangelism. Coming to terms with the horrors of the Holocaust has proved extraordinarily difficult, as has dealing with anti-Jewish attitudes.

Darwin and parts of north-western Australia were heavily bombed by the Japanese, but the full horror of destruction was felt in the Solomon Islands, and New Guinea, with Japanese forces coming within 50 kilometres of Port Moresby. Many local people were killed and wounded in a struggle of which they had no comprehension. Others were conscripted and forced to labour by both sides. Australian forces showed little sympathy for those forced to work for the Japanese, treating them as collaborators rather than conscripts.

The war also caused enormous physical destruction in the Solomon Islands and New Guinea, which was very testing for the churches. A number of missionaries who remained were murdered by the Japanese, some died of illness and privations in prison camps, and others died at sea on prison ships sunk or bombed by Allied action. Many local Christians also died, and had their commitment dramatically tested by the invaders, for they were suspected of collaboration with the Allies. Many thousands suffered greatly and were given an insight into a different kind of colonial conquest. Australians were harsh recruiters of porters and labourers, though some Papuans were happy to volunteer for service for they knew some of the dangers of invasion, even if they were miserably paid by the Australia New Guinea Administrative Unit. Some 37,000 were serving in 1944. Several thousand served as soldiers and orderlies for fourpence weekly, and no pension. Fijians served with distinction in the Solomons, proudly reviving their warrior traditions, as did the Maori Battalion in North Africa and Europe.

While the precise number may never be known, over 300 mission workers and local Christians were killed by the Japanese and, most tragically, on 6 February 1944, by Allied bombing of a ship, the *Yorishimi Maru*, carrying a number of prisoners of war.[121] Another, the *Montevideo Maru*, with a similar body of missionaries, was torpedoed with total loss of life. Many local Christians risked their lives to shelter missionaries and troops, or to smuggle food to them when they were imprisoned, while others like the notable Fijian missionary Usaia Sotutu travelled long distances to guide them to safety behind the

---

[121] T. Aerts (ed.), *The Martyrs of Papua New Guinea* (Port Moresby, 1994) 37–44 for lists. Aerts' bibliography is invaluable. He also prints a moving apology from Japan by Bishop Soma, who served in Rabaul, 244–6.

lines. Some were put to death because they refused to obey Japanese orders to forsake Christianity.

One of the most remarkable of these was the catechist Peter To Rot Burua of Rokunai, born in 1912, whose father refused him permission to study for the priesthood. He was beatified on the occasion of Pope John Paul II's visit to Australasia in 1995. He was killed by the Japanese in 1945 for continuing to call people to worship, and performing pastoral work, despite four warnings, imprisonment, and beatings. He had collected traditional songs. All other catechists gave up the *lotu* because of Japanese pressure. His wife, Paula, suggested he live as an ordinary man. He replied, 'This is not your business. It is fitting that I die for the Name of God the Father, the Son and the Holy Spirit . . . and for the sake of my people.'[122]

War, and the removal of European leadership, created serious problems for the churches, especially in Papua New Guinea. In Brisbane, Otto Theile negotiated skilfully with the Australian authorities to preserve the New Guinea missions run by Lutherans. Some Germans were interned, but Theile's contacts and ecumenical connections were vital to minimizing disruption. The worship and witness of the loyal congregations, led by evangelists and teachers, kept the churches growing even though they suffered heavy physical losses. The relationship with missionaries was changed as local leaders grew in confidence and demonstrated that missionaries were not indispensable.

The Divine Word fathers lost Bishops Loerks and Wolf, but they, too, were surprised to find how faithful congregations had continued their work and worship, led by catechists. Sacred Heart fathers and the Daughters of Our Lady of the Sacred Heart showed great fortitude in prison. Bishop Scharmach was a courageous and inspiring spiritual leader during internment. Indeed, such experience greatly contributed to the breaking down of denominational suspicions, as prisoners found that their unity in Christ was something that transcended national, cultural, and religious differences. The later strength of ecumenism in Papua New Guinea and the Solomons owed much to the shared experience of suffering. Bishops Strong in Papua and Baddeley in the Solomons also gave notable leadership to Anglicans, refusing to desert their flock.

Though French Polynesia and New Caledonia were not invaded by the Japanese, the war brought other problems, especially how to be

---

[122] C. G. To Vaninara, *The Life of Peter To Rot* (Vunapope, 1975) 29.

related to the rival French regimes of Vichy and De Gaulle.[123] Both territories opted for De Gaulle. Australian missionaries in Korea had a different kind of struggle with the Japanese administration. Faced with the demand that Koreans pay homage to the emperor Hirohito, the Presbyterian mission staff was divided between those who saw this as a civil matter, like James Mackenzie, and those, like Dr Charles McLaren, who believed that it was idolatry which demanded non-compliance. He went to prison for a time, but many Korean Christians suffered cruelly as a consequence of their refusal to pay divine homage to the emperor.[124]

In war-torn China, Australian and New Zealand missionaries had varying fates.[125] Some were captured by the Japanese and interned for the duration. Such contacts helped to keep Christians aware of the wider world, and to remind them of their community role. Burgmann, passionately committed to the spiritual foundations of democracy, suggested that 'great tasks need high-souled unselfish people. It's here that the Church comes in. If the Church fails, the State will probably fail also. The making of a nation needs the free and vigorous co-operation of both Church and State. Australia has never yet felt the power of a mighty religious impulse and therefore it has no culture that is at all distinctive.'[126]

Dealing with the power of atomic weapons was a great challenge. To harness atomic power for life and not death has proved as difficult for Christians to cope with as their societies, as has the use of other major technological advances like computing. Scientific reason has outpaced moral and political capacity, and enhanced the power of the exploitative mentality which has been so potent in the region. The testing of rockets at Woomera caused concerns for Aborigines. Professor Elkin defended government policy. 'To talk of firing atomic bombs is simply nonsense.'[127] He was under-informed by his high-level government contacts, for his support was politically important. Later governments had to pay heavily for clearing the fall-out from the British atomic tests at Maralinga.[128]

---

[123] Garrett, *Footsteps in the Sea*, 366, 421–3.

[124] H. Mackenzie, *Mackenzie, Man of Mission* (Melbourne, 1995) 212–13.

[125] T. Newnham, *He Min Qing: Life of Kathleen Hall* (Beijing, 1992); G. Ogilvie, *Little Feet in a Big Room* (Christchurch, 1994); A. James, *I was in Prison* (Christchurch, 1952). She described the courage of Chinese Christians who supported her.

[126] *Southern Churchman*, Jan. 1944, 1.   [127] Ibid., July 1947, 12.

[128] C. Duguid, *The Rocket Range, Aborigines and War* (Melbourne, 1947) was a withering denunciation of government overlooking the needs of the Aborigines affected.

The first decades of the twentieth century had shown how strongly the region's churches had shaped individual, community, and national life. Serious limitations in their Australian and New Zealand witness were emerging, for the number disconnected from the churches was slowly growing. This did not mean such people saw themselves always as unbelievers. They remained committed to aspects of Christian morality, which for many was *the* defining feature of authentic Christianity. Issues of theodicy remained critical for many of those who disbelieved. They could not reconcile the power of evil with Christian claims about the goodness of God.

6

CREATING NEW SOCIETIES

The whole region saw major changes between 1960 and 80.[1] Australia and New Zealand both rejected wartime Labor/Labour governments for a less controlled economic regime, but turned back to their policies with the leadership of Gough Whitlam, confirmed Anglican, Bob Hawke, a Congregational minister's son, and David Lange, a Methodist lay preacher, each of whom brought a new style of politics representing the generational and social shifts which occurred after peace in 1945. A number of Pacific countries were granted independence or were moving towards it, access to information was improving, but only a privileged minority had access to wealth and political power. Regional population grew rapidly, both by natural increase and by large migration schemes. In 1947 Australia had 7,518,000 people. Between 1947 and 1983, 3.25 million immigrants came to Australia, of whom 46 per cent were British. Between 1964 and 1984, 152,160 people emigrated from New Zealand to Australia. Some 180,000 a year were travelling overseas and bringing back new perspectives.

For the churches here, as in other parts of the world, it was initially a time of optimistic expansion and post-war rebuilding, whether in the Highlands of New Guinea, or with large building programmes in growing suburbs and new towns. In all the Pacific churches, signs of desire for local control gathered momentum, supported by younger missionaries, though village Christianity appeared outwardly the same, but was changing within. Leaders believed that tried and tested worship, theology, pastoral care, and religious education only needed to be applied, for the churches as institutions seemed to have a secure social place.

Leaders were still convinced that the interests of religion and the interests of the nation coincided. The churches' place seemed secure in all parts of the region. Providing buildings for worship, education, and recreation in new areas seemed the best way of ministering to those who wanted to create a better society. There was a steady expan-

[1] J. Molony, *History of Australia* (Melbourne, 1988); K. Sinclair (ed.), *Oxford Illustrated History of New Zealand* (Auckland, 1990).

sion of aged care and hospitals. Many Christians were hopeful about the role of the United Nations, and Dr Evatt, an Anglican, a Labor leader, and a jurist from Sydney, used a number of clergy to advise him there. Almost continuous prosperity in the Menzies period under-pinned these developments, with full employment making the terrible Depression seem light years away. Despite the bitterness created by war, the Australian Board of Missions ministry to Japan, which began with Frank Coaldrake, was a sign that some Australian Christians were prepared to make new beginnings to overcome the hatreds of war.

Another sign was education. Both tertiary and secondary education expanded. One of the most important developments in Australia, from the 1960s, was growth of the Catholic school system, rapid growth of government secondary schools, and the steady expansion of state aid to church schools. The Presbyterian Church of Queensland Public Questions Committee deplored the latter 'as not in the best interests of national unity or the Protestant standards of morality'.[2] Some clergy concerned for national harmony called for an end to class war in the strife-torn 1940s. In his presidential address to the Association of Sociology, Kenneth Henderson showed how class-bound he was, when he pled for individuals to take 'tide turning initiatives back from class war to the co-operative spirit'.[3] He had clearly never worked for an unscrupulous employer. A generation grew up with no real knowledge of unemployment, or war. The possibilities for human improvement seemed endless, though nuclear testing began a long-term poisoning of the environment, and other forms of ecological deterioration accelerated until Rachel Carson's *Silent Spring* sounded a warning.

Many migrants to Australia brought with them a different experience from those from an Anglo-Celtic heritage, deep hatreds of totalitarian regimes, economic energy, and gratitude for opportunities to start a new life. They included 35,000 Jewish Holocaust survivors who have transformed Jewish–Christian relationships by rejecting the assimilationist model. Others, like the Cook Islander migrants to New Zealand, came simply for social and economic advancement, rather than as refugees from war and ancient hatreds. In 1944, the first Cook Islands minister, the Revd Tariu Teaia, arrived in Auckland to work amongst those who felt marginalized in New Zealand. He was followed in 1948 by the Revd R. L. Challis, who helped to create an

[2] GAQ *Proceedings* (1957) 128.
[3] K. T. Henderson, *Is Class War Still Necessary?* (Sydney, 1946) 9.

inter-island Congregational church which did not take sufficient account of Islander loyalties, but which was vital in the early years of adjustment to New Zealand.

Though wars broke out regularly during this period, they were localized and sometimes related to the Cold War between the Soviet bloc and what was optimistically called the 'Free World'. True believers in communism and capitalism both insisted they held the key to the future, but voters chose interventionist governments. Bitter struggles in the Australian trade unions, major strikes in the 1940s, attempts to ban communism, and the conviction of many Roman Catholics that defeat of communism was essential to Australia's survival as a democracy, brought a major political upheaval in the 1950s, which split both the Roman Catholic Church and the Australian Labor Party.

In 1951, a referendum to ban the Communist Party of Australia failed. There were sharp divisions among Christians about which way to vote. In Perth, Kim Beazley of the Labor Party was highly critical of his fellow Anglican Bishop Burgmann's 'toleration' of the Communist Party, and allegedly buying their lie that the Labor Party was domi-nated by Roman Catholics.[4] There was controversy about Doctor Hromadka's visit and his pleas for co-operation with socialism based on his Czech experience. Some migrants saw him as a despicable collaborator. Many ideas which once were considered 'socialist' became mainstream, and 'leftish' views spread widely among church leaders, even though they did not have the optimism of Alexander Gosman's Socialism in the 1890s. Beneath these conflicts, and the polarization in New Zealand caused by the 151-day-long 1951 water-front strike, many wished for a home of their own, opportunities for their children which had been denied to them by depression and war, and secure employment in a fair society shaped by a broad Christian ethos. Perhaps it was a limited society, but it offered a basic civility absent in many more sophisticated societies.

Criticism of suburban life by some self-appointed intellectuals is fashionable fifty years later, but what many achieved in the 1950s and 1960s was a summit of social ambition, with carpets, electric stoves, washing machines, fridges, even a car.[5] Opportunities for leisure grew

---

[4] St Mark's Library, L.C. Webb papers, Beazley–Burgmann, 13 Oct. 1952.
[5] D. Edwards, *Mirimar Dog* (Auckland, 1998) for an amusing account of suburban sectarian hostilities in the 1950s. D. Hilliard, 'Church, family and sexuality in Australia in the 1950s', *AHS* 109 (1997) 133–56; 'The religious crisis of the 1960s', *JRH* 21 (1997) 209–27.

with the introduction of the 40-hour week, family benefits, and the expansion of a safety net against misfortune and illness. Some women wanted to improve family life and widen female roles in society. In 1952, Winifred Kiek headed the Australian Council of Churches Commission of Enquiry into the work of women in the Church. Simone de Beauvoir's *The Second Sex* had just been published in 1953, but few foresaw that reformism would be insufficient, even though Queen Elizabeth had succeeded to the throne in the same year, and provided a fresh model of Christian family life. Marriage guidance was beginning to be an influential movement. W. G. Coughlan became Executive Officer of the organization in New South Wales in 1954 but did not envisage re-examination of marriage and family life.

Secondary education expanded dramatically, with the raising of school leaving age to fifteen and then to sixteen, but Islander children still lacked adequate education. Universities grew rapidly, and offered young Australians and New Zealanders opportunities for advancement independent of income and class, without deepening spiritual depth and wisdom. Music, drama, and publishing expanded in both the cities and smaller towns with more than a little help from European migrants, providing additional leisure pursuits besides sport, drinking, fishing, and hunting, and bringing a major change in culture for Australians and New Zealanders.[6] Pacific Island capitals also expanded, especially in New Caledonia and French Polynesia, reflecting policy changes in Paris. British colonial policy was also changing, with expanded spending on education, health, and public works.

LEADERSHIP CHANGES

The Anglican Church in the region was still formally led by English-born bishops in the metropolitan sees and many rural ones. During 1962–6, there was significant turnover in the episcopate. Ten Australian bishops out of twenty-five were newly appointed. In New Zealand, English bishops were no longer a majority. Though English-ness was still revered, local clergy and laity increasingly shaped parish life. Attachment to the Crown was still strong, reinforced by royal visits. The Revd J. P. Haldane-Stevenson claimed that, 'Royalty has something transcendental about it, representing a spiritual sphere,

[6] M. Lewis, *Ngaio Marsh* (London, 1991) 114–89 describes some of these through the influence of an Anglophile New Zealander who described herself as 'a wobbly Anglican'.

where differences fade away before a glowing and living unity . . . The King is exalted but you are ennobled by your relationship to him as a co-worker for Britain and Christ.'[7] Though there was still a strong sense of Christian society, that was not always defined as bishops would have liked, though they symbolized its importance. There were already signs that growth in communicant membership was slowing. In Newcastle Anglican Diocese only about twenty new communicant members a year were joining, according to a report on the decline in churchgoing which was published in 1951, noting also that just over half of the Anglican constituency did not attend worship.

In Sydney, Archbishop Mowll gave important leadership in a rapidly expanding community, fundraising for church extension, recruiting for ministers, but never losing sight of the need to nurture the diocese's Evangelical identity, through expanding mission work internationally. Mowll emphasized that 'A unique opportunity has been given to us, as representatives of the British way of life and of the Christian faith, to influence 1160 million of the world's population living close to our shores.'[8] The vision for a Christian society was also voiced at the 1962 General Synod by the governor-general, Viscount De L'Isle, who said, 'Here the duties of a Christian in his capacity as a citizen and his responsibility for helping to sustain an ordered society are not at all in conflict with his supreme duty to God.'[9]

Mowll and his gifted wife, Dorothy, mixed easily with people in parishes, and he laid the foundations for lasting expansion. As primate, he showed that he could meet colleagues of very different views when he visited other dioceses. His contributions to the acceptance of a revised constitution for General Synod was decisive, for there were articulate opponents in Sydney, but they could not convince their synod that it was a victory for Anglo-Catholics when Mowll supported change, along with T. C. Hammond.[10]

At a time when any contact with China was seen as 'communist', Mowll had, in 1956, the courage to lead a party of bishops, clergy, Francis James, the flamboyant editor of *The Anglican*, and Mrs

---

[7] La Trobe MS 7583 Box 544 Stevenson Papers.

[8] M. Loane, *Archbishop Mowll* (London, 1960); GSA *Proceedings* (1950) 21; S. Judd and K. J. Cable, *Sydney Anglicans*, (Sydney, 1987) 225–66.

[9] GSA *Proceedings* (1962) 31.

[10] Hammond was also involved in the Red Book case, an Evangelical attempt to limit 'advanced' worship. R. Teale, 'The Red Book case', *JRH* 12 (1982) 74–89; B. F. Pigeon, 'The Bathurst Case and the legal nexus', *CQ* 14/3 (1949) 16–22; St Mark's Library, Webb Papers LCW–R. B. Peagram, 4 July 1972.

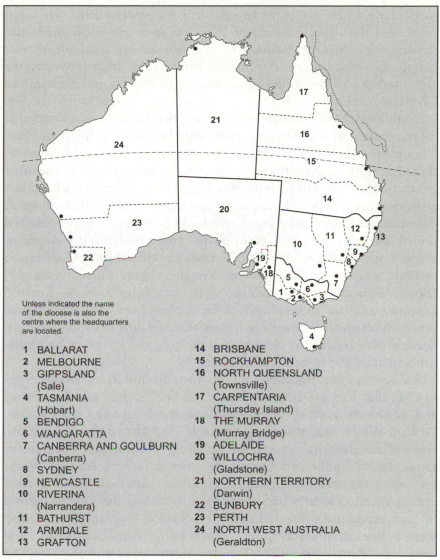

Unless indicated the name of the diocese is also the centre where the headquarters are located.

1	BALLARAT	14	BRISBANE
2	MELBOURNE	15	ROCKHAMPTON
3	GIPPSLAND	16	NORTH QUEENSLAND
	(Sale)		(Townsville)
4	TASMANIA	17	CARPENTARIA
	(Hobart)		(Thursday Island)
5	BENDIGO	18	THE MURRAY
6	WANGARATTA		(Murray Bridge)
7	CANBERRA AND GOULBURN	19	ADELAIDE
	(Canberra)	20	WILLOCHRA
8	SYDNEY		(Gladstone)
9	NEWCASTLE	21	NORTHERN TERRITORY
10	RIVERINA		(Darwin)
	(Narrandera)	22	BUNBURY
11	BATHURST	23	PERTH
12	ARMIDALE	24	NORTH WEST AUSTRALIA
13	GRAFTON		(Geraldton)

Australia: Anglican dioceses (1995). (*Source: The Australian Anglican Directory,* Melbourne, 1995, pp. 4–5. With permission of Angela Grutzner.)

Mowll to revisit Szechwan, where he had been bishop in 1923–33, re-establishing contacts which were to be invaluable for Chinese and Australian Christians alike. His vision for a renewed church, his straightforward approach, and his capacity to translate vision into reality, gave Sydney Anglicanism an impetus which it has not lost, particularly in its attraction to gifted and energetic laity. He even persuaded the diocese to invest £30,000 in a television company. 'Unless television can be used to convey, in due measure, to our people, the ethical spiritual influence on which Christianity rests, we are entering a phase of life which may well mark a grave decline in Christian values.'[11]

In addition, Mowll was involved in the beginnings of the ecumenical movement in Australia, especially after becoming primate in 1947. Though not personally interested in theological scholarship, he was skilled at nurturing promising young men, who provided the next generation of leadership for the diocese, as well as for Evangelical outposts in other dioceses. There were also ties with Wycliffe College in Toronto and Canadian Evangelicals. Links were also being established with bishops to the north through the first South Pacific Anglican council, which met in May 1966. Sydney provided bishops for Nelson in New Zealand until the 1960s. Yet there were unresolved issues about Anglican identity which were raised by a New Zealand academic migrant to Canberra, who deplored the lack of historical sense which underlay Anglican failure to agree on a new constitution, because of 'a lack of any clear idea of the essential nature of Anglicanism and of its role in Australian society'.[12]

Sydney was the largest diocese in Australia and its leadership from key families like the Begbies, Langford-Smiths, Knoxes, Horderns, and Taubmans gave it unique status in the Anglican Communion. Dr Paul White, one of the most notable Christians of his generation, was not involved in Synod, but was hugely influential through his *Jungle Doctor* books and broadcasts, and university student work. He was a founder of Pilgrim, a significant international Christian communication agency in Sydney. Yet there was also a strong group of laity, especially lawyers like Minton-Taylor, Gee, and Mann, who were better described as Low Church rather than Evangelical, and were very careful about legal and constitutional powers, sceptical about privilege, and carried weight with laity in synods. Minton-Taylor briefed counsel in the Red Book case. They were a reminder that not only bishops defined the church.

Sydney Anglicans included a number of the distinguished judges and senior lawyers who played an important part in the synods and parishes, as well as highly placed business people. C. R. Walsh, the

[11] GSA *Proceedings* (1955) 26.
[12] L. Webb, *The Conciliar Element in the Anglican Tradition* (Canberra, 1957) 20.

registrar and diocesan secretary for twenty years, had his fingers in every conceivable pie. He was followed by H.V. Archival, 1948–58, who was an Evangelical activist and a skilful manager in Synod. He was an unyielding defender of the faith. Walter Gee, from St Paul's, Chatswood, disliked Anglo-Catholicism intensely and specialized in cutting down episcopal aspirations in the General Synod. Not all Sydney Anglican lawyers were Evangelical. A. B. Kerrigan of St James's, King Street, was Chancellor of Newcastle and used his influence in the General Synod against Sydney and its positions.

Differences between Sydney and Melbourne tantalize historians. Their religious ethos is certainly different, affecting all the major churches, especially the Anglicans. In Melbourne, Archbishop Booth was much more cautious, but he had a common touch due to being orphaned, winning recognition through struggle after education at Ridley College. He was a fine chaplain in the First World War and was awarded the Military Cross, returning to be a successful parish minister, and fundraiser extraordinary. Becoming co-adjutor to Archbishop Head, he again served as chaplain in the Second World War until recalled when Head died, then becoming archbishop. He laid foundations for rapid parochial expansion, was a wise steward of Melbourne's slender finances, began a network of hospital chaplaincies, and demonstrated that an Evangelical could respect other patterns of churchmanship. He was also committed to the development of a comprehensive and authentically Australian Anglican Church, which made Melbourne's variety unusual amidst a church of largely monochrome dioceses.[13]

The English connection was also represented by Sharp in Brisbane, Moline in Perth, Robin in Adelaide, and Batty in Newcastle. Despite the social strength of Anglican networks the problem of nominalism was growing. In 1955, an Air Force chaplain reported that of seventy-nine Anglicans in the intake, four were confirmed, thirteen unbaptized, forty-one did not know their parish priest's name. That went alongside Moline's language about Australia as a 'forward base of the Kingdom of Heaven in the Southern Hemisphere', and building a Christian nation in Western Australia.[14]

Australian-born bishops were beginning to exercise national leadership. So was Averill in New Zealand. Hart at Wangaratta and Moyes

[13] A. De Q. Robin, *Making Many Rich* (Melbourne, 1978).
[14] Battye MS MN 112/1174A Perth Diocesan Registry; Perth Synod, *Proceedings* (1951) 9–10, 51.

at Armidale were both equipped with keen minds. Moyes had abilities larger than his diocese, and helped Lambeth in 1958 take a more sympathetic view on contraception.[15] Similarly, T. T. Reed was elected Archbishop of Adelaide when Reindorp refused to let his name go forward from Southwark, and Reed became the first Australian-born metropolitan. New Zealand Anglican bishops had no one of the stature of the Australian metropolitans, though West-Watson in Christchurch was certainly the equal of the smaller diocesans in Australia.

The Roman Catholic Church on both sides of the Tasman was dominated by long-lived archbishops, Mannix in Melbourne and Duhig in Brisbane, Liston in Auckland and McKeefry in Wellington, all of whom had taken office in the early twentieth century.[16] An occasional Australian became a New Zealand bishop, but none went in the opposite direction. Duhig was genial and outgoing, actively involved in civic and university affairs, but never neglected visiting his parishes, or defending Catholic interests, though he rejected Mannix's republicanism. He was knighted in 1959. Known as James the Builder, he sought to make the churches and schools more accessible to his people, adding over thirty-two new parishes to the existing seventy-seven, founding thirty primary and eighteen secondary schools, and bringing in thirty-five new orders and congregations to staff the diocesan expansion, as well as building two university colleges, and a splendid seminary at Banyo. He also gave some encouragement to Catholic women.[17]

Mannix was a master of biting sarcasm and thinly veined irony which could cause great offence to Protestants, so that he was both reviled and revered for his oratory. He published very little. Prayerful and intensely ascetic, he was an isolated figure who scorned the Melbourne establishment, but had close relations with widely read and strongly committed laity like Arthur Calwell and Bob Santamaria, who were later bitter political enemies to each other. A wide reader, he was not a deep thinker. Assiduous in episcopal duties, he attended

---

[15] P. Lamb, *The Conscience of the Church. John Stoward Moyes* (Armidale, 1997); A. O'Brien, 'The case of the cultivated man', *AHS* 107 (1996) 242–56.

[16] B. A. Santamaria, *The Quality of Leadership* (Melbourne, 1984). The *ADB* article by J. Griffin offers a counterview. C. Kiernan, 'Reflections on historical biography: the case of Daniel Mannix', *Australian Studies* 3 (1989) 36–44; R. M. Sweetman, 'Second thoughts on historical biography', *Australian Studies* 6 (1992) 81–5.

[17] T. P. Boland, *James Duhig* (Brisbane, 1986); R. Daley, 'The Catholic Women's League in Queensland', *BCHS* 4 (1994) 35–46.

innumerable functions, and presided over a huge expansion of the diocese after 1945. His political influence is difficult to assess, since all his papers were destroyed, but he was a key player in the Catholic Social Study Movement which contributed to 'The Split' in the Australian Labor Party in 1954–5, and the later formation of the Democratic Labor Party which divided the Labor vote until 1972.[18]

Though The Grail was still suspect to many bishops and clergy, its life-changing impact on women can be seen in the career of Rosemary Goldie, whose career in teaching French literature changed direction because of the contacts she had through the movement. She became instead an influential figure in the Roman Catholic lay apostolate, one of the few lay auditors at Vatican II, and a respected ecumenical speaker on the role of the laity, as well as a professor at the Pontifical Lateran University from 1977 to 1986. She stands in a different place from advocates of women's ordination to the priesthood, but argues for the partnership of men and women.[19]

In 1937, Archbishop Gilroy of Sydney was the first Australian to be appointed to a metropolitan Catholic diocese.[20] In 1934–7 he was bishop in Port Augusta, then co-adjutor to Kelly, whom he succeeded in 1940. He had a speedy climb to responsibility both because of his administrative gifts, and also because he was well known in Rome. He gained his doctorate there, and was a friend of Montini, later Paul VI. His appointment as cardinal gave him a great deal of influence in Rome, which he used to good effect to defeat the supporters of the Movement, including Mannix and his allies. He was knighted in 1969. Gilroy did not approve of independent laity, whether the Knights of the Southern Cross or the National Civic Council, and kept his clergy on a tight rein, insisting on very detailed accountability regarding their administration. He approved a new hymnal in 1959, so long as James McAuley's name was left out.[21] His administration was, like his personal life, frugal, but that meant that he husbanded diocesan resources skilfully for the huge post-war expansion, with sixty-four new parishes by 1958. In 1971 there were almost 3,000 women religious, but only 522 men. He built a very competent administrative

[18] P. Cleary, *Cleary Independent* (Melbourne, 1998) gives a vivid account of the rivalries in Coburg between supporters of the DLP and ALP.

[19] R. Goldie, *From a Roman Window* (Melbourne, 1998) 218–35.

[20] J. J. Luttrell, 'Norman Thomas, Cardinal Gilroy as Archbishop of Sydney', Ph.D. thesis (Sydney, 1998). See also T. P. Boland's *ADB* article.

[21] Luttrell, 'Norman Thomas, Cardinal Gilroy', 89.

team of consultants around him, and was very skilful in relations to the wider community and its leaders.

Though he cultivated the image of reluctant bishop and simple priest, he was astute politically, and influential in the early stages of Vatican II as one of the council of presidency. The huge theological and canonical changes which followed left him bemused, and he had no sympathy for those who questioned what were, for him and his generation, the basic verities of faith. His hope in the 1940s for a Catholic university had been strongly resisted by Protestants like T. C. Hammond and was not realized in his lifetime, but he had the faculty at Manly recognized as a pontifical one in 1954.[22] His 1971 invitation to Opus Dei to run Warrane College at the University of New South Wales shows his commitment to traditional Catholicism. That kind of mindset can also be seen in the young John Bathersby, later Archbishop of Brisbane, in Goondiwindi, Queensland, who baptized a devout dying Anglican who had already had his own vicar's ministry. 'We thought we'd done a marvellous job for this poor and good man—that we'd secured the salvation of his immortal soul.'[23]

DEALING WITH REGIONAL SOCIETIES' CONCERNS

A move to leftish political sympathies among younger Protestant clergy saw a Christian critique of capitalism, which expected an interventionist style of government but was not so good at encouraging economic innovations, and was sometimes blind to the follies of socialism. Nineteenth-century praise of capitalists by churchmen had disappeared by the late twentieth century. Catholics like Vincent Buckley and James McAuley, both notable teachers of English literature sought to rescue Australia from Protestant liberalism and its secularizing tendencies. On both sides of the Tasman, the churches and their leaders remained important contributors to national and local identity, and received many political favours from governments.[24]

Church leaders regularly commented on public issues, usually with

[22] K. J. Walsh, *Yesterday's Seminary* (Sydney, 1998) studies Manly till 1968.
[23] *In Unity* 44/3 (1997) 1; D. Hughes, *Don't You Sing! Memories of a Catholic Boyhood* (Sydney, 1994) gives a lay perspective.
[24] J. Evans, 'Church–state relations in New Zealand 1940–90', Ph.D. thesis (Dunedin, 1993).

a conservative bias, but upholding the widespread conviction that society was still broadly Christian. Many newspapers had clergy as regular columnists and leader writers, but only a few papers had a regular religion correspondent like Alan Gill on the *Sydney Morning Herald*, who acquired real authority in commenting on church affairs. The Australian Broadcasting Corporation's religion staff contributed greatly to the intelligent public discussion of religious matters. Christians were also active in local government. In New Plymouth, the Town Clerk, F. T. Bellringer, was from a staunch Methodist family. He prepared an installation ceremony for the Council, for 'we believe that in local and international affairs a recognition of God as our Creator and Guide and our strength is in itself essential. Holding this belief, it is fitting that the council's new term of office should commence with prayer.'[25]

Leading Protestant clergy combined with judges in the 1951 'Call to Australia' to summon the nation to renewed moral and religious commitment.[26] The Catholic bishops weighed in with a more apocalyptic and pessimistic vision in *The Future of Australia* in 1951, but saw Australia's destiny as a Christian commonwealth. Many Christians were deeply concerned about the threat of communism. Santamaria and the Lutheran Dr Fred Schwarz were two of its articulate Christian opponents, mocked by some for being too extreme, but who took the religious challenge of Marxism seriously. Dealing with issues which were deemed 'political' was more controversial, for Christians disagreed sharply about the placement of that boundary. In New Zealand, the difficulties of finding a common Christian voice were well shown in the work of the Inter-Church Council for Public Affairs, founded in 1941, and even including Roman Catholics. It agreed that no public pronouncement would be made unless the representatives of its constituents were unanimous. Its silences meant it was little-known. Nevertheless, it made submissions to governments on a wide range of issues, helped by the number of parliamentarians with church connections. Bishop Burgmann saw the Church as a critic of the state, what he called 'a standing opposition' in the great parliament of man.[27]

Ecumenism was slowly creating a new atmosphere. The formation

[25] Taranaki Museum Bellringer MS.
[26] D. Hilliard, 'Church, family and sexuality in the 1950s', *Australian Historical Studies* 109 (1997) 133–46; Hunt, *This Side of Heaven* (Adelaide, 1985) 395–6.
[27] *Southern Churchman*, May 1955.

of the New Zealand Council for Christian Education in 1949 and the appointment of the Methodist Les Clements as the first Justice Department prison chaplain in 1951 were signs of a new ecumenical climate. The growing impact of television, from 1956 in Australia, and 1961 in New Zealand, developed that. Controversial issues were dealt with more and more publicly. Media clergy such as Malcolm Mackay in Sydney, and Bob Lowe, the genial vicar of Fendalton, Christchurch, with his Open Pulpit, reached far beyond church walls in dealing with a variety of public issues. Media personalities such as Bobby Limb in Australia showed how Christian convictions and entertainment could be combined.

Bridging the Catholic–Protestant divide was more difficult. 'Educational justice' was still a matter of deep concern for Catholics, especially in Australian dioceses where rapidly rising school rolls placed an almost unbearable burden on parishes and religious congregations which dealt with teaching.[28] Approximately 20 per cent of Australia's school population were at Catholic schools in the 1950s. Many Protestants were unsympathetic and quite unable to see the cogency of Catholic views, for their youth movements were flourishing without the assistance of denominational schools. In Goulburn, the diocesan newspaper feared 'the consequences of this policy if Roman Catholic schools turn out a politically disciplined body within the state'.[29] Some Catholics were discussing the closure of their schools, and developing religious instruction, along Protestant lines, for Catholic pupils in state schools, a process already operating in a small way. The Knights of the Southern Cross, however, pressed strongly for educational justice in Australia, as did the Holy Name Society in New Zealand.

In New Zealand, the Holy Name Society unsuccessfully petitioned for aid in 1956. The Currie Commission in 1962 recommended that the secular principle be upheld in primary schools, but noted that the 1877 Act did not apply to secondary schools. An amendment to the Education Act in 1964 permitted religious instruction at more flexible times. Religious instruction and prayers at assemblies were permissible, but that depended on the willingness of teachers and school committees to deal with objections.[30] In 1975 a major change

[28] I. Breward, *A History of the Australian Churches* (Sydney, 1993) 160–2.
[29] *Southern Churchman*, Oct. 1956, 3.
[30] R. P. Davis, *Guide to State Aid in Tasmania* (Hobart, 1974); B. Gilling (ed.), *Godly Schools* (Hamilton, 1993); J. Woodward, 'The turmoil of state aid', *BCHS* 1 (1989) 52–62.

occurred. The government invited church schools to integrate with the national system. Almost all Catholic schools accepted.

Some Australian Catholics in Western Australia and Queensland also argued strongly for state aid, but politicians were hard of hearing, fearing a Protestant reaction. A group of parents in Goulburn, New South Wales, showed the collapse of the Catholic school system would create greater difficulties for government schools. Fed up with some bureaucratic needling over toilet facilities, they closed the schools and sent their children to state schools. It made a dramatic point, even though it was speedily over.[31] It showed that if the Catholic school system collapsed, state schools could not possibly cope with the resulting influx of pupils.

Education was constitutionally a state matter, but the Menzies' federal government had already made loans available for the development of church schools in Canberra, as more and more public servants moved there from Sydney and Melbourne. Grants for the development of science teaching followed nationally, and not just in the Australian Capital Territory. Church protest was muted, and Protestant independent schools accepted the grants, despite some Protestants being passionately opposed. Clearly there was scope for further aid and, in the process, attracting votes and preferences away from the Australian Labor Party. State governments also began to make grants.

Similar partnerships between the authorities and missions on education occurred in colonial territories. In Papua New Guinea, the Australian government steadily increased its expenditure on schools and medical services, for the United Nations made it plain that independence for the trust territory of New Guinea must have a timetable. Papua, which was legally part of Australia, also shared in the process, despite its leaders' suspicion of swamping by Highlanders. Similar developments were occurring in British, French, and New Zealand colonial territories. In the Solomon Islands, Britain found that many people on Malaita were no longer willing to be subjects of the old-style colonial regime. Maasina Rule (1944–52) sought to create an alternative government, and encouraged refusal to pay taxes to the colonial authorities.[32] The leadership of the movement was strongly influenced by members of the SSEM. After some violence and prison sentences, the British authorities were persuaded to permit local

[31] T. Cullinane, 'Goulburn for the record', *ACR* 61–3 (July 1984 to June 1986).
[32] H. Laracy (ed.), *Pacific Protest* (Suva, 1983).

participation in government. This was the first post-war sign of restiveness about colonial rule outside New Guinea, where a number of adjustment cults undertook some political activity alongside their eschatological hopes for a new economic order. By the 1970s such political turbulence was especially obvious in New Caledonia and French Polynesia.

DEVELOPING RESOURCES

All the churches had to develop their fundraising capacity to cope with migration and increases in birth rates. The methods of the American, Colonel Wells, were amazingly successful. St Andrew's Anglican Church in Brighton, Victoria, trebled its giving per head to £15 a year. In Wellington, Bishop Reginald Owen launched the Advancing Church Campaign in 1948 to raise a modest £10,000 for site purchase. New Zealand Presbyterians in 1948 aimed for £500,000 by 1958 to finance expansion, and founded sixty-six new parishes, as well as building institutions, and expanding overseas missions. Growing prosperity helped these aims, but the Presbyterian New Life Movement, led by Tom Steele, Norman Perry, and a dynamic team of young businessmen, transformed the church from 1949, giving it a fresh vision for evangelism, expansion, and service to the nation.[33] New Life programmes were held in one out of three parishes and extended into Stewardship campaigns which raised giving sharply and were copied by many Presbyterian congregations in Australia. Methodists in New Zealand set up a Spiritual Advance Committee in 1947 and then ran a Crusade for Christ and His Kingdom from 1949 to 1952, which aimed to increase membership by 5,000 from the many census Methodists who were not attached to circuits. For a short time the gap between regular worshippers, those under pastoral care, and the census figures of adherence significantly narrowed for all the major churches. The most successful restructure of church finances was in the Anglican Diocese of Sydney under Archbishop Hugh Gough in the 1960s. Methodists in Australia had their Mission to the Nation, led by Alan Walker. He had ministered successfully in a mining community in New South Wales. His energy, flair, business contacts, and capacity to communicate with people from all walks of life made a

[33] R. D. McEldowney (ed.), *Presbyterians in Aotearoa* (Wellington, 1990) 122–6.

huge impact, with thousands attending meetings, and gaining new confidence in their Christian identity.[34]

In some places, young ministers were watching American developments like the Ecumenical Institute and changes in education with interest, and wondering whether the multiplication of geographically based parishes was the best model for the future urban ministry. Study and visits to the United States dramatically grew from the 1950s.[35] Australian innovators crossed the Tasman. Ted Buckle, an Australian who had worked in the Snowy Mountains Scheme amongst thousands of New Australians, came to the Auckland Anglican diocese, and introduced strategic thinking about the future shape of ministry, later becoming a respected bishop. In Dunedin, Sydney Smale, who had been involved in similar forward planning in Victoria, challenged Presbyterian colleagues to think afresh about ministry, especially in the centre of the city, before he returned to Melbourne. Methodists in Auckland remodelled their City Mission, and Alan Walker conducted several New Zealand evangelistic campaigns which reminded many Methodists of their origins, and the desirability of modernizing their heritage.[36]

SEARCHES FOR UNITY

The visit of the Southern Baptist Billy Graham in 1959 came at a time when the vitality and expansion of Protestantism seemed assured.[37] In New Zealand, his visit was cautiously backed by the National Council of Churches, though Anglo-Catholics on both sides of the Tasman were dismissive of his theology and methods. Archbishop Halse, of Brisbane, welcomed the reawakening of interest in spiritual values, but claimed that it was hard to estimate 'how many thoughtful people have been "put off" by the over-simplicity of the fundamentalist approach to the Bible'.[38] In each centre Graham visited, an interdenominational committee was formed, training instituted for counsellors, and relay facilities set up. For Protestants it was an opportunity to savour the excitement of huge gatherings like the brilliantly

[34] D. Wright, *Alan Walker* (Adelaide, 1997) 93–119.
[35] N. Buch, 'American influences on Protestantism in Queensland since 1945', Ph.D. thesis (Brisbane, 1994).
[36] Wright, ibid., 120–48.
[37] S. Piggin, *Evangelical Christianity in Australia* (Melbourne, 1996) 154–71.
[38] *Church Chronicle*, Aug. 1959, 227.

managed Catholic Eucharistic Congresses. For many it brought a deepening renewal of commitment. The huge crowds seemed to indicate confirmation of the essentials of the Christian message and the timeless offer of salvation. Critics had to recognize that Graham's appeal rested on much more than emotion. Many were searching for deeper experiences of spiritual reality than was provided by their local congregation and denomination. Baptists especially benefited because other Protestant churches did not always deal adequately with those who were changed by the crusades. Numbers offering for ministry and missionary service rose sharply. Evangelicals were given fresh heart and saw little need for the ambitious plans for Protestant reunion which were being pursued in Australia between Congregationalists, Methodists, and Presbyterians, with Anglicans and Churches of Christ also involved in New Zealand.[39]

In many local gatherings, Congregationalists, Methodists, and Presbyterians found that discussion of reunion in the 1950s gave them a new understanding of their heritage and the possibilities of united Christian witness in their community. They began to work towards local co-operation long before their leaders had reached agreement. Such ecumenical possibilities in new housing areas, and declining inner-city and scattered rural congregations excited young ministers desirous of working on the frontiers of Christian witness.

Here and there, warning signals emerged. Dutch Reformed migrants founded the Reformed Church in 1952–3 after finding Presbyterians too liberal. Pacific Island migrants to New Zealand from LMS churches naturally gravitated to the Congregational Union, which soon found itself numerically dominated by the newcomers. The Union leadership and some of the Pacific missionaries who had come to New Zealand saw this as an opportunity to create a new kind of partnership between Christians who had so much in common. Tensions between Cook Islanders, Niueans, Samoans, and Tokelauans were overcome in some contexts by wise leadership, and careful attention to the sensibilities of each group. In Auckland, a group of Samoans, led by Konese Fuimaono Ta'ala, decided in late 1962 and early 1963 that they did not want their children to grow up in a church where the Samoan heritage was devalued. They asked to become part of the Congregational Christian Church of Samoa. 'One cannot get full satisfaction out of worshipping when one has to sing in a language

---

[39] A. Black, 'Church union in Canada and Australia', *Australian–Canadian Studies* 1 (1983) 44–56.

one does not fully understand.' Or as Elder Pastor Ieriko said, 'Samoan culture is one hundred percent better than any other culture in the world. Samoa exists in respect.'

Complicated issues of status, family rivalry, and personalities quickly emerged, and the church in Samoa found it difficult to know how to resolve the matter, for some could see that there were financial advantages in having New Zealand congregations as well as those in California and Hawaii. Few could have seen that by 1993 20 per cent of the Congregational Christian Church of Samoa's income would come from New Zealand, as did 20 per cent of its giving for missions. The upshot was a chain reaction of splits throughout New Zealand which violently divided families.[40] Some Cook Islanders took similar action. The New Zealand Congregational leadership simply could not understand the power of ethnicity in migrant churches, or appreciate that Samoans were also setting up similar churches in the United States, and disliked their gifts going to other groups. Schism and switching denominations were long established in Samoa, an important way of resolving disputes in the name of high principle, and thus enhancing family status. By 1969, there were over 30,000 Islanders in New Zealand, somewhat resented by the Maori. While most joined the Presbyterian Church in 1970, the ten Samoan–related churches grew steadily in spread and numbers. By 1991, Islander numbers had grown to over 130,000, concentrated in Auckland and Wellington.

Christianity and ethnicity are at their most complex amongst the Orthodox churches.[41] In Australia in 1947, they numbered 17,000 members. By 1971 they had grown to 338,632, moving towards 3 per cent of the population. Canonically, there can only be one bishop in one place, but ethnic and regional loyalties run so strongly that the sacrifice required to achieve such a suitable result is simply not possible for the foreseeable future. So far it has proved impossible even to set up a forum where all the Australian or the far fewer New Zealand Orthodox can meet together. The Greek Orthodox joined the Australian Council of Churches in 1958. Because of jurisdictional rivalries and political divisions from the communist era, some bishops cannot meet, though informal conversations occur through state

---

[40] D. Ioka, 'Origin and beginning of the Congregational Christian Church of Samoa in Aotearoa, New Zealand', Ph.D. thesis (Dunedin, 1998) 227 gives an admirable discussion which adds a great deal to the earlier analysis of U. F. Nokise. On 586–628, Ioka prints documents on disputes between various groups.

[41] H. L. N. Simmons, *Orthodoxy in Australia* (Brookline, 1986); N. Doumanis, 'Eastern Orthodoxy and migrant conflict: the Greek Church schism in Australia', *JRH* 17 (1972) 60–7.

councils of churches. Even the largest community, the Greek Orthodox, is seriously divided between jurisdictions, with some communities refusing to recognize the authority of the bishops in communion
with the Ecumenical Patriarch in Constantinople. The history of
Orthodoxy in North America suggests that historic ethnic divisions
will remain, even if there is limited co-operation through ecumenical
bodies.

Institutionally, the Australian and New Zealand churches reached
their peak in the 1960s in terms of the absolute numbers worshipping.
In proportion to the total population, all the major churches, except
Roman Catholics, were slowly declining, though that did not seem
important until the 1960s and 1970s. The impact of television, the
collapse of censorship, and the changes in education brought about a
challenge to the practice and theology of the churches, felt most
keenly by those in their twenties who found the churches out of touch
with their aspirations and their search for a better life than their tedious
parents enjoyed. Maori reaction was different. In New Zealand in
1951, 32 per cent of Maori were Anglican, 14 per cent Roman
Catholic, 20 per cent Ratana, and 6 per cent Ringatu.

Many experiments in new forms of Christian witness occurred. In
Sydney, Alan Walker was by far the best-known innovator. His
development of Life Line was very successful in reaching the lonely
with timely phone counselling, and it spread internationally. Arthur
Preston in Brisbane, and then in Melbourne's Central Methodist
Mission, encouraged service for forgotten groups like those with
Huntington's Disease, for whom there was little care.[42] Harry Squires
of the Anglican City Mission in Wellington, from 1939 to 1954,[43] and
George Jefferies of St James Presbyterian Church in Auckland, from
1957 to 1981, both worked effectively with marginal people who
slipped outside the welfare net provided by government. Specialist
counselling agencies, like the Cairnmillar Centre in Melbourne (led
by Dr Francis MacNab) and the Campbell Centre in Christchurch,
provided service to those who would not approach parish clergy.
Marriage Guidance also became another important community
service, working ecumenically, with help from British mentors like
David Mace and Jack Dominian, and including Christians and non-
Christians alike from the 1960s. In country towns, however, churches

---

[42] R. Howe and S. Swain, *The Challenge of the City* (Melbourne, 1993) narrates the history
of the Central Mission in Melbourne.

[43] W. P. Morrell, *The Anglican Church in New Zealand* (Dunedin, 1993) 226–7.

continued to give important contributions to community life. Dr Bill Bossence's diary of life in Kyabram gives a vivid picture of such Methodism.[44]

The polarization between Protestant and Roman Catholic, liberal and Evangelical was still very real. In 1950, some New Zealand Presbyterians formed the Westminster Fellowship to defend historic theology. In Catholic seminaries, Protestant Bible colleges, and smaller theological colleges, and in countless homilies and sermons, long-standing divisions were reinforced, and worldliness kept out. Catholic seminarians were denied access to newspapers. Dr Leslie Rumble MSC, of Sydney, was a skilled apologist for classical Catholicism, both on radio and in his collection of *Radio Replies*, which sold in tens of thousands, though his assured approach was increasingly dated by the 1960s. Some Catholics became Protestants, but there was a traffic the other way amongst those who wanted more than personal opinion as a basis for living. In Sydney, James McAuley, a lapsed Anglican, and Catherine MacKellar, a questioning Presbyterian, both went over to Rome, becoming articulate advocates for their authoritative new religious home. Mrs MacKellar's children were showing some Protestant children round their church. 'In clear and precise terms they were expounding the true faith. Here you have to genuflect. . . . Unlike you Protestants, we know that Jesus is really and truly here.'[45]

One of the most fascinating people involved in this search for a more authentic identity was James Baxter, a fine New Zealand poet whose sexual and alcoholic adventures were notorious. Until he became a Roman Catholic, he had no particular religious allegiance, but once the choice was made he became a *guru* for many young people who were searching for a new way of life. At Jerusalem, on the Wanganui River, he and others attempted to create a Christian community. Baxter speedily absorbed Catholic spirituality, theology, and culture, and wrote some of the best popular regional theology of the 1970s in *The Flowering Cross*. Barefooted, bearded, and ill-dressed, he moved freely in the worlds of cathedral and commune. His own personal struggles helped him to guide young New Zealanders whose desire to experiment had broken family relationships and their own sense of self-worth. He was an uncomfortable conscience. A series of unpublished letters on the priesthood expanded the dilemmas of

[44] La Trobe MS 11239/Box 2732 Bossence Papers.
[45] W. Dalton, *Seeking the Word* (Melbourne 1996) 89.

celibacy and obedience with rare compassion about the dualistic world which many priests could not integrate, and about their problems of sexuality and loneliness.

A different insight into Catholicism came from Morris West,[46] almost a Christian Brother, who became one of Australia's most influential bestselling authors. He owed more than a little to the Christian Brothers. His insight into the ironies, tragedies, and meaninglessness of life is suffused with moments of grace and communion, but unlike Baxter's is expressed in prose rather than poetry. He was aware of the inadequacies of reason for definition of God or understanding the mysteries of living. For West, faith was an affirmation that light can triumph over darkness. He was critical of the way the Church was so slow to admit failure.

Theologians like Drs Siegfried Hebart and Hermann Sasse in Adelaide, and Broughton Knox in Sydney, Lutherans and Anglican respectively, skilfully defended classic Protestant orthodoxy. Lutherans with their confessional heritage showed that ministers could be contemporary, but intelligently interpret their heritage. Others whose lives showed the tensions between heritage and contemporary relevance were Bill Hobbin and Dudley Hyde, both Australian Methodists.[47] Hobbin came from a poor family, which appeared to rule out academic study, despite his passion for ministry. His doubts about the adequacy of traditional theology were raised in Newcastle, by the inability of leading Methodists to apply the Gospel to business. He began study at Leigh College in 1929, and was concerned to find that a clergyman was evicting his tenants in Newtown. Throughout his ministry he continually angered conservative Methodists in his position as Director of the Department of Public Questions and Social Service. Within two years of his appointment in 1949, he was in trouble for starting a home for intellectually disabled children without conference permission. Other similar homes followed. He acted as industrial chaplain at Email and Imperial Chemical Industries, and served with World Refugee Year in 1959, as well as being President of Freedom from Hunger and raising over $3 million (A) for that cause. His critics constantly complained that he was too involved in secular activities, but he was unrepentant about the timeliness of liberal philosophy and theology.

One of the most difficult issues Australians and New Zealanders had

[46] M. West, *A View from the Ridge* (Melbourne, 1996).
[47] W. Ward, *Men Ahead of their Time* (Melbourne, 1996) 15–46.

to deal with was the implicit racism which marginalized Aborigines and Maori. Politics and religion intersected in a very painful way. Professor Thomas Jollie Smith of Melbourne put it forcefully in a previous generation. 'They should not, and they cannot be assimilated by the white community. They must live apart . . . So far as one can see, these men will not become the equals of the white man.'[48] Presbyterians in New Zealand unsuccessfully requested the Rugby Union in 1958 to choose a team to tour South Africa on merit only. In 1960, eight church leaders issued a statement supporting this stand, but the Anglican Bishop of Wellington, the Primate R. H. Owen, rejected such reasoning, arguing paternalistically that it was better for Maori not to go.[49] Assimilation was the ideal. Maori increasingly rejected this. In the Waikato diocese, Canon Wi Te Tau Huata showed that separate pastoral work on *marae* was successful, compared with the notion that every Anglican parish should care for the Maori in its bounds. The General Synod in 1966 set up a Commission on Ministry among Maori, in light of the falling Maori affiliation to Anglicanism. Some in the Waikato Synod were doubtful about the value of Huata's work and what seemed excessive travel.

Many influential Australians were still convinced of white superiority. At the 1960 General Synod, the Bishop of Carpentaria called for mining leases over reserves to be granted without Aborigines being granted a share of the royalties.[50] In New South Wales, Charles Perkins, an Aboriginal activist, and Ted Noffs, a radical Methodist minister, organized a freedom ride in 1963 through country towns to alert people to the segregation of baths, theatres, and schools.[51] Many churchgoers were angered by this head-on activism. In some cases freedom riders were violently abused, even run off the road, but in many cases the publicity forced councils to change their policy. It was an important step along the partnership road, and a reminder that younger Aborigines were no longer prepared to be passive and invisible.

There was still a great deal of racism in both Australia and Papua New Guinea. The Australian Labor Party was persuaded by Don Dunstan to remove the White Australia Policy from its platform, though the legal end did not come till 1972. Liberals had already

---

[48] *ABM Review* (1923) 151.
[49] A. K. Davidson, *Christianity in Aotearoa* (Wellington, 1991) 158–9.
[50] GSA *Proceedings* (1960) 20.
[51] C. Perkins, *A Bastard Like Me* (Sydney, 1975).

modified migration policy significantly.[52] In 1940, T. C. Hammond
had warned that if the White Australia Policy was changed, and there
was a large incursion of non-Christians, it would 'alter the whole
character of our people, and destroy our witness in the Pacific as
effectively as if we had come under the heel of Nazism . . . We are
British, and we want to remain British, but if our heritage is worthy,
our contribution must be noble.'[53] Christian attitudes had also been
changing. By the 1970s some Christians such as Professor J. Zubrzycki
were arguing that increased migration was an ethical imperative for
survival as a nation. The dismantling of discriminatory entry requirements for migrants was another step in making both Australia and
New Zealand less British in their stance, and more able to move to a
recognition of diversity as a vital part of national identity where
removal of legal barriers to indigenous equality could also begin.
France took hesitant steps in the same direction in its Pacific territories.

Similar racist ideas were influential in New Zealand, but the
churches were moving in a different direction. Baptists set up a Maori
Department in 1954. When the 1961 Hunn Report argued strongly for
integration of Maori and Pakeha, a perceptive set of criticisms came
from the Presbyterian Maori Synod which had been given full synodal
authority in 1956. In addition, a Presbyterian theological college
began in Whakatane, under L. M. Rogers, to make theological education possible in a Maori context. The New Zealand churches were
quite blind to the need for Maori on the Joint Commission for Church
Union set up in 1964, until 1967, when the Methodist Rua Rakena was
appointed. No Aborigine or Islander sat on the similar body in
Australia. The New Zealand Anglican General Synod did not give the
Bishop of Aotearoa constitutional equality in Synod with other
bishops until 1964, and in 1978 established a diocesan council.
Methodists set up a Maori Division in 1973, with Rua Rakena elected
as Conference President in 1975. Catholics did not take similar steps
till 1983.

Churches were also equally slow to notice how they marginalized
women, both reflecting and reinforcing general social patterns.[54]
'Despite women's historical exclusion from the top jobs in the church,

[52] K. Betts, *The Great Divide* (Sydney, 1999) 160–76.
[53] Moore College, T. C. Hammond Papers, Box 6, 1940.
[54] R. Begg, *Jean Begg* (Wellington, 1974); N. Turner, *Ways of Belonging: Stories of Catholics
1910–90* (Melbourne, 1993); M. Hutchinson and E. Campion (eds.), *Long Patient Struggle:
Essays on Women and Gender in Australian Christianity* (Sydney, 1994); R. Else, *Women Together*
(Wellington, 1997); N. De Courcy (ed.), *History of the Catholic Women's League of New*

they have been religion's most able and effective agents.'[55] Significant parts of female activity have been outside male frames of reference. Much more research is needed on motherhood, because many talented women chose this gladly. Janet Holmes A'Court and Jean Penman were high-profile examples of this commitment. The former was married to a leading Perth businessman, the other wife of a New Zealand Anglican missionary who later became Archbishop of Melbourne. It was only after their husbands' deaths that they emerged as significant public figures in their own right. Women could be politically conservative or radical, but not always in male ways. Australian women were expected to resign from teaching, the civil service, deaconess ministry, and missionary work if they married, for marriage was identified with homemaking full-time. Legislative changes came in the 1960s and 1970s, with slow progress towards equal pay and recognition of the realities of marriage breakdown. All the Protestant churches moved slowly on this issue, supported by their women's organizations, not wanting to undermine family stability.

Men and women worked in separate structures for their churches. Women raised money and men spent it. Occasionally women were able to break out of traditional roles. All the Protestant churches were slow to recognize the gifts women had to offer at every level of church life.[56] Anglicans in some Australian dioceses began to admit women to their synod, but that was patchy. Attitudes to the ministerial status of deaconesses were slowly changing worldwide. Methodists had forgotten the role played by women in the founding years of their history. Phyllis Guthardt was ordained in 1959 by the New Zealand Methodist conference, but that did little to change relations between women and men in the denomination as a whole. Indeed focus on ordination for women sometimes diverted attention from the wider issues of partnership, though it was of enormous symbolic importance. Congregationalists in New Zealand accepted Nancie Ward in 1951

Zealand, 1931–90 (Dunedin, 1990); B. Archer et al., *A History of the Mothers' Union and the Association of Anglican Women in New Zealand* (Wellington, 1983); A. Matheson, *History of the Mothers' Union in Australia* (Melbourne, 1992). I am indebted to Dr Anne O'Brien for a preliminary paper, given in 1998, on the Mothers' Union. J. Simpson, 'Liberal Christianity and the changing role of women in New Zealand Society', Ph.D. thesis (Dunedin, 1992).

[55] A. O'Brien, 'Sins of omission', *AHS* 108 (1997) 127.
[56] G. G. Carter, *Valuable Beyond Price (Lina Jones 1890–1979)* (Auckland, 1985); V. Whittington, *Sister on Patrol* (Rabaul, n.d.) on Sister Dorothy Pederick; E. Simon, *Through My Eyes* (Melbourne, 1978); E. Roughsey, *An Aboriginal Mother Tells of the Old and the New* (Melbourne, 1984).

when she came already ordained from Scotland, and Presbyterians reflected worldwide discussion in Reformed churches when, after an intensive process of study and discussion, women were ordained to the eldership in 1955. Margaret Reid became the first woman to be ordained as a minister by New Zealand Presbyterians in 1965. Baptists ordained their first woman minister in 1973. Progress across the Tasman was much slower for Methodists and Presbyterians because of the difficulties of reunion negotiations, due in part to a strong conservative Presbyterian bloc and a Methodist desire not to move too far ahead of the British Conference.

The situation of deaconesses remained anomalous. Although contact with the worldwide movement widened deaconesses' horizons and reopened questions on their status, there was still dispute whether they should be ordained, or merely commissioned.[57] In 1968, the Lambeth Conference resolved that both men and women could be admitted to the diaconate, ending a debate which had gone on for decades about whether the ministry of deaconess was a distinctive apostolic ministry. Australian Anglicans moved slowly on this, but the 1970 New Zealand General Synod passed a canon admitting women to the diaconate, as well as asking for a report on the ordination of women to the priesthood. That resulted in ordinations in 1977. Glenys Lewis was one of several deaconesses ordained as presbyters in 1978. It would take time for attitudes to change. The Presbyterian Church of New Zealand decided that since women were eligible for ordination to ministry of word and sacrament, there was no need for a diaconate. The ministry of deaconess was therefore terminated in 1975, and existing deaconesses offered ordination to ministry of word and sacrament.

Indigenous people were much more conservative about the role of women. Many Maori refused to permit women to speak on their *marae*. For women to exercise ministerial or priestly functions was deemed unthinkable. Some Presbyterian deaconesses were ordained, but could only exercise a limited ministry. In 1913, Kirihihi Iraia was the first to train as a Presbyterian deaconess, but had to leave for an arranged marriage. In 1963, Meri Kahukuru was ordained deaconess, and then to ministry of word and sacrament in 1973, combining that with marriage. A Methodist deaconess from the Tainui people, Heeni

[57] Davidson, *Christianity in Aotearoa*, 149; G. M. R. Haworth, *Anglican Deaconesses in New Zealand* (Auckland, n.d.); G. Lewis, *Kept by the Power* (Christchurch, 1999); N. Tress, *Caught for Life* (Araluen, 1993); B. Champness (ed.), *The Servant Ministry* (Melbourne, 1996); C. Ritchie et al., *Not to be Ministered Unto* (Melbourne, 1998).

Wharemaru, was very influential in Waikato. Even though many Maori women had no sphere for leadership, in 1951 they set up the Maori Women's Welfare League, with Whina Cooper, a Catholic, as first president, and Miraka Szaszy, an Anglican, as secretary from 1952.[58] They were both from Northland, with great ability and authority. Later they both were made DBE for their services. The League was an important forum for a wide range of matters and gave many women opportunity to serve their community more effectively and to further their gifts for leadership.

VATICAN II

The 1960s saw enormous changes in the churches of the region, coming from parent bodies and partner churches elsewhere in the world. The first was the unexpected calling of the Second Vatican Council, which, in 1962–5, changed the course of Christian history in the twentieth century, opening up communication with the world and other churches in a way that only the wildest dreamers could have envisaged. In 1960, Archbishop Fisher privately visited the Pope, amidst significant Protestant perturbation. Archbishop Ramsey's visit in 1966 was accepted quite differently. Vatican II redefined the relation of society and the sacred. Initial submissions from regional bishops showed little sense that change was needed.[59] Vatican II introduced them to a church they were unaware of, for most of them were conscientious administrators, with little time for reflective reading or concern about signs of diminishing Australian Mass attendance, with a fall from 44 per cent to 36 per cent between 1962 and 1971.

The elderly amongst them, like Archbishop O'Donnell in Brisbane, introduced the decrees obediently, but with little enthusiasm. Guilford Young, the youngest of the Australian bishops, was the evangelist for the Council, especially in matters of liturgy.[60] Joint working groups were quickly set up by the Roman Catholic bishops with the Australian Council of Churches and the New Zealand

---

[58] M. King, *Whina* (Auckland, 1983); M. King, *Te Puea* (Auckland, 1977); M. Duffie, *Heeni* (Auckland, 1997).

[59] W. Ryder, 'The Australian bishops' proposals for Vatican II', *ACR* 65 (1988) 62–76.

[60] W. T. Southerwood, *Wisdom of Guilford Young* (Hobart, 1989); F. R. Rush, 'Brisbane and the spirit of Vatican II', *BCHS* 1 (1988) 19–26; P. Martin, 'Archbishop Patrick Mary O'Donnell', *BCHS* 3 (1992) 78–86; 'The Brisbane church before and after Vatican II', *BCHS* 5 (1996) 38–53.

National Council of Churches (1969), exploring sensitive issues of sacramental theology, authority, and salvation which had divided western Christianity since the sixteenth century. Dialogue groups with individual churches resulted.

What quickly became clear was that many laity welcomed the changes, which made it possible to worship ecumenically and to share family rites of passage without priestly permission. The Englishing of the liturgy and the introduction of contemporary music made many feel strangers, for the old patterns of devotion seemed no longer to fit. Nor did the regular discipline of fasting, eating fish on Fridays, and regular confession. Weekly rhythms were less influenced by the great themes of expiation and atonement. Much traditional Catholic piety simply died. Religious broadcasting became much more inclusive.

Seminary education changed swiftly. Bells and rules disappeared, and some who had known the rigidity of the old found the new freedom unbearable, or dizzyingly liberating. A young priest, later archbishop of Brisbane, John Bathersby, found in 1969 while studying in Rome that his faith was collapsing. 'I had a terrible feeling that I had been deceived in my belief and I had been deliberately misled by the church. I lived in that chaos for the best part of six months before I woke one morning and things seemed to come together once again . . . Convinced it was the prayers of others, and having found God again in the midst of that, I had a firm conviction I would never lose God again.'[61]

The Marist faculty at Greenmeadows in New Zealand, its most notable graduate being Gerald Arbuckle, remained somewhat conservative. George Duggan wrote a sharp critique of Professor Hans Küng, who typified a new Catholic approach to theology, accusing him of obscuring all Catholic distinctives, and indulging in spurious ecumenism. 'For the truth is that the Catholic Church is the one true Church, to which dissidents must return, and the Church would be false to herself and the dissidents if she failed to proclaim, quite unambiguously, this truth.'[62] Rome vainly tried to keep control of ecumenical experiments. Ian Sanders, the Rector of Holy Cross College, Mosgiel, circumvented this by reporting a joint degree at Otago University on the last pages of his annual report to Rome. It was not noticed for several years and, when challenged, he simply said

---

[61] *In Unity* 44/3 (1997) 1–2.
[62] G. Duggan, *Hans Küng* (Cork, 1964) 87; P. Norris, *Southernmost Seminary* (Dunedin, 1999) deals with Holy Cross.

that he had assumed Roman approval, since he had reported so long ago without any Roman comment.

Formation of women religious also began to include the major theological disciplines. Sisters moved away from many traditional roles, but some continued teaching music. One of the most internationally significant was an Auckland Mercy Sister, Dame Mary Leo, whose pupils like Mina Foley, Malvina Major, and Kiri Te Kanawa made her a household name from the 1960s. After exams she sent the girls to thank God for closing examiners' ears to their mistakes![63]

For a hierarchical church to move from monarchy to consultation, and even a touch of democracy, was a sea change. Many bishops were reluctant to consult their priests, and were angered when clergy formed their own associations. Laity were unused to being consulted by their parish priests.[64] Many clergy and bishops did little to honour the letter or spirit of the decree on the laity, but where partnership began to emerge the results were very positive. Seen from the perspective of thirty years later, the magnitude of the change is obvious. So are the limitations, and the amount which remains to be achieved. Change is usually more ambiguous than reformers anticipate, and can confirm conservatives' worst fears.

The dramatic fall in priestly and religious vocations has changed many parishes decisively, and given laity more responsibilities. In Melbourne an average of only five secular priests a year have been ordained since 1977.[65] Schools and hospitals are now staffed mainly by laity. Ecumenical partnership has changed forever. It can no longer be conversation among like-minded Protestants, anxious to minimize their heritage for the sake of contemporary relevance. Nor can it be only Anglo-European. Asians and Pacific Islanders want the integrity of their translations of Christianity recognized. The union of the Presbyterian Church of New Zealand with the Congregational Union of New Zealand in 1969 did not achieve this, and Pacific Island congregations felt marginalized. Until a Synod was approved in 1994 and implemented in 1998, they felt left outside of biculturalism. In 1963, the Evangelical Church in French Polynesia became autonomous, as part of the devolution of central authority that was taking place in many formerly mission-controlled Pacific churches. The formation of the Pacific Council of Churches in 1966 and the

---

[63] M. Lovell-Smith, *The Enigma of Sister Mary Leo* (Auckland, 1998) 79.
[64] N. Turner, *Catholics in Australia* (Melbourne, 1992) 2. 41–4 for reactions to a parish council in Maitland, NSW.   [65] Ibid., 2. 245.

Melanesian Council of Churches in 1965 gave Islanders a forum to voice their own concerns comparable to the regional ecumenical bodies in other former mission countries.

HERESY AND ORTHODOXY

Even within the Protestant churches, the 1960s saw major changes, though they were not of the magnitude of Roman experience. They came from several sources. One was the theological earthquake caused by John Robinson's *Honest to God*, published in 1963, and a runaway bestseller. For those who had kept up their theological reading, it attractively packaged liberal theological answers to questions which had been around for several decades. In February 1948, in Western Australia, Walter Murdoch claimed nobody who thinks at all believes in the resurrection of the body. Challenged publicly by the Anglican Archbishop Moline, he recognized the need for a living faith. 'Surely we may ask the Church to reconsider, not any of its essential teachings, but the phrases and formulae which drive so many from its doors.'[66] For many laity, *Honest to God* was a shock introduction to the way in which liberal theology and modern biblical scholarship had changed the Christian landscape, while pewsitters had assumed little had altered. Judging by parish programmes they were right.

The post-war generation had been brought up to believe that new was true, and that what was relevant was right. In New Zealand the tensions caused by this shift were dramatically revealed in the controversy ignited by Principal Geering's Easter articles in *The Outlook* in 1966, from April to October. Traditionally minded Presbyterians found his reinterpretation of Jesus' resurrection unacceptable.[67] Others with questions about the meaning of faith found it liberating to be able to discuss their concerns without being written off as atheists. Geering's 'trial' at Assembly in November was highly dramatic, attracting intense public interest. Anglican opponents of the proposals for reunion used Presbyterian divisions skilfully and somewhat unscrupulously.[68]

Between 1967 and 1972, a number of significant books appeared

[66] *West Australian*, 26 Feb. 1948.
[67] *Stimulus* 5/2 (1997) gives comments from some of the participants. J. A. Veitch, 'Will nothing ever be the same again?', D.Th. thesis (Sydney, 1999). *GANZ Proceedings* (1966) 42–8.
[68] R. J. Nicholson, *The Plan for Union: Truth and Unity* (Selwyn Society No. 3, 1972).

exploring the issues, accompanied by many newspaper articles.[69] Veitch, who has made a special study of the controversy, argues that it was ultimately a victory for the conservatives, for though the liberals won the first battle when the General Assembly ruled that no doctrinal error had been established, they were unable to offer unitive answers to the religiously pluralist New Zealand community. Their strength in the Presbyterian Church has steadily diminished, with conservatives winning power, and offering parishioners guidance for troubled times which was religiously more satisfying. That reflected the re-emergence of Evangelicals into the Protestant mainstream in Britain and North America, and the rapid growth of Pentecostal churches and the associated charismatic movement which began to affect all the churches in the 1960s and beyond, creating a new pattern of division.[70] Jesus' people and communitarians attempted to capture the disillusioned Christians of the 1970s for a modern expression of faith. Few of the communities lasted more than a decade. One of the most significant, the House of the Gentle Bunyip in Melbourne, closed in 1998.

PENTECOSTALS AND CHARISMATICS

The emergence of Pentecostals from 1906 attracted only small numbers in the region. Their growth in North America and elsewhere can only be described as extraordinary from the 1960s onwards. That was obvious in both Australia and New Zealand and then in many Pacific churches. Healing, prophecy, speaking in tongues, exciting participatory worship with contemporary music, offered meetings with God in a way which traditional churches had no desire to match. Itinerant evangelists, like the Holts from Melbourne, international figures like David Du Plessis, Dennis Bennett (1966), Derek Prince (1968), Graham Pulkingham (1972 and 1975) helped Australian and New Zealand Christians to feel part of a worldwide movement of

---

[69] C. G. Brown, 'The end of Anglican innocence', in J. Veitch (ed.), *Faith in an Age of Turmoil* (London, 1990).

[70] B. Chant, *Heart of Fire* (Adelaide, 1984) is a preliminary study, with a fuller one due in 1999. J. Worsfold, *History of the Charismatic Movements in New Zealand* (Bradford, 1974); B. Knowles, '*Vision of the Disinherited?*', in B. Gilling (ed.),'*Be Ye Separate*' (Hamilton, 1992) 107–41; 'Some aspects of the history of New Life Churches of New Zealand, 1960–90', Ph.D. thesis (Dunedin, 1994); A. F. F. Van der Linden, 'Church planting', research essay (Melbourne, 1996).

renewal, even though they had a rough time in local congregations, and were condemned in a number of official reports from major churches, such as the Anglicans in 1976 in New Zealand. Leaders deplored naïve reading of the Bible, unbalanced teaching, and even claimed to detect the presence of Satan, but offered no comparable religious energy. In Auckland, St Paul's Anglican Church was an influential centre for renewal. David and Dale Garratt, members there, put together *Songs of Praise* (1971), which became one of the most influential resources for the movement, and still sells well, despite rapid change in musical styles.[71] Christian Advance Ministries from 1973 fostered influential conferences for charismatics and sponsored international visitors to New Zealand.

Baptists, Churches of Christ, and Brethren, who were inclined to believe that they were the most authentic form of Christianity, also found that a number of their most ardent members left. The long-standing boundaries of party and denominationalism were literally crumbling, hit by change, from above through Vatican II, and by Pentecostalism from below. Anglo-Catholicism had lost its energy, and was left floundering by the dramatic changes in Rome. Moving from avant-garde to an out-of-touch minority was a difficult change for parishes like Christ Church-St Laurence in Sydney, All Saints in Brisbane, St Peter's, Melbourne, or St Michael's in Christchurch.[72]

Conflicting voices about the path ahead led many out of the churches into various para-church groups and self-improvement networks, or into translations of Hinduism and Buddhism, packaged by astute gurus for culturally Christian seekers after personal fulfilment, who often lost their critical facilities when they converted to New Age groups. Billy Graham's second visit in 1969 did not have the impact of his first. For those who sought chemical ecstasy, marijuana, heroin, and LSD offered far more in individual peak experiences than the churches and their tired worship. The movement to libertarian individualism gathered momentum with the help of trendy clergy, television, and the collapse of censorship. Liberal Christians were sometimes astonishingly naïve. The Revd Norman Webb, briefly

---

[71] P. J. Lineham, 'Tongues must cease in the Brethren and the charismatic movement', *CBRFJ* 96 (1982) 1–48. Baptists in New Zealand issued a report on neo-Pentecostalism in 1969. N. F. H. Merritt, *To God Be the Glory* (Auckland, 1981) narrates the St Paul's beginnings.

[72] C. Holden, *From Tories at Prayer to Socialists at Mass: A History of St Peter's, Eastern Hill, Melbourne* (Melbourne, 1997) 245–68; M. Peters, *Christchurch St Michael's* (Christchurch, 1986) 190–2.

master of Wesley College, Sydney, in the 1960s, believed that 'life is groping forward in the right direction'.[73] He reduced Christianity to caring and sensitive relationships. The life of the college fell apart. Attempts by the churches to uphold a traditional position on sexuality, divorce, and abortion, in carefully argued reports, had little denominational impact, and even less in the community, though Patricia Bartlett's Society for the Protection of Community Standards, founded in 1970, caused considerable controversy in New Zealand.

MAINLINE RENEWAL

For Australian Anglicans, the 1962 new Constitution for General Synod led to far-reaching changes at national and diocesan levels, because it made possible work towards a new Prayer Book, published in 1978, reflecting the international liturgical change which had built up irresistible pressures in all churches except the Pentecostal and the Orthodox. Institutionally, little changed in parishes, for whom the General Synod was very remote, but the Australian Prayer Book ended 300 years of shared liturgy. The new climate was symbolized by the election of Marcus Loane as Archbishop of Sydney in 1966, the first Australian to hold the office. He and his successor, Donald Robinson, had influenced students at the diocese's Moore College to rethink their understanding of the church as local gathering, rather than hierarchic and institutional.[74] In practice, both were very ecclesiastical in their administration. The doctrinal commitment of Sydney Evangelicalism was unshaken, but its energies began to move in varied directions in response to huge population growth in Sydney's west, and the need for new ministries and kinds of social service through the Home Mission Society.

A combination of increased diocesan income through Gough's reforms and local initiative was a heady mixture. Loane was a low-profile and judicious leader, with an endearingly dry wit, but the capacity to act decisively when necessary, as he did in a confrontation with the prime minister, in 1972. That led to the Henderson Enquiry, which attempted to define poverty in a way which made remedies

---

[73] N. Webb, *Heresies* (Sydney, n.d.) 53.

[74] W. J. Lawton, *That Woman Jezebel* (Sydney, 1981). M. Loane and P. Jensen, *Broughton Knox* (Sydney, 1994) notes the large influence Knox had in shaping generations of Sydney clergy, Moore is still the most influential Anglican theological college in the region.

possible. That has not been overly successful. Twenty years later there are still deep differences in churches and community on how to deal with poverty. An American theologian, Michael Novak, and some local economists attacked the welfarist mentality of church leaders. The Round Table in New Zealand has taken the same free-market line, as have business-sponsored research organizations in Australia like the Centre for Independent Studies in Sydney.[75] Loane's reputation was high among Evangelicals, but other Anglican groups did not look to him for leadership. He had the confidence of key clergy and the loyalty of the laity, and chose a talented Evangelical team to work through the next decades.

Developments in the mission churches with which Australians and New Zealanders were involved also brought pressure to rethink the fundamentals of the Christian message, and to translate them effectively for the post-war generation whose idealism was directed towards personal freedom, hostility to racism, and opposition to involvement in Vietnam's civil war. New Zealand and Australia both began withdrawal in 1972. In the Northern Territory, the 1968 meeting of the United Church took a strong stand on Aboriginal land ownership 'as understood from time immemorial'.[76] Thoughtful Australian Christians noted the absence of an Aboriginal church comparable to the strong and increasingly independent Pacific churches. Gradualism was no longer acceptable as a reason to claim that Aborigines were not ready for ordination and lay leadership.[77] Independent groups like the United Aborigines Mission and the Aboriginal Inland Mission had nurtured evangelists from the 1930s. So had the Lutherans in Central Australia, where the first ordinations of Peter Bulla and Conrad Raberabe occurred in 1964. Methodists began ordinations with Lazarus Lamilami in 1966, Presbyterians and Anglicans followed suit in 1969 with Patrick Brisbane and Alan Polgen. Patrick Dodson, the first Roman Catholic Aboriginal priest was ordained in 1975, but soon left because of an unsympathetic bishop who did not encourage enculturation. Dodson and his brother Mick had become national leaders by the 1990s.

    [75] P. Harris and L. Tuiname, *First Knights* (Auckland, 1998); S. Gregg (ed.), *In Praise of the Free Economy* (Sydney, 1999).

    [76] Northern Territory Archives UCNA File 5143:2; J. Harris, *We Wish We'd Done More*, (Adelaide, 1998) 429–89.

    [77] K. Cole, *From Mission to Church* (Bendigo, 1985) narrates the Anglican process. J. Harris, *One Blood* (Sydney, 1990) 855–64; J. Kabida, 'The Methodist Mission and the emerging Aboriginal Church in Arnhem Land, 1916–77', Ph.D. thesis (Darwin, 1998).

Few missionaries were willing to allow Aboriginal painting or dance to be used inside church buildings. Aboriginal culture was deemed worthless. The idea that Christianity could be effectively enculturated seemed out of the question to most missions. Rules for discipline approved in February 1967 by the North Australia Methodist District Synod could have come straight out of the nineteenth century. Completion of discipline was marked by a service of restoration. For those with eyes to see, there was plenty of evidence that change was taking place. In the Northern Territory, the Aputala community wrote to the United Church of North Australia, precursor of the Uniting Church. 'We are like leafy branches of a tree. We should become one with the Church which is like the butt of the tree, therefore we now ask to become one with the United Church.' The letter was signed 'Jesus' relations', a significant combination of clan loyalties and ecclesiology.[78] On Bathurst Island, the Catholic Church had a cross of spears by Benny Tipungwuti and an altar on posts which evoked a ceremony to break the power of the taboos surrounding death.

Beginnings in enculturation were made by Sacred Heart missionaries, such as Frank Fletcher in the Northern Territory, and by Pallotines, in North Western Australia. Beulah Lowe had insight into Aboriginal society which many male Methodist missionaries lacked. Few saw the importance of evangelism in tribal languages. Thoughtful missionaries like Margaret Bain took a different line, arguing for evangelism in the vernacular at Ernabella.[79] Other missionaries disagreed with her. Edgar Wells and his wife, Anne, were Methodists well along the path of cultural understanding, and were amazed at the depth of the oral traditions which were cautiously revealed to them at Milingimbi and Yirrkala.[80] When Wells designed a totemic window at Milingimbi, 'the elders went back to camp and wept again for joy that something of their own art had been found worthy of use'.[81]

Those Aborigines who had become Christians took little account of denominational boundaries, and were deeply influenced by Evangelical hymns and choruses, and the drama of personal salvation

---

[78] Northern Territory Archives UCNA, *Standing Committee Minutes*, 1971–77, Letter, 1 Feb. 1974.

[79] Mitchell MS 1893, Bain letters. UCA Further records. 20 Jan. 1964, 3 Aug. 1966.

[80] J. Martin, 'The Bark Petition and Edgar Almond Wells', *PUCHSV* 3/2 (1996) 6–10.

[81] A. Wells, *Milingimbi* (Sydney, 1963) 223.

expressed in testimony of changed lives from alcohol abuse, gambling, and fighting. Douglas Nicholls in Melbourne was exercising a notable ministry as a Churches of Christ pastor.[82] Helped by his fame in sport, he became a quiet but very effective advocate for his people.

Protestant co-operation took new shape following the creation of the New Zealand National Council of Churches (NCC) in 1941 and the Australian Council for the World Council of Churches (ACC) in 1946.[83] Alan Brash, one of New Zealand's foremost ecumenists, began work for the NCC in 1947.[84] Brash played a boldly pioneering role in developing relations with the East Asia Council of Churches in 1959, long before Asia was politically fashionable. Attempts to raise aware-ness of racism, and disagreements over involvement in Vietnam and atomic testing in the Pacific, gave the Council a reputation for taking up causes which were of little interest to its more conservative member churches. One of the oldest ecumenical partnerships was the Melbourne College of Divinity, founded in 1910, which took on a new lease of life in 1972 when it incorporated Roman Catholics and Churches of Christ as members, providing a model for other theo-logical consortia in the region.

MELANESIAN CHANGES

Churches working in Melanesia had a huge task to rebuild schools, hospitals, and churches that had been destroyed by war. Some missions were skilled at using buildings, boats, vehicles, and supplies left behind by the Allies.[85] Catholic bishops in Papua New Guinea had to replace priests and religious who had been lost in the war years. Invitations were issued to a number of new orders. Capuchins arrived in 1954, Dominicans went to the Solomons in 1956, and Montfortians came from Quebec in 1959, together with Marianhill Fathers. American Marists not only filled gaps left by French Marists, they also helped to staff expansion after 1945. By 1981, fifty-five had gone to the Pacific,

---

[82] M. T. Clark, *Pastor Doug* (Melbourne, 1975).

[83] F. Engel, *Times of Change* (Melbourne, 1993) 198–230.

[84] C. G. Brown, *Forty Years On* (Christchurch, 1981); R. O'Grady, *Alan Brash* (Auckland, 1991).

[85] J. Waldersee, *Neither Eagles nor Saints* (Sydney, 1995) 317–32; H. Nelson, *Taim Bilong Masta* (Sydney, 1982) for a survey of Papua New Guinea under Australian rule; T. Aerts (ed.), *Memorial Volume of the Catholic Church in Papua 1885–1985* (Port Moresby, 1985) is a brief general survey. D. Hilliard, 'The SSEM in the Solomon Islands', *JPH* 4 (1969) 41–64.

including the Canadian Louis Beauchemin, to Samoa, who was an important ecumenist and translator.[86]

Marists also influenced the setting up of trusts like the Foundation for the Peoples of the South Pacific, founded in New York during 1966, the result of Marists working with Betty Silverstein, the Australian-born wife of the president of MGM. Able to draw both on private generosity and on public funding, it has become a major source of finance for regional development. Gerald Arbuckle, a noted Marist from New Zealand, prepared the important report *Socio-economic Guidance to Missionaries in the South Pacific* (1967) under the Foundation's aegis. He has been a very influential writer on strategies for the post-Vatican II world, using his expertise in both the social sciences and theology. The Marist connection has opened up opportunities for postgraduate study by Pacific students in the USA, as well as in Europe and Australasia.[87]

The Roman Catholic Church grew very dramatically in the postwar years.[88] Providing more schools, hospitals, clinics, and church buildings was a large task. So was provision of personnel. Australian volunteers were strongly represented amongst the 140 lay auxiliaries who met crucial personnel needs between 1947 and 1972. There was a growing Australian interest in missions, with 1,278 Roman Catholic missionaries by 1972, up from 278 in 1948, with an increase in development projects.

The growth of Catholic and Methodist communities on Bougainville was strong. By 1956, the population totalled over 51,000, of whom just over 36,000 were Catholics. Six hundred and eight catechists led lively village ministries, and thirty-five sisters made up a local community. Bishop Thomas Wade, an American Marist, set up a minor seminary at Chabai which produced outstanding priests like John Momis and Gregory Singkai. European wealth was still a mystery, and two catechists set up the Hahalis Welfare Society in the 1950s, which had both cargo and Catholic elements, showing how fluid religious boundaries were at local level. Methodist ministers played a considerable role. David Pausu was a notable peacemaker,

[86] J. W. Lynch, *Island Adventure* (Rome, 1977) on Beauchemin; B. Tourigny, *Mémoires du Père Ben* (Montreal, 1992); H. Laracy, 'Maine, Massachusetts and the Marists: American Catholic missionaries in the South Pacific', 15–16. I am indebted to Dr Laracy for providing a copy of his unpublished paper. C. Hally, *Australia's Missionary Effort* (Melbourne, 1973) 28–30 provides figures of Roman Catholics in missionary service in 1972; see p. 24.

[87] Laracy, 'Maine, Massachusetts and the Marists', 17.

[88] Waldersee, *Neither Eagles nor Saints*, 569–601.

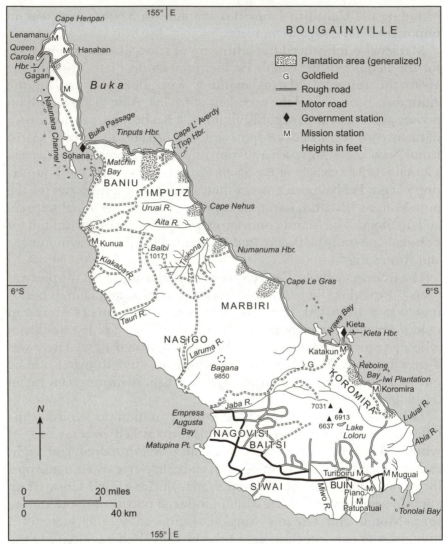

Bougainville (1944). (*Source:* Naval Intelligence Division, British Admiralty, *Pacific Islands*, 5 vols., London, 1939–45, vol. 3, p. 671. © British Crown Copyright/MOD. Reproduced with the permission of Her Britannic Majesty's Stationery Office.)

cultural authority, translator, and mentor. Many Solomon Islanders were educated in Methodist schools in Australia and New Zealand. When the United Church was formed, Sione Taufa from Tonga became Bishop of Bougainville.

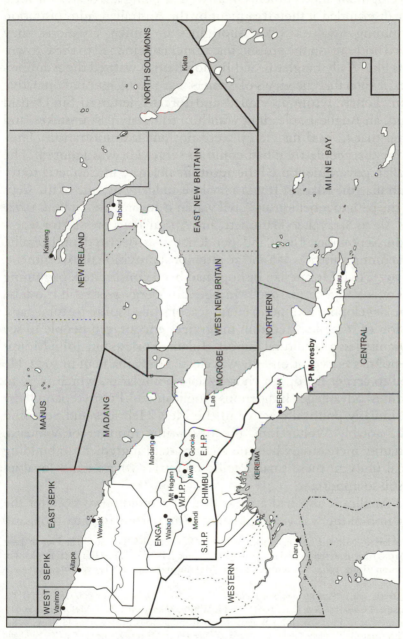

Papua New Guinea: Roman Catholic dioceses (1985). (*Source*: T. Aerts (ed.), *Memorial Volume of the Roman Catholic Church in Papua 1885–1985*, Port Moresby, 1985, p. 7.)

On Buka and Bougainville, Marists made important contributions to development and ecumenism, as well as being advocates for local people disgruntled at their treatment by the Australian Administration over mining royalties. Like Aborigines in similar situations, they received nothing, on the ground that minerals belonged to the Crown. Marists like Wally Fingleton and Bishop Lemay warned the Administration in 1966 that the views of owners were being ignored on native custom. Lemay wrote a detailed and forceful letter to Sir Donald Cleland, an Anglican, pleading with him to rectify past mistakes, and insisting that he and his clergy were not anti-administration. They were for the people they had come to serve. He was ignored. The Australian government used the apostolic delegate in Canberra to try to neutralize the Marists. It was a fatal misjudgement, one of the steps along the path to rebellion and civil war in Bougainville. In June 1974, priests Alexis Saray, Leo Hammett, and Apasai Toga pressed for secession. In September 1975, independence was declared unilaterally, until a compromise in 1976 and an attempt at provisional government.

By 1973, five Melanesian bishops had been consecrated, beginning with Louis Vangeke in 1970.[89] Indigenous clergy were still too few, but the development of permanent deacons filled some pastoral gaps. Inclusion of some local custom in services encouraged people to see Christianity less as a cultural import. Talented priests like John Momis chose politics as a vocation—he was elected to Parliament in 1972. He refused to accept European church/state boundaries, which were to the whites' advantage. Indigenous Anglican and Presbyterian clergy were similarly politically active in the New Hebrides and Solomon Islands, notably Walter Lini, the first prime minister of Vanuatu. Christianity increasingly became an important ingredient in building national unity in these small Pacific countries where tribal loyalties were still so important.

The Anglicans also had a great deal of rebuilding to do after the destruction of the war years.[90] Nancy White, from 1948 to 1968, and

[89] Waldersee, *Neither Eagles nor Saints*, 365–7 on Vangeke. K. McGhee, *The First 50 Years* (Sidera, 1982) discusses the Sacred Heart work in Papua. J. Barnes, 'The church triumphant in the Solomon islands 1964–67', research paper (Melbourne, 1990) is a lay volunteer perspective.

[90] T. Aerts (ed.), *Romans and Anglicans in Papua New Guinea* (Goroka/Lae, 1991) 59; T. Kinahan, *A Church is Born* (Lae, 1991); N. H. White, *Sharing the Climb* (Melbourne, 1991). She was mentor to Professor John Waiko, the first indigenous Professor of History, 1985. J. M. Titterington, *Strongly Grows the Modawa Tree* (Port Moresby, 1991); *God's Wonderful Treasures* (Port Moresby, 1991); *The Anglican Story* (Port Moresby, 1991); C. Garland, *Centenary History of the Diocese of Popondetta* (Port Moresby, 1985).

Peggy De Bibra taught in very primitive conditions, and produced their own reading materials. The government gave twelve sticks of chalk a month! Both skilfully countered sorcery through fostering deeper faith in their pupils, who in turn passed this insight on to their children. Bishop Strong wanted twelve more clergy and forty others to expand adult literacy into unmissionalized areas. Though his hope was not entirely fulfilled, one of the recruits was David Hand, who became an outstanding pioneer in the Highlands, and in New Britain, which was transferred from the Melanesian Mission. He became bishop in 1950 and archbishop from 1977 to 1983. Secondary schools for boys and girls were set up, and a theological college founded in 1951. Paramedical training began in 1950. The terrible eruption of Mt Lamington on 21 January 1951 killed over 3,000 people, and wiped out almost all the Anglican indigenous leaders. Eighteen were killed while attending a course. Australian and English churches generously supported rebuilding, but replacing people was to take much longer. Anglicans established a synod in 1971, and cut their ties with the province of Queensland in 1977, creating a local province, with an archbishop and four other bishops. George Ambo was the first Papuan to be consecrated bishop, in 1960. He was then archbishop from 1983 until 1990. Though the ethos of the Anglican Church in Papua New Guinea was strongly Anglo–Catholic, it has been deeply committed to ecumenism.[91]

The LMS held its first Papuan Assembly in 1950. Initially its role was advisory, but by 1962 the Papuan District Committee run by missionaries was dissolved, and incorporated in the Assembly of the Ekalesia. Samoans, who were used to a much larger degree of partnership, helped Papuans see the possibilities of meeting simultaneously with the missionaries each year in May. That began in 1945. Missionaries like Percy Chatterton, Bert Brown, and the Rankins saw the importance of congregational meetings in each village as training grounds for responsibility.[92] In 1968, the Ekalesia, Methodists, and the United Church at Ela Beach (which was linked with the United Church of Northern Australia), formed the United Church. Its regional bishops initially included missionaries like Graham Smith and Frank Butler, but it speedily moved to localize leadership. The new church made it clear some missionaries were no longer welcome. New relations were

[91] T. Aerts (ed.), *Romans and Anglicans in Papua New Guinea* (Port Moresby, 1991).

[92] N. D. Oram, 'The LMS pastorate and the emergence of an educated elite in Papua', *JPH* 6 (1971) 115–32; A. H. Voyce, *Peacemakers* (Coromandel, 1979) 29.

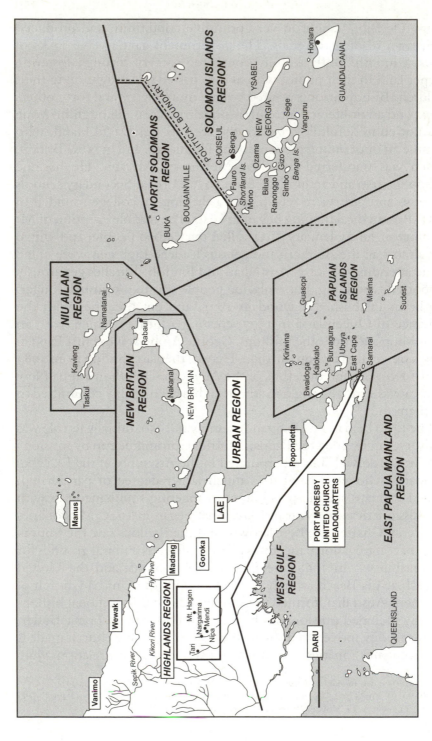

Papua New Guinea and Solomon Islands: United Church Regions (no date). (With permission of the United Church.)

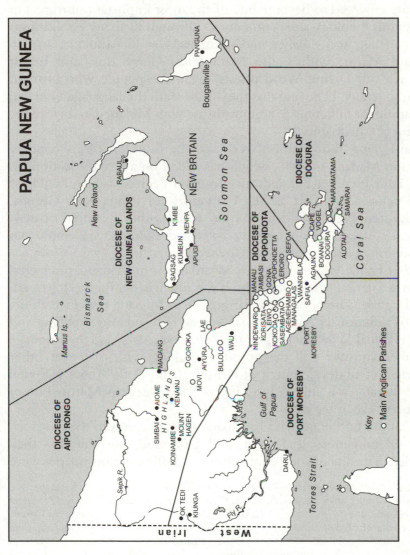

Papua New Guinea: Anglican dioceses (1991). (*Source*: T. Aerts (ed.), *Romans and Anglicans in Papua New Guinea*, Port Moresby, 1991, p. 66.)

finalized in 1972, with the Revd Morehu Te Whare from New Zealand playing an important part in the delicate negotiations.

Catholic religious superiors began orientation courses for newly arrived workers in 1968. From small beginnings, the Melanesian Institute emerged to become one of the most important nurturers of indigenous theology and ecumenism[93] through its many publications such as *Point*, and *Catalyst*, and seminars. Gerald Arbuckle, a New Zealand Marist, with Ennio Mantovani, Gerry Bus, and Ernest Bradewie, all Divine Word priests, were the people who brought dream to reality, believing that they must learn the language God had been using for millennia to communicate with Melanesians before the coming of Christianity.

The Divine Word fathers were also the founders of a secondary school in Madang in 1968, which has added on a tertiary section. In 1994, Parliament gave it authority to grant degrees, which could see the development of a Catholic University for Papua New Guinea. The Kristen Press founded in 1969 was another example of ecumenical co-operation, which by 1975 had eighty-seven employees and published a wide variety of Christian literature.

Father Frank Mihalic, a Divine Word father in Madang, pioneered pidgin as a national language, which was much easier for locals to learn than English. There were 175 languages in Madang province alone. His 1957 dictionary and grammar helped to standardize spelling and usage. *Wantok*, a *tok pisin* paper, has 100,000 readers, and the language is spoken by over half the population along with over 800 other languages. The development of Kristen Radio in the 1960s was vital while literacy was still so low. It has been based in Martin Luther Seminary, Lae, since 1978.[94]

It was the Lutherans who had made most progress in the development of indigenous leadership, and grounding the churches they founded in the life of local communities.[95] Lutheran missionaries were

[93] *Divine Word Missionaries*, 119–26, Zocca describes the Institute. N. Z. Kenung, *Local Ecumenism* (Goroka, 1980); C. Renali, *Roman Catholic Participation in the Ecumenical Movement in PNG* (Rome, 1991).   [94] G. Baskett, *Islands and Mountains* (Sydney, n.d.) 172 ff.

[95] R. Pech, 'The acts of the apostles in PNG', *Point* 7 (1983) 17–71; G. Fugmann (ed.), *Birth of an Indigenous Church* (Goroka, 1985); G. Renck, *Contextualization of Christianity* (Erlangen, 1990); P. Lawrence, 'Lutheran mission influence on Madang societies', *Oceania* 27 (1956) 73–89; R. J. Meshanko, 'The gospel among the Huli', MA thesis (Washington, 1985) 127–32 has valuable material on adaptation to Huli custom. H. R. Hannemann, *Mission Work* (Lutheran Archives, Lae) 199–200 gives a report of local people about A. Schafer in 1947, who reportedly told them that Lutheran teaching was not good and that their dogs and pigs would die. 'But if I teach you . . . the people will be very well off'; ibid., 201–7.

often acute observers of custom and, like the Divine Word fathers, produced a number of indispensable ethnographic writings, recording myths and ceremonies, thereby providing some benchmarks against which progress in Christian acculturation could be measured. Education was a desperate need at all levels with only half the eligible children at primary school. In United Church Gulf and East Papua regions, of 143 ordinands, only half had been formally trained. The foundation of a new college at Rarongo, with a five-year course, gradually raised professional standards. There were interesting cultural problems. A pastor who visited, instead of people coming to him, was thought to be looking for girls. In preaching, it was culturally forbidden to reprimand people outside their own clan.

Work in the Highlands was demanding but expanded steadily, despite sectarian rivalries. One *luluai* called Bumbu divided his people into Protestants and Roman Catholics to see who prospered more, but was very dissatisfied with his treatment by Roman Catholic catechists. Most of the population had become Christian by the end of the 1970s. A strong movement of renewal through the Holy Spirit also swept through the region, through the work of Solomon Island ministers. A New Zealand Maori evangelist, Muri Thompson, was a key figure, for his ability to translate his own vital faith into the culture of the Solomon Islanders helped them in turn to communicate with Christians of Papua New Guinea. The first Lutheran baptism came in 1948 out of a different structure of decision-making, because of powerful chiefs who looked for the best religious deal, making Keysser's communal approach less viable.[96] Expansion occurred in coastal areas, with more local pastors and stations subdivided. Locals began sharing the deliberations of missionaries' field conferences from 1951. A constituting synod held in 1956 marked the landing of Flierl 70 years before, and set up the Evangelical Lutheran Church of New Guinea with John Kuder as first bishop, until 1973. This was a dramatic change in authority, and many were uncertain about their role in the new structures. Local leaders soon began to make their presence felt.

Christianity often began from local religious movements, which preceded missionaries. Clan rivalries could impede or help. At Mondosugl, Roman Catholics chopped down a Lutheran house, and the *kiap* forced them to rebuild. In defence, they claimed Fr Bodner

[96] H. Wagner and H. Reiner (eds.), *The Lutheran Church in Papua New Guinea* (Adelaide, 1987) 273–301 for work among the Enga.

had paid them two pearl shells for the task. Wambalipi and his brothers began a religious movement in 1940, which grew until he and others were gaoled, because the administration regarded it as a cargo cult.[97] They taught ritual cleansing, had communal meals, were pan-tribal, and rejected spirits, seeking to worship a higher power. Wambalipi is now a Lutheran, and believes that the movement had important preparatory functions for the coming of Christianity. Clan leaders like Minjuku Yasima and Looa Waimane played an important part in inviting Lutheran missionaries to eastern Enga-territory. Yangomane Yakoya's father had a vision. 'When someone comes with "white skin", the people will live in peace and have plenty. They will find the way to the skyland, and fulfil all of their longings.'[98] Kate missionaries were important, as were locals like Teoc, a skilled teacher from Siassi, and Pokon, from Ogelbeng, the first author of Enga language hymns. By 1968, the Wabag Lutheran Church had a baptized membership of 37,000. In 1978, it became the Gutnius Church with five bishops. It was a huge task to provide for all expectations in education and health, as well as for pastors. Agreement on places for synods could be contentious.

The 1952 Education Ordinance placed a new emphasis on English. By 1959, only about half of the 700,000 children eligible to attend were at school. The Lutherans kept some schools which were unaided, because they wanted religious education and retention of the children's local languages. In 1964–5, 189,000 children were in mission schools, costing $2 million (A), with 67,000 pupils in government schools costing $8 million (A). Only 0.2 per cent of the population had secondary education.

Georg Vicedom, a Lutheran missiological leader, in 1965 made important theological comments on becoming indigenous, and the dangers that needed to be faced. The church was renamed in 1976 as the Evangelical Lutheran Church of Papua New Guinea. Lutherans rejected any compromise with pre-Christian practices.[99] There was a dispute over dress at the Dagle ancestral festival. Mr Gauci, the *kiap*, wanted Christians to take off their loincloths. Kundie, a *tultul*, refused, even though Gauci threatened to take his office away. 'I was baptised so I could become good.' Eventually the people decided that the traditional feathers could be worn both at baptism and to welcome

[97] H. Wagner and H. Reiner (eds.), *The Lutheran Church in Papua New Guinea*, 275–6.
[98] Ibid., 278.
[99] Hannemann, *Mission Work*, 423–4.

visitors at festivals to denote joy.[100] The Melanesian Institute and an international Lutheran team carried out an evaluation in 1977, exposing many big issues. How to be an internally united and national church, without financial dependence on overseas churches, was crucial. The problem of schools and hospitals was immense, with one-third of the Lutheran budget spent on medical work by the 1960s. People do not see financing national organizations as their responsibility.

The interaction of local culture with Christianity in Melanesia has taken a variety of forms, all the more interesting because of the varied length of time over which Christianity has become known. Some areas have been Christian for over 150 years, others have been exploring the implications of Christianity only in the last thirty years, especially in the New Guinea Highlands. Studies of the relation of religion and culture have underlined how durable and powerful traditional religious ideas have been, shaping local Christianity in ways which have eluded or baffled missionaries and anthropologists, without being readily analysable through rational categories. A party of coastal evangelists, when a Kamara man had died, escaped death due to a downpour, which prevented the Kamara people killing them, to stop the spirit of the dead man taking revenge on neglectful kin.[101] No single hermeneutic category is a key to understanding the whole of Melanesian religion. Culture determines some things, psychological forces shape others, and individuals and what Herdt and Stephen describe as 'autonomous imagination' yet others.[102] Each culture and region will have a different mix, depending on the nature of the local culture, the quality of indigenous leadership in adapting European Christian models, and the authority of the missionaries and European officials.

Cargo cults or adjustment religions (which is perhaps a better name) indicate the success of Melanesians in integrating Christian and traditional religion. They underline that religious change was far more than missionary colonialism, though the mediation of missionaries in tribal warfare complemented the desire of European governments to secure peace and economic development. Each needed the other, for

---

[100] Ibid., 428–36; G. Reitz, *The Contribution of ELCONG to Development in PNG* (Lae, 1975).

[101] Hannemann, *Mission Work*, 116.

[102] R. Radford, 'Burning the spears', *JPH* 12 (1977) 40–54; G. H. Herdt and M. Stephen (eds.), *The Religious Imagination* (New Brunswick, 1989); M. Stephen, *Sorcerer and Witch* (New Brunswick, 1987) 55–63.

they had different roles in the pacification process. Australian, British, and French administrations had different objectives, but all showed serious misunderstandings of Melanesian culture in their policies towards these adjustment movements, whose aspirations were an important part of religious and other changes, as people sought religious renewal on their own terms.

Varied hypotheses have been offered for such adjustment movements, but they remain larger than academic explanations.[103] Magical elements, traditional cosmology, incipient nationalism, and struggles for power and wealth have been involved. Many anthropologists give less weight to religious factors, for if religion is only an extension of social relationships, the supernatural necessarily has to be described in this-worldly categories. In many cases that has advanced understanding of the movements and their social context, suggesting that 'religion' is a technology to ensure well-being and harmonious relationships between the living and the dead. The absence of a transcendent God in many of the Melanesian mythologies can lend support to this theory of religion as human construct and projection, without doing justice to the appeal of Christianity as a much wider system of transcendent explanation, or to personal and communal experience of the sacred. Dreams and visions are part of the way in which many Melanesians attempt to describe a reality beyond the terrestrial, where every happening may have spiritual meaning. Shaman-type activities have great prestige, often evoking fear and anxiety, but are accepted as evidence of another world of meaning, to which Christianity also bears witness while offering a very different set of explanations. The spiritual world is intensely real to Melanesians.

Trompf argues that it is unhelpful to push such Melanesian movements into European or African categories. Observers need to recognize the particularity of each group, while recognizing that there is a strong tension between the old order and the new, for the impact of Western culture has been difficult enough for tribal societies to cope with. Conversion is a many-layered process, involving both

---

[103] The literature on these movements is enormous. G. Trompf, *Melanesian Religion* (Melbourne, 1991) gives a very comprehensive account. His classic study *Payback* (Melbourne, 1994) explores patterns for settling conflict over exchange and other aspects of community life. P. Lawrence and M. J. Megitt (eds.), *Gods, Ghosts and Men in Melanesia* (Melbourne, 1965) 8–18 is an example of the terrestrial explanation of 'religious' phenomena. F. Hermann, 'The Yali movement in retrospect', *Oceania* 63 (1992) 55–71; B. Douglas, 'Autonomous and controlled spirits: traditional ritual and early interpretations on Tanna, Aneityum and the Isle of Pines in comparative perspective', *JPS* 98 (1989) 7–48.

modernization and also reassessment of custom, its mythological foundations and justification.[104] Such movements are reminders of the need for examination of primal myths and religion, and how Melanesians use them to create meaning as they become Christians. The role of spirits, sin sniffers, dreams, public criticism of sins, healing, all pick up elements of custom for village people. They raise important issues about foci of power in worship and congregational life. Given the evident excitement about Bible study, and the role women have been playing, such movements indicated significant displacement of custom. Churches have also provided space and support for Melanesian aspirations. The Evangelical Church of Papua New Guinea, which grew far beyond its foundations by the Unevangelized Fields Mission in the Fly River region, demonstrates how movement to indigenous control brought up issues which meant departure from the decisions of pioneer missionaries. Similar trends can be seen among Baptists, the United Church, and Brethren assemblies.[105]

The importance of the Bible translation into local languages has been vital for the development of indigenous churches throughout the Pacific. The Wycliffe Bible Translators held their first Australian course in 1950 with thirty-six students, and began work in Papua New Guinea in 1956. By 1997, there were 100 translations in Papua New Guinea. The impact of translation on the life of the Binumarien people in the Eastern Highlands, whose numbers had been reduced from over 3,000 to 111 in 1959 because of tribal fighting, is a case study in the way a community, riven by mistrust, rebuilt its life by making quite deliberate religious choices.[106] They had been first reached by Pilhofer in 1922, but the first Lutheran missionaries left after unremitting hostility. Winia, a Kate, came and stayed for forty years, stopping warfare, and introducing literacy. Sorcery continued, as did the deceit which was ingrained in their culture.

Two New Zealanders, the Oatridges from Taranaki, spent twenty-six years from 1958 in the community translating the whole Bible.

[104] A. Lattas, 'Memory, forgetting and the New Tribes Mission', *Oceania* 65 (1994) 286–304; W. Kempf, 'The second coming of the Lord', *Oceania* 63 (1992) 72–96.

[105] J. and M. Prince, *No Fading Vision* (Melbourne, 1981); *A Church is Born* (Melbourne, 1991); J. Fountain, *To Teach Others Also* (Wellington, 1999); W. Flannery (ed.), *Religious Movements in Melanesia* (Goroka, 1983) 116 ff. for renewal among Enga Baptists 1967–78 at Baiyer River. In the Gulf, the Calverts, missionaries from New Zealand, brought in Christian Life Crusade speakers in the late 1970s and early 1980s. The United Church leaders were divided about the value of this initiative.

[106] L. Oates, *Hidden People* (Sydney, 1992) 120–4, 171–2, 215–18.

Initially the community, fearing their language would be stolen, decided not to divulge key elements of their language, like verb endings. There was an extraordinary reaction to the translation of Jesus' genealogy, for the people suddenly realized he was like them, unlike spirits, who have no ancestors. The publication of Matthew's Gospel in 1965 caused huge excitement, as did the translation of Genesis. Not only did these books challenge their view that there was no religious place for women, it underlined that the Hebrews were rather like themselves. The previously used Kate translation of John 3: 16 used 'man' in the sense of 'male', not 'human'. The idea that wives could share eternal life was amazing to women, and offensive to men. By the end of 1977, the New Testament translation was complete, and it was published in 1984. Burials without sorcery were becoming common, and the old fears were in decline. 'Cargo' ideas were diminishing.[107] Population was increasing, and the community was using their Bible to reorder their individual and communal life.

PENTECOSTAL MISSIONS

Dealing with the traditional beliefs about help by spirits to secure well-being is a long-term task. Melanesian Christians keep the old religion and the new in creative partnership, especially in times of crisis, for they are very pragmatic about results. The Christian view of creation is radically different from traditional cosmology. Concepts of truth, justification, and grace are hard to grasp because of the cultural importance of payback. Nothing was seen as accidental, for sorcery was always blamed for death and illness. That has worked in favour of the various forms of Pentecostalism, for it provides space for experience of dreams, visions, healing, power encounters, and prophecies. Pastors are believed to be endowed with magical powers.

The first Assemblies of God missions from Australia began in India, through the leadership of C. L. Greenwood of the Richmond Temple in Melbourne, in 1937. It was not until 1947 that Hugh Davidson, a worker with Aborigines, went to explore possibilities in the Sepik, and was joined by the Hoveys and the Westbrooks at Maprik. Over the next fifteen years, the Westbrooks planted twenty-three churches, taught literacy, and reduced infant mortality by tetanus immunizations

---

[107] L. Oates, *Hidden People* , 230–5, 259–60; G. Trompf, *Melanesian Religion* (Melbourne, 1991).

against infection from the dirty bamboo knives used to cut the umbilical cord, all for a stipend of $20 per week. The style of Pentecostal worship was appealing, and teaching on the power of the Holy Spirit had provided cultural resonances with custom belief about spirits, even though missionaries were occasionally bemused by women's visions and claims to be able to smell evil spirits. Pentecostals did not themselves encourage women's ministry, but Elva Shum showed that long-term female missionaries could exert great influence by modelling new roles for women.[108]

Pentecostals attempted to develop local leadership from the 1960s. The first National Conference was held in 1962, and the church was incorporated in 1973 with nationals as president and secretary. Assemblies have spread into every province. Difficulties over local culture included polygamy. In 1959 a heated debate occurred at the Twelfth Commonwealth Conference over polygamy. Monogamy was upheld by 32 votes to 15. When Jack Easton baptized one of a pagan's wives after she had received the Spirit, he was suspended. By 1961, that was rescinded, though polygamists were banned from holding office. Many theologically conservative missionaries, like Pentecostals, learnt the hard way that their perception of what was Christian was very culture-bound. Despite this, 27 per cent of the population in East Sepik province had become Pentecostals. By 1965, there were ninety-seven churches in East Sepik. Local control was established in 1975, with a resulting reduction of expatriate staff. In 1977, the Australian budget for missionary giving of $500,000 was achieved. In 1979, Assemblies had aimed for 1 million dollars (A). By 1993, they achieved over 6 million dollars, spent in nineteen countries. Papua New Guinea was only a part of Pentecostal work in twenty-six countries, but important because key leaders, like Andrew Evans of the Paradise Assembly in South Australia, who had worked in Papua New Guinea, saw their methods blessed and confirmed, and helped to expand missionary thinking as their denomination grew.

BAPTIST PIONEERS

Baptist work amongst the Highlanders of Papua New Guinea began as a result of a number of Australian servicemen being struck by the spiritual needs of Papua New Guinea during their military service.

[108] A. Davies, *Invading Paradise* (Melbourne, 1991) 25–7.

They included Alan Prior, later President of the Union in New South Wales. Though there was little extra money available, the Baptist Missionary Society went ahead and sent several missionaries into the Baiyer-Lumasa area of the Highlands in the early 1950s. The area had been pacified, but the legacy of tribal war was debilitating, infant mortality was high, malaria, yaws, pneumonia, and leprosy were endemic. In 1952, the Tinsley Health Centre was established, serving 35,000 people, run by Sr Betty Crouch. Many lived fourteen days' walk from the nearest nurse. This medical work had a large impact. She set up a simple health insurance scheme. There was initial progress, then a breakdown as the missionaries left just before independence in 1975, because there had been too little grounding. Enga felt deserted when the missionaries were withdrawn so that leadership of the indigenous church could develop.

The 1970s revival also brought changes. The Enga word for 'revival' means to shake, utter strange noises, speak in tongues, and leap about. Special prayer places, where 'prayer power' men led, were established, sometimes on former places of sacrifice to the sky spirits. They were connected by the Enga to the Old Testament holy of holies. Prophecy was important. Marching in line, dancing, and traditional-style oratory were all part of the expression of faith.

Pii Nalu described how 'as the months went by and I learned more about this God they loved and served I found the alternative I had been looking for, the other path in life, that led to peace, security, and loving one another instead of fighting and killing'.[109] Others were more conscious of the tools the visitors had, and the strange gabble of their language, not to mention their unpleasant smell. Aeroplanes still roused fear and amazement. Those who worked for the strangers found there were many difficulties. Missionaries called them by name, which was dangerous, because the spirits could overhear. In marriage services, one missionary devised vows which did not mention couple's names.[110] Curiously, the whites had no fear of spirits, and did not need medicine men to mediate for them with God. New medical treatments helped to break taboos over birth and death. They gradually lost faith in the old beliefs, and accepted what the newcomers were teaching. This was crucial in area after area.

[109] N. and S. Draper, *Daring to Believe* (Melbourne, 1990) 32; R. Ansoul, *Beautiful Feet: Australian Baptists Enter Papua New Guinea* (Melbourne, 1981); A. C. Prior, *Into the Land that Time Forgot* (Melbourne, 1951).

[110] K. M. Ridgway, *Feet upon the Mountains* (Melbourne, 1976) 67.

The people found the story of Jesus' death very affecting. 'Then we heard that Jesus had also broken the power of death, which we feared so much, and had risen to a new life! We wanted this new life too.' When some bold young men requested baptism, the elders were deeply disturbed that this would upset the cosmic order, for the gardens would not grow if they went against the elders' advice. After paying their debts and confessing their sins, they felt clean inside. When they came out of the water, watched by thousands of the curious, they also felt clean on the outside 'and ready to begin a new life of following Christ's teachings'. Motives for being baptized varied from testing out the new God, to overcoming terrible fear about the river being a place of evil spirits. Some also wanted to sacrifice pigs to the deity Serango, so that other members of the family would not be harmed. There were still powerful emotional links to traditional placatory rituals. People did not appreciate the difference between the Holy Spirit and capricious traditional spirits.

Leaving behind the old order was very demanding. Some continued to carry weapons to church. Some converts found it difficult to give up the protection of carrying around ancestors' bones, though gradually, as the old fears subsided, magical practices no longer aroused such anxiety and spirit houses were destroyed. Papua New Guinea, however, is one of the few countries in the region where people can still be tried in the courts for sorcery. Sorcerors tried to cast spells on missionaries. Their failure undermined their authority. Some continued to consult ancestral skulls in times of stress, or to pray on ground where ancestral spirits had been consulted. Dreams continued to be very real, as were cases of spirit possession, and fears that unusual events were warnings. One young man had a pig born without a tail. His family insisted that he kill it, or he would be killed by Semano, the death spirit. Instead, he dedicated the piglet to God. It grew splendidly. That was a decisive factor in persuading him of the power of the Christian God, and led him to become a Christian.

Meeting for worship, with women present, was considered initially to be potentially very dangerous. Some did not wash, because they feared water spirits. People still felt vulnerable to spirits of other tribes when they left their own territory, but gradually came to appreciate the freedom without such fears, or from the danger of being attacked and killed by their enemies. Missionaries seemed immoral because they shared their house with their wife. Miki Maningiwa gave a vivid description of the terrible impact of fighting, but recognized the

difficulty of being Christian. At times he deeply regretted the end of
pig exchanges and all the excitement of such days, which meant that
the young no longer learnt the obligations of hospitality.[111]

Medical work was sometimes dangerous because of different
cultural views. Sister Joyce Walker, a Methodist, nearly lost her life
when she took a starving baby to her house, after its grandmother
refused permission to take it to hospital. Fortunately, skilled feeding
restored the baby to health, and the vengeful relatives were most
impressed. They had assumed that because she was single, she had
wanted to steal a baby. There were also confusions over tinned baby
food. People were used to tins with pictures of fruit, vegetables, and
animals. Not unnaturally, they concluded that tins with a smiling baby
indicated tinned baby. The obligations to relatives and to the church
could clash painfully. Members of Smith's baptism class were caught in
a series of payback killings in 1966. They were released for their
baptisms and returned to prison.[112] In the Solomon Islands, the South
Seas Evangelical Church also experienced a dramatic revival movement in 1964.

The Missionary Aviation Fellowship (MAF) was another invaluable
contributor to both missions and country, for they were able to fly
people, supplies, and medicine, or to take ill people out for care, in
journeys over impossible terrain that might take weeks.[113] Len Buck,
a genial and visionary Methodist businessman involved in many
Christian activities in Australia and beyond, saw the potential and
formed a Melbourne branch in 1947, and another in New Zealand the
same year. MAF began flying in Papua New Guinea in 1951. The conditions were very dangerous, but the number of fatal crashes has been
remarkably small. Airstrips were primitive, but made access easier to
the Highlands and Sepik regions. By 1963 there were twenty-one
field staff, and six planes. The numbers doubled in 1971, for other
churches saw the value of the service and joined in with financial
support. They expanded into Irian Jaya, Borneo, and Timor, and then
into Northern Australia. Professional help from other airlines was
invaluable, but it was the quality of leadership by Sir John Nimmo,
Bill Clack, and Bruce Redpath which gave the Fellowship the
financial viability it needed. Indigenous staff steadily increased, and a
Papua New Guinea Board has ensured sensitivity to local concerns.

---

[111] Draper, *Daring to Believe*, 46, 69–80.
[112] G. Smith, *Mendi Memories* (Melbourne, 1974) 21–2, 116–20, 125–6.
[113] V. Ambrose, *Balus Bilong Mipela* (Melbourne, 1987).

MOVES TO INDEPENDENCE

Decolonization significantly affected all the Pacific churches, making the development of local leadership essential, for missionary control, however wisely exercised, was not any more politically appropriate. French territories had an elected legislature by 1957. De Gaulle had said the French would stay in the Pacific. Local churches also had to find ways to deal with urbanization in all the capital cities of the former colonies, with accompanying problems of alcohol abuse, family breakdown, unemployment, poor housing, health, and violence from dislocated young men. Though women remained subordinate, those with education or influential spouses exerted considerable influence, first in Polynesia and then increasingly in Melanesia from the 1950s. Churches slowly began to admit women to their government. Samoan Congregationalists began in 1956, as did the Evangelical Church in New Caledonia, with Solomon Island Methodists the following year, and the Tongans in 1966. Organizations like the YWCA, uniformed organizations like the Girls' Brigade, and National Councils for Women reflected Australian and New Zealand patterns. Fetaui Mata'afa was one of the most high-profile women to emerge. Wife of one of the major Samoan titleholders, she became Chair of the Pacific Council of Churches in 1971, while Lorine Tevi of Fiji became the general secretary in 1977. The Pacific Council of Churches and its Papua New Guinea counterpart, the Melanesian Council of Churches have been very important in fostering a sense of Pacific identity, opposing survivals of colonialism, finding strategies to deal with tourism, economic development, and speaking out against the testing of atomic weapons in the Pacific.[114] Roman Catholics joined the Pacific Council of Churches in 1972, after joining the Melanesian Council of Churches in 1970.

In 1962, Western Samoa was the first Pacific state to gain independence. Samoans had long experience in managing church affairs and governing their own villages.[115] The constitution made it plain that the nation was founded on God. Influential ministers, like Mila Sapolu, had been important in the process of its drafting. The Congregational Church had already gone through a process of

---

[114] C. W. Forman, *The Voice of Many Waters* (Suva, 1986); R. Adler (ed.), *Religious Cooperation in the Pacific Islands* (Suva, 1983).
[115] L. Kamu, *Samoan Culture and Christian Gospel* (Suva, 1996).

assessment since 1953, and planning for the Constitution of the Congregational Church in 1961. A slight thawing of relationships with Methodists meant that they agreed to support jointly a Boys' Brigade organizer. The Commission drafting the Constitution attempted to check the lifelong covenant between pastor and village, with retirement imposed at the age of seventy-five. Women were to be deacons in 250 churches. Initially, the small parliament was elected by chiefs only, though of course that meant a great deal of consultation at village level, and brokering of votes. Significant changes occurred in the major churches. Led by Dr John Bradshaw, the innovative principal of Malua College in 1954–65, Congregationalists prepared a fresh doctrinal statement, patterns of ministerial education were updated 'for the pastor must be better educated than his congregation',[116] and new hymns were written by influential ministers such as Vavae Toma.

The most able Congregational students were sent to Pacific Theological College, which opened with 22 students in Suva in 1966. Generously funded by the Theological Education Fund of the World Council of Churches, which gave $100,000 (US) whilst the Pacific churches gave $65,000 (US), it was led by George Knight, a notable Old Testament scholar with experience in Hungary, New Zealand, and the United States, as well as in his native Scotland. Alan Quigley, from New Zealand, followed him in fostering contextual theology. When graduates returned to their home churches, they found that applying their knowledge of a wide theological world to traditional villages was difficult. Chiefs and older pastors found their confidence annoying and disliked their advocacy of change, for that threatened their authority.

Mormons doubled their membership to nearly 17,000 between 1951 and 1961, and built schools and chapels which caused alarm among Samoan Christians, who could not match the financial resources of Salt Lake City. By the 1960s, a Stake had been established, followed by a Temple. Seventh-day Adventists were barely 1,000 in number, but Sauni Kiuresa, a member, wrote the national anthem. They too had access to outside funds in a way that was not open to Methodists and Congregationalists.[117]

The Samoan vicariate became a diocese in 1966, with Pio Taofinu'u as first bishop, in 1968, and cardinal in 1973.[118] In 1982, further

---

[116] Congregational Church of Samoa Commission, *Report* (n.d.) 52.
[117] J. Garrett, *Where Nets Were Cast* (Suva, 1997) 251–3.
[118] J. Heslin, *History of the Catholic Church in Samoa* (Apia, 1995) 89.

jurisdictional changes occurred when John Weitzel became bishop of American Samoa, and Pio of Western Samoa and Tokelau. During the 1960s, new religious congregations, like the Sisters of Mercy, the Salesians, Maryknoll Fathers, the Little Sisters of the Poor, and the Sisters of Our Lady of Nazareth, came to help with the expanding needs for education, health, and pastoral care. Pope Paul visited in 1970, and gave Samoans a sense of belonging to the world church. Disagreements with other churches did not disappear, but were greatly moderated by the ecumenism which changed relationships. At the Independence Feast Day, Congregationalists and Roman Catholics disagreed over who should say grace. The food was finally blessed by the organizing committee saying grace in unison, which ensured that no one's status was devalued.

Methodism's presence is marked by a large church in the centre of Apia, built by Australians, and opened with great celebrations in October 1953.[119] After a number of years of preparation, a Samoan Conference was set up in July 1964, after being approved by the Australian Conference the previous year. The first president was Russell Maddox. It was set up on the same basis as the state conferences, with Tonga and Fiji also sending delegates to the triennial general Australian conference. In 1975, a Samoan congregation in New Zealand was made a district of the conference, underlining how strongly Samoan Christians uphold their unity across national boundaries. The United States became a similar district. In 1966, Kamu Tagaolo became the first Samoan president. Succeeding a long line of Australians, Lene Milo became principal of the Piula College from 1962, and Samoans also became principals of the church high schools. Ron Allardice of Melbourne continued to be a respected elder statesman until his death in 1990. In retirement he produced a valuable dictionary, and encouraged Samoans to study and serve overseas so that they could share in the insights of the world church.

The relation of Christianity, local culture, and political power was most obvious in Tonga. Bishop John Rodgers, consecrated in 1953 after many years teaching, nurtured local leaders like Patelisio Finau and Sione Foliaki, becoming with them an authority on Tongan history, and a greatly admired orator in Tongan.[120] His body was returned from New Zealand for burial in January 1997. He helped to strengthen Tongan links with New Zealand. Occasional New

---

[119] R. Allardice, *The Methodist Story in Samoa 1828–1984* (Malifa, 1984) 33–5.
[120] D. Mullins, *Bishop Patelisio Finau* (Auckland, 1994).

Zealand Methodists came, but ties were strongest with the Australian Conference.

Finau was consecrated as Bishop of Tonga, in Rome, in 1972. Along with Sione Havea and Lopeti Taufa, both Free Wesleyans, he fostered ecumenical partnership and brought his people into the new era opened by Vatican II. That gave Catholics an alternative to the wave of Pentecostalism which came in the 1960s and powerfully appealed to many Methodists. By the 1970s, Pentecostalism had seriously begun to influence Tongan Christianity. Claims to inspiration by the Holy Spirit made by young women had interesting parallels with the *avanga* beliefs about spirit possession in traditional Tongan society. Mormons were also consolidating their influence, especially through their schools.

Dr Sione Havea, a man of great stature, physically and personally, brought a sharp mind to theological education as Principal of Pacific Theological College, and challenged students to think their faith through in a Pacific context. With Setareki Tuilovoni of Fiji, he also played an important part in the development of ecumenism, through the Pacific Council of Churches and the Tongan Council of Churches. Their international experience, spiritual depth, and know-ledge of their heritage enabled them to encourage Christians from every island to share their faith and to reflect on what it meant to be Pacific Christians. Sharp division remained over the boundaries of gospel and culture. Bishop Leslie Boseto argued that 'our Melanesian and Polynesian culture with its animistic religions have given us a general revelation of God'.[121]

FRANCOPHONE CHRISTIANS

Anglophone Christians did not have a monopoly on that debate. Churches in French Polynesia, the New Hebrides, and New Caledonia also had important contributions to make.[122] In New Caledonia, the Kanaks were driven off the most fertile land and severely disadvantaged until 1945. The huge presence of US troops had an immense impact. By 1949, the racist administrative decrees had been removed. Kanaks have grown from around 19,000 in 1921 to 40,000 in 1976.

[121] L. Boseto (ed.), *Partnership in Mission and Development* (Lae, 1979) 10.
[122] Garrett, *Where Nets Were Cast*, 65–77, 207–21, 365–78; C. W. Forman, 'Regional co-operation', in J. Barker (ed.), *Christianity in Oceania* (Lanham, 1994).

Land ownership is a burning issue, but little attempt has yet been made to redress the loss of Kanak land last century to settlers and land companies. Land and business ownership by those of French descent is heavily concentrated in a few families, and senior positions in business and government are dominated by the French. Universal suffrage was granted in 1957, but bitter disputes destabilized the government, and hindered the development of a broadly based political system and removal of racial inequalities in employment, government, and education. Another major problem was the migration from the 1960s to 1980s, which reduced the proportion of Kanaks in the population to 44 per cent, with another 24 per cent from other French Pacific territories, especially Wallis and Futuna, with 32 per cent of French or mixed descent. By 1989 the population was 164,000.

Protestantism, which is roughly a quarter of the population, heavily influences the Loyalty Islands, and retains its seminary there at Chépénhé on Lifou. Roman Catholics are almost 70 per cent of the population. Some French priests support the rightist settlers and the continued association with France. Marists remain influential, though Kanak, Indo-Chinese, and Wallisian clergy are increasing, and staff some important parishes. New Caledonia retains a French archbishop. Protestants have been actively involved in the politics of Kanak self-determination, especially younger ministers. The deacons and older ministers have been much more cautious, but the Evangelical Church's positive attitude to custom has been deeply influenced by the pioneering work of the great missionary Maurice Leenhardt. Some Roman Catholic priests have also incorporated his insights into their pastoral work and used his educational methods.

A very talented younger missionary, Raymond Charlemagne, further sought to encourage Kanak self-determination, but fell out of favour with the older leaders of the Paris Mission. He took out a quarter of the church's membership into the Free Evangelical Church of New Caledonia in 1959. The Evangelical Church was granted autonomy by missionaries in 1960. He had also followed Leenhardt's emphasis on indigenous missionaries, and began work in 1962 on Malekula, where another of Leenhardt's disciples, Jean Guiart, had been working as an anthropologist.

His work was partly supported by Roman Catholic funds given to foster literacy in French. Presbyterian missionaries from Australia and New Zealand were irritated because they had not been consulted, and some unjustly suspected him as an agent of renewed French imperialism in the Condominium. Mission sources in Paris and some influential Kanak pastors like Elia Thidjine, the general secretary of the Evangelical Church from 1957, became increasingly uneasy. Charlemagne was suspended in 1959. It was a tragic schism which showed how fluid were the boundaries between religion and politics. Educational standards for clergy of both major churches continued to rise, linking Kanak aspirations with French radicalism and liberation theology. Thidjine led a campaign to improve church schools from 1958, with some WCC assistance by the 1980s, which led to twenty-three primary schools, seven colleges, and two lycées by 1994.

Vatican II also fostered emphasis on indigenization, which dismayed conservative Catholics. Pierre Martin, bishop from 1957 to 1970, who had been imprisoned in Buchenwald, cautiously implemented the Vatican decrees. He was followed by Xavier Marie Klein MSC (1972–81), from Papua New Guinea, then Michel Calvet SM (1981–). The first local priests had been ordained in 1946, but the establishment of a major seminary at Paita in 1947, which moved to Noumea in 1967, gave promising young men like Jean-Marie Tjibaou, Apollinaire Ataba, Eloi Machoro, and Alphonse Diaou the academic grounding which enabled them to study further in France. There they absorbed the ferment of ideas in the 1960s, including socialist notions which deeply alarmed more conservative Catholics. They became leaders in the independence struggle of the 1980s. Protestants who studied in France, or at the Pacific Theological College, also came back, stirred by the possibilities other Pacific Christians had to shape their political and religious destiny.

In French Polynesia, such graduates fostered increasingly strong currents of interest in the Maohi heritage, supported by some very knowledgeable French Protestant missionaries like Henri Vernier, who worked there from 1955 to 1986, shaping many generations of ministers who were educated in the Hermon seminary, founded in 1927. Occasional schisms occurred, led by graduates of Pacific Theological College.[123] By 1969, the Roman Catholic community had grown to 20,000 compared with 34,000 Protestants. Paul Mazé was vicar apostolic, and then bishop from 1939 to 1968. One of his most important decisions was to found a seminary in 1940. Michel Coppenrath, from a local family, succeeded him as archbishop and has given regional Catholicism new energy.

Though there were no obvious personal connections between

---

[123] Garrett, *Where Nets Were Cast*, 257–69.

Tahitian and New Caledonian Christians, Kanak ideas were very similar to those emerging among Maohi. Daniel Mauer and Philippe Rey-Lescure (Leenhardt's nephew) were important cultural mediators for French Polynesian Protestants. In addition to conceptualizing Christianity in local terms, later missionaries like Georges Preiss worked out forms of polity for a church rather than a mission with the co-operation of leaders in Paris. Local leaders, like Samuel Raapoto, who became the church's first President in 1963, were able to live in both a Maohi and a French world, and played a vital part in the transition. Deacons in local congregations exercised considerable authority over their pastors, whereas in New Caledonia the Synod of the Evangelical Church appointed pastors. The finances of the church are generously supported.

Deciding the boundaries of relation with France was a difficult task for both Protestants and Catholics, which was not made easier by the vacillations of French governments about the powers of local government and the possibility of self-determination. The building of facilities for atomic testing made French presence even more economically important, and distorted island politics.[124] Maohi leaders such as Pouvanaa a Oopa, initially an Evangelical Church deacon, wanted autonomy in some form; he was exiled to France from 1959 to 1968, but was elected to the Senate in 1971 until his death in 1975. Mormons in French Polynesia, as in other parts of the Pacific, were brought firmly under Salt Lake City control, with erring disciples sternly disciplined, so that a clean-cut, clean-living image became a badge of identity. The Reorganized Mormons, based in Missouri, were much more sensitive to local context, compared with the larger groups.

Slight interest was taken in connecting Mormon beliefs and Pacific cultures, even though the foundation of 'stakes' permitted a degree of local devolution within a clearly defined set of guidelines. By contrast, among Roman Catholics in Papua New Guinea in the Goilala area, a pig is killed for every person baptized. Otherwise people believe that the baptism has no power. In Vanuatu, Sethy Regenvanu insisted that, 'The church must use indigenous music, instruments, drama, art, hymns and styles of church buildings in order to bring the Christian gospel nearer to the people in a way they recognise and know.'[125]

---

[124] B. Saura, *Politique et religion à Tahiti* (Papeete, 1993).
[125] C. Wright (ed.), *New Hebridean Culture and Christian Faith* (Melbourne, 1979) 15; N. Besnier, 'Christianity, authority and personhood. Sermonic discourse on Nukulaelae atoll', *JPS* 103 (1994) 339–78, deals with similar issues in Tuvalu.

Though these changes were, in one sense, local responses to changes in Rome and in the ecumenical movement, into which Pacific Christians had little direct input, they were part of a worldwide Christian interest in contextualizing worship, theology, ministry, and social ethics that affected Africa, Asia, Australia, and New Zealand, as well as the Pacific Islands. A campaign for a nuclear-free Pacific was one controversial consequence which ultimately persuaded both American and French governments to cease nuclear weapons testing.

Local people were often cautious over liturgical change. Missionary definitions of sacred/common boundaries were still very potent because they had been internalized. Christians everywhere were challenged by the need to explore the relation between heritage and context, for the long-accepted 'languages' no longer carried the same conviction. That was to be a demanding task for the rest of the century. At some points Christian rites and local culture interact powerfully. Bishop Pogo points out that, in a society where memories of ritual cannibalism are still present, 'by eating the flesh and drinking the blood . . . of our Lord at the Eucharistic Feast, we are taking to ourselves something of the mana of Christ'.[126]

---

[126] E. L. Pogo, 'Culture and liturgy', *AJL* 6 (1998) 193.

7

SEARCHING FOR CREDIBILITY

The last three decades of the twentieth century have been very testing for all the churches in the region. Major changes have been caused by scientific developments over which Christianity has had no control, and which have undermined the community identity which is vital for the region's churches. The development of electronic media, the Internet, and interaction through telecommunications has begun an information revolution. Many Christians are at a loss to know how to deal with either the negative or positive implications of these changes. Rising divorce rates, dramatic growth in abortions, the emergence of a large group of *de facto* marriages and single-parent families have changed the context of family life in Australia and New Zealand. Pacific village life has also eroded. Emphasis on personal freedom and rights has escalated, with many seeking chemical rather than religious ecstasy, but finding only emptiness. That is one of the causes of very high rates of youth suicide in Australia and New Zealand.

The churches' historic role has been called into question by the desertion of hundreds of thousands of former members in Australia and New Zealand. In the 1996 New Zealand Census, 1,150,503 people, or 30 per cent, claimed no religion or objected to stating their religious allegiance. In the Australian Census of 1996 the figure was 4,553,637 or 25.6 per cent. Patterns of worship have changed significantly. By 1993, only 16 per cent of the population in New Zealand and 17 per cent in Australia were weekly attenders. These figures are lower than in North America, but higher than in Europe. Even in the Pacific Islands, there are signs that the communal nature of the churches is breaking down, but not so dramatically as elsewhere.

The proportional sizes of churches has also changed. The Roman Catholic Church now has the largest number of attenders in Australia, New Caledonia, New Zealand, and Papua New Guinea. In Australia it is the single largest church, at 26 per cent of the population of 19 million. In New Zealand the percentage is 13. Doctrinal emphases have changed dramatically, and attempts at enhancing Christian unity have had ambiguous results. Bitter political conflicts in Fiji, Papua

New Guinea, and the Solomon Islands have underlined the inability of churches to transcend ethnic and tribal loyalties. Paradoxically, Christianity has helped to create new national identities in emerging Pacific nations, as rival elites constructed a history of common purpose to overcome tribal and regional rivalries.

Though the process of change has been painful, many churches have shown their capacity to change on issues of ethnicity, gender, and sexuality. The major churches are also important employers, with substantial budgets that place them in the major league of corporates. The Uniting Church in 1999 had a community service budget of c.$800 million (A). The Brisbane Anglican Archdiocese Diocesan Fund stood at $200 million (A) in December 1997.[1] The Victorian Uniting Church in Australia controls investments of $280 million (A), the New South Wales Uniting Church manages $408 million (A). The Anglican Diocese of Sydney has $380 million (A) invested, the Salvation Army $190 million (A). Roman Catholics are very reticent about their assets, which are hard to track because they are dispersed so widely.

A number of religious institutions have changed or disappeared. The last thirty years have seen the demise of many church newspapers and religious bookshops. Those churches with large spending budgets needed executive staff with considerable authority, for government funding for educational and social services performed by the churches grew significantly.[2] So have stringent conditions for funding and accountability. Some church executives hand pick their management committee, which can improve expertise, but can equally exclude alternative views.

So senior officers of the Uniting Church in Australia were shocked, in 1983, when *The Bulletin* published a political analysis, by Dr Tim Duncan, of its leaders, suggesting that the key committees had been captured by leftist proponents of liberation theology and ecumenism, who were quite unrepresentative of the view of church members.[3] Though the thesis had limitations, it was a reminder that the theology of an inner group can shape decisions and elections.

One of the most striking signs of change was the development of other world religions in Australia because of migration. Judaism, which formed its first synagogue in Hobart in 1843, was greatly

---

[1] *The Bulletin*, 14 April 1998, 20–4.
[2] *Financial Review*, 17–20 Dec. 1991.
[3] *The Bulletin*, 25 Jan. 1983.

strengthened numerically by an influx of 35,000 Holocaust survivors. Orthodox Judaism now accounts for 40 per cent of the Jewish population, a major shift from the more liberal and reformist tradition. Australian Jews have become important business, professional, and cultural leaders, as well as being noted for their philanthropy. They have been very critical of some aspects of Christian public ethics. Islam, which was very small until the 1950s, has now become a significant group of over 200,000 because of migration from Turkey, Lebanon, and the former Yugoslavia. The dominant ethos is Sunni, though other groups are also present. Buddhism is also now significant because of migration from Indo-China. In Fiji, Muslims, Hindus, and Sikhs provide an important alternative to majority Christianity. In Australia they have challenged long-held assumptions about Australia basically being a Christian society, assisted by secular-minded intellectuals who dismiss religion.[4]

ARCHITECTURE FOR WORSHIP

By the 1980s, important liturgical changes were making themselves felt in Protestant churches. They stemmed from the liturgical writing of Catholic scholars and the work of Protestants who were also rediscovering their Catholic and Reformation heritage. Two major themes emerged—a rediscovery of the classic form of worship beneath the additions of the centuries, and a fresh insight into the Church as the people of God gathered around Word and Sacraments. Those historical and theological perceptions, in turn, led to questions being raised about the Gothic form of Christian architecture and church interiors. The wholesale destruction of European church buildings during the 1939–45 war offered architects and clergy opportunity to build anew. Many exciting new buildings were erected, which awakened interest in design among Australians and New Zealanders who were facing the challenges of suburban expansion in the 1950s.

Louis Williams of Melbourne designed more than 130 churches, mainly in Victoria. Churches like St Andrew's Anglican at Brighton, Victoria, showed his mastery of space and light.[5] Availability of new building materials and techniques made it possible to break with the cruciform and rectangular Gothic shapes which had been so

---

[4] A. W. Ata (ed.), *Religion and Ethnic Identity* (3 vols., Melbourne, 1988).
[5] La Trobe MS 9965, Williams papers.

dominant.[6] Altered church interiors were needed in order to reflect the community celebration of worship, without distance between clergy and people.

Preaching auditoria remained important for Baptists and the newly prominent large Pentecostal churches, with little concern for liturgical atmosphere, and suspicions of any traditional forms which limited the freedom of the Spirit. Individual and movable seating made possible a variety of service, impossible with fixed pews. So did the use of electronic organs, and instruments like the guitar and drums, which became a symbol of adaptation to pop music. Traditional hymnody was challenged by choruses sung to folksy tunes. Mobile microphones made congregational participation in prayers and testimony possible in new ways. Overhead projectors and television monitors made the singing of new hymns much easier. At the same time the international emergence of charismatic worship, and the 1960s rejection of formality and boundaries, freed congregations for less ordered services right across the Christian spectrum. Australians and New Zealanders began to write hymns in unprecedented numbers.

New Zealand also saw a resurgence of building in the post-war era, financed by Wells Way and the Stewardship campaigns, because of the dramatic growth of population. Many of the new churches were very functional, with no pretensions to architectural distinction, but created light, airy interiors with congregations gathered around a small sanctuary area, as in the Wakari Union Church, Dunedin, creating a feeling of community which reflected liturgical changes. Miles Warren's chapel at College House, Christchurch, was unabashedly modern externally, but internally traditional and awkward for worship. John Scott's chapel, at Futuna House, Wellington, was a masterpiece of design, with a numinous interior.[7] The Hukarere School Chapel in Napier had rich Maori symbolism through the partnership of Sir Apirana Ngata and the principal Isla Hunter.

Extensions to Anglican cathedrals in Dunedin and Auckland caused some controversy by blending old with new, in very different ways. E. J. McCoy's soaring clear windows in the modern chancel in Dunedin create a feeling of space and lightness, while the hanging perspex panel and multi-coloured cross focus attention on the altar. In

    [6] J. Freeland, *Melbourne Churches* (Melbourne, 1963); T. T. Reed, *Historic Churches of Australia* (Melbourne, 1978); E. Walker, 'Sources of Protestant church design', *PUCHSV* 3/2 (1996) 84–97.
    [7] R. Walden, *Voices of Silence: New Zealand's Chapel of Futuna* (Wellington, 1987).

Auckland, Professor E. J. Toy was the brains behind the move of the fine wooden old pro-cathedral across the road to be linked with the stark modern section. This achieved important financial savings, as well as winning over some who loved the old building and were glad to see it used. Architectural opinion is divided about the combination of styles. Malcolm McKenzie, who was dismissed as architect when the money ran out in 1969, called it a monstrosity.[8] In Brisbane, the completion of the Anglican cathedral is expected in the new millennium. It makes no changes in the basic neo-Gothic design.

In the Cook Islands, Tonga, and Western Samoa, migrants to New Zealand sent back money which made possible a church-building boom there, nourished by village competition. Furnishings and fittings were eclectic, but created ownership of new buildings by key families. They also built in their adopted country, for there are about 180,000 Pacific Islanders in New Zealand, with over 90 per cent in Auckland and Wellington. Roman Catholics in Port Moresby built a cathedral incorporating indigenous features. At Martin Luther Seminary, Lae, the chapel has striking carving. The chapel at Siatoutai Theological College, Tonga, adapts house architecture to Christian worship. Most Pacific churches are still very simply furnished and often with open sides. The Flierl Memorial Lutheran Church at Sambang was a bold attempt at enculturation built like a men's house, which contained a sanctuary area for ancestors.

KEEPING FAITH AND UNITY

Buildings convey insight into identity, but sustaining a common purpose can be difficult when views of the sacred fracture. The Presbyterian Church of New Zealand found how difficult it could be to contain schism amongst its Pacific Islanders.[9] In Otara, South Auckland, Matofu Fuimaono's leadership divided his large congregation. The pastoral tie was dissolved at the 1985 Assembly. The moderator's personal announcement of the decision at the church was greeted with abuse by Fuimaono's supporters. Attempts to deal in-house with the disputes failed, and the result was a complex and expensive legal case in which the Assembly Sessional Conference of

[8] *New Zealand Herald*, 7 Jan. 1993.
[9] GANZ *Proceedings* (1985) 143–4; P. Culbertson (ed.), *Counselling Issues and South Pacific Communities* (Auckland, 1997) 93–106 Tonga; 117–34 Cook Islands; 161–88 Samoa; 135–60 Niue.

1985 was declared invalid by Mr Justice Thorp in 1986. A Special Commission met in February 1987 and issued a very careful report.[10] This did nothing to move people from their entrenched positions. Cultural differences were underlined, as were financial irregularities, poorly kept minutes, and questions over ministerial style. Some left, disillusioned, and moved to other denominations. Fuimaono resigned in February 1987 and went to Sydney. The case was a reminder of the power of the Congregationalist ethos and the difficulty of aligning European and Islander models of authority and administration.

The Greek Orthodox Church in Australia provides another angle on the tensions between unity and schism. Archbishop Stylianos wants all the Greek churches in Australasia to be united under his authority. Even though he is an acute cultural critic, unfortunately his leadership has created many opponents. In addition, a number of schisms had riven the Greek community before he arrived, aided by bishops who are out of communion with Constantinople, such as Bishop Laios in Adelaide. Communities which have raised money to build a local church, which they run by elected committees, are not willing to give up their property and to have no further say in administration. Factions have changed locks and excluded their rivals.

The Orthodox model of unity has a strong theological and historical appeal. In practice, it is undermined by ethnic and personal rivalries and unable to take major initiatives in building relations with Protestants and Roman Catholics. Any suspicion of proselytism is inflammatory to the Orthodox. They remain very critical of aspects of western civilization. 'Our knowledge is death, our science is death, our individual and social morality is death.'[11]

The Roman Catholic approach to unity has changed significantly over the last thirty years.[12] There has been a slow recognition of the importance of Uniates, Maronites, and Melkites, as Orthodoxy becomes more important. Return to Rome is no longer seen in crude terms of submission to the one true church. Dialogues with other churches, and other faiths, which occur internationally and regionally, have shown many advances in understanding on baptism, mixed marriages, and areas of doctrine like justification, even when partners are still not wholly agreed about shared eucharist.

[10] PCNZ Special Assembly *Report*, 3 Apr. 1987.
[11] Archbishop Stylianos, 'Easter musings, 1986', *Voice of Orthodoxy* (1986); J. Murray (ed.), *Would You Believe?* (Alexandria, 1997) 41–8 for a brief biography.
[12] John Paul II, *Ut unum sint* (1995).

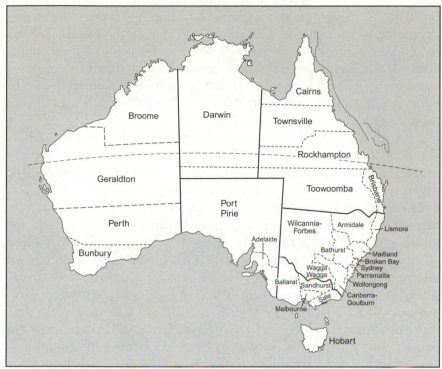

Australia: Catholic dioceses (1991). (*Source: Official Directory of the Catholic Church in Australia*, Sydney, 1991, pp. 8–9. With permission of E. J. Dwyer.)

In both Australia and New Zealand, the Roman Catholic Church became a full member of the national ecumenical body, thereby bringing new credibility to the decisions of the Council of Churches of Aotearoa New Zealand (CCANZ) and the National Council of Churches in Australia (NCCA), and providing further impetus to the forging of closer relationships and more effective networks. That has been sadly undermined by the Roman Catholic decision of late 1998 to move out of the CCANZ because there is not enough commitment to faith issues. Lutherans joined the NCCA in 1998.

Any further corporate reunions appear to be out of the question for the present. The international and local climate has changed. In New Zealand the attempt to create a united Church of Christ foundered on Anglican nervousness about losing their heritage. The General Synod in 1974 failed by two votes to gain a two-thirds majority in the house of clergy. The scheme was finally rejected in 1976 when the Dunedin, Nelson, and Wellington dioceses refused assent. Thousands of ordinary Christians in the negotiating churches were deeply disappointed when the 1980 General Synod saw the House of Bishops fail to reach the required majority for a unification of ministries.[13] Some of the conservative Presbyterians, who had hoped to become a continuing and purer church, found it frustrating to have to live on in what they regarded as a liberally dominated church which did not take them seriously.

Evangelicals had another approach to union, which can best be described as conciliar and local. They rejected the need for corporate reunion and any union which was based on sacrifice of their version of doctrinal integrity. Their great concern was unity of effort in mission overseas, local evangelism, and service. Part of that concern was focused in the work of the Evangelical Alliances and in networks for co-operation between the many missionary societies which worked all over the globe. Living and studying together within an agreed doctrinal framework reinforced a sense of unity and permissible diversity which has had a long-lasting impact in local churches and overseas mission work. That has been reinforced by the Christian radio network developed in New Zealand by Keith Berry and others under the name Radio Rhema, which finally obtained a licence by a combination of prayer and very skilled lobbying and has grown considerably since 1973.

One of the most influential and high-profile of these Evangelical networks was World Vision, an American agency which, from small beginnings in Melbourne in August 1966, with 307 child sponsors, has grown to become the largest Australian and New Zealand development and relief agency. In Australia it raised $100 million in 1998–9. It is unashamedly Christian, but is respected right across the national community on either side of the Tasman.[14] They have appealed to the generosity and fairness of the whole community. Another example of Christians' practical compassion, Community Aid Abroad, now combined with Freedom from Hunger and Oxfam, was founded by the Anglican Father G. K. Tucker. TEAR Fund of the Evangelical Alliance and the funds of denominations have also made important contributions to bringing disaster relief and development to commu-

[13] B. Davis, *The Way Ahead* (Christchurch, 1995) 176–80.

[14] G. Irvine, *Best Things in Worst Times* (Wilsonville, 1996); B. Barron, 'How World Vision Australia came into existence', 1993 address, typescript; P. Hunt, *Journeys to Justice* (Melbourne, 1996); G. Bryant, *Pathways of Hope* (Palmerston North, 1996); S. Blackburn, *Practical Visionaries* (Melbourne, 1993).

nities all around the world. Adventists, in proportion to their size, are the most generous givers to relief overseas.

For a time in the 1980s a series of ecumenical statements were issued in Australia, but that caused dissatisfaction amongst the participating churches. Indeed the Australian Catholic Bishops' Conference disbanded the Commission on Social Justice, and set up a new group which they closely controlled. Tensions about the extent to which social justice and charitable activity should interact also deeply divided the St Vincent de Paul movement in the mid-1990s in Australia, with a more conservative emphasis triumphing. The New Zealand Catholic bishops issued a careful response to the difficulty of those on low incomes, but on some occasions joint statements were made with Anglicans, or with the Catholic bishops of Oceania on subjects like nuclear testing in 1995, after the French tests resumed.[15]

The Anglican General Synod in Australia has published many statements on important policy issues, but individual dioceses also speak on matters germane to their territory. Sydney has been more active than most, because it is better resourced, but Melbourne produced a fine report on multiculturalism, *A Garden of Many Colours*, in 1985. Its 1998 report on education brought a strong response from the state government which claimed the report was seriously flawed. More conservative churches like Baptists, Lutherans, and Churches of Christ rarely comment on political and economic matters, because of the way they separate the divine tasks of church and state. The Salvation Army comments regularly on welfare issues. The peak bodies of all churches comment on spiritual and theological matters to their members, though such statements are less noticed by the media than twenty-five years ago.[16]

An example of cross-cultural unity can be seen in the remote North West, where John Jobst SAC was consecrated vicar apostolic in 1959, when Bishop Rauble retired. He had served with distinction in the German Army and was awarded the Iron Cross (and a CBE in 1981). The challenges of ministering to fewer than 2,000 Catholics in a million square kilometres taxed all his abilities. In 1930, Sydney diocese gave only £19 to work in Western Australia. The missions were dreadfully run-down, and were dependent on parsimonious

---

[15] C. Osman and P. Swart (eds.), *Church in the World* (Wellington, 1997); M. Newport (ed.), *Australian Catholic Bishops Statements, 1985–95* (Sydney, 1997).

[16] D. Hilliard, 'The ties that used to bind: a fresh look at the history of Australian Anglicanism', *Pacifica* 11/3 (1998) 265–80.

government funding for 85 per cent of their income. Aborigines in the diocese were marginal, and little attempt had been made to break with generations of paternalism. Jobst fostered further anthropological study, pioneered by Fr Ernst Worms, broke with the past to connect more adequately with traditional culture, raised £120,000 nationally, and sought to develop an Aboriginal church, giving Aborigines title to most of the diocese's land. The vicariate became a diocese in 1967, when government spending on major development projects, like the Ord River dam, brought population to the region, without benefiting Aborigines. Jobst had to cope with many tensions, not least a confrontation with Aborigines at Turkey Creek in 1979, but he and his religious managed to bring positive results out of turmoil. In 1890, the church had arrived in the region. In 1984, a great gathering at Beagle Bay celebrated that, and brought together the coastal and inland tribes for the first time.[17]

THEOLOGICAL DEVELOPMENTS

Australian and New Zealand theological scholars have become better known internationally since the 1970s.[18] So have a small number of Melanesian and Polynesian Christian leaders, like the Lutheran Wesley Kigasung and Bishop Leslie Boseto from the Solomon Islands Region of the United Church of Papua New Guinea, Bishop Finau, and Sir Sione Havea of Tonga, whose work on international confessional and ecumenical bodies has reminded Christians to the north that contextualizing Christianity in this region is of more than local significance.

One of the most notable Australian theologians is the botanist Charles Birch of Sydney, whose work on the boundaries of science, theology, and ethics won him the Templeton Prize in 1990. Strongly influenced by the SCM and South Australian Methodism, he began to explore the writings of process theologians in order to try and find a scientifically credible basis for ecological ethics. Active in the Club of Rome and the World Council of Churches in the 1970s, he has continued to challenge Australian Christians to re-examine their theological foundations and to connect with the methods of scientists.

---

[17] M. Zucker, *From Patrons to Partners* (Perth, 1994) 167–72.

[18] Rainbow Spirit Elders, *Rainbow Spirit Theology* (Melbourne, 1998); A. Pattel-Gray (ed.), *Martung Upah* (Melbourne, 1996); C. Sherlock, 'Theology in Australia', in A. McGrath (ed.), *Blackwell Encyclopaedia of Modern Christian Thought* (Oxford, 1993) 672.

Paul Davies, an Adelaide physicist, also won a Templeton Prize for his work on understanding God.[19] He is not a theist in the same sense as Birch, and is not so concerned to connect his hypothesis with classical or modern Christian theology. In Auckland, the Anglican zoologist John Morton made useful contributions to the debates after Geering, as well as exploring links between theology and environmental issues, which has helped to provide some bases for eco-theology being developed by Clive Pearson in Sydney, and Ray Galvin in Auckland, two lively younger theologians. Paul Collins has also addressed this in an ABC TV series, *God's Earth*, in 1998. He is the first Australian Catholic theologian formally to be proceeded against in Rome, because of his 1997 book *Papal Power*, which proposed serious constitutional reforms to the papacy.

Australian theological scholarship has several denominational strands. Strong biblical, historical, and theological scholarship has emerged in each of the Australian mainland capital cities, with Catholic, Orthodox, and Protestant scholars sharing in ecumenical dialogues and having their writings published internationally. A modest number of scholarly journals provide a context for debate and local dissemination of ideas. In New Zealand, Auckland and Dunedin have small theological faculties who vigorously explore matters of faith, but Australian scholars with international reputations, such as Peter Carnley, Brendan Byrne, Leon Morris, Francis Moloney, Tony Kelly, Gerry O'Collins, Eric Osborn, Dorothy Lee, Elaine Wainwright, and Peter Matheson, indicate that the region does not simply respond to northern agendas but is beginning to mark out its own priorities.

Australians and New Zealanders have also made their mark internationally on witness for justice. They include Fr Brian Gore, deported by the Marcos regime; Viv Grigg of the Servants of the Poor in the Philippines; and Michael Lapsley in Southern Africa, who was the victim of an Afrikaaner bomb. Sir Garfield Todd, a Churches of Christ missionary from New Zealand between 1934 and 1946, then a member of parliament in 1946–58, was for a time prime minister in Southern Rhodesia.[20] During the Smith regime he was often under house arrest, or in prison for his convictions about the importance of a

---

[19] C. Birch, *Liberating Life* (Maryknoll, 1990); *Biology and the Riddle of Life* (Sydney, 1999); P. Davies, *The Mind of God* (New York, 1992).

[20] B. Wurth, *Justice in the Philippines* (Sydney, 1985); V. Grigg, *Companion to the Poor* (Sydney, 1990); M. Worsnip, *Michael Lapsley* (Melbourne, 1996).

society based on equality before God. A number of Christians from the region have served in the ecumenical movement or in their own denomination as international leaders. John Denton chaired the Anglican Consultative Council between 1979 and 1984. General Eva Burrows led the Salvation Army during 1986–93. Dr Noel Vose headed the Baptist World Alliance from 1985 to 1990. Alan Brash, Jean Skuse, and David Gill have been influential in the WCC, the most visible members of a wide regional and ecumenical network. Margaret Rodgers, a Sydney Anglican deaconess with a keen theological mind, has won respect in the Christian Conference of Asia for her role in the Praesidium. Hundreds continue to serve as missionaries and fraternal workers in every continent, carrying with them something of the practicality and modesty which characterize this region's Christianity at its best. Occasionally, it can be controversial, but it has strengthened regional ties significantly.

MUSIC AND LITURGY

Shared music was another common bond, as was the movement of organists and choirmasters. They have never been constrained by denominational or geographical boundaries. In St Andrew's Uniting Church, Brisbane, Guy Jansen in the 1990s built on a long-standing choral tradition, by including his experience over many years with the Festival Singers in Wellington. He is an outstanding musical educator at the University of Queensland, able to work in a variety of styles, and has helped Queenslanders appreciate the liveliness of the choral tradition, both old and new. From the Anglican tradition, Peter Godfrey, from Auckland and Wellington, spent a period with the Canterbury Fellowship at Trinity College, Melbourne, while next door at Ormond College, Douglas Lawrence has built a world class choir since 1982. The reputation of Robert Boughen at the Anglican cathedral in Brisbane extends far beyond his home territory, as does that of Roger Heagney at St Francis', Melbourne. All-male cathedral choirs still flourish on both sides of the Tasman. *The Australian Hymn Book* took on a New Zealand form as *With One Voice*, with an important supplement of Polynesian hymns. A new hymnal, *Together in Song,* appeared during 1999 in Australia, with a wide ecumenical selection.

Every part of worship came under scrutiny, as radicals and conservatives struggled to decide what should be changed and what was non-negotiable. The Englishing of Roman Catholic liturgy in Australia and New Zealand, and its translation into other regional languages, has ended the reign of Latin as the liturgical language of the largest of the world's Christian churches, though older Catholics deeply regret its passing. Deciding on new translation has been difficult. An interesting example of the political implications can be seen in the translations of some words in the Psalms of the 1989 *A New Zealand Prayer Book*, as well as in some omissions on theological grounds. At the request of migrant Arab Anglicans who felt totally marginalized in Israel, alternatives to 'Zion' were found. That, in turn, provoked a strong protest from members of the Jewish community in New Zealand, who objected to what they regarded as misleading translations and excisions, arguing that references to Zion did not have a contemporary political link with Zionism. From another angle, David Frost, of Newcastle, made telling criticisms of the Psalms translation in the Australian Prayer Book. More recently, Barry Spurr was highly critical of the new Australian Anglican Prayer Book. 'Masquerading as liturgy, volumes such as AAPB derive from ideas about worship which are profoundly anti-liturgical.'[21]

An articulate group of women were also increasingly angered at their exclusion from liturgy by the use of exclusively male language for God and for the Christian community's members.[22] The experience and insight of half of the human race is only slowly being recognized in some of the region's churches. Amongst Orthodox, many Roman Catholics, Lutherans, conservative Protestants, and most Pentecostals, such linguistic changes appear merely to reflect modern secularizing influences, which have no place in a religion of revelation. Yet even in the Pentecostal churches, women like Bunty Collins and Florrie Mortimer quietly exerted influence in Australian Assemblies of God. Women Aglow and Women who Want to be Women are parachurch groups which celebrate traditional female roles and reject feminist theologies and demands for share in leadership.

Growth of Pentecostalism and charismatic renewal have led to the production of a number of new collections of songs and choruses which have become a kind of ecumenical musical currency, in books like *The Sound of Living Waters* and even in the more mainstream *Alleluia Aotearoa* (1992). One of the reasons for the success of such

[21] B. Spurr, 'A preface sensitized', *AJL* 6 (1997) 25.
[22] E. Smith, *Bearing Fruit in Due Season* (Collegeville, 1999); V. Webb, *Why We're Equal* (St Louis, 1999); J. Nelson, *Let Us Pray* (Melbourne, 1999) offer alternatives.

songs is the way in which the music is much closer to folk idioms and what people hear electronically.

Geoff Bullock, Trish Watts, Natalie Yule Yeoman, and John McRae are among those who write for this region's popular audience.[23] Some mainstream hymn writers, like the Methodist Colin Gibson of Dunedin, a professor of English, are also talented composers, but write in a different idiom from pop tunes. The new hymnals produced by major churches overseas or groups like the Iona Community in Scotland have also been influential. A number of significant hymn writers have emerged in the last thirty years, such as James McAuley, Robin Mann, Jim Minchin, Elizabeth Smith, Digby Hannah, Annie Judd, Shirley Murray, and Ross Langmead, the quality of whose work is recognized by publication internationally. Fr Bill Jordan of Melbourne edited *The Catholic Worship Book* in 1985, with many Australian inclusions.

In Papua New Guinea, the publication of *tok pisin* hymnals, which translate European hymns, also demonstrates the vitality of local Christians who have written hymns to catchy modern tunes, often with a charismatic flavour.[24] Aborigines and Torres Strait Islanders in Australia likewise draw on the songs and choruses of Evangelical Protestantism, but without forgetting indigenous chants and accompaniment, though these have rarely been published. Parish choirs have been in decline since the 1960s, and musical standards have slid, although congregational singing has stayed vigorous where ministers and organists have successfully educated people for musical change. The virtual disappearance of broadcast services in Australia and New Zealand has also removed an incentive to keep standards of congregational singing high, but Gospel music from North America has quite a following on some radio stations.

The 1993 Catholic Congress in Melbourne was very significant, popularizing Gelineau and opening up many new musical perspectives. Few major modern composers regard setting the eucharist to music as an opportunity to offer their gifts in worship, as was still happening in the nineteenth century with composers like Tchaikovsky. Malcolm Williamson, Master of the Queen's Music

[23] G. Bullock, *Hands of Grace* (Sydney, 1998) 6–7 describes an experience of brokenness, by a leading Pentecostal composer and hymn writer, which has transformed his writing for Hillsong music.

[24] M. H. Webb, 'Pipal Bilong Musik tru', 'A truly musical people', Ph.D. thesis (Middletown, 1995). M. P. B. Felde, 'Song and stance', Ph.D. thesis (Chicago, 1984) is an invaluable study of music and hymns in the Evangelical Lutheran Church of New Guinea.

since 1995, has produced some fine church music, but it is rarely performed in his homeland. Anglicans Peter Paviour of Goulburn and Rosalie Bonython of Ballarat have produced eucharistic settings, while the latter has composed cantatas and settings for responsorial psalms. Christopher Willcock SJ in Melbourne made an especially important contribution to setting Psalms for differing instruments. He has had close links with Roger Heagney and the St Francis choir.[25]

Douglas K. Mews migrated to Auckland in 1969 and was appointed Director of Music at St Patrick's Cathedral, Auckland, a position he held until 1982. Settling in New Zealand enabled his musical creativity to flourish. As Director of Music, he built up a choir accomplished in singing both great works of the Latin choral repertoire and his own prolific output of polyphonic compositions with English texts, as well as arrangements of traditional hymns, spirituals, and songs. He wanted congregations to sing easily learnt refrains to music which might be led either by a cantor or by a choir. Not the least of his gifts was an infectious enthusiasm, by which he could get any kind of congregation to raise its voice in song.

Music can be profoundly moving, but music and active bodily movement have not been connected with European worship for many centuries. Religious dance was a vital part of many Pacific Island societies, performed and sung by both men and women as a way of embodying relationship with the gods, ancestors, and the land, and evoking the sacred in a most powerful way that took the dancers out of everyday life into an ecstasy of motion. Aborigines likewise have an extremely rich heritage of dance which is deeply religious, even though missionaries tried to stamp out corroborees. In his Annual Report of 1874–5, Hagenauer, a Moravian in Victoria, said, 'Through the general filthy appearance, often with painted faces, the yelling noises during whole nights about the townships and continual indolence they were at best only considered a great nuisance and good for nothing, by the increasing white population.'[26] European Christians

---

[25] N. Ancell, 'Christopher Willcock, Australian liturgical composer', MA thesis (Monash, 1992), which offers a valuable discussion of the relation between liturgy and music. I am indebted to Dr Constant Mews for material on his late father. N. Small, 'Music in the Roman Catholic Church after Vatican II', BA Hons. thesis (Brisbane, 1991) on St Stephen's Roman Catholic cathedral in Brisbane.

[26] D. Horton (ed.), *Encyclopaedia of Aboriginal Australia* (Canberra, 1994) 'Dance'; La Trobe MS 3343 Hagenauer Letter Books. E. F. Hannemann, *Papuan Dances and Dancing* (Martin Luther Seminary Library TS, 1935) 27 noted that to be a dancer you needed to be both heathen and Christian. Dancing honoured ancestors and also indicated how the tribe can be propagated.

have found it difficult to integrate this with their understanding of worship as bodily immobility in the sacred space of a church. Many of the Pacific Island dances were banned because of their overt sexuality and links with traditional religion. Sometimes this was missionary initiative, but converts also believed that their new-found faith and traditional dancing were incompatible. Some purified dances survived, but they were invariably performed outside sacred space and never on Sunday. Night dancing was especially suspect.

One of the most important pioneers of a different approach has been Shona Dunlop MacTavish of Dunedin. Equipped with a keen mind, a deep faith, and a lively social conscience, as well as great gifts for dance, she has given religious dance a new meaning. She was a pupil and colleague of Professor Gertrud Bodenwieser in Vienna before the Anschluss. After returning to Dunedin, she began teaching choreography and working with other dancers until, in 1961 at the Harvest Festival Service in Maori Hill Presbyterian Church, she asked Tom Corkill, the minister, if the congregation was thanking God or saluting human consumerism. She suggested instead young girls dancing their offering. That was what happened next year and began an astonishingly creative period of dancing in the worship of churches up and down New Zealand which inspired some and bemused others.

Because I am so aware of the power of dance, which apart from the sheer joy of bodily movement, gives one the heightened feeling of being totally alive, I also see it as a kind of living sermon. It is also capable of speaking upon issues of our time with devastating clarity.[27]

Slowly in other parts of Australasia, other Christians such as Wendy Bytheway and Ian Ferguson, a Uniting Church minister, have also been recovering the spiritual power of dance. The same recovery can be seen amongst Roman Catholics in Papua New Guinea and New Caledonia, where the opening of the Tjibaou Centre in 1998 saw a renaissance of traditional dance. However, for many Islanders, dancing must be performed outside the church, even if it includes biblical themes. Nihi Vini reported that during one Christmas service 'our music got so good that we began dancing, even though we were in church'.[28] Much misunderstanding still remains to be broken down, so that mind, body, and spirit can combine, in a total worship of God that breaks down the barriers of time, and opens up new humanity. Pentecostals have been partly successful in this.

[27] S. Dunlop MacTavish, *Leap of Faith* (Dunedin, 1997) 233.
[28] *Point* (1973) 109.

LIBERAL DECLINE

Some strands of liberal theology in the major Protestant churches have withered since the 1980s with great biblical themes such as eschatology reduced to a view that the future would be better than the present. Liberals no longer set the theological agenda as they did till the 1970s. They have not persuaded those on the boundaries of the churches, who have left because the life, worship, and teaching they experienced resonated less and less with them. They lacked a doctrine of authority which united the disparate elements of the Catholic heritage. So many new intellectual worlds have developed, rising and falling in and out of fashion so rapidly that it is difficult to relate the Christian faith to any one in a significant way.

Francis MacNab of Melbourne is one of the most influential liberals who combined the insights of Christianity and various schools of psychotherapy. As well as establishing the innovative Cairnmillar Institute for counselling and life education, he restored life to an inner Melbourne parish, Collins Street Independent Church, now named St Michael's. It has one of the largest inner-city Protestant congregations in Australia, unified by MacNab's charismatic personality and remark-able communication gifts. A different approach to correlation can be seen in Archbishop Brian Davis, Dr Bruce Kaye, Bishop Bruce Wilson, Bishop Brian Carrell, and Bishop Paul Barnett, who attempt to be loyal to their Anglican heritage, while at the same time communi-cating with their contemporary context.[29]

Amongst Sydney Anglicans, keeping the faith is bound up with many other factors besides commitment to the Evangelical ethos. A number of families like the Begbies and Knoxes have played a key role for several generations. To be born into one of these families, or to be kin, means involvement in groups like Childrens' Special Service Missions, Evangelical Union, Crusaders, Scripture Union, CMS. They provide invaluable formation for the young, and keep them from worldly influences and also from serious encounter with other Christian traditions, even those claiming to be Evangelical in other denominations. Loyalty to Moore College and its biblical interpreta-tion is important, as is being in a parish with a 'sound' rector. Rejection

---

[29] B. Kaye, *Church Without Walls* (Melbourne, 1996); B. Wilson, *Reasons of the Heart* (Sutherland, 1998); B. Carrell, *Moving Between Times* (Auckland, 1998); P. Barnett, *The Logic of History* (Grand Rapids, 1997).

of liberalism and Catholicism is important, and to outsiders Sydney Anglicans have a preoccupation with stereotypes and boundaries.

Sydney women were and are expected to be helpmates, submissive to the convictions of their husbands, and shapers of their children's piety, like 'Granny' Knox, wife of Canon D. J. Knox, who was seen as a model of a fine Evangelical, even though she had some non-conforming children. Such women were expected to be loyal parish workers, with community involvement, but they have not exercised significant leadership in parishes or diocesan affairs. Headmistresses were an exception, though they were never Evangelical hardliners. They were too conscious of the need to mould an inclusive school community.

Talented lawyers and judges have always been important in Sydney's Synod and its committees. The chancellor of Sydney Diocese, Mr Justice Handley, a key member of the Appellate Tribunal, has been a sage adviser of successive archbishops, bishops, and primates, and a loyal supporter of his rector. While he could not be described as an Evangelical activist, his integration of faith and life is respected in the legal world. A judge of an older generation, Athol Richardson, a former Salvationist, prior to his election to Parliament, ruled diocesan committees with a firm hand, speaking afterwards to people if their behaviour in committee did not measure up to his standards. Such attitudes are anathema to freer spirits but liberating to others.[30]

Some liberal ideas are akin to the movements loosely called post-modern, or New Age, which are accommodationist and seek individualistically to synthesize insights from all kinds of religion and philosophies. Sometimes remaining strongly theistic with a core of Christian nostalgia, in other cases they moved romantically into varieties of Buddhism, with occasional forays into Hinduism.[31] These are religious counterparts to other progeny of liberalism, the various humanisms and spiritualities which provide a framework for those who find Christian exclusivism and dogma no longer helpful or meaningful. Philip Adams, agnostic son of a Congregational minister, is one of the most articulate of this group, whose regular demolition of religious follies in the Australian media has quite a wide following.[32] For the more politically inclined, the emergence of multiculturalism

---

[30] A. Kerr, *A Guided Journey* (Gundaroo, 1998).

[31] D. Millikan and N. Drury, *Worlds Apart* (Sydney, 1991); J. Roe, 'Dayspring: Australia and New Zealand as Setting for the New Age from the 1890s to Nimbin', *SCH* (1997/8) 170–87; H. Carey, *Believing in Australia* (Sydney, 1996) 177.

[32] T. Lane, *As the Twig is Bent* (Melbourne, 1980) 105–18.

in Australia, and biculturalism in New Zealand, has been one way of creating a new national identity, without Christianity or any other religion able to provide a focus for unity.

Including an adequate account of local congregational life in a general history is an impossible task, but study of parishes is a vital way of understanding how Christianity is embodied in both constructive and limiting ways, even though parish life is under some pressure.[33] In the Roman Catholic Church, fewer than thirty would-be diocesan priests entered seminary in Australia in 1999, while the Uniting and Anglican Churches have had hard choices about closures when finances fall short. Frome Presbytery in South Australia has no serving ministers, but has developed local lay leadership. Such micro-history is a vital complement to the study of leaders and the impact of international change.

A few examples of Australasian parish life in the 1980s and 1990s must suffice. In Kingswood, Adelaide, a solid suburban community, the transition to a new style of parish life after Vatican II had its bumps, but was greatly helped by Fr Cronin's leadership and the initiatives of loyal and gifted laity.[34] Appointed in 1964 and retiring in 1998 aged 75, he served on the senate and diocesan council of priests, chairing the latter in 1991–2, as well as being a consultor. A parish pastoral council was begun in 1968 and the financial strain of running a parish school was removed by state aid. The Josephite sisters have remained, but widened their role into pastoral work, as well as moving to a more general educational role. A parish worker was appointed in 1982, and a liturgy co-ordinator in 1991.

Laity from the parish replaced the traditional sodalities with the Christian Life Movement, a housing co-operative, a home help service, while the St Vincent de Paul Conference became inclusive, with women admitted in 1985. Parishioners have sat on key diocesan committees, as well as ensuring the relevance of parish programmes. A strong youth ministry emerged, and giving rose steadily in real terms, despite inflation, as people identified new needs. David Cappo, the director of the Australian Catholic Social Welfare Commission from 1992 to 1997, is a priest born in the parish, now with additional responsibilities for implementing guidelines on avoiding sexual

---

[33] K. Stephens, *A Day in the Life of the Bendigo Churches* (Bendigo, 1993) surveys the worship and preaching of all denominations.

[34] D. Hilliard, *Catholics in Kingswood* (1994) has kindly permitted me to use this excellent history. See also M. Peters, *Christchurch St Michael's* (Christchurch, 1983); R. Sweetman, *Spire on the Hill* (Auckland, 1996).

harassment. Jan Ruff-O'Herne, a parishioner, was courageous enough to tell the appalling story of her treatment as a prisoner and 'comfort woman' for the Japanese in the Second World War, in an ABC documentary on 2 October 1994.

Introducing and managing local change in religion can be most demanding and divisive. The priests at St Joseph's Catholic parish in Benalla, Victoria, who succeeded a well-loved priest discovered that quickly. Monsignor O'Reilly had managed the changes required by Vatican II with great skill and sustained a flourishing parish with Mass attendances of over 1,200 on a Sunday. He retired in Benalla and was replaced by a team of three. In February 1990, a fire severely damaged the interior of the church and a bitter struggle broke out about the form of the restoration, which was aggravated by the dislike of some very articulate parishioners for some of the liturgical changes introduced by the modernizing team. Informality was seen as irreverence, but appeals to the bishop had no effect and the dissatisfied were dismissed as ignorant fanatics. Mass attendances fell from 1,200 to 700.

To make matters worse, the dissentients felt that the reconstructed interior looked like a Methodist church. Monsignor O'Reilly was bitter about the changes, suggesting that they were an insult to the labours of previous Irish priests. The protestors were especially angered by the destruction of the splendid traditional altar and its replacement by a large block of wood. The conflict vividly illustrated the deep emotional identification parishioners could feel for furnishings and the ambience they created. Their disappearance created another kind of sacred space in which they no longer felt God was present. Some neatly avoided the passing of the peace by kneeling in prayer. The strength of the feelings aroused indicated a conflict between two Catholicisms, which appeared much more widely in the late 1990s.[35]

The story of the O'Connor Uniting Church in Canberra was very different.[36] Formerly Methodist, it was a flourishing smaller congregation under the ministry of Perry and Doreen Smith from 1966 to 1972. Its members tithed, a few members had Pentecostal associations, but it was a typical Methodist church with a warm piety and plenty of activities. Harry Westcott came in 1973 and became an ardent and entrepreneurial charismatic minister. He established very successful services in the Lakeside Hotel which attracted hundreds, and was

[35] R. McGrade, *Death of a Parish* (Benalla, 1995).
[36] W. and S. Emilsen, *O'Connor* (Sydney, 1997).

frequently away with teams of members encouraging others to follow their example of renewal. Ross Kingham became an associate minister in 1977, but soon found Westcott very difficult to work with. The latter believed that his leadership was anointed by the Spirit, and expected to be followed, not questioned. Tensions with the presbytery grew over re-baptism and pleas for authorization of lay presidents for communion services. Westcott left in 1981 and was replaced by Dan Armstrong, also a strong evangelist who travelled widely, leaving elders to lead worship and foster pastoral care. A school had begun in 1980 which had thirty-five teachers and 410 pupils, part of the burgeoning Christian School movement in Australia and New Zealand, which followed North American models and was usually linked with Pentecostal and charismatic churches. Many came briefly to worship, but about 20 per cent left every year, a not uncommon figure for many charismatic and pentecostal congregations during the 1980s.

Tensions with the Uniting Church grew, especially after the 1985 Assembly forbade ministers from re-baptizing those who claimed their baptism as infants was not a real baptism. Grace Christian Ministries was set up to hold the property of the school and Nagle Centre, which was bought for $500,000 (A) in 1993. In 1994, 234 members voted to leave the Uniting Church, thirty-four disagreed and stayed. Settling property issues was complex, and the Uniting Church found dealing with mobile searchers for peak experiences of God very difficult. They were unwilling to accept presbytery authority, but readily accepted strong ministerial guidance when it accorded with their own ideas.

Rural and small-town congregations were less volatile, and continued their worship, education, and community service without fanfare. A different and more predictable story can be told about Tapanui Presbyterian church from the late 1960s, including the fundraising for a new manse, the commencement of a Week of Prayer for Christian Unity, and the first Christmas Eve service in 1972. Alex Barton, the minister, served two terms as mayor, nominated by the Anglican and Catholic priests of the town, a formidable ecumenical combination in a predominantly Presbyterian community. The parish generously supported social service and missionary work, but was not enthusiastic over church union proposals. The Association of Presbyterian Women supported Professor Beryl Howie at Ludhiana Hospital in India, and raised money for disabled work in Indonesia, a well in Botswana, and the Helena Goldie hospital in the Solomon Islands, as well as making eighty pairs of red boxer shorts for pupils at a school in the New Hebrides. Sunday schools and Bible classes continued their tasks of education and socialization, though numbers had declined by the 1980s.[37]

The rapid and continuing development of an alternative Christian conservative school system in Australia and New Zealand, often linked with Pentecostal congregations, is one Protestant attempt to deal with ethical relativism. Roman Catholic schools are still, for many Catholics, a vital part of moral and religious education. That has been complemented by the development of teachers' colleges and, most recently, by the Australian Catholic University in the eastern states and Notre Dame University in Perth.

In 1998, the Revd Dr Peter Elliott, a former Anglican, was given the task of reversing well-established school curricula as part of Archbishop Pell's concern to establish Catholic identity in Melbourne more clearly.

POLITICAL CHRISTIANITY

There have been sharpening differences over identity and the boundaries of modernization. Phillip Jensen of St Matthias, Paddington, in the Anglican diocese of Sydney, and Stuart Lange of the Presbyterian Church of New Zealand, are each trying to reshape major denominations by reassertion of a distinctive reading of the biblical and Reformation heritage, and the creation of an alternative network to exert pressure for change, so as to subvert rival views.

Another more dramatic way of dealing with the tensions between modernization and the apparent certainties of previous generations has been to take military action. This happened dramatically in Fiji in 1987. Colonel Rabuka described his skilfully executed coups in May and September as *No other way*.[38] He was determined that the Indian community would not have political power through the Bavandra coalition elected in April 1987. He acted the day after their swearing-in. His position was that, like the land, the political power must remain with the Fijians, the *taukei*. Their nationalism erupted violently with gangs terrorizing Indian communities while the police did nothing.

---

[37] M. Bathgate, *Into the Second Century* (Tapanui, 1984).

[38] Y. Chand and V. Naidu, *Fiji: Coups, Crises and Reconciliation, 1987–97* (Suva, 1997); E. Dean and S. Ritova, *Rabuka* (Sydney, 1988).

Rabuka spoke often about Fiji being a Christian country, and said Indian-born Fijians needed to become Christian if they were to have a future there.[39] Some 30,000 migrated. Those remaining were excluded from almost every position of influence. Some of the Council of Chiefs used the coup for their own ends and the 1990 Constitution entrenched their power. Rabuka's religious allies, Lasaro and Caucau, captured the Methodist Conference, evicting the elected leaders, and refused to budge even when Chief Justice Tuivaga ruled against them and in favour of Josateki Kori. Some legality returned when Dr Sevati Tuwere became president in 1996. Rabuka also expelled some American Columban missionaries whose social justice commitments annoyed traditional Fijians.

After a decade, Rabuka had discovered that, far from creating a more Christian Fiji or delivering prosperity to his supporters, the economy had gone backwards. Military expenditure had grown from $15 million (Fijian) in 1986 to nearly $50 million by 1995. Sir Paul Reeves of New Zealand headed a commission to draft a new constitution, which was only partly acceptable to the militant Fijians. Agreement was reached in 1997 which entrenched Fijian political dominance, while allowing Indians some political status although the 1999 government was headed by a Fijian Indian, Mahendra Chaudry, who was removed in 2000 with another coup by treasonous soldiers and corrupt business interests. The coups against a legally elected government were the end of political innocence for the region. A further reminder of the power of military force emerged in the mutiny led by Brigadier General Jerry Singirok, a Christian in the Papua New Guinea Defence Force which brought down the government of Sir Julius Chan in 1997, because of the contract with Sandline to end the Bougainville War. He lost his job, but was reinstated late in 1998.[40]

Another hotly debated area of contention, where some believe modernization to have been inappropriate and where historic theology and contemporary ideas conflict, was in feminist theology, which has had major impact on church politics. Internationally influential writers like Mary Daly and Daphne Hampson insist that Christianity cannot be an adequate religion for women, for it is irremediably oppressive. Some Australian and New Zealand women, influenced by these critiques, have attempted to develop a womanist religion drawing on the religion of the goddess, or on reconstructed ideas about

[39] J. Bush, 'Claiming a Christian state where none exists', *Pacifica* 12 (1999) 55–68.
[40] S. Dorney, *The Sandline Affair* (Sydney, 1998); V. Lal, *Coups in Paradise* (London, 1989).

wicca, as has Audrey Sharp, a former Methodist influenced by Lea Holford of the USA, who came to Australia in 1984. An influential group in Sydney, including Marie Tulip and Erin White, formed Woman-Church to break out of male structures.[41]

The diversity of women's responses since the 1970s has led some men, like Michael Gilchrist, to try to discredit the whole movement as another example of secular ideologies being used politically to corrupt and subvert revealed Christianity. Some Anglicans opposed to women priests used disgraceful language to discredit 'uppity' women, whose dignified response put the masculinists to shame. Muriel Porter's historical work discredited many of their wilder assertions. The issues are, in fact, more complex. Important reports from the Australian Council of Churches in 1974, and the National Council of Churches in New Zealand in 1975, made it clear that there were serious inconsistencies between the policy of the churches, the teaching of the New Testament, and the responsibilities given to women, who were a majority of worshippers in most churches. By the 1990s, they were 65 per cent of membership in the major churches. Archbishop Arnott of Brisbane saw no theological argument against women priests, 'The main question is when the time is ripe.'[42] Orthodox, Roman Catholics, Lutherans, and most Pentecostals vigorously disagreed.

The issue of ordination was one major concern, and a number of men, like the New Zealanders Ian Fraser (Presbyterian), John Mullane (Anglican), and Allan Smart (Presbyterian) in Sydney, and John Gaden (Anglican) in Melbourne, played an important part in opening up the theological issues which ultimately led to Anglicans, Methodists, and Presbyterians ordaining women to the ministry of Word and Sacraments. By 1975 in Sydney, Zandra Wilson and Colleen O'Reilly formed Anglican Women Concerned to foster constructive discussion.

In New Zealand, Carole Graham and Margaret Wood were ordained Anglican priests in 1977, without the polarization which occurred in Australia. In Melbourne, Archbishop Penman licensed Susan Adams, an Australian ordained in the USA, to preside at Holy Communion in May 1986. The Australian Anglican battle for ordination was finally won in 1992 in General Synod after a series of legal

---

[41] B. Cain (ed.), *Australian Feminism: A Companion* (Melbourne, 1998) has a valuable essay 'Religion and spirituality'. L. Hume, *Witchcraft and Paganism in Australia* (Melbourne, 1997).

[42] Brisbane Diocese, *Year Book* (1972) 280; M. Porter, *Women in the Church* (Melbourne, 1988).

issues were settled. Anglican women clergy had a difficult first decade. Ballarat, Sydney, and Wangaratta dioceses have refused to ordain women to the priesthood, and strongly resisted attempts led by Muriel Porter in 1998 at the General Synod to set procedures in motion which would make the election of women to the episcopate possible in the future. There has been an Evangelical counterattack pressing for lay presidency and denying the importance of ordination, which is anathema to Anglo-Catholics. In 1998, Archbishop Harry Goodhew of Sydney, however, indicated that he might not veto Synod legislation approving women's ordination to the priesthood. In 1989, Dianne Miller Keeley, originally a Baptist, became the first woman archdeacon in New Zealand. Marjorie McGregor was similarly appointed from 1995 to 1998 in Melbourne.

Dr Jamieson (1942–), the first woman diocesan bishop in the Anglican Communion, has broken a great deal of new ground, though a bitter dispute over the cathedral choir in 1998 has soured relationships.[43] She became a priest in 1983. From 1982 to 1990 she worked in parishes before her unexpected election to Dunedin, a very traditional Anglo-Catholic diocese, on 26 November 1989. The intellectual equal of any of the male New Zealand bishops, she has made important contributions to the General Synod and to the whole New Zealand Christian community. Her personal and academic credentials enabled her to mix equally with diocesans and clergy opposed to a woman bishop. Her consecration was boycotted by the Maori Bishop Vercoe of Aotearoa and she found some senior clergy difficult to work with. Her close friendship with the primus of the Episcopal Church in Scotland, Richard Holloway, has enabled her to have mentoring from one of the ablest British bishops.[44]

Ecumenically, it was easier to appoint women to positions of leadership. Jean Skuse made a notable contribution to the Australian Council of Churches and the World Council of Churches. The New Zealand Presbyterian Joan Anderson has also been ecumenically important. In Victoria, Sr Mary Lou Moorhead became the first female secretary of the Victorian Council of Churches, offering a different style of leadership from her male predecessors, as did Jocelyn Armstrong in the New Zealand National Council of Churches from 1985.[45] Other Christians simply demonstrated how effectively women

---

[43] *Listener*, 15 Jan. 1990 for interview; C. H. Brett, 'The choir', *North and South*, Oct. 1998, 57–66. [44] P. Jamieson, *Living at the Edge* (London, 1997).
[45] M. Porter, 'Laity in the aisles', *Eureka Street*, June/July 1994, 26–8; M. L. Moorhead,

led. Dr Phyllis Guthardt, a notable New Zealand Methodist minister, has become chancellor of the University of Canterbury. Charity Majiza, a refugee from South Africa, returned to be secretary of the South African Council of Churches in 1997 after serving in the UCA in Victoria for a number of years. Though now retired, Dame Mira Szaszy, the first Maori woman graduate in New Zealand, has been an important leader in Anglican parish and national synod affairs, as well as in the Maori Women's Welfare League since 1952, and a member of many government and community organizations.[46] She supported Jewish objections to the new Prayer Book. Though there is a place for Maori women to gain high status, as yet, their leadership has not been fully used in the churches. Dame Rangimarie Hetet, another Anglican and a founding member of the Maori Women's Welfare League, has been a leader in the revival of arts and crafts in Maoridom.[47]

In Adelaide, Joan Vandersman, from a cultured Dutch family, attempted unsuccessfully to study theology in the local Catholic seminary. She was a notable music teacher, a peace activist, and translator of Hans Küng, and better read in theology than many clergy and bishops. Such women are a reminder that advocacy for partnership does not mean disloyalty, despite a Catholic bishop in Canberra refusing communion in 1998 to a parishioner because of her support for women's ordination. In the Pacific churches also, women have quietly moved out of traditional gender roles, especially if they had tertiary education and high social status.[48]

A number of women in all the churches rejected the strategy of seeking ordination, arguing that the battle lines were elsewhere. Ordination was bound up with patriarchal domination. They were concerned for a much more radical exploration of partnership and inclusiveness. In the Roman Catholic Church, women's roles have widened. Religious such as Margaret Jenkin CSB, Joan Nowotny IBVM, Maryanne Confoy RSC, Elaine Wainwright RSM, Carmel Walsh OP, Rosa McGinley PBVM, and Pauline O'Regan RSM, are now teaching in theological faculties. Others are sharing in parish work in ways which would have been impossible thirty years ago.

'The ecumenical movement in the Roman Catholic Church', M.Th. thesis (Melbourne, 1990).

[46] A. Rogers and M. Simpson (eds.), *Te Timatangu Tatua Tatua* (Auckland, 1993) gives an account of the league's origin and development.

[47] R. Paki-Titi, *Rangimarie* (Wellington, 1998).

[48] C. W. Forman, 'Sing to the Lord a new song: women in the churches of Oceania', in D. O'Brien and S. Tiffany (eds.), *Rethinking Women's Roles* (Berkeley, 1984).

Roman Catholic women religious were especially innovative in ministry, new constitutions, and governance.

WATAC (Women and the Australian Church), set up in 1982 by major superiors, continues its witness for equality, but lay leaders, like Patricia Gillard, a theology graduate of Melbourne, who have pressed for the ordination of women, have found that their principled stand has had disadvantages for their children, like being refused admission to the parish school.[49] In New Zealand, the bishops commissioned a major report on women in the Church, *Made in God's Image* (1990), and then in 1991 made a detailed theological response[50] without yielding much ground in practice. The Australian Catholic bishops produced a report, *Woman and Man,* on women's role in the Church in 1999. The polarization over the issues was shown by Cardinal Clancy of Sydney being cheered by conservatives and booed by liberals when he launched the report.

LAND AND RELIGION

Reconciling the traditional religious heritage of land amongst Polynesians, Melanesians, and Aborigines with the claims of economic development is difficult. Aboriginal land claims are hugely complex. Some in the Lutheran Church opposed land rights legislation, for they saw problems of locally translating it into effective policy, and recognized how the role of the Aboriginal and Torres Strait Islander Commission could clash with locally based groups like the proposed Anmatjeri Land Council.[51]

In Australia, the Blackburn judgement of 1970 upheld the view that Aborigines had no title. Hugh Morgan, chief executive of Western Mining and an Anglican, rejected Aboriginal religion and views on land. Following this attack, Djiniyini Gondarra, a Uniting Church minister, said, 'If the law of our fathers and fellow fathers is desecrated and destroyed, will we still hear the word which created us in the beginning? . . . Our feelings about the land are so unique: when the land is raped we feel like a man whose wife has been raped. We still

---

[49] *The Age*, 24 June 1999. N. McManus (ed.), *A Remarkable Absence of Passion* (Melbourne, 1991) collects Catholic women's stories.

[50] C. Orsman and P. Zwart (eds.), *Church in the World* (Wellington, 1997) 109–41; J. McLeay, 'Establishing a Voice for Women', research essay (Melbourne, 1995).

[51] I am indebted to Paul Albrecht for material on this.

love her, but we feel ashamed of ourselves that we have not protected her.'[52]

When land title was misunderstood by mining company negotiators, strong churches were unable to prevent insurrection on Bougainville, which has cost some 10–20,000 lives, destroying most infrastructure, and causing great trauma and hardship to thousands of others. A striking example of the intersection of religion, politics, and development, its roots lie in the era before independence when the Australian administration treated local people with the same paternalism as Aborigines over mining development, which began in 1964.[53] The huge copper mine began producing in 1972. Some owners were compensated, others were not. No recognition was given to the dislike local people had for the 'redskins' of the mainland, or their sense of kinship with Solomon Islanders from whom they had been divided with no consultation. Pleas for independence were dismissed, for the mineral wealth of the island was crucial for the newly independent state of Papua New Guinea.

Bougainvilleans like Fr John Momis tried to solve the problem through a constitution which granted substantial power to provinces, but that was not enough and feelings of anger grew as the scale of the mining became apparent, and its diverse environmental effects grew, especially through tons of tailings a day. Few locals were employed and the Panguna mine operators had no awareness of local anger. Nor did the government heed the warnings of the local Roman Catholic bishop, Gregory Singkai, before Bougainville independence was unilaterally declared in May 1990. Francis Ona, a reclusive Catholic, in co-operation with Sam Kauona, who had left the Defence Force and formed the Bougainville Revolutionary Army, had by mid-1989 forced the closure of the mine by skilful sabotage. Government attempts to solve the problems militarily failed, especially in the 'final' solution proposed in 1997 with the help of professional soldiers from an English company—Sandline. Both rebel and government forces committed atrocities, broke agreements, and terrorized civilians. A number of moderates and would-be mediators were killed.

The Catholic bishop has given qualified support to the rebels, but the dominance of Christianity on the island has not lessened the

---

[52] *Crucible*, 25 July 1984.

[53] R. West, *River of Tears* (London, 1972) gave a prescient forecast of conflict in his study of Rio Tinto Zinc. J. Griffin, *Bougainville: A Challenge to the Churches* (Sydney, 1995); S. Dorney, *The Sandline Affair* (Sydney, 1998); Joint Standing Committee on Foreign Affairs, Defence and Trade, *Bougainville: The Peace Process and Beyond* (Canberra, 1999).

ferocity of the resistance or the demand for independence. Women fed up with war played an important part in the lead-up to negotiations in 1997–8. Brokered in New Zealand and supported by Australian peacekeepers, talks have opened up fragile possibilities of settlement, even though the independence issue remains unresolved. The United Church's Bishop Tutmoano worked through the Trauma Counselling Institute (Roman Catholic, United Church, and Seventh-day Adventist) to bring Australian expertise to assist with the huge task of rebuilding community, helped by AusAid and Caritas. Despite such ecumenical partnership, tensions were again boiling over in early 1999, with hopeful signs of agreement emerging by the end of 2000. The Papua New Guinea government cannot afford to let one region leave, for that could lead to other provinces demanding the same right. Nor can it afford the continued cost of a military struggle and the risks of the conflict spilling over into the Solomon Islands. Guadalcanal landowners dispossessed thousands from Malaita. The resulting armed conflict was ended in October 2000 by a signed agreement, confirmed by singing a hymn.

In New Zealand a different path was chosen for the vexed issues of land claims by Maori and changing definitions of their identity.[54] The Kirk Labour government passed a Race Relations Act in 1971, and added to its 1973 declaration on partnership in 1975 by giving the Treaty of Waitangi unequivocal legal authority. A tribunal was set up under Chief Judge Edward Durie, a leading Anglican, in 1981 to deal with claims. The tribunal's power was dramatically expanded in 1985 with power to deal with disputes from 1840. That decisively changed the political climate in New Zealand and led to a new kind of bi-cultural partnership. Though the meaning of key terms in the treaty is disputed, some hugely important decisions have been made, such as the recognition of Maori rights to fisheries in 1992, which in turn led to disputes between coastal and inland tribes, and claims by women that their position had been ignored.

[54] A. Sharp, *Justice and the Maori*, 2nd edn. (Auckland, 1997) 73–180 for an analysis of the legal authority of the tribunal. H. Evison, *The Long Dispute* (Christchurch, 1997); R. Spence, *Whakaaria Mai: Canon Wiremu Wi Te Tau Huata* (Palmerston North, 1994); A. Fieras and J. L. Elliott, *The Nations Within* (Toronto, 1992) offers a useful comparative perspective on Canada, New Zealand, and the USA's policies to indigenous peoples. J. Crawford (ed.), *Church and State* (Auckland, 1998) 56–65 notes that many Maori read the treaty in such a way as to marginalize women. Bishop Walters argues that the treaty creates a new meaning for 'rangatira-tanga', 66–74, because there are no longer commoners and slaves as in 1840. D. Graham, *Trick or Treaty?* (Wellington, 1997) 68–86 for the ministerial side of several key settlements. Many meetings began and ended with prayers, indicating the spiritual realities behind Maori claims.

The Honourable Doug Graham's unequivocal commitment to negotiation has been vital. Tainui grievances were at last recognized in May 1995 and some 16,000 hectares returned. At the end of 1997, the Ngai Tahu claim to their lands in the South Island was substantially recognized. Though the Waitangi Tribunal is under-resourced and has a backlog of claims, its care for due process has won respect, if not universal praise. Maori attachment to land as the source of their identity is still not understood rationally or emotionally by many Pakeha, who found the great 1975 Land March, led by Whina Cooper, frankly a fuss about nothing. The occupation of Auckland's Bastion Point in 1978 and Moutua Gardens, Wanganui, in 1995 indicated that some Maori were no longer willing to rely on law to make land claims. Far from disappearing, tribal loyalties were increasing and transcending place, as more and more became urban—90 per cent by the 1980s, as compared to 11 per cent in the 1930s.

The most dramatic initiative was taken by the Anglican Church. John Paterson, from 1995 Bishop of Auckland, and primate since 1998, was secretary of the Bi-cultural Commission from 1984 to 1986. He had gained fluency in Maori at Waimate in 1971–6 and was widely trusted. After a careful consultative process, a new constitutional structure of three *tikanga* was implemented, which gave Maori and the Diocese of Polynesia equal status with Pakeha in decision-making.[55] No decision could be made without their agreement as part of the church's commitment to biculturalism. Methodists and Presbyterians did not create such a complex constitutional structure, but have adopted Maori procedure for making some key decisions. Four Anglican Maori bishops and a female Maori theological college principal indicate how the balance of partnership is changing.

In Australia, self-described Aborigines and Torres Strait Islanders number well over 300,000 in a nation of 19 million. They have no direct representation in the lower house of the federal parliament, and are absent from most state parliaments, though they have some electoral weight in the Northern Territory. Senator Aden Ridgeway, a Democrat and Catholic, took his seat only in 1999, some years after Queensland Senator Neville Bonner lost his seat. The elected Aboriginal and Torres Strait Islander Commission has only partly met the representation issues. Aborigines carry little weight in the peak church bodies and it is only in the last twenty years that they have begun to share in decision-making, rather than be the recipients

---

[55] GSNZ *Proceedings* (1986) 185–254 for the constitutional proposals.

of what white Christians thought appropriate. A start in giving Aboriginal views legal form was made in the Aboriginal Land Rights (Northern Territory) Act 1976, but the process of alignment is proving very difficult. The Mabo (1992) and Wik (1996 and 2000) high court judgements had dramatic impact on business and pastoralists. Aborigines' views on the sacredness of land are little understood by other Australians.[56]

Each of the major churches has now established a semi-autonomous body, like the Aboriginal and Islander Christian Congress within the Uniting Church founded in 1985.[57] This was modelled on the Maori Synod of the New Zealand Presbyterian Church. Even more important has been the flowering of distinct styles of Aboriginal Christianity following the revival which began on Elcho Island in the 1970s and which has spread to most communities throughout Australia, crossing denominational and tribal boundaries. Though some white Christians attempted to use it for their own purposes, Aborigines have developed their own leaders. So have Torres Strait Islanders, who expressed concern at the lowly status of Bishop Dai and the incorporation of Carpentaria diocese into North Queensland in 1996. Their 1998 schism over Bishop Ted Mosby's appointment by Bishop Clyde Wood shows that clan loyalties are still powerful.[58] It was claimed that most theology students and clergy had left. Bishops Gayai Hankin and David Passi now lead the Church of Torres Strait, consecrated by a schismatic bishop in Easter 1998, linked with the Traditional Anglican Communion. A bitter property dispute has emerged, but many of the laity have not left the Anglican Church, creating all sorts of local problems of jurisdiction and pastoral care.

RETHINKING MINISTRIES

Ministry by laity has steadily increased in importance, with ordained ministries diversifying through the growth of chaplaincy. New patterns of non-stipendiary ministry have modified clergy authority, as have changes in the diaconate and increasing use of lay workers who have developed important new networks in the region. There have

---

[56] G. Yunupingu (ed.), *Our Land Is Our Life* (Brisbane, 1997); G. Goosen, 'Christian and Aboriginal interface in Australia', *Theological Studies* 60 (1999) 72–94; J. Harris, *We Wish We'd Done More* (Adelaide, 1998) 429–96.
[57] W. Emilsen, 'The vision was born in my spirit', *UCS* 5 (1999) 33–52.
[58] *The Age*, 14 Feb. 1998.

been many Australians and New Zealanders working in the Pacific, strengthening regional ties. Much of Australia and New Zealand's overseas aid goes to the Pacific. Numerous Island clergy have studied in Australian and New Zealand theological colleges.

A number of Anglican and some Catholic dioceses have established permanent deacons. The Anglican Diocese of Sydney has restricted their ministry, so that if they speak in worship, they do not speak with authority. In the Methodist Church in New Zealand and in the Uniting Church, a new kind of diaconate emerged, which was much more wide-ranging in its scope than the ministry of deaconesses or traditional deacons. The theological rationales were different, but both were attempts to deal with a rapidly changing social context and to provide a focused ministry which had something of the transforming power that the refounding of diaconal ministry had in the nineteenth century, where a gendered and voluntarist focus was inescapable. The changes also reflected shifts in international discussions on ministry. Among Maori, Anglicans in New Zealand developed a non-stipendiary ministry, invaluable for small rural communities. There are now over 300 such ministers. Presbyterian Maori created similar ministers called *Amorangi*, partly to break down hierarchy, partly to recreate Maori identity.[59]

PENTECOSTALS AND CHARISMATICS

A different view of ministry emerged in the Pentecostal churches where a number of new churches were begun by men with no ministerial education, claiming the personal calling of the Holy Spirit. They simply established churches, without credentials except success. They appealed to those seeking a deeper religious experience, and it was no accident that they grew most rapidly from the 1960s when the major churches were confused about their priorities, and defection was widespread. Strong American influence was obvious in this growth, but the movement had origins in both Australia and New Zealand. Percentage-wise, the movement was strongest in Papua New Guinea with 7 per cent of the population of 3.6 million in 1990.

The Assemblies of God in Australia were so named in 1937. By 1972

---

[59] D. Edwards, *Vows: Nuns and Priests Speak Out* (Auckland, 1997) offers a variety of portraits of those in ministry and those out of it in the Catholic Church. J. Graham, *Breaking the Habit* (Dunedin, 1992); C. Ritchie, *Not to be Ministered Unto* (Melbourne, 1998) 235–53, for Bev Fabb's account.

there were about 120 churches, each independent. Some, like the Richmond Temple in Melbourne,[60] went back to 1925, but disputes led to schism, and a fresh beginning for some groups in 1937. Smith Wigglesworth in 1927 had created small groups of followers, as did various Elim and Apostolic itinerants. By the 1970s, some gifted leaders like Andrew Evans in Paradise, South Australia, had emerged, who built congregations which were large by Australian standards. In Mt Gravatt, Queensland, Reginald Kliminiok began in 1968 with 100 people and by 1982 had a building seating over 2,000 people, and ministries which included television, a theological school, counselling, a book shop, and a vigorous outreach. The Christian Life Centre in Darlinghurst, Sydney, which was led by Frank Houston, from New Zealand, grew from nine people in 1977 to over 1,300 by 1982.[61] Between 1961 and 1996 Australian Pentecostals increased from 16,572 to 174,720, just under 1 per cent of the total population. The figures in New Zealand were almost 2 per cent in 1996 at 69,182.

The breakdown of historic patterns of church life and theology in the 1960s, major cultural changes focusing on self-fulfilment, the emergence of Jesus people, who rejected everything between Jesus' time and their own, and the desire for more authentic religious experience, gave the Pentecostal churches opportunities for rapid growth, especially in South Australia and Queensland. The Christian Revival Crusade with its prophetic vision of a transformed nation, and Britain as Israel was founded by Leo Harris in the early 1940s. Its major growth came later, when the religious climate changed. By his death in 1977, the Crusade had spread beyond Australia into Papua New Guinea, and Asia. Like many of the other groups, this association had divisions, but has retained its vitality and capacity for growth.[62]

At a time when some major Protestant churches were in decline, the Pentecostal churches were almost doubling every five years. In 1976 they had 388 ministers, but by 1982 there were 690, and by 1984 there were 890.[63] More than one-third of these worked in Queensland, where the population percentage of Pentecostals is highest, due in part to high migration rates and also to a long Evangelical Protestant tradition.

[60] Anon., *70 Years* (Melbourne, 1995).

[61] B. Chant, *Heart of Fire* (Adelaide, 1984) 145; J. Worsfold, *A History of the Charismatic Movements in New Zealand* (Bradford, 1974); J. Blacker, *When God Makes It Happen* (Melbourne, 1997) 133–5 for Alan Yorke's insight; H. Houston, *Being Frank* (London, 1989).

[62] Chant, *Heart of Fire*, 181–99.

[63] Ibid., 220.

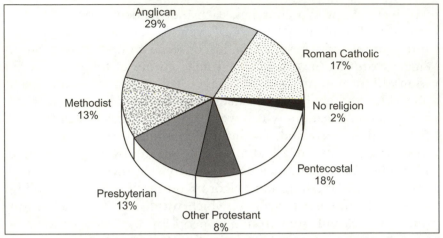

Fig. 1. Australia: origins of Pentecostal affiliates. (*Source:* T. Blombery and P. Hughes, *Faith Without the Church*, Melbourne, 1993, p. 40. With the permission of P. Hughes.)

The large congregations they have built up provide a different range of worship and education from the small congregations which are still such a substantial presence in rural and small-town Australia. The excitement of singing, dancing, and speaking in the Spirit, with entertaining speakers able to captivate large audiences by their selectively biblical and personalized message, and use of electronic aids, has undoubtedly been attractive to many. By 1991, 31 per cent of incomers have been Anglicans, 26 per cent Methodist and Presbyterian, and 17 per cent Catholic. So have the small groups for fellowship and ethnic churches like Sicilians, who migrated because of persecution. Personal conversion and self-improvement are fundamental. The decision of Darren Beadman, one of Australia's leading jockeys, to become a Pentecostal minister in 1997 was a sensation in the racing world, and had begun with the healing of a child and the passage through a bleak professional period.[64] But the Wimber emphasis on miracles, the so-called Toronto Blessing, and the preoccupation with numbers raise questions about the relative priority of power and love, as does prosperity theology espoused by Peter Daniels, a former bricklayer. Bogus healings and exorcisms also have created serious problems, leading to deaths in 1993 and 1999 and a Melbourne trial where difficult questions of law and rationality were unresolved.

[64] D. Beadman, *Daylight Ahead: The Darren Beadman Story* (Sydney, 1998).

There have been many splits, with congregations briefly thriving and then collapsing when expectations are not met by satisfying feelings of fragile egos. There is little on being crucified with Christ, or testing claims of religious experience, and weak pastoral accountability has been a continual problem. In New Zealand, New Life churches, under Peter Morrow in Christchurch and Rob Wheeler in Auckland, had no unity with the Assemblies of God despite Ian Clark's attempts to create a Pentecostal federation in the 1970s.[65] Australian Assemblies of God have an increasingly firm national leadership structure, with Brian Houston of Sydney the secretary, but with no leader of the stature of the now retired Andrew Evans yet emerging.

Pentecostals cannot be understood without understanding how local congregations are established and led. André van der Linden migrated from the Netherlands to New Zealand in 1960, found New Zealand Catholicism most unwelcoming, and became a Pentecostal. He was a talented tenor and speech therapist, and with his wife June, a skilled musician, became involved in starting a new Assembly in 1968, which was very demanding along with his teaching post. Then in 1969 he purchased property in Mangere East, before he pioneered churches at Matamata, Te Aroha, Te Kuiti, and Papakura, part of the growth, in the 1970s, of the Pentecostal Assemblies in almost all New Zealand towns.

In 1979, he went to Australia, where he linked up with Ken Chant, but decided to focus on Melbourne not Sydney, and started the Glen Waverley Christian Fellowship Centre. This attracted new converts, and people from divided churches. Some financial support came from Matamata, but the first few years were very difficult. Van der Linden decided not to link with the Assemblies of God, as they had been unhelpful to him in New Zealand. In Victoria, the Assemblies of God held all properties in trust, which gave significant central control. He wished to remain independent.

Van der Linden's congregation was ruled by elders on Brethren lines, but grew into new understanding of pastoral authority through a visit of the United Kingdom's Arthur Wallis (1986/87). Glen Waverley had 165 attenders giving $2,500 each week, and expanded into Malvern and Clayton in 1984. Dissension was not easily handled,

[65] T. Blomberg and P. Hughes, *Faith Without the Church* (Melbourne, 1993) 40; B. Knowles, 'Some aspects of the history of New Life churches of New Zealand 1960–90', Ph.D. thesis (Dunedin, 1994); K. Stephens, *A Day in the Life of the Bendigo Churches* (Bendigo, 1993) 122–48 describes Pentecostal worship in a variety of settings.

and ministers were expected to be superperformers. Expansion into Asia saw the church go to Singapore, the Philippines, Malaysia, and Indonesia, giving it a fascinating international dimension. A crisis broke out in 1990, with a personality dispute, and quarrels over assets. A new cause was nevertheless begun in Berwick. Gradually van der Linden came to see the importance of women's ministry as a result of meeting a woman pastor in the Philippines. His twenty-seven years of ministry offer a window into the energy and fractiousness of the Assemblies of God on both sides of the Tasman.[66]

The success of the Pentecostal churches has been a challenge to other denominations with Evangelical convictions. After initial rejection and some painful splits, Baptists, Brethren, and Churches of Christ learned from Pentecostals about more open styles of worship, new music, and the value of developing large congregations which can offer a variety of activities and ministries. Te Atatu Gospel Chapel under Brian Hathaway took that path. At Rockingham, Western Australia, Gordon Bassett's Baptist Church grew from forty-four to 660 members between 1979 and 1992. Similarly, at Wollongong, New South Wales, a Church of Christ developed under the leadership of Barry McMurtrie, with a theological college that has begun to challenge the official college at Woolwich, and a large complex opened in 1991, capable of servicing a wide range of needs. There are a minority whose charismatic experiences have taken them into a new synthesis of evangelism and social concern. Viv Grigg from Hillsborough Baptist Church, Auckland, was an engineer until he responded to a call to be minister to the squatters in Metro-Manila.[67]

MOVING PASTORAL FRONTIERS

There has been a move to 'user pays' in social services in the 1990s as governments dismantled tax funding to discourage welfare dependency.[68] Lange and Douglas in New Zealand brought huge changes,

---

[66] A. Black (ed.), *Religion in Australia* (Sydney, 1991), 'Australian Pentecostal renewal in comparative perspective', 106–20; A. P. F. van der Linden, 'Church planting: a journey of faith', research essay (Melbourne, 1996) covers 1968–95. I am indebted to him for permission to use his work.

[67] V. Grigg, *Companions to the Poor* (Sydney, 1990); B. Hathaway, *Beyond Renewal* (Milton Keynes, 1990).

[68] D. Thompson, *A World Without Welfare* (Auckland, 1998); J. Kelsey, *The New Zealand Experiment* (Auckland, 1995); A. Melrose, 'Politicised clergy', *ARSR* 7 (1995) 35–40.

which forced churches to rethink their community service priorities and financial commitments. On 28 February 1993, a Social Justice Statement was read from the pulpit of all major New Zealand churches in an attempt to challenge the National government to change direction. The impact was considerable, though leaseholders of Anglican land in Auckland said this was hypocrisy since the church had put up the cost of 21-year leases dramatically. In Australia, the Catholic bishops also issued a number of statements on social justice and the cost of privatizing public services. Archbishop Peter Hollingworth, of Brisbane and formerly of the Brotherhood of St Laurence in Melbourne for twenty-five years, had not only unique knowledge of the problems of poverty, but the capacity for challenging contributions to public debates which politicians needed to notice. His successor, Bishop Michael Challen, had the same gift, without falling into the sometimes ill-informed criticisms which some Protestants liked to think were prophetic.

The energy which had once gone into anti-gambling campaigns had declined by the 1970s and steady expansion of gambling outlets occurred, although there was still energy in Victoria to restrict this in the 1980s, because of the threats it posed to family life and to the work ethic. By the 1990s, the Victorian economy had suffered severely and the Labor premier, Mrs Joan Kirner, spoke of a gambling-led recovery. Opposition to the huge Crown casino and large numbers of poker machines approved by the Kennett government, and which opened in 1997, was spiritedly led by Tim Costello, a civically minded Baptist minister, together with more cautious condemnation from other heads of churches.[69] Between 1991/2 and 1995/6, gambling spending in Victoria grew from $902 million to $25 billion (A). Opposition to this did not compare with the support in the churches earlier in the century for strict legislative controls on gambling, although economists have pointed out the serious consequences of such heavy spending.

The conviction that the churches could Christianize the nation by the quality of their spiritual witness and judicious legislation against threats to Christian social ethics and personal morality was in decline, but not dead. There was sharp conflict between liberal church leaders

---

[69] D. Grant, *On a Roll* (Wellington, 1996) gives a comprehensive history of gambling in New Zealand; J. O'Hare, *A Mug's Game* (Kensington, 1998) on gambling in Australia; T. Costello, *Streets of Hope* (Sydney, 1998); P. Culbertson (ed.), *Counselling Issues* (Auckland, 1997) provides an invaluable pastoral angle from varied Polynesian perspectives.

claiming to be prophetic and the federal conservative coalition government over involvement in Vietnam. A few church leaders such as the Archbishop of Sydney supported involvement, and many church members felt betrayed by other leaders who implied that they were less Christian in supporting what was defended as a struggle against communism. Many younger clergy and members marched in support of disengagement. It was in Melbourne that the Moratorium Marches with over 100,000 participants raised most massive public support. Governments could no longer ignore these protests as simply a minority opinion. Response to Vietnam was another example of the way traditional boundaries were no longer helpful predictors of behaviour. Deep wounds remain, though not to the same extent as in the United States. A number of Roman Catholics were disillusioned by their bishops' active campaign for involvement and failure to listen to what they believed was reasoned argument against involvement. That added to scepticism about authority already fuelled by *Humanae vitae* and cynicism about some episcopal support given to the Democratic Labor Party.[70] Similar tensions existed in New Zealand, but not so divisively as in Australia.

Discussions of sexuality have proved very divisive in the churches. Serious pastoral problems have come to light, as unethical clerical sexual behaviour has become the subject of criminal charges.[71] Between 1993 and 1997, nineteen Australian Catholic priests were sentenced, plus thirteen religious and nine lay teachers. In the Anglican Church of Melanesia, the Bishop of Malaita was forced to resign in 1989. In July 1994, the vicar general of Palmerston North was sentenced to four years. Roman Catholic bishops and leaders of related institutions issued a pastoral letter of apology on 26 April 1996, and then *Towards Healing*, on 31 March 1997. The Catholic Episcopal Conference in 1997 issued a series of very firm guidelines designed to prevent sexual harassment and criminal behaviour, making it clear swift and appropriate action would be taken, making Fr David Cappo full-time officer to deal with its implementation. The Anglican and

---

[70] V. Noone, *Disturbing the War* (Melbourne, 1993).

[71] *Boys of St Vincent* (1993) was a powerful film based on a Canadian case. S. Hamilton-Byrne, *Unseen, Unheard, Unknown* (Melbourne, 1995) gives a harrowing account of life inside a community run by Ms Hamilton-Byrne, a protégé of a former master of Queens College, Melbourne. P. Hollingworth, *Public Thoughts of an Archbishop* (Brisbane, 1996) 86–7; G. Windsor, *Heaven where the Bachelors Sit* (Brisbane, 1996); P. May, 'Sexual discoveries in the Society of Jesus', MA thesis (Melbourne, 1997); D. Hilliard, 'Sydney Anglicans and homosexuality', *Journal of Homosexuality* 33 (1997) 101–23.

Uniting Churches produced similar documents and took action where professional standards had been breached.

The Uniting Church spent a good deal of time in making and discussing reports on the subject of homosexuality in the 1980s and 1990s, as did the Presbyterian Church in New Zealand, where the debates were made more volatile by the massive petition of 855,000 against parliamentary proposals to decriminalize homosexual activity between consenting adults in 1985. The law was changed in 1986. Methodist and Presbyterian bodies supported it, whilst Cardinal Tom Williams opposed it, as did the Assemblies of God, Lutherans, and Dean John Rymer, a leading Anglican. Was homosexual practice sinful, or part of a spectrum of normal behaviour? That was the question on which Christians could not agree because of their differing biblical exegesis, even though most churches recognized that their pastoral care of homosexuals had been very inadequate.

In New Zealand, the Methodist Conference in 1997 finally re-admitted Dr David Brommell, a minister who changed his sexual orientation, but faced conservative resistance led by the Revd George Bryant. The Wesleyan Methodist Church was formed after the 1999 Conference. The Presbyterian Church's General Assembly was equally divided and the referendum held in 1997 was ambiguous, for a significant number of members chose not to vote.[72]

CONSERVATIVE LEADERS

In the Presbyterian Church of New Zealand, Affirm networks secured the election of a talented charismatic minister, Peter Willsman in 1996, rather than the system of 'turns' which had characterized the process of selection by presbytery votes. The appointment of Basil Meeking to Christchurch Diocese and George Pell as Archbishop of Melbourne in 1996 was another signal of Rome's concern for less variety and more uniformity. Though the processes behind nomination are obscure, as consultation was very selective, conservative groups in the Roman Catholic Church had been lobbying Rome for years against those clergy and religious who were seen as subversive modernizers. The

---

[72] D. McRae-McMahon, *Ordinary Passions* (Sydney, 1998); G. Bryant, *Why a Wesleyan Methodist Movement?* (n.p., 1998); S. M. Mead, *Landmarks, Bridges and Visions* (Wellington, 1997) discusses the *rahui* and its application, pp. 167–78.

1998 Synod of Bishops from Oceania indicated growing unease in Rome about democratic and egalitarian tendencies in the region.[73]

One of the most interesting and influential of the conservative laity was B. A. Santamaria, who was accorded the rare honour of a state funeral in 1998, despite never having been elected to public office. Small of stature but large in intellect, Santamaria's self-effacing commitment to family and friends, ability to analyse issues, and to create networks, and his gifts as a speaker and writer meant that he remained a widely known public figure through the media until debilitated by a brain tumour, outliving many of his enemies and rewriting history. Santamaria's ideas on political action were published in the *Bombay Examiner* in 1956, a 'speculative thesis' creating a furore in Australia. He also drafted bishops' statements on social justice. He confused the roles of church and state at times. His most controversial role was in The Movement, a secret network which defeated Communists in many key trade unions in the 1940s and 1950s. At times his anti-Communism led to serious misjudgements and his contribution to The Split in 1954 has remained unforgiven in sections of the Labor Party.

Up until his last year, he remained an astute and sometimes acerbic national media commentator on the follies of reformers, politicians, and business people. Revered by admirers and hated by his political opponents, he won the grudging respect of some erstwhile opponents in later years, just as he respected people with strong principles, even when he disagreed with them and did his best to destabilize their influence. He was a Catholic intellectual of a type not uncommon in Europe, but unusual in Australia. He was utterly scornful of religious liberalizers and those whom he believed undermined the family and Australian sovereignty. His criticisms of Communist penetration and deceit about receiving aid from Moscow, and the political danger the Communist Party of Australia represented to democracy, were mocked by many supporters of Marxism and social democracy in the Labor Party and media, but the partial opening of Soviet archives in the 1990s has made it clear that Santamaria was more right than his critics. He never sought to enrich himself and remained a very modest man, with deep convictions about what was right in religion and morality, unwavering in his belief that Christianity was for the whole of life.

---

[73] *Jesus Christ and the Peoples of Oceania* (Sydney, 1997) set out issues for the Synod's attention. *Compass* 33/1 (1999) 1–12 discusses the Synod.

A different kind of layman who has had an influential ministry among Pentecostals and charismatics has been a former New Zealand Anglican, Bill Subritzky, descended from a pioneering family in Northland. A lawyer and developer, he became a wealthy man, but devoted a great deal of time and energy to conducting missions, healing, and exorcizing.[74] In Ethiopia, Dr Catherine Hamlin and her late husband Reginald worked with fistula victims since 1959. Their ministry of simple surgery has transformed the lives of thousands of women who were rejected by society because of the injuries they suffered giving birth. The story of the churches in the region cannot be understood without recognizing the impact of such public service nationally and internationally, and lay witness to Jesus at every level of society, even though much of it will never be recorded in published histories.

POLITICS AND CHURCHES

The intersections of Christianity and politics are many-levelled, though often informal and personal, rather than public and institutional as they are in European countries, where Christianity has been politically and culturally formative for centuries. Some clergy still are seen as symbolic leaders in the community, but that is rarely translated into votes. The Christian Heritage Party, formed in 1988, gained only 0.53 per cent of the 1990 vote in New Zealand. Insufficient votes for a Christian coalition in 1996 meant it did not win a single seat. Yet Archbishop George Pell and the Reverend Tim Costello were movers of key motions at the Constitutional Convention in Canberra in February 1998, for they were not identified with any party and were seen as influential spiritual leaders.

In the New Hebrides there were growing tensions between French- and English-speaking areas. The French Residency supported Union des Communautés des Nouvelles Hébrides and the National Party. Both French and British administrators in Vila were trying to slow the process of devolution, uneasy about Vanuatu Pati demands for independence. M. Dijoud of the French government worked closely with Fr Gerard Leymang to safeguard minority rights for French culture. In the 1979 election, the Vanuatu Pati won twenty-six out of thirty-nine seats, but the French government clandestinely

---

[74] W. Subritzky, *On the Cutting Edge* (Auckland, 1993).

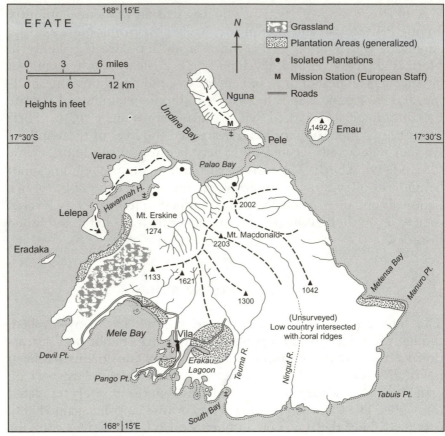

Efate (1944). (*Source:* Naval Intelligence Division, British Admiralty, *Pacific Islands*, 5 vols., London, 1939–45, vol. 3, p. 574. © British Crown Copyright/MOD. Reproduced with the permission of Her Britannic Majesty's Stationery Office.)

supported minority Francophone groups, fearing a spill-over to Kanaks in New Caledonia if independence was granted. In May 1980, the Republic of Venerama was declared by custom chief Jimmy Stevens on Santo, with covert support from the French and the active backing of the right-wing American group—the Phoenix Foundation. Heavy pressure was brought on the Lini government, as the French refused to pay their share of civil service salaries, and delayed promised aid, and their share of electoral costs. Both the leading French officials in Vila had been in the Comoros Islands, which had voted for independence until France executed a military coup to keep

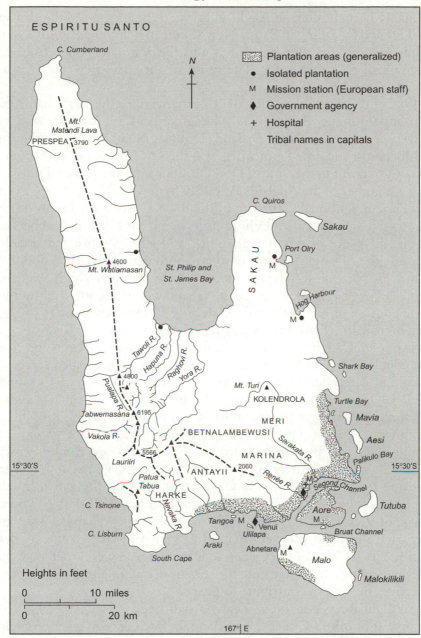

ESPIRITU SANTO

C. Cumberland

N

Plantation areas (generalized)
● Isolated plantation
M Mission station (European staff)
◆ Government agency
+ Hospital
Tribal names in capitals

Mt.
Matendi Lava
PRESPEA 3790

C. Quiros

Sakau

▲4600
Mt. Watiamasan

St. Philip and
St. James Bay

S
A
K
A
U

Port Olry
M

Hog Harbour

M

Shark Bay

Tawoli R.
Hapuna R.
Raghoïi R.
Yora R.

▲4800

Mt. Turi ▲
KOLENDROLA

Turtle Bay

Mavia

Pualapa R.

Tabwemasana ▲6195

MERI

Aesi

Vakola R.

BETNALAMBEWUSI

Sarakata R.

Palikulo Bay

15°30'S

▲5566

Lauriiri

MARINA

2060

Renée R.

Segond Channel

15°30'S

ANTAYII ▲

Patua
Tabua

HARKE

Aore
M

Tutuba

C. Tsinone

Nevaka R.

Tangoa M

Venui
Ulilapa

Bruat Channel

C. Lisburn

Araki

Abnetare M ▲

Malo

South Cape

Malokilikili

Heights in feet

0   10 miles

0   20 km

167° E

Espiritu Santo (1944). (*Source:* Naval Intelligence Division, British
Admiralty, *Pacific Islands*, 5 vols., London, 1939–45, vol. 3, p. 583. © British
Crown Copyright/MOD. Reproduced with the permission of Her
Britannic Majesty's Stationery Office.)

Mayotte French. Lini, an Anglican priest, outmanoeuvred the British and French by calling in Papua New Guinean help on 6 August 1980. They speedily defeated the rebels and the Vanuatu police finished the task of restoring order. The unity of the small new nation was saved.

One of the most interesting developments since the 1970s has been the appointment of clergy as state governors in Australia and as governor general in New Zealand. Douglas Nicholls, a Churches of Christ pastor and noted sportsman, was the first Aborigine[75] to become a state governor in the time of Don Dunstan as premier. Don Dunstan was a member of the Adelaide Anglican Synod for several years, even if an unconventional Christian, but had left Christianity by his death in 1999. It was a very symbolic appointment, for Nicholls had been a strong advocate of Aboriginal rights, and all the more remarkable because the Aboriginal community in South Australia had no political status. He was followed from 1977 to 1982 by the Revd Keith Seaman, who had been a civil servant (1937–54) and was then known across the state because of his work in the Adelaide Central Mission (1958–77) and his role in religious broadcasting.

Davis McCaughey, an Irish Presbyterian, who had been the first president of the Uniting Church in 1977, had a distinguished career as theological teacher in Melbourne and then as master of Ormond College, from 1959 to 1979. He had a unique range of contacts in the Victorian and national community and was famous for his preaching at funerals, and as a witty and provoking speaker to a variety of community and professional groups. Few could use English more elegantly and arrestingly in the service of civic Christianity.[76] He became governor of Victoria for 1986–9, making the office much more accessible, and continuing to build relations with an even wider range of Victorians. His wife Jean was an authority on social issues in her own right and was very helpful to varied service groups by her patronage. Dr McCaughey's Anzac Day addresses were small masterpieces, dealing adequately with the tradition, but opening up new perspectives in ways to contribute to peace.

Sir Paul Reeves in New Zealand had been a teacher of church history at St John's College, Auckland, before becoming successively Bishop of Waiapu, Auckland, and primate. He was steadily more aware of the importance of his mother's Maori heritage and became a

[75] M. T. Clark, Pastor Doug (Melbourne, 1977).
[76] J. D. McCaughey, Tradition and Dissent (Melbourne, 1997).

notable interpreter of biculturalism before it was fashionable. His mother's *marae* in Taranaki was called 'confiscation'. Some were nervous when he became governor general in 1985, for he had been identified with some radical causes like Citizens and Clergy for Rowling in 1975; but while he always spoke freely he never politicized his role.[77] After a short time as representative of the Anglican Communion at the United Nations in 1991, a post specially created for him, he returned to lead the College of St John in its Maori section, but when invited to head a committee drawing up a new constitution for divided Fiji, took up that vital task. Few New Zealand clergy have had a wider role in public life.

A few clergy have held high elected office. Sir Arnold Nordmeyer, a Presbyterian, was leader of the New Zealand Labour Party from 1963 to 1965 and a notable minister of finance from 1957 to 1960. He had been one of the pioneers of social security. Russell Marshall, a Methodist minister, was a minister from 1984–1990 in a later Labour government, while in Australia Brian Howe, a Uniting Church minister, became deputy prime minister in the Hawke government, and initiated a number of reforms in housing and social welfare before retiring in 1998. Lay Christianity has had many representatives in parliaments, whose unobtrusive religion is an important indicator of what Christianity means in politics, as distinct from church leaders' definitions. Those whose Christianity was seen as too obtrusive, like Sir Joh Bjelke-Petersen in Queensland, were more admired for their political skills than their faith. One of his strongest opponents, Gough Whitlam, Labor prime minister from 1972 to 1975, described him as 'a Bible-bashing bastard'. Many state politicians had strong Christian connections, as did Pacific parliamentarians. They played an important part in the transition from colonial dependence to self-government.[78] Many Pacific Island colonies became independent from the 1960s—Western Samoa (1962), Cook Islands (1965), Tonga and Fiji (1970), Solomon Islands and Tuvalu (1978), Kiribati (1979), Vanuatu (1980).

In the Solomon Islands, which became independent in 1978, with 97 per cent of its population Christian, the British had left a modest infrastructure of administration, health, and education, with significant

---

[77] An editorial in *The New Zealand Herald*, 21 March 1985, stated that 'The symbolism of a churchman as head of state is wrong.'

[78] Murray, *Would You Believe?*, 215–25 on Tate. C. Court, *The Early Years* (Fremantle, 1995) tells the story of a Western Australian premier.

numbers of local staff. The challenge in the period of transition was to prepare locals for senior responsibility, for the numbers attending tertiary and technical education in Fiji, Australia, and New Zealand were small, and the costs of increasing numbers were beyond the local economy. Christians have been important political leaders since independence, but have not necessarily followed church directives.

Expatriate leadership was by no means the only feature of Solomon Islands Christianity before independence. Catechists educated at Nazareth Apostolic Centre were very influential. Moro of Makaruka on Guadalcanal, claiming inspiration by the Holy Spirit, began a movement with some cargo elements, but which challenged Catholic clergy to attend more carefully to development and justice issues, even though the possibility of self-government seemed utterly remote in the 1960s.

Another sign of local initiative was the formation of the Solomon Islands Christian Association in 1967 by the Anglican, Methodist, and Roman Catholic Churches. The South Seas Evangelical Mission also had people at the meeting but they did not join, although Sir Peter Kenilorea, one of its members, the first prime minister, had been at the opening meeting. One of the first actions of the association was to devise a religious education syllabus. Though its effectiveness has fluctuated, the association has provided an important forum for discussion of common problems.

The South Seas Evangelical Church was more easily indigenized than the other major churches, because of its strong local leadership. Though its missionary leaders had taken a firm stand against some aspects of custom, members and village pastors remained in the ambit of spirit beliefs and traditional culture, given that some areas of Malaita remained strongly attached to traditional religion. Their Christianity was therefore strongly oriented to dealing with the cultural conflicts that were thereby set up. The church protected its members against dangerous spiritual powers by insisting on the strict observance of rules, which served the same social function as the traditional taboos.[79]

Such significant developments are not just to be seen as adaptations of Western Christianity, but must be judged in their own right as legitimate developments using the Christian way, so that European values would not disrupt their society. Christianity has many of the social functions of the old religion, but with the Christian God

[79] B. Burt, *Tradition and Christianity* (Chur, 1994) 270. A. Griffiths, *Fire in the Islands* (Wheaton, 1973).

exercising far more universal functions than the spirits. Christianity has both changed 'custom' and been affected by it, because of the Evangelical emphasis on personal conversion.[80]

In French Pacific territories, the intersection of politics and religion took a different form. In New Caledonia, the nickel boom (40 per cent of the world's resources) in the early 1970s attracted many migrants from other French Pacific territories, reducing the Kanak share of the population to 44 per cent. Not all that number supported the growing pressure for independence. Kanaks were offered more of a share in government and its agencies. A former priest, Jean-Marie Tjibaou (1936–89), entered the Territorial Assembly in 1979–84 after being laicized in 1972, and serving as Mayor of Hienghene in 1977. He was university educated in France (1961–71) but was passionately Kanak, and became president of the Provisional Kanaky.

Conservative settlers (Caldoches) were hostile to any serious changes and found Kanak use of themes of liberty, equality, and fraternity utterly distasteful. They were successfully able to persuade the Roman Catholic authorities to rid the Catholic school system of radical teachers. M. Dijoud in Paris wanted large French migration so there would be 400,000 people in New Caledonia by 2000. Archbishop Pierre Martin, who had survived Buchenwald and Dachau, was appointed to Noumea in 1966, and had a difficult path to walk with his divided French and Kanak followers. Pierre Declercq, a former teacher, supporter of independence and important member of the Assembly was assassinated on 19 September 1981. A new Governing Council was appointed in 1982. Caldoches demonstrated violently on 22 July 1982 against the assembly when it attempted to debate procedures for dealing with Kanak land claims against unjust dispossession. Land reform had begun in 1980. The French government attempted to deal with growing polarization by a conference in Nainville-les-Roches in July 1983, which recognized Kanak rights to independence, provided other inhabitants were adequately consulted. Without electoral reform, Kanaks could not achieve a majority vote. They boycotted the 1984 elections. In 1979 the Evangelical Church,

---

[80] J. Robbins, 'Dispossessing the spirits: Christian transformations of desire and ecology among the Urapmin of Papua New Guinea', *Ethnology* 24 (1995) 211–24. H. Whitehouse, 'Rites of terror', *Journal of the Royal Anthropological Institute* NS 2 (1996) 703–16; B. Burt, *Living Tradition* (London, 1997); F. Osifelo, *Reconciliation through Melanesian Eyes* (Holy Spirit Seminary, 1995) explores how Baegu clan obligations can be incorporated into the rite of reconciliation, so that both ancestors and wronged individuals are compensated, concluding in a peace-meal.

which has over thirty schools, had officially supported independence, but not armed struggle.

The churches were unable to prevent the violence which escalated at the end of 1984. Tjibaou and the FLNKS (Kanak National Liberation Front) formed a provisional government. Eduard Pisani arrived from Paris in December to try and resolve the tensions, but that was stymied by the Caldoche killing of ten unarmed Kanaks at Hienghene on 5 December. On 12 January 1985, E. Machoro and M. Nonaro were killed by gendarmes in very dubious circumstances. On 6 March 1985, Roman Catholic and Evangelical Church leaders drew up a statement on Reconciliation, but despite such initiatives, in 1985 the Evangelical Church's Lycée Dokalo in Noumea was bombed. Caldoches rioted against Pisani's proposals for devolution in association with France and a referendum in 1987. The proposals were for four Regional Councils, with Kanaks controlling three, whose members made up a Territorial Assembly. A violent confrontation in April 1988 led to deaths of two police, and nineteen Kanaks on Ouvea, who were holding hostages. Tjibaou and Yeiwene Yeiwene were assassinated on 4 May 1989, by Djubelly Wea, a former Protestant pastor, and a political rival who rejected the Matignon Accords of 26 June 1988. He in turn was shot by Tjibaou's supporters.

Tjibaou's family knew the power of death. His grandmother was killed by the French in 1917. Her infant son survived to become Tjibaou's father. Two of his brothers were murdered unarmed in December 1984. Their killers were acquitted on the grounds they had acted in self-defence! The killings were a tragedy for Kanaky. Tjibaou was one of the most gifted of the Pacific's political leaders. Not only did he have notable political skills, he led an intellectual and cultural renaissance for his people, taking 'canaque', a term of contempt in the mouths of the colonialists, and turning it into a name of honour with roots in traditional culture.

He was a key organizer, with Jacques Iekawe, of Melanesia 2000. This Pacific-wide cultural festival enabled Kanaks to display their heritage and give it new life. He co-authored *Kanaké: The Melanesian Way* in 1978, a fruit of his reflection on this heritage in the light of social science. His major book, *La Présence Kanak*, is a profound philosophical exposition of Kanak culture, without intellectual equivalent anywhere else in the Pacific. As he noted, 'The hardest thing to do is to stay alive and feel like a stranger in your own land.' Whether a Kanak was Catholic or Protestant 'deep inside himself, he seems to have kept a safe passage to the ancestors'.[81] He created the belief that the Kanak path to decolonization was more powerful than European representations of them as savages.

Some land was redistributed in 1993. Kanaks, both Protestants and Roman Catholics, sought independence. In April and November 1998 a 20-year process was agreed in Noumea before a final vote on independence, after steady devolution of power by France. A victory for negotiation, it has left many Kanaks dissatisfied. Crucial issues of land have not yet been addressed.[82]

In Papua New Guinea, there is still heavy economic dependence on Australia. In 1976, 22 per cent of Australian investment was in the newly independent country, providing 40 per cent of its government's expenditure. Two-thirds of the population were illiterate. The Australian government now gives 15 per cent of the Papua New Guinean income, providing major opportunity for politicians to help their *wantoks*. The changes since independence on 16 September 1975 have been startling for all the churches, as they share in the task of building a sense of nationhood amongst tribes who are still deeply suspicious of those who are not their *wantoks*. Even Evangelical Baptist churches are organized on blood lines, and it requires great courage to minister out of one's tribal area. The churches managed the transition to local responsibility very well, though overseas aid is still financially vital for national work.

The Evangelical Lutheran Church of Papua New Guinea (ELCONG) finances local ministry, while the Neuendettelslau mission still finances German specialist workers and some projects. Locals are responsible for implementation. In 1985, the Evangelical Church of Bavaria gave 400,000 Kina and the Lutheran Church of Australia gave 444,000 Kina, out of a local budget of 1 million Kina. The New Guinea Coordinating Committee 1980–1989 Minutes indicate how significant such partners were. For many, Christianity remains local, part of the fabric of living in a subsistence economy where European technology and economic patterns are only slowly being absorbed, with constant problems over maintenance of projects and corruption. In 1975 an international Lutheran team visited and

[81] A. Bensa and E. Wittersheim (eds.), *Cibau, Cibau* (Noumea, 1998) 58. J.-M. Tjibaou, *La Présence Kanak* (Paris, 1996) is a powerful contemporary account of traditional Kanak culture and its spiritual value.

[82] H. Fraser, *Your Flag's Blocking Our Sun* (Sydney, 1970); M. Lyon, *Totem and Tricolour* (Sydney, 1986); M. Spender et al., *New Caledonia* (Brisbane, 1988); J. Dahlem, *Nouvelle Calédonie* (Paris, 1996).

Table 1. *Papua New Guinea: The 1990 Census*

A summary of the 1990 Census, showing the total population by religion and age groups is available from the National Census Office. Church numbers, in descending order of size, are shown to be:

			%
1.	Roman Catholics	1,023,139	28.40
2.	Evangelical Lutherans	832,933	23.10
3.	United	456,994	12.70
4.	Evangelical Alliance	315,416	8.70
5.	Seventh-day Adventists	290,067	8.04
6.	Pentecostal	253,844	7.00
7.	Anglican	142,590	3.95
8.	Salvation Army	7,493	0.21
	Other Christians	155,928	4.33
	Total Christians	3,489,891	96.40
	Other Religions	11,487	0.30
	No Religion/Not stated	118,063	3.30
	Total	3,607,954	100.00

Source: T. Aerts and P. Ramsden, *Studies and Statements on Romans and Anglicans in Papua New Guinea*, No. 1, Port Moresby, 1995, p. 38.

made a searching report on the collapse of Kumau Holdings, in the Chimbu area, which had circumvented Lae Head Office control and lost large sums with the same mix of poor administration and endemic cronyism which brought the nation to the brink of bankruptcy by 1999.

Conversion could bring local, but not systemic changes. The corrupt prime ministership of Bill Skate illustrated that, as did Richmond Tamanabae of Popondetta, who was awakened by the Christian Revival Crusade in Port Moresby and threw away his magical objects. He returned to his village and they burnt theirs too. There were real tensions with the Anglican majority there.[83] Pastoral issues of spirits,

[83] J. K. Daimoi, 'Nominalism in Papua New Guinea', M.Theol. thesis (Pasadena, 1986) 67–71; E. L. Spruth, 'And the Word of God spread', D.Miss. thesis (Pasadena, 1981) is invaluable on the Guitnuis Church. R. W. Robin, 'Revival movements in the South Highlands Province', *Oceania* 52 (1982) 320–43.

sorcery, and illness still abound.[84] Fighting re-emerged in the 1980s and 1990s in the Highlands. Bishop Boniepe was vital in solving tribal fights in Simbu in the 1980s for the Lutheran Church. Localizing leadership has meant that some church leaders conform to patterns of 'big man' behaviour, enhancing their status and authority by securing grants for lavish buildings, scholarships for promising students, and refusing to retire, but doing little for politically unimportant and remote villages where pastors and catechists are still poorly paid, often not for months.

Clergy can become very influential. Fr Ignatius Kilage left the priesthood because of clan pressure and eventually became governor general. Archbishop Louis Vangeke, Bishop Z. K. Zurenuo (ELCONG), Bishop Getake Gam, head Lutheran bishop from 1991, and Leslie Boseto, a Solomon Islander bishop of the United Church, now a Member of Parliament and minister of home affairs, are listened to with respect, as was the Catholic Bishop Singkai of Bougainville. The first Anglican archbishop, James Ayong, was appointed in 1995.[85] Leaders follow Melanesian style and do not take a high profile in advocacy which would be interpreted as anti-government, though they can influence single issues. In 1987, the major churches lobbied for amendments in the Mass Media Tribunal Bill and secured changes.

City congregations offer pastoral and social support to their members, as well as transcending tribal loyalties. For many village people churches offer valuable experience of self-government and financial responsibility in a political system where corruption is a serious problem. The self-study programme of the Roman Catholic Church in the 1970s provided a great deal of useful information about how to move forward after independence. The United Church also did a similar kind of survey, though without the same expatriate resources to plan implementation and follow-through.

The major group not included in ecumenical partnership is the Adventists. In 1989 in French Polynesia there were 2,910, in Western Samoa 4,770, in Fiji 11,005, and in Vanuatu 5,831. In some regions of

---

[84] C. C. McDonnell, 'Networks and associations in urban mission', Ph.D. thesis (Pasadena, 1970); L. Oates, *Not in the Common Mould* (Kangaroo Ground, 1997) 155 for healing, 212–15 for defeat of sorcery.

[85] F. Steinbauer, *Shaping the Future* (Madang, 1974) 141–4 (Vangeke), 155–60 (Kilage); L. A. Cupit, 'Ecumenical Relations in Papua New Guinea', M.Theol. thesis (Melbourne, 1974); M. K. Rankin, *No Chance to Panic* (Mountain View, 1980) describes the lead up to independence from an Adventist pastor's view. A. Davies, *Invading Paradise* (Melbourne, 1991).

the Highlands, Adventists are now the major church. By 1900, Adventists had 23 per cent of the population in areas such as the East Highlands province of Papua New Guinea. Begun in 1934, they greatly outnumber their co-religionists in Australia and New Zealand, and have members in a number of important positions nationally, a novel experience for a very separatist church which has rejoiced in being a remnant looking forward to Jesus' second coming. Sir James Donald in the 1920s was one of the few Adventist public figures in New Zealand. The denomination is kept under Sydney control, and thus avoided clan conflicts. Dealing with the challenges of being a folk church with 8 per cent of the population instead of a small sectarian minority poses challenges for the regional leadership which are quite novel.[86]

In 1994, the members of the South Pacific Division and the Papua New Guinea Union Mission Development Advisory Committee of the Seventh-day Adventists published an important report based on two years' work, addressing the changes expected by the end of the century. Growth has been very rapid, especially in the Highlands, where there were 67,000 members and over 51,000 adherents. In the country as a whole, there were over 86,000 members and 132,000 claimed adherents. Twenty-eight per cent were in the Eastern High-lands Province, 10 per cent in Enga, 14 per cent in the Gulf, 19 per cent in Manus, and 12 per cent in the national capital. They were found in 550 churches and 1,519 'hand' or branch churches, the latter of which had a huge number of people waiting to be gathered into full membership. It was an urgent task to provide them with the necessary leadership and teaching to prevent them from being attracted away to other independent groups. The hand churches had an anomalous status. Many had become larger than the parent church, but lacked leadership, education, and suitable pastoral care. Ministers and leading laity were impossibly overstretched. In one mission, on average, a minister looked after fifteen to sixteen churches. In another, a Samoan minister looked after eleven churches and fifteen hand churches. In another, a layman cared for seven churches and sixteen hand churches. Rivalry with other denominations could be strong. In one village, Roman Catholics tried to drown the Seventh-day

[86] H. Jebens, *Wege Zum Himmel; Katholiken, Siebenten Tags-Adventisten und der Einfluss der traditionellen Religion in Paraidu* (Bonn, 1995) is a perceptive study of inter-relationships. M. Ernst, *Role of Social Change* (Hamburg, 1996) 53, notes that in the Solomon Islands, Adventists are over 10 per cent of the population. M. K. Rankin, *I Hear Singing* (Mountain View, 1976) tells the story of one family's conversion.

Adventist service by singing. The Seventh-day Adventists outsang them.

The Development Advisory Committee noted that between 1988 and 1992, at least 13,115 had 'apostatized' or left. Such figures were recognized to be very inadequate. The committee suspected that with accurate figures it might be the case that the equivalent of the current membership had been lost over a decade. To counter this, regional meetings were to be held for all members to attend, religious instruction teaching courses introduced into ministerial education, systematic visitation undertaken according to a schedule, suitable men encouraged to prepare for ordination, and upgrading organized for Sonoma College ministerial graduates. Given that as many as 80 per cent of the Papua New Guinea population is only partly literate, careful attention needs to be given to suitable education materials in English, pidgin, and Motu. Teaching needed to be given on drug-related issues, gambling, dancing, and tribal fighting, so that a positive Christian lifestyle could be promoted. Land needed to be identified for future worship buildings, with simple plans for rural and urban churches.

While there was no consideration given by the report to the content of the Adventist message, careful attention was paid to reorganizing administration at national, regional, and local levels, fostering stewardship and clarifying the position of voluntary workers. They expected growth to over 100,000 members by 2000, mostly in the Eastern and Western Highlands missions in the last quinquennium of 1995–2000.[87]

The growth of the Adventist church in some areas of Papua New Guinea is a fascinating phenomenon. Rejection of pigs, a central feature of local culture, would seem to be a recipe for disaster, with the emergence of a small sectarian church the most likely result. Yet on the contrary, the last few decades have seen explosive growth in some regions, which has made Seventh-day Adventism the fourth largest church in the nation.

Changes within the Adventists have produced a more Evangelical

---

[87] I owe this information to the South Pacific Division, Sydney. G. J. Humble, *An Accurate Picture of the Eastern Highlands–Simbu Mission of the Seventh-day Adventists* (Pasadena, 1991) notes that membership in 1953 was 758, while in 1990 it was 44,119. In 1953 there were 12 members per minister, in 1990 there were 527. M. Ernst, *Winds of Change* (Suva, 1994); P. Gesch (ed.), *Culture, Gospel and Church* (Madang, 1994); J. D. May, *Christus Initiator* (1990); G. Herdt and M. Stephen (eds.), *The Religious Imagination in New Guinea* (New Brunswick, 1984).

theology, following the bitter disputes over justification by faith in the 1960s and 1970s sparked by the critiques of Mrs White by Desmond Ford, an Australian Adventist scholar.[88] They have been cautiously moving out of their separatism, developing informal and occasional links with the ecumenical Melanesian Institute, but steering clear of application for membership of the Melanesian Council of Churches. The sharp criticisms of other churches as apostate have diminished as Adventists have cautiously begun attending some academic theological conferences and exploring their relationship with the Evangelical networks that have some parallel beliefs. Their attacks on other churches have perhaps even helped them in Papua New Guinea, for that appeals to the combativeness of the Highland cultures, where their impact has been most striking. Adventists' repute as the 'clean' church, their strong commitment to health, their honesty, and their education have helped members and adherents fit into the opportunities for employment in post-independence Papua New Guinea.

In other parts of the Pacific, other religious movements like Pentecostals, as well as more exotic groups like the Bahais, who claimed to be the definitive world religion, offer alternatives to the historic churches, along with the Mormons, who have been growing steadily because of the education they offer and the fine facilities for worship and recreation. Their temples also offer an important link with ancestors, and their strict rules on morality offer some barrier against the breakdown of traditional sanctions, even though they show little interest in linking their faith with local culture, insisting instead on American definitions laid down by the leadership in Salt Lake City. In Tahiti's islands they increased from 2,000 in 1962 to 12,000 by 1992.[89]

In French Polynesia, Protestants have increasingly sought to recover their Maohi heritage, even though the French authorities have been reluctant to allow the Maohi language to be used in education or broadcasting.[90] The *Buka Himene* (1974) contains some hymns sung to traditional tunes and sung in parts. On Rapa, songs akin to the Cook Islands *uapou* are specially composed, using well-known tunes. In Tahiti, *tuaroi*, held on the evening of the first Sunday of the month, are

[88] P. Ballis, *Leaving the Adventist Ministry* (Westport, 1999). Adventists were demonized in the aftermath of Azaria Chamberlain's tragic killing by a dingo. F. Moorhouse, 'The Azaria Chamberlain case (1980–1986)', *ACH* (1993) 160–75.

[89] J. Garrett, *Where Nets Were Cast* (Suva, 1997) 416; M. Ernst, *Winds of Change* (Suva, 1994).

[90] B. Saura, *Politique et religion à Tahiti* (Pirae, 1993); *Les sanito, te mau sanito* (Independence, 1994).

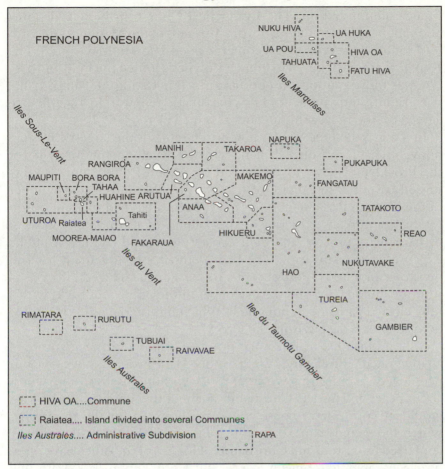

French Polynesia (1983). (*Source:* R. Crocombe (ed.), *Politics in Polynesia*, Suva, 1983, p. 191. With permission of the Institute for Pacific Studies.)

discussions of texts with *himene tarava* contests in eloquence. Singing in worship is unaccompanied.

A number of younger pastors have studied at Pacific Theological College in Suva and become aware of the wider issues affecting the region. Several founded separatist churches. John Doom has been an ecumenical leader, as well as secretary of the Evangelical Church since 1971, before moving to Geneva as secretary for the Pacific. In 1982, the church publicly opposed further nuclear testing and skilfully used the WCC and Pacific Council of Churches (PCC) to bring their concerns before the international community, to the chagrin of the

French administration. The Evangelical Church in New Caledonia also sought to widen international awareness of the Matignon Accords by a round-table ecumenical conference on Lifou in May 1994.[91] The Roman Catholic Church in French Polynesia joined the PCC in 1976, but was more cautious in opposing nuclear testing in Tahiti. It has been significantly influenced by charismatic renewal. In 1992 France agreed to stop nuclear testing, but resumed in 1995–6.

In Tonga, the Free Wesleyan Church remains the largest Christian body, but has faced some challenges by the development since 1987 of the Pro-Democracy Movement led by Akelisi Pohiva, unjustly dismissed as a public servant in 1985, a local preacher and elected member of the Tongan Parliament since 1987. Pohiva has had spells in prison for his remorseless criticism of the failings of the nobles, abuse of parliamentary process, and their capacity to spend lavishly at public expense on overseas trips. The Pro-Democracy Movement has had divisions since 1995. Pohiva wants to see Tonga changed into a constitutional monarchy and the privileges of the nobles cut back, with a fully elected parliament, not one in which ministerial office is a noble perquisite or royal gift from the Crown.

Bishop Finau has made similar points. He was a strong advocate of an integrated Christianity. 'We are indeed false prophets if we give our people Jesus' comforting words of peace without his disturbing words about peace and justice. Christianity is about the whole of life.'[92] That would of course have considerable implications for the monarchy, which has sacred status, based on long-standing titles and authority conferred by custom and Christianity. Holders of the office have often been very able, like Queen Salote, but King Tupou IV's death will create some succession problems.

Tongan Methodism has produced a number of ecumenical leaders like Sione Havea and Lopeti Taufa. Church leadership is linked with chiefly families. Village Christians practise their faith with an energy and enthusiasm which amazes visitors, especially on the Sabbath. British Methodism and Tongan traditional culture have been closely integrated with a strongly Christocentric devotion; this has some fascinating links with primal religious understanding of the sacred and prophetic inspiration, which can include women. Drs Meleana Puloka and Asinate Samate are two important educators, out of the six women ministers. Christianity provides the framework of authority

---

[91] R. Weingartner (ed.), *Nouvelle Calédonie* (Geneva, 1994).
[92] D. Mullins, *He Spoke the Truth in Love* (Auckland, 1994) 9.

for every aspect of village life. Recent charismatic emphases have resonances with the Methodist heritage but have proved subversive of the unitive sacral order.

So has another group led by the Reverend Senetuli Koloi and known as the Maamafo'ou movement. This grew out of his leadership in the Scripture Union and his appeal to the emotional elements in Tongan Methodism, from which he broke away in 1978 with a number of followers. By 1979 he ended his links with Scripture Union and formed the Tokaikolo Fellowship with its own college. The Free Wesleyan Church in May 1979 expelled both him and Sione Taufa, a former bishop of the United Church in Papua New Guinea. Koloi built up migrant support in Australia, New Zealand, and the United States. He died unexpectedly in February 1980.

Liufau Vailea succeeded as leader, continuing the emphasis on personal faith, the need to break away from Tongan custom, as well as distrust of institutions. Some 4,000 members left the Free Wesleyan Church, including 112 local preachers. A very successful school continued and ministers were ordained. Makisi Finau suggests that the schism might have been contained within the Free Wesleyans if the president had been less authoritarian, but Koloi undoubtedly appealed because of his dedication, his fasting, healing, and example of new life, which contrasted with the settled ways of the majority church. Once the break occurred, the dynamics of Tongan society ensured that return would be very unlikely.[93]

CHRISTIAN ART AND LITERATURE

In Europe and North America there has been a long tradition of Christian art, though its boundaries have been challenged over the last century by movements which refuse any framework of meaning except individual creativity. For those nurtured in the European tradition, Polynesian and Melanesian art, like Aboriginal art, did not fit easily into any recognized set of boundaries, except to be classed as 'primitive'. Early missionaries banished anything which had association with traditional religion, and converts also were well aware of the sacred power of some religious artefacts. To portray Jesus or Mary as

[93] I. C. Campbell, *Island Kingdom: Tonga Ancient and Modern* (Christchurch, 1992); P. van der Grijp, 'Christian confrontation in paradise', *Anthropos* 88 (1993) 135–52; M. Finau et al., *Island Churches: Challenge and Change* (Suva, 1992) 141–206.

anything other than European was offensive, even though the European tradition ignored Jesus' Semitic context. Recognition of the importance of Pacific art, as well as change in missiology, have made possible the use of indigenous art, music, and dance in a new way.

Melanesia has many varieties of art, some of which are not intended to be permanent, like body painting, masks, and even elaborate wooden buildings which have a short life because of termites. Tools for working stone were rare, or demanded an enormous labour input. First-generation Christians did little to translate their traditional arts into Christian contexts. They simply accepted European religious pictures, buildings, and furnishings as part of the Christian cultural package. By the 1950s, however, an exhibition of Christian art in Rome from all over the world was a reminder that the Pacific did have a recognizable tradition with vitality and power. Occasional examples of indigenous themes are found in churches. The Catholic parish of Koumac on Grande Terre contrasts strikingly with the cathedral in Noumea, which is devoid of any recognition of Kanak culture. By contrast, the Catholic cathedral in Port Moresby is obviously contextual, in a way that the Anglican one at Dogura is not.[94]

Many books have been published on Aboriginal, Melanesian, and Polynesian art, but, as yet, few Christians of recent migrant origins in Australia and New Zealand appreciate the possibilities for cultural connection and translation offered by indigenous art, or what it means to be the people of the land. A strong Protestant suspicion of art lies close to the surface in the region. In 1951 Felix Arnott and Michael Scott, a Jesuit, were leading movers in setting up the Blake Prize for Australian religious art, hoping that this would help to give form to the meaning of theological thought and convey religious inspiration in a manner which was helpful to viewer as well as to artist. The meaning of 'religious' has become rather wider than they intended, but some significant paintings have been produced. Many Australians were surprised at the range of local religious painting displayed at an exhibition in 1988.

Melbourne in 1997 saw a divisive confrontation about the acceptable boundaries of art, and what constituted blasphemy. An exhibition of the works of the American photo artist Andre Serrano, a former

---

[94] T. Aerts, 'Christian art from Melanesia', in Bettscheider et al., *Divine Word Mission*, 189–230; Comité Paroissial, *Koumac et Son Eglise* (Noumea, 1994); H. Wagner and H. Reiner, *The Lutheran Church in Papua New Guinea* (Adelaide, 1987) 451–67 on sculptures and paintings; G. Fugman, *David Anam* (Minneapolis, 1986).

Roman Catholic, at the National Gallery of Victoria, included 'piss Christ', which a number of Christians found grossly offensive, including the Anglican and Roman Catholic archbishops. While Archbishop Rayner was not prepared to take his protest as far as seeking a legal injunction, Archbishop Pell was.[95] Though his plea was not upheld, he made it clear that blasphemy was still a concern for many Christians. The matter was ended when two teenagers, who found the depiction offensive, smashed the photo with a hammer. The gallery closed the exhibition, although Serrano's other pornographic exhibition, in a private gallery, remained open so that members of the public could decide in what sense Serrano's work was artistic. Sr Rosemary Crumlin's superb 1998 Melbourne exhibition of religious art was a reminder of what was painfully authentic, without being blasphemous.

In literature there is a Christian presence, certainly not dominant and sometimes devalued by the literary lions. It has similarities with Christian presence in the region as a whole. Sometimes it is very public and obvious. In other cases it is subtle, where Christian resonances can only be detected by sharp ears for broad themes. Fine religious poetry has been anthologized, going back into colonial times. That tradition is continued by Les Murray and Kevin Hart, notable converts to Catholicism. Patrick White's novels have an ambiguous relation with his family Anglicanism, but explore human dilemmas with great power.[96] The Anglican Tim Winton comes from a Churches of Christ family, and writes with great sensitivity about the links of people and environment.[97] Elizabeth Jolley is fascinated by the links of spirituality and life while Gillian Bouras' books wryly comment about the interaction of Orthodoxy and Protestantism. Many Catholic authors are quite explicit in their religious commitment, nourished by a number of literary magazines like Victoria's *Eureka Street*. In New Zealand, James Baxter and Ian Cross, in different ways, showed how deeply Catholicism had intersected with New Zealand life, though Baxter

[95] 'The Pope's man', *Bulletin*, 27 April 1999, 25–31; A. C. Moore, *Arts in the Religions of the Pacific* (London, 1994); H. Zahn, *Missions and Music* (Port Moresby, 1996); R. Crumlin, *Images of Religion in Australian Art* (Sydney, 1988); *Aboriginal Art and Spirituality* (Melbourne, 1995); *Beyond Belief* (Melbourne, 1998); Windsor, *Heaven where the Bachelors Sit*, 168 ff. for Michael Scott.

[96] E. V. Thomas, 'Patrick White and the purification of atheism', *Theology* 101 (1998) 36–43; M. Zylstra (ed.), *The Deep End* (Melbourne, 1989) 5–20 on Winton.

[97] E. Guy, 'Tim Winton', in M. Griffith and J. Tulip (eds.), *Religion, Literature and the Arts* (Sydney, 1996) 88–97.

maintained that the bedrock of Kiwi consciousness was Calvinist.[98] Actors like Ruth Cracknell and Jacqui Weaver, and singers like Dame Joan Sutherland or Dame Kiri Te Kanawa, acknowledge the influence of their Christian backgrounds.

Christian festivals—Christmas and Easter—have become the property of the whole community, often in ways of which church leaders deeply disapprove. They are a reminder that Christianity can take deep roots through lay convictions rather than church teaching. Whether that process can continue and the churches retain their identity remains a question which will have to be answered more definitely in the twenty-first century.

[98] M. Williams (ed.), *The Source of the Song* (Wellington, 1995) 7–22 gives an introduction to Catholic writing. E. Isichei, 'Dark vocation', in Griffith and Tulip, *Religion, Literature and the Arts*, 19–34.

CONCLUSION

When the first religious contacts with Europeans occurred, Aborigines and Pacific Islanders did not dream of religious choice. Now all are challenged to develop a more inclusive Christianity since there is such variety. Traditional society and its way of life was interwoven with deep convictions about the nature of the sacred, and appropriate propitiation of the gods and spirits. Religion was communal and the religious practices of these strange incomers appeared bizarre. Yet their critique of war, slavery, cannibalism, and human sacrifice gradually won support. Two centuries later, that communalism has been significantly eroded by the combined impacts of colonialism, capitalism, education, electronic and print media, and the aftermath of independence. Local identity remains important, even though new forms of political and regional identity have emerged. Christianity provided an important context for Islanders and Aborigines to modernize their communities and to widen choices on their own terms. Choice was not always possible because of the destructive power of invasive systems, especially when land was lost, history only partly remembered, and traditional authority undermined. Regional Christians now face similar pressures from globalization, which undermines cherished forms of community, without any unitive religious alternative.

In many villages in the nineteenth century, Christian communalism replaced pre-contact forms of social organization. The boundaries of the sacred were redefined, but religion remained at the heart of culture. Leaders fought against threats to village unity, invoking a variety of punitive sanctions. In January 1999 that was highlighted in New Caledonia. Two women from Chépénéhé on Lifou had become Jehovah's Witnesses and were expelled. From their viewpoint, this was unjustified, especially when their refusal to leave was followed by a severe beating ordered by the local chief. They appealed to the courts, which ruled that their legal right to religious freedom had been infringed. Likewise, numbers of young people escape communal authority by migrating to towns, or to other countries, or by joining a new religion where religious and secular authority are not so obtrusively related, thus fundamentally changing traditional forms of religious authority.

Missionaries, settlers, and colonizers differed in their attitudes to social change. Most did not want religious pluralism unless it suited their own interests. British Christians resolved the problem of diversity versus social cohesion by the creation of denominations. Recreated by missionaries in Oceania by the 1870s, they provided, for a century, continuity and a vision of Christian nationhood in Britain's colonies. These churches maintained unity by common doctrine, worship, and ethical norms. Deviants were severely dealt with to uphold the myth of national and religious unity. Maintenance of British national unity was achieved by Protestant hegemony and the attempted exclusion of Roman Catholics from privilege and power. The Crown was the focus for this symbolic unity, enhanced by the conviction of many Protestants that the Catholic Irish were so 'other' that they could not be trusted as citizens. While such stereotyped views were possible in the United Kingdom with its Protestant establishment before 1829, they were incompatible with the demography of the Australasian colonies, massive internal migration, and universal suffrage by the early twentieth century, despite the militant anti-Catholicism of many colonial Protestant churches and their agencies. In the Pacific Islands, comity agreements and varied village choices of competing Christianities gave pluralism in practice, but maintained a local unitive sacred order, which was an essential part of the construction of society.

In the colonies of settlement, other currents were eroding the ancient foundations of religious, moral, and political unity. Fear of a primitive deity steadily declined with growing Protestant emphasis on the love of God. A new consensus emerged, integrating the social order and lending moral authority to the state for over a century till the 1960s. The Protestant insistence on the right of private judgement made unified biblical interpretation impossible as new views of philosophy and history widened hermeneutic possibilities, and challenged traditional correlations with culture. Allied with vigorously exchanged views in the press and pulpit, with social reform, and liberal opposition to censorship, these new versions of Christianity made the traditional creeds, confessions, and liturgies look dated and a brake on religious progress. From the mid-nineteenth century to the 1960s, religious liberalism was an influential form of Protestantism, allied with expansion of education, and political and social reform. Anglo-Catholicism was another important form of Protestantism, despite its members' convictions that they were creating a form of Christianity free of the defects of Protestantism and Roman Catholicism. Individual choice stood at its heart, despite communitarian rhetoric and appeals to an idealized Catholic England. Evangelicalism was the other major Protestant movement, upholding biblical authority and conversion, and rejecting modernizing theology, but allied with many forms of change, especially in liturgy, business, and the professions. It was also resolutely committed to work as a sacred vocation, to self-improvement, and to separation of church and government. It stimulated missionary effort, evangelism, and lay generosity. Steer, founded in 1961, has since given $23 million to Christian causes. Where pluralism prevented churches influencing legislation, Christian citizens were encouraged to work for legislation which protected a sacred order and the family, limited the abuse of alcohol and gambling, and upheld broadly conceived notions of Christian morality. Polynesian and Melanesian Christians did not necessarily share the same priorities in upholding sacred order.

During the first five decades of the twentieth century, Australian and New Zealand Protestantism was mildly polarized between Evangelicals and liberals, each seeking answers to the challenges posed by scientific and philosophical ideas, without the bitterness and schism of the United States and Canada. Differing attitudes to the authority and interpretation of the Bible; the nature of sin and need for atonement; incarnation, and resurrection; the work of the Holy Spirit, evangelism, and the character of the Kingdom, cut deeply. Evangelicals created a subculture of conventions, magazines, Bible colleges, and faith missions which rejected the priorities of the liberals. Liberals regarded such views as marginal—even intellectually bankrupt. The early 1900s emergence of Pentecostal groups seemed to them the nadir of this dated and irrelevant Protestantism. Conservative and Evangelical Protestants, however, saw liberals as betrayers of the faith, who kept the form of words, but denied the supernatural and revelatory character of historic Christianity. Such stereotyping did little to clarify the issues. Nor did conservative Presbyterian attempts to try leading liberals for heresy, for they were widely trusted for their intelligence, judgement, and denominational commitment. They were far from uncritical modernizers and stood for careful adaption of the Christian heritage to the best of modern thought—a recipe for religious and moral change which was unitive and progressive.

A vocal minority of free thinkers, atheists, and rationalists wanted the abolition of Christianity, believing passionately that their versions of reason and tolerance were the foundations of democratic societies. A small group of sectarian Protestants looked for the Second Coming of Christ to end all compromises with evil, and to the Kingdom of God on earth. In some regions of Australia and New Zealand they created a small powerful subculture largely separate from surrounding society.

Most colonists and their descendants retained varying degrees of adherence to Christianity. The churches were immensely important in shaping communities, because of their leaders' links with ruling elites—locally and nationally. The major Protestant churches claimed the support of over two-thirds to three-quarters of the population of Australia and New Zealand, depending on the number of Roman Catholics. Though their participation rates were lower than those of Catholics, they stayed remarkably stable until the 1960s and 1970s.

Catholics formed a sharp alternative to Protestant definitions of Christian normality by their union with Rome, their significantly Irish ethnicity, and their determination to retain a distinctive Christian identity, which for them was the only form acceptable to the Almighty. They were little affected by the Protestant theological and ethical modernizers, due to the papal imposition of an anti-Modernist oath required of all clergy until the 1960s. The Latin liturgy had remained substantially unchanged since the Middle Ages and no participation in Protestant worship was permitted. About 50 per cent of Catholic children attended Catholic schools and experienced the additional reinforcement of identity they offered. In the Pacific Islands, Catholics often formed tightly-knit entities with French and German missionary leadership. While indicators of Catholics' practice were higher than in many parts of Europe, they had moved markedly closer by 2000.

Yet life in a predominantly Protestant society presented alternative values and attitudes ranging from grudging recognition to those who cherished the Christian plurality offered in Australia and New Zealand. This favourably compared with the unyielding religious hostilities of the United Kingdom and independent Irish Republic from the 1920s. Above all, Catholics insisted they were loyal Australians and New Zealanders. Certainly their civic commitment was a key foundation for regional democracy and cautious religious tolerance, even if they were sometimes republicans. Few of the laity

showed much enthusiasm for calls to convert their Protestant neighbours or to create a Catholic Australia, even though they turned out in
their tens of thousands for Eucharistic Congresses and other demon-
strations of Catholic solidarity. In Papua New Guinea and New
Caledonia, Roman Catholicism had become the largest Christian
community by the mid-twentieth century and significant in many
other Pacific Islands, with occasional islands like Wallis and Futuna
totally Catholic. Where regions were religiously plural, occasionally
tribal and kin obligations triumphed over confessional separateness, a
reminder that there were deeper religious commitments than those
imported from Europe.

Amongst Protestants in Australia and New Zealand, modernizers
had captured the national and regional institutions for church government, though the pace of change was too slow for many influenced by
the Student Christian Movement. They were committed to ecumenism, new theological ideas, and shared worship. Many of the
twentieth-century leaders in the major Protestant churches were
deeply affected by their experiences of religious partnership in the
Student Christian Movement and its hopes for a new international
order, based on universal missionary proclamation of the Kingdom of
God. At the heart of the movement was passionate commitment to
study of the Bible and radical following of Jesus. Another reformist
movement with less intellectual appeal was Moral Rearmament,
whose commitment to absolutes appeared in surprising places. Most
young Protestants, however, were socialized in their discipleship by
Sunday schools and the large youth movements which were very
influential until the 1960s. Now fewer than 10 per cent of eligible
children in New South Wales attend Sunday schools. Some church-
related Protestant schools and colleges also shaped the piety of elites,
but local congregations were often led by members whose piety was
thoughtful but pre-critical. The liberals did not win their allegiance
and many lived comfortably with a religion where deep spiritual
experience did not correlate with their vocational skills in a liberal
manner.

There was a tension at the heart of liberal Protestantism over the
definition of Jesus. For traditionally minded Christians, whether
Catholic or Protestant, Jesus was the incarnate Son of God, uniquely
embodying the divine and the human. Liberal Christians were
increasingly attracted by the humanity of Jesus as 'Elder Brother', or
'Exemplar'. In their teaching, writing, and preaching they simply

placed traditional definitions on the sideline. They did this with the best of intentions, seeking to make Jesus a contemporary of those who were shaped by modern culture and who saw the traditional theology as a burden on conscience, or even as an affront to reason in a scientific era.

There was no agreement about the best way of testing new theological translations, for heresy trials were abhorrent to those of a liberal mind. Instead trust was placed in the free marketplace of ideas to sort the wheat from the chaff. Liberals who rejected the identification of the Bible with the Word of God, insisted that the Bible contained the Word of God, but left identification to the individual Christian. Gradually the shape of belief changed, especially because new attitudes to the Bible undermined the pious reading and meditation on the Bible as God's Word which had been one of the foundations of Protestantism since the sixteenth century. Some managed to combine that with the fashionably critical approaches to the Bible, but they were few. A quiet polarization took place in the major Protestant churches between those who heard the Bible as the authoritative Word of God and those who read it for wise counsel from those in other centuries, and correlated that with what passed for the wisdom of the time.

Anglican Evangelicals in the Dioceses of Sydney and Melbourne rejected liberalism, safeguarding their heritage by insisting on the appointment of sound men to teach ordinands in Moore and Ridley Colleges, but that option was not open to Methodists and Presbyterians whose colleges were dominated by teachers with liberal sympathies. Churches of Christ, Baptists, and Lutherans were as firm as Roman Catholics in excluding modernizing theologians from their theological colleges. Others preferred to attend Bible colleges, where classical views of the Bible, and commitment to evangelism and to overseas mission still dominated. Majority Protestantism was increasingly uneasy about any of these three emphases, even though conversionism survived in Sunday schools and youth movements, where Evangelicals were still well represented.

In the Pacific Island churches, modern theological ideas were hardly known and the nineteenth-century doctrine, piety, worship, and ethics imparted by the missionaries acquired a sacredness which made change neither necessary nor desirable—even in ministerial dress. That was true for Catholics and Protestants alike. There was often strong resistance to attempts by Mormons and Seventh-day Adventists to lure villagers from their traditional religious loyalties. Roman Catholic attempts at proselytism in Protestant areas met similar resistance, unless there had been failures in leadership, which opened a way to changed loyalties. The rhythms of Christian time and Island time were interwoven in a powerfully creative way.

In the Highlands of New Guinea, the expansion of the churches was dramatic. Translations of the Christian message were built on experience in other parts of the Pacific and the conviction of French and German missionaries that interaction of the new religion with the patterns of the old was essential. Their ethnography, and their ability to cope with the pressures generated by adjustment religions, helped ground the Lutheran and Roman Catholic versions of Christianity among large numbers of tribes. They saw the new religion not only as superior to the old. Education, technology, health care, and new methods of farming were seen as doors into the tantalizing wealth of the Europeans. Cautious beginnings had been made in adapting traditional arts and architecture to Christian purposes, but the more conservative Christian missions such as the Christian Brethren, Unevangelized Fields Mission, Pentecostals, and the Adventists were still inclined to identify primal religion with Satan, and to ask for both personal and social repudiation of the old order.

Fresh translations of the Christian message were also needed for film, radio, and television. Churches in Australia and New Zealand were unable to provide the financial resources needed for effective and large-scale TV programmes. Regionally they did much better with radio. Some Protestants attempted to combine Christian songs and pop music, but most Christians remained wedded to the hymnody and music of the past.

The rise in absolute numbers through migration and natural increase after 1945 placed great strains on denominational finances, but did not challenge conventional wisdom. Liturgy, doctrine, and practice were apparently satisfactory to the large majority of the population. Erection of new buildings in the burgeoning suburbs, and recruitment of clergy and ancillary workers such as deaconesses, religious educators, and missionaries, continued apace in the Protestant churches, while Catholic religious orders and dioceses built large new complexes to accommodate the increased numbers of vocations to religious life and the priesthood. In the 1950s optimism about the future was palpable in all the churches throughout the region, for even in isolated islands and villages changes in centuries-old patterns were emerging.

THE HINGE YEARS

The history of the churches up until the 1960s could be summed up as cautious modernization and sharp disagreement about the principles and boundaries of change. While a few church leaders sounded warnings about the increase of secularism and unbelief and suggested links between godlessness and immorality, statistics of religious adherence and attendance at worship, Sunday school, and youth groups suggested only a slow proportional decline until the 1960s.

From then on till 2000 political and social pressures were to lead to the dismantling of censorship, the loosening of controls on use of alcohol and gambling, the decline in prohibition of sport, entertainment, and commerce on Sundays, and a significant rise in divorce, and numbers of single-parent families, all of which eroded the century-old consensus about the foundations of religious and social order.

Nowhere was change more obvious than in the Roman Catholic Church. Massive post-war migration to Australia and high birth-rates had boosted numbers considerably. The call by John XXIII for a council to renew the church took regional Christians by surprise, for the existing recipes for success seemed assured. Catholics faced change to an extent without parallel in history, following the Second Vatican Council. The heritage of the Middle Ages in such matters as worship, attitudes to other churches and religions, formation of priests and religious, and the responsibilities expected of the laity was swiftly replaced by a new generosity of spirit and willingness for partnership. This amazed the rest of the Christian world. The implications of that change wrought from the centre of authority brought an undreamt-of pluralism into the regional Roman Catholic Church. It forced its leaders and members to deal with issues which had divided Protestants for over a century. The absence of any resolution created an ecumenism of puzzlement.

From the 1960s, Protestants were also faced with sharp challenges about the content and principles of their faith.. Doctrinal issues which had been earnestly discussed in theological faculties for over fifty years suddenly became public through the writings of John Robinson, Bishop of Woolwich. *Honest to God* was written in 1963 after careful consultation with young Anglican clergy who were wrestling with the challenges of ministry to an English population which was less inclined to identify with orthodox doctrine, Prayer Book liturgy, and time-honoured church institutions and organizations. Robinson believed that new language had to be found in order effectively to witness to Jesus and the Gospel. The little book was symptomatic of the conviction that change was needed, especially as it coincided with new styles in music and the emergence of a youth culture which wanted to question everything.

The student revolutions of the 1960s assumed that all the old had to be destroyed for something new to emerge, without seeing that the self-discipline imposed by institutions and voluntary societies could only be replaced by law, if society was not to collapse into anarchy and dictatorship by minorities. Churches which had lived by relevance and gradual acculturation suddenly found themselves left hopelessly behind by the speed of change. The old paradigms were in disarray. The bewildering variety of cultural options unleashed by the information explosion fostered the conviction that there were no boundaries for the exploration and expression of the self. Consciousness–expanding drugs, a sexual revolution built on the contraceptive pill, and a burgeoning interest in other religions made the churches and their message merely one option amongst many to consumers in the religious marketplace. The collapse of a unitive culture since the 1960s led to further privatization of religion and morality, because of dramatic expansion of cultural choices. The processes were slower in the Pacific Islands, but equally inexorable.

The acceptance of universal meaning systems had collapsed into a myriad of individual choices. Whether the process was described as privatization or secularization of belief made no difference. Purchasers of the old religious packages declined. Family religious allegiance shrank and ecumenism did not create strong new loyalties. The churches in the region were all affected by changes originating in Europe and North America. They could only respond with initiatives taken from the source of the disease. Jesus people, Pentecostals, charismatics, liberation theologians, Christian schools, all found enthusiastic supporters in the region, each claiming that they held the solution to the reclamation of Christian authority and influence. Yet while vocations to religious life and priesthood dramatically collapsed, as did candidacy for ministry and missionary service in the major Protestant churches, the number of laity studying theology grew rapidly. Many Christians who once would have taken up a religious vocation found outlets for their faith in social service.

Liberal Protestants had been predicting the demise of Evangelical and Pentecostal churches since early in the century. Suddenly they found themselves deserted by some of their most committed members, for despised subcultures whose rapid growth threatened to reduce the mainline churches to sideline churches. They had impressive structures and considerable corporate wealth, but a dramatically declining membership, which stripped away the post-war gains with bewildering speed. Advocates of pluralism for the sake of liberty of conscience found themselves unable to cope with the new situation. Writing new statements of faith solved nothing without agreed criteria. Too many leaders alienated their constituents by uncritical alliances with trendy causes. A new census phenomenon emerged in the 1970s—those listing no religious allegiance, whose numbers by the 1990s almost exactly matched those who no longer identified with the major churches. The cause of the fallout has been too little researched, but its demographic implications are alarming, for it affects all voluntary organizations. The Country Women's Association has lost two-thirds of its members since 1945. The once major Protestant churches—Anglicans, Methodists, Presbyterians, and the Uniting Church in Australia—have lost large numbers of members, especially from the crucial under-forties. Though Roman Catholics have not suffered to the same extent, their Mass attendance has also slumped, now little different from the 1830s.

The liberal synthesis cracked wide open in the 1960s and 1970s. Despite the decline of sectarianism and growth of ecumenism, liberal Christianity was unable to deal with radicals who wished wholly to remake society, government, and churches—who appealed to liberty of the individual as the supreme value. The churches' leaders were tolerant and incapable of seeing the institutional havoc the new views could wreak. Some of the changes in attitudes to mission, gender, and social justice were overdue, and can now be seen as in accord with some of the deepest imperatives of the Christian faith. But liberal and reformist leaders, whether Catholic or Protestant, were not able to deal adequately with conservative political or theological views. They often identified with the views of the moderate left in politics, ignoring the deep antipathies this roused in parts of their membership, who often felt frustrated with the inability of leaders to see that there might be a conservative political position which could be responsibly held by Christians.

Church leaders were angered when their views were called into question, especially when it was demonstrated by opposing lay analysts

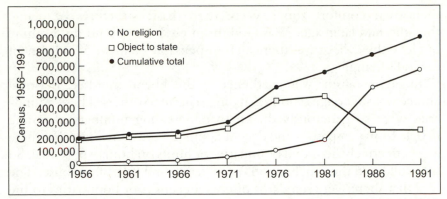

Fig. 2. New Zealand: no religion/not stated 1956–91. (*Source:* B. Patrick (ed.), *New Vision, New Zealand*, Auckland, 1993, p. 99. With the permission of Vision New Zealand.)

Table 2. *Australia: the religious 'nones'. Non-church categories in Australian Census 1911–86*

Year	No Religion		Not Stated		Population
	Persons	%	Persons	%	
1911	16,668	0.4	119,117	2.67	4,455,005
1921	28,932	0.5	92,258	1.70	5,435,734
1933	15,417	0.2	848,948	12.80	6,629,839
1947	26,328	0.4	824,824	10.88	7,579,358
1954	23,684	0.2	855,819	9.52	8,986,530
1961	37,550	0.4	1,102,929	10.50	10,508,186
1966	96,104	0.8	1,159,474	10.00	11,550,462
1971	855,676	6.7	781,247	6.10	12,755,639
1976	1,130,330	8.3	1,593,959	11.80	13,548,440
1981	1,576,718	10.8	1,595,195	10.90	14,576,330
1986	1,977,464	12.7	1,863,642	11.90	16,602,156

Source: Australian Bureau of Statistics. In T. Blomberg and P. Hughes, *Faith without the Church*, Melbourne, 1993, p. 45.

that their views in politics, economics, and ethics were seriously defective and partisan. Underneath such conflict lay a much deeper theological issue—what was the nature of Christianity? Was it a revelation which demanded a radical obedience, or was it fundamentally a human construct in which individuals could tailor the historic faith to their own comfort zone? Were there basic structures of being, thought, and language? Was God infinitely loving, who did nothing but love the evil, or was there an indispensable element of judgement in God's being?

'Judgementalism' was anathema to the liberal mindset. Personal choice was sovereign so long as it did no harm to others. These boundaries were so generously drawn that increasing numbers of young people from prosperous and decent families were convinced that there were effectively no moral boundaries or limits on human potential. So they followed their inclinations in sexuality and substance abuse. The idea that there were standards of civic decency, or boundaries to the portrayal of human behaviour in art, literature, and music, was dissolved by the subjective idiosyncrasy that such standards were only the imposition of powerful elites. Multiculturalism also undermined Anglo-Celtic religious certainties, along with the core Anglomorph culture.

By the 1980s, faced with indisputable evidence of social breakdown and the consequential financial costs, some Christians began to speak about reclaiming the past. They redrew boundary lines and repudiated the conviction that Christianity was simply the creation of multifarious individual choices. But will this response suffice? Undoing the last thirty years promises to be a long process. The task of translating interest in spirituality into Christian institutional loyalty is huge. Some churches with packaged answers have been able to attract members, or retain them. Winning back market share for historic churches from New Age philosophies is likely to be a demanding task, taxing the wisdom and energy of an ageing leadership and membership.

It is the Pentecostal churches that have grown in the changed religious climate since the 1970s. They have attracted those seeking a more authentic piety, contemporary idiom, and participatory worship. Some who rejected the churches as institutions which do not speak to their condition have partly fitted into the variety of movements loosely categorized as New Age. Others would want still to describe themselves as Christians, but they do not fit into approved denominational categories. They could perhaps be described as ultimate Protestants, liberal, tolerant to a fault, trusting in private judgement, but divorced from historic piety and worship. They are still strongly committed to the Christian ethic, but are often silent about its religious roots and do not want to impose their beliefs on their children, who too often grow up in a relativist vacuum.

By contrast a number of groups have sought to deal with these challenges by a rediscovery of traditional Christianity. The most sophisticated form of that is centred in Rome's Congregation for the Doctrine of the Faith. They are seeking to restore committed Catholicism by reassertion of classical dogma and ecclesiastical authority as a mark of Catholic identity. Appointment of conservative bishops, discipline of theologians deemed disloyal, refusal to change attitudes to homosexual behaviour, or to modify rules on priestly celibacy, let alone consider women sharing the priestly role, have already affected Catholicism in the region. That impact is likely to grow, following the decisions of the 1998 Synod of Oceania in Rome and support from well-organized lay groups hostile to modernization. Alienation will also increase, for many Catholics have been angered by renewed emphases on authority.

In the New Zealand Protestant churches, a group called Affirm has created a network of Christians who have set out to challenge liberal dominance of church bodies. Stuart Lange of the Presbyterian Church in New Zealand ran a sustained campaign to clarify the Assembly's decision on homosexuality and to make it clear that ordination of practising homosexuals was rejected. He and his allies were partially successful, but neither he nor his liberal opponents had the numbers for a decisive majority decision in 1999. From the other end of the theological spectrum the liberal leadership of the Uniting Church in Australia had likewise to admit that consensus on such a controversial matter was impossible.

Another strategy was adopted by Phillip Jensen, of St Matthias Church in Sydney, who created a startlingly effective network of like-minded Christians who sit lightly on the Anglican label in several capital cities, and are literally a church within a church. His congregation has provided the majority of students for Moore College for a number of years and his influence on students at the University of New South Wales through the Christian Union has been very significant.

Liberal responses to the new religious situation have included the Sea of Faith networks, which explore the significance of all religions, and the Ephesus Group in New Zealand, which produces thoughtful booklets. No one has emerged to give a strong critique of the assumptions of contemporary culture comparable to Lesslie Newbigin in Britain. The Deepsight Trust founded by Dr Harold Turner in Auckland is seeking to provide that kind of long-term critique. Turner has had a remarkable career as Presbyterian minister in Dunedin, and as an authority on West African independent churches and new religious movements, working in Aberdeen and Birmingham. Returning for a second retirement in New Zealand, he has taken issue with the liberal fashions, while insisting on the importance of informed scholarship.

The real impact of adaptation to modernity has to be investigated in the sermons preached across the church spectrum each week and over a year, not just for what they say, but for what they emphasize and what they omit from historic Christianity. Perceptions of the nature of God have changed, moving towards an always loving and accepting deity, a psychotherapist in the sky. The great themes of atonement and judgement, hopes for a new world and life-changing encounter with the transcendent One who elects to salvation, have been secularized and privatized, so that the Church and its sacraments are no longer deemed necessary to the Christian life. These trends are also observable in deliberately conservative groups as well as in the self-consciously relevant and modern, for few now assume that the historic message of Christianity is an essential component of public life. Conservative Christians have also changed the historic contours of their faith by selective emphasis on the past.

These tendencies can be identified in the nineteenth century, but they have gathered momentum dramatically since the 1960s. The house of faith has not only been renovated from within, its external appearance has changed. Some churches have been more successful than others in living out Christian Tradition. The Orthodox churches, which are now a significant minority in Australia, with almost 4 per cent of the population, because of massive migration, have yet to face the consequences of living with pluralism, a more subtle and dangerous opponent than the persecution with which they have lived for centuries.

Similarly, the Pacific churches have retained their heritage in countless villages which have been little touched by modernity. The spread of migration, education, new religious movements, and media culture indicate clearly that the young are attracted by the new and impatient at the conservatism of their elders, who resist change in order to protect what is holy. The effects of new sectarian options, especially Pentecostalism, have yet to be fully evaluated. Many young people find it attractive because it corresponds to the media culture, with a strong emphasis on entertainment. It also promises a life free from the destructive elements of alcohol, violence, and promiscuity which

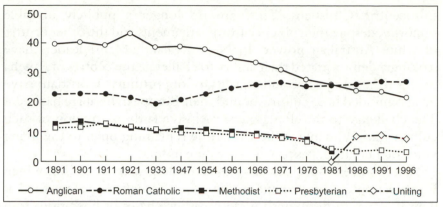

Fig. 3. Australia: major denominations as a percentage of all religious affiliates, 1891–1996. (*Source:* I. Breward, *A History of the Australian Churches*, Sydney, 1993, p. 235. With the permission of the author.)

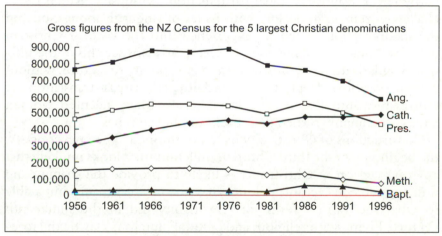

Fig. 4. New Zealand: major denominations' changing affiliation, 1956–96. (*Source:* B. Patrick (ed.), *New Vision, New Zealand*, Auckland, 1993, p. 98. With the permission of Vision New Zealand.)

characterize the urban cultures in rapidly growing Pacific towns, like Port Moresby, Honiara, Lae, Suva, or Auckland.

Aboriginal communities also have suffered the same accelerated destruction since the 1970s. They have also produced impressive leaders whose ability to reinterpret law and culture, often in conjunction with a vital adaptation of Christianity and skilful use of the media and courts in pursuit of justice over land, has dismayed and angered

Eurocentric Christians. They are no longer a publicly invisible minority, despite their absence from parliaments and the other centres of white Australian power. In New Zealand, Maori leaders have strikingly demonstrated their ability to challenge the centres of Pakeha power to secure justice and equality of opportunity. Christians have been reminded how culture-bound their European heritage has been. The challenge to develop a more inclusive faith in a region of such cultural variety, while at the same time remaining open to the living voice of Tradition, has proved very demanding.

That has been especially obvious in dealing with feminism, which became a potent movement by the 1970s, sometimes categorized as Third Wave, to distinguish it from earlier phases of liberation from patriarchy. Though it has some Christian roots, not least in the prophetic rage of Germaine Greer, whose Catholic education must not be ignored in evaluating her feminism, its challenge has been only partly felt in claims for equal participation in ministry. Much larger challenges remain in dealing with issues of language about God and the incorporation of female experience into the core of Christian belief and practice. Some conservative Christians see this as the ultimate secularization of Christianity and its captivity to culture, without recognizing how deeply their own faith reflects past translations of Christianity into European cultural terms. Many talented women have consequently turned their backs on the churches.

Constructions of Christianity have not finished. They never do. At the beginning of the third Christian millennium, it looks unlikely that any one version of Christianity is likely to provide the shaping and unifying force in Oceanic cultures over the new century, comparable to what the various forms of Christianity did in the nineteenth century. Living with religious and cultural pluralism may be the foreseeable future, but individualism should not be taken as a final solution. Even the short history of Christianity in the region indicates how the hopes of the powerful are subverted by the unexpected, for the God of the Bible is full of surprises. Catholicity has always demanded more inclusivity than Christians have been willing to grant. Their notions of unity are too earth- and time-bound, confused with uniformity rather than the richly textured divine variety of language, religious experience, and culture which is the most striking feature of the region. Churches which fail to adapt suffer from the powerful weapons of switching or drop-out. The Uniting Church suffered a 12 per cent attendance drop between 1991 and 1996.

Table 3. *Australian weekly attendance at church compared to religious identification*

	No. of people (Census)	Attendance in an average week (NCLS/CCLS)	Per cent attending of people identifying (%)
Anglican	3,909,324	181,500	5
Baptist	295,178	103,800	35
Brethren	22,063	12,000	54
Catholic	4,798,950	875,000	18
Congregational	6,186	1,700	27
Church of the Nazarene	1,619	1,200	74
Churches of Christ	75,023	42,000	56
Lutheran	249,989	44,100	18
Pentecostal	174,720	183,000	105
Presbyterian & Reformed	675,534	43,200	6
Salvation Army	74,145	30,100	41
Seventh-day Adventist	52,655	35,500	67
Uniting	1,334,917	142,900	11
Wesleyan Methodist	3,700	4,100	111

Source: 1996 National Church Life Survey, 1996 Catholic Church Life Survey, and 1996 Census of Population and Housing.
Note: 'Pentecostal' includes estimates for non-participating Pentecostal denominations.

Table 4. *New Zealand: Who goes where*

	1991 Census	1991/2 attendance	Attend/ Census	Attend/ NZ popl'n
GROUP A: mainline				
Anglican	732,000	44,500	6%	1.4%
Methodist	138,700	16,000	12%	0.5%
Presbyterian	540,700	54,300	10%	1.7%
Other	19,800	6,000	30%	0.2%
Sub-totals	1,431,200	120,800	8%	0.2%

Table 4. (*cont.*):

	1991 Census	1991/2 attendance	Attend/ Census	Attend/ NZ popl'n
GROUP B: baptistic				
Baptist Union	70,200	31,000	44%	0.9%
Churches of Christ	4,900	2,800	57%	0.1%
Seventh day Adventist	13,000	7,000	54%	0.2%
Salvation Army	16,800	7,500	45%	0.2%
Brethren	20,000	15,000	75%	0.5%
Other	400	3,200	800%	0.1%
Sub-totals	125,300	66,500	53%	2%
GROUP C: pentecostal				
Assemblies of God	17,200	22,000	128%	0.7%
Apostolic	6,800	9,700	143%	0.3%
Elim	2,400	5,800	242%	0.2%
Other	21,500	20,800	97%	0.6%
Sub-totals	47,900	58,300	122%	2%
GROUP D: catholic				
Roman Catholic	497,700	124,500	25%	4%
Other	4,300			
Sub-total	502,000			
Totals A–D	2,106,400	371,600	18%	11%
GROUP E: other				
Ratana and Ringatu	56,000			
Other 'christian'	105,200			
Other religion	122,400			
No religion or object	979,000			

Sub-total 1,267,500 plus A–D above = 3,373,900

Source: B. Patrick (ed.), *New Vision, New Zealand* (Auckland, 1993) 123.

If Australasian Christianity has anything distinctive to offer to the worldwide Christian movement it must have inclusivity which values tribalism, oral culture, and land as a spiritual resource, while offering the wealth of the Catholic heritage to those who wish to build communities and nations which are more than local. The task of translation and correction of partial insight is a never-ending one. Common prayer may be an impossible dream in a highly plural society with no will to enforce religious or ideological conformity or intrusively to make windows in souls.

Yet Aboriginal, Melanesian, and Polynesian tribalism and intense sense of place have striking commonalities. There are similar signs of search for commonalities and meaning in our restless electronic and capitalist culture, but as yet the Christians of the region have not convincingly connected these with the great themes of the Christian heritage and personal piety. They should not look to the Christians of Europe and North America for the answers, though their voices cannot be ignored, because they are so important in world Christianity. Christianity in this region has also to take account of the presence of all the major world religions.

The countries of the region have been strongly influenced by Christianity, but its impact should not just be measured by European and North American standards. Even those groups and individuals who reject formal association with Christianity value the religious toleration which emerged from the struggle of Catholics and Protestants against an Establishment mentality, and also from the Catholic struggle against an unjust Protestant hegemony. Sectarianism may have left a bitter legacy, but also fostered fresh attempts to construct new Christianities. The virtue of compassion still flourishes in ways that indicate a residual Christianity is still formative. So does the conviction that politics, justice, and morality are connected. Powerful though individualism is, there are still deep desires for realistic community which owe much to Christian memories. Religious and political liberty are still cherished in ways that are indebted to Catholic and Reformed versions of Christianity, with their long heritage of resistance to injustice and passion for a new community. The foundations of law remain deeply influenced by the Judaeo-Christian heritage.

Though these convictions can be described as secular as well as Christian, the churches still have a vital role to play in offering alternatives to those proposed by current powerbrokers. Within the courts, media, and voluntary organizations of many kinds they bear witness to the importance of balancing pluralism and overarching convictions about unity, which demand sacrifice of individual interests for the common good. Settling for only one translation of the Gospel is a terrible sin, just as is forgetfulness about the capacity of the best to be corrupted by human sin and evil. Much remains to be explored in the relationship of Gospel and culture, with organizations like Zadok in Melbourne, the New Zealand Christian Brethren Research Association, and the Deepsight Trust beginning this task, along with the Melanesian Institute in Goroka.

In a number of the Pacific Islands, the majority status of the churches, and their cultural importance, gives them major political impact and dangerous power as guardians of traditional identity and constructors of the future. Drawing fixed boundaries between the sacred and the secular distorts perception. Aborigines, Melanesians, and Polynesians have a much more holistic view. That makes generalizations about the region perilous, because there is so much variety. Even though the Australian and New Zealand churches do not have the direct political influence they have had at some periods of the last two centuries, Christian influences still impinge through deep-rooted archetypes, the convictions of individual parliamentarians, and their ability to form networks such as the Lyons Forum in the Australian federal parliament. Formal parties such as the Christian Coalition in New Zealand or the Call to Australia attract only small votes. The decreased influence of leading clergy and bishops is not the end of a Christian society, merely a sign that regional Christian witness takes different forms than European ones.

In Australasia the asset-rich churches continue to be major players in education and social service in partnership with government, spending huge sums of money annually and providing many jobs. The Catholic Education Office in Melbourne had a budget of over $1 billion (A) for 500 schools in 1999. Anglicare in Sydney had an income of $42 million (A) in 1998—much from government contracts, as is true of most church welfare agencies. Locally, countless Christians serve with community volunteers in humanitarian agencies and voluntary organizations, which greatly enrich the quality of community life. It is physically and financially impossible for governments and non-government agencies to meet all the demands for welfare services to the needy. The churches continue to inspire individuals and groups for such service, and to sustain their energy through worship and fellowship. Much of this civic activism is so normal that it is taken for granted by the community and exploited by governments.

The institutional fragility of the churches in some parts of the region, and the ageing of active members, will inevitably diminish the possibilities of community service on the present scale, unless there is a major influx of younger people shaped by encounter with the risen Christ and prepared to serve sacrificially without financial reward. Currently only 20 per cent of Australians are involved in volunteer activity. Privatized belief and morality, electronic communication and the self-protection possible for the rich do not provide the human care necessary in any truly civilized society, where the quality of life of the least important citizens is the acid test of the priorities of the rich and powerful. Paradoxically, an atomized society benefits from a strong religious community to carry the heritage of the past, and to challenge the self-interest of the present. New forms of regional and religious unity have developed, but have been unable to counter resurgent tribalism.

This region has a different religious ethos from North America, even though that influence is powerful. It may yet move in the direction of a marketplace of competing religious options as the electronic revolution bites deeper and further undermines long-term social and religious commitment. New voices and options continue to emerge, indicating that the Christian tradition still has creative vitality and voices which are heard amidst so many competing claims to religious authority. Even if absolute numbers are lower than attendances at sporting events and cinemas, they are large. Styles of leadership have become more consensual, even anonymous, on national and regional issues. Explanatory models of Christian cultural influence taken from European history can only lead to nostalgia for a world that never was here, except in some of the Pacific Islands which still have strongly theocratic and sacred societies. Political and social leverage is no longer related to size, but to ability to shape opinion and apply pressures to sensitive spots in the body politic through the media.

In two centuries, Christians of varied convictions have built surprisingly effective local and national institutions which have carried the Christian message in good times and bad, along with fluctuating levels of public involvement. Disappearance of legal establishment in the nineteenth century has forced a certain modesty on Christian leaders, instead of reliance on inherited privilege and status. Influence has not been so obvious at the level of high culture, but in local community and folk religion Christianity has exercised considerable influence, even if historians and social scientists have not been able to delineate it very accurately.

Writing history from below with careful attention to tribe, village, and congregation will help Christians in the region to see that there is more to Christian history than the activities of the powerful and the decisions of church courts. Translations of the Christian message have varied in their effectiveness and there are encouraging signs that Christians in the region are beginning to recognize their identity within the world movement. Searching questions will need to be asked and answered about the principles and embodiment of translation if the rich variety of the region is to be unitive and not divisive. The story of the last fifty years indicates that the task has begun. To sustain it will demand both freedom and growing deeper into the Christian heritage.

BIBLIOGRAPHY

There are a number of useful resources for Australia in I. Breward, *History of the Australian Churches* (Sydney, 1993), 257–8. For New Zealand P. J. Lineham's regularly updated *New Zealand: A Religious Bibliography* (Palmerston North, 1993–) is very comprehensive. J. Thawley, *Australia and South Pacific Islands Bibliography* (Lanham, 1997) updates the classic older bibliographies such as P. O'Reilly's works. Primary source material on individual Pacific Islands is found in Pacific Manuscripts Bureau, *Printed Document Series: Short Title Catalogue and Index to Microfilms* (Canberra, 1998). Anglican material is calendared by R. Teale et al., *Anglicans in the Antipodes* (Westport, 1999).

The *Australasian Religion Index* (Wagga Wagga, 1989–) covers almost all the significant religious periodicals, while the *Yearbook of Australian Churches* (Melbourne, 1991–) has an annual bibliography. The Bureau of Immigration and Multicultural Affairs, Canberra, published in 1996–7 a useful series, *Religious Community Profiles*, on all the major Australian religious bodies. They are edited by P. J. Hughes. Important material on New Age groups is covered by H. Carey, *Believing in Australia* (Sydney, 1996) and R. Ellwood, *Islands of the Dawn* (Honolulu, 1993). G. Bouma, *Many Religions, All Australian* (Melbourne, 1996) and G. Goosen, *Religion in Australian Culture* (Sydney, 1997) update earlier sociological studies. From a different angle P. Kaldor et al., *Build My Church* and *Taking Stock* (Adelaide, 1999), analyse the results of the National Church Life Survey. A. Webster et al., *Values and Beliefs in New Zealand* (Palmerston North, 1992) made comparable comments on New Zealand material, which needs to be supplemented by B. Patrick (ed.), *New Vision, New Zealand* (2 vols., Auckland, 1993, 1997) and by P. Donovan, *Religions of New Zealand* (Palmerston North, 1990). Useful and succinct historical information on important individuals is found in *The Australian Dictionary of Biography* (Melbourne, 1966–) and the *Dictionary of New Zealand Biography* (Wellington, 1990–), and B. Dickey, *Australian Dictionary of Evangelical Biography* (Sydney, 1993). A. Turner (ed.), *Historical Dictionary of Papua New Guinea* (Metuchen, 1994) makes a beginning on the very complex history of that country. Unfortunately, the bibliographies in D. Denoon et al., *The Cambridge History of Pacific Islanders* (Cambridge, 1997) are very brief.

J. Garrett's three magisterial volumes on Christianity in Oceania have very thorough bibliographies, which I have occasionally supplemented. *To Live Among the Stars*, *Footsteps in the Sea*, and *Where Nets were Cast* (Suva, 1982–97), are indispensable reading. A. K. Davidson, *Christianity in Aotearoa,* 2nd edn. (Wellington, 1997) has a full bibliography, as does P. O'Farrell, *The Catholic Church and Community*, 3rd edn. (Sydney, 1992). M. King, *God's Farthest Outpost* (Auckland, 1997) and R. Wiltgen, *The Founding of the Roman Catholic Church in Oceania* (Canberra, 1979) should now be supplemented by F. Angleviel, *Les missions à Wallis et Futuna au XIXème siècle* (Bordeaux, 1994); P. Hodée, *Tahiti 1834–1984* (Papeete 1983); the books by G. Delbos, *The Mustard Seed* (Port Moresby, 1985), *L'Eglise Catholique en Nouvelle Calédonie* (Paris, 1993), *Nous Mourons de te voir!* (Paris, 1993); and J. Waldersee, *Neither Eagles nor Saints* (Sydney, 1995). P. Steffen, *Die Anfänge der Rheinischer, Neuendetteslauer und Steyler Missionsarbeit in Neuguinea* (Rome, 1993) is a unique comparative study.

H. Wagner and H. Reiner (eds.), *The Lutheran Church in Papua New Guinea* (Adelaide, 1987) and D. Wetherell, *Reluctant Mission: The Anglican Church in Papua New Guinea, 1891–1942* (Brisbane, 1977) have valuable bibliographies, as does D. Hilliard, *God's Gentlemen* (Brisbane, 1978); A. Tippett, *Solomon Islands Christianity* (New York, 1967); B. Burt, *Tradition and Christianity* (Chur, 1994); H. Laracy, *Marists and Melanesians* (Canberra, 1976). M. Ernst, *The Role of Social Change in the Rise and Development of New Religious Groups in the Pacific Islands* (Hamburg, 1996) has valuable material.

MANUSCRIPT SOURCES

Alexander Turnbull Library, Wellington
Battye Library, Perth
Fryer Library, University of Queensland, Brisbane
La Trobe Library, Melbourne
Lutheran Archives, Lae
Mitchell Library, Sydney
Moore College, Sydney
Moravian Archives, Herrnhut, Germany
Northern Territory Archives, Darwin
Oxley Library, Brisbane
St Mark's Library, Canberra
Taranaki Archives, New Plymouth

AUSTRALASIA AND GENERAL

Monographs and Articles

BARKER, J. (ed.), *Christianity in Oceania* (Lanham, 1990).

BURRIDGE, K., *'In the Way': A Study of Christian Missionary Endeavours* (Vancouver, 1991).

CHENOWETH, V., *Sing-Sing: Communal Singing and Dancing* (Christchurch, 1999).

CROCOMBE, R. G., et al., *The New South Pacific* (Wellington, 1973).

CROCOMBE, R. G., et al., *Polynesian Missions in the Pacific* (Suva, 1992).

DOUGLAS, B., *Across the Great Divide* (Amsterdam, 1998).

ERNST, M., *Winds of Change: Rapidly Growing Religious Groups in the Pacific Islands* (Suva, 1994).

—— *The Role of Social Change in the Rise and Development of New Religious Groups in the Pacific Islands* (Hamburg, 1996).

FINAU, M., et al., *Island Churches: Challenge and Change* (Suva, 1992).

GRIMSHAW, P., 'Problems in writing women's history in the Pacific', *PS* 15 (1992) 156–70.

JANSSEN, H., 'Neue religiose Bewegungen in Melanesia', *ZMW* 77 (1993) 35–49.

MOORE, A. C., *Arts in the Religions of the Pacific* (London, 1994).

MUNRO, D. and THORNLEY, A. (eds.), *The Covenant Makers: Islander Missionaries in the Pacific* (Suva, 1996).

NOKISE, U. F., 'The role of the LMS Samoan missionaries in the evangelisation of the South-west Pacific', Ph.D. thesis (Canberra, 1992).

RICKARDS, R. S., *In their Own Tongues: The Bible in the Pacific* (Canberra, 1996).

SMITH, L. T., *Decolonizing Methodologies: Research and Indigenous Peoples* (Dunedin, 1999).

STELEY, D., 'Unfinished: The Seventh-Day Adventist mission in the South Pacific, excluding Papua New Guinea, 1886–1986', Ph.D. thesis (Auckland, 1989).

SWAIN, T. and TROMPF, G. (eds.), *The Religions of Oceania* (London, 1995).

TEALE, R., WITHYCOMBE, R., FRAPPELL, L., and NOBBS, R. (eds.), *Anglicans in the Antipodes* (Westport 1999).

THOMAS, N., *In Oceania: Visions, Artifacts, Histories* (Durham, North Carolina, 1997).

THOMPSON, R., *Australia in the Pacific Islands in the Twentieth Century* (Melbourne, 1999).

VAN DER HEYDEN, U. and LIEBAU, H. (eds.), *Missionsgeschichte* (Berlin, 1996).

WHITEHOUSE, H., 'Strong words and forceful winds: religious experience and political process in Melanesia', *Oceania* 65 (1994) 40–58.

AUSTRALIA

Manuscripts

National Library, Canberra
Australian Inland Mission Papers (1908–77) MS 5574.
T. S. Forsaith Diaries MS 3369.

Northern Territory Archives
UCNA Standing Committee Minutes 1971–7 MS 5143.

Printed Primary Sources

GOOD SAMARITAN SISTERS, *Letters of John Bede Polding* (2 vols., Sydney, 1994–6).
KERR N. (ed.), *Australian Catholic Bishops' Statements since Vatican II* (Sydney, 1985).
NEWPORT, M. (ed.), *Australian Catholic Bishops' Statements 1985–95* (Sydney, 1997).

Monographs and Articles

ANON., 'Mary MacKillop number', *ACR* 72 (1995).
ARMITAGE, A., *Comparing the Policy of Aboriginal Assimilation: Australia, Canada, New Zealand* (Vancouver, 1995).
BALLIS, P., *Leaving Adventist Ministry* (Westport, 1999).
BLACK, A. (ed.), *Religion in Australia* (Sydney, 1991).
BLACKET, J., *Fire in the Outback* (Sutherland, 1997).
BOLAND, T. P., *Thomas Carr, Archbishop of Melbourne* (Melbourne, 1997).
BRENNAN, F., *One Land One Nation* (Brisbane, 1995).
BUCH, N., 'American influences on Protestantism in Queensland since 1945', Ph.D. thesis (Brisbane, 1994).
CAREY, H., 'Women's peculiar mission to the heathen', in M. Hutchinson and E. Campion (eds.), *Long Patient Struggle* (Sydney, 1994).
—— 'Companions in the wilderness? Missionary wives in colonial Australia', *JRH* 19 (1995) 227–48.
CATHOLIC BISHOPS' CONFERENCE, *Woman and Man* (Melbourne, 1999).
CHANT, B., *Studying Pentecost in Australia* (Sydney, 1994).
COLLINS, E., 'Hardly a proper thing for genteel children: education through Sabbath Schools and Bands of Hope in nineteenth century Victoria', M.Ed. thesis (Melbourne, 1989).
COOPER, A., *A Little By Ourselves: Oblates of Mary Immaculate Australia 1884–1994* (Melbourne, 1994).
CUNNINGHAM, A. E., '"Under the Banner of the Cross": Catholic Episcopal

and Consultorial Relations in New South Wales 1865–85', Ph.D. thesis (Sydney, 1998).

DAVIES, P., *The Mind of God* (New York, 1992).

DENIS, S. M. (ed.), *Mother Mary's Circulars to the Sisters* (Sydney, 1976).

DEVENISH, B., *Man of Energy and Compassion* (Fremantle, 1994).

DUKE, G., 'Science, biblical criticism, and the Protestant churches in Victoria', Th.D. thesis (Melbourne, 1999).

EDWARDS, W., *Moravian Aboriginal Missions in Australia, 1850–1919* (Adelaide, 1999.

EMILSEN, S. and W. (eds.), *Marking Twenty Years: The Uniting Church in Australia 1977–1997* (Sydney, 1997).

EMILSEN, W., ' "The Vision was Born in my Spirit": The Origins of the Uniting Aboriginal and Islander Christian Congress', *Uniting Church Studies* 5 (1999) 33–52.

FOALE, M. T., *The Josephite Story* (Sydney, 1989).

FRAPPELL, R. M., 'Anglican ministry to the unsettled rural districts of Australia *c.*1890–1940', Ph.D. thesis (Sydney, 1991).

—— 'The Australian Bush Brotherhoods and their English origins', *JEH* 47 (1996) 82–97.

GARDINER, P., *Mary MacKillop* (Adelaide, 1994).

GOODEN, R. M., 'Awakened women: initial formative influences among Australasian Baptist women in overseas mission, 1864–1913', M.Th. thesis (Melbourne, 1998).

GREEN, N., *The Forrest River Massacres* (Fremantle, 1995).

GRIFFIN, G. M., *They Came to Care* (Melbourne, 1993).

HABEL, N., *Reconciliation* (Melbourne, 1999).

HALSE, C., 'The Rev. Ernest Gribble and race relations in Northern Australia', Ph.D. thesis (Brisbane, 1992).

HARRIS, J., *One Blood,* 2nd edn. (Sutherland, 1994).

—— *We Wish We'd Done More* (Adelaide, 1998).

HILLIARD, D., 'God in the suburbs: the religious culture of Australian cities in the 1950s', *AHS* 97 (1991) 399–419.

—— 'The Anglo-Catholic tradition in Australian Anglicanism', *SMR* 158 (1994) 14–22.

—— 'The church, family and sexuality in Australia in the 1950s', *AHS* 109 (1997) 133–56.

—— 'The ties that used to bind: a fresh look at the history of Australian Anglicanism', *Pacifica* 11 (1998) 265–80.

—— The Anglican schism at Port Lincoln 1928–55', *JHSSA* 23 (1995) 51–69.

—— 'Sydney Anglicans and homosexuality', *Journal of Homosexuality* 33 (1997) 101–23.

—— 'The religious crisis of the 1960s', *JRH* 21 (1997) 209–27.

HOLDEN, C., *From Tories at Prayer to Socialists at Mass: A History of St Peter's, Eastern Hill, Melbourne* (Melbourne, 1997).

—— *Ritualist on a Tricycle* (Perth, 1997).

HOWARD-WRIGHT, M., *Hearts Hands and Voices: Celebrating the Diocese of Perth Centenary of Mothers' Union* (Perth, 1999).

HOWE, R. and SWAIN, S.,*The Challenges of the City: Centenary History of Wesley Central Mission* (Melbourne, 1993).

HUNT, A., *This Side of Heaven* (Adelaide, 1985).

HUTCHINSON, M. and CAMPION, E. (eds.), *Long, Patient Struggle* (Sydney, 1998).

HUTCHINSON, M. and CAMPION, E. (eds.), *Revisioning Australian Colonial Christianity* (Sydney, 1994).

HUTCHINSON, M. and PIGGIN, S. (eds)., *Reviving Australia* (Sydney, 1994).

HUTCHINSON, M. and TRELOAR, G. R. (eds.), *Australian Christianity and Culture* (Sydney, 1998).

HUTCHINSON, M. and TRELOAR, G. R. (eds.), *This Gospel shall be Preached* (Sydney, 1998).

HUTCHINSON, M. and TRELOAR, G. R. (eds.), *Ties that Bind: Australian and Canadian Communities of Faith* (Sydney, 1998).

INGLIS, K., *Sacred Places* (Melbourne, 1999).

JARRATT, P., *Ted Noffs* (Sydney, 1997).

JUDD, S. and CABLE, K. J., *Sydney Anglicans* (Sydney, 1987).

KABIDA, J., 'The Methodist Mission and the emerging Aboriginal Church in Arnhem Land 1916–77', Ph.D. thesis (Darwin, 1998).

KALDOR, P., *Winds of Change* (Sydney, 1994).

—— *Shaping the Future* (Adelaide, 1997).

KALDOR, P. et al., *Build My Church: Trends and Possibilities for Australian Churches* (Adelaide, 1999).

KALDOR, P. et al., *Taking Stock: A Profile of Australian Church Attenders* (Adelaide, 1999).

KERR, A., *Guided Journey* (Aynderoo, 1999).

KIDD, A. P., 'The Brisbane episcopate of St Clair Donaldson, 1904–21', Ph.D. thesis (Brisbane, 1996).

—— 'The Brisbane episcopate of William Wand', MA thesis (Brisbane, 1990).

LACK, J. (ed.), *Anzac Remembered: Selected Writings of K. S. Inglis* (Melbourne, 1998).

LAKE, M., *Getting Equal: The History of Australian Feminism* (Sydney, 1999).

LAMB, M., *Going it Alone* (Sydney, 1995).

LAMB, P., *The Conscience of the Church: John Stoward Moyes* (Armidale, 1997).

LILBURNE, G., 'Australian theology: Protestant contributions', *Colloquium* 28/2 (1996) 19–30.

LINES, W. J., *All Consuming Passion* (Sydney, 1994).

Loos, N., *Edward Koiki Mabo* (Brisbane, 1996).

Luttrell, J. J., 'Norman Thomas, Cardinal Gilroy as Archbishop of Sydney', Ph.D. thesis (Sydney, 1998).

McGinley, M. R., *Dynamic of Hope: Institutes of Women Religious* (Sydney, 1996).

McIntosh, I., 'Anthropology, self-determination and Aboriginal belief in the Christian God', *Oceania* 67 (1997) 273–88.

Manley, K., *Shapers of our Australian Baptist Identity* (Melbourne, 1998).

Massam, K., *Sacred Threads* (Sydney, 1997).

Moore, R. K., *All Western Australia is My Parish* (Perth, 1996).

Moses, J. A., 'Canon David Garland and the Anzac tradition', *SMR* (1993) 12–21.

O'Brien, A., 'A church full of men: masculinism and the church in Australian history', *AHS* 102 (1993) 437–57.

—— 'The case of the cultivated man: class, gender and the Church of the Establishment in Interwar Australia', *AHS* 107 (1996) 242–56.

—— 'Sins of omission? Women in the history of Australian religion and religion in the history of Australian women', *AHS* 108 (1997) 277–93.

O'Connor, T. M., 'Wesleyan Methodism and the paedogogics of Christian formation in Victoria 1836–1901', Ph.D. thesis (Melbourne, 1995).

Orpwood, M., *Chappo* (Sydney, 1997).

Pattel-Gray, A. (ed.), *Martung Upah: Black and White Australians Seeking Partnership* (Melbourne, 1996).

Phillips, W. W., *James Jefferis* (Melbourne, 1993).

Piggin, S., *Evangelical Christianity in Australia* (Melbourne, 1996).

Porter, B. (ed.), *Melbourne Anglicans* (Melbourne, 1997).

Rainbow Spirit Elders, *Rainbow Spirit Theology* (Melbourne, 1997).

Rajowski, P., *Linden Girl* (Perth, 1995).

Reynolds, H., *Why Weren't We Told* (Melbourne, 1999).

Ritchie, C. I., *Not to be Ministered Unto . . . The Story of Presbyterian Deaconesses Trained in Melbourne* (Melbourne, 1998).

Rintoul, S., *The Wailing: A National Black Oral History* (Melbourne, 1993).

Ryan, L., *Aboriginal Tasmanians,* 2nd edn. (Sydney, 1996).

Santamaria, B. A., *Memoirs* (Melbourne, 1997).

Sharpe, N., *Stars of Tagai* (Canberra, 1993).

Simmons, H. L. N., *Orthodoxy in Australia* (Brookline, 1986).

Swain, T., *A Place for Strangers* (Melbourne, 1993).

—— *Interpreting Aboriginal Religion* (Adelaide, 1995).

Theobald, M., *Knowing Women: The Origins of Women's Education in Nineteenth Century Australia* (Cambridge, 1996).

Thompson, R. C., *Religion in Australia* (Melbourne, 1994).

Treloar, G. R. (ed.), *The Furtherance of Religious Beliefs* (Sydney, 1997).

TRESS, N., *Caught for Life: A Story of the Anglican Deaconess Order in Australia* (Araluen, 1993).

TURNER, N., *Ways of Belonging: Stories of Catholics 1910–90* (Melbourne, 1993).

WALSH, K., *Yesterday's Seminary* (Sydney, 1998).

WARD, G., *Unna you Fullas* (Broome, 1991).

WEST, J., *Daughters of Freedom* (Sutherland, 1997).

WETHERELL, D., 'From Samuel McFarlane to Stephen Davies: Continuity and change in the Torres Strait Island churches', *PS* 16 (1993) 1–32.

WILLIAMSON, R. K. (ed.), *Stages on the Way* (Melbourne, 1993).

WILSON, B., *Reasons of the Heart* (Sutherland, 1998).

WILSON, D., *The Cost of Crossing Bridges* (Melbourne, 1998).

WINDSOR, G., *Heaven Where the Bachelors Sit* (Brisbane, 1996).

YARWOOD, A. T., *Samuel Marsden,* 2nd edn. (Melbourne, 1996).

YENGOYAN, A. A., 'Religion, morality and prophetic traditions', in R.W. Hefner (ed.), *Conversion to Christianity* (Berkeley, 1993).

CONGREGATIONAL AND PARISH HISTORIES

ANON., *Centenary History of Zion Lutheran Congregation* (Walla Walla, 1969).

CABLE, K. and ANNABLE, R., *St James 1824–1999* (Sydney, 1999).

HIMBURY, D. M., *The Theatre of the Word* (Melbourne, 1993).

McGRADE, R. M., *Death of a Parish* (Benalla, 1995).

SWEETMAN, R., *Spire on the Hill* (Auckland, 1996).

COOK ISLANDS

BUCK, P., *Mangaia and the Mission* (Suva, 1993).

CROCOMBE, R. and M., *Cannibals and Converts* (Suva, 1983).

SIIKALA, J., *Cult and Conflict in Tropical Polynesia* (Helsinki, 1982).

—— *Akatokamanava* (Auckland, 1991).

TANGATATUTAI, T., 'Ministry to migrants: a case study in Cook Islands Christians in Melbourne from the early 80s to the present', M.Min. thesis (Melbourne, 1993).

FIJI AND ROTUMA

CHAND, Y. and NAIDU, V., *Fiji: Coups, Crises and Reconciliation 1987–97* (Suva, 1997).
FISON, L., *Old Sephania* (London, 1896).
RATAWA, W., 'Fijian Methodist music', *SPJMS* 13 (1995) 11–25.
THORNLEY, A., 'Fijian Methodism, 1874–1945', Ph.D. thesis (Canberra, 1979).
—— *From When to Where* (Suva, 1997).
TUWERE, I. S., 'Making sense of *vanua* (land) in the Fijian context', Th.D. thesis (Melbourne, 1992).
VULAMO, T. (ed.), *Mei Kia Ki Vei: Stories of Methodism in Fiji and Rotuma* (Suva, 1996).

FRENCH POLYNESIA

NICOLE, J., *Au pied de L'Écriture* (Papeete, 1988).
SAURA, B., *Les bûchers de Faaite* (Papeete, 1990).
—— *Politique et Religion à la Tahiti* (Pirae, 1993).
TOULLELAN, P. Y., *Missionaires au quotidien à Tahiti* (Leiden, 1995).
ZORN, J. F., *Le grand Siècle d'une Mission Protestante* (Karthala, 1993).

NEW CALEDONIA, WALLIS AND FUTUNA

DAUPHINE, J., *Christianisation et politique en Nouvelle Calédonie au XIXème siècle* (Noumea, 1996).
IZOULET, J., *Mekete Poun* (Paris, 1996).
TJIBAOU, J.-M. and MISSOTTE, P., *Kanake* (Papeete, 1978).
—— *La Présence Kanak* (Paris, 1996).
WEINGARTNER, R. (ed.), *Nouvelle Calédonie* (Geneva, 1994).

NEW ZEALAND

Printed Primary Sources

CHOUVET, J. M., *A Marist Missionary in New Zealand* (Whakatane, 1985).
HOGAN, H. (ed.), *Renate's Journey* (Christchurch, 1994).

PORTER, F. (ed.) and McDONALD, C. (eds.), *My Hand will Write what my Heart Dictates* (Auckland, 1996).

TUNNICLIFF, S. (ed.), *Selected Letters of Mary Hobhouse* (Wellington, 1992).

Monographs and Articles

ALLAN, V., *Nurse Maude* (Christchurch, 1996).

ARNOLD, R., 'A shepherded sheep: a harrowed toad: an experience of Presbyterian lay protest', *Stimulus* 5/2 (1997) 6–18.

BELICH, J., *Making of Peoples* (Auckland, 1996).

BOLITHO, E., 'Women in the New Zealand churches', *Stimulus* 1/3–4 (1993) 25–32, 28–37.

BUTT, P., *The Cross and the Stars* (Wellington, 1993).

CARRELL, B., *Moving between Times* (Auckland, 1998).

CHRISTCHURCH METHODIST MISSION, *Your Kingdom Come on Earth: Methodist Social Concerns in New Zealand* (Christchurch, 1999).

CROSBY, R., *The Musket Wars* (Auckland, 1999).

CULBERTSON, P. (ed.), *Counselling Issues and South Pacific Communities* (Auckland, 1997).

DAVIDSON, A. K., *Selwyn's Legacy: The College of St John the Evangelist* (Auckland, 1993).

EVANS, J., 'Church–state relations in New Zealand 1940–90', Ph.D. thesis (Dunedin, 1993).

FRASER, L., *From Tara to Holyhead* (Auckland, 1997).

GLEN, R. (ed.), *Mission and Moko: Aspects of the Work of the CMS in New Zealand 1814–82* (Christchurch, 1992).

HORRELL, S., *Forging a Workplace Mission* (Red Beach, 1995).

HOWE, E., 'Caught in the crossfire', M.Th. thesis (Melbourne, 1998).

IKITOELAGI, D., 'Pacific Islanders Church: Pacific Islands Presbyterians in Aotearoa New Zealand', M.Th. thesis (Dunedin, 1994).

IRWIN, J., 'The rise and fall of a vision: Maori in the midst of Pakeha in the Presbyterian Church of New Zealand', Ph.D. thesis (Wellington, 1994).

IOKA, D., 'Origin and beginning of the Congregational Christian Church of Samoa in Aotearoa New Zealand', Ph. D. thesis (Dunedin, 1997).

KEEN, D., 'The Role of Sunday schools in the socialisation of children in Otago and Southland 1848–1901', Ph.D. thesis (Dunedin, 1999).

KIRK, M. D., *Remembering your Mercy* (Auckland, 1998).

KNOWLES, B., 'Some aspects of the New Life Churches of New Zealand, 1960–90', Ph.D. thesis (Otago, 1994).

LEWIS, G., *Kept by the Power* (Christchurch, 1999).

LOVELL-SMITH, M., *No Turning Back* (Christchurch, 1986).

—— *Plain Living High Thinking* (Christchurch, 1994).

—— *The Enigma of Sr Mary Leo* (Auckland, 1998).

McEldowney, R. D. (ed.), *Presbyterians in Aotearoa* (Wellington, 1990).

Maclean, C., *For Whom the Bells Toll* (Wellington, 1998).

Ng, J., *Windows on a Chinese Past* (4 vols., Dunedin, 1993–2000).

Norris, P., *Southernmost Seminary* (Dunedin, 1999).

O'Farrell, P., *Vanished Kingdoms: The Irish in Australia and New Zealand* (Sydney, 1990).

O'Grady, R., *Alan Brash* (Auckland, 1991).

O'Regan, P., *There is Hope for a Tree* (Auckland, 1995).

Orsman, C. and Zwart, P. (eds.), *Church in the World: Statements on Social Issues 1979–1997 by New Zealand's Catholic Bishops* (Wellington, 1997).

Philipson, G., ' "The thirteenth apostle": Bishop Selwyn and the transplantation of Anglicanism to New Zealand', Ph.D. thesis (Otago, 1992).

Simpson, J. M. R., 'Liberal Christianity and the changing role of women in New Zealand society: a study of the National Council of Churches and the League of Mothers 1939–59', Ph.D. thesis (Dunedin, 1992).

—— 'Women, religion and society in New Zealand', *JRH* 18 (1994) 198–218.

—— 'Io as Supreme Being: intellectual colonization of the Maori', *History of Religions* 37 (1997) 50–85.

Strevens, D., 'The Sisters of St Joseph of Nazareth, New Zealand, 1880–1965', M.Th. thesis (Melbourne, 1995).

Sweetman, R., 'New Zealand Catholicism, war, politics and the Irish issue, 1912–22', Ph.D. thesis (Cambridge, 1990).

—— *Bishop in the Dock: The Sedition Trial of James Liston* (Auckland, 1997).

Thomson, D., *World without Welfare* (Auckland, 1998).

Tiatia, J., *Caught between Cultures* (Auckland, 1998).

Troughton, C., 'Christianity and community: aspects of religious life and attitudes in the Wanganui-Manawatu region 1870–85', MA thesis (Palmerston North, 1996).

Van der Kroght, C., 'More a part than apart: the Catholic community in New Zealand society ,' Ph.D. thesis (Palmerston North, 1994).

—— 'Exercising the utmost vigilance', *JRH* (1998) 320–35.

Van der Linden, A. F. F., 'Church planting', research essay (Melbourne, 1996).

Van Mejl, T., 'Historicizing Maoritanga', *JPS* 105 (1996) 311–46.

Veitch, J. (ed.), 'Will nothing ever be the same again? New Zealand Presbyterians in conflict', Th.D. thesis (Sydney, 1998).

Walsh, C., 'Michael Verdon', M.Th. thesis (Melbourne, 1995).

PAPUA NEW GUINEA

Monographs and Articles

AERTS, T. (ed.), *Memorial Volume of the Catholic Church in Papua, 1885–1985: Papers Prepared for the Visit of Pope John Paul II, 1985* (Port Moresby, 1985).
—— (ed.), *Romans and Anglicans in Papua New Guinea* (Port Moresby, 1991).
—— *The Martyrs of Papua New Guinea* (Port Moresby, 1994).
—— (ed.), *Religious Freedom in Papua New Guinea* (Port Moresby, 1994).
BARKER, J., 'We are Ekalesia: conversion in Kiakes, Papua New Guinea', in J. Carrier (ed.), *History and Tradition in Melanesian Ethnography* (Berkeley, 1992) 199–32.
BATLEY, G. R., 'A study of the Emic Christian theologising taking place among the Samban people of Papua New Guinea', Th.D. thesis (Melbourne, 1999).
BROWN, P., *Beyond a Mountain Valley* (Honolulu, 1995).
DRAPER, N. and S. (eds.), *Daring to Believe* (Melbourne, 1990).
FOUNTAIN, J., *'To Touch Others Also': The Bible Schools of the Christian Brethren in Papua New Guinea* (Wellington, 1999).
GESCH, P. (ed.), *Culture, Gospel and Church* (Madang, 1994).
HUMBLE, G. J., 'An accurate picture of the Eastern Highlands–Simbu mission of the Seventh-Day Adventists', MA thesis (Pasadena, 1991).
JEBENS, H., *Wege zum Himmel* (Bonn, 1995).
KEAYS, S. C., 'Sinabada or Misis', Ph.D. thesis (Brisbane, 1995).
LATUKEFU, S. and TROMPF, G., *Christian Missions and Development in Papua New Guinea* (Suva, 1995).
LENSSEN, F., *History of the Diocese of Lae, 1959–91* (Rome, 1992).
MATANE, P., *My Childhood in New Guinea* (Port Moresby, 1972).
—— *To Serve with Love* (Melbourne, 1995).
POORT, W. A., *The Pacific between Indigenous Culture and Exogenous Worship* (Hilvaranbeek, 1983).
PRINCE, J. and M., *No Fading Vision* (Melbourne, 1981).
—— *A Church is Born* (Melbourne, 1991).
RENALDI, C., *The Roman Catholic Church's Participation in the Ecumenical Movement in Papua New Guinea* (Rome, 1991).
RENCK, G., *Contextualization of Christianity and Christianisation of Language* (Erlangen, 1990).
ROBBINS, J., 'Dispossessing the spirits: Christian transformations of desire and ecology among the Urapmin of Papua New Guinea', *Ethnology* 24 (1995) 211–24.
SCHAEFER, A., *Cassowary of the Mountains* (Rome, 1991).
TOURIGNY, B., *Mémoires du Père Ben* (Montreal, 1992).
TROMPF, G. (ed.), *Cargo Cults and Melanesian Movements* (Berlin, 1990).

—— *Melanesian Religion* (Melbourne, 1991).

—— *Payback* (Melbourne, 1994).

WETHERELL, D., *Charles Abel and the Kwato Mission, 1891–1975* (Melbourne, 1996).

WHITE, N., *Sharing the Climb* (Melbourne, 1991).

ZAHN, H., *Missions and Music* (Port Moresby, 1996).

SAMOA, TOKELAU, TUVALU, KIRIBATI, AND NIUE

DOBBYN, K. P., 'Iaoni Kaiwara', M.Th. thesis (Melbourne, 1996).

FA'ALAFI, F. T., 'A century in the making of the Samoan Church 1828–1928', Th.D. thesis (Melbourne, 1994).

HAMILTON, A., 'Nineteenth century French missionaries and Fa'a Samoa', *JPH* 33 (1998) 163–77.

HESLIN, J., *A History of the Roman Catholic Church in Samoa, 1845–1995* (Apia, 1995).

HUNTSMAN, J. and HOOPER, A., *Tokelau* (Honolulu, 1996).

KAMU, L., *The Samoan Culture and the Christian Gospel* (Suva, 1996).

MAKANI, K.-T., 'Ekalesia Niue: an indigenous church in the making', M.Th. thesis (Suva, 1993).

O'MEARA, J. T., *Samoan Planters* (Fort Worth, 1990).

TA'ASE, E. T., 'The Congregational Church in Samoa 1818–1928', Ph.D. thesis (Pasadena, 1995).

SOLOMON ISLANDS

DAVIDSON, A. K. (ed.), *Semisi Nau: The Story of My Life* (Suva, 1996).

EARLY, L., 'If we win the women', Ph.D. thesis (Dunedin, 1996).

FEINBERG, R., 'Christian Polynesians and pagan spirits: Anuta, Solomon Islands', *JPS* 104 (1995) 267–301.

LITTLE, J., 'And God sent women: women in the SSEM', M.Th. thesis (Suva, 1993).

OSIFELO, F., 'Reconciliation through Melanesian eyes', Baccalaureate essay (Bomana, 1995).

O'BRIEN, C., *A Greater than Solomon Here: The Story of the Catholic Church in the Solomon Islands* (Honiara, 1995).

WHITE, G., *Identity through History: Living Stones in a Solomon Islands Society* (Cambridge, 1991).

WHITE, G. and LINDSTROM, L. (eds.), *Custom Today: Anthropological Forum* (1993).

TONGA

CAMPBELL, I. C., *Island Kingdom* (Christchurch, 1992).
DONALD, S. L., *In Some Sense the Work of an Individual* (Red Beach, 1994).
WOOD-ELLEM, E., *Queen Salote of Tonga* (Auckland, 1998).
VAN DER GRIJP, P., 'Christian confrontation in paradise', *Anthropos* 88 (1993) 135–52.

VANUATU

BOLTON, L., 'Chief Willie Bonmatur Maldo and the role of chiefs in Vanuatu', *JPH* 33 (1998) 179–95.
BONNEMAISON, J., *The Tree and the Canoe: History and Ethnography of Tanna* (Honolulu, 1994).
MONNIER, P., *Cent ans de mission: L'Église Catholique au Vanuatu 1887–1987* (Port Vila, 1987–92).
PARSONSON, G. S., *The Gospel in the Southern New Hebrides, 1839–1958* (Dunedin, 1985).
PRIOR, R. G., 'The relationship between Gospel and culture: a missiological critique of the Rev. John Geddie', M.Th. thesis (Melbourne, 1992).
TONKINSON, R., 'Church and Kastom in Southern Ambryn', in M. Allen (ed.), *Vanuatu* (Sydney, 1981) 237–67.

GLOSSARY

aitu	spirits, ghosts, sometimes malign.
ariki	first-born male or female from high-ranking family. High chief, includes priestly power.
atua	supernatural beings; sometimes with malign or disagreeable meaning.
avanga	sickness or mental condition caused by spirits.
cargo	general term for the goods promised by Melanesian prophetic leaders in a new world, where European secrets for gaining wealth are revealed to followers.
faife'au	the term for ministers in Samoa.
fa'a Samoa	Samoan custom and culture.
Fono Tele	annual meeting of Congregational Church in Polynesia, held in May.
hapu	section of large tribal group.
karakia	precisely worded prayers.
kava	mildly narcotic drink used in ceremonial and social occasions, especially in Fiji and Polynesia.
kawanatanga	gubernatorial authority, used in the Treaty of Waitangi.
kiap	pidgin term for government patrol officials in Papua New Guinea.
kumara	purple-skinned sweet potato grown widely by Islanders.
lotu	term for worship and prayer and for denomination. As a verb, to pray and be religious.
luluai	local chief in Papua New Guinea. Originally fight leader.
makutu	sorcery, spell.
mana	power, privilege, spiritual power, effective authority.
Maohi	the indigenous people of French Polynesia.
Maori	normal, usual, human being. Applied by natives of New Zealand to themselves as distinct from Pakeha, by the 1850s.
maoritanga	Maori culture and custom.
marae	space for tribal activities, sometimes with sacred associations.
matai	titled chief in Samoan extended family, elected, but also master.
mihinare	missionary.

moa   generic term for bird, but particularly applied in New Zealand to a large flightless bird, now extinct.

noa   common, destroys what is sacred and holy.

nu'u   Village in Samoa.

pa   fortified Maori village

Pakeha   foreign, European, sometimes with uncomplimentary meaning, but now regularly used in New Zealand.

rahui   warning of danger area, sometimes used to protect property and food sources.

rangatira   chief, master or mistress.

talatala   one who is sent, used in Fiji of ministers.

tapu   sacred, set apart, authority, closely linked with *mana*.

taukei   people of the land in Fiji.

tikanga   authority, based on custom and rightness.

toea'ina   senior pastor in Samoa, or old man.

tohunga   priest, shaman with sacred powers, often of chiefly birth.

tok pisin   the common vernacular in Papua New Guinea and Melanesia, with local variations.

tuka   a cult which combined traditional Fijian religion with some Christian elements.

tukutuku   decorative work in lattice panels, varied in colours.

tulafale   chiefly orators who speak for *matai*.

tultul   assistant village chief appointed by government in Papua New Guinea.

uapou   Cook Island services with singing specially composed for the occasion.

utu   satisfaction, reparation.

waiata   traditional song or chant.

wantok   Melanesian term for people of same language and custom, often related.

whare   house or hut.

INDEX